Civil

Aircraft Markings

1988

LONDON

IAN ALLAN LTD

Alan J. Wright

Contents

This thirty-ninth edition published 1988

ISBN 0 7110 1763 8

Published by Ian Allan Ltd, Shepperton, Surrey;
and printed by Ian Allan Printing Ltd at their works
at Coombelands in Runnymede, England.

Cover: *Boeing 747-230B D-ABYT of Lufthansa.* Lufthansa

Introduction

The 'G' prefixed four letter registration system was adopted in 1919 after a short-lived spell of about three months with serial numbers beginning at K-100. Until July 1928 the UK allocations were in the G-Exxx range, but as a result of further International agreements, this series was ended at G-EBZZ, the replacement being G-Axxx. From this point the registrations were issued in a reasonably orderly manner through to G-AZZZ, reached in July 1972. There were two exceptions. To avoid possible confusion with signal codes, the G-AQxx sequence was omitted, while G-AUxx was reserved for Australian use originally. In recent years however, an individual request for a mark in the latter range has been granted by the Authorities.

Although the next logical sequence was started at G-Bxxx, it was not long before the strictly applied rules relating to aircraft registration began to be relaxed. Permission was readily given for personalised marks to be issued incorporating virtually any four letter combination, while re-registration has also become a common feature, a practice almost unheard of in the past. In this book, where this has taken place at some time, the previous UK civil identity appears in parenthesis after the owner's/operator's name. An example of this is One-Eleven G-BBMG which originally carried G-AWEJ.

Some aircraft have also been allowed to wear military markings without displaying their civil identity. In this case the serial number actually carried is shown in parenthesis after the type's name. For example Gladiator G-AMRK flies as L8082 in RAF colours. As an aid to the identification of these machines, a military conversion list is provided.

Other factors caused a sudden acceleration in the number of registrations allocated by the Civil Aviation Authority in the early 1980s. The first surge came with the discovery that it was possible to register plastic bags and other items even less likely to fly, on payment of the standard fee. This erosion of the main register was checked in early 1982 by the issue of a special sequence for such devices commencing at G-FYAA. Powered hang-gliders provided the second glut of allocations as a result of the decision that these types should be officially registered. Although a few of the early examples penetrated the normal in-sequence register, the vast majority were given marks in other special ranges, this time G-MBxx, G-MGxx, G-MJxx, G-MMxx, G-MNxx, G-MTxx with G-MVxx, G-MWxx, G-MYxx and G-MZxx reserved for future use. At first it was common practice for microlights to ignore the requirement to carry their official identity. However the vast majority now display their registration somewhere on the structure, the size and position depending on the dimensions of the component to which it is applied.

Throughout the UK section of this book, there are many instances where the probable base of the aircraft has been included. This is positioned at the end of the owner/operator details preceded by an oblique stroke. It must of course be borne in mind that changes do take place and that no attempt has been made to record the residents at the many private strips. The base of airline equipment has been given as the company's headquarter's airport, although frequently aircraft are outstationed for long periods.

Non-airworthy preserved aircraft are shown with a star after the type.

Any new registrations issued by the CAA after this publication went to press will inevitably not be included until the next edition. To aid the recording of later marks logged, grids have been provided at the end of the book.

The three-letter codes used by airlines to prefix flight numbers are included for those carriers appearing in the book. Radio frequencies for the larger airfields/airports are also listed.

Acknowledgements

Once again thanks are extended to the Registration Department of the Civil Aviation Authority for their assistance and allowing access to their files. The comments and amendments flowing from Wal Gandy have as always proved of considerable value, while Ian Checkley, Neil Chadwick, Duncan Cummings and Howard Curtis also contributed useful facts. The help given by numerous airlines or their information agencies has been much appreciated. The work of A. S. Wright and C. P. Wright during the update of this edition must not go unrecorded, since without it, deadlines would probably become impossible.   **AJW**

International Civil Aircraft Markings

A2-	Botswana	P-	Korea (North)
A3-	Tonga	P2-	Papua New Guinea
A5-	Bhutan	PH-	Netherlands
A6-	United Arab Emirates	PJ-	Netherlands Antilles
A7-	Qatar	PK-	Indonesia and West Irian
A9-	Bahrain	PP-, PT-	Brazil
A40-	Oman	PZ-	Surinam
AP-	Pakistan	RDPL-	Laos
B-	China/Taiwan	RP-	Philippine Republic
C-F, C-G	Canada	S2-	Bangladesh
C2-	Nauru	S7-	Seychelles
C3	Andora	S9-	São Tomé
C5-	Gambia	SE-	Sweden
C6-	Bahamas	SP-	Poland
C9-	Mozambique	ST-	Sudan
CC-	Chile	SU-	Egypt
CCCP-*	Soviet Union	SX-	Greece
CN-	Morocco	T2	Tuvalu
CP-	Bolivia	T3-	Kiribati
CR-	Portuguese Overseas Provinces	T7-	San Marino
CS-	Portugal	TC-	Turkey
CU-	Cuba	TF-	Iceland
CX-	Uruguay	TG-	Guatemala
D-	German Federal Republic (West)	TI-	Costa Rica
D2-	Angola	TJ-	United Republic of Cameroon
D4	Cape Verde Islands	TL-	Central African Republic
D6-	Comores Islands	TN-	Republic of Congo (Brazzaville)
DDR-	German Democratic Republic (East)	TR-	Gabon
DQ-	Fiji	TS-	Tunisia
EC-	Spain	TT-	Chad
EI-, EJ-	Republic of Ireland	TU-	Ivory Coast
EL-	Liberia	TY-	Benin
EP-	Iran	TZ-	Mali
ET-	Ethiopia	V2-	Antigua
F-	France, Colonies and Protectorates	V3-	Belize
G-	United Kingdom	V8-	Brunei
H4-	Solomon Islands	VH-	Australia
HA-	Hungarian People's Republic	VN-	Vietnam
HB-	Switzerland and Liechtenstein	VP-F	Falkland Islands
HC-	Ecuador	VP-LKA/	
HH-	Haiti	LLZ	St Kitts-Nevis
HI-	Dominican Republic	VP-LMA/	
HK-	Colombia	LUZ	Montserrat
HL-	Korea (South)	VP-LVA/	
HP-	Panama	LZZ	Virgin Islands
HR-	Honduras	VQ-T	Turks & Caicos Islands
HS-	Thailand	VR-B	Bermuda
HZ-	Saudi Arabia	VR-C	Cayman Islands
I-	Italy	VR-G	Gibraltar (not used: present
J2-	Djibouti		Gibraltar Airways aircraft
J3-	Grenada		registered G-)
J5-	Guinea Bissau	VR-H	Hong Kong
J6-	St Lucia	VT-	India
J7-	Dominica	XA-, XB-,	
J8-	St Vincent	XC-,	Mexico
JA-	Japan	XT-	Upper Volta
JY-	Jordan	XU-	Kampuchea
LN-	Norway	XY-, XZ-	Burma
LQ-, LV-	Argentine Republic	YA-	Afghanistan
LX-	Luxembourg	YI-	Iraq
LZ-	Bulgaria	YJ-	Vanuatu
MI-	Marshall Islands	YK-	Syria
N-	United States of America	YN-	Nicaragua
OB-	Peru	YR-	Romania
OD-	Lebanon	YS-	El Salvador
OE-	Austria	YU-	Yugoslavia
OH-	Finland	YV-	Venezuela
OK-	Czechoslovakia	Z-	Zimbabwe
OO-	Belgium	ZA-	Albania
OY-	Denmark	ZK-	New Zealand

* Cyrillic letters for SSSR.

8

ZP-	Paraguay	6O-	Somalia
ZS-	South Africa	6V-, 6W-	Senegal
3A-	Monaco	6Y-	Jamaica
3B-	Mauritius	7O-	Democratic Yemen
3C-	Equatorial Guinea	7P-	Lesotho
3D-	Swaziland	7Q-	Malawi
3X-	Guinea	7T-	Algeria
4R-	Sri Lanka	8P-	Barbados
4W-	Yemen Arab Republic	8Q-	Maldives
4X-	Israel	8R-	Guyana
4YB	Jordanian-Iraqi Co-op Treaty	9G-	Ghana
5A-	Libya	9H-	Malta
5B-	Cyprus	9J-	Zambia
5H-	Tanzania	9K-	Kuwait
5N-	Nigeria	9L-	Sierra Leone
5R-	Malagasy Republic (Madagascar)	9M-	Malaysia
5T-	Mauritania	9N-	Nepal
5U-	Niger	9Q-	Zaïre
5V-	Togo	9U-	Burundi
5W-	Western Somoa (Polynesia)	9V-	Singapore
5X-	Uganda	9XR-	Rwanda
5Y-	Kenya	9Y-	Trinidad and Tobago

Aircraft Type Designations

(eg PA-28 Piper Type 28)

A.	Beagle, Auster	GY	Gardan
AA-	American Aviation, Grumman American	H	Helio
		HM.	Henri Mignet
AB	Agusta-Bell	HP.	Handley Page
AS	Aerospatiale	HR.	Robin
A.S.	Airspeed	H.S.	Hawker Siddeley
A.W.	Armstrong Whitworth	IL	Ilyushin
B.	Blackburn, Bristol Boeing, Beagle	J.	Auster
		L.	Lockheed
BAC	British Aircraft Corporation	L.A.	Luton
BAe	British Aerospace	M.	Miles, Mooney
BAT	British Aerial Transport	MBB	Messerschmitt-Bölkow-Blohm
BN	Britten-Norman	M.S.	Morane-Saulnier
Bo	Bolkow	P.	Hunting (formerly Percival), Piaggio
Bu	Bucker	PA-	Piper
C.H.	Chrislea	PC.	Pilatus
CLA	Comper	R.	Rockwell
CP.	Piel	S.	Short, Sikorsky
D.	Druine	SA., SE, SO.	Sud-Aviation, Aérospatiale, Scottish Aviation
DC-	Douglas Commercial		
D.H.	de Havilland	SCD	Side Cargo Door
D.H.C.	de Havilland Canada	S.R.	Saunders-Roe, Stinson
DR.	Jodel (Robin-built)	ST	SOCATA
EoN	Elliotts of Newbury	T.	Tipsy
EP	Edgar Percival	Tu	Tupolev
F.	Fairchild, Fokker	UH.	United Helicopters (Hiller)
G.	Grumman	V.	Vickers-Armstrongs, BAC
GA	Gulfstream American	V.S.	Vickers-Supermarine
G.A.L.	General Aircraft	W.S.	Westland
G.C.	Globe	Z.	Zlin

† False registration

Notes	Reg.	Type	Owner or Operator
	G-EACN	BAT BK23 Bantam (KI23) ★	Shuttleworth Trust/O. Warden
	G-EASO	Bristol Babe (replica) (BAPC87)★	Bomber Command Museum
	G-EAVX	Sopwith Pup (B1807)	K. A. M. Baker
	G-EBHX	D.H.53 Humming Bird	Shuttleworth Trust/O. Warden
	G-EBIA	S.E.5A (F904)	Shuttleworth Trust/O. Warden
	G-EBIB	S.E.5A (F939) ★	Science Museum
	G-EBIC	S.E.5A (F938) ★	RAF Museum
	G-EBIR	D.H.51	Shuttleworth Trust/O. Warden
	G-EBJE	Avro 504K (E449)★	RAF Museum
	G-EBJG	Parnall Pixie III ★	Midland Aircraft Preservation Soc
	G-EBJO	ANEC II ★	Shuttleworth Trust/O. Warden
	G-EBKY	Sopwith Pup (N5180)	Shuttleworth Trust/O. Warden
	G-EBLV	D.H.60 Cirrus Moth	British Aerospace/Hatfield
	G-EBMB	Hawker Cygnet I ★	RAF Museum
	G-EBNV	English Electric Wren	Shuttleworth Trust/O. Warden
	G-EBQP	D.H.53 Humming Bird ★	Russavia Collection/Duxford
	G-EBWD	D.H.60X Hermes Moth	Shuttleworth Trust/O. Warden
	G-EBYY	Cierva C.8L ★	Musée de l'Air, Paris
	G-EBZM	Avro 594 Avian IIIA ★	Greater Manchester Museum of Science & Technology
	G-AAAH	D.H.60G Gipsy Moth (replica) (BAPC 168) ★	Hilton Hotel/Gatwick
	G-AAAH	D.H.60G Gipsy Moth ★	Science Museum
	G-AACN	H.P.39 Gugnunc ★	Science Museum/Wroughton
	G-AADR	D.H.60GM Moth	H. F. Moffatt
	G-AAHY	D.H.60M Moth	Parker Airways Ltd/Denham
	G-AAIN	Parnall Elf II	Shuttleworth Trust/O. Warden
	G-AAMX	D.H.60GM Moth	R. J. Parkhouse
	G-AAMY	D.H.60M Moth	R. Twisleton-Wykeham Fiennes
	G-AAMZ	D.H.60G Moth	C. C. & J. M. Lovell
	G-AANF	D.H.60M Moth	A. Lloyd
	G-AANG	Blériot XI	Shuttleworth Trust/O. Warden
	G-AANH	Deperdussin Monoplane	Shuttleworth Trust/O. Warden
	G-AANI	Blackburn Monoplane	Shuttleworth Trust/O. Warden
	G-AANJ	L.V.G.-C VI (7198/18)	Shuttleworth Trust/O. Warden
	G-AANL	D.H.60M Moth	D. & P. Ellis
	G-AANM	Bristol 96A F.2B (D7889)	Aero Vintage Ltd
	G-AANV	D.H.60G Moth	D. H. Ellis
	G-AAOK	Curtiss Wright Travel Air 12Q	Shipping & Airlines Ltd/Biggin Hill
	G-AAOR	D.H.60G Moth (EM-01)	J. A. Pothecary/Shoreham
	G-AAPZ	Desoutter I (mod.) ★	Shuttleworth Trust/O. Warden
	G-AAUP	Klemm L.25-1A	J. I. Cooper
	G-AAVJ	D.H.60GMW Moth	R. W. Livett/Sywell
	G-AAWO	D.H.60G Gipsy Moth	J. F. W. Reid
	G-AAXK	Klemm L.25-1A	C. C. Russell-Vick
	G-AAYX	Southern Martlet	Shuttleworth Trust/O. Warden
	G-AAZP	D.H.80A Puss Moth	R. P. Williams
	G-ABAA	Avro 504K (H2311) ★	RAF Museum/Henlow
	G-ABAG	D.H.60G Moth	Shuttleworth Trust/O. Warden
	G-ABDW	D.H.80A Puss Moth (VH-UQB) ★	Museum of Flight/E. Fortune
	G-ABDX	D.H.60G Moth	M. D. Souch
	G-ABEE	Avro 594 Avian IVM (Sports) ★	Aeroplane Collection Ltd
	G-ABEV	D.H.60G Moth	Wessex Aviation & Transport Ltd
	G-ABLM	Cierva C.24 ★	Mosquito Aircraft Museum
	G-ABLS	D.H.80A Puss Moth	R. C. F. Bailey
	G-ABMR	Hart 2 (J9941)★	RAF Museum
	G-ABNT	Civilian C.A.C.1 Coupe	Shipping & Airlines Ltd/Biggin Hill
	G-ABNX	Redwing 2	J. Pothecary
	G-ABOI	Wheeler Slymph ★	Midland Air Museum
	G-ABOX	Sopwith Pup (N5195)	Museum of Army Flying/Middle Wallop
	G-ABSD	D.H.60G Moth	M. E. Vaisey
	G-ABTC	CLA.7 Swift	P. Channon/Biggin Hill
	G-ABUS	CLA.7 Swift	R. C. F. Bailey
	G-ABUU	CLA.7 Swift	H. B. Fox/Booker
	G-ABVE	Arrow Active 2	J. D. Penrose
	G-ABWP	Spartan Arrow	R. E. Blain/Barton
	G-ABXL	Granger Archaeopteryx ★	Shuttleworth Trust/O. Warden
	G-ABYA	D.H.60G Gipsy Moth	Dr I. D. C. Hay & J. F. Moore
	G-ABZB	D.H.60G-III Moth Major	R. E. & B. A. Ogden

Reg.	Type	Owner or Operator	Notes
G-ACBH	Blackburn B.2 ★	R. Coles	
G-ACCB	D.H.83 Fox Moth ★	Midland Aircraft Preservation Soc	
G-ACDC	D.H.82A Tiger Moth	Tiger Club Ltd/Redhill	
G-ACDJ	D.H.82A Tiger Moth	F. J. Terry	
G-ACEJ	D.H.83 Fox Moth	J. I. Cooper	
G-ACGT	Avro 594 Avian IIIA ★	Yorkshire Light Aircraft Ltd/Leeds	
G-ACIT	D.H.84 Dragon ★	Science Museum/Wroughton	
G-ACLL	D.H.85 Leopard Moth	D. C. M. & V. M. Stiles	
G-ACMA	D.H.85 Leopard Moth	S. J. Filhol/Sherburn	
G-ACMN	D.H.85 Leopard Moth	H. D. Labouchere	
G-ACOJ	D.H.85 Leopard Moth	M. J. Abbott	
G-ACOL	D.H.85 Leopard Moth	M. J. Abbott	
G-ACSP	D.H.88 Comet ★	W. B. Hosie & ptnrs/Bodmin	
G-ACSS	D.H.88 Comet	Shuttleworth Trust/Hatfield	
G-ACTF	CLA.7 Swift	A. J. Chalkley/Booker	
G-ACUS	D.H.85 Leopard Moth	T. P. A. Norman/Panshanger	
G-ACUU	Cierva C.30A ★	G. S. Baker/Duxford	
G-ACUX	S.16 Scion (VH-UUP) ★	Ulster Folk & Transport Museum	
G-ACVA	Kay Gyroplane ★	Glasgow Museum of Transport	
G-ACWM	Cierva C.30A ★	J. Eagles	
G-ACWP	Cierva C.30A (AP507) ★	Science Museum	
G-ACXE	B.K.L-25C Swallow	D. G. Ellis	
G-ACYK	Spartan Cruiser III ★	Museum of Flight (front fuselage)/ E. Fortune	
G-ACZE	D.H.89A Dragon Rapide	Wessex Aviation & Transport Ltd (G-AJGS)	
G-ADAH	D.H.89A Dragon Rapide ★	Museum of Flight/E. Fortune	
G-ADCG	D.H.82A Tiger Moth	D. A. Lowe (*stored*)	
G-ADEL	Spartan Cruiser III ★	Museum of Flight/E. Fortune	
G-ADEV	Avro 504K (H5199)	Shuttleworth Trust (G-ACNB)/ O. Warden	
G-ADFO	Blackburn B-2 ★	R. Cole	
G-ADFV	Blackburn B-2 ★	Humberside Aircraft Preservation Soc	
G-ADGP	M.2L Hawk Speed Six	R. Souch	
G-ADGT	D.H.82A Tiger Moth	D. R. & Mrs M. Wood	
G-ADGV	D.H.82A Tiger Moth	K. J. Whitehead	
G-ADHA	D.H.83 Fox Moth	Wessex Aviation & Transport Ltd	
G-ADIA	D.H.82A Tiger Moth	Mithril Racing Ltd/Goodwood	
G-ADJJ	D.H.82A Tiger Moth	J. M. Preston	
G-ADKC	D.H.87B Hornet Moth	L. E. Day/Carlisle	
G-ADKK	D.H.87B Hornet Moth	C. P. B. Horsley & R. G. Anniss	
G-ADKL	D.H.87B Hornet Moth	L. J. Rice	
G-ADKM	D.H.87B Hornet Moth	L. V. Mayhead	
G-ADLY	D.H.87B Hornet Moth	P. & A. Wood	
G-ADMT	D.H.87B Hornet Moth	M. A. Livett	
G-ADMW	M.2H Hawk Major (DG590) ★	RAF Museum/Henlow	
G-ADND	D.H.87B Hornet Moth	Shuttleworth Trust/O. Warden	
G-ADNE	D.H.87B Hornet Moth	R. Twisleton-Wykeham Fiennes/ Biggin Hill	
G-ADNZ	D.H.82A Tiger Moth	R. W. & Mrs. S. Pullan	
G-ADOT	D.H.87B Hornet Moth ★	Mosquito Aircraft Museum	
G-ADPJ	B.A.C. Drone	P. G. Dunnington	
G-ADPR	P.3 Gull ★	Shuttleworth Trust *Jean*/O. Warden	
G-ADPS	B.A. Swallow 2	Wessex Aviation & Transport Ltd	
G-ADRA	Pietenpol Aircamper	A. J. Mason & R. J. Barrett	
G-ADRC	K. & S. Jungster J-1	J. J. Penney & L. R. Williams	
G-ADRG†	Mignet HM.14 replica (BAPC77) ★	Cotswold Aircraft Restoration Group	
G-ADRH	D.H.87B Hornet Moth	I. M. Callier	
G-ADRY†	Mignet HM.14 replica (BAPC29) ★	Brooklands Museum	
G-ADUR	D.H.87B Hornet Moth	Wessex Aviation & Transport Ltd	
G-ADWO	D.H.82A Tiger Moth (BB807)	Wessex Aviation Soc	
G-ADXS	Mignet HM.14 ★	Rebel Air Museum/Earls Colne	
G-ADXT	D.H.82A Tiger Moth	J. & J. M. Pothecary/Shoreham	
G-ADYS	Aeronca C.3	B. Cooper	
G-AEBB	Mignet HM.14 ★	Shuttleworth Trust/O. Warden	
G-AEBJ	Blackburn B-2	British Aerospace/Brough	
G-AEDB	B.A.C. Drone 2	M. C. Russell/Duxford	
G-AEDT	D.H.90 Dragonfly	Wessex Aviation & Transport Ltd	
G-AEEG	M.3A Falcon	Vintage Aircraft Magazine Ltd/Denham	
G-AEEH	Mignet HM.14 ★	RAF/St Athan	
G-AEFG	Mignet HM.14 (BAPC75) ★	N. Ponsford	
G-AEFT	Aeronca C-3	C. E. Humphreys & ptnrs/Henstridge	

Notes	Reg.	Type	Owner or Operator
	G-AEGV	Mignet HM.14 ★	Midland Aircraft Preservation Soc
	G-AEHM	Pou-du-Ciel ★	Science Museum/Wroughton
	G-AEJZ	Mignet HM.14 (BAPC120) ★	Bomber County Museum/Cleethorpes
	G-AEKR	Mignet HM.14 (BAPC121) ★	S. Yorks Aviation Soc
	G-AEKV	Kronfield Drone	M. L. Beach/Booker
	G-AELO	D.H.87B Hornet Moth	S. N. Bostock
	G-AEML	D.H.89 Dragon Rapide	I. Jones
	G-AENP	Hawker Hind (K5414) (BAPC78)	Shuttleworth Trust/O. Warden
	G-AEOA	D.H.80A Puss Moth	P. & A. Wood/O. Warden
	G-AEOF†	Mignet HM.14 (BAPC22) ★	Aviodome/Schiphol, Holland
	G-AEOF	Rearwin 8500	Shipping & Airlines Ltd/Biggin Hill
	G-AEOH	Mignet HM.14 ★	Midland Air Museum
	G-AEPH	Bristol F.2B (D8096)	Shuttleworth Trust/O. Warden
	G-AERV	M.11A Whitney Straight ★	Ulster Folk & Transport Museum
	G-AESE	D.H.87B Hornet Moth	J. G. Green/Redhill
	G-AESZ	Chilton D.W.1	R. E. Nerou
	G-AETA	Caudron G.3 (3066) ★	RAF Museum
	G-AEUJ	M.11A Whitney Straight	R. E. Mitchell
	G-AEVS	Aeronca 100	A. J. E. Smith
	G-AEVZ	B. A. Swallow 2	E. H. S. Warner
	G-AEXD	Aeronca 100	Mrs M. A. & R. W. Mills
	G-AEXF	P.6 Mew Gull	J. D. Penrose/Old Warden
	G-AEXT	Dart Kitten II	A. J. Hartfield
	G-AEXZ	Piper J-2 Cub	Mrs M. & J. R. Dowson/Leicester
	G-AEYY	Martin Monoplane ★	Martin Monoplane Syndicate/Hatfield
	G-AEZF	S.16 Scion 2 ★	Southend Historic Aircraft Soc
	G-AEZJ	P.10 Vega Gull	R. N. Goode & C. R. Wilson
	G-AFAP†	C.A.S.A. C.352L ★	Aerospace Museum/Cosford
	G-AFAX	B. A. Eagle 2	J. G. Green
	G-AFBS	M.14A Hawk Trainer ★	G. D. Durbridge-Freeman (G-AKKU)/ Duxford
	G-AFCL	B. A. Swallow 2	A. M. Dowson/O. Warden
	G-AFDX	Hanriot HD.1 (75) ★	RAF Museum
	G-AFEL	Monocoupe 90A	Fortune Holdings Ltd/Barton
	G-AFFD	Percival Q-6 ★	B. D. Greenwood
	G-AFFH	Piper J-2 Cub	M. J. Honeychurch
	G-AFFI	Mignet HM.14 replica (BAPC76) ★	Bomber County Museum/Cleethorpes
	G-AFGC	B. A. Swallow 2	H. Plain
	G-AFGD	B. A. Swallow 2	A. T. Williams & ptnrs/Shobdon
	G-AFGE	B. A. Swallow 2	G. R. French
	G-AFGH	Chilton D.W.1.	M. L. & G. L. Joseph
	G-AFGI	Chilton D.W.1. ★	J. E. McDonald
	G-AFGM	Piper J-4A Cub Coupé	A. J. P. Marshall/Carlisle
	G-AFHA	Mosscraft M.A.1. ★	C. V. Butler
	G-AFIN	Chrislea Airguard ★	Aeroplane Collection Ltd
	G-AFIU	Parker C.A.4 Parasol (LA-3 Minor)	Aeroplane Collection Ltd/Warmington
	G-AFJA	Watkinson Dingbat ★	K. Woolley
	G-AFJB	Foster-Wickner G.M.1. Wicko (DR613) ★	K. Woolley
	G-AFJR	Tipsy Trainer 1	M. E. Vaisey
	G-AFJV	Mosscraft MA.2	C. V. Butler
	G-AFLW	M.17 Monarch	N. I. Dalziel/Biggin Hill
	G-AFNG	D.H.94 Moth Minor	R. W. Livett/Sywell
	G-AFNI	D.H.94 Moth Minor	B. M. Welford
	G-AFOB	D.H.94 Moth Minor	Wessex Aviation & Transport Ltd
	G-AFOJ	D.H.94 Moth Minor	R. M. Long
	G-AFPN	D.H.94 Moth Minor	J. W. & A. R. Davy/Carlisle
	G-AFPR	D.H.94 Moth Minor	J. A. Livett
	G-AFRZ	M.17 Monarch	R. E. Mitchell (G-AIDE)
	G-AFSC	Tipsy Trainer 1	R. V. & M. H. Smith
	G-AFSV	Chilton D.W.1A	R. Nerou
	G-AFSW	Chilton D.W.2 ★	R. I. Souch
	G-AFTA	Hawker Tomtit (K1786)	Shuttleworth Trust/O. Warden
	G-AFTN	Taylorcraft Plus C2 ★	Leicestershire County Council Museums
	G-AFVE	D.H.82 Tiger Moth	P. E. Swinstead
	G-AFVN	Tipsy Trainer 1	W. Callow & ptnrs
	G-AFWH	Piper J-4A Cub Coupé	J. R. Edwards
	G-AFWI	D.H.82A Tiger Moth	N. E. Rankin & ptnrs
	G-AFWT	Tipsy Trainer 1	J. S. Barker/Redhill
	G-AFYD	Luscombe 8E Silvaire	J. D. Iliffe
	G-AFYO	Stinson H.W.75	R. N. Wright
	G-AFZA	Piper J-4A Cub Coupé	J. Catley

Reg.	Type	Owner or Operator	Notes
G-AFZE	Heath Parasol	K. C. D. St Cyrien	
G-AFZL	Porterfield CP.50	P. G. Lucas & ptnrs/White Waltham	
G-AFZN	Luscombe 8A Silvaire	R. V. Smith	
G-AGAT	Piper J-3F-50 Cub	Wessex Aviation & Transport Ltd	
G-AGBN	G.A.L.42 Cygnet 2 ★	Museum of Flight/E. Fortune	
G-AGEG	D.H.82A Tiger Moth	T. P. A. Norman	
G-AGFT	Avia FL.3	P. A. Smith	
G-AGIV	Piper J-3C-65 Cub	P. C. & F. M. Gill	
G-AGJG	D.H.89A Dragon Rapide	Russavia Ltd/Duxford	
G-AGLK	Auster 5D	W. C. E. Tazewell	
G-AGNV	Avro 685 York 1 (MW100) ★	Aerospace Museum/Cosford	
G-AGOH	J/1 Autocrat	Leicestershire County Council Museums	
G-AGOS	R.S.4 Desford Trainer (VZ728)	Scottish Aircraft Collection/Perth	
G-AGOY	M.48 Messenger 3 (U-0247)	P. A. Brooks	
G-AGPG	Avro 19 Srs 2 ★	Brenzett Aviation Museum	
G-AGRU	V.498 Viking 1A ★	Aerospace Museum/Cosford	
G-AGSH	D.H.89A Dragon Rapide 6	Specialist Flying Training Ltd/Carlisle	
G-AGTM	D.H.89A Dragon Rapide 6 (NF875)	Russavia Ltd/Duxford	
G-AGTO	J/1 Autocrat	M. J. Barnett & D. J. T. Miller/Duxford	
G-AGTT	J/1 Autocrat	R. Farrer	
G-AGVG	J/1 Autocrat	RN Aviation (Leicester Airport) Ltd	
G-AGVN	J/1 Autocrat	S. Thursfield & K. E. Eld/Leicester	
G-AGVV	Piper L-4H Cub	A. R. W. Taylor & D. Lofts/Sleap	
G-AGWE	Avro 19 Srs 2 ★	Phoenix Aviation Museum	
G-AGXN	J/1N Alpha	I. R. Walters/Cranwell	
G-AGXT	J/1N Alpha ★	Nene Valley Aircraft Museum/Sibson	
G-AGXU	J/1N Alpha	R. J. Guess/Sibson	
G-AGXV	J/1 Autocrat	B. S. Dowsett & K. Mitchell	
G-AGYD	J/1N Alpha	P. Herring & ptnrs/Dishforth	
G-AGYH	J/1N Alpha	G. E. Twyman & P. J. Rae	
G-AGYK	J/1 Autocrat	D. A. Smith	
G-AGYL	J/1 Autocrat ★	WWII Aircraft Preservation Society/ Lasham	
G-AGYT	J/1N Alpha	P. C. Davies & ptnrs/Lee-on-Solent	
G-AGYU	DH.82A Tiger Moth (DE208)	P. & A. Wood	
G-AGYY	Ryan ST.3KR	D. S. & I. M. Morgan	
G-AGZZ	D.H.82A Tiger Moth	G. P. LaT. Shea-Simonds/Netheravon	
G-AHAL	J/1N Alpha	Skegness Air Taxi Services Ltd/ Ingoldmells	
G-AHAM	J/1 Autocrat	D. W. Philp/Goodwood	
G-AHAN	D.H.82A Tiger Moth	G. L. Owens	
G-AHAP	J/1 Autocrat (Rover) ★	V. H. Bellamy	
G-AHAU	J/1 Autocrat	J. F. Smith	
G-AHAV	J/1 Autocrat	C. J. Freeman/Headcorn	
G-AHBL	D.H.87B Hornet Moth	Dr Ursula H. Hamilton	
G-AHBM	D.H.87B Hornet Moth	P. A. & E. P. Gliddon	
G-AHCK	J/1N Alpha	P. A. Woodman/Shoreham	
G-AHCR	Gould-Taylorcraft Plus D Special	D. E. H. Balmford & D. R. Shepherd/ Yeovil	
G-AHEC	Grumman G.44 Widgeon (1411)	M. Dunkerley/Biggin Hill	
G-AHED	D.H.89A Dragon Rapide (RL962) ★	RAF Museum (Cardington)	
G-AHGD	D.H.89A Dragon Rapide (Z7258)	M. R. L. Astor/Booker	
G-AHGW	Taylorcraft Plus D (LB375)	C. V. Butler/Coventry	
G-AHGZ	Taylorcraft Plus D	S. J. Ball/Leicester	
G-AHHH	J/1 Autocrat	H. A. Jones/Norwich	
G-AHHK	J/1 Autocrat	C. Johns	
G-AHHN	J/1 Autocrat	KK Aviation	
G-AHHP	J/1N Alpha	D. J. Hutcheson (G-SIME)	
G-AHHT	J/1N Alpha	R.A.E. Aero Club/Farnborough	
G-AHHU	J/1N Alpha ★	L. Groves & I. R. F. Hammond	
G-AHIP	Piper J-3C-65 Cub	R. E. Nerou/Coventry	
G-AHIZ	D.H.82A Tiger Moth	C.F.G. Flying Ltd/Cambridge	
G-AHKX	Avro 19 Srs 2	British Aerospace PLC/Woodford	
G-AHKY	Miles M.18 Series 2	Scottish Aircraft Collection/Perth	
G-AHLI	Auster 3	G. A. Leathers	
G-AHLK	Auster 3	E. T. Brackenbury/Leicester	
G-AHLT	D.H.82A Tiger Moth	R. C. F. Bailey	
G-AHMJ	Cierva C.30A (K4235) ★	Shuttleworth Trust/O. Warden	
G-AHMN	D.H.82A Tiger Moth (N6985)	George House (Holdings) Ltd	

Notes	Reg.	Type	Owner or Operator
	G-AHOO	D.H.82A Tiger Moth	G. W. Bisshopp
	G-AHRI	D.H.104 Dove 1 ★	Lincolnshire Aviation Museum
	G-AHRO	Cessna 140	R. H. Screen/Kidlington
	G-AHSA	Avro 621 Tutor (K3215)	Shuttleworth Trust/O. Warden
	G-AHSD	Taylorcraft Plus D	A. Tucker
	G-AHSO	J/1N Alpha	Skegness Air Taxi Services Ltd/ Ingoldmells
	G-AHSP	J/1 Autocrat	D. S. Johnstone & ptnrs
	G-AHSS	J/1N Alpha	Parker Airways Ltd/Denham
	G-AHST	J/1N Alpha	C. H. Smith
	G-AHSW	J/1 Autocrat	K. W. Brown/Coventry
	G-AHTE	P.44 Proctor V	J. G. H. Hassell
	G-AHTW	A.S.40 Oxford (V3388) ★	Skyfame Collection/Duxford
	G-AHUF	D.H.82A Tiger Moth	D. S. & I. M. Morgan
	G-AHUG	Taylorcraft Plus D	D. Nieman
	G-AHUI	M.38 Messenger 2A ★	Berkshire Aviation Group
	G-AHUJ	M.14A Hawk Trainer 3 (R1914)	Vintage Aircraft Team
	G-AHUN	Globe GC-1B Swift	B. R. Rossiter/White Waltham
	G-AHUV	D.H.82A Tiger Moth	W. G. Gordon
	G-AHVU	D.H.82A Tiger Moth (T6313)	Parker Airways Ltd/Denham
	G-AHVV	D.H.82A Tiger Moth	R. Jones
	G-AHWJ	Taylorcraft Plus D	A. Tucker
	G-AHXE	Taylorcraft Plus D (LB312)	Museum of Army Flying/Middle Wallop
	G-AIBE	Fulmar II (N1854) ★	F.A.A. Museum/Yeovilton
	G-AIBH	J/1N Alpha	M. J. Bonnick
	G-AIBM	J/1 Autocrat	J. K. Avis
	G-AIBR	J/1 Autocrat ★	A. Topen
	G-AIBW	J/1N Alpha	W. E. Bateson/Blackpool
	G-AIBX	J/1 Autocrat	Wasp Flying Group/Panshanger
	G-AIBY	J/1 Autocrat	D. Morris/Sherburn
	G-AIDL	D.H.89A Dragon Rapide 6	Snowdon Mountain Aviation Ltd
	G-AIDS	D.H.82A Tiger Moth	K. D. Pogmore & T. Dann
	G-AIEK	M.38 Messenger 2A (RG333)	J. Buckingham
	G-AIFZ	J/1N Alpha	C. P. Humphries
	G-AIGD	J/1 Autocrat	A. G. Batchelor
	G-AIGF	J/1N Alpha	A. R. C. Mathie
	G-AIGM	J/1N Alpha	Wickenby Flying Club Ltd
	G-AIGT	J/1N Alpha	B. D. Waller
	G-AIGU	J/1N Alpha	T. Pate
	G-AIIH	Piper J-3C-65 Cub	J. A. de Salis
	G-AIJI	J/1N Alpha ★	Humberside Aircraft Preservation Soc
	G-AIJM	Auster J/4	N. Huxtable
	G-AIJR	Auster J/4	B. A. Harris/Halfpenny Green
	G-AIJS	Auster J/4 ★	stored
	G-AIJT	Auster J/4 srs 100	Aberdeen Auster Flying Group
	G-AIJZ	J/1 Autocrat	stored
	G-AILL	M.38 Messenger 2A	H. Best-Devereux
	G-AIPR	Auster J/4	MPM Flying Group/Booker
	G-AIPV	J/1 Autocrat	J. Linegar
	G-AIPW	J/1 Autocrat	B. Hillman
	G-AIRC	J/1 Autocrat	A. G. Martlew/Barton
	G-AIRI	D.H.82A Tiger Moth	E. R. Goodwin
	G-AIRK	D.H.82A Tiger Moth	R. C. Teverson & ptnrs
	G-AISA	Tipsy B Srs 1	J. W. Thomson & R. P. Aston
	G-AISB	Tipsy B Srs 1	D. M. Fenton
	G-AISC	Tipsy B Srs 1	Wagtail Flying Group
	G-AISD	M.65 Gemini 1A	J. E. Homewood
	G-AISS	Piper J-3C-65 Cub	K. R. Nunn
	G-AIST	V.S.300 Spitfire IA (AR213)	The Hon A. M. M. Lindsay/Booker
	G-AISX	Piper J-3C-65 Cub	R. I. Souch
	G-AITB	A.S.10 Oxford (MP425) ★	RAF Museum/Cardington
	G-AITP	Piper J-3C-65 Cub	L. E. Svensson
	G-AIUA	M.14A Hawk Trainer 3 ★	P. A. Brook
	G-AIUL	D.H.89A Dragon Rapide 6	I. Jones
	G-AIXA	Taylorcraft Plus D	A. A. & M. J. Copse
	G-AIXD	D.H.82A Tiger Moth	Sark International Airways/Guernsey
	G-AIXN	Benes-Mraz M.1c Sokol	J. F. Evetts & D. Patel
	G-AIYR	D.H.89A Dragon Rapide	C. D. Cyster
	G-AIYS	D.H.85 Leopard Moth	Wessex Aviation & Transport Ltd
	G-AIZE	F.24W Argus 2 ★	RAF Museum/Henlow
	G-AIZF	D.H.82A Tiger Moth ★	stored
	G-AIZG	V.S. Walrus (L2301) ★	F.A.A. Museum/Yeovilton
	G-AIZU	J/1 Autocrat	C. J. & J. G. B. Morley

Reg.	Type	Owner or Operator	Notes
G-AIZY	J/1 Autocrat	B. J. Richards	
G-AIZZ	J/1 Autocrat ★	S. E. Bond	
G-AJAB	J/1N Alpha	Air Farm Ltd	
G-AJAC	J/1N Alpha	R. C. Hibberd	
G-AJAD	Piper J-3C-65 Cub	R. A. C. Hoppenbrouwers	
G-AJAE	J/1N Alpha	M. G. Stops	
G-AJAJ	J/1N Alpha	R. B. Lawrence	
G-AJAM	J/2 Arrow	D. A. Porter	
G-AJAO	Piper J-3C Cub	T. G. Dixon	
G-AJAS	J/1N Alpha	C. J. Baker	
G-AJCP	D.31 Turbulent	H. J. Shaw	
G-AJDW	J/1 Autocrat	D. R. Hunt	
G-AJDY	J/1 Autocraft ★	stored	
G-AJEB	J/1N Alpha ★	Aeroplane Collection Ltd/Warmingham	
G-AJEE	J/1 Autocrat	A. R. C. De Albanoz/Bournemouth	
G-AJEH	J/1N Alpha	A. Beswick & N. Robinson	
G-AJEI	J/1N Alpha	Skegness Air Taxi Services Ltd/ Ingoldmells	
G-AJEM	J/1 Autocrat	B. Weare	
G-AJES	Piper J-3C-65 Cub (330485)	P. Crawford	
G-AJGJ	Auster 5 (RT486)	S. C. Challis & J. Lawless	
G-AJHJ	Auster 5	stored	
G-AJHO	D.H.89A Dragon Rapide ★	East Anglian Aviation Soc Ltd	
G-AJHS	D.H.82A Tiger Moth	Machine Music Ltd/Redhill	
G-AJHU	D.H.82A Tiger Moth	F. P. Le Coyte	
G-AJID	J/1 Autocrat	D. J. Ronayne/Headcorn	
G-AJIH	J/1 Autocrat	T. Boyd & A. H. Diver	
G-AJIS	J/1N Alpha	A. Tucker	
G-AJIT	J/1 Kingsland Autocrat	Kingsland Aviation Ltd	
G-AJIU	J/1 Autocrat	A. Mirfin/Doncaster	
G-AJIW	J/1N Alpha	N. A. Roberts	
G-AJJP	Jet Gyrodyne (XJ389) ★	Aerospace Museum/Cosford	
G-AJJS	Cessna 120	L. G. Sharkey	
G-AJOA	D.H.82A Tiger Moth (T5424)	F. P. Le Coyte	
G-AJOC	M.38 Messenger 2A ★	Ulster Folk & Transport Museum	
G-AJOE	M.38 Messenger 2A	J. Eagles & P. C. Kirby/Staverton	
G-AJON	Aeronca 7AC Champion	B. A. Bower & C. S. Keeping	
G-AJOV	Sikorsky S-51 ★	Aerospace Museum/Cosford	
G-AJOZ	F.24W Argus 2 ★	Lincolnshire Aviation Museum	
G-AJPI	F.24R-41a Argus 3	J. F. Read/White Waltham	
G-AJPZ	J/1 Autocrat ★	Wessex Aviation Soc	
G-AJRB	J/1 Autocrat	S. C. Luck/Sywell	
G-AJRC	J/1 Autocrat	S. W. Watkins & ptnrs	
G-AJRE	J/1 Autocrat (Lycoming)	R. Gammage/Headcorn	
G-AJRH	J/1N Alpha	Leicestershire County Council Museums	
G-AJRS	M.14A Hawk Trainer 3 (P6382)	Shuttleworth Trust/O. Warden	
G-AJTW	D.H.82A Tiger Moth	J. A. Barker	
G-AJUD	J/1 Autocrat	C. L. Sawyer	
G-AJUE	J/1 Autocrat	P. H. B. Cole	
G-AJUL	J/1N Alpha	M. J. Crees	
G-AJVE	D.H.82A Tiger Moth	M. J. Abbot & I. J. Jones/Dunkeswell	
G-AJVT	Auster 5	I. N. M. Cameron	
G-AJXC	Auster 5	J. E. Graves	
G-AJXV	Auster 4 (NJ695)	P. C. J. Farries/Tollerton	
G-AJXY	Auster 4	G. B. Morris	
G-AJYB	J/1N Alpha	P. J. Shotbolt	
G-AKAA	Piper L-4H Cub	P. Raggett	
G-AKAT	M.14A Magister (T9738)	A. J. E. Smith	
G-AKAZ	Piper J-3C-65 Cub	S. J. Johnstone	
G-AKBM	M.38 Messenger 2A ★	Bristol Plane Preservation Unit	
G-AKBO	M.38 Messenger 2A	B. Du Cros	
G-AKDN	D.H.C. 1A Chipmunk 10	K. R. Nunn/Seething	
G-AKEL	M.65 Gemini 1A ★	Ulster Folk & Transport Museum	
G-AKER	M.65 Gemini 1A ★	Berkshire Aviation Group	
G-AKEZ	M.38 Messenger 2A (RG333) ★	Torbay Aircraft Museum	
G-AKGD	M.65 Gemini 1A ★	Berkshire Aviation Group	
G-AKGE	M.65 Gemini 3C ★	Ulster Folk & Transport Museum	
G-AKHP	M.65 Gemini 1A	P. G. Lee	
G-AKHW	M.65 Gemini 1A	Vintage Aircraft Magazine Ltd/Denham	
G-AKHZ	M.65 Gemini 7 ★	Berkshire Aviation Group	
G-AKIB	Piper J-3C-65 Cub (480015)	M. C. Bennett	
G-AKIF	D.H.89A Dragon Rapide	Airborne Taxi Services Ltd/Booker	

Notes	Reg.	Type	Owner or Operator
	G-AKIN	M.38 Messenger 2A	A. J. Spiller/Sywell
	G-AKIU	P.44 Proctor V ★	N. Weald Aircraft Restoration Flight
	G-AKJU	J/1N Alpha	R. C. Lewis
	G-AKKB	M.65 Gemini 1A	S.A.C. Bristol Ltd
	G-AKKH	M.65 Gemini 1A	M. C. Russell/Duxford
	G-AKKR	M.14A Magister (T9707) ★	Greater Manchester Museum of Science & Technology
	G-AKKY	M.14A Hawk Trainer 3 (BAPC44)★	G. H. R. Johnston
	G-AKLW	SA.6 Sealand 1 ★	Ulster Folk & Transport Museum
	G-AKOE	D.H.89A Dragon Rapide 4	J. E. Pierce
	G-AKOT	Auster 5 ★	C. Baker
	G-AKOW	Auster 5 (TJ569) ★	Museum of Army Flying/Middle Wallop
	G-AKPF	M.14A Hawk Trainer 3 (N3788) ★	L. N. D. Taylor
	G-AKPI	Auster 5 (NJ703)	B. H. Hargrave/Sherburn
	G-AKRA	Piper J-3C-65 Cub	W. R. Savin
	G-AKSZ	Auster 5	A. R. C. Mathie
	G-AKTH	Piper L-4J Cub	A. L. Wickens
	G-AKTI	Luscombe 8A Silvaire	C. C. & J. M. Lovell
	G-AKUE	D.H.82A Tiger Moth	S. J. Ellis
	G-AKUW	C.H.3 Super Ace	C. V. Butler (stored)
	G-AKVF	C.H.3 Super Ace	P. V. B. Longthorp/Bodmin
	G-AKVZ	M.38 Messenger 4B	Shipping & Airlines Ltd/Biggin Hill
	G-AKWS	Auster 5-160	J. E. Homewood
	G-AKWT	Auster 5 (MT360) ★	Humberside Aircraft Preservation Soc
	G-AKXP	Auster 5	F. E. Telling
	G-AKXS	D.H.82A Tiger Moth	P. A. Colman
	G-AKZN	P.34A Proctor 3 (Z7197) ★	RAF Museum/St Athan
	G-ALAH	M.38 Messenger 4A (RH377) ★	RAF Museum/Henlow
	G-ALAX	D.H.89A Dragon Rapide ★	Durney Aeronautical Collection
	G-ALBJ	Auster 5	R. H. Elkington
	G-ALBK	Auster 5	S. J. Wright & Co (Farmers) Ltd
	G-ALBN	Bristol 173 (XF785) ★	RAF Museum/Henlow
	G-ALCK	P.34A Proctor 3 (LZ766) ★	Skyfame Collection/Duxford
	G-ALCS	M.65 Gemini 3C ★	Stored
	G-ALCU	D.H.104 Dove 2 ★	Midland Air Museum
	G-ALDG	HP.81 Hermes 4 ★	Duxford Aviation Soc (Fuselage only)
	G-ALEH	PA-17 Vagabond	A. D. Pearce/Redhill
	G-ALFA	Auster 5	Alpha Flying Group
	G-ALFM	D.H.104 Devon C.2	N. J. Taaffe & A. D. Hemley
	G-ALFT	D.H.104 Dove 6 ★	Torbay Aircraft Museum
	G-ALFU	D.H.104 Dove 6 ★	Imperial War Museum/Duxford
	G-ALGA	PA-15 Vagabond	M. J. Markey/Biggin Hill
	G-ALGT	V.S.379 Spitfire 14 (RM689)	Rolls-Royce Ltd
	G-ALIJ	PA-17 Vagabond	RFC Flying Group/Popham
	G-ALIW	D.H.82A Tiger Moth	D. I. M. Geddes & F. Curry/Booker
	G-ALJF	P.34A Proctor 3	J. F. Moore/Biggin Hill
	G-ALJL	D.H.82A Tiger Moth	C. G. Clarke
	G-ALNA	D.H.82A Tiger Moth	A. W. Kennedy
	G-ALND	D.H.82A Tiger Moth (N9191)	Arrow Air Services (Engineering) Ltd/ Shipdham
	G-ALNV	Auster 5 ★	stored
	G-ALOD	Cessna 140	J. R. Stainer
	G-ALRH	EoN Type 8 Baby	P. D. Moran
	G-ALRI	D.H.82A Tiger Moth (T5672)	Wessex Aviation & Transport Ltd
	G-ALSP	Bristol 171 (WV783) Sycamore ★	RAF Museum/Henlow
	G-ALSS	Bristol 171 (WA576) Sycamore ★	E. Fortune
	G-ALST	Bristol 171 (WA577) Sycamore ★	N.E. Aircraft Museum/Usworth
	G-ALSW	Bristol 171 (WT933) Sycamore ★	Newark Air Museum
	G-ALSX	Bristol 171 (G-48-1) Sycamore ★	British Rotorcraft Museum/Duxford
	G-ALTO	Cessna 140	J. E. Cummings/Popham
	G-ALTW	D.H.82A Tiger Moth ★	A. Mangham
	G-ALUC	D.H.82A Tiger Moth	D. R. & M. Wood
	G-ALVP	D.H.82A Tiger Moth ★	V. & R. Wheele (stored)
	G-ALWB	D.H.C.1 Chipmunk 22A	M. L. & J. M. Soper/Perth
	G-ALWC	Dakota 4	Visionair (International Aviation) Ltd
	G-ALWF	V.701 Viscount ★	Viscount Preservation Trust/Duxford
	G-ALWS	D.H.82A Tiger Moth ★	Airwork Services Ltd
	G-ALWW	D.H.82A Tiger Moth	F. W. Fay & ptnrs/Long Marston
	G-ALXT	D.H.89A Dragon Rapide ★	Science Museum/Wroughton
	G-ALXZ	Auster 5-150	B. J. W. Thomas & R. A. E. Witheridge
	G-ALYB	Auster 5 ★	S. Yorks Aviation Soc
	G-ALYG	Auster 5D	A. L. Young
	G-ALYW	D.H.106 Comet 1 ★	RAF Exhibition Flight (fuselage converted to Nimrod)

Reg.	Type	Owner or Operator	Notes
G-ALZE	BN-1F ★	M. R. Short	
G-ALZO	A.S.57 Ambassador★	Duxford Aviation Soc	
G-AMAW	Luton LA-4 Minor	R. H. Coates	
G-AMBB	D.H.82A Tiger Moth	J. Eagles	
G-AMCA	Dakota 3	Air Atlantique Ltd/Coventry	
G-AMCM	D.H.82A Tiger Moth	G. C. Masterton	
G-AMDA	Avro 652A Anson 1 (N4877)★	Skyfame Collection/Duxford	
G-AMEN	PA-19 Super Cub 95	A. Lovejoy & ptnrs	
G-AMHF	D.H.82A Tiger Moth	L. Mayhead	
G-AMHJ	Dakota 6	Atlantic Air Transport Ltd/Coventry	
G-AMIU	D.H.82A Tiger Moth	R. & Mrs J. L. Jones	
G-AMKU	J/1B Aiglet	Southdown Flying Group/Slinfold	
G-AMLZ	P.50 Prince 6E ★	J. F. Coggins/Coventry	
G-AMMS	J/5F Aiglet Trainer	V. Long	
G-AMOE	V.701 Viscount (G-WHIZ) ★	Saltwell Park/Gateshead	
G-AMOG	V.701 Viscount ★	Aerospace Museum/Cosford	
G-AMPG	PA-12 Super Cruiser	R. Simpson	
G-AMPI	SNCAN Stampe SV-4C	J. Hewett	
G-AMPO	Dakota 4	Aces High Ltd/North Weald	
G-AMPP	Dakota 3 (G-AMSU) ★	Dan-Air Preservation Group/Lasham	
G-AMPW	J/5B Autocar ★	R. Neal (stored)	
G-AMPY	Dakota 4	Air Atlantique Ltd/Coventry	
G-AMPZ	Dakota 4	Harvest Air Ltd/Southend	
G-AMRA	Dakota 6	Air Atlantique Ltd/Coventry	
G-AMRF	J/5F Aiglet Trainer	A. I. Topps/E. Midlands	
G-AMRK	G.37 Gladiator (L8032)	Shuttleworth Trust/O. Warden	
G-AMSG	SIPA 903	S. W. Markham	
G-AMSV	Dakota 4	Air Atlantique Ltd/Coventry	
G-AMTA	J/5F Aiglet Trainer	H. J. Jauncey/Rochester	
G-AMTD	J/5F Aiglet Trainer	C. I. Fray	
G-AMTK	D.H.82A Tiger Moth ★	A. Topen (stored)	
G-AMTM	J/1 Autocrat	R. Stobo & D. Clewley	
G-AMUF	D.H.C.1 Chipmunk 21	Redhill Tailwheel Flying Club Ltd	
G-AMVD	Auster 5	R. F. Tolhurst	
G-AMVP	Tipsy Junior	A. R. Wershat/Popham	
G-AMVS	D.H.82A Tiger Moth	P. A. Crawford	
G-AMXT	D.H.104 Sea Devon C.20	Scoteroy Ltd/Southampton	
G-AMYA	Zlin Z.381	D. M. Fenton	
G-AMYD	J/5L Aiglet Trainer	G. H. Maskell	
G-AMYJ	Dakota 6	Harvest Air Ltd/Southend	
G-AMYL	PA-17 Vagabond	P. J. Penn-Sayers/Shoreham	
G-AMZI	J/5F Aiglet Trainer	J. F. Moore/Biggin Hill	
G-AMZT	J/5F Aiglet Trainer	D. Hyde & J. W. Saull/Cranfield	
G-AMZU	J/5F Aiglet Trainer	J. A. Longworth & ptnrs	
G-ANAP	D.H.104 Dove 6 ★	Brunel Technical College/Lulsgate	
G-ANCS	D.H.82A Tiger Moth (R4907)	M. F. Newman	
G-ANCX	D.H.82A Tiger Moth	D. R. Wood/Biggin Hill	
G-ANDE	D.H.82A Tiger Moth	A. J. & P. B. Borsberry	
G-ANDI	D.H.82A Tiger Moth	P. J. Jefferies & ptnrs	
G-ANDM	D.H.82A Tiger Moth	J. G. Green	
G-ANDP	D.H.82A Tiger Moth	A. H. Diver	
G-ANDX	D.H.104 Devon C.2	L. Richards	
G-ANEC	D.H.82A Tiger Moth ★	(stored)	
G-ANEF	D.H.82A Tiger Moth (T5493)	RAF College Flying Club Co Ltd/ Cranwell	
G-ANEH	DH.82A Tiger Moth ★	A. Topen/Cranfield	
G-ANEL	D.H.82A Tiger Moth (N9238)	Chauffair Ltd	
G-ANEM	D.H.82A Tiger Moth	P. J. Benest	
G-ANEW	D.H.82A Tiger Moth	A. L. Young	
G-ANEZ	D.H.82A Tiger Moth	C. D. J. Bland & T. S. Warren/Sandown	
G-ANFC	D.H.82A Tiger Moth (DE363) ★	Mosquito Aircraft Museum	
G-ANFH	Westland S-55 ★	British Rotorcraft Museum	
G-ANFI	D.H.82A Tiger Moth (DE623)	D. H. R. Jenkins	
G-ANFL	D.H.82A Tiger Moth	R. P. Whitby & ptnrs	
G-ANFM	D.H.82A Tiger Moth	S. A. Brook & ptnrs/Booker	
G-ANFP	D.H.82A Tiger Moth ★	Mosquito Aircraft Museum	
G-ANFU	Auster 5 ★	N.E. Aircraft Museum	
G-ANFV	D.H.82A Tiger Moth (DF155)	R. A. L. Falconer/Inverness	
G-ANFW	D.H.82A Tiger Moth	G. M. Fraser/Denham	
G-ANHK	D.H.82A Tiger Moth	J. D. Iliffe	
G-ANHR	Auster 5	C. G. Winch	

Notes	Reg.	Type	Owner or Operator
	G-ANHS	Auster 4	C. E. Tyers
	G-ANHX	Auster 5D	D. J. Baker
	G-ANHZ	Auster 5	D. W. Pennell
	G-ANIE	Auster 5 (TW467)	S. A. Stibbard
	G-ANIJ	Auster 5D	Museum of Army Flying/Middle Wallop
	G-ANIS	Auster 5	J. Clarke-Cockburn
	G-ANJA	D.H.82A Tiger Moth (N9389)	J. J. Young
	G-ANJD	D.H.82A Tiger Moth	H. J. Jauncey/(stored)
	G-ANJK	D.H.82A Tiger Moth	A. D. Williams
	G-ANJV	Westland S-55 Srs 3 (VR-BET)★	British Rotorcraft Museum
	G-ANKK	D.H.82A Tiger Moth (T5854)	P. W. Crispe/Halfpenny Green
	G-ANKT	D.H.82A Tiger Moth (T6818)	Shuttleworth Trust/O. Warden
	G-ANKZ	D.H.82A Tiger Moth (N6466)	Fortune Services Ltd/Barton
	G-ANLD	D.H.82A Tiger Moth	D. P. Parks
	G-ANLH	D.H.82A Tiger Moth	The Aeroplane Co (Hamble) Ltd
	G-ANLS	D.H.82A Tiger Moth	P. A. Gliddon
	G-ANLW	W.B.1. Widgeon (MD497) ★	Helicopter Hire Ltd (stored)
	G-ANLX	D.H.82A Tiger Moth	B. J. Borsberry & ptnrs
	G-ANMO	D.H.82A Tiger Moth	E. Lay
	G-ANMY	D.H.82A Tiger Moth	D. J. Elliott
	G-ANMV	D.H.82A Tiger Moth (T7404)	J. W. Davy/Cardiff
	G-ANNK	D.H.82A Tiger Moth	P. J. Wilcox/Cranfield
	G-ANNN	D.H.82A Tiger Moth	T. Pate
	G-ANOA	Hiller UH-12A ★	Redhill Technical College
	G-ANOD	D.H.82A Tiger Moth	D. R. & M. Wood
	G-ANOH	D.H.82A Tiger Moth	D. H. Parkhouse & ptnrs/White Waltham
	G-ANOK	S.91 Safir ★	Strathallan Aircraft Collection
	G-ANOM	D.H.82A Tiger Moth	P. A. Colman
	G-ANON	D.H.82A Tiger Moth (T7909)	A. C. Mercer/Sherburn
	G-ANOO	D.H.82A Tiger Moth	T. J. Hartwell & ptnrs
	G-ANOR	D.H.82A Tiger Moth	G. A. Black & C. L. Keith-Lucas
	G-ANOV	D.H.104 Dove 6 ★	Museum of Flight/E. Fortune
	G-ANPK	D.H.82A Tiger Moth	The D. & P. Group
	G-ANPP	P.34A Proctor 3	C. P. A. & J. Jeffery
	G-ANRF	D.H.82A Tiger Moth	C. D. Cyster
	G-ANRM	D.H.82A Tiger Moth	R. J. Walker
	G-ANRN	D.H.82A Tiger Moth	J. J. V. Elwes
	G-ANRP	Auster 5 (TW439)	C. T. K. Lane
	G-ANRX	D.H.82A Tiger Moth ★	Mosquito Aircraft Museum
	G-ANSM	D.H.82A Tiger Moth	J. W. & A. J. Davy
	G-ANTE	D.H.82A Tiger Moth	T. I. Sutton & B. J. Champion/ Chester
	G-ANTK	Avro 685 York ★	Duxford Aviation Soc
	G-ANTS	D.H.82A Tiger Moth (N6532)	J. G. Green
	G-ANUO	D.H.114 Heron 2D	Topflight Aviation Ltd/Fairoaks
	G-ANUW	D.H.104 Dove 6 ★	Civil Aviation Authority/Stansted
	G-ANWB	D.H.C.1 Chipmunk 21	G. Briggs/Blackpool
	G-ANWO	M.14A Hawk Trainer 3 ★	P. A. Brook
	G-ANWX	J/5L Aiglet Trainer	Applied Fastenings & Components
	G-ANXB	D.H.114 Heron 1B ★	Newark Air Museum
	G-ANXC	J/5R Alpine	C. J. Repek & ptnrs
	G-ANXR	P.31C Proctor 4 (RM221)	L. H. Oakins/Biggin Hill
	G-ANYP	P.31C Proctor 4 (NP184) ★	Torbay Aircraft Museum
	G-ANZJ	P.31C Proctor 4 (NP303) ★	A. Hillyard
	G-ANZT	Thruxton Jackaroo ★	J. D. Illiffe (stored)
	G-ANZU	D.H.82A Tiger Moth	P. A. Jackson/Sibson
	G-ANZZ	D.H.82A Tiger Moth	IBC Transport Containers Ltd
	G-AOAA	D.H.82A Tiger Moth	Tiger Club Ltd/Redhill
	G-AOAR	P.31C Proctor 4 (NP181) ★	Historic Aircraft Preservation Soc
	G-AOBG	Somers-Kendall SK.1 ★	stored
	G-AOBH	D.H.82A Tiger Moth (T7997)	C. H. A. Bott
	G-AOBO	D.H.82A Tiger Moth	P. A. Brook
	G-AOBU	P.84 Jet Provost ★	Shuttleworth Trust/O. Warden
	G-AOBV	J/5P Autocar	P. E. Champney
	G-AOBX	D.H.82A Tiger Moth	M. Gibbs/Redhill
	G-AOCP	Auster 5 ★	C. Baker (stored)
	G-AOCR	Auster 5D	J. M. Edis
	G-AOCU	Auster 5	S. J. Ball/Leicester
	G-AODA	Westland S-55 Srs 3	Bristow Helicopters Ltd
	G-AODT	D.H.82A Tiger Moth	N. A. Brett & A. H. Warminger
	G-AOEH	Aeronca 7AC Champion	M. Weeks & ptnrs
	G-AOEI	D.H.82A Tiger Moth	C.F.G. Flying Ltd/Cambridge
	G-AOEL	D.H.82A Tiger Moth (N9510) ★	Museum of Flight/E. Fortune

Reg.	Type	Owner or Operator	Notes
G-AOES	D.H.82A Tiger Moth	A. Twemlow & G. A. Cordery/Redhill	
G-AOET	D.H.82A Tiger Moth	Glylynn Ltd	
G-AOEX	Thruxton Jackaroo	A. T. Christian	
G-AOFE	D.H.C.1 Chipmunk 22A	M. L. Sargeant	
G-AOFJ	Auster 5	Miss M. R. Innocent/Perth	
G-AOFM	J/5P Autocar	Micro Rent Aviation Ltd	
G-AOFS	J/5L Aiglet Trainer	J. K. Avis	
G-AOGA	M.75 Aries ★	Irish Aviation Museum *(stored)*	
G-AOGE	P.34A Proctor 3	N. I. Dalziel/Biggin Hill	
G-AOGI	D.H.82A Tiger Moth	W. J. Taylor	
G-AOGR	D.H.82A Tiger Moth	H. C. Adkins & E. Shipley/N. Denes	
G-AOGV	J/5R Alpine	ABH Aviation	
G-AOHL	V.802 Viscount ★	British Air Ferries (Cabin Trainer)/ Southend	
G-AOHM	V.802 Viscount	British Air Ferries *Viscount Sir George Edwards*/Southend	
G-AOHT	V.802 Viscount	British Air Ferries/Southend	
G-AOHZ	J/5P Autocar	M. R. Gibbons & G. W. Brown	
G-AOIL	D.H.82A Tiger Moth	J. O. Souch	
G-AOIM	D.H.82A Tiger Moth	R. M. Wade & F. J. Terry	
G-AOIR	Thruxton Jackaroo	Stevenage Flying Club/O. Warden	
G-AOIS	D.H.82A Tiger Moth	V. B. & R. G. Wheele/Shoreham	
G-AOIY	J/5G Autocar	P. E. Scott	
G-AOJC	V.802 Viscount ★	Wales Aircraft Museum/Cardiff	
G-AOJH	D.H.83C Fox Moth	J. S. Lewery/Bournemouth	
G-AOJJ	D.H.82A Tiger Moth (DF128)	E. Lay	
G-AOJK	D.H.82A Tiger Moth	L. J. Rice	
G-AOJT	D.H.106 Comet 1 ★	Mosquito Aircraft Museum	
G-AOKH	P.40 Prentice 1	J. F. Moore/Biggin Hill	
G-AOKL	P.40 Prentice 1 (VS610)	J. R. Batt/Southend	
G-AOKO	P.40 Prentice 1 ★	J. F. Coggins/Coventry	
G-AOKZ	P.40 Prentice 1 (VS623) ★	Midland Air Museum	
G-AOLK	P.40 Prentice 1	Hilton Aviation Ltd/Southend	
G-AOLU	P.40 Prentice 1 (VS356) ★	Scottish Aircraft Collection/Perth	
G-AORB	Cessna 170B	G. Lawry	
G-AORW	D.H.C.1 Chipmunk 22A	D. C. Budd/Netherthorpe	
G-AOSK	D.H.C.1 Chipmunk 22	A. M. S. Cullen	
G-AOSO	D.H.C.1 Chipmunk 22	Aviation Advisory Services Ltd/ Stapleford	
G-AOSU	D.H.C.1 Chipmunk 22 (Lycoming)	RAFGSA/Bicester	
G-AOSY	D.H.C.1 Chipmunk 22	Fletcher Aviation Ltd	
G-AOSZ	D.H.C.1 Chipmunk 22A	J. Dempsey	
G-AOTD	D.H.C.1 Chipmunk 22 (WB588)	Shuttleworth Trust/O. Warden	
G-AOTF	D.H.C.1 Chipmunk 23 (Lycoming)	RAFGSA/Bicester	
G-AOTI	D.H.114 Heron 2D	Topflight Aviation Ltd/Fairoaks	
G-AOTK	D.53 Turbi	The T. K. Flying Group/Hatfield	
G-AOTR	D.H.C.1 Chipmunk 22	P. W. B. & M. A. R. Spearing	
G-AOTY	D.H.C.1 Chipmunk 22A	West London Aero Services Ltd/ White Waltham	
G-AOUJ	Fairey Ultra-Light ★	British Rotorcraft Museum	
G-AOUO	D.H.C.1 Chipmunk 22 (Lycoming)	RAFGSA/Bicester	
G-AOUP	D.H.C.1 Chipmunk 22	Wessex Flying Group	
G-AOUR	D.H.82A Tiger Moth ★	Ulster Folk & Transport Museum	
G-AOVF	B.175 Britannia 312F ★	Aerospace Museum/Cosford	
G-AOVT	B.175 Britannia 312F ★	Duxford Aviation Soc	
G-AOVW	Auster 5	B. Marriott/Cranwell	
G-AOXG	D.H.82A Tiger Moth (XL717)	FAA Museum/Yeovilton	
G-AOXN	D.H.82A Tiger Moth	S. L. G. Darch	
G-AOYG	V.806 Viscount	British Air Ferries/Virgin Atlantic	
G-AOYL	V.806 Viscount	British Air Ferries *Viscount Churchill*/ Southend	
G-AOYN	V.806 Viscount	British Air Ferries *Viscount Jersey*/ Southend	
G-AOYP	V.806 Viscount	British Air Ferries	
G-AOYR	V.806 Viscount	British Air Ferries *Viscount Gatwick*/ Southend	
G-AOZB	D.H.82A Tiger Moth	Structure Flex Ltd/Redhill	
G-AOZH	D.H.82A Tiger Moth (K2572)	V. B. & R. G. Wheele/Shoreham	
G-AOZL	J/5Q Alpine	E. A. Taylor/Southend	
G-AOZP	D.H.C.1 Chipmunk 22	M. E. Darlington	
G-APAA	J/5R Alpine ★	L. A. Groves *(stored)*	

Notes	Reg.	Type	Owner or Operator
	G-APAH	Auster 5	Executive Flying Services Ltd
	G-APAL	D.H.82A Tiger Moth (N6847)	L. H. Smith & D. S. Chapman
	G-APAM	D.H.82A Tiger Moth	R. P. Williams
	G-APAO	D.H.82A Tiger Moth	C. K. Irvine
	G-APAP	D.H.82A Tiger Moth	R. A. Slade
	G-APAS	D.H.106 Comet 1XB ★	Aerospace Museum/Cosford
	G-APBD	PA-23 Apache 160 ★	E. A. Clack & T. Pritchard (stored)
	G-APBE	Auster 5	G. W. Clark/O. Warden
	G-APBI	D.H.82A Tiger Moth (EM903)	R. Devaney & ptnrs/Audley End
	G-APBO	D.53 Turbi	H. C. Cox
	G-APBW	Auster 5	N. Huxtable
	G-APCB	J/5Q Alpine	M. J. Wilson/Redhill
	G-APCC	D.H.82A Tiger Moth	L. J. Rice/Henstridge
	G-APDB	D.H.106 Comet 4 ★	Duxford Aviation Soc
	G-APDT	D.H.106 Comet 4 ★	Fire School/Heathrow
	G-APEG	V.953C Merchantman	Air Bridge Carriers Ltd/E. Midlands
	G-APEJ	V.953C Merchantman	Air Bridge Carriers Ltd/E. Midlands
	G-APEK	V.953C Merchantman	Air Bridge Carriers Ltd Dreadnought/ E. Midlands
	G-APEM	V.953C Merchantman	Elan International Ltd Agamemnon/ E. Midlands
	G-APEP	V.953C Merchantman	Air Bridge Carriers Ltd/E. Midlands
	G-APES	V.953C Merchantman	Air Bridge Carriers Ltd Swiftsure (withdrawn)/E. Midlands
	G-APET	V.953C Merchantman	Air Bridge Carriers Ltd Temeraire/ E. Midlands
	G-APEY	V.806 Viscount	British Air Ferries/Virgin Atlantic Dublin Lady
	G-APFA	D.54 Turbi	A. Eastelow & F. J. Keitch/Dunkeswell
	G-APFG	Boeing 707-436 ★	Instructional airframe/Stansted
	G-APFJ	Boeing 707-436 ★	Aerospace Museum/Cosford
	G-APFU	D.H.82A Tiger Moth	J. W. & A. R. Davy/Carlisle
	G-APGM	D.H.82A Tiger Moth	H. A. N. Orde-Powlett
	G-APHV	Avro 19 Srs 2 (VM360) ★	Museum of Flight/E. Fortune
	G-APIE	Tipsy Belfair B	P. A. Smith
	G-APIG	D.H.82A Tiger Moth	A. M. Handley
	G-APIH	D.H.82A Tiger Moth (R5086)	A. J. Ditheridge
	G-APIK	J/1N Alpha	T. D. Howe/Redhill
	G-APIM	V.806 Viscount	British Air Ferries Viscount Stephen Piercey/Southend
	G-APIT	P.40 Prentice 1 (VR192) ★	WWII Aircraft Preservation Soc/Lasham
	G-APIU	P.40 Prentice 1 ★	J. F. Coggins/Coventry
	G-APIY	P.40 Prentice 1 (VR249) ★	Newark Air Museum
	G-APIZ	D.31 Turbulent	M. J. Abbott
	G-APJB	P.40 Prentice 1 ★	City Airways/Coventry
	G-APJJ	Fairey Ultra-light ★	Midland Aircraft Preservation Soc
	G-APJO	D.H.82A Tiger Moth	D. R. & Mrs M. Wood
	G-APKH	D.H.85 Leopard Moth	P. Franklin (G-ACGS)
	G-APKN	J/1N Alpha	Felthorpe Auster Group
	G-APKY	Hiller UH-12B	D. A. George
	G-APLG	J/5L Aiglet Trainer	G. R. W. Brown
	G-APLO	D.H.C.1 Chipmunk 22A (WD379)	Channel Islands Aero Holdings Ltd
	G-APMB	D.H.106 Comet 4B ★	Gatwick Handling Ltd (ground trainer)
	G-APMH	J/1U Workmaster	R. E. Neal & E. R. Stevens
	G-APML	Dakota 6	Air Atlantique Ltd
	G-APMM	D.H.82A Tiger Moth (K2568)	R. K. J. Hadlow
	G-APMX	D.H.82A Tiger Moth	For rebuild
	G-APMY	PA-23 Apache 160 ★	Kelsterton College (instructional airframe)/Deeside
	G-APNJ	Cessna 310 ★	Chelsea College/Shoreham
	G-APNS	Garland-Bianchi Linnet	Paul Penn-Sayers Model Services Ltd
	G-APNT	Currie Wot	R. A. Bowes
	G-APNZ	D.31 Turbulent	Tiger Club Ltd/Redhill
	G-APOA	J/1N Alpha	Bristow Helicopters Ltd
	G-APOD	Tipsy Belfair	L. F. Potts
	G-APOI	Saro Skeeter Srs 8	F. F. Chamberlain/Inverness
	G-APOL	D.36 Turbulent	T. A. S. Rayner
	G-APPL	P.40 Prentice 1	Miss S. J. Saggers/Biggin Hill
	G-APPM	D.H.C.1 Chipmunk 22	J. D. Frankel
	G-APRF	Auster 5	R. Giles & ptnrs/Clacton
	G-APRJ	Avro 694 Lincoln B.2 ★	Aces High Ltd/North Weald
	G-APRL	AW.650 Argosy 101 ★	Midland Air Museum
	G-APRR	Super Aero 45 (A1+BT)	M. C. Searle/Elstree
	G-APSA	Douglas DC-6A	Instone Air Line Ltd/Coventry

Reg.	Type	Owner or Operator	Notes
G-APSO	D.H.104 Dove 5 ★	*Stored*/Shobdon	
G-APSR	J/1U Workmaster	D. & K. Aero Services Ltd/Shobdon	
G-APSZ	Cessna 172	M. J. Butler & ptnrs/Barton	
G-APTH	Agusta-Bell 47J	R. Windley	
G-APTP	PA-22 Tri-Pacer 150	A. J. Corr	
G-APTR	J/1N Alpha	C. J. & D. J. Baker	
G-APTS	D.H.C.1 Chipmunk 22A	Wycombe Air Centre Ltd	
G-APTU	Auster 5	Tango Uniform Group/Leicester	
G-APTW	W.B.1 Widgeon ★	Cornwall Aero Park/Helston	
G-APTY	Beech G.35 Bonanza	G. E. Brennand & J. M. Fish	
G-APTZ	D.31 Turbulent	H. W. Raith/Wick	
G-APUD	Bensen B.7M (modified) ★	Manchester Air & Space Museum	
G-APUE	L-40 Meta Sokol	S. E. & M. J. Aherne	
G-APUK	J/1 Autocrat	P. L. Morley	
G-APUP	Sopwith Pup (N5182) (replica)★	RAF Museum	
G-APUR	PA-22 Tri-Pacer 160	G. A. Allen & ptnrs	
G-APUW	J/5V-160 Autocar	Anglia Auster Syndicate	
G-APUY	D.31 Turbulent	C. Jones & ptnrs/Barton	
G-APUZ	PA-24 Comanche 250	S. D. Quigley	
G-APVF	Putzer Elster B	K. P. Rusling	
G-APVG	J/5L Aiglet Trainer	Cranfield Institute of Technology	
G-APVN	D.31 Turbulent	R. Sherwin/Shoreham	
G-APVS	Cessna 170B	N. Simpson	
G-APVU	L-40 Meta-Sokol	D. Kirk	
G-APVV	Mooney M-20A	Telcom Associates/Barton	
G-APVW	Beech A35 Bonanza	R. A. O'Neill	
G-APVY	PA-25 Pawnee 150	KK Aviation	
G-APVZ	D.31 Turbulent	A. F. Bullock/Staverton	
G-APWJ	HPR-7 Herald 201 ★	Duxford Aviation Soc	
G-APWN	WS-55 Whirlwind 3 ★	Midland Air Museum	
G-APWR	PA-22 Tri-Pacer 160	Airads/Goodwood	
G-APWY	Piaggio P.166 ★	Science Museum/Wroughton	
G-APWZ	EP.9 Prospector ★	Museum of Army Flying/Middle Wallop	
G-APXJ	PA-24 Comanche 250	T. Wildsmith/Netherthorpe	
G-APXR	PA-22 Tri-Pacer 160	A. Troughton	
G-APXT	PA-22 Tri-Pacer 150	J. W. & I. Daniels	
G-APXU	PA-22 Tri-Pacer 125	C. G. Stone/Biggin Hill	
G-APXW	EP.9 Prospector ★	Museum of Army Flying/Middle Wallop	
G-APXX	D.H.A.3 Drover 2 (VH-FDT) ★	WWII Aircraft Preservation Soc/ Lasham	
G-APXY	Cessna 150	Merlin Flying Club Ltd/Hucknall	
G-APYB	T.66 Nipper 2	B. O. Smith	
G-APYD	D.H.106 Comet 4B ★	Science Museum/Wroughton	
G-APYG	D.H.C.1 Chipmunk 22	E. J. I. Musty & P. A. Colman	
G-APYI	PA-22 Tri-Pacer 135	G. K. Hare	
G-APYN	PA-22 Tri-Pacer 160	W. D. Stephens	
G-APYT	7FC Tri-Traveller	R. W. Brown	
G-APYU	7FC Tri-Traveller	K. Collins (*stored*)	
G-APYW	PA-22 Tri-Pacer 150	Fiddian Ltd	
G-APZG	PA-24 Comanche 250	Jewelbarron Ltd/Goodwood	
G-APZJ	PA-18 Super Cub 150	Southern Sailplanes	
G-APZK	PA-18 Super Cub 95	W. T. Knapton	
G-APZL	PA-22 Tri-Pacer 160	M. R. Coward & R. T. Evans	
G-APZR	Cessna 150 ★	*Engine test-bed*/Biggin Hill	
G-APZS	Cessna 175A	G. A. Nash/Booker	
G-APZU	D.H.104 Dove 6	RSA Parachute Club Ltd (*stored*)/Exeter	
G-APZX	PA-22 Tri-Pacer 150	L. A. Thompson/Sywell	
G-ARAM	PA-18 Super Cub 150	I. M. & D. S. Morgan	
G-ARAN	PA-18 Super Cub 150	A. P. Docherty/Kidlington	
G-ARAO	PA-18 Super Cub 95	G. Ashmore & ptnrs	
G-ARAP	7EC Traveller ★	P. J. Heron	
G-ARAS	7EC Tri-Traveller	I. D. Daniels	
G-ARAT	Cessna 180C	R. E. Styles & ptnrs	
G-ARAU	Cessna 150	S. Lynn/Sibson	
G-ARAW	Cessna 182C Skylane	P. Channon	
G-ARAX	PA-22 Tri-Pacer 150	P. Fabish	
G-ARAY	H.S.748 Srs 1	Dan-Air Services Ltd/Gatwick	
G-ARAZ	D.H.82A Tiger Moth (R4959)	M. V. Gauntlett/Goodwood	
G-ARBE	D.H.104 Dove 8	A. Freeman	
G-ARBG	T.66 Nipper 2	Felthorpe Tipsy Group	
G-ARBN	PA-23 Apache 160	H. Norden & H. J. Liggins	
G-ARBO	PA-24 Comanche 250	D. M. Harbottle/Blackpool	
G-ARBP	T.66 Nipper 2	A. Cambridge & D. B. Winstanley	

Notes	Reg.	Type	Owner or Operator
	G-ARBS	PA-22 Tri-Pacer 160	T. R. G. Barney & M. A. Sherry/Redhill
	G-ARBV	PA-22 Tri-Pacer 150	P. J. Kember
	G-ARBZ	D.31 Turbulent	D. G. H. Hilliard/Bodmin
	G-ARCC	PA-22 Tri-Pacer 150	RFC Flying Group/Popham
	G-ARCF	PA-22 Tri-Pacer 150	A. L. Scadding (stored)
	G-ARCH	Cessna 310D ★	Instructional airframe/Perth
	G-ARCI	Cessna 310D	Sandtoft Air Services Ltd
	G-ARCS	Auster D6/180	E. A. Matty/Shobdon
	G-ARCT	PA-18 Super Cub 95	M. Kirk
	G-ARCV	Cessna 175A	Michael Gardner Ltd
	G-ARCW	PA-23 Apache 160	E. M. Brain & R. Chew/St Just
	G-ARCX	AW Meteor 14 ★	Museum of Flight/E. Fortune
	G-ARDB	PA-24 Comanche 250	R. A. Sareen/Booker
	G-ARDD	CP.301C1 Emeraude	F. P. L. Clauson & C. V. Samuel
	G-ARDE	D.H.104 Dove 6	R. J. H. Small/Cranfield
	G-ARDG	EP.9 Prospector ★	Museum of Army Flying/Middle Wallop
	G-ARDJ	Auster D.6/180	RN Aviation (Leicester Airport) Ltd
	G-ARDO	Jodel D.112	P. J. H. McCraig
	G-ARDP	PA-22 Tri-Pacer 150	G. M. Jones
	G-ARDS	PA-22 Caribbean 150	D. V. Asher/Leicester
	G-ARDT	PA-22 Tri-Pacer 160	A. A. Whiter
	G-ARDV	PA-22 Tri-Pacer 160	B. & J. Hillman
	G-ARDY	T.66 Nipper 2	M. T. Groves
	G-ARDZ	Jodel D.140A	G. K. & C. J. Verser
	G-AREA	D.H.104 Dove 8	British Aerospace/Hatfield
	G-AREB	Cessna 175B Skylark	R. J. Postlethwaite & ptnrs/Wellesbourne
	G-AREE	PA-23 Aztec 250	W. C. C. Meyer/Biggin Hill
	G-AREF	PA-23 Aztec 250 ★	Southall College of Technology
	G-AREH	D.H.82A Tiger Moth	T. Pate
	G-AREI	Auster 3 (MT438)	R. Alliker & ptnrs/Bodmin
	G-AREJ	Beech 95 Travel Air	D. Huggett/Stapleford
	G-AREL	PA-22 Caribbean 150	H. H. Cousins/Fenland
	G-AREO	PA-18 Super Cub 150	Lasham Gliding Soc Ltd
	G-ARET	PA-22 Tri-Pacer 160	P. & V. Slatterey
	G-AREV	PA-22 Tri-Pacer 160	Spatrek Ltd/Barton
	G-AREX	Aeronca 15AC Sedan	R. J. Middleton-Turnbull & P. Lowndes
	G-AREZ	D.31 Turbulent	J. St. Clair-Quentin/Shobdon
	G-ARFB	PA-22 Caribbean 150	C. T. Woodward & ptnrs
	G-ARFD	PA-22 Tri-Pacer 160	G. Cormack/Glasgow
	G-ARFG	Cessna 175A Skylark	C. S. & Mrs B. A. Frost/Panshanger
	G-ARFH	Forney F-1A Aircoupe	R. A. Nesbitt-Dufort
	G-ARFH	PA-24 Comanche 250	L. M. Walton
	G-ARFL	Cessna 175B Skylark	R. T. L. Arkell
	G-ARFN	Cessna 150A ★	Instructional airframe/Perth
	G-ARFO	Cessna 150A	Moray Flying Club Ltd
	G-ARFT	Jodel DR. 1050	R. Shaw
	G-ARFV	T.66 Nipper 2	C. G. Stone/Biggin Hill
	G-ARGB	Auster 6A ★	C. Baker (stored)
	G-ARGG	D.H.C.1 Chipmunk 22	B. Hook
	G-ARGO	PA-22 Colt 108	B. E. Goodman/Liverpool
	G-ARGV	PA-18 Super Cub 150	Deeside Gliding Club (Aberdeenshire) Ltd/Aboyne
	G-ARGZ	D.31 Turbulent	A. N. Burgin/Rochester
	G-ARHC	Forney F-1A Aircoupe	A. P. Gardner/Elstree
	G-ARHF	Forney F-1A Aircoupe	R. A. Nesbitt-Dufort
	G-ARHI	PA-24 Comanche 180	W. H. Entress/Swansea
	G-ARHL	PA-23 Aztec 250	J. J. Freeman & Co Ltd/Headcorn
	G-ARHM	Auster 6A	D. Hollowell & ptnrs/Finmere
	G-ARHN	PA-22 Caribbean 150	D. B. Furniss & A. Munro/Doncaster
	G-ARHP	PA-22 Tri-Pacer 160	W. Wardle
	G-ARHR	PA-22 Caribbean 150	J. A. Hargraves/Fairoaks
	G-ARHT	PA-22 Caribbean 150 ★	Moston Technical College
	G-ARHU	PA-22 Tri-Pacer 160	N. Kirk & ptnrs
	G-ARHW	D.H.104 Dove 8	Davis, Gibson Advertising Ltd
	G-ARHZ	D.62 Condor	C. G. Jarvis/Andrewsfield
	G-ARIA	Bell 47G ★	Museum of Army Flying/Middle Wallop
	G-ARID	Cessna 172B	L. A. Buckley & ptnrs/Leeds
	G-ARIE	PA-24 Comanche 250	W. Radwanski (stored)/Coventry
	G-ARIF	Orde-Hume O-H.7 Minor Coupe	A. W. J. G. Orde-Hume
	G-ARIH	Auster 6A (TW591)	R. Larder
	G-ARIK	PA-22 Caribbean 150	C. J. Berry
	G-ARIL	PA-22 Caribbean 150	G. N. Richardson Motors/Shobdon

Reg.	Type	Owner or Operator	Notes
G-ARIN	PA-24 Comanche 250	S. J. Savage	
G-ARIV	Cessna 172B	C. Taylor & ptnrs	
G-ARIW	CP.301B Emeraude	CJM Flying Group/Wellesbourne	
G-ARJB	D.H.104 Dove 8 ★	J. C. Bamford (stored)	
G-ARJE	PA-22 Colt 108	J. Souch	
G-ARJF	PA-22 Colt 108	M. J. Collins	
G-ARJH	PA-22 Colt 108	M. M. Wallis & T. A. Hodges	
G-ARJR	PA-23 Apache 160 ★	Instructional airframe/Kidlington	
G-ARJS	PA-23 Apache 160	Bencray Ltd/Blackpool	
G-ARJT	PA-23 Apache 160	Hiveland Ltd	
G-ARJU	PA-23 Apache 160	Chantaco Ltd/Biggin Hill	
G-ARJV	PA-23 Apache 160	Smart Estates Ltd/Bristol	
G-ARJW	PA-23 Apache 160	Gordon King (Aviation) Ltd/Biggin Hill	
G-ARJZ	D.31 Turbulent	N. H. Jones	
G-ARKG	J/5G Autocar	M. M. James & C. M. G. Ellis	
G-ARKJ	Beech N35 Bonanza	T. Hasleden	
G-ARKK	PA-22 Colt 108	A. W. Baxter/Tollerton	
G-ARKM	PA-22 Colt 108	L. E. Usher	
G-ARKN	PA-22 Colt 108	J. H. Underwood & A. J. F. Tabenor	
G-ARKP	PA-22 Colt 108	C. J. & J. Freeman/Headcorn	
G-ARKR	PA-22 Colt 108	D. J. Nethersole	
G-ARKS	PA-22 Colt 108	J. Dickenson	
G-ARLD	H-395 Super Courier	Active Airsports Ltd	
G-ARLG	Auster D.4/108	Auster D4 Group	
G-ARLK	PA-24 Comanche 250	M. Walker & C. Robinson	
G-ARLO	A.61 Terrier 1 ★	stored	
G-ARLP	A.61 Terrier 1	T. L. Gray & ptnrs	
G-ARLR	A.61 Terrier 2	A. Kennedy & D. Delaney	
G-ARLU	Cessna 172B Skyhawk ★	Instructional airframe/Irish AC	
G-ARLV	Cessna 172B Skyhawk	P. D. Lowdon	
G-ARLW	Cessna 172B Skyhawk	S. Lancashire Flyers Ltd/Barton	
G-ARLX	Jodel D.140B	Shipping & Airlines Ltd/Biggin Hill	
G-ARLY	J/5P Autocar	P. J. Elliott & G. Green/Leicester	
G-ARLZ	D.31A Turbulent	R. S. Hatwell	
G-ARMA	PA-23 Apache 160 ★	Instructional airframe/Kidlington	
G-ARMB	D.H.C.1 Chipmunk 22A (WB660)	P. A. Layzell/Goodwood	
G-ARMC	D.H.C.1 Chipmunk 22A	W. London Aero Services Ltd/ White Waltham	
G-ARMD	D.H.C.1 Chipmunk 22A ★	K. & L. Aero Services (stored)	
G-ARMG	D.H.C.1 Chipmunk 22A	Chipmunk Preservation Group Ltd/ Wellesbourne	
G-ARMI	PA-23 Apache 160 ★	Stapleford Flying Club Ltd	
G-ARML	Cessna 175B Skylark	R. C. Convine	
G-ARMN	Cessna 175B Skylark ★	Southall College of Technology	
G-ARMO	Cessna 172B Skyhawk	Sangria Designs Ltd & BRM Plastics Ltd/Booker	
G-ARMP	Cessna 172B	Ryders Express Services Ltd/ Birmingham	
G-ARMR	Cessna 172B Skyhawk	G. Burns & ptnrs	
G-ARMZ	D.31 Turbulent	A. J. Cooke	
G-ARNA	Mooney M.20B	R. Travers/Blackpool	
G-ARNB	J/5G Autocar	M. T. Jeffrey	
G-ARND	PA-22 Colt 108	A. M. & D. Fitton/Barton	
G-ARNE	PA-22 Colt 108	T. D. L. Bowden/Shipdham	
G-ARNI	PA-22 Colt 108	H. D. Batchelor	
G-ARNJ	PA-22 Colt 108	MKM Flying Group/Leavesden	
G-ARNK	PA-22 Colt 108	A. R. Cameron	
G-ARNL	PA-22 Colt 108	J. A. & J. A. Dodsworth/White Waltham	
G-ARNO	A.61 Terrier 1	M. B. Hill	
G-ARNP	A.109 Airedale	P. A. Gunn	
G-ARNY	Jodel D.117	D. J. Lockett	
G-ARNZ	D.31 Turbulent	P. L. Cox & ptnrs	
G-AROA	Cessna 172B Skyhawk	D. E. Partridge/Andrewsfield	
G-AROD	Cessna 175B	Medical Co Hospital Supplies Ltd	
G-AROE	Aero 145	Gooney Bird Aviation Ltd	
G-AROF	L.40 Meta-Sokol	B. G. Barber	
G-AROJ	A.109 Airedale ★	D. J. Shaw (stored)	
G-AROM	PA-22 Colt 108	G. J. Romanes	
G-ARON	PA-22 Colt 108	R. W. Curtis	
G-AROO	Forney F-1A Aircoupe	W. J. McMeekan/Newtownards	
G-AROW	Jodel D.140B	Kent Gliding Club Ltd/Challock	
G-AROY	Stearman A.75N.1	W. A. Jordan	
G-ARPD	H.S.121 Trident 1C ★	CAA Fire School/Teesside	
G-ARPH	H.S.121 Trident 1C ★	Aerospace Museum, Cosford	

Notes	Reg.	Type	Owner or Operator
	G-ARPK	H.S.121 Trident 1C ★	Manchester Airport Authority
	G-ARPL	H.S.121 Trident 1C ★	British Airports Authority/Edinburgh
	G-ARPN	H.S.121 Trident 1C ★	British Airports Authority/Aberdeen
	G-ARPO	H.S.121 Trident 1C ★	CAA Fire School/Teesside
	G-ARPP	H.S.121 Trident 1C ★	British Airports Authority/Glasgow
	G-ARPR	H.S.121 Trident 1C ★	CAA Fire School/Teesside
	G-ARPW	H.S.121 Trident 1C ★	CAA Fire School/Teesside
	G-ARPX	H.S.121 Trident 1C ★	Airwork Services Ltd/Perth
	G-ARPZ	H.S.121 Trident 1C ★	RFD Ltd/Dunsfold
	G-ARRE	Jodel DR.1050	S. J. Pugh & M. Ridsdale
	G-ARRF	Cessna 150A	A. W. Humphries/Bodmin
	G-ARRI	Cessna 175B Skylark	C. L. Thomas
	G-ARRL	J/1N Alpha	G. N. Smith & C. Webb
	G-ARRM	Beagle B.206-X ★	Shoreham Airport Museum
	G-ARRP	PA-28 Cherokee 160	M. J. Flynn/Cardiff
	G-ARRS	CP.301A Emeraude	E. H. Booker/Sibson
	G-ARRT	Wallis WA-116-1	K. H. Wallis
	G-ARRU	D.31 Turbulent	J. R. Edwards & D. D. Smith
	G-ARRY	Jodel D.140B	A. J. E. Ditheridge
	G-ARRZ	D.31 Turbulent	R. J. Grimstead/Redhill
	G-ARSB	Cessna 150A	B. T. White/Andrewsfield
	G-ARSG	Roe Triplane Type IV replica	Shuttleworth Trust/O. Warden
	G-ARSJ	CP.301-C2 Emeraude	J. R. Ware
	G-ARSL	A.61 Terrier 2	R. A. Hutchinson & P. T. M. Hardy
	G-ARSP	L.40 Meta-Sokol	Classic Aeroplane Ltd/Staverton
	G-ARSU	PA-22 Colt 108	P. C. Riggs
	G-ARSW	PA-22 Colt 108	R. W. Rushton & ptnrs
	G-ARSX	PA-22 Tri-Pacer 160	M. J. Blanchard
	G-ARTD	PA-23 Apache 160	Dr. D. A. Jones
	G-ARTF	D.31 Turbulent	J. R. D. Bygraves/O. Warden
	G-ARTG	Hiller UH-12C ★	White Hart Inn/Stockbridge
	G-ARTH	PA-12 Super Cruiser	A. Horsfall
	G-ARTJ	Bensen B.8 ★	Museum of Flight/E. Fortune
	G-ARTL	D.H.82A Tiger Moth (T7281)	P. A. Jackson
	G-ARTT	M.S.880B Rallye Club	R. N. Scott
	G-ARTW	Cessna 150B ★	*Instructional airframe*/Perth
	G-ARTX	Cessna 150B ★	*Instructional airframe*/Perth
	G-ARTY	Cessna 150B ★	*Instructional airframe*/Perth
	G-ARTZ	McCandless M.4 Gyrocopter	W. E. Partridge (*stored*)
	G-ARUG	J/5G Autocar	J. Cantellow & D. Hulme/Biggin Hill
	G-ARUH	Jodel DR.1050	PFA Group/Denham
	G-ARUI	A.61 Terrier	Crossford Hotels (Dunfermline) Ltd
	G-ARUL	Cosmic Wind	P. G. Kynsey/Redhill
	G-ARUO	PA-24 Comanche 180	Uniform Oscar Group/Elstree
	G-ARUR	PA-28 Cherokee 160	The G-ARUR Group/Redhill
	G-ARUV	CP.301A Emeraude	J. Tanswell
	G-ARUY	J/1N Alpha	D. L. Webley
	G-ARUZ	Cessna 175C Skylark	J. E. Sansome & J. T. Gout/Luton
	G-ARVF	V.1101 VC10 ★	Hermeskeil Museum (nr Trier)/ W. Germany
	G-ARVM	V.1101 VC10 ★	Aerospace Museum/Cosford
	G-ARVO	PA-18 Super Cub 95	Mona Aviation Ltd
	G-ARVS	PA-28 Cherokee 160	Skyscraper Ltd/Stapleford
	G-ARVT	PA-28 Cherokee 160	C. R. Knapton
	G-ARVU	PA-28 Cherokee 160	G. R. Outwin & ptnrs/Doncaster
	G-ARVV	PA-28 Cherokee 160	G. E. Hopkins
	G-ARVW	PA-28 Cherokee 160	R. W. L. Norman/Southend
	G-ARVZ	D.62B Condor	C. Watson & W. H. Cole/Redhill
	G-ARWB	D.H.C.1 Chipmunk 200	Pulsegrove Ltd/Shoreham
	G-ARWC	Cessna 150B	Worldwide Wheels Ltd/Biggin Hill
	G-ARWH	Cessna 172C Skyhawk ★	Pizza Express, Golders Green Rd
	G-ARWM	Cessna 175C	J. Taylor
	G-ARWO	Cessna 172C Skyhawk	A. Philip & ptnrs/Bodmin
	G-ARWR	Cessna 172C Skyhawk	The Devanha Flying Group Ltd
	G-ARWS	Cessna 175C Skylark	E. N. Skinner
	G-ARWW	Bensen B.8M	B. McIntyre
	G-ARXD	A.109 Airedale	D. Howden
	G-ARXF	PA-23 Aztec 250B	Weendy Aviation (UK)
	G-ARXG	PA-24 Comanche 250	I. M. Callier
	G-ARXH	Bell 47G	A. B. Searle
	G-ARXN	T.66 Nipper 2	Griffon Flying Group/Hucknall
	G-ARXP	Luton LA-4A Minor	W. C. Hymas
	G-ARXT	Jodel DR.1050	T. P. Jenkinson & K. Ambrose-Hunt/ Elstree

Reg.	Type	Owner or Operator	Notes
G-ARXU	Auster 6A	Bath & Wilts Gliding Club Ltd	
G-ARXW	M.S.885 Super Rallye	M. A. Jones	
G-ARXX	M.S.880B Rallye Club	M. S. Bird	
G-ARYB	H.S.125 Srs 1★	British Aerospace PLC/Hatfield	
G-ARYC	H.S.125 Srs 1★	The Mosquito Aircraft Museum	
G-ARYD	Auster AOP.6 (WJ358) ★	Museum of Army Flying/Middle Wallop	
G-ARYF	PA-23 Aztec 250	I. J. T. Branson/Biggin Hill	
G-ARYH	PA-22 Tri-Pacer 160	Filtration (Water Treatment Engineers) Ltd	
G-ARYI	Cessna 172C	Michael Gardner Ltd	
G-ARYK	Cessna 172C	D. C. Barker/Sandown	
G-ARYR	PA-28 Cherokee 180	M. L. Allford/Kidlington	
G-ARYS	Cessna 172C Skyhawk	P. H. Preston & ptnrs/Birmingham	
G-ARYV	PA-24 Comanche 250	P. Meeson	
G-ARYZ	A.109 Airedale	J. D. Reid	
G-ARZA	Wallis WA-116 Srs 1	N. D. Z. de Ferranti	
G-ARZB	Wallis WA-116 Srs 1	K. H. Wallis	
G-ARZE	Cessna 172C ★	Parachute jump trainer/Cockermouth	
G-ARZF	Cessna 150B	M. M. James	
G-ARZM	D.31 Turbulent	Tiger Club Ltd/Redhill	
G-ARZN	Beech N35 Bonanza	Beech Aircraft Ltd/Elstree	
G-ARZP	A.109 Airedale	G. B. O'Neill/(stored)/Booker	
G-ARZW	Currie Wot	J. H. Blake	
G-ARZX	Cessna 150B	M. D. Corbett	
G-ASAA	Luton LA-4A Minor	D. F. Lingard	
G-ASAI	A.109 Airedale ★	A. C. Watt	
G-ASAJ	A.61 Terrier 2 (WE569)	S. J. B. White & V. M. Howard	
G-ASAK	A.61 Terrier 2	Rochford Hundred Flying Group/Southend	
G-ASAL	SAL Bulldog 120	British Aerospace/Prestwick	
G-ASAM	D.31 Turbulent	Tiger Club Ltd/Redhill	
G-ASAN	A.61 Terrier 2	D. R. Godfrey	
G-ASAT	M.S.880B Rallye Club	A. Noble	
G-ASAU	M.S.880B Rallye Club	W. J. Armstrong	
G-ASAV	M.S.880B Rallye Club	A. L. Averill & ptnrs	
G-ASAX	A.61 Terrier 2	G. Strathdee	
G-ASBA	Currie Wot	M. A. Kaye	
G-ASBB	Beech 23 Musketeer	D. Silver/Southend	
G-ASBH	A.109 Airedale	D. T. Smollett	
G-ASBY	A.109 Airedale	M. J. Barnett & ptnrs	
G-ASCC	Beagle E.3 AOP Mk 11	G. G. L. Janes	
G-ASCM	Isaacs Fury II (K2050)	D. Calabritto	
G-ASCU	PA-18A-150 Super Cub	Farm Aviation Services Ltd	
G-ASCZ	CP.310A Emeraude	Hylton Flying Group/Newcastle	
G-ASDA	Beech 65-80 Queen Air	Parker & Heard Ltd/Biggin Hill	
G-ASDF	Edwards Gyrocopter ★	B. King	
G-ASDK	A.61 Terrier 2	M. L. Rose	
G-ASDL	A.61 Terrier 2	T. J. Rilley & C. E. Mason	
G-ASDO	Beech 95-A55 Baron ★	No 2498 Sqn ATC/Jersey	
G-ASDY	Wallis WA-116/F	K. H. Wallis	
G-ASEA	Luton LA-4A Minor	C. W. N. Huke	
G-ASEB	Luton LA-4A Minor	S. R. P. Harper	
G-ASEG	A.61 Terrier	J. A. Stott	
G-ASEO	PA-24 Comanche 250	Planetalk Ltd	
G-ASEP	PA-23 Apache 235	Arrowstate Ltd/Denham	
G-ASEU	D.62A Condor	W. Grant & D. McNicholl	
G-ASEV	PA-23 Aztec 250	Selexpress Ltd	
G-ASFA	Cessna 172D	The Dakota Flying Club/Cranfield	
G-ASFD	L-200A Morava	M. Emery/Shoreham	
G-ASFK	J/5G Autocar	D. N. K. & M. A. Symon/Aberdeen	
G-ASFL	PA-28 Cherokee 180	E. W. Pinchbeck & D. F. Ranger/Popham	
G-ASFR	Bo.208A1 Junior	S. T. Dauncey	
G-ASFX	D.31 Turbulent	E. F. Clapham & W. B. S. Dobie	
G-ASGC	V.1151 Super VC10 ★	Imperial War Museum/Duxford	
G-ASHA	Cessna F.172D	R. Soar & ptnrs	
G-ASHB	Cessna 182F	Lincoln Parachute Centre Ltd/Sturgate	
G-ASHD	Brantly B-2A ★	British Rotorcraft Museum/Weston	
G-ASHH	PA-23 Aztec 250	Leicestershire Thread & Trimming Manufacturers Ltd	
G-ASHS	Stampe SV-4B	L. W. Gruber & ptnrs/Goodwood	
G-ASHT	D.31 Turbulent	J. T. Taylor	
G-ASHU	PA-15 Vagabond	G. J. Romanes	
G-ASHV	PA-E23 Aztec 250	R. J. Ashley & G. O'Gorman	

Notes	Reg.	Type	Owner or Operator
	G-ASHX	PA-28 Cherokee 180	Telepoint Ltd/Manchester
	G-ASIB	Cessna F.172D	A. T. Jay
	G-ASII	PA-28 Cherokee 180	Worldwide Wheels Ltd & ptnrs/Lulsgate
	G-ASIJ	PA-28 Cherokee 180	Precision Products Ltd & Stormweld Ltd
	G-ASIL	PA-28 Cherokee 180	N. M. Barker & ptnrs/Leicester
	G-ASIS	Jodel D.112	E. F. Hazell
	G-ASIT	Cessna 180	A. & P. A. Wood
	G-ASIY	PA-25 Pawnee 235	RAFGSA/Bicester
	G-ASJL	Beech H.35 Bonanza	P. M. Coulton
	G-ASJM	PA-30 Twin Comanche 160 ★	Via Nova Ltd (stored)
	G-ASJO	Beech B.23 Musketeer	G-Air Ltd/Goodwood
	G-ASJV	V.S.361 Spitfire IX (MH434)	Nalfire Aviation Ltd/Booker
	G-ASJY	GY-80 Horizon 160	A. D. Hemley
	G-ASJZ	Jodel D.117A	V. K. Hardy & R. B. Spink/Barton
	G-ASKC	D.H.98 Mosquito 35 (TA719) ★	Skyfame Collection/Duxford
	G-ASKH	D.H.98 Mosquito T.3 (RR299)	British Aerospace/Chester
	G-ASKK	HPR-7 Herald 211 ★	Norwich Aviation Museum
	G-ASKL	Jodel D.150A	J. M. Graty
	G-ASKP	D.H.82A Tiger Moth	Tiger Club Ltd/Redhill
	G-ASKS	Cessna 336 Skymaster	M. J. Godwin
	G-ASKT	PA-28 Cherokee 180	W. A. Webb/Biggin Hill
	G-ASKV	PA-25 Pawnee 235	Southdown Gliding Club Ltd
	G-ASLF	Bensen B.7	S. R. Hughes
	G-ASLH	Cessna 182F	Celahurst Ltd/Southend
	G-ASLK	PA-25 Pawnee 235	Crop Aviation Ltd/Wyberton
	G-ASLL	Cessna 336 ★	stored
	G-ASLR	Agusta-Bell 47J-2	D. Jack
	G-ASLV	PA-28 Cherokee 235	C.S.E. Aviation Ltd/Kidlington
	G-ASLX	CP.301A Emeraude	K. C. Green/Panshanger
	G-ASMA	PA-30 Twin Comanche 160	B. D. Glynn/Redhill
	G-ASMC	P.56 Provost T.1.	W. Walker/Kidlington
	G-ASME	Bensen B.8M	R. K. Williamson
	G-ASMF	Beech D.95A Travel Air	Hawk Aviation Ltd
	G-ASMG	D.H.104 Dove 8	Hall & Clarke (Insurance Consultants) Ltd/Elstree
	G-ASMJ	Cessna F.I72E	J. E. Tribe & Z. W. Jakubowski/ Cambridge
	G-ASML	Luton LA-4A Minor	R. L. E. Horrell
	G-ASMM	D.31 Tubulent	K. A. Browne
	G-ASMN	PA-23 Apache 160	W. London Aero Services Ltd/ White Waltham
	G-ASMO	PA-23 Apache 160 ★	Aviation Enterprises/Fairoaks
	G-ASMS	Cessna 150A	K. R. & T. W. Davies
	G-ASMT	Fairtravel Linnet 2	A. F. Cashin
	G-ASMU	Cessna 150D	Telepoint Ltd/Barton
	G-ASMV	CP.1310-C3 Super Emeraude	P. F. D. Waltham/Leicester
	G-ASMW	Cessna 150D	Yorkshire Light Aircraft Ltd/Leeds
	G-ASMY	PA-23 Apache 160	Hanseviter Aviation/Ipswich
	G-ASMZ	A.61 Terrier 2 (VF516)	Museum of Army Flying/Middle Wallop
	G-ASNA	PA-23 Aztec 250	Margate Motors Plant & Aircraft Hire Ltd
	G-ASNB	Auster 6A (VX118)	M. Pocock & ptnrs
	G-ASNC	Beagle D.5/180 Husky	Peterborough & Spalding Gliding Club/ Crowland
	G-ASND	PA-23 Aztec 250	Commercial Air (Woking) Ltd/ Fairoaks
	G-ASNE	PA-28 Cherokee 180	J. L. Dexter
	G-ASNH	PA-23 Aztec 250	D. C. H. Crouch
	G-ASNI	CP.1310-C3 Super Emeraude	D. Chapman
	G-ASNK	Cessna 205	Woodvale Parachute Centre
	G-ASNU	H.S.125 Srs. 1	Flintgrange Ltd
	G-ASNW	Cessna F.172E	J. A. Gibbs
	G-ASNY	Bensen B.8M	D. L. Wallis
	G-ASNZ	Bensen B.8M	W. H. Turner
	G-ASOC	Auster 6A	J. A. Rayment/Finmere
	G-ASOH	Beech B.55A Baron	J. S. Goodsir & J. Mason/Biggin Hill
	G-ASOI	A.61 Terrier 2	R. H. Jowett
	G-ASOK	Cessna F.172E	Okay Flying Group/Denham
	G-ASOM	A.61 Terrier 2 ★	stored
	G-ASON	PA-30 Twin Comanche 160	Follandbeech Ltd
	G-ASOO	PA-30 Twin Comanche 160	Cold Storage (Jersey) Ltd
	G-ASOX	Cessna 205A	Dorglen Ltd/Wellesbourne
	G-ASPF	Jodel D.120	W. S. Howell
	G-ASPI	Cessna F.172E	Icarus Flying Group/Rochester

Reg.	Type	Owner or Operator	Notes
G-ASPK	PA-28 Cherokee 140	Westward Airways (Lands End) Ltd/ St Just	
G-ASPP	Bristol Boxkite replica	Shuttleworth Trust/O. Warden	
G-ASPS	Piper J-3C-90 Cub	A. J. Chalkley/Blackbushe	
G-ASPU	D.31 Turbulent	I. Maclennan	
G-ASPV	D.H.82A Tiger Moth	B. S. Charters/Shipdham	
G-ASPX	Bensen B-8S	R. Williams	
G-ASRB	D.62B Condor	Tiger Club Ltd (stored)/Redhill	
G-ASRC	D.62B Condor	P. S. Milner	
G-ASRF	Jenny Wren	G. W. Gowland	
G-ASRH	PA-30 Twin Comanche 160	Island Aviation & Travel Ltd	
G-ASRI	PA-23 Aztec 250 ★	Graham Collins Associates Ltd	
G-ASRK	A.109 Airedale ★	M. J. Barnett & R. Skingley	
G-ASRO	PA-30 Twin Comanche 160	A. G. Perkins/Halfpenny Green	
G-ASRR	Cessna 182G	G. J. Richardson/Bourn	
G-ASRT	Jodel D.150	H. M. Kendall	
G-ASRW	PA-28 Cherokee 180	K. R. Deering/Shoreham	
G-ASRX	Beech 65 A80 Queen Air	Aero Charter (Midlands) Ltd	
G-ASSB	PA-30 Twin Comanche 160	Air Charter Scotland Ltd/Glasgow	
G-ASSE	PA-22 Colt 108	J. B. King/Goodwood	
G-ASSF	Cessna 182G Skylane	Burbage Farms Ltd/Leicester	
G-ASSP	PA-30 Twin Comanche 160	The Mastermix Engineering Co Ltd/ Coventry	
G-ASSR	PA-30 Twin Comanche 160	Rangebury Ltd	
G-ASSS	Cessna 172E	D. H. N. Squires/Bristol	
G-ASST	Cessna 150D	F. R. H. Parker	
G-ASSU	CP.301A Emeraude	R. W. Millward (stored)/Redhill	
G-ASSW	PA-28 Cherokee 140	C. J. Plummer/Biggin Hill	
G-ASTA	D.31 Turbulent	D. C. R. Writer	
G-ASTH	Mooney M.20C ★	E. Martin (stored)	
G-ASTI	Auster 6A	M. Pocock	
G-ASTL	Fairey Firefly 1 (Z2033) ★	Skyfame Collection/Duxford	
G-ASTP	Hiller UH-12C	L. Goddard	
G-ASTV	Cessna 150D (tailwheel) ★	stored	
G-ASUB	Mooney M.20E Super 21	A. Smith	
G-ASUD	PA-28 Cherokee 180	S. E. Hobbs & Co Ltd	
G-ASUE	Cessna 150D	D. Huckle/Panshanger	
G-ASUG	Beech E18S ★	Museum of Flight/E. Fortune	
G-ASUH	Cessna F.172E	G. H. Willson & E. Shipley/Felthorpe	
G-ASUI	A.61 Terrier 2	M. Durand	
G-ASUL	Cessna 182G Skylane	Parafreight Ltd/Halfpenny Green	
G-ASUP	Cessna F.172E	GASUP Air/Cardiff	
G-ASUR	Dornier Do 28A-1	Sheffair Ltd	
G-ASUS	Jurca MJ.2B Tempete	D. G. Jones/Coventry	
G-ASVG	CP.301B Emeraude	K. R. Jackson	
G-ASVM	Cessna F.172E	A. P. D. Hynes & ptnrs/Cambridge	
G-ASVN	Cessna U.206 Super Skywagon	British Skysports	
G-ASVO	HPR-7 Herald 214	British Air Ferries Herald Tribune/ Southend	
G-ASVP	PA-25 Pawnee 235	Aquila Gliding Club Ltd	
G-ASVZ	PA-28 Cherokee 140	B. W. & S. A. Presslie	
G-ASWB	A.109 Airedale	C. Gene & G. Taylor/Tees-side	
G-ASWF	A.109 Airedale	C. Baker	
G-ASWH	Luton LA-5A Major	D. G. J. Chisholm/Coventry	
G-ASWJ	Beagle 206 Srs 1 (8449M) ★	RAF Halton	
G-ASWL	Cessna F.172F	C. Wilson	
G-ASWN	Bensen B.8M	D. R. Shepherd	
G-ASWP	Beech A.23 Musketeer	H. Mendelssohn & ptnrs	
G-ASWW	PA-30 Twin Comanche 160	Bristol & Wessex Flying Club Ltd/ Bristol	
G-ASWX	PA-28 Cherokee 180	A. F. Dadds	
G-ASXB	D.H.82A Tiger Moth	P. B. Borsberry & ptnrs	
G-ASXC	SIPA 901	B. L. Proctor	
G-ASXD	Brantly B.2B	Brantly Enterprises	
G-ASXI	T.66 Nipper 2	M. R. Holden/Biggin Hill	
G-ASXJ	Luton LA-4A Minor	J. S. Allison	
G-ASXR	Cessna 210	S. G. Brady (stored)	
G-ASXS	Jodel DR.1050	R. A. Hunter	
G-ASXU	Jodel D.120A	R. W. & J. Thompsett	
G-ASXX	Avro 683 Lancaster 7 (NX611) ★	RAF Scampton Gate Guard	
G-ASXY	Jodel D.117A	P. A. Davies & ptnrs/Cardiff	
G-ASXZ	Cessna 182G Skylane	P. M. Robertson/Perth	
G-ASYD	BAC One-Eleven 670	British Aerospace	
G-ASYG	A.61 Terrier 2 ★	stored	

27

Notes	Reg.	Type	Owner or Operator
	G-ASYJ	Beech D.95A Travel Air	Crosby Aviation (Jersey) Ltd
	G-ASYK	PA-30 Twin Comanche 160	E. W. Pinchback & D. F. Ranger
	G-ASYL	Cessna 150E	D. Mallinson
	G-ASYP	Cessna 150E	J. R. Payne
	G-ASYW	Bell 47G-2	Bristow Helicopters Ltd
	G-ASYZ	Victa Airtourer 100	R. Fletcher/Coventry
	G-ASZB	Cessna 150E	Exmoor Flying Syndicate/Exeter
	G-ASZD	Bo 208A2 Junior	A. J. Watson & ptnrs/O. Warden
	G-ASZE	A.61 Terrier 2	P. J. Moore
	G-ASZJ	S.C.7 Skyvan 3A-100	GEC Avionics Ltd
	G-ASZR	Fairtravel Linnet	H. C. D. & F. J. Garner
	G-ASZS	GY.80 Horizon 160	W. F. Bower/Blackbushe
	G-ASZU	Cessna 150E	T. H. Milburn
	G-ASZV	T.66 Nipper 2	R. L. Mitcham/Elstree
	G-ASZX	A.61 Terrier 1	C. A. Bailey
	G-ATAD	Mooney M.20C	M. R. Burr/Swansea
	G-ATAF	Cessna F.172F	F. R. Pearson/Shipdham
	G-ATAG	Jodel DR. 1050	T. J. N. H. Palmer & G. W. Oliver
	G-ATAI	D.H.104 Dove 8	M. Gaye/Exeter
	G-ATAS	PA-28 Cherokee 180	D. R. Wood/Biggin Hill
	G-ATAT	Cessna 150E	The Derek Pointon Group
	G-ATAU	D.62B Condor	M. A. Peare/Redhill
	G-ATAV	D.62C Condor	The Condor Syndicate
	G-ATBF	F-86E Sabre 4 (XB733) ★	T. Bracewell (stored)
	G-ATBG	Nord 1002 (17)	L. M. Walton
	G-ATBH	Aero 145	P. D. Aberbach
	G-ATBI	Beech A.23 Musketeer	R. F. G. Dent/Staverton
	G-ATBJ	Sikorsky S-61N	British International Helicopters Ltd
	G-ATBL	D.H.60G Moth	M. E. Vaisey/O. Warden
	G-ATBP	Fournier RF-3	M. J. Aherne & ptnrs
	G-ATBS	D.31 Turbulent	N. W. & B. R. Woodwood/Booker
	G-ATBU	A.61 Terrier 2	P. R. Anderson
	G-ATBW	T.66 Nipper 2	N. J. Newbold & ptnrs/Fenland
	G-ATBX	PA-20 Pacer 135	G. D. & P. M. Thomson
	G-ATBZ	W.S-58 Wessex 60 ★	Sykes Aviation Ltd (stored)
	G-ATCC	A.109 Airedale	J. F. Moore & ptnrs/Biggin Hill
	G-ATCD	D.5/180 Husky	Oxford Flying & Gliding Group/Enstone
	G-ATCE	Cessna U.206	J. Fletcher & D. Hickling/Langar
	G-ATCI	Victa Airtourer 100	B. & C. Building Materials (Canvey Island) Ltd
	G-ATCJ	Luton LA-4A Minor	R. M. Sharphouse
	G-ATCL	Victa Airtourer 100	A. D. Goodall
	G-ATCN	Luton LA-4A Minor	J. C. Gates & C. Neilson
	G-ATCR	Cessna 310 ★	Holly Hill Service Station/ Swanton Novers
	G-ATCU	Cessna 337	University of Cambridge
	G-ATCX	Cessna 182H Skylane	K. J. Fisher/Bodmin
	G-ATDA	PA-28 Cherokee 160	D. E. Siviter (Motors) Ltd/Coventry
	G-ATDB	Nord 1101 Noralpha	J. B. Jackson
	G-ATDN	A.61 Terrier 2 (TW641)	S. J. Saggers/Biggin Hill
	G-ATDO	Bo 208C Junior	D. L. Elite
	G-ATDS	HPR-7 Herald 209	Channel Express/Bournemouth
	G-ATEF	Cessna 150E	M. Smith & ptnrs/Blackbushe
	G-ATEG	Cessna 150E	A. W. Woodward/Biggin Hill
	G-ATEM	PA-28 Cherokee 180	G. Wyles & W. Adams
	G-ATEP	EAA Biplane ★	E. L. Martin (stored)/Guernsey
	G-ATES	PA-32 Cherokee Six 260 ★	Parachute jump trainer/Ipswich
	G-ATEV	Jodel DR. 1050	B. A. Mills & G. W. Payne
	G-ATEW	PA-30 Twin Comanche 160	Air Northumbria Group/Newcastle
	G-ATEX	Victa Airtourer 100	Medway Victa Group
	G-ATEZ	PA-28 Cherokee 140	J. A. Burton/E. Midlands
	G-ATFA	Bensen B.8	J. Butler (stored)
	G-ATFD	Jodel DR. 1050	A. D. Edge
	G-ATFF	PA-23 Aztec 250	Topflight Aviation Ltd
	G-ATFG	Brantly B.2B	R. J. Chapman Ltd (stored)
	G-ATFK	PA-30 Twin Comanche 160	L. J. Martin/Redhill
	G-ATFL	Cessna F.172F	R. L. Beverley/Bournemouth
	G-ATFM	Sikorsky S-61N	British International Helicopters Ltd/ Aberdeen
	G-ATFR	PA-25 Pawnee 150	W. A. Braim Ltd
	G-ATFU	D.H.85 Leopard Moth	A. H. Carrington & C. D. Duthy-James
	G-ATFV	Agusta-Bell 47J-2A	Alexander Warren & Co Ltd
	G-ATFW	Luton LA-4A Minor	C. Kirk

Reg.	Type	Owner or Operator	Notes
G-ATFX	Cessna F.172G	M. J. J. Fenwick	
G-ATFY	Cessna F.172G	H. Bennett & P. McCabe	
G-ATGE	Jodel DR.1050	S. T. & B. J. Dangar	
G-ATGG	M.S.885 Super Rallye	B&C Plant Hire Ltd/Southend	
G-ATGH	Brantly B.2B	T. C. Barry	
G-ATGO	Cessna F.172G	Planetalk Ltd	
G-ATGP	Jodel DR.1050	W. M. Haley/Tees-side	
G-ATGY	GY.80 Horizon	P. W. Gibberson/Birmingham	
G-ATGZ	Griffiths GH-4 Gyroplane	G. Griffiths	
G-ATHA	PA-23 Apache 235	Avon Aviation Services Ltd (stored)	
G-ATHD	D.H.C.1 Chipmunk 22	Spartan Flying Group Ltd/Denham	
G-ATHF	Cessna 150F ★	Lincolnshire Aircraft Museum	
G-ATHG	Cessna 150F	G. T. Williams	
G-ATHI	PA-28 Cherokee 180 ★	Instructional airframe/Dublin	
G-ATHK	Aeronca 7AC Champion	A. Corran	
G-ATHL	Wallis WA-116/F	W. Vinten Ltd	
G-ATHM	Wallis WA-116 Srs 1	Wallis Autogyros Ltd	
G-ATHN	Nord 1101 Noralpha	E. L. Martin (stored)	
G-ATHR	PA-28 Cherokee 180	Britannia Airways Ltd/Luton	
G-ATHT	Victa Airtourer 115	H. C. G. Munroe	
G-ATHU	A.61 Terrier 1	J. A. L. Irwin	
G-ATHV	Cessna 150F	P. P. D. Howard-Johnston/Edinburgh	
G-ATHX	Jodel DR. 100A	T. S. & L. M. Wilkins	
G-ATHZ	Cessna 150F	E. & R. D. Forster	
G-ATIA	PA-24 Comanche 260	India Alpha Partnership/Sywell	
G-ATIC	Jodel DR.1050 ★	stored	
G-ATID	Cessna 337	M. R. Tarrant	
G-ATIE	Cessna 150F ★	Parachute jump trainer/Chetwynd	
G-ATIG	HPR-7 Herald 214	Nordic Oil Services Ltd/South East Air	
G-ATIN	Jodel D.117	D. R. Upton & J. G. Kay/Barton	
G-ATIR	Stampe SV-4C	D. T. Kaberry/Barton	
G-ATIS	PA-28 Cherokee 160	S. Boon	
G-ATIZ	Jodel D.117	R. Frith & ptnrs	
G-ATJA	Jodel DR.1050	S. J. Kew/Booker	
G-ATJC	Victa Airtourer 100	D. G. Palmer & D. C. Giles	
G-ATJG	PA-28 Cherokee 140	Royal Aircraft Establishment Dept/ Thurleigh	
G-ATJL	PA-24 Comanche 260	M. J. Berry/White Waltham	
G-ATJM	Fokker DR.1 replica (152/17)	R. Lamplough/Duxford	
G-ATJN	Jodel D.119	R. F. Bradshaw/Sibson	
G-ATJR	PA-E23 Aztec 250	W. A. G. Willbond	
G-ATJT	GY.80 Horizon 160	P. J. Stephenson	
G-ATJV	PA-32 Cherokee Six 260	Doncaster Aero Club Ltd	
G-ATKF	Cessna 150F	P. Sumner/Netherthorpe	
G-ATKH	Luton LA-4A Minor	H. E. Jenner	
G-ATKI	Piper J-3C-65 Cub	A. C. Netting	
G-ATKS	Cessna F.172G	Blois Aviation Ltd	
G-ATKT	Cessna F.172G	N. Y. Souster	
G-ATKU	Cessna F.172G	W. J. & S. K. Boettcher/Doncaster	
G-ATKX	Jodel D.140C	M. P. F. Norman	
G-ATKZ	T.66-2 Nipper	M. W. Knights/Felthorpe	
G-ATLA	Cessna 182J Skylane	Shefford Transport Engineers Ltd/ Luton	
G-ATLB	Jodel DR.1050-M1	Tiger Club Ltd/Redhill	
G-ATLC	PA-23 Aztec 250 ★	Alderney Air Charter Ltd (stored)	
G-ATLG	Hiller UH-12B	Bristow Helicopters Ltd	
G-ATLM	Cessna F.172G	Yorkshire Flying Services Ltd/Leeds	
G-ATLP	Bensen B.8M	C. D. Julian	
G-ATLR	Cessna F.172G	A. Wood & R. F. Patmore/Andrewsfield	
G-ATLT	Cessna U-206A	Lincoln Parachute Centre Ltd/Sturgate	
G-ATLV	Jodel D.120	G. Dawes	
G-ATLW	PA-28 Cherokee 180	Lima Whisky Flying Group	
G-ATMB	Cessna F.150F	Mickey Bravo Group 84/Barton	
G-ATMC	Cessna F.150F	H. E. Peacock	
G-ATMG	M.S.893 Rallye Commodore 180	F. W. Fay & ptnrs/Wellesbourne	
G-ATMH	D.5/180 Husky	Devon & Somerset Gliding Club Ltd	
G-ATMI	H.S.748 Srs 2A	Dan-Air Services Ltd/Gatwick	
G-ATMJ	H.S.748 Srs 2A	Dan-Air Services Ltd/Gatwick	
G-ATML	Cessna F.150F	N. Grantham/Conington	
G-ATMM	Cessna F.150F	DJH Aviation Ltd/Biggin Hill	
G-ATMT	PA-30 Twin Comanche 160	D. H. T. Bain/Newcastle	
G-ATMU	PA-23 Apache 160	Southend Flying Club	
G-ATMW	PA-28 Cherokee 140	Bencray Ltd/Blackpool	
G-ATMX	Cessna F.150F	H. M. Synge	

Notes	Reg.	Type	Owner or Operator
	G-ATMY	Cessna 150F	C. F. Read/Doncaster
	G-ATNB	PA-28 Cherokee 180	R. F. Hill
	G-ATNE	Cessna F.150F	R. Gray/Leicester
	G-ATNI	Cessna F.150F	Telepoint Ltd/Barton
	G-ATNJ	Cessna F.150F ★	*Instructional airframe*/Perth
	G-ATNK	Cessna F.150F	Pegasus Aviation Ltd
	G-ATNL	Cessna F.150F	S. M. Kemp & ptnrs
	G-ATNV	PA-24 Comanche 260	B. S. Reynolds & P. R. Fortescue
	G-ATNX	Cessna F.150F	P. Jenkins
	G-ATOA	PA-23 Apache 160	S. J. Green
	G-ATOE	Cessna F.150F	S. Armstrong
	G-ATOF	Cessna F.150F ★	*Instructional airframe*/Perth
	G-ATOG	Cessna F-150F ★	*Instructional airframe*/Perth
	G-ATOH	D.62B Condor	E. D. Burke
	G-ATOI	PA-28 Cherokee 140	O. & E. Flying Ltd/Stapleford
	G-ATOJ	PA-28 Cherokee 140	Liteflight Ltd/Kidlington
	G-ATOK	PA-28 Cherokee 140	P. Randall
	G-ATOL	PA-28 Cherokee 140	L. J. Nation & G. Alford
	G-ATOM	PA-28 Cherokee 140	R. D. Bowerman & R. P. Synge
	G-ATON	PA-28 Cherokee 140	R. G. Walters
	G-ATOO	PA-28 Cherokee 140	P. J. Stead/Cark
	G-ATOP	PA-28 Cherokee 140	P. R. Coombs/Blackbushe
	G-ATOR	PA-28 Cherokee 140	T. A. J. Morgan & ptnrs/Shobdon
	G-ATOS	PA-28 Cherokee 140	AFT Craft Ltd/Halfpenny Green
	G-ATOT	PA-28 Cherokee 180	J. B. Waterfield & G. L. Birch
	G-ATOU	Mooney M.20E Super 21	P. R. & M. R. Parr
	G-ATOY	PA-24 Comanche 260 ★	Museum of Flight/E. Fortune
	G-ATOZ	Bensen B.8M	J. Jordan
	G-ATPD	H.S.125 Srs 1B	Euroguard Ltd
	G-ATPE	H.S.125 Srs 1B	Colt Executive Aviation Ltd/Staverton
	G-ATPJ	BAC One-Eleven 301	Dan-Air Services Ltd/Gatwick
	G-ATPK	BAC One-Eleven 301	Dan-Air Services Ltd/Gatwick
	G-ATPL	BAC One-Eleven 301	Dan-Air Services Ltd/Gatwick
	G-ATPM	Cessna F.150F	Dan-Air Flying Club/Lasham
	G-ATPN	PA-28 Cherokee 140	R. W. Harris & A. Jahanfar/Southend
	G-ATPT	Cessna 182J Skylane	Western Models Ltd/Redhill
	G-ATPV	JB.01 Minicab	J. Bryant & ptnrs
	G-ATRC	Beech B.95A Travel Air	Hispech (Holdings) Ltd
	G-ATRG	PA-18 Super Cub 150	Lasham Gliding Soc Ltd
	G-ATRI	Bo 208C Junior	W. H. Jones/Shoreham
	G-ATRK	Cessna F.150F	A. B. Mills
	G-ATRL	Cessna F.150F	Loganair Ltd/Glasgow
	G-ATRM	Cessna F.150F	J. W. C. A. Coulcutt
	G-ATRO	PA-28 Cherokee 140	390th Flying Group
	G-ATRR	PA-28 Cherokee 140	Manx Flyers Aero Club Ltd
	G-ATRU	PA-28 Cherokee 180	L. D. Lawrence & ptrns/Luton
	G-ATRW	PA-32 Cherokee Six 260	Eastern Enterprises
	G-ATRX	PA-32 Cherokee Six 260	Comet Flying Group/Panshanger
	G-ATSI	Bo 208C Junior	T. M. H. Paterson
	G-ATSL	Cessna F.172G	D. Le Cheminant/Guernsey
	G-ATSM	Cessna 337A	Anglo-European Trustees Ltd
	G-ATSR	Beech M.35 Bonanza	Alstan Aviation Ltd
	G-ATSU	Jodel D.140B	B. M. O'Brien & P. J. Sellar
	G-ATSX	Bo 208C Junior	N. M. G. Pearson/Bristol
	G-ATSY	Wassmer WA41 Super Baladou IV	Acorn Aviation Services Ltd/Newcastle
	G-ATTB	Wallis WA-116-1 (XR944)	D. A. Wallis
	G-ATTD	Cessna 182J Skylane	K. M. Brennan & ptnrs
	G-ATTF	PA-28 Cherokee 140	S. J. & H. Y. George
	G-ATTG	PA-28 Cherokee 140	Arrow Air Services Engineering Ltd/ Shipdham
	G-ATTI	PA-28 Cherokee 140	D. Newman & C. Babb
	G-ATTK	PA-28 Cherokee 140	G-ATTK Flying Group/Southend
	G-ATTM	Jodel DR.250-160	R. W. Tomkinson
	G-ATTP	BAC One-Eleven 207	Dan-Air Services Ltd/Gatwick
	G-ATTR	Bo 208C Junior 3	S. Luck
	G-ATTU	PA-28 Cherokee 140	Lion Flying Group/Elstree
	G-ATTV	PA-28 Cherokee 140	D. R. Winder
	G-ATTX	PA-28 Cherokee 180	A. Gray & ptnrs
	G-ATTY	PA-32 Cherokee Six 260	Onustech Engineering Ltd
	G-ATUB	PA-28 Cherokee 140	R. H. Partington & M. J. Porter
	G-ATUC	PA-28 Cherokee 140	Executive Communications Ltd/Booker
	G-ATUD	PA-28 Cherokee 140	E. J. Clempson
	G-ATUF	Cessna F.150F	C. J. Lynn/Sibson

Reg.	Type	Owner or Operator	Notes
G-ATUG	D.62B Condor	C. B. Marsh & D. J. R. Williams	
G-ATUH	T.66 Nipper Srs 1	G. L. Winterbourne	
G-ATUI	Bo 208C Junior	G. Clarke & N. P. Bruce	
G-ATUL	PA-28 Cherokee 180	R. F. W. Warner	
G-ATVF	D.H.C.1 Chipmunk 22	RAFGSA/Bicester	
G-ATVH	BAC One-Eleven 207	Dan-Air Services Ltd *City of Newcastle-upon-Tyne*/Gatwick	
G-ATVK	PA-28 Cherokee 140	JRB Aviation Ltd/Southend	
G-ATVL	PA-28 Cherokee 140	West London Aero Services Ltd/White Waltham	
G-ATVO	PA-28 Cherokee 140	Firefly Aviation Ltd/Glasgow	
G-ATVP	F.B.5 Gunbus (2345) ★	RAF Museum	
G-ATVS	PA-28 Cherokee 180	Marshalls Woodflakes Ltd/Bristol	
G-ATVW	D.62B Condor	J. P. Coulter & J. Chidley/Panshanger	
G-ATVX	Bo 208C Junior	M. J. Porter	
G-ATWA	Jodel DR.1050	M. A. Hook	
G-ATWB	Jodel D.117	Andrewsfield Flying Club Ltd	
G-ATWE	M.S.892A Rallye Commodore	D. I. Murray	
G-ATWJ	Cessna F.172F	C. J. & J. Freeman/Headcorn	
G-ATWP	Alon A-2 Aircoupe	H. Dodd & I. Wilson	
G-ATWR	PA-30 Twin Comanche 160	Lubair (Transport Services) Ltd E. Midlands	
G-ATWZ	M.S.892A Rallye Commodore	Wessex Torran Purchase	
G-ATXA	PA-22 Tri-Pacer 150	R. C. Teverson	
G-ATXD	PA-30 Twin Comanche 160	Alphameric Systems Ltd	
G-ATXF	GY-80 Horizon 150	A. I. Milne	
G-ATXJ	H.P.137 Jetstream 300 ★	British Aerospace (*display mock-up*)/ Prestwick	
G-ATXM	PA-28 Cherokee 180	J. Khan/Ipswich	
G-ATXN	Mitchell-Proctor Kittiwake	D. W. Kent	
G-ATXO	SIPA 903	M. Hillam/Sherburn	
G-ATXR	AFB 1 gas balloon	C. M. Bulmer	
G-ATXZ	Bo 208C Junior	J. Dyson & M. Hutchinson	
G-ATYM	Cessna F.150G	J. F. Perry & Co	
G-ATYN	Cessna F.150G	Skegness Air Taxi Services Ltd	
G-ATYS	PA-28 Cherokee 180	R. V. Waite	
G-ATZA	Bo 208C Junior	R. Wilder/Jersey	
G-ATZG	AFB2 gas balloon	Flt Lt S. Cameron *Aeolis*	
G-ATZK	PA-28 Cherokee 180	BI Aviation Services/Blackbushe	
G-ATZM	Piper J-3C-65 Cub	R. W. Davison	
G-ATZS	Wassmer WA41 Super Baladou IV	DSH Aviation Ltd/Biggin Hill	
G-ATZY	Cessna F.150G	P. P. D. Howard-Johnston/Edinburgh	
G-ATZZ	Cessna F.150G	Routair Aviation Services Ltd/Southend	
G-AUTO	Cessna 441 Conquest	Faresavers Ltd	
G-AVAA	Cessna F.150G	A. C. Garrett	
G-AVAJ	Hiller UH-12B	R. White & P. Lancaster	
G-AVAK	M.S.893A Rallye Commodore 180	W. K. Anderson (*stored*)/Perth	
G-AVAO	PA-30 Twin Comanche 160	Ghan-Air	
G-AVAP	Cessna F.150G	Seawing Flying Club Ltd/Southend	
G-AVAR	Cessna F.150G	J. A. Rees & F. Doncaster	
G-AVAU	PA-30 Twin Comanche 160	L. Batin/Fairoaks	
G-AVAW	D.62B Condor	Avato Flying Group	
G-AVAX	PA-28 Cherokee 180	Three Counties Flying Group	
G-AVBG	PA-28 Cherokee 180	Transknight Ltd/Booker	
G-AVBH	PA-28 Cherokee 180	C. Ellerbrook & T. Smith	
G-AVBP	PA-28 Cherokee 140	Bristol & Wessex Aeroplane Club Ltd/Bristol	
G-AVBS	PA-28 Cherokee 180	S. L. Robinson/St Just	
G-AVBT	PA-28 Cherokee 180	P. O. Hire & D. J. Spicer/Denham	
G-AVBZ	Cessna F.172H	J. Seville	
G-AVCC	Cessna F.172H	Charlie Charlie Flying Group/Elstree	
G-AVCE	Cessna F.172H	Damon Products	
G-AVCM	PA-24 Comanche 260	F. Smith & Sons Ltd/Stapleford	
G-AVCS	A.61 Terrier 1	A. Topen/Cranfield	
G-AVCT	Cessna F.150G	DJH Aviation Ltd/Biggin Hill	
G-AVCU	Cessna F.150G	P. R. Moss/Alderney	
G-AVCV	Cessna 182J Skylane	University of Manchester Institute of Science & Technology/Woodford	
G-AVCX	PA-30 Twin Comanche 160	F. J. Stevens/Leicester	
G-AVCY	PA-30 Twin Comanche 160	M. Dukes/Biggin Hill	

Notes	Reg.	Type	Owner or Operator
	G-AVDA	Cessna 182K Skylane	J. W. Grant
	G-AVDE	Turner Gyroglider Mk 1	J. S. Smith
	G-AVDF	Beagle Pup 100 ★	Shoreham Airport Museum
	G-AVDG	Wallis WA-116 Srs 1	K. H. Wallis
	G-AVDR	Beech B80 Queen Air	Shoreham Flight Simulation/Bournemouth
	G-AVDS	Beech B80 Queen Air	Shoreham Flight Simulation/Bournemouth
	G-AVDT	Aeronca 7AC Champion	D. Cheney & J. G. Woods
	G-AVDV	PA-22 Tri-Pacer 150 (modified to Pacer)	S. C. Brooks/Slinfold
	G-AVDW	D.62B Condor	Essex Aviation/Andrewsfield
	G-AVDY	Luton LA-4A Minor	D. E. Evans & ptnrs
	G-AVEB	Morane MS 230 (1076)	The Hon A. M. M. Lindsay/Booker
	G-AVEC	Cessna F.172H	W. H. Ekin (Engineering) Co Ltd
	G-AVEF	Jodel D.150	Tiger Club Ltd/Redhill
	G-AVEH	SIAI-Marchetti S.205	P. D. Winborne
	G-AVEM	Cessna F.150G	D. E. Bedford
	G-AVEN	Cessna F.150G	N. J. Budd/Aberdeen
	G-AVEO	Cessna F.150G	Computaplane Ltd/Glasgow
	G-AVER	Cessna F.150G	Telepoint Ltd/Manchester
	G-AVET	Beech 95-C55A Baron	Tunstall Telecom Ltd
	G-AVEU	Wassmer WA.41 Baladou	Baladou Flying Group/Aberdeen
	G-AVEX	D.62B Condor	Cotswold Roller Hire Ltd/Long Marston
	G-AVEY	Currie Super Wot	A. Eastelow/Dunkeswell
	G-AVFB	H.S.121 Trident 2E ★	Imperial War Museum/Duxford
	G-AVFE	H.S.121 Trident 2E ★	Belfast Airport Authority
	G-AVFH	H.S.121 Trident 2E ★	Mosquito Aircraft Museum (Fuselage only)
	G-AVFK	H.S.121 Trident 2E ★	Metropolitan Police Training Centre/Hounslow
	G-AVFM	H.S.121 Trident 2E ★	Brunel Technical College/Bristol
	G-AVFP	PA-28 Cherokee 140	H. D. Vince Ltd/Woodvale
	G-AVFR	PA-28 Cherokee 140	J. J. Ballagh/Newtownards
	G-AVFS	PA-32 Cherokee Six 300	A. V. Brown/Cambridge
	G-AVFU	PA-32 Cherokee Six 300	Couesnon Ltd/Biggin Hill
	G-AVFX	PA-28 Cherokee 140	J. D. Palfreman
	G-AVFY	PA-28 Cherokee 140	D. R. Davidson/Bournemouth
	G-AVFZ	PA-28 Cherokee 140	R. S. Littlechild & V. B. G. Childs
	G-AVGA	PA-24 Comanche 260	W. B. Baillie/Tees-side
	G-AVGB	PA-28 Cherokee 140	D. Jenkins & ptnrs/Swansea
	G-AVGC	PA-28 Cherokee 140	B. A. Bennett/Redhill
	G-AVGD	PA-28 Cherokee 140	L. J. Fisher/Southend
	G-AVGE	PA-28 Cherokee 140	H. H. T. Wolf
	G-AVGH	PA-28 Cherokee 140	G. S. Mimms/Bristol
	G-AVGI	PA-28 Cherokee 140	K. Hope & ptnrs/Barton
	G-AVGJ	Jodel DR.1050	S. T. Gilbert & G. W. Camp
	G-AVGK	PA-28 Cherokee 180	MRK Aviation Ltd/Liverpool
	G-AVGP	BAC One-Eleven 408	British Airways County of Nottinghamshire/Birmingham
	G-AVGV	Cessna F.150G	J. P. Lassey
	G-AVGY	Cessna 182K Skylane	Clifford F. Cross (Wisbech) Ltd/Fenland
	G-AVGZ	Jodel DR.1050	Gordonair Ltd/Enstone
	G-AVHF	Beech A.23 Musketeer	R. W. Neale/Coventry
	G-AVHH	Cessna F.172H	V. W. Wharton & ptnrs/Goodwood
	G-AVHJ	Wassmer WA.41 Baladou	D. G. Pickering & ptnrs
	G-AVHL	Jodel DR.105A	G. L. Winterbourne/Redhill
	G-AVHM	Cessna F.150G	M. Tosh/Panshanger
	G-AVHN	Cessna F.150F	RGR High Service Ltd
	G-AVHT	Auster AOP.9 (WZ711)	M. Somerton-Rayner/Middle Wallop
	G-AVHY	Fournier RF.4D	R. Swinn & J. Conolly
	G-AVIA	Cessna F.150G	Cheshire Air Training School (Merseyside) Ltd/Liverpool
	G-AVIB	Cessna F.150G	D. W. Horton/Humberside
	G-AVIC	Cessna F.172H	Pembrokeshire Air/Haverfordwest
	G-AVID	Cessna 182J	T. D. Boyle
	G-AVIE	Cessna F.172H	M. P. Parker
	G-AVII	AB-206A JetRanger	Bristow Helicopters Ltd
	G-AVIL	Alon A.2 Aircoupe	D. W. Vernon/Woodvale
	G-AVIN	M.S.880B Rallye Club	D. R. F. Sapte & D. A. Greife/Elstree
	G-AVIO	M.S.880B Rallye Club	A. R. Johnston/Popham
	G-AVIP	Brantly B.2B	Cosworth Engineering Ltd
	G-AVIR	Cessna F.172H	Anglian Flight Training Ltd/Norwich
	G-AVIS	Cessna F.172H	Jon Paul Photography Ltd/Rochester

Reg.	Type	Owner or Operator	Notes
G-AVIT	Cessna F.150G	Shropshire Aero Club Ltd/Sleap	
G-AVIZ	Scheibe SF.25A Motorfalke	D. C. Pattison & D. A. Wilson	
G-AVJE	Cessna F.150G	P. R. Green & ptnrs/Booker	
G-AVJF	Cessna F.172H	J. A. & G. M. Rees	
G-AVJG	Cessna 337B	P. R. Moss/Bournemouth	
G-AVJH	D.62 Condor	Lleyn Flying Group/Mona	
G-AVJI	Cessna F.172H	J. R. Pearce/Compton Abbas	
G-AVJJ	PA-30 Twin Comanche 160	A. H. Manser Ltd/Staverton	
G-AVJK	Jodel DR.1050 M.1	G. Wylde	
G-AVJO	Fokker E.III Replica (422-15)	Personal Plane Services Ltd/Booker	
G-AVJV	Wallis WA-117 Srs 1	K. H. Wallis (G-ATCV)	
G-AVJW	Wallis WA-118 Srs 2	K. H. Wallis (G-ATPW)	
G-AVKB	MB.50 Pipistrelle	R. A. Fairclough	
G-AVKD	Fournier RF-4D	Lasham RF4 Group	
G-AVKE	Gadfly HDW.1 ★	British Rotorcraft Museum	
G-AVKG	Cessna F.172H	P. E. P. Sheppard	
G-AVKI	Nipper T.66 Srs 3	P. Archer	
G-AVKJ	Nipper T.66 Srs 3	N. M. Yeo	
G-AVKK	Nipper T.66 Srs 3	C. Watson	
G-AVKN	Cessna 401	Strand Furniture Ltd/E. Midlands	
G-AVKP	A.109 Airedale	Bobbington Estates Ltd	
G-AVKR	Bo 208C Junior	P. E. Hinkley/Redhill	
G-AVKY	Hiller UH-12E	Agricopters Ltd/Chilbolton	
G-AVKZ	PA-23 Aztec 250C	Distance No Object Ltd/Stansted	
G-AVLA	PA-28 Cherokee 140	L. P. & I. Keegan/Perth	
G-AVLB	PA-28 Cherokee 140	J. A. Overton Ltd/Andrewsfield	
G-AVLC	PA-28 Cherokee 140	F. C. V. Hopkins/Swansea	
G-AVLD	PA-28 Cherokee 140	Lion Flying Group/Elstree	
G-AVLE	PA-28 Cherokee 140	Hambrair Ltd	
G-AVLF	PA-28 Cherokee 140	W. London Aero Services Ltd/ White Waltham	
G-AVLG	PA-28 Cherokee 140	R. Friedlander	
G-AVLH	PA-28 Cherokee 140	P. Preece/Goodwood	
G-AVLI	PA-28 Cherokee 140	Peter Collier Aviation Ltd	
G-AVLJ	PA-28 Cherokee 140	E. Berks Boat Company Ltd	
G-AVLM	B.121 Pup 2	R. Towle	
G-AVLN	B.121 Pup 2	P. Wilkinson	
G-AVLO	Bo 208C Junior	J. A. Webb & K. F. Barnard/Popham	
G-AVLP	PA-23 Aztec 250	Survey Data Ltd	
G-AVLR	PA-28 Cherokee 140	Peter Dolan & Co Ltd/Conington	
G-AVLS	PA-28 Cherokee 140	G. C. Stewart/Humberside	
G-AVLT	PA-28 Cherokee 140	R. W. Harris & ptnrs/Southend	
G-AVLU	PA-28 Cherokee 140	I. K. George/Fairoaks	
G-AVLW	Fournier RF-4D	P. J. Sellar & B. M. O'Brien/Redhill	
G-AVLY	Jodel D.120A	P. Cawkwell	
G-AVMA	GY-80 Horizon 180	B. R. & S. Hildick	
G-AVMB	D.62B Condor	J. C. Mansell	
G-AVMD	Cessna 150G	T. E. Aviation (W. Yorkshire) Ltd	
G-AVMF	Cessna F. 150G	J. F. Marsh & M. J. Oliver	
G-AVMH	BAC One-Eleven 510	British Airways *County of Cheshire/* Manchester	
G-AVMI	BAC One-Eleven 510	British Airways *County of Avon/* Manchester	
G-AVMJ	BAC One-Eleven 510	British Airways *Strathclyde Region/* Manchester	
G-AVMK	BAC One-Eleven 510	British Airways *County of Kent/* Manchester	
G-AVML	BAC One-Eleven 510	British Airways *County of Surrey/* Manchester	
G-AVMM	BAC One-Eleven 510	British Airways *County of Antrim/* Manchester	
G-AVMN	BAC One-Eleven 510	British Airways *County of Essex/* Manchester	
G-AVMO	BAC One-Eleven 510	British Airways *Lothian Region/* Manchester	
G-AVMP	BAC One-Eleven 510	British Airways *Bailiwick of Jersey/* Manchester	
G-AVMR	BAC One-Eleven 510	British Airways *County of Tyne & Wear/* Manchester	
G-AVMS	BAC One-Eleven 510	British Airways *County of West Sussex/* Manchester	
G-AVMT	BAC One-Eleven 510	British Airways *County of Berkshire/* Manchester	
G-AVMU	BAC One-Eleven 510	British Airways *County of Dorset/* Manchester	

Notes	Reg.	Type	Owner or Operator
	G-AVMV	BAC One-Eleven 510	British Airways *County of Powys*/ Manchester
	G-AVMW	BAC One-Eleven 510	British Airways *Grampian Region*/ Manchester
	G-AVMX	BAC One-Eleven 510	British Airways *County of East Sussex*/ Manchester
	G-AVMY	BAC One-Eleven 510	British Airways *County of Derbyshire*/ Manchester
	G-AVMZ	BAC One-Eleven 510	British Airways *County of Lancashire*/ Manchester
	G-AVNB	Cessna F.150G	BLS Aviation Ltd/Elstree
	G-AVNC	Cessna F.150G	J. Turner
	G-AVNM	PA-28 Cherokee 180	Brands Hatch Circuit Ltd/Biggin Hill
	G-AVNN	PA-28 Cherokee 180	Barum Alloys Ltd
	G-AVNO	PA-28 Cherokee 180	Allister Flight Ltd/Stapleford
	G-AVNP	PA-28 Cherokee 180	R. W. Harris & ptnrs
	G-AVNR	PA-28 Cherokee 180	L. R. Davies/Biggin Hill
	G-AVNS	PA-28 Cherokee 180	A. Walton/Conington
	G-AVNU	PA-28 Cherokee 180	F. E. Gooding/Biggin Hill
	G-AVNW	PA-28 Cherokee 180	Len Smith's School & Sports Ltd
	G-AVNX	Fournier RF-4D	O. C. Harris & C. G. Masterman
	G-AVNY	Fournier RF-4D	M. P. Dentith/Biggin Hill
	G-AVNZ	Fournier RF-4D	Aviation Special Developments (ASD) Ltd/Biggin Hill
	G-AVOA	Jodel DR.1050	D. A. Willies/Cranwell
	G-AVOD	Beagle D5/180 Husky	D. Bonsall & ptnrs/Netherthorpe
	G-AVOH	D.62B Condor	J. E. Hobbs/Sandown
	G-AVOM	Jodel DR.221	M. A. Mountford/Headcorn
	G-AVON	Luton LA-5A Major	G. R. Mee
	G-AVOO	PA-18 Super Cub 150	London Gliding Club Ltd/ Dunstable
	G-AVOZ	PA-28 Cherokee 180	J. R. Winning/Booker
	G-AVPC	D.31 Turbulent	J. Sharp (*stored*)
	G-AVPD	D.9 Bebe	S. W. McKay (*stored*)
	G-AVPE	H.S.125 Srs 3B	British Aerospace/Filton
	G-AVPH	Cessna F.150G	W. Lancashire Aero Club/Woodvale
	G-AVPI	Cessna F.172H	R. W. Cope
	G-AVPJ	D.H.82A Tiger Moth	C. C. Silk
	G-AVPK	M.S.892A Rallye Commodore	B. A. Bridgewater/Halfpenny Green
	G-AVPM	Jodel D.117	J. Houghton/Breighton
	G-AVPN	HPR-7 Herald 213	Nordic Oil Services Ltd
	G-AVPO	Hindustan HAL-26 Pushpak	A. & R. Rimington
	G-AVPR	PA-30 Twin Comanche 160	Cold Storage (Jersey) Ltd
	G-AVPS	PA-30 Twin Comanche 160	Solitair Aviation Ltd
	G-AVPT	PA-18 Super Cub 150	Tiger Club Ltd/Redhill
	G-AVPV	PA-28 Cherokee 180	R. W. Harris & ptnrs/Southend
	G-AVRF	H.S.125 Srs 3B	S. Gill
	G-AVRK	PA-28 Cherokee 180	S. R. Culley Developments Ltd
	G-AVRN	Boeing 737-204	Britannia Airways Ltd *Capt James Cook*/Luton
	G-AVRP	PA-28 Cherokee 140	K. Cooper & N. D. Douglas/ Halfpenny Green
	G-AVRS	GY-80 Horizon 180	Horizon Flyers Ltd/Denham
	G-AVRT	PA-28 Cherokee 140	F. Clarke/Stapleford
	G-AVRU	PA-28 Cherokee 180	H. B. Holden & ptnrs/Biggin Hill
	G-AVRW	GY-20 Minicab	R. B. Pybus
	G-AVRY	PA-28 Cherokee 180	Roses Flying Group/Barton
	G-AVRZ	PA-28 Cherokee 180	Briglea Engineering Ltd/Guernsey
	G-AVSA	PA-28 Cherokee 180	E. Barrow & J. Walker/Barton
	G-AVSB	PA-28 Cherokee 180	White House Garage Ashford Ltd
	G-AVSC	PA-28 Cherokee 180	W. London Aero Services Ltd/ White Waltham
	G-AVSD	PA-28 Cherokee 180	Landmate Ltd
	G-AVSE	PA-28 Cherokee 180	Yorkshire Light Aircraft Ltd/Leeds
	G-AVSF	PA-28 Cherokee 180	Goodwood Terrena Ltd
	G-AVSI	PA-28 Cherokee 140	W. London Aero Services/White Waltham
	G-AVSP	PA-28 Cherokee 180	Trig Engineering Ltd
	G-AVSR	Beagle D 5/180 Husky	A. L. Young
	G-AVTB	Nipper T.66 Srs 3	B. A. Wright
	G-AVTC	Nipper T.66 Srs 3	M. K. Field
	G-AVTJ	PA-32 Cherokee Six 260	A. W. Chapman/Southend
	G-AVTK	PA-32 Cherokee Six 260	Mannix Aviation Ltd/E. Midlands

Reg.	Type	Owner or Operator	Notes
G-AVTP	Cessna F.172H	J. H. A. Clarke & ptnrs	
G-AVTT	Ercoupe 415D	Wright's Farm Eggs Ltd/Andrewsfield	
G-AVTV	M.S.893A Rallye Commodore	D. B. Meeks	
G-AVUA	Cessna F.172H	Recreational Flying Centre (Popham) Ltd	
G-AVUD	PA-30 Twin Comanche 160B	F. M. Aviation/Biggin Hill	
G-AVUG	Cessna F.150H	Skyways Flying Group/Netherthorpe	
G-AVUH	Cessna F.150H	C. D. Brack	
G-AVUL	Cessna F.172H	D. H. Stephens & D. J. Reason/Elstree	
G-AVUS	PA-28 Cherokee 140	R. Groat/Glasgow	
G-AVUT	PA-28 Cherokee 140	Bencray Ltd/Blackpool	
G-AVUU	PA-28 Cherokee 140	R. W. Harris	
G-AVUZ	PA-32 Cherokee Six 300	Ceesix Ltd/Jersey	
G-AVVB	H.S. 125 Srs 3B	Hitchens (Hatfield) Ltd	
G-AVVC	Cessna F.172H	Kestrel Air Ltd/Swansea	
G-AVVE	Cessna F.150H ★	R. Windley (stored)	
G-AVVF	D.H.104 Dove 8	Sparline Agencies Ltd/Cranfield	
G-AVVI	PA-30 Twin Comanche 160B	Tindon Ltd/Little Snoring	
G-AVVJ	M.S.893A Rallye Commodore	Herefordshire Gliding Club Ltd/ Shobdon	
G-AVVL	Cessna F.150H	Osprey Air Services Ltd/Cranfield	
G-AVVO	Avro 652A Anson 19 (VL348) ★	Newark Air Museum	
G-AVVS	Hughes 269B	W. Holmes	
G-AVVT	PA-23 Aztec 250	Kayglynn Investment Holdings Ltd	
G-AVVV	PA-28 Cherokee 180	Courtrun Ltd/Redhill	
G-AVVX	Cessna F.150H	Hatfield Flying Club	
G-AVVY	Cessna F.150H	Telepoint Ltd/Manchester	
G-AVWA	PA-28 Cherokee 140	W. London Aero Services Ltd/ White Waltham	
G-AVWD	PA-28 Cherokee 140	Telepoint Ltd	
G-AVWE	PA-28 Cherokee 140	W. C. C. Meyer/Biggin Hill	
G-AVWG	PA-28 Cherokee 140	Bencray Ltd/Blackpool	
G-AVWH	PA-28 Cherokee 140	P. Elliott/Biggin Hill	
G-AVWI	PA-28 Cherokee 140	L. M. Veitch	
G-AVWJ	PA-28 Cherokee 140	M. J. Steer/Biggin Hill	
G-AVWL	PA-28 Cherokee 140	Bristol & Wessex Aeroplane Club Ltd/ Bristol	
G-AVWM	PA-28 Cherokee 140	N. Jahanfar/Southend	
G-AVWN	PA-28R Cherokee Arrow 180	Vawn Air Ltd/Jersey	
G-AVWO	PA-28R Cherokee Arrow 180	P. D. Cahill/Biggin Hill	
G-AVWR	PA-28R Cherokee Arrow 180	D. J. Cooper/Netherthorpe	
G-AVWT	PA-28R Cherokee Arrow 180	Yorkshire Light Aircraft Ltd/Leeds	
G-AVWU	PA-28R Cherokee Arrow 180	Horizon Flyers Ltd/Denham	
G-AVWV	PA-28R Cherokee Arrow 180	Mapair Ltd/Birmingham	
G-AVWY	Fournier RF-4D	ASD Formaero Ltd	
G-AVXA	PA-25 Pawnee 235	Agricultural Aerial Services Ltd	
G-AVXB	Lovegrove PL-1 gyrocopter	A. Stone	
G-AVXC	Nipper T.66 Srs 3	T. P. W. Hyde	
G-AVXD	Nipper T.66 Srs 3	D. A. Davidson	
G-AVXF	PA-28R Cherokee-Arrow 180	J. G. Stewart & I. M. S. Ferriman/ Cranfield	
G-AVXI	H.S.748 Srs 2A	Civil Aviation Authority/Stansted	
G-AVXJ	H.S.748 Srs 2A	Civil Aviation Authority/Stansted	
G-AVXV	Bleriot XI (BAPC 104) ★	Imperial War Museum/Duxford	
G-AVXW	D.62B Condor	A. J. Cooper/Rochester	
G-AVXX	Cessna FR.172E	Hadrian Flying Group/Newcastle	
G-AVXY	Auster AOP.9 (XK417) ★	R. Windley (stored)	
G-AVXZ	PA-28 Cherokee 140 ★	ATC Hayle (instructional airframe)	
G-AVYB	H.S.121 Trident 1E-140 ★	SAS training airframe/Hereford	
G-AVYE	H.S.121 Trident 1E-140 ★	Science Museum/Wroughton	
G-AVYK	A.61 Terrier 3	G. J. Busby	
G-AVYL	PA-28 Cherokee 180	N. J. Allcoat	
G-AVYM	PA-28 Cherokee 180	Carlisle Aviation (1985) Ltd/Crosby	
G-AVYP	PA-28 Cherokee 140	T. D. Reid (Braids) Ltd/Newtownards	
G-AVYR	PA-28 Cherokee 140	D.R. Flying Club Ltd/Staverton	
G-AVYS	PA-28R Cherokee Arrow 180	E. W. Passmore	
G-AVYT	PA-28R Cherokee Arrow 180	H. Stephenson/Tees-side	
G-AVYV	Jodel D.120	Long Mountain Aero Group	
G-AVYX	AB-206A JetRanger	D. A. C. Pipe	
G-AVZB	Aero Z-37 Cmelak	ADS (Aerial) Ltd/Southend	
G-AVZC	Hughes 269B	LRC Mail Order Ltd	
G-AVZE	D.62B Condor	J. Sweeney	
G-AVZI	Bo 208C Junior	C. F. Rogers	
G-AVZM	B.121 Pup 1	ARAZ Group/Elstree	

Notes	Reg.	Type	Owner or Operator
	G-AVZN	B.121 Pup 1	W. E. Cro & Sons Ltd/Shoreham
	G-AVZP	B.121 Pup 1	T. A. White
	G-AVZR	PA-28 Cherokee 180	W. E. Lowe/Halfpenny Green
	G-AVZU	Cessna F.150H	E. J. R. McDowell
	G-AVZV	Cessna F.172H	Bencray Ltd/Blackpool
	G-AVZW	EAA Model P Biplane	R. G. Maidment & G. R. Edmundson/ Goodwood
	G-AVZX	M.S.880B Rallye Club	M. Atkins & G. Harris
	G-AWAA	M.S.880B Rallye Club	P. A. Cairns/Dunkeswell
	G-AWAC	GY-80 Horizon 180	R. D. Harper
	G-AWAD	Beech D 55 Baron	Aero Lease Ltd/Bournemouth
	G-AWAH	Beech D 55 Baron	B. J. S. Grey
	G-AWAI	Beech D 55 Baron	Alibear Ltd/Booker
	G-AWAJ	Beech D 55 Baron	Standard Hose Ltd/Leeds
	G-AWAO	Beech D 55 Baron	D. W. Clark/Wellesbourne
	G-AWAT	D.62B Condor	Tarwood Ltd/Redhill
	G-AWAU	Vickers F.B.27A Vimy (replica) (F8614) ★	Bomber Command Museum/Hendon
	G-AWAW	Cessna F.150F	G. M. White
	G-AWAZ	PA-28R Cherokee Arrow 180	C. J. Chapman
	G-AWBA	PA-28R Cherokee Arrow 180	March Flying Group/Stapleford
	G-AWBB	PA-28R Cherokee Arrow 180	J. Calverley
	G-AWBC	PA-28R Cherokee Arrow 180	G. K. Furneaux/Blackbushe
	G-AWBE	PA-28 Cherokee 140	Arle Building & Construction Co Ltd/ Staverton
	G-AWBG	PA-28 Cherokee 140	D. J. Smith
	G-AWBH	PA-28 Cherokee 140	R. C. A. Mackworth
	G-AWBJ	Fournier RF-4D	M. G. Fountain
	G-AWBL	BAC One-Eleven 416	British Airways *County of Leicestershire*/Birmingham
	G-AWBM	D.31 Turbulent	J. P. Taylor
	G-AWBN	PA-30 Twin Comanche 160	Stourfield Investments Ltd/Jersey
	G-AWBP	Cessna 182L Skylane	Bournemouth Aviation
	G-AWBS	PA-28 Cherokee 140	W. London Aero Services Ltd/ White Waltham
	G-AWBT	PA-30 Twin Comanche 160	Fridaythorpe Feeds Ltd
	G-AWBU	Morane-Saulnier N (replica) (M.S.50)	Personal Plane Services Ltd/Booker
	G-AWBV	Cessna 182L Skylane	Hunting Surveys & Consultants Ltd/ Manchester
	G-AWBW	Cessna F.172H ★	Brunel Technical College/Bristol
	G-AWBX	Cessna F.150H	D. F. Ranger & ptnrs/Popham
	G-AWCD	CEA DR.253	D. H. Smith
	G-AWCH	Cessna F.172H	Tindon Ltd/Little Snoring
	G-AWCL	Cessna F.150H	Signtest Ltd
	G-AWCM	Cessna F.150H	Telepoint Ltd/Manchester
	G-AWCN	Cessna FR.172E	LEC Refrigeration Ltd
	G-AWCP	Cessna F.150H (tailwheel)	C. E. Mason/Shobdon
	G-AWCW	Beech E.95 Travel Air	H. W. Astor/White Waltham
	G-AWCY	PA-32 Cherokee Six 260	J. Harvey
	G-AWDA	Nipper T.66 Srs. 3	J. A. Cheesebrough
	G-AWDD	Nipper T.66 Srs. 3	T. D. G. Roberts/Inverness
	G-AWDI	PA-23 Aztec 250	Air Foyle Ltd/Luton
	G-AWDO	D.31 Turbulent	R. Watling-Greenwood
	G-AWDP	PA-28 Cherokee 180	B. H. & P. M. Illston/Shipdham
	G-AWDR	Cessna FR.172E	Levendene Ltd
	G-AWDU	Brantly B.2B	S. N. Cole
	G-AWEF	Stampe SV-4B	Tiger Club Ltd/Redhill
	G-AWEI	D.62B Condor	M. A. Pearce/Redhill
	G-AWEL	Fournier RF-4D	A. B. Clymo/Halfpenny Green
	G-AWEM	Fournier RF-4D	B. J. Griffin/Wickenby
	G-AWEN	Jodel DR.1050	L. G. Earnshaw & ptnrs
	G-AWEO	Cessna F.150H	Banbury Plant Hire Ltd
	G-AWEP	JB-01 Minicab	F. Davies
	G-AWER	PA-23 Aztec 250	Woodgate Air Services (IOM) Ltd
	G-AWET	PA-28 Cherokee 180	Broadland Flying Group Ltd/ Swanton Morley
	G-AWEV	PA-28 Cherokee 140	Smith Engineering/Shipdham
	G-AWEX	PA-28 Cherokee 140	R. Badham
	G-AWEZ	PA-28R Cherokee Arrow 180	BTG Plant Hire & Repairs Ltd/Stapleford
	G-AWFB	PA-28R Cherokee Arrow 180	Luke Aviation Ltd/Bristol
	G-AWFC	PA-28R Cherokee Arrow 180	K. A. Goodchild/Southend
	G-AWFD	PA-28R Cherokee Arrow 180	C. A. Robbins

Reg.	Type	Owner or Operator	Notes
G-AWFF	Cessna F.150H	DJH Aviation Ltd/Biggin Hill	
G-AWFJ	PA-28R Cherokee Arrow 180	W. F. van Schoten/Sherburn	
G-AWFK	PA-28R Cherokee Arrow 180	J. A. Rundle (Holdings) Ltd/Kidlington	
G-AWFN	D.62B Condor	A. F. Bullock	
G-AWFO	D.62B Condor	T. A. Major	
G-AWFP	D.62B Condor	Blackbushe Flying Club	
G-AWFR	D.31 Turbulent	L. W. Usherwood	
G-AWFT	Jodel D.9 Bebe	W. H. Cole	
G-AWFW	Jodel D.117	F. H. Greenwell	
G-AWFX	Sikorsky S-61N	British International Helicopters Ltd/ Aberdeen	
G-AWFZ	Beech A23 Musketeer	R. Sweet & B D. Corbett	
G-AWGA	A.109 Airedale	RAFGSA/Bicester	
G-AWGD	Cessna F.172H	Brook Shaw Ltd	
G-AWGJ	Cessna F.172H	J. & C. J. Freeman/Headcorn	
G-AWGK	Cessna F.150H	G. R. Brown/Shoreham	
G-AWGM	Arkle Kittiwake 2	A. F. S. Caldecourt	
G-AWGN	Fournier RF-4D	R. H. Ashforth/Staverton	
G-AWGR	Cessna F.172H	P. Bushell/Liverpool	
G-AWGZ	Taylor JT.1 Monoplane	A. Hill	
G-AWHV	Rollason Beta B.2A	Tiger Club Ltd/Redhill	
G-AWHW	Rollason Beta B.2A	V. S. E. Norman	
G-AWHX	Rollason Beta B.2	J. J. Cooke/White Waltham	
G-AWII	V.S.349 Spitfire VC (AR501)	Shuttleworth Trust/Duxford	
G-AWIN	Campbell-Bensen B.8MC	M. J. Cuttel & J. Deane	
G-AWIP	Luton LA-4A Minor	J. Houghton	
G-AWIR	Midget Mustang	K. E. Sword/Leicester	
G-AWIT	PA-28 Cherokee 180	H.M. Air Ltd	
G-AWIV	Airmark TSR.3	C. J. Jesson/Redhill	
G-AWIW	Stampe SV-4B	R. E. Mitchell	
G-AWIY	PA-23 Aztec 250	B. Anderson/Belfast	
G-AWJA	Cessna 182L Skylane	D. Penny	
G-AWJC	Brighton gas balloon	P. D. Furlong *Slippery William*	
G-AWJE	Nipper T.66 Srs. 3	N. McArthur & T. Mosedale	
G-AWJF	Nipper T.66 Srs. 3	R. Wilcock/Shoreham	
G-AWJI	M.S.880B Rallye Club	D. V. Tyler/Southend	
G-AWJV	D.H.98 Mosquito TT Mk 35 (TA634) ★	Mosquito Aircraft Museum	
G-AWJX	Z.526 Akrobat	Aerobatics International Ltd	
G-AWJY	Z.526 Akrobat	Elco Manufacturing Co/Redhill	
G-AWKB	M.J.5 Sirocco F2/39	G. D. Claxton	
G-AWKD	PA-17 Vagabond	A. T. & M. R. Dowie/ White Waltham	
G-AWKM	B.121 Pup 1	D. M. G. Jenkins/Swansea	
G-AWKO	B.121 Pup 1	Golden Lion Flying Group/Redhill	
G-AWKP	Jodel DR.253	R. C. Chandless	
G-AWKT	M.S.880B Rallye Club	D. C. Strain	
G-AWKX	Beech A65 Queen Air	Keeler Air Transport Service/Shoreham	
G-AWLA	Cessna F.150H	Royal Artillery Aero Club Ltd/ Middle Wallop	
G-AWLE	Cessna F.172H	H. Mendelssohn & H. I. Shott	
G-AWLF	Cessna F.172H	Osprey Air Services Ltd	
G-AWLG	SIPA 903	S. W. Markham	
G-AWLI	PA-22 Tri-Pacer 150	H. J. W. Ellison/Biggin Hill	
G-AWLL	AB-206B JetRanger 2	F. Lloyd (Penley) Ltd	
G-AWLM	Bensen B.8MS	C. J. E. Ashby	
G-AWLO	Boeing N2S-5 Kaydet	N. D. Pickard	
G-AWLP	Mooney M.20F	Petratek Ltd	
G-AWLR	Nipper T. 66 Srs. 3	J. D. Lawther	
G-AWLS	Nipper T. 66 Srs. 3	Stapleford Nipper Group	
G-AWLY	Cessna F.150H	Banbury Plant Hire Ltd	
G-AWLZ	Fournier RF-4D	E. V. Goodwin & C. R. Williamson	
G-AWMD	Jodel D.11	K. Dawson & E. Chandler/Stapleford	
G-AWMF	PA-18 Super Cub 150	Airways Aero Associations Ltd/Booker	
G-AWMI	Glos-Airtourer 115	Airtourer Group 86/Cardiff	
G-AWMK	AB-206B JetRanger	Bristow Helicopters Ltd	
G-AWMM	M.S.893A Rallye Commodore 180	Tug 83 Group/Perranporth	
G-AWMN	Luton LA-4A Minor	R. E. R. Wilks	
G-AWMP	Cessna F.172H	W. Rennie-Roberts/Ipswich	
G-AWMR	D.31 Turbulent	K. Wales	
G-AWMT	Cessna F.150H	R. V. Grocott/Sleap	
G-AWMZ	Cessna F.172H ★	*Parachute jump trainer*/Cark	
G-AWNA	Boeing 747-136	British Airways *City of Peterborough*/ Heathrow	

Notes	Reg.	Type	Owner or Operator
	G-AWNB	Boeing 747-136	British Airways *City of Newcastle*/Heathrow
	G-AWNC	Boeing 747-136	British Airways *City of Belfast*/Heathrow
	G-AWND	Boeing 747-136	British Airways *City of Leeds*/Heathrow
	G-AWNE	Boeing 747-136	British Airways *City of Southampton*/Heathrow
	G-AWNF	Boeing 747-136	British Airways *City of Westminster*/Heathrow
	G-AWNG	Boeing 747-136	British Airways *City of London*/Heathrow
	G-AWNH	Boeing 747-136	British Airways *City of Elgin*/Heathrow
	G-AWNJ	Boeing 747-136	British Airways *City of Sheffield*/Heathrow
	G-AWNL	Boeing 747-136	British Airways *City of Nottingham*/Heathrow
	G-AWNM	Boeing 747-136	British Airways *City of Bristol*/Heathrow
	G-AWNN	Boeing 747-136	British Airways *City of Leicester*/Heathrow
	G-AWNO	Boeing 747-136	British Airways *City of Durham*/Heathrow
	G-AWNP	Boeing 747-136	British Airways *City of Portsmouth*/Heathrow
	G-AWNT	BN-2A Islander	Hunting Surveys & Consultants Ltd/Leavesden
	G-AWOA	M.S.880B Rallye Club	E. & M. Craven/Barton
	G-AWOE	Aero Commander 680E	J. M. Houlder/Elstree
	G-AWOF	PA-15 Vagabond	E. J. & S. McEntee/White Waltham
	G-AWOH	PA-17 Vagabond	K. M. & H. Bowen
	G-AWOL	Bell 206B JetRanger 2	J. Palmer
	G-AWOT	Cessna F.150H	J. M. Montgomerie & J. Ferguson
	G-AWOU	Cessna 170B	P. Chaplin/Booker
	G-AWOX	W.S-58 Wessex 60 ★	Sykes Aviation Ltd (*stored*)
	G-AWPH	P.56 Provost T.1	J. A. D. Bradshaw
	G-AWPJ	Cessna F.150H	W. J. Greenfield
	G-AWPN	Shield Xyla	T. Brown
	G-AWPS	PA-28 Cherokee 140	Jakecourt Ltd/Bournemouth
	G-AWPU	Cessna F.150J	Light Planes (Lancashire) Ltd/Barton
	G-AWPW	PA-12 Super Cruiser	J. E. Davies/Sandown
	G-AWPX	Cessna 150E	W. R. Emberton/Southampton
	G-AWPY	Bensen B.8M	J. Jordan
	G-AWPZ	Andreasson BA-4B	J. M. Vening
	G-AWRK	Cessna F.150J	Southern Strut Flying Club/Shoreham
	G-AWRL	Cessna F.172H	T. Hayselden (Doncaster) Ltd
	G-AWRS	Avro 19 Srs. 2 ★	N. E. Aircraft Museum
	G-AWRY	P.56 Provost T.1 (XF836)	Slymar Aviation & Services Ltd/Popham
	G-AWRZ	Bell 47G-5	Hammond Aerial Spraying Ltd
	G-AWSA	Avro 652A Anson 19 (VL349) ★	Norfolk & Suffolk Aviation Museum
	G-AWSD	Cessna F.150J	British Skysports
	G-AWSL	PA-28 Cherokee 180D	Fascia Ltd/Southend
	G-AWSM	PA-28 Cherokee 235	Firecrest Aviation Ltd/Leavesden
	G-AWSN	D.62B Condor	J. Leader
	G-AWSP	D.62B Condor	R. Q. & A. S. Bond/Wellesbourne
	G-AWSS	D.62C Condor	G. Bruce
	G-AWST	D.62B Condor	Humberside Aviation/Doncaster
	G-AWSV	Skeeter 12 (XM553)	Maj. M. Somerton-Rayner/Middle Wallop
	G-AWSY	Boeing 737-204	Britannia Airways Ltd *General James Wolfe*/Luton
	G-AWTA	Cessna E.310N	Heliscott Ltd
	G-AWTJ	Cessna F.150J	Metropolitan Police Flying Club/Biggin Hill
	G-AWTL	PA-28 Cherokee 180D	S. J. Lambden/Southend
	G-AWTR	Beech A.23 Musketeer	J. & P. Donoher
	G-AWTS	Beech A.23 Musketeer	M. Corbett & ptnrs
	G-AWTV	Beech A.23 Musketeer	A. Johnston/Blackbushe
	G-AWTW	Beech B.55 Baron	Ingham Aviation Ltd/Bristol
	G-AWTX	Cessna F.150J	R. D. & E. Forster
	G-AWUA	Cessna P.206D	Balmar Aviation/Thruxton
	G-AWUB	GY-201 Minicab	H. P. Burrill

Reg.	Type	Owner or Operator	Notes
G-AWUE	Jodel DR.1050	S. Bichan	
G-AWUG	Cessna F.150H	P. P. D. Howard-Johnston/Edinburgh	
G-AWUH	Cessna F.150H	Airtime (Hampshire) Ltd	
G-AWUJ	Cessna F.150H	W. Lawton/Doncaster	
G-AWUL	Cessna F.150H	E. I. Bett	
G-AWUN	Cessna F.150H	Northamptonshire School of Flying Ltd/ Sywell	
G-AWUO	Cessna F.150H	K. A. Ellis/Sibson	
G-AWUP	Cessna F.150H	R. H. Timmis	
G-AWUS	Cessna F.150J	Recreational Flying Centre (Popham) Ltd	
G-AWUT	Cessna F.150J	L. Salmon/Tollerton	
G-AWUW	Cessna F.172H	B. Stewart/Panshanger	
G-AWUX	Cessna F.172H	V. Gray & ptnrs/Headcorn	
G-AWUZ	Cessna F.172H	March Microwave Ltd/Andrewsfield	
G-AWVA	Cessna F.172H	C. F. Bishop	
G-AWVB	Jodel D.117	C. M. & T. R. C. Griffin	
G-AWVC	B.121 Pup 1	S. W. Bates	
G-AWVE	Jodel DR.1050M.I	E. A. Taylor/Southend	
G-AWVF	P.56 Provost T.1 (XF877)	J. Harper/Bourn	
G-AWVG	AESL Airtourer T.2	C. J. Schofield & G. M. Gearing	
G-AWVN	Aeronca 7AC Champion	Bowker Air Services Ltd/Rush Green	
G-AWVZ	Jodel D.112	D. C. Stokes/Dunkeswell	
G-AWWE	B.121 Pup 2	J. M. Randle/Coventry	
G-AWWF	B.121 Pup 1	N. M. Morris & Keef & Co Ltd	
G-AWWI	Jodel D.117	R. L. Sambell/Coventry	
G-AWWM	GY-201 Minicab	J. S. Brayshaw	
G-AWWN	Jodel DR.1051	T. W. M. Beck & ptnrs	
G-AWWO	Jodel DR.1050	Whiskey Oscar Group/Barton	
G-AWWP	Aerosport Woody Pusher III	M. S. Bird & R. D. Bird	
G-AWWT	D.31 Turbulent	M. A. Sherry & J. Tring/Redhill	
G-AWWU	Cessna FR.172F	Westward Airways (Lands End) Ltd	
G-AWWW	Cessna 401	Westair Flying Services Ltd/Blackpool	
G-AWWX	BAC One-Eleven 509	Dan-Air Services Ltd/Gatwick	
G-AWWZ	BAC One-Eleven 509	British Island Airways PLC *Island Empress*/Gatwick	
G-AWXA	Cessna 182M	P. Cannon	
G-AWXO	H.S.125 Srs. 400B	Twinjet Aircraft Sales Ltd/Luton	
G-AWXR	PA-28 Cherokee 180D	J. D. Williams	
G-AWXS	PA-28 Cherokee 180D	Rayhenro Flying Group/Shobdon	
G-AWXU	Cessna F.150J	B. B. Burtenshaw & ptnrs	
G-AWXV	Cessna F.172H	BAe Warton Flying Club	
G-AWXX	W.S.58 Wessex Mk. 60 Srs. 1	Sykes Group Co Ltd/Bournemouth	
G-AWXY	M.S.885 Super Rallye	Arrow Group/Shipdham	
G-AWXZ	SNCAN SV-4C (D88)	Personal Plane Services Ltd/Booker	
G-AWYB	Cessna FR.172F	C. W. Larkin/Southend	
G-AWYE	H.S.125 Srs 1B	Flamebird Ltd/Jersey	
G-AWYF	G.159 Gulfstream 1	Ford Motor Co Ltd/Stansted	
G-AWYJ	B.121 Pup 2	H. C. Taylor	
G-AWYL	Jodel DR.253B	Clarville Ltd/Headcorn	
G-AWYO	B.121 Pup 1	B. R. C. Wild/Popham	
G-AWYR	BAC One-Eleven 501	BCal/British Airways *Isle of Tiree*/ Gatwick	
G-AWYS	BAC One-Eleven 501	BCal/British Airways *Isle of Bute*/ Gatwick	
G-AWYT	BAC One-Eleven 501	BCal/British Airways *Isle of Barra*/ Gatwick	
G-AWYU	BAC One-Eleven 501	BCal/British Airways *Isle of Colonsay*/Gatwick	
G-AWYV	BAC One-Eleven 501	BCal/British Airways *Isle of Harris*/Gatwick	
G-AWYX	M.S.880B Rallye Club	Joy M. L. Edwards/Exeter	
G-AWYY	T.57 Camel replica (B6401)	FAA Museum/Yeovilton	
G-AWZE	H.S.121 Trident 3B ★	*Instructional airframe*/Heathrow	
G-AWZJ	H.S.121 Trident 3B ★	British Airports Authority/Prestwick	
G-AWZK	H.S.121 Trident 3B ★	*Ground trainer*/Heathrow	
G-AWZM	H.S.121 Trident 3B ★	Science Museum/Wroughton	
G-AWZN	H.S.121 Trident 3B ★	Cranfield Institute of Technology	
G-AWZO	H.S.121 Trident 3B ★	British Aerospace/Hatfield	
G-AWZP	H.S.121 Trident 3B ★	Greater Manchester Museum of Science & Technology (*nose only*)	
G-AWZR	H.S.121 Trident 3B ★	CAA Fire School/Teesside	
G-AWZU	H.S.121 Trident 3B ★	British Airports Authority/Stansted	
G-AWZX	H.S.121 Trident 3B ★	BAA Fire Services/Gatwick	

Notes	Reg.	Type	Owner or Operator
	G-AWZZ	H.S.121 Trident 3B ★	Airport Fire Services/Birmingham
	G-AXAB	PA-28 Cherokee 140	Bencray Ltd/Blackpool
	G-AXAK	M.S.880B Rallye Club	R. L. & C. Stewart
	G-AXAN	D.H.82A Tiger Moth (EM720)	Comarket Aviation Ltd/Staverton
	G-AXAO	Omega 56 balloon	P. D. Furlong
	G-AXAS	Wallis WA-116T	K. H. Wallis (G-AVDH)
	G-AXAT	Jodel D.117A	J. F. Barber & ptnrs/Southend
	G-AXAU	PA-30 Twin Comanche 160C	Bartcourt Ltd
	G-AXAV	PA-30 Twin Comanche 160C	P. S. King/Guernsey
	G-AXAW	Cessna 421A	P. J. McGoldrick/Stansted
	G-AXAX	PA-23 Aztec 250D	J. G. Woods/Shoreham
	G-AXBB	BAC One-Eleven 409	British Island Airways PLC Island Entente/Gatwick
	G-AXBF	Beagle D.5/180 Husky	C. H. Barnes
	G-AXBH	Cessna F.172H	Photoair Ltd/Sibson
	G-AXBJ	Cessna F.172H	K. M. Brennan & C. Mackay/Leicester
	G-AXBW	D.H.82A Tiger Moth (T5879)	R. Venning
	G-AXBZ	D.H.82A Tiger Moth	D. H. McWhir
	G-AXCA	PA-28R Cherokee Arrow 200	N. D. Douglas
	G-AXCG	Jodel D.117	D. R. Lindy
	G-AXCI	Bensen B.8M ★	Loughborough & Leicester Aircraft Museum
	G-AXCL	M.S.880B Rallye Club	Long Marston Flying Group
	G-AXCM	M.S.880B Rallye Club	Avcom Developments Ltd/Denham
	G-AXCN	M.S.880B Rallye Club	J. E. Compton
	G-AXCX	B.121 Pup 2	R. S. Blackman/Elstree
	G-AXCY	Jodel D.117	J. Gillespie
	G-AXDB	Piper L-4B Cub	J. R. Wraight
	G-AXDC	PA-23 Aztec 250D	N. J. Lilley/Bodmin
	G-AXDE	Bensen B.8	T. J. Hartwell
	G-AXDH	BN-2A Islander	J. P. Lewington
	G-AXDI	Cessna F.172H	M. F. & J. R. Leusby/Conington
	G-AXDK	Jodel DR.315	P. J. Checketts & T. J. Thomas
	G-AXDM	H.S.125 Srs 400B	Ferranti Ltd/Edinburgh
	G-AXDN	BAC-Sud Concorde 01 ★	Duxford Aviation Soc
	G-AXDU	B.121 Pup 2	R. Wilson/Cambridge
	G-AXDV	B.121 Pup 1	C. N. G. Hobbs & J. J. Teagle
	G-AXDW	B.121 Pup 1	Cranfield Institute of Technology
	G-AXDY	Falconar F-II	J. Nunn
	G-AXDZ	Cassutt Racer Srs IIIM	A. Chadwick/Little Staughton
	G-AXEB	Cassutt Racer Srs IIIM	G. E. Horder/Redhill
	G-AXEC	Cessna 182M	H. S. Mulligan & E. R. Wilson
	G-AXED	PA-25 Pawnee 235	Wolds Gliding Club Ltd
	G-AXEH	B.121 Pup ★	Museum of Flight/E. Fortune
	G-AXEI	Ward Gnome ★	Lincolnshire Aviation Museum
	G-AXEO	Scheibe SF.25B Falke	Newcastle & Tees-side Gliding Club Ltd
	G-AXES	B.121 Pup 2	P. A. G. Field/Nairobi
	G-AXEV	B.121 Pup 2	T. D. Staveker/Birmingham
	G-AXFD	PA-25 Pawnee 235	J.E.F. Aviation Ltd
	G-AXFE	Beech B.90 King Air	T. S. Grimshaw Ltd/Cardiff
	G-AXFH	D.H.114 Heron 1B/C	Topflight Aviation Co Ltd
	G-AXFN	Jodel D.119	T. Peil & ptnrs/Woodvale
	G-AXGC	M.S.880B Rallye Club	Ian Richard Transport Services Ltd
	G-AXGE	M.S.880B Rallye Club	R. P. Loxton
	G-AXGG	Cessna F.150J	A. R. Nicholls
	G-AXGP	Piper L-4B Cub	W. K. Butler
	G-AXGR	Luton LA-4A Minor	J. M. Kellett & A. J. E. Tiley
	G-AXGS	D.62B Condor	Tiger Club Ltd/Redhill
	G-AXGT	D.62B Condor	P. J. Simpson & ptnrs
	G-AXGU	D.62B Condor	Tiger Club Ltd/Redhill
	G-AXGV	D.62B Condor	R. J. Wrixon
	G-AXGZ	D.62B Condor	Lincoln Condor Group/Sturgate
	G-AXHA	Cessna 337A	G. Evans
	G-AXHC	Stampe SV-4C	BLS Aviation Ltd/Denham
	G-AXHE	BN-2A Islander	NW Parachute Centre/Cark
	G-AXHI	M.S.880B Rallye Club	J. M. Whittard
	G-AXHO	B.121 Pup 2	L. W. Grundy/Stapleford
	G-AXHP	Piper L-4H Cub	R. Giles
	G-AXHR	Piper L-4H Cub (329601)	I. S. Hodge
	G-AXHS	M.S.880B Rallye Club	D. Horne & ptnrs
	G-AXHT	M.S.880B Rallye Club	J. A. Levey
	G-AXHV	Jodel D.117A	D. M. Cashmore & K. R. Payne
	G-AXHX	M.S.892A Rallye Commodore	D. W. Weever

Reg.	Type	Owner or Operator	Notes
G-AXIA	B.121 Pup 1	Cranfield Institute of Technology	
G-AXIE	B.121 Pup 2	I. J. Ross & D. I. McBride	
G-AXIF	B.121 Pup 2	T. G. Hiscock/Elstree	
G-AXIG	B.125 Bulldog 104	George House (Holdings) Ltd	
G-AXIO	PA-28 Cherokee 140B	W. London Aero Services Ltd/ White Waltham	
G-AXIR	PA-28 Cherokee 140B	M. F. L. Purse/Weston Zoyland	
G-AXIT	M.S.893A Rallye Commodore 180	South Wales Gliding Club Ltd	
G-AXIW	Scheibe SF.25B Falke	Kent Motor Gliding & Soaring Centre/ Manston	
G-AXIX	Glos-Airtourer 150	G. C. Thomas	
G-AXIY	Bird Gyrocopter	E. N. Grace	
G-AXJB	Omega 84 balloon	Hot-Air Group Jester	
G-AXJH	B.121 Pup 2	J. S. Chillingworth	
G-AXJI	B.121 Pup 2	Cole Aviation Ltd/Southend	
G-AXJJ	B.121 Pup 2	The Bumpf Group/Crosland Moor	
G-AXJK	BAC One-Eleven 501	BCal/British Airways Isle of Staffa/Gatwick	
G-AXJM	BAC One-Eleven 501	BCal/British Airways Isle of Islay/ Gatwick	
G-AXJN	B.121 Pup 2	D. M. Jenkins/Shoreham	
G-AXJO	B.121 Pup 2	J. A. D. Bradshaw	
G-AXJR	Scheibe SF.25B Falke	D. R. Chatterton	
G-AXJV	PA-28 Cherokee 140B	Mona Aviation Ltd	
G-AXJW	PA-28 Cherokee 140B	S. A. Vale & P. C. Dimond/Shoreham	
G-AXJX	PA-28 Cherokee 140B	I. R. Smith/Barton	
G-AXJY	Cessna U-206D	Hereford Parachute Club Ltd/Shobdon	
G-AXKD	PA-23 Aztec 250D	P. P. D. Howard-Johnston/Edinburgh	
G-AXKH	Luton LA-4A Minor	M. E. Vaisey	
G-AXKI	Jodel D.9 Bebe	A. F. Cashin	
G-AXKJ	Jodel D.9 Bebe	J. R. Surbey	
G-AXKK	Westland Bell 47G-4A	Bristow Helicopters Ltd	
G-AXKO	Westland Bell 47G-4A	Bristow Helicopters Ltd	
G-AXKR	Westland Bell 47G-4A	Robert & Hewett Agriculture Ltd	
G-AXKS	Westland Bell 47G-4A	Museum of Army Flying/Middle Wallop	
G-AXKU	Westland Bell 47G-4A	Bristow Helicopters Ltd	
G-AXKX	Westland Bell 47G-4A	Bristow Helicopters Ltd	
G-AXKY	Westland Bell 47G-4A	Bristow Helicopters Ltd	
G-AXLG	Cessna 310K	Smiths (Outdrives) Ltd	
G-AXLI	Nipper T.66 Srs 3	N. J. Arthur/Finmere	
G-AXLL	BAC One-Eleven 523FJ	BCal/British Airways/Gatwick	
G-AXLN	BAC One-Eleven 523FJ	British Island Airways PLC Island Enterprise/Gatwick	
G-AXLS	Jodel DR.105A	E. Gee/Southampton	
G-AXLZ	PA-19 Super Cub 95	J. C. Quantrell/Shipdham	
G-AXMA	PA-24 Comanche 180	Tegrel Products Ltd/Newcastle	
G-AXMB	Slingsby T.7 Motor Cadet 2	I. G. Smith/Langar	
G-AXMD	Omega 20 balloon ★	British Balloon Museum	
G-AXME	SNCAN SV-4C	D. W. Hawthorne/Oporto	
G-AXMG	BAC One-Eleven 518	British Island Airways PLC Island Emblem/Gatwick	
G-AXMN	J/5B Autocar	A. Phillips	
G-AXMP	PA-28 Cherokee 180	P. Taylor	
G-AXMS	PA-30 Twin Comanche 160C	Ernest Green International Ltd	
G-AXMU	BAC One-Eleven 432	British Island Airways PLC/Gatwick	
G-AXMW	B.121 Pup 1	DJP Engineering (Knebworth) Ltd	
G-AXMX	B.121 Pup 2	Susan A. Jones/Cannes	
G-AXNA	Boeing 737-204C	Britannia Airways Ltd Robert Clive of India/Luton	
G-AXNB	Boeing 737-204C	Britannia Airways Ltd Charles Darwin/ Luton	
G-AXNC	Boeing 737-204	Britannia Airways Ltd Isambard Kingdom Brunel/Luton	
G-AXNJ	Wassmer Jodel D.120	Clive Flying Group/Sleap	
G-AXNK	Cessna F.150J	Fowler Aviation Ltd/Leavesden	
G-AXNL	B.121 Pup 1	D. C. Barber/St Just	
G-AXNM	B.121 Pup 1	D. F. Ranger/Old Sarum	
G-AXNN	B.121 Pup 2	Romney Marsh Flying Group/Lydd	
G-AXNP	B.121 Pup 2	J. W. & K. E. Ellis	
G-AXNR	B.121 Pup 2	P. A. Jackson & ptnrs	
G-AXNS	B.121 Pup 2	T. Wood	
G-AXNW	SNCAN SV-4C	C. S. Grace	
G-AXNX	Cessna 182M	P. Reid/Halfpenny Green	

Notes	Reg.	Type	Owner or Operator
	G-AXNZ	Pitts S.1C Special	W. A. Jordan
	G-AXOG	PA-23 Aztec 250D	R. W. Diggens/Denham
	G-AXOH	M.S.894 Rallye Minerva	Bristol Cars Ltd/White Waltham
	G-AXOI	Jodel D.9 Bebe	P. R. Underhill
	G-AXOJ	B.121 Pup 2	K. Fitzsimons
	G-AXOL	Currie Wot	A. Kennedy & ptnrs/Andrewsfield
	G-AXOR	PA-28 Cherokee 180D	Axor Aviation Ltd/Compton Abbas
	G-AXOS	M.S.894A Rallye Minerva	T. E. H. Simmons & S. L. Laker
	G-AXOT	M.S.893 Rallye Commodore 180	P. Evans & D. Riley
	G-AXOV	Beech B55A Baron	S. Brod/Elstree
	G-AXOX	BAC One-Eleven 432	British Island Airways PLC *Island Endeavour*/Gatwick
	G-AXOZ	B.121 Pup 1	Arrow Air Centre Ltd/Shipdham
	G-AXPB	B.121 Pup 1	C. N. Carter
	G-AXPD	B.121 Pup 1	C. A. Thorpe
	G-AXPF	Cessna F.150K	Y. Newell/Booker
	G-AXPG	Mignet HM-293	W. H. Cole (*stored*)
	G-AXPM	B.121 Pup 1	M. J. Coton
	G-AXPN	B.121 Pup 2	Isohigh Ltd
	G-AXPZ	Campbell Cricket	W. R. Partridge
	G-AXRA	Campbell Cricket	L. E. Schnurr
	G-AXRC	Campbell Cricket	K. W. Hayr (*stored*)
	G-AXRK	Practavia Sprite 115	E. G. Thale
	G-AXRL	PA-28 Cherokee 160	T. W. Clark/Headcorn
	G-AXRO	PA-30 Twin Comanche 160C	Lydd Air Training Centre Ltd
	G-AXRP	SNCAN SV-4C	C. C. Manning
	G-AXRR	Auster AOP.9 (XR241) ★	British Aerial Museum/Duxford
	G-AXRT	Cessna FA.150K (tailwheel)	W. R. Pickett/Southampton
	G-AXRU	Cessna FA.150K	Arrival Enterprises Ltd/Denham
	G-AXSC	B.121 Pup 1	T. R. Golding & C. Spencer
	G-AXSD	B.121 Pup 1	A. C. Townend
	G-AXSF	Nash Petrel	Nash Aircraft Ltd/Lasham
	G-AXSG	PA-28 Cherokee 180	Shropshire Aero Club Ltd/Sleap
	G-AXSM	Jodel DR.1051	C. Cousten/White Waltham
	G-AXSV	Jodel DR.340	Leonard F. Jollye Ltd/Panshanger
	G-AXSW	Cessna FA.150K	Furness Aviation Ltd/Walney Island
	G-AXSZ	PA-28 Cherokee 140B	N. Cureton & ptnrs/Sandown
	G-AXTA	PA-28 Cherokee 140B	P. Barry & I. Cameron/Shoreham
	G-AXTC	PA-28 Cherokee 140B	B. Mellor & J. Hutchinson
	G-AXTD	PA-28 Cherokee 140B	G. R. Walker/Southend
	G-AXTH	PA-28 Cherokee 140B	W. London Aero Services Ltd/ White Waltham
	G-AXTI	PA-28 Cherokee 140B	I. K. George/Fairoaks
	G-AXTJ	PA-28 Cherokee 140B	A. P. Merrifield/Stapleford
	G-AXTL	PA-28 Cherokee 140B	P. Murphy & R. Flower/Blackbushe
	G-AXTO	PA-24 Comanche 260	J. L. Wright
	G-AXTP	PA-28 Cherokee 180	E. R. Moore/Elstree
	G-AXTX	Jodel D.112	J. J. Penney
	G-AXUA	B.121 Pup 1	F. R. Blennerhassett & C. Wedlake/ Tees-side
	G-AXUB	BN-2A Islander	Headcorn Parachute Club
	G-AXUC	PA-12 Super Cruiser	J. J. Bunton
	G-AXUE	Jodel DR.105A	L. Lewis
	G-AXUF	Cessna FA.150K	A. J. Redknap
	G-AXUI	H.P.137 Jetstream 1	Cranfield Institute of Technology
	G-AXUJ	J/1 Autocrat	R. G. Earp & J. W. H. Lee/Sibson
	G-AXUK	Jodel DR.1050	Ambassadeur Flying/Bicester
	G-AXUM	H.P.137 Jetstream 1	Cranfield Institute of Technology
	G-AXUW	Cessna FA.150K	Coventry Air Training School
	G-AXVB	Cessna F.172H	C. Gabbitas/Staverton
	G-AXVC	Cessna FA.150K	V. F. Lynn/Sibson
	G-AXVK	Campbell Cricket	L. W. Harding
	G-AXVM	Campbell Cricket	D. M. Organ
	G-AXVN	McCandless M.4	W. R. Partridge
	G-AXVU	Omega 84 balloon	Brede Balloons Ltd *Henry VIII*
	G-AXVV	Piper L-4H Cub	J. MacCarthy
	G-AXVW	Cessna F.150K	R. A. Nichols/Elstree
	G-AXVX	Cessna F.172H	Judgenote Ltd
	G-AXWA	Auster AOP.9 (XN437)	T. Platt/Biggin Hill
	G-AXWB	Omega 65 balloon	A. Robinson & M. J. Moore *Ezekiel*
	G-AXWF	Cessna F.172H	Red Fir Aviation Ltd/Clacton
	G-AXWH	BN-2A Islander	Midland Parachute Centre Ltd
	G-AXWP	BN-2A Islander	Aurigny Air Services/Guernsey

Reg.	Type	Owner or Operator	Notes
G-AXWR	BN-2A Islander	Aurigny Air Services/Guernsey	
G-AXWT	Jodel D.11	R. C. Owen	
G-AXWV	Jodel DR.253	J. R. D. Bygraves/O. Warden	
G-AXWZ	PA-28R Cherokee Arrow 200	R. F. Grute & M. K. Taylor	
G-AXXC	CP.301B Emeraude	J. R. R. Gale & J. Tetley	
G-AXXG	BN-2A Islander	Van Diemen International Racing Services Ltd	
G-AXXJ	BN-2A Islander	Air Wight Ltd/Bembridge	
G-AXXV	D.H.82A Tiger Moth (DE992)	J. I. Hyslop	
G-AXXW	Jodel D.117	D. J. & M. Watson	
G-AXYA	PA-31-300 Navajo	W. R. M. C. Foyle/Luton	
G-AXYD	BAC One-Eleven 509	Dan-Air Services Ltd/Gatwick	
G-AXYK	Taylor JT.1 Monoplane	C. Oakins	
G-AXYM	BN-2A Islander	A1 Skydiving Centre Ltd/Bassingbourn	
G-AXYY	WHE Airbuggy	R. A. A. Chiles	
G-AXYZ	WHE Airbuggy	W. B. Lumb	
G-AXZA	WHE Airbuggy	B. Gunn	
G-AXZB	WHE Airbuggy	D. R. C. Pugh	
G-AXZD	PA-28 Cherokee 180E	M. D. Callaghan & ptnrs	
G-AXZF	PA-28 Cherokee 180E	E. P. C. & W. R. Rabson/Southampton	
G-AXZK	BN-2A Islander	Atlantic Air Transport Ltd/Coventry	
G-AXZM	Slingsby Nipper T.66 Srs 3	G. R. Harlow	
G-AXZO	Cessna 180	A. R. Brett	
G-AXZP	PA-E23 Aztec 250C	Aviation East Ltd	
G-AXZT	Jodel D.117	H. W. Baines	
G-AXZU	Cessna 182N	Earthlogic Ltd	
G-AYAA	PA-28 Cherokee 180E	Briskloom Ltd/Manchester	
G-AYAB	PA-28 Cherokee 180E	J. A. & J. C. Cunningham	
G-AYAC	PA-28R Cherokee Arrow 200	Fersfield Flying Group	
G-AYAI	Fournier RF-5	Exeter RF Group	
G-AYAJ	Cameron O-84 balloon	E. T. Hall *Flaming Pearl*	
G-AYAL	Omega 56 balloon	British Balloon Museum	
G-AYAN	Slingsby Motor Cadet Mk III	I. Stevenson	
G-AYAP	PA-28 Cherokee 180E	Gala Air Holidays Ltd/Stapleford	
G-AYAR	PA-28 Cherokee 180E	C. H. Campbell/Elstree	
G-AYAT	PA-28 Cherokee 180E	P. J. Messervy/Norwich	
G-AYAU	PA-28 Cherokee 180E	Tiarco Ltd	
G-AYAV	PA-28 Cherokee 180E	Bawtry Road Service Station Ltd/Netherthorpe	
G-AYAW	PA-28 Cherokee 180E	Wizard Air Services Ltd/Coventry	
G-AYBD	Cessna F.150K	D. G. & W. B. Adams	
G-AYBG	Scheibe SF.25B Falke	D. J. Rickman	
G-AYBK	PA-28 Cherokee 180E	Firecrest Aviation Ltd/Leavesden	
G-AYBO	PA-23 Aztec 250D	Twinguard Aviation Ltd/Elstree	
G-AYBP	Jodel D.112	Fairwood Flying Group/Swansea	
G-AYBU	Western 84 balloon	D. R. Gibbons	
G-AYBV	Chasle YC-12 Tourbillon	B. A. Mills	
G-AYCC	Campbell Cricket	K. W. E. Denson	
G-AYCE	CP.301C Emeraude	R. A. Austin/Bodmin	
G-AYCF	Cessna FA.150K	E. J. Atkins/Popham	
G-AYCG	SNCAN SV-4C	N. Bignall/Booker	
G-AYCJ	Cessna TP.206D	H. O. Holm/Bournemouth	
G-AYCM	Bell 206A JetRanger	W.R. Finance Ltd	
G-AYCN	Piper L-4H Cub	W. R. & B. M. Young	
G-AYCO	CEA DR.360	L. M. Gould/Jersey	
G-AYCP	Jodel D.112	D. J. Nunn	
G-AYCT	Cessna F.172H	Fife Airport Management & Kontrox Ltd/Glenrothes	
G-AYDG	M.S.894A Rallye Minerva	Hills Office Equipment Ltd & AFS Printing Ltd/Stapleford	
G-AYDI	D.H.82A Tiger Moth	R. B. Woods & ptnrs	
G-AYDR	SNCAN SV-4C	R. A. Phillips	
G-AYDV	Coates SA.II-1 Swalesong	J. R. Coates/Rush Green	
G-AYDW	A.61 Terrier 2	J. S. Harwood	
G-AYDX	A.61 Terrier 2	G. W. & M. M. Bisshopp	
G-AYDY	Luton LA-4A Minor	T. Littlefair & N. Clark	
G-AYDZ	Jodel DR.200	F. M. Ward	
G-AYEB	Jodel D.112	B. Ibbott	
G-AYEC	CP.301A Emeraude	Snowdon Aviation/Mona	
G-AYED	PA-24 Comanche 260	C. A. Saville	
G-AYEE	PA-28 Cherokee 180E	D. J. Beale	
G-AYEF	PA-28 Cherokee 180E	L. Cheetham	
G-AYEG	Falconar F-9	A. G. Thelwall	

Notes	Reg.	Type	Owner or Operator
	G-AYEH	Jodel DR.1050	R. O. F. Harper & P. R. Skeels/Barton
	G-AYEI	PA-31-300 Navajo	G-Air Ltd/Goodwood
	G-AYEJ	Jodel DR.1050	J. M. Newbold
	G-AYEK	Jodel DR.1050	I. Shaw & B. Hanson/Sherburn
	G-AYEN	Piper L-4H Cub	P. Warde & C. F. Morris
	G-AYES	M.S.892A Rallye Commodore 150	Waveney Flying Group (stored)/ Seething
	G-AYET	M.S.892A Rallye Commodore 150	Osprey Flying Club/Cranfield
	G-AYEU	Brookland Hornet	M. G. Reilly
	G-AYEV	Jodel DR.1050	L. G. Evans/Headcorn
	G-AYEW	Jodel DR.1051	Taildragger Group/Halfpenny Green
	G-AYEY	Cessna F.150K	B&M Motors/Goodwood
	G-AYFA	SA Twin Pioneer 3	Flight One Ltd/Shobdon
	G-AYFC	D.62B Condor	R. A. Smith/Redhill
	G-AYFD	D.62B Condor	Tiger Club Ltd/Redhill
	G-AYFE	D.62C Condor	J. Abbess/Andrewsfield
	G-AYFF	D.62B Condor	A. F. S. Caldecourt/Fairoaks
	G-AYFG	D.62C Condor	S. R. Winder
	G-AYFJ	M.S.880B Rallye Club	E. P. Browne/Sibson
	G-AYFP	Jodel D.140	S. K. Minocha/Sherburn
	G-AYFT	PA-39 Twin Comanche C/R	Subtec Aviation Ltd
	G-AYFV	Crosby BA-4B	A. Fines/Norwich
	G-AYFX	AA-1 Yankee	P. A. Ellway & R. M. Bainbridge
	G-AYFZ	PA-31-300 Navajo	P. M. Doran
	G-AYGA	Jodel D.117	R. L. E. Horrell
	G-AYGB	Cessna 310Q	Airwork Services Ltd/Perth
	G-AYGC	Cessna F.150K	Alpha Aviation/Manchester
	G-AYGD	Jodel DR.1051	I. G. & M. Glenn
	G-AYGE	SNCAN SV-4C	The Hon A. M. J. Rothschild/Booker
	G-AYGG	Jodel D.120	R. F. Sothcott
	G-AYGK	BN-2A Islander	Pathcircle Ltd/Langar
	G-AYGN	Cessna 210K	J. W. O'Sullivan/Jersey
	G-AYGX	Cessna FR.172G	J. A. Edwards/Blackpool
	G-AYHA	AA-1 Yankee	D. L. Harrisberg & I. J. Widger/ Elstree
	G-AYHI	Campbell Cricket	J. F. MacKay
	G-AYHX	Jodel D.117A	L. J. E. Goldfinch
	G-AYHY	Fournier RF-4D	Tiger Club Ltd/Redhill
	G-AYIA	Hughes 369HS	G. D. E. Bilton/Sywell
	G-AYIB	Cessna 182N Skylane	R. M. Clarke/Leicester
	G-AYIF	PA-28 Cherokee 140C	The Hare Flying Group/Elstree
	G-AYIG	PA-28 Cherokee 140C	Snowdon Mountain Aviation Ltd
	G-AYIH	PA-28 Cherokee 140C	B. Lince/Elstree
	G-AYII	PA-28R Cherokee Arrow 200	Devon Growers Ltd & A. L. Bacon/ Exeter
	G-AYIJ	SNCAN SV-4B	K. B. Palmer/Headcorn
	G-AYIO	PA-28 Cherokee 140C	Frontline Aviation Ltd
	G-AYIT	D.H.82A Tiger Moth	R. L. H. Alexander & ptnrs/Newtownards
	G-AYJA	Jodel DR.1050	G. I. Doaks & R. J. Bleakley
	G-AYJB	SNCAN SV-4C	F. J. M. & J. P. Esson/Middle Wallop
	G-AYJD	Alpavia-Fournier RF-3	C. Wren/Southend
	G-AYJE	BN-2A-26 Islander	Headcorn Parachute Club Ltd
	G-AYJP	PA-28 Cherokee 140C	RAF Brize Norton Flying Club Ltd
	G-AYJR	PA-28 Cherokee 140C	RAF Brize Norton Flying Club Ltd
	G-AYJS	PA-28 Cherokee 140C	W. R. Griffiths & Sons (Office Furnishers) Ltd
	G-AYJT	PA-28 Cherokee 140C	Jennifer M. Lesslie/Leicester
	G-AYJU	Cessna TP-206A	Balmar Aviation/Thruxton
	G-AYJY	Isaacs Fury II	A. V. Francis
	G-AYKA	Beech 95-B55A Baron	Morris Cohen (Underwear) Ltd
	G-AYKD	Jodel DR.1050	B. P. Irish & A. W. Humphries
	G-AYKF	M.S.880B Rallye Club	Kilo Fox Flying Group/Bodmin
	G-AYKJ	Jodel D.117A	G. R. W. Monksfield/Stapleford
	G-AYKK	Jodel D.117	D. M. Whitham
	G-AYKL	Cessna F.150L	Aero Group 78/Netherthorpe
	G-AYKS	Leopoldoff L-7	C. E. & W. B. Cooper
	G-AYKT	Jodel D.117	G. Wright/Leeds
	G-AYKV	PA-28 Cherokee 140C	A. Wright/Liverpool
	G-AYKW	PA-28 Cherokee 140C	A. Jahanfar & R. W. Harris/Southend
	G-AYKX	PA-28 Cherokee 140C	M. J. Garland & ptnrs/Woodford
	G-AYKZ	SAI KZ-8	R. E. Mitchell/Coventry
	G-AYLA	Glos-Airtourer 115	R. E. Parker
	G-AYLB	PA-39 Twin Comanche C/R	Mercia Aviation/Wellesbourne

Reg.	Type	Owner or Operator	Notes
G-AYLE	M.S.880B Rallye Club	B. Butler	
G-AYLF	Jodel DR.1051	A. C. Frost & ptnrs/Cranfield	
G-AYLG	H.S.125 Srs 400B	British Aerospace PLC	
G-AYLL	Jodel DR.1050	B. R. Cornes	
G-AYLO	AA-1 Yankee	J. A. & A. J. Boyd/Cardiff	
G-AYLP	AA-1 Yankee	D. Nairn & E. Y. Hawkins	
G-AYLV	Jodel D.120	R. E. Wray/Stapleford	
G-AYLX	Hughes 269C	Feastlight Ltd/Sywell	
G-AYLY	PA-23 Aztec 250	British Island Airways PLC/Shoreham	
G-AYLZ	Super Aero 45 Srs 2	A. Topen	
G-AYME	Fournier RF-5	R. D. Goodger/Biggin Hill	
G-AYMG	HPR-7 Herald 213	Securicor Ltd/Birmingham	
G-AYMK	PA-28 Cherokee 140C	The Piper Flying Group	
G-AYML	PA-28 Cherokee 140C	J. M. Bendle/Elstree	
G-AYMN	PA-28 Cherokee 140C	H. W. Smith	
G-AYMO	PA-23 Aztec 250	RFS Transport Ltd	
G-AYMP	Currie Wot Special	H. F. Moffatt	
G-AYMR	Lederlin 380L Ladybug	J. S. Brayshaw	
G-AYMT	Jodel DR.1050	Merlin Flying Club Ltd/Hucknall	
G-AYMU	Jodel D.112	M. R. Baker	
G-AYMV	Western 20 balloon	G. F. Turnbull & ptnrs *Tinkerbelle*	
G-AYMW	Bell 206A JetRanger 2	London & Sheffield Industrial Finance Co Ltd	
G-AYMX	Bell 206A JetRanger	W. Holmes	
G-AYMZ	PA-28 Cherokee 140C	T. E. & M. G. Weetman/Prestwick	
G-AYNA	Currie Wot	J. M. Lister	
G-AYNC	Wessex Mk 60 Srs 1	Sykes Group Co Ltd	
G-AYND	Cessna 310Q	Source Premium & Promotional Consultants Ltd/Fairoaks	
G-AYNF	PA-28 Cherokee 140C	R. Foster & ptnrs	
G-AYNJ	PA-28 Cherokee 140C	G. F. Ettridge	
G-AYNN	Cessna 185B Skywagon	Bencray Ltd/Blackpool	
G-AYNP	Westland S-55 Srs 3	Bristow Helicopters Ltd	
G-AYOC	BN-2A-8 Islander	Region Airways Ltd/Southend	
G-AYOD	Cessna 172	E. N. Simmons	
G-AYOM	Sikorsky S-61N Mk 2	British International Helicopters Ltd/ Aberdeen	
G-AYOP	BAC One-Eleven 530	BCal/British Airways *Isle of Hoy*/Gatwick	
G-AYOW	Cessna 182N Skylane	C. H. Royal	
G-AYOY	Sikorsky S-61N Mk 2	British International Helicopters Ltd/ Aberdeen	
G-AYOZ	Cessna FA.150L	Exeter Flying Club Ltd	
G-AYPB	Beech C-23 Musketeer	Martlets Flying Group/Goodwood	
G-AYPD	Beech 95-B55 Baron	Sir W. S. Dugdale/Birmingham	
G-AYPE	Bo 209 Monsun	Papa Echo Ltd/Biggin Hill	
G-AYPF	Cessna F.177RG	H.W. Structures Ltd/Southend	
G-AYPG	Cessna F.177RG	D. Davies	
G-AYPH	Cessna F.177RG	D. Hewerdine & J. G. Collins	
G-AYPI	Cessna F.177RG	Cardinal Aviation Ltd/Guernsey	
G-AYPJ	PA-28 Cherokee 180	Mona Aviation Ltd	
G-AYPM	PA-19 Super Cub 95	D. H. Pattison	
G-AYPO	PA-19 Super Cub 95	R. T. Love	
G-AYPR	PA-19 Super Cub 95	J. W. Hollingsworth	
G-AYPS	PA-19 Super Cub 95	Tony Dyer Television	
G-AYPT	PA-19 Super Cub 95	P. Shires	
G-AYPU	PA-28R Cherokee Arrow 200	Alpine Ltd/Jersey	
G-AYPV	PA-28 Cherokee 140D	R. S. Mennie/Newcastle	
G-AYPZ	Campbell Cricket	A. Melody	
G-AYRF	Cessna F.150L	Northern Auto Salvage/Inverness	
G-AYRG	Cessna F.172K	W. I. Robinson	
G-AYRH	M.S.892A Rallye Commodore 150	J. D. Watt	
G-AYRI	PA-28R Cherokee Arrow 200	E. P. Van Mechelen & Delta Motor Co (Windsor) Sales Ltd/White Waltham	
G-AYRK	Cessna 150J	K. A. Learmonth/Southend	
G-AYRM	PA-28 Cherokee 140D	E. S. Dignam/Biggin Hill	
G-AYRN	Schleicher ASK-14	V. J. F. Falconer/Dunstable	
G-AYRO	Cessna FA.150L Aerobat	Thruxton Flight Centre	
G-AYRP	Cessna FA.150L Aerobat	Andrewsfield Flying Club Ltd	
G-AYRS	Jodel D.120A	J. H. Tetley & G. C. Smith/Sherburn	
G-AYRT	Cessna F.172K	W. Gibson/Thruxton	
G-AYRU	BN-2A-6 Islander	Joint Services Parachute Centre/ Netheravon	
G-AYSA	PA-23 Aztec 250C	J. M. Yendall & R. Greenhill	

Notes	Reg.	Type	Owner or Operator
	G-AYSB	PA-30 Twin Comanche 160C	R. Fotheringham & Finrad Ltd/Biggin Hill
	G-AYSD	Slingsby T.67A Falke	N. J. Heaton
	G-AYSH	Taylor JT.1 Monoplane	C. J. Lodge
	G-AYSK	Luton LA-4A Minor	P. F. Bennison & ptnrs/Barton
	G-AYSX	Cessna F.177RG	Nasaire Ltd/Liverpool
	G-AYSY	Cessna F.177RG	Bernard Vermilio & Co
	G-AYSZ	Cessna FA.150L	D. J. Forest
	G-AYTA	M.S.880B Rallye Club	Kemps Corrosion Services Ltd
	G-AYTC	PA-E23 Aztec 250C	New Guarantee Trust Finance Ltd/ E. Midlands
	G-AYTJ	Cessna 207 Super Skywagon	Foxair/Perth
	G-AYTN	Cameron O-65 balloon	P. G. Hall & R. F. Jessett *Prometheus*
	G-AYTR	CP.301A Emeraude	D. J. Knight
	G-AYTT	Phoenix PM-3 Duet	Gp Capt A. S. Knowles
	G-AYTV	MJ.2A Tempete	Tempete Group/Barton
	G-AYTY	Bensen B.8	J. H. Wood (*Stored*)
	G-AYUB	CEA DR.253B	D. J. Brook
	G-AYUH	PA-28 Cherokee 180F	M. S. Bayliss/Coventry
	G-AYUI	PA-28 Cherokee 180	Routair Aviation Services Ltd/Southend
	G-AYUJ	Evans VP-1 Volksplane	P. D. Shand & R. D. Davidson/Perth
	G-AYUL	PA-23 Aztec 250E	Northern Executive Aviation Ltd/ Manchester
	G-AYUM	Slingsby T-61A Falke	The Burn Gliding Club
	G-AYUN	Slingsby T-61A Falke	C. W. Vigar & R. J. Watts
	G-AYUP	Slingsby T-61A Falke	Cranwell Gliding Club
	G-AYUR	Slingsby T-61A Falke	W. A Urwin
	G-AYUS	Taylor JT.1 Monoplane	R. R. McKinnon & A. D. Lincoln/ Southampton
	G-AYUT	Jodel DR.1050	R. Norris
	G-AYUV	Cessna F.172H	Klingair Ltd/Conington
	G-AYUW	BAC One-Eleven 476FM	Mediterranean Express Ltd/Luton
	G-AYUX	D.H.82A Tiger Moth (PG651)	Ardentland Ltd/Booker
	G-AYUY	Cessna FA.150L Aerobat	G. C. B. Weir
	G-AYVA	Cameron O-84 balloon	A. Kirk *April Fool*
	G-AYVI	Cessna T.210H	R. H. Laing/Glasgow
	G-AYVO	Wallis WA120 Srs 1	K. H. Wallis
	G-AYVP	Woody Pusher	J. R. Wraight
	G-AYVT	Brochet MB.84 ★	Dunelm Flying Group (*stored*)
	G-AYVU	Cameron O-56 balloon	Shell-Mex & B.P. Ltd *Hot Potato*
	G-AYVY	D.H.82A Tiger Moth (PG617)	R. C. Button/Tollerton
	G-AYWA	Avro 19 Srs 2 ★	Strathallan Aircraft Collection
	G-AYWB	BAC One-Eleven 531FS	British Island Airways PLC *Island Envoy*/Gatwick
	G-AYWD	Cessna 182N	Trans Para Aviation Ltd
	G-AYWE	PA-28 Cherokee 140	Sound Properties Ltd
	G-AYWH	Jodel D.117A	J. M. Knapp & ptnrs
	G-AYWM	Glos-Airtourer Super 150	The Star Flying Group/Staverton
	G-AYWT	Stampe SV-4B	B. K. Lecomber/Denham
	G-AYWW	PA-28R Cherokee Arrow 200D	Acorn Aviation Ltd/Coventry
	G-AYXO	Luton LA-5A Major	A. C. T. Broomcroft
	G-AYXP	Jodel D.117A	G. N. Davies
	G-AYXS	SIAI-Marchetti S205-18R	D. P. & P. A. Dawson
	G-AYXT	Westland Sikorsky S-55 Srs 2	J. E. Wilkie/Blackpool
	G-AYXU	Champion 7KCAB Citabria	H. Fould & ptnrs
	G-AYXV	Cessna FA.150L	*Wreck*/Popham
	G-AYXW	Evans VP-1	J. S. Penny/Doncaster
	G-AYYD	M.S.894A Rallye Minerva	P. D. Lloyd & ptnrs
	G-AYYF	Cessna F.150L	Falcon Aero Club/Swansea
	G-AYYK	Slingsby T-61A Falke	Cornish Gliding & Flying Club Ltd/ Perranporth
	G-AYYL	Slingsby T-61A Falke	C. Wood
	G-AYYO	Jodel DR.1050/M1	Bustard Flying Club Ltd/Old Sarum
	G-AYYT	Jodel DR.1050/M1	Sicile Flying Group/Sandown
	G-AYYU	Beech C23 Musketeer	R. L. C. Appleton/Staverton
	G-AYYW	BN-2A Islander	Foster Yeoman Ltd/Biggin Hill
	G-AYYX	M.S.880B Rallye Club	S. N. T. Dempsey & ptnrs
	G-AYYY	M.S.880B Rallye Club	T. W. Heffer/Panshanger
	G-AYYZ	M.S.880B Rallye Club	R. R. & M. Mackay
	G-AYZE	PA-39 Twin Comanche 160 C/R	J. E. Balmer/Staverton
	G-AYZH	Taylor JT.2 Titch	K. J. Munro
	G-AYZI	Stampe SV-4C	W. H. Smout & C. W. A. Simmons
	G-AYZJ	Westland Sikorsky S-55 (XM685) ★	Newark Air Museum

Reg.	Type	Owner or Operator	Notes
G-AYZK	Jodel DR.1050/M1	G. Kearney & D. G. Hesketh	
G-AYZN	PA-E23 Aztec 250	International Institute of Tropical Agriculture	
G-AYZS	D.62B Condor	P. E. J. Huntley & M. N. Thrush	
G-AYZT	D.62B Condor	J. Abbess	
G-AYZU	Slingsby T-61A Falke	The Falcon Gliding Group/Enstone	
G-AYZW	Slingsby T-61A Falke	J. A. Dandie & R. J. M. Clement	
G-AZAB	PA-30 Twin Comanche 160	T. W. P. Sheffield/Humberside	
G-AZAD	Jodel DR.1051	I. C. Young & J. S. Paget/Bodmin	
G-AZAJ	PA-28R Cherokee Arrow 200B	Driscoll Tyres Ltd & J. McHugh & Son (Civil Engineers) Ltd/Stapleford	
G-AZAV	Cessna 337F	W. T. Johnson & Sons (Huddersfield) Ltd	
G-AZAW	GY-80 Horizon 160	G. A. P. N. Barlow	
G-AZAZ	Bensen B.8M	FAA Museum/Yeovilton	
G-AZBA	Nipper T.66 Srs 3	I. McKenzie	
G-AZBB	MBB Bo 209 Monsun 160FV	G. N. Richardson/Staverton	
G-AZBC	PA-39 Twin Comanche 160 C/R	Tenison Air Ltd	
G-AZBE	Glos-Airtourer Super 150	S. E. Marples	
G-AZBI	Jodel D.150	T. A. Rawson & W. H. Milner	
G-AZBK	PA-E23 Aztec 250E	Qualitair Engineering Ltd/Blackbushe	
G-AZBL	Jodel D.9 Bebe	West Midlands Flying Group	
G-AZBN	AT-16 Harvard 2B (FT391)	The Old Flying Machine Co Ltd/ Duxford	
G-AZBT	Western O-65 balloon	D. J. Harris *Hermes*	
G-AZBU	Auster AOP.9	K. H. Wallis	
G-AZBY	Westland Wessex 60 Srs 1 ★	Sykes Aviation Ltd (*stored*)	
G-AZBZ	Westland Wessex 60 Srs 1 ★	Sykes Aviation Ltd (*stored*)	
G-AZCB	Stampe SV-4B	M. J. Cowburn/Redhill	
G-AZCI	Cessna 320A Skyknight	Landsurcon (Air Survey) Ltd	
G-AZCK	B.121 Pup 2	K. E. Barrett	
G-AZCL	B.121 Pup 2	Cameron Rainwear Ltd/Lympne	
G-AZCP	B.121 Pup 1	Pup Group 87/Elstree	
G-AZCT	B.121 Pup 1	P. & P. A. Smith/Sywell	
G-AZCU	B.121 Pup 1	Leyline Aviation Ltd/Tees-side	
G-AZCV	B.121 Pup 2	N. R. W. Long	
G-AZCZ	B.121 Pup 2	P. R. Moorehead	
G-AZDA	B.121 Pup 1	G. H. G. Bishop/Shoreham	
G-AZDD	MBB Bo 209 Monsun 150FF	Double Delta Flying Group/Biggin Hill	
G-AZDE	PA-28R Cherokee Arrow 200B	Electro-Motion UK (Export) Ltd/ E. Midlands	
G-AZDF	Cameron O-84 balloon	K. L. C. M. Busemeyer	
G-AZDG	B.121 Pup 2	D. J. Sage	
G-AZDK	Beech B55 Baron	Forbury Foods Ltd	
G-AZDX	PA-28 Cherokee 180F	S. D. Quigley & K. J. Gallagher/ Prestwick	
G-AZDY	D.H.82A Tiger Moth	J. B. Mills	
G-AZED	BAC One-Eleven 414EG	—	
G-AZEE	M.S.880B Rallye Club	P. L. Clements	
G-AZEF	Jodel D.120	J. R. Legge	
G-AZEG	PA-28 Cherokee 140D	Ashley Gardner Flying Club Ltd	
G-AZER	Cameron O-42 balloon	M. P. Dokk-Olsen & P. L. Jaye *Shy Tot*	
G-AZEU	B.121 Pup 2	P. Tonkin & R. S. Kinman	
G-AZEV	B.121 Pup 2	G. P. Martin/Shoreham	
G-AZEW	B.121 Pup 2	J. T. Reynolds	
G-AZEY	B.121 Pup 2	G. Huxtable/Elstree	
G-AZFA	B.121 Pup 2	K. F. Plummer	
G-AZFC	PA-28 Cherokee 140D	A. H. Lavender/Biggin Hill	
G-AZFF	Jodel D.112	P. D. Smoothy/Cranfield	
G-AZFI	PA-28R Cherokee Arrow 200B	Sherburn Aero Club Ltd	
G-AZFM	PA-28R Cherokee Arrow 200B	Linco Poultry Machinery Ltd/Biggin Hill	
G-AZFO	PA-39 Twin Comanche 160 C/R	Handhorn Ltd/Blackpool	
G-AZFP	Cessna F.177RG	Somet Ltd/Goodwood	
G-AZFR	Cessna 401B	S. Shorrock/Blackpool	
G-AZFZ	Cessna 414	Redapple Ltd/Fairoaks	
G-AZGA	Jodel D.120	G. B. Morris	
G-AZGB	PA-E23 Aztec 250D	Qualitair Engineering Ltd/Blackbushe	
G-AZGC	Stampe SV-4C (No 120)	The Hon A. M. M. Lindsay	
G-AZGE	Stampe SV-4A	M. R. L. Astor/Booker	
G-AZGF	B.121 Pup 2	K. Singh	
G-AZGI	M.S.880B Rallye Club	J. & S. Cattle/Newcastle	

Notes	Reg.	Type	Owner or Operator
	G-AZGJ	M.S.880B Rallye Club	P. Rose
	G-AZGL	M.S.894A Rallye Minerva	The Cambridge Aero Club Ltd
	G-AZGY	CP.301B Emeraude	Rodingair Flying Group/Stapleford
	G-AZGZ	D.H.82A Tiger Moth	F. R. Manning
	G-AZHB	Robin HR.100-200	C. & P. P. Scarlett/Sywell
	G-AZHC	Jodel D.112	J. A. Summer & A. Burton/Netherthorpe
	G-AZHD	Slingsby T-61A Falke	J. Sentance
	G-AZHH	SA 102.5 Cavalier	D. W. Buckle
	G-AZHI	Glos-Airtourer Super 150	H. J. Douglas/Biggin Hill
	G-AZHJ	S.A. Twin Pioneer Srs 3	Flight One Ltd/Staverton
	G-AZHR	Piccard Ax6 balloon	G. Fisher
	G-AZHT	Glos-Airtourer T.3	D. G. Palmer & D. C. Giles/Glasgow
	G-AZHU	Luton LA-4A Minor	W. Cawrey/Netherthorpe
	G-AZIB	ST-10 Diplomate	Wilmslow Audio Ltd/Wickenby
	G-AZID	Cessna FA.150L	Exeter Flying Club Ltd
	G-AZII	Jodel D.117A	J. S. Brayshaw
	G-AZIJ	Jodel DR.360	Rob Airway Ltd/Guernsey
	G-AZIK	PA-34-200 Seneca	C.S.E. Aviation Ltd/Kidlington
	G-AZIL	Slingsby T-61A Falke	D. W. Savage
	G-AZIO	Stampe SV-4C (Lycoming) ★	/Booker
	G-AZIP	Cameron O-65 balloon	Dante Balloon Group Dante
	G-AZJC	Fournier RF-5	J. J. Butler/Biggin Hill
	G-AZJE	Ord-Hume JB-01 Minicab	J. B. Evans/Sandown
	G-AZJI	Western O-65 balloon	W. Davison Peek-a-Boo
	G-AZJN	Robin DR.300/140	Wright Farm Eggs Ltd
	G-AZJV	Cessna F.172L	J. A. & A. J. Boyd/Cardiff
	G-AZJW	Cessna F.150L	A. J. Fletcher/Elstree
	G-AZJY	Cessna FRA.150L	Shropshire Aero Club Ltd/Sleap
	G-AZJZ	PA-23 Aztec 250E	Encee Services Ltd/Cardiff
	G-AZKC	M.S.880B Rallye Club	L. J. Martin/Redhill
	G-AZKD	M.S.880B Rallye Club	P. Feeney/Kidlington
	G-AZKE	M.S.880B Rallye Club	B. S. Rowden & W. L. Rogers
	G-AZKG	Cessna F.172L	Nultree Ltd/Blackbushe
	G-AZKK	Cameron O-56 balloon	Gemini Balloon Group Gemini
	G-AZKN	Robin HR.100/200	J. G. Bell/Aberdeen
	G-AZKO	Cessna F.337F	Crispair Aviation Services Ltd
	G-AZKP	Jodel D.117	J. Lowe
	G-AZKR	PA-24 Comanche 180	K. W. Brigden
	G-AZKS	AA-1A Trainer	D. K. Jackson
	G-AZKV	Cessna FRA.150L	Penguin Flight/Bodmin
	G-AZKW	Cessna F.172L	Banbury Plant Hire Ltd/ Hinton-in-the-Hedges
	G-AZKZ	Cessna F.172L	R. Hill Farms Ltd/Swanton Morley
	G-AZLE	Boeing N2S-5 Kaydet	Parker Airways Ltd/Denham
	G-AZLF	Jodel D.120	B. J. Edwards
	G-AZLH	Cessna F.150L	Skegness Air Taxi Service Ltd/Boston
	G-AZLL	Cessna FRA.150L	Airwork Ltd/Perth
	G-AZLM	Cessna F.172L	J. F. Davis
	G-AZLN	PA-28 Cherokee 180F	D. H. L. Wigan
	G-AZLV	Cessna 172K	D. Chapman
	G-AZLY	Cessna F.150L	Cleveland Flying School Ltd/Tees-side
	G-AZLZ	Cessna F.150L	Exeter Flying Club Ltd
	G-AZMB	Bell 47G-3B	Trent Air Services Ltd/Cranfield
	G-AZMC	Slingsby T-61A Falke	Essex Gliding Club Ltd
	G-AZMD	Slingsby T-61C Falke	R. A. Rice
	G-AZMF	BAC One-Eleven 530	BCal/British Airways Isle of Raasay/ Gatwick
	G-AZMH	Morane-Saulnier M.S.500 (ZA+WN)	Wessex Aviation & Transport Ltd
	G-AZMJ	AA-5 Traveler	R. T. Love/Bodmin
	G-AZMK	PA-23 Aztec 250	Andrew Edie Aviation/Shoreham
	G-AZMN	Glos-Airtourer T.5	Troypine Ltd
	G-AZMV	D.62C Condor	Ouse Gliding Club Ltd/Rufforth
	G-AZMX	PA-28 Cherokee 140 ★	Kelsterton College (instructional airframe)/Deeside
	G-AZMZ	M.S.893A Rallye Commodore 150	P. J. Wilcox/Cranfield
	G-AZNA	V.813 Viscount	British Midland Airways Ltd/E. Midlands
	G-AZNC	V.813 Viscount	British Aerospace (withdrawn)
	G-AZNF	Stampe SV-4C	H. J. Smith/Shoreham
	G-AZNI	S.A.315B Lama	Dollar Air Services Ltd (G-AWLC)/ Coventry
	G-AZNK	Stampe SV-4A	R. H. Reeves/Barton
	G-AZNL	PA-28R Cherokee Arrow 200D	Medical-Assist Ltd

Reg.	Type	Owner or Operator	Notes
G-AZNO	Cessna 182P	M&D Aviation/Bournemouth	
G-AZNT	Cameron O-84 balloon	N. Tasker	
G-AZOA	MBB Bo 209 Monsun 150FF	R. J. O. Walker & R. P. Wilson	
G-AZOB	MBB Bo 209 Monsun 150FF	G. N. Richardson	
G-AZOD	PA-23 Aztec 250D	Falcon Flying Services/Biggin Hill	
G-AZOE	Glos-Airtourer 115	R. J. Zukowski	
G-AZOF	Glos-Airtourer Super 150	Lands End Flying Club/St Just	
G-AZOG	PA-28R Cherokee Arrow 200D	J. G. Collins/Cambridge	
G-AZOH	Beech 65-B90 Queen Air	Clyde Surveys Ltd/White Waltham	
G-AZOL	PA-34-200 Seneca	MTV Design Ltd/Bournemouth	
G-AZON	PA-34-200-2 Seneca	Willowvale Electronics Ltd/Elstree	
G-AZOO	Western O-65 balloon	Southern Balloon Group *Carousel*	
G-AZOR	MBB Bo 105D	Bond Helicopters Ltd/Bourn	
G-AZOS	MJ.5-F1 Sirocco	B. W. Davies	
G-AZOT	PA-34-200-2 Seneca	L. G. Payne/Elstree	
G-AZOU	Jodel DR.1051	T. W. Jones & ptnrs/Slinfold	
G-AZOZ	Cessna FRA.150L	L. C. Cole/Netherthorpe	
G-AZPA	PA-25 Pawnee 235	Black Mountain Gliding Co Ltd	
G-AZPC	Slingsby T-61C Falke	B. C. Dixon	
G-AZPF	Fournier RF-5	R. Pye/Blackpool	
G-AZPH	Craft-Pitts S-1S Special	N. M. Bloom	
G-AZPV	Luton LA-4A Minor	J. Scott/(*Stored*)	
G-AZPX	Western O-31 balloon	E. R. McCosh	
G-AZPZ	BAC One-Eleven 515	BCal/British Airways Ltd *City of Glasgow*/Gatwick	
G-AZRA	MBB Bo 209 Monsun 150FF	Alpha Flying Ltd/Denham	
G-AZRD	Cessna 401B	Spring Valley Trading Co Ltd	
G-AZRG	PA-23 Aztec 250D	Woodgate Aviation (IOM) Ltd/ Ronaldsway	
G-AZRH	PA-28 Cherokee 140D	Newcastle-upon-Tyne Aero Club Ltd	
G-AZRI	Payne balloon	G. F. Payne *Shoestring*	
G-AZRK	Fournier RF-5	Thurleigh Flying Group	
G-AZRL	PA-19 Super Cub 95	B. J. Stead	
G-AZRM	Fournier RF-5	R. S. A. Lloyd-Bostock/Shoreham	
G-AZRN	Cameron O-84 balloon	C. A. Butter & J. J. T. Cooke	
G-AZRP	Glos-Airtourer 115	Torfaen Self Drive Hire Ltd	
G-AZRR	Cessna 310Q	Routarrow Ltd/Norwich	
G-AZRS	PA-22 Tri-Pacer 150	E. A. Harrhy/Shoreham	
G-AZRU	AB-206B JetRanger 2	Dollar Air Services Ltd/Coventry	
G-AZRV	PA-28R Cherokee Arrow 200B	Designed for Sound Ltd	
G-AZRW	Cessna T.337C	R. C. Frazle/Southend	
G-AZRX	GY-80 Horizon 160	P. S. Cottrell	
G-AZRZ	Cessna U.206F	Army Parachute Association/ Netheravon	
G-AZSA	Stampe SV-4B	J. K. Faulkner/Biggin Hill	
G-AZSC	AT-16 Harvard IIB	Machine Music Ltd/Fairoaks	
G-AZSD	Slingsby T.29B Motor Tutor	R. G. Boynton	
G-AZSF	PA-28R Cherokee Arrow 200D	W. T. Northorpe & R. J. Mills/Coventry	
G-AZSG	PA-28 Cherokee 180E	Cherokee Flying Group/Netherthorpe	
G-AZSH	PA-28R Cherokee Arrow 180	C. R. Hayward	
G-AZSK	Taylor JT.1 Monoplane	R. R. Lockwood	
G-AZSN	PA-28R Cherokee Arrow 200	Jetstream Air Couriers Ltd/Bristol	
G-AZSU	H.S.748 Srs 2A	Dan-Air Services Ltd/Gatwick	
G-AZSW	B.121 Pup 1	Northamptonshire School of Flying Ltd/Sywell	
G-AZSZ	PA-23 Aztec 250	Ravenair/Manchester	
G-AZTA	MBB Bo 209 Monsun 150FF	R. S. Perks/Elstree	
G-AZTD	PA-32 Cherokee Six 300	Presshouse Publications Ltd/Enstone	
G-AZTF	Cessna F.177RG	J. Bolson & Son Ltd/Bournemouth	
G-AZTI	MBB Bo 105D	Bond Helicopters Ltd/Bourn	
G-AZTK	Cessna F.172F	M. J. Steele/Clacton	
G-AZTM	Glos-Airtourer 115	I. J. Smith	
G-AZTO	PA-34-200-2 Seneca	Bulldog Aviation Ltd	
G-AZTR	SNCAN SV-4C	P. G. Palumbo/Booker	
G-AZTS	Cessna F.172L	J. F. Morgan/Humberside	
G-AZTV	Stolp SA.500 Starlet	V. Long	
G-AZTW	Cessna F.177RG	R. M. Clarke/Leicester	
G-AZUK	BAC One-Eleven 476FM	Mediterranean Express Ltd/Luton	
G-AZUM	Cessna F.172L	L. B. Rapkins	
G-AZUO	Cessna F.177RG	Newbury Sand and Gravel Co Ltd	
G-AZUP	Cameron O-65 balloon	R. S. Bailey & ptnrs	
G-AZUT	M.S.893A Rallye Commodore 180	Rallye Flying Group	
G-AZUV	Cameron O-65 balloon ★	British Balloon Museum	

Notes	Reg.	Type	Owner or Operator
	G-AZUX	Western O-56 balloon	H. C. J. & Mrs S. L. G. Williams *Slow Djinn*
	G-AZUY	Cessna E.310L	ATL Holdings Ltd
	G-AZUZ	Cessna FRA.150L	D. J. Parker/Netherthorpe
	G-AZVA	MBB Bo 209 Monsun 150FF	K. H. Wallis
	G-AZVB	MBB Bo 209 Monsun 150FF	P. C. Logsdon/Dunkeswell
	G-AZVE	AA-5 Traveler	R. N. Morant
	G-AZVF	M.S.894A Rallye Minerva	R. J. Cole & W. G. Gregory
	G-AZVG	AA-5 Traveler	R. W. Somerville & A. F. Reid
	G-AZVH	M.S.894A Rallye Minerva	Bristol Cars Ltd/White Waltham
	G-AZVI	M.S.892A Rallye Commodore	W. A. McCartney & T. A. Pugh
	G-AZVJ	PA-34-200-2 Seneca	Business Air Travel Ltd/Lydd
	G-AZVL	Jodel D.119	Forest Flying Group/Stapleford
	G-AZVM	Hughes 369HS	Diagnostic Reagents Ltd
	G-AZVP	Cessna F.177RG	R. G. Saunders/Biggin Hill
	G-AZVT	Cameron O-84 balloon	Sky Soarer Ltd *Jules Verne*
	G-AZWB	PA-28 Cherokee 140	Avon Flying Group/Bristol
	G-AZWD	PA-28 Cherokee 140	Airways Aero Associations Ltd/Booker
	G-AZWE	PA-28 Cherokee 140	Airways Aero Associations Ltd/Booker
	G-AZWF	SAN Jodel DR.1050	R. A. Jarvis
	G-AZWS	PA-28R Cherokee Arrow 180	J. E. Shepherd
	G-AZWT	Westland Lysander III (V9441)	Strathallan Aircraft Collection
	G-AZWW	PA-23 Aztec 250E	Phoenix Aviation (Bedford) Ltd/ Cranfield
	G-AZWY	PA-24 Comanche 260	Keymer Son & Co Ltd/Biggin Hill
	G-AZXA	Beechcraft 95-C55 Baron	F.R. Aviation Ltd/Bournemouth
	G-AZXB	Cameron O-65 balloon	London Balloon Club Ltd *London Pride II*
	G-AZXC	Cessna F.150L	R. W. Cope/Netherthorpe
	G-AZXD	Cessna F.172L	Birdlake Ltd/Wellesbourne
	G-AZXE	Jodel D.120A	Kestrel Flying Group/Hucknall
	G-AZXG	PA-23 Aztec 250	K. J. Le Fevre/Norwich
	G-AZXR	BN-2A-9 Islander	Stanton Aircraft Management Ltd
	G-AZYA	GY-80 Horizon 160	T. Poole & ptnrs/Sywell
	G-AZYD	M.S.893A Rallye Commodore	Deeside Gliding Club
	G-AZYF	PA-28 Cherokee 180	J. C. Glynn/E. Midlands
	G-AZYM	Cessna E.310Q	Kingswinford Engineering Co Ltd
	G-AZYS	CP.301C-1 Emeraude	J. R. Hughes/Stapleford
	G-AZYU	PA-E23 Aztec 250	L. J. Martin/Biggin Hill
	G-AZYV	Burns O-77 balloon	B. F. G. Ribbans *Contrary Mary*
	G-AZYX	M.S.893A Rallye Commodore	Black Mountain Gliding Co Ltd
	G-AZYY	Slingsby T-61A Falke	J. A. Towers
	G-AZYZ	WA.51A Pacific	A. E. O'Broin
	G-AZZF	M.S.880B Rallye Club	I. C. Davies/Swansea
	G-AZZG	Cessna 188 Agwagon	*Wreck*/Southend
	G-AZZH	Practavia Pilot Sprite 115	K. G. Stewart
	G-AZZK	Cessna 414	D. O. McIntyre
	G-AZZO	PA-28 Cherokee 140	R. J. Hind
	G-AZZP	Cessna F.172H	D. Bishop/Exeter
	G-AZZR	Cessna F.150L	J. B. Small/Swansea
	G-AZZS	PA-34-200-2 Seneca	Robin Cook Aviation/Shoreham
	G-AZZT	PA-28 Cherokee 180 ★	*Ground instruction airframe*/Cranfield
	G-AZZV	Cessna F.172L	Cleveland Flying School Ltd/Tees-side
	G-AZZW	Fournier RF-5	Aviation Special Developments
	G-AZZX	Cessna FRA.150L	J. E. Uprichard & ptnrs/Newtownards
	G-AZZZ	D.H.82A Tiger Moth	S. W. McKay
	G-BAAD	Evans Super VP-1	R. W. Husband/Netherthorpe
	G-BAAF	Manning-Flanders MF1 replica	Aviation Film Services Ltd/Booker
	G-BAAH	Coates SA.III Swalesong	J. R. Coates
	G-BAAI	M.S.893A Rallye Commodore	R. D. Taylor/Thruxton
	G-BAAK	Cessna 207	Balmar Aviation/Thruxton
	G-BAAL	Cessna 172A	B. Earl/St Just
	G-BAAP	PA-28R Cherokee Arrow 200	Shirley A. Shelley/Biggin Hill
	G-BAAT	Cessna 182P Skylane	J. B. Anderson/Newtownards
	G-BAAU	Enstrom F-28C-UK	M. Upton
	G-BAAW	Jodel D.119	S. W. Ward/Ipswich
	G-BAAX	Cameron O-84 balloon	The New Holker Estate Co Ltd *Holker Hall*
	G-BAAY	Valtion Viima II (VI-3)	P. H. McConnell/White Waltham
	G-BAAZ	PA-28R Cherokee Arrow 200D	A. W. Rix/Guernsey
	G-BABB	Cessna F.150L	E. Shipley
	G-BABC	Cessna F.150L	Suffolk Aero Club Ltd/Ipswich
	G-BABD	Cessna FRA.150L	Phoenix Aviation (Bedford) Ltd/ Cranfield

Reg.	Type	Owner or Operator	Notes
G-BABE	Taylor JT.2 Titch	P. D. G. Grist/Sibson	
G-BABG	PA-28 Cherokee 180	P. D. Foster	
G-BABH	Cessna F.150L	Skyviews & General Ltd/Leeds	
G-BABK	PA-34-200-2 Seneca	D. F. J. & N. R. Flashman/Biggin Hill	
G-BABY	Taylor JT.2 Titch	R. E. Finlay	
G-BACA	BAC Petrel	British Aircraft Corporation Ltd/ Warton	
G-BACB	PA-34-200-2 Seneca	London Flight Centre (Stansted) Ltd	
G-BACC	Cessna FRA.150L	Osprey Air Services Ltd/Cranfield	
G-BACE	Fournier RF-5	R. W. K. Stead/Perranporth	
G-BACH	Enstrom F.28A	Rotor Enterprises Ltd/Coventry	
G-BACJ	Jodel D.120	Wearside Flying Association/Newcastle	
G-BACL	Jodel D.150	G. R. French	
G-BACN	Cessna FRA.150L	Airwork Ltd/Perth	
G-BACO	Cessna FRA.150L	H. G. & V. Fawkes/Bodmin	
G-BACP	Cessna FRA.150L	B. A. Mills	
G-BADC	Luton Beta B.2A	H. M. Mackenzie	
G-BADH	Slingsby T.61A Falke	E. M. Andrew & ptnrs/Old Sarum	
G-BADI	PA-E23 Aztec 250	W. London Aero Services Ltd/ White Waltham	
G-BADJ	PA-E23 Aztec 250	CKS Air Ltd/Southend	
G-BADK	BN-2A-8 Islandser	Harvest Air Ltd/Southend	
G-BADL	PA-34-200-2 Seneca	Cartographical Services (Southampton) Ltd/Birmingham	
G-BADO	PA-32 Cherokee Six 300	B. J. Haylor & ptnrs/Southampton	
G-BADP	Boeing 737-204	Britannia Airways Ltd *Sir Arthur Whitten Brown*/Luton	
G-BADR	Boeing 737-204	Britannia Airways Ltd *Capt Robert Falconer Scott*/Luton	
G-BADT	Cessna 402B	British Aircraft Corp Ltd/Warton	
G-BADU	Cameron O-56 balloon	J. Philp *Dream Machine*	
G-BADV	Brochet MB-50	P. A. Cairns/Dunkeswell	
G-BADW	Pitts S-2A Special	R. E. Mitchell/Coventry	
G-BADZ	Pitts S-2A Special	A. L. Brown & ptnrs/Wellesbourne	
G-BAEB	Robin DR.400/160	W. D. Nightingale/Bodmin	
G-BAEC	Robin HR.100/210	Autographics Ltd/Booker	
G-BAED	PA-E23 Aztec 250	Trial Rapid Ltd/Norwich	
G-BAEE	Jodel DR.1050/M1	J. B. Randle	
G-BAEF	Boeing 727-46	Dan-Air Services Ltd/Gatwick	
G-BAEM	Robin DR.400/125	Store Equipment (London) Ltd	
G-BAEN	Robin DR.400/180	Trans Europe Air Charter Ltd/Booker	
G-BAEP	Cessna FRA.150L	J. Calverley	
G-BAER	Cosmic Wind	R. S. Voice/Redhill	
G-BAES	Cessna 337A	Page & Moy Ltd & High Voltage Applications Ltd/Leicester	
G-BAET	Piper L-4H Cub	C. M. G. Ellis	
G-BAEU	Cessna F.150L	Skyviews & General Ltd	
G-BAEV	Cessna FRA.150L	B. F. Axford/Bournemouth	
G-BAEW	Cessna F.172M	Northamptonshire School of Flying Ltd/ Sywell	
G-BAEY	Cessna F.172M	R. Fursman/Southampton	
G-BAEZ	Cessna FRA.150L	J. C. Glynn/E. Midlands	
G-BAFA	AA-5 Traveler	C. F. Mackley/Stapleford	
G-BAFD	MBB Bo 105D	Gleneagle Helicopter Services (Scotland) Ltd	
G-BAFG	D.H.82A Tiger Moth	J. E. Shaw & ptnrs	
G-BAFH	Evans VP-1	R. H. W. Beath	
G-BAFI	Cessna F.177RG	Grandsystem Ltd/Bristol	
G-BAFL	Cessna 182P	Ingham Aviation Ltd/Lulsgate	
G-BAFM	AT-16 Harvard IIB (FS728)	Parker Airways Ltd/Denham	
G-BAFP	Robin DR.400/160	N. R. Haines	
G-BAFS	PA-18 Super Cub 150	M. D. Morris/Sandown	
G-BAFT	PA-18 Super Cub 150	Cambridge University Gliding Trust Ltd/ Duxford	
G-BAFU	PA-28 Cherokee 140	Goshawk Aviation Ltd/Southend	
G-BAFV	PA-18 Super Cub 95	P. Elliott	
G-BAFW	PA-28 Cherokee 140	H. T. Boal & ptnrs/Cambridge	
G-BAFX	Robin DR.400/140	Nicholas Advertising Ltd	
G-BAGB	SIAI-Marchetti SF.260	British Midland Airways Ltd/ E. Midlands	
G-BAGC	Robin DR.400/140	Hempalm Ltd/Headcorn	
G-BAGF	Jodel D.92 Bebe	G. R. French & J. D. Watt	
G-BAGG	PA-32 Cherokee Six 300E	Hornair Ltd	
G-BAGI	Cameron O-31 balloon	D. C. & S. J. Boxall	

Notes	Reg.	Type	Owner or Operator
	G-BAGL	SA.341 G. Gazelle Srs 1	Autokraft Ltd
	G-BAGN	Cessna F.177RG	M. L. Rhodes/Halfpenny Green
	G-BAGO	Cessna 421B	Donington Aviation Ltd/E. Midlands
	G-BAGR	Robin DR.400/140	F. C. Aris & J. D. Last/Mona
	G-BAGS	Robin DR.400/180 2+2	Headcorn Flying School Ltd
	G-BAGT	Helio H.295 Courier	B. J. C. Woodall Ltd
	G-BAGU	Luton LA-5A Major	J. Gawley
	G-BAGV	Cessna U.206F	Scottish Parachute Club/Perth
	G-BAGX	PA-28 Cherokee 140	D. Marriott/Conington
	G-BAGY	Cameron O-84 balloon	P. G. Dunnington *Beatrice*
	G-BAHD	Cessna 182P Skylane	S. Brunt (Silverdale Staffs) Ltd/Sleap
	G-BAHE	PA-28 Cherokee 140	A. H. Evans & A. O. Jones/Sleap
	G-BAHF	PA-28 Cherokee 140	S. J. Green/Halfpenny Green
	G-BAHG	PA-24 Comanche 260	Friendly Aviation (Jersey) Ltd
	G-BAHH	Wallis WA-121	K. H. Wallis
	G-BAHI	Cessna F.150H	M. D. Barrow/Exeter
	G-BAHJ	PA-24 Comanche 250	M. D. Faiers/Staverton
	G-BAHL	Robin DR.400/160	Norvett Electronics Ltd
	G-BAHN	Beech 58 Baron	British Midland Airways/E. Midlands
	G-BAHO	Beech C.23 Sundowner	G-ATJG Private Aircraft Syndicate Ltd
	G-BAHP	Volmer VJ.22 Sportsman	W. St G. V. Stoney
	G-BAHS	PA-28R Cherokee Arrow 200-II	A. A. Wild & ptnrs
	G-BAHU	Enstrom F-28A	Allen Timpany Racing
	G-BAHX	Cessna 182P	D. Best/Blackpool
	G-BAHZ	PA-28R Cherokee Arrow 200-II	Rutland Properties Ltd/Leicester
	G-BAIA	PA-32 Cherokee Six 300E	Langham International (Aircraft) Ltd/Southend
	G-BAIB	Enstrom F-28A	VIP Air Ltd
	G-BAIH	PA-28R Cherokee Arrow 200-II	J. Pemberton/Cambridge
	G-BAII	Cessna FRA.150L	Airwork Ltd/Perth
	G-BAIK	Cessna F.150L	Wickenby Aviation Ltd
	G-BAIL	Cessna FR.172J	D. R. Elphick/O. Warden
	G-BAIM	Cessna 310Q	Airwork Ltd/Perth
	G-BAIN	Cessna FRA.150L	Airwork Ltd/Perth
	G-BAIP	Cessna F.150L	W. D. Cliffe & J. F. Platt/Wellesbourne
	G-BAIR	Thunder Ax7-77 balloon	P. A. & Mrs M. Hutchins
	G-BAIS	Cessna F.177RG	I. H. Bewley
	G-BAIU	Hiller UH-12E (Soloy)	Heliwork Finance Ltd/Thruxton
	G-BAIW	Cessna F.172M	Humber Aviation Ltd
	G-BAIX	Cessna F.172M	JG Aviation Ltd
	G-BAIY	Cameron O-65 balloon	Budget Rent A Car (UK) Ltd *Lady Budget*
	G-BAIZ	Slingsby T.61A Falke	W. L. C. O'Neill & ptnrs
	G-BAJA	Cessna F.177RG	Don Ward Productions Ltd/Biggin Hill
	G-BAJB	Cessna F.177RG	K. D. Horton/Staverton
	G-BAJC	Evans VP-1	J. R. Clements/Rochester
	G-BAJE	Cessna 177 Cardinal	J. E. Cull
	G-BAJN	AA-5 Traveler	Janacrew Ltd/Sherburn
	G-BAJO	AA-5 Traveler	A. Townson/Blackpool
	G-BAJR	PA-28 Cherokee 180	G-Air Ltd/Goodwood
	G-BAJT	PA-28R Cherokee Arrow 200-II	P. H. Tavener
	G-BAJW	Boeing 727-46	Dan-Air Services Ltd/Gatwick
	G-BAJY	Robin DR.400/180	F. Birch & K. J. Pike/Sturgate
	G-BAJZ	Robin DR.400/125	Rochester Aviation Ltd
	G-BAKD	PA-34-200-2 Seneca	Andrews Professional Colour Laboratories/Elstree
	G-BAKF	Bell 206B JetRanger 2	M. J. K. Belmont/Coventry
	G-BAKG	Hughes 269C	W. K. MacGillivray
	G-BAKH	PA-28 Cherokee 140	Woodgate Air Services (IoM) Ltd/Ronaldsway
	G-BAKJ	PA-30 Twin Comanche 160	M. F. Fisher & M. Geliot/Biggin Hill
	G-BAKK	Cessna F.172H ★	*Parachute jump trainer*/Coventry
	G-BAKL	F.27 Friendship 200	Loganair Ltd/Glasgow
	G-BAKM	Robin DR.400/140	MKS Syndicate
	G-BAKN	SNCAN SV-4C	M. Holloway
	G-BAKO	Cameron O-84 balloon	D. C. Dokk-Olsen *Pied Piper*
	G-BAKP	PA-E23 Aztec 250	J. J. Woodhouse
	G-BAKR	Jodel D.117	A. B. Bailey/White Waltham
	G-BAKS	AB-206B JetRanger 2	Dollar Air Services Ltd/Coventry
	G-BAKT	AB-206B JetRanger 2	Gleneagle Helicopter Services (Scotland) Ltd
	G-BAKV	PA-18 Super Cub 150	Pounds Marine Shipping Ltd/Goodwood

Reg.	Type	Owner or Operator	Notes
G-BAKW	B.121 Pup 2	The KW Group/Shoreham	
G-BAKY	Slingsby T.61C Falke	G. Hill & P. Shepherd	
G-BALA	Stampe SV-4C	Full Bore Productions Ltd	
G-BALC	Bell 206B JetRanger 2	Dollar Air Services Ltd/Coventry	
G-BALF	Robin DR.400/140	F. A. Spear/Panshanger	
G-BALG	Robin DR.400/180	R. Jones	
G-BALH	Robin DR.400/140B	J. D. Copsey	
G-BALI	Robin DR.400 2+2	R. A. Gridley	
G-BALJ	Robin DR.400/180	D. Batt & ptnrs/Headcorn	
G-BALK	SNCAN SV-4C	L. J. Rice	
G-BALM	Cessna 340	Manro Transport Ltd/Manchester	
G-BALN	Cessna T.310Q	O'Brien Properties Ltd/Shoreham	
G-BALS	Nipper T.66 Srs 3	L. W. Shaw	
G-BALT	Enstrom F-28A	D. W. C. Holmes	
G-BALW	PA-28R Cherokee Arrow 200-II	Cresthale Group Ltd	
G-BALX	D.H.82A Tiger Moth (N6848)	Toadair	
G-BALY	Practavia Pilot Sprite 150	A. L. Young	
G-BALZ	Bell 212	B.E.A.S. Ltd/Redhill	
G-BAMB	Slingsby T.61C Falke	Universities of Glasgow & Strathclyde Gliding Club/Strathaven	
G-BAMC	Cessna F.150L	D. F. Smith	
G-BAME	Volmer VJ-22 Sportsman	T. M. Kidd/Glasgow	
G-BAMF	MBB Bo 105D	Bond Helicopters Ltd/Bourn	
G-BAMG	Avions Lobet Ganagobie	J. A. Brompton	
G-BAMJ	Cessna 182P	Graham Cook Aviation Ltd/Shoreham	
G-BAML	Bell 206A JetRanger	Peter Scott Agriculture Ltd	
G-BAMM	PA-28 Cherokee 235	Holmfield Wakefield Ltd	
G-BAMR	PA-16 Clipper	H. Royce	
G-BAMS	Robin DR.400/160	G-BAMS Ltd/Headcorn	
G-BAMU	Robin DR.400/160	The Alternative Flying Group/Sywell	
G-BAMV	Robin DR.400/180	W. J. Gooding/Rochester	
G-BAMY	PA-28R Cherokee Arrow 200-II	G. R. Gilbert & ptnrs/Birmingham	
G-BANA	Robin DR.221	G. T. Pryor	
G-BANB	Robin DR.400/180	Time Electronics Ltd/Biggin Hill	
G-BANC	GY-201 Minicab	J. T. S. Lewis & J. E. Williams	
G-BAND	Cameron O-84 balloon	Mid-Bucks Farmers Balloon Group *Clover*	
G-BANE	Cessna FRA.150L	Osprey Air Services Ltd/Cranfield	
G-BANF	Luton LA-4A Minor	D. W. Bosworth	
G-BANG	Cameron O-84 balloon	R. F. Harrower	
G-BANK	PA-34-200-2 Seneca	Cleveland Flying School Ltd/Teesside	
G-BANL	BN-2A-8 Islander	Loganair Ltd/Glasgow	
G-BANS	PA-34-200-2 Seneca	G. Knowles/Halfpenny Green	
G-BANT	Cameron O-65 balloon	M. A. Dworski & R. M. Bishop	
G-BANU	Wassmer Jodel D.120	C. E. McKinney	
G-BANV	Phoenix Currie Wot	K. Knight	
G-BANW	CP.1330 Super Emeraude	J. D. McCracken & ptnrs/Turnhouse	
G-BANX	Cessna F.172M	T. Edwards	
G-BAOB	Cessna F.172M	Gordon King (Aviation) Ltd/ Biggin Hill	
G-BAOG	M.S.880B Rallye Club	Thruxton Flight Centre Ltd	
G-BAOH	M.S.880B Rallye Club	S. P. Bryant & ptnrs/Shobdon	
G-BAOJ	M.S.880B Rallye Club	B. J. Clark & D. J. Stevenson	
G-BAOM	M.S.880B Rallye Club	D. W. Brown/Seething	
G-BAOP	Cessna FRA.150L	Falcon Flying Services/Biggin Hill	
G-BAOS	Cessna F.172M	F. W. Ellis & ptnrs	
G-BAOT	M.S.880B Rallye Club	E. J. Morris & Son	
G-BAOU	AA-5 Traveler	W. H. Ingram/St Just	
G-BAOV	AA-5A Cheetah	R. E. Pettit/Southend	
G-BAOW	Cameron O-65 balloon	P. I. White *Winslow Boy*	
G-BAOY	Cameron S-31 balloon	Shell-Mex BP Ltd *New Potato*	
G-BAPA	Fournier RF-5B Sperber	Black Mountain Gliding Co Ltd	
G-BAPB	D.H.C.1 Chipmunk 22	R. C. P. Brookhouse/Redhill	
G-BAPC	Luton LA-4A Minor	Midland Aircraft Preservation Soc	
G-BAPF	V.814 Viscount	Sean T. Hully (Sales) Ltd	
G-BAPG	V.814 Viscount	Sean T. Hully (Sales) Ltd	
G-BAPI	Cessna FRA.150L	Industrial Supplies (Peterborough) Ltd	
G-BAPJ	Cessna FRA.150L	M. D. Page/Manston	
G-BAPK	Cessna F.150L	Andrewsfield Flying Club Ltd	
G-BAPL	PA-23 Aztec 250E	Merlin Marine Investments Ltd	
G-BAPM	Fuji FA.200-160	Papa Mike Group/Swansea	
G-BAPN	PA-28 Cherokee 180	Park Display Ltd	
G-BAPP	Evans VP-1	K. McNaughton	
G-BAPR	Jodel D.11	R. G. Marshall	

Notes	Reg.	Type	Owner or Operator
	G-BAPS	Campbell Cougar ★	British Rotorcraft Museum
	G-BAPT	Fuji FA.200-180	J. F. Thurlow & J. H. Pickering/Ipswich
	G-BAPV	Robin DR.400/160	J. D. Millne & ptnrs/Brunton
	G-BAPW	PA-28R Cherokee Arrow 180	G. & R. Consultants Ltd
	G-BAPX	Robin DR.400/160	R. R. Hall & R. H. Richards
	G-BAPY	Robin HR.100/210	J. Westermann
	G-BARB	PA-34-200-2 Seneca	H. McC. Clarke
	G-BARC	Cessna FR.172J	G. N. Hopcraft
	G-BARD	Cessna 337C	Jadealto Ltd
	G-BARF	Jodel D.112 Club	A. F. Scott
	G-BARG	Cessna E.310Q	Sally Marine Ltd
	G-BARH	Beech C.23 Sundowner	T. R. Sage
	G-BARJ	Bell 212	Autair International Ltd/Panshanger
	G-BARN	Taylor JT.2 Titch	R. G. W. Newton
	G-BARP	Bell 206B JetRanger 2	S.W. Electricity Board/Bristol
	G-BARS	D.H.C.1. Chipmunk 22	T. I. Sutton/Chester
	G-BARV	Cessna 310Q	Old England Watches Ltd/Elstree
	G-BARY	CP.301A Emeraude	J. J. Butler & B. Hill
	G-BARZ	Scheibe SF.28A Tandem Falke	J. A. Fox & ptnrs/Dishforth
	G-BASB	Enstrom F-28A	Blades Helicopters Ltd/Goodwood
	G-BASD	B.121 Pup 2	C. C. Brown/Leicester
	G-BASE	Bell 206B JetRanger 2	Air Hanson Ltd/Brooklands
	G-BASG	AA-5 Traveler	D. Hepburn
	G-BASH	AA-5 Traveler	M. J. Metham/Blackbushe
	G-BASI	PA-28 Cherokee 140	Telepoint Ltd/Blackpool
	G-BASJ	PA-28 Cherokee 180	Guildhaven Ltd/Staverton
	G-BASL	PA-28 Cherokee 140	Air Navigation & Trading Ltd/Blackpool
	G-BASM	PA-34-200-2 Seneca	Poplar Aviation/Ipswich
	G-BASN	Beech C.23 Sundowner	M. F. Fisher
	G-BASO	Lake LA-4 Amphibian	E. P. Beck
	G-BASP	B.121 Pup 1	Northamptonshire School of Flying Ltd/ Sywell
	G-BASU	PA-31-350 Navajo Chieftain	Streamline Aviation/E. Midlands
	G-BASX	PA-34-200-2 Seneca	Willowvale Electronics Ltd/Elstree
	G-BATC	MBB Bo 105D	Bond Helicopters Ltd/Swansea
	G-BATJ	Jodel D.119	E. G. Waite/Shobdon
	G-BATM	PA-32 Cherokee Six 300	Patgrove Ltd/Bolney
	G-BATN	PA-E23 Aztec 250	Marshall of Cambridge Ltd
	G-BATS	Taylor JT.1 Monoplane	J. Jennings
	G-BATT	Hughes 269C	Keith Sutcliffe & Sons Ltd
	G-BATU	Enstrom F-28A-UK	Rotor Enterprises Ltd/Coventry
	G-BATV	PA-28 Cherokee 180D	The Scoreby Flying Group/Sherburn
	G-BATW	PA-28 Cherokee 140	B. J. Willett
	G-BATX	PA-23 Aztec 250E	Tayside Aviation Ltd/Dundee
	G-BAUA	PA-E23 Aztec 250	David Parr & Associates Ltd/Shobdon
	G-BAUC	PA-25 Pawnee 235	Southdown Gliding Club Ltd
	G-BAUD	Robin DR.400/160	R. E. Delvis/Shoreham
	G-BAUE	Cessna 310Q	A. J. Dyer/Elstree
	G-BAUH	Jodel D.112	G. A. & D. Shepherd
	G-BAUI	PA-E23 Aztec 250	SFT Aviation Ltd/Bournemouth
	G-BAUJ	PA-E23 Aztec 250	Express Aviation Services Ltd/ Biggin Hill
	G-BAUK	Hughes 269C	Curtis Engineering (Frome) Ltd
	G-BAUR	F.27 Friendship Mk 200	Air UK Ltd/Norwich
	G-BAUV	Cessna F.150L	Smiths Harlow (Aerospace) Ltd
	G-BAUW	PA-E23 Aztec 250	R. E. Myson
	G-BAUY	Cessna FRA.150L	B. M. Murray
	G-BAUZ	Nord NC.854S	W. A. Ashley & D. Horne
	G-BAVB	Cessna F.172M	Hudson Bell Aviation
	G-BAVC	Cessna F.150L	Metronote Aviation Ltd/Biggin Hill
	G-BAVE	Beech A.100 King Air	Northern Executive Aviation Ltd/ Manchester
	G-BAVF	Beech 58 Baron	Gama Aviation Ltd/Fairoaks
	G-BAVH	D.H.C.1 Chipmunk 22	Portsmouth Naval Gliding Club/ Lee-on-Solent
	G-BAVL	PA-E23 Aztec 250	Haynes Holiday Homes/Thruxton
	G-BAVO	Boeing Stearman N2S (26)	A. A. Hodgson
	G-BAVR	AA-5 Traveler	Rabhart Ltd/Carlisle
	G-BAVS	AA-5 Traveler	V. J. Peake/Headcorn
	G-BAVU	Cameron A-105 balloon	J. D. Michaelis
	G-BAVX	HPR-7 Herald 214	British Air Ferries Ltd/Southend
	G-BAVZ	PA-E23 Aztec 250	Merseyside Air Charter Ltd/Liverpool
	G-BAWB	PA-E23 Aztec 250	Sutaberry Ltd/Rochester
	G-BAWG	PA-28R-200-2 Cherokee Arrow	Solent Air Ltd

Reg.	Type	Owner or Operator	Notes
G-BAWI	Enstrom F-28A-UK	Southern Air Ltd/Shoreham	
G-BAWK	PA-28 Cherokee 140	Newcastle-Upon-Tyne Aero Club Ltd	
G-BAWN	PA-30C Twin Comanche 160	Status Mail Order Services Ltd/ Manchester	
G-BAWR	Robin HR.100/210	Yarmouth Marine Service/Sandown	
G-BAWU	PA-30 Twin Comanche 160	C. P. Francis	
G-BAWV	PA-E23 Aztec 250	Woodvale Aviation Co Ltd & J. Lincoln	
G-BAWW	Thunder Ax7-77 balloon	M. L. C. Hutchins *Taurus*/Holland	
G-BAWX	PA-28 Cherokee 180	I. D. Slack & ptnrs/Leeds	
G-BAXD	BN-2A Mk III Trislander	Aurigny Air Services/Guernsey	
G-BAXE	Hughes 269A	Reethorpe Engineering Ltd	
G-BAXF	Cameron O-77 balloon	R. D. Sargeant & M. F. Lasson	
G-BAXH	Cessna 310Q	D. A. Williamson	
G-BAXJ	PA-32 Cherokee Six 300	UK Parachute Services/Ipswich	
G-BAXK	Thunder Ax7-77 balloon	Newbury Balloon Group *Jack O'Newbury*	
G-BAXL	H.S.125 Srs 3B	Dennis Vanguard International (Switchgear) Ltd/Coventry	
G-BAXP	PA-E23 Aztec 250	Subtec Aviation Ltd	
G-BAXS	Bell 47G-5	Helicopter Supplies & Engineering Ltd/ Bournemouth	
G-BAXT	PA-28R-200 Cherokee Arrow	Williams & Griffin Ltd	
G-BAXU	Cessna F.150L	W. Lancs Aero Club Ltd/Woodvale	
G-BAXY	Cessna F.172M	Merrett Aviation Ltd	
G-BAXZ	PA-28 Cherokee 140	H. Martin & D. Norris/Halton	
G-BAYC	Cameron O-65 balloon	D. Whitlock & R. T. F. Mitchell	
G-BAYL	Nord 1203/III Norecrin	D. M. Fincham/Bodmin	
G-BAYO	Cessna 150L	Cheshire Air Training School Ltd/ Liverpool	
G-BAYP	Cessna 150L	Three Counties Aero Club Ltd/ Blackbushe	
G-BAYR	Robin HR.100/210	Gilbey Warren Co Ltd/Stapleford	
G-BAYV	SNCAN 1101 Noralpha (1480)★	Booker Aircraft Museum	
G-BAYY	Cessna 310C	Specialist Flying Training Ltd/Carlisle	
G-BAYZ	Bellanca 7GC BC Citabria	Cambridge University Gliding Trust Ltd/ Duxford	
G-BAZB	H.S.125 Srs 400B	Short Bros PLC/Sydenham	
G-BAZC	Robin DR.400/160	Sherburn Robin Group	
G-BAZG	Boeing 737-204	Britannia Airways Ltd *Florence Nightingale*/Luton	
G-BAZH	Boeing 737-204	Britannia Airways Ltd *Sir Frederick Handley Page*/Luton	
G-BAZI	Boeing 737-204	Airways International Cymru Ltd/ Cardiff	
G-BAZJ	HPR-7 Herald 209 ★	Guernsey Airport Fire Services	
G-BAZM	Jodel D.11	Bingley Flying Group/Leeds	
G-BAZS	Cessna F.150L	Sherburn Aero Club Ltd	
G-BAZT	Cessna F.172M	M. Fraser/Exeter	
G-BAZU	PA-28R-200 Cherokee Arrow	S. C. Simmons	
G-BBAE	L.1011-385 TriStar	British Airtours *Torbay*/Gatwick	
G-BBAF	L.1011-385 TriStar	British Airways *Babbacombe Bay*/ Heathrow	
G-BBAG	L.1011-385 TriStar	British Airways *Bridgwater Bay*/ Heathrow	
G-BBAH	L.1011-385 TriStar	British Airways *Lyme Bay*/Heathrow	
G-BBAI	L.1011-385 TriStar	British Airways *St Brides Bay*/Heathrow	
G-BBAJ	L.1011-385 TriStar	British Airtours *Holyhead Bay*/Gatwick	
G-BBAK	M.S.894A Rallye Minerva	W. G. Henderson/Glenrothes	
G-BBAW	Robin HR.100/210	Scoba Ltd/Goodwood	
G-BBAX	Robin DR.400/140	S. R. Young	
G-BBAY	Robin DR.400/140	G. A. Pentelow & D. B. Roadnight	
G-BBAZ	Hiller UH-12E	John Holborn (Helicopters) Ltd	
G-BBBC	Cessna F.150L	T. Hayselden (Doncaster) Ltd	
G-BBBI	AA-5 Traveler	C. B. Dew	
G-BBBK	PA-28 Cherokee 140	Bencray Ltd/Blackpool	
G-BBBM	Bell 206B JetRanger 2	D. M. Leasing Co	
G-BBBN	PA-28 Cherokee 180	Avon Aircraft Sales Ltd/Bristol	
G-BBBO	SIPA 903	J. S. Hemmings	
G-BBBW	FRED Series 2	D. L. Webster/Sherburn	
G-BBBX	Cessna E310L	Atlantic Air Transport Ltd/Coventry	
G-BBBY	PA-28 Cherokee 140	R. A. E. Tremlett/Guernsey	
G-BBCA	Bell 206B JetRanger 2	Hecray Ltd/Southend	
G-BBCB	Western O-65 balloon	M. Westwood *Cee Bee*	

Notes	Reg.	Type	Owner or Operator
	G-BBCC	PA-E23 Aztec 250	Dorglen Ltd/Coventry
	G-BBCD	Beech 95-B55 Baron	L. M. Tulloch
	G-BBCF	Cessna FRA.150L	Yorkshire Light Aircraft Ltd/Leeds
	G-BBCH	Robin DR.400/2+2	Headcorn Flying School Ltd
	G-BBCI	Cessna 150H	N. R. Windley
	G-BBCJ	Cessna 150J	Ingham Aviation Ltd/Bristol
	G-BBCK	Cameron O-77 balloon	R. J. Leathart The Mary Gloster
	G-BBCM	PA-E23 Aztec 250	Peak Aviation Services Ltd
	G-BBCN	Robin HR.100/210	K. T. G. Atkins
	G-BBCP	Thunder Ax6-56 balloon	J. M. Robinson Jack Frost
	G-BBCS	Robin DR.400/140	J. A. Thomas
	G-BBCW	PA-E23 Aztec 250	JDT Holdings Ltd/Sturgate
	G-BBCY	Luton LA-4A Minor	C. H. Difford
	G-BBCZ	AA-5 Traveler	Stronghill Flying Group/Bournemouth
	G-BBDA	AA-5 Traveler	R. E. Pettitt & J. R. Parkham
	G-BBDB	PA-28 Cherokee 180	T. D. Strange/Newtownards
	G-BBDC	PA-28 Cherokee 140	P. E. Quick/Popham
	G-BBDD	PA-28 Cherokee 140	Midland Air Training School
	G-BBDE	PA-28R-200-2 Cherokee Arrow	R. L. Coleman
	G-BBDG	Concorde 100	British Aerospace PLC/Filton
	G-BBDH	Cessna F.172M	A. E. & G. R. Garner Ltd/Mona
	G-BBDI	PA-18 Super Cub 150	Scottish Gliding Union Ltd
	G-BBDJ	Thunder Ax6-56 balloon	S. W. D. & H. B. Ashby Jack Tar
	G-BBDK	V.808C Viscount Freightmaster	British Air Ferries Viscount Linley/ Southend
	G-BBDL	AA-5 Traveler	A. M. Truslove
	G-BBDM	AA-5 Traveler	J. Pettit/Stapleford
	G-BBDN	Taylor JT.1 Monoplane	T. Barnes
	G-BBDO	PA-E23 Aztec 250	R. Long/Bristol
	G-BBDP	Robin DR.400/160	Jarrett & Plumb Aviation (Rochester) Ltd
	G-BBDS	PA-31 Navajo	Broad Oak Air Services/Rochester
	G-BBDT	Cessna 150H	J. M. McCloy/Sherburn
	G-BBDU	PA-31 Navajo	G-Air Ltd/Goodwood
	G-BBDV	SIPA S.903	W. McAndrew
	G-BBEA	Luton LA-4A Minor	R. T. Callow
	G-BBEB	PA-28R-200-2 Cherokee Arrow	R. D. Rippingale/Thruxton
	G-BBEC	PA-28 Cherokee 180	J. H. Kimber
	G-BBED	M.S.894A Rallye Minerva 220	Sky-Ad Ltd/Birmingham
	G-BBEF	PA-28 Cherokee 140	Air Navigation & Trading Co Ltd/ Blackpool
	G-BBEI	PA-31 Navajo	BKS Surveys Ltd/Exeter
	G-BBEL	PA-28R Cherokee Arrow 180	W. A. L. Mitchell/Glasgow
	G-BBEN	Bellanca 7GCBC Citabria	Ulster Gliding Club Ltd
	G-BBEO	Cessna FRA.150L	Granair Ltd
	G-BBEV	PA-28 Cherokee 140	Telepoint Ltd/Manchester
	G-BBEW	PA-E23 Aztec 250	Air Furness/Walney Island
	G-BBEX	Cessna 185A Skywagon	Cabair Air Taxis Ltd/Elstree
	G-BBEY	PA-23 Aztec 250	D. W. Higgins
	G-BBFC	AA-1B Trainer	R. C. Gillingham & G. Mobey/Lydd
	G-BBFD	PA-28R-200-2 Cherokee Arrow	Delta Sound Services Ltd/Fairoaks
	G-BBFL	GY-201 Minicab	C. W. Thomas
	G-BBFS	Van Den Bemden gas balloon	A. J. F. Smith Le Tomate
	G-BBFV	PA-32 Cherokee Six 260	Southend Securities Ltd
	G-BBFW	PA-E23 Aztec 250B	T. Bartlett/Stapleford
	G-BBFZ	PA-28R-200-2 Cherokee Arrow	Larkfield Garage (Chepstow) Ltd
	G-BBGB	PA-E23 Aztec 250	Keeler Air Transport Service (Air Taxis) Ltd/Shoreham
	G-BBGC	M.S.893E Rallye Commodore 180	A. Somerville
	G-BBGE	PA-E23 Aztec 250	Dollar Air Services Ltd/Coventry
	G-BBGF	Cessna 340	ADM Air Services Ltd
	G-BBGH	AA-5 Traveler	J. W. Skene/Biggin Hill
	G-BBGI	Fuji FA.200-160	J. J. Young/Seething
	G-BBGJ	Cessna 180	Med-Co Hospital Supplies Ltd
	G-BBGL	Baby Great Lakes	F. Ball
	G-BBGR	Cameron O-65 balloon	M. L. & L. P. Willoughby
	G-BBGX	Cessna 182P Skylane	H. I. Williams & ptnrs/Sleap
	G-BBGZ	CHABA 42 balloon	G. Laslett & ptnrs
	G-BBHB	PA-31-300 Navajo	Kondair/Stansted
	G-BBHC	Enstrom F-28A	Blades Helicopters Ltd/Goodwood
	G-BBHD	Enstrom F-28A	Farm Supply Co (Thirsk) Ltd
	G-BBHF	PA-23 Aztec 250E	Bevan Lynch Aviation Ltd/Birmingham
	G-BBHG	Cessna E310Q	Delta Aviation Ltd/Elstree

Reg.	Type	Owner or Operator	Notes
G-BBHI	Cessna 177RG	Independent Tape Duplicators Ltd	
G-BBHJ	Piper J-3C-65 Cub	R. V. Miller & R. H. Heath	
G-BBHK	AT-16 Harvard IIB	Bob Warner Aviation/Exeter	
G-BBHL	Sikorsky S-61N Mk II	Bristow Helicopters Ltd *Glamis*	
G-BBHM	Sikorsky S-61N Mk II	Bristow Helicopters Ltd *Braemar*	
G-BBHW	SA.341G Gazelle 1	McAlpine Aviation Ltd/Hayes	
G-BBHX	M.S.893E Rallye Commodore	H. H. Elder/Exeter	
G-BBHY	PA-28 Cherokee 180	Air Operations Ltd/Guernsey	
G-BBIA	PA-28R-200 Cherokee Arrow	A. G. (Commodities) Ltd/Stapleford	
G-BBIC	Cessna 310Q	Angus Motor Co/Dundee	
G-BBID	PA-28 Cherokee 140	R. K. Tamlinson/Elstree	
G-BBIF	PA-E23 Aztec 250	Northern Executive Aviation Ltd/ Manchester	
G-BBIH	Enstrom F-28A	Rivaldouble Ltd	
G-BBII	Fiat G-46-3B	The Hon A. M. M. Lindsay/Booker	
G-BBIL	PA-28 Cherokee 140	D. Arlette/Stapleford	
G-BBIN	Enstrom F28A	Jarogate Ltd/Redhill	
G-BBIO	Robin HR.100/210	R. A. King/Headcorn	
G-BBIT	Hughes 269B	Contract Development & Projects (Leeds) Ltd	
G-BBIV	Hughes 269C	W. R. Finance Ltd	
G-BBIX	PA-28 Cherokee 140	R. J. Hill/Biggin Hill	
G-BBJB	Thunder Ax7-77 balloon	St Crispin Balloon Group *Dick Darby*	
G-BBJI	Isaacs Spitfire	A. N. R. Houghton & ptnrs	
G-BBJU	Robin DR.400/140	J. C. Lister	
G-BBJV	Cessna F.177RG	Pilot Magazine/Biggin Hill	
G-BBJW	Cessna FRA.150L	Coventry School of Flying Ltd	
G-BBJX	Cessna F.150L	Yorkshire Flying Services Ltd/Leeds	
G-BBJY	Cessna F.172M	J. Lucketti/Barton	
G-BBJZ	Cessna F.172M	Burks, Green & ptnrs	
G-BBKA	Cessna F.150L	Sherburn Aero Club Ltd	
G-BBKB	Cessna F.150L	Shoreham Flight Simulation/ Bournemouth	
G-BBKC	Cessna F.172M	W. F. Hall	
G-BBKE	Cessna F.150L	Wickenby Aviation Ltd	
G-BBKF	Cessna FRA.150L	Compton Abbas Airfield Ltd	
G-BBKG	Cessna FR.172J	Cabledraw Ltd/Lydd	
G-BBKI	Cessna F.172M	B. C. Lemon & D. Godfrey/ Fenland	
G-BBKL	CP.301A Emeraude	R. Wells	
G-BBKR	Scheibe SF.24A Motorspatz	P. I. Morgans	
G-BBKU	Cessna FRA.150L	Balgin Ltd/Bourn	
G-BBKV	Cessna FRA.150L	Skegness Air Taxi Service Ltd	
G-BBKX	PA-28 Cherokee 180	P. E. Eglington	
G-BBKY	Cessna F.150L	Telepoint Ltd/Manchester	
G-BBKZ	Cessna 172M	Exeter Flying Club Ltd	
G-BBLA	PA-28 Cherokee 140	Woodgate Aviation Co Ltd/Woodvale	
G-BBLE	Hiller UH-12E	Agricopters Ltd/Chilbolton	
G-BBLH	Piper O-59A Grasshopper	Shipping & Airlines Ltd/Biggin Hill	
G-BBLL	Cameron O-84 balloon	University of East Anglia Hot-Air Ballooning Club *Boadicea*	
G-BBLM	M.S.880 Rallye 100 Sport	R. J. Lewis & P. Walker	
G-BBLP	PA-E23 Aztec 250D	Donnington Aviation Ltd/E. Midlands	
G-BBLS	AA-5 Traveler	Turnhouse Flying Club/Edinburgh	
G-BBLU	PA-34-200-2 Seneca	F. Tranter/Manchester	
G-BBMB	Robin DR.400/180	G. A. Mason	
G-BBME	BAC One-Eleven 401	British Airways *County of Shropshire* (G-AZMI)/Birmingham	
G-BBMF	BAC One-Eleven 401	British Airways *County of Worcestershire* (G-ATVU)/ Birmingham	
G-BBMG	BAC One-Eleven 408	British Airways *County of Gloucestershire* (G-AWEJ)/ Birmingham	
G-BBMH	E.A.A. Sports Biplane Model P.1.	K. Dawson	
G-BBMJ	PA-E23 Aztec 250	Tindon Ltd/Little Snoring	
G-BBMK	PA-31-300 Navajo	Steer Aviation Ltd/Biggin Hill	
G-BBMN	D.H.C.1 Chipmunk 22	R. Steiner/Panshanger	
G-BBMO	D.H.C.1 Chipmunk 22	A. J. Hurst/Holland	
G-BBMR	D.H.C.1 Chipmunk T.10 ★ (WB763)	Southall Technical College	
G-BBMT	D.H.C.1 Chipmunk 22	A. T. Letts & ptnrs/Dunstable	
G-BBMV	D.H.C.1 Chipmunk 22 (WG348)	M. F. Newman	
G-BBMW	D.H.C.1 Chipmunk 22	M. S. Evans	

Notes	Reg.	Type	Owner or Operator
	G-BBMX	D.H.C.1 Chipmunk 22	A. L. Brown & P. S. Murchison
	G-BBMZ	D.H.C.1 Chipmunk 22	Wycombe Gliding School Syndicate/Booker
	G-BBNA	D.H.C.1 Chipmunk 22 (Lycoming)	Coventry Gliding Club Ltd/Husbands Bosworth
	G-BBNC	D.H.C.1 Chipmunk T.10 ★ (WP790)	Mosquito Aircraft Museum
	G-BBND	D.H.C.1 Chipmunk 22	A. J. Organ/Bourn
	G-BBNG	Bell 206B JetRanger 2	Helicopter Crop Spraying Ltd
	G-BBNH	PA-34-200-2 Seneca	Lawrence Goodwin Machine Tools Ltd Wellesbourne
	G-BBNI	PA-34-200-2 Seneca	Colnenay Ltd/Guernsey
	G-BBNJ	Cessna F.150L	Sherburn Aero Club
	G-BBNN	PA-E23 Aztec 250D	J. W. B. Wimble
	G-BBNO	PA-E23 Aztec 250E	Hedley & Ellis Ltd/Conington
	G-BBNR	Cessna 340	J. Lipton/Elstree
	G-BBNT	PA-31-350 Navajo Chieftain	Northern Executive Aviation Ltd/Manchester
	G-BBNV	Fuji FA.200-160	C.S.E. Aviation Ltd/Kidlington
	G-BBNX	Cessna FRA.150L	General Airline Ltd
	G-BBNY	Cessna FRA.150L	Air Tows Ltd/Lasham
	G-BBNZ	Cessna F.172M	Andrews & Associates
	G-BBOA	Cessna F.172M	J. W. J. Adkins/Southend
	G-BBOB	Cessna 421B	R. F. Gregory/Cardiff
	G-BBOC	Cameron O-77 balloon	J. A. B. Gray
	G-BBOE	Robin HR.200/100	Aberdeen Flying Group
	G-BBOH	Pitts S-1S Special	P. Meeson
	G-BBOI	Bede BD-5B	Heather V. B. Wheeler
	G-BBOJ	PA-23 Aztec 250 ★	*Instructional airframe*/Cranfield
	G-BBOK	PA-23 Aztec 250	J. J. Anglin
	G-BBOL	PA-18 Super Cub 150	Lakes Gliding Club Ltd
	G-BBOO	Thunder Ax6-56 balloon	K. Meehan *Tigerjack*
	G-BBOR	Bell 206B JetRanger 2	Land Air Ltd
	G-BBOX	Thunder Ax7-77 balloon	R. C. Weyda *Rocinante*
	G-BBOY	Thunder Ax6-56A balloon	N. C. Faithfull *Eric of Titchfield*
	G-BBPJ	Cessna F.172M	B. W. Aviation Ltd/Cardiff
	G-BBPK	Evans VP-1	P. D. Kelsey
	G-BBPM	Enstrom F-28A	Wardell Holdings Ltd
	G-BBPN	Enstrom F-28A	D. S. Chandler/Shoreham
	G-BBPO	Enstrom F-28A	J. Morton & E. Ryan
	G-BBPP	PA-28 Cherokee 180	Hartmann Ltd
	G-BBPS	Jodel D.117	A. Appleby/Redhill
	G-BBPU	Boeing 747-136	British Airways *City of Dundee*/Heathrow
	G-BBPW	Robin HR.100/210	The Character Premium Co Ltd
	G-BBPX	PA-34-200-2 Seneca	Richel Investments Ltd/Guernsey
	G-BBPY	PA-28 Cherokee 180	George Hill (Oldham) Ltd
	G-BBRA	PA-E23 Aztec 250E	W. London Aviation Services/White Waltham
	G-BBRB	D.H.82A Tiger Moth (DF198)	R. Barham/Biggin Hill
	G-BBRC	Fuji FA.200-180	W. & L. Installations & Co Ltd/Fairoaks
	G-BBRH	Bell 47G-5A	Helicopter Supplies & Engineering Ltd
	G-BBRI	Bell 47G-5A	Camlet Helicopters Ltd/Fairoaks
	G-BBRN	Procter Kittiwake	Vari-Prop (GB) Ltd/Exeter
	G-BBRV	D.H.C.1 Chipmunk 22	HSA (Chester) Sports & Social Club
	G-BBRW	PA-28 Cherokee 140	P. R. Wernham/Elstree
	G-BBRX	SIAI-Marchetti S.205-18F	P. R. Gabriel/Stapleford
	G-BBRZ	AA-5 Traveler	C. P. Osbourne
	G-BBSA	AA-5 Traveler	K. Lynn
	G-BBSB	Beech C23 Sundowner	Sundowner Group/Manchester
	G-BBSC	Beech B24R Sierra	Beechcombers Flying Group
	G-BBSE	D.H.C.1 Chipmunk 22	Felthorpe Flying Group Ltd
	G-BBSM	PA-32 Cherokee Six 300	R. Robson/Biggin Hill
	G-BBSS	D.H.C.1A Chipmunk 22	Northumbria Tug Group
	G-BBSU	Cessna 421B	Hamdanair Ltd
	G-BBSV	Cessna 421B	World Carrier (London) Ltd
	G-BBSW	Pietenpol Air Camper	J. K. S. Wills
	G-BBTB	Cessna FRA.150L	Compton Abbas Airfield Ltd
	G-BBTG	Cessna F.172M	D. H. Laws
	G-BBTH	Cessna F.172M	S. Gilmore/Newtownards
	G-BBTJ	PA-E23 Aztec 250E	GCA Survey Group Ltd/Shoreham
	G-BBTK	Cessna FRA.150L	Airwork Ltd/Perth
	G-BBTL	PA-E23 Aztec 250C	Air Navigation & Trading Co Ltd/Blackpool

Reg.	Type	Owner or Operator	Notes
G-BBTS	Beech V35B Bonanza	Charles Lock Motors Ltd/Stapleford	
G-BBTU	ST-10 Diplomate	P. Campion/Stapleford	
G-BBTW	PA-31P Navajo	M. G. Tyrell & Co Ltd/Leavesden	
G-BBTX	Beech C23 Sundowner	Celahurst Ltd	
G-BBTY	Beech C23 Sundowner	Torlid Ltd/Biggin Hill	
G-BBTZ	Cessna F.150L	Woodgate Air Services Ltd	
G-BBUD	Sikorsky S-61N Mk II	British International Helicopters Ltd/ Aberdeen	
G-BBUE	AA-5 Traveler	S. J. Southwell-Gray/Blackpool	
G-BBUF	AA-5 Traveler	W. J. Brogan	
G-BBUG	PA-16 Clipper	A. G. Palmer/Coventry	
G-BBUJ	Cessna 421B	Expressflight Ltd/Southend	
G-BBUL	Mitchell-Procter Kittiwake 1	R. Bull	
G-BBUO	Cessna 150L	Exeter Flying Club Ltd	
G-BBUT	Western O-65 balloon	Wg. Cdr. G. F. Turnbull & Mrs K. Turnbull *Christabelle II*	
G-BBUU	Piper L-4B Cub	Cooper Bros/Little Snoring	
G-BBUY	Bell 206B JetRanger 2	Hecray Ltd/Southend	
G-BBVA	Sikorsky S-61N Mk II	Bristow Helicopters Ltd *Vega*	
G-BBVE	Cessna 340	R. M. Cox Ltd/Biggin Hill	
G-BBVF	SA Twin Pioneer III ★	Museum of Flight/E. Fortune	
G-BBVG	PA-23 Aztec 250D	R. F. Wanbon & P. G. Warmerdan/ Panshanger	
G-BBVH	V.807 Viscount	GB Airways Ltd/Gibraltar	
G-BBVI	Enstrom F-28A ★	*Ground trainer*/Kidlington	
G-BBVJ	Beech B24R Sierra	Beech Sierra Group/Netherthorpe	
G-BBVM	Beech A.100 King Air	Northern Executive Aviation Ltd/ Manchester	
G-BBVO	Isaacs Fury II	D. Silsbury	
G-BBVP	Westland-Bell 47G-3B1	CKS Air Ltd/Southend	
G-BBWM	PA-23 Aztec 250E	Guernsey Air Search Ltd	
G-BBWN	D.H.C.1 Chipmunk 22	B. E. Simpson/Booker	
G-BBXB	Cessna FRA.150L	M. L. Swain/Bourn	
G-BBXG	PA-34-200-2 Seneca	London Flight Centre (Stansted) Ltd	
G-BBXH	Cessna FR.172F	H. H. Metal Finishing (Wales) Ltd	
G-BBXK	PA-34-200-2 Seneca	Aerobatic Displays Ltd	
G-BBXL	Cessna E310Q	Chatsworth Studios Ltd/Newcastle	
G-BBXO	Enstrom F-28A	Southern Air Ltd/Shoreham	
G-BBXR	PA-31-350 Navajo Chieftain	W. R. M. C. Foyle/Luton	
G-BBXS	Piper J-3C-65 Cub	M. J. Butler (G-ALMA)/Langham	
G-BBXT	Cessna F.172M	I. B. Wilkens/Netherthorpe	
G-BBXU	Beech B24R Sierra	B. M. Russell/Coventry	
G-BBXV	PA-28-151 Warrior	London Flight Centre (Stansted) Ltd	
G-BBXW	PA-28-151 Warrior	Shropshire Aero Club Ltd	
G-BBXX	PA-31-350 Navajo Chieftain	Natural Environment Research Council	
G-BBXY	Bellanca 7GCBC Citabria	J. Turner/Shoreham	
G-BBXZ	Evans VP-1	J. D. Kingston	
G-BBYB	PA-18 Super Cub 95	J. Taylor	
G-BBYE	Cessna 195	R. J. Willies	
G-BBYH	Cessna 182P	Sanderson (Forklifts) Ltd	
G-BBYK	PA-23 Aztec 250	Kraken Air/Cardiff	
G-BBYL	Cameron O-77 balloon	Buckingham Balloon Club *Jammy*	
G-BBYM	H.P.137 Jetstream 200	British Aerospace PLC (G-AYWR)/ Woodford	
G-BBYO	BN-2A Mk III Trislander	Aurigny Air Services (G-BBWR)/ Guernsey	
G-BBYP	PA-28 Cherokee 140	A. J. Bamrah/Biggin Hill	
G-BBYS	Cessna 182P Skylane	Traffic Management Services	
G-BBYU	Cameron O-56 balloon	C. J. T. Davey *Chieftain*	
G-BBYW	PA-28 Cherokee 140	C.S.E. Aviation Ltd/Kidlington	
G-BBZF	PA-28 Cherokee 140	J. L. Yourell	
G-BBZH	PA-28R-200 Cherokee Arrow	Mightycraft Ltd	
G-BBZI	PA-31-310 Navajo	Airways International Cymru Ltd/Cardiff	
G-BBZJ	PA-34-200-2 Seneca	Three Counties Aero Club Ltd/ Blackbushe	
G-BBZK	Westland-Bell 47G-3B1	Autair Helicopters Ltd/Cranfield	
G-BBZN	Fuji FA.200-180	J. Westwood & P. D. Wedd	
G-BBZO	Fuji FA.200-160	D. G. Lewendon/Bournemouth	
G-BBZS	Enstrom F-28A	Southern Air Ltd/Shoreham	
G-BBZV	PA-28R Cherokee Arrow 200-2	Unicol Engineering/Kidlington	
G-BCAC	M.S.894A Rallye Minerva 220	R. S. Rogers/Cardiff	
G-BCAH	D.H.C.1 Chipmunk 22 (WG316)	G. Lacey	
G-BCAN	Thunder Ax7-77 balloon	Wessex Hot-Air Team	

Notes	Reg.	Type	Owner or Operator
	G-BCAP	Cameron O-56 balloon	S. R. Seager
	G-BCAR	Thunder Ax7-77 balloon	T. J. Woodbridge/Australia
	G-BCAT	PA-31-310 Turbo Navajo	Hubbardair Ltd
	G-BCAZ	PA-12 Super Cruiser	A. D. Williams
	G-BCBD	Bede BD-5B	Brockmore-Bede Aircraft (UK) Ltd/ Shobdon
	G-BCBG	PA-E23 Aztec 250	M. J. L. Batt/Booker
	G-BCBH	Fairchild 24R-46A Argus III	Bluegale Ltd/Biggin Hill
	G-BCBJ	PA-25 Pawnee 235	Deeside Gliding Club (Aberdeenshire) Ltd
	G-BCBK	Cessna 421B	Sullivan Management Control Ltd
	G-BCBL	Fairchild 24R-46A Argus III (HB751)	J. Turner/Shoreham
	G-BCBM	PA-23 Aztec 250	S. Lightbrown & M. Kavanagh
	G-BCBP	M.S.880B Rallye 100S Sport	A. A. Thomas/Dunkeswell
	G-BCBR	AJEP/Wittman W.8 Tailwind	I. McMillan
	G-BCBW	Cessna 182P	E. Reed
	G-BCBX	Cessna F.150L	J. Kelly/Newtownards
	G-BCBY	Cessna F.150L	Scottish Airways Flyers (Prestwick) Ltd
	G-BCBZ	Cessna 337C	Westward Airways (Land End) Ltd/ St Just
	G-BCCB	Robin HR.200/100	P. J. Howard
	G-BCCC	Cessna F.150L	J. C. Glynn
	G-BCCD	Cessna F.172M	Lota Ltd
	G-BCCE	PA-E23 Aztec 250	Hymore Hodson Antiques
	G-BCCF	PA-28 Cherokee 180	J. T. Friskney Ltd/Skegness
	G-BCCG	Thunder Ax7-65 balloon	N. H. Ponsford
	G-BCCK	AA-5 Traveler	Prospect Air Ltd/Barton
	G-BCCP	Robin HR. 200/100	Northampton School of Flying Ltd/ Sywell
	G-BCCR	CP.301B Emeraude	A. B. Fisher/Dishforth
	G-BCCU	BN-2A Mk III-1 Trislander	Kondair/Stansted
	G-BCCX	D.H.C.1 Chipmunk 22 (Lycoming)	RAFGSA/Dishforth
	G-BCCY	Robin HR.200/100	D. S. Farler/Bristol
	G-BCDA	Boeing 727-46	Dan-Air Services Ltd/Gatwick
	G-BCDB	PA-34-200-2 Seneca	A. & G. Aviation Ltd/Bournemouth
	G-BCDC	PA-18 Super Cub 95	ALY Aviation Ltd
	G-BCDJ	PA-28 Cherokee 140	J. A. Renelt/Southend
	G-BCDK	Partenavia P.68B	Nottingham Offshore Marine
	G-BCDL	Cameron O-42 balloon	D. P. & Mrs B. O. Turner Chums
	G-BCDN	F.27 Friendship Mk 200	Air UK/Norwich
	G-BCDO	F.27 Friendship Mk 200	Air UK Lord Butler/Norwich
	G-BCDR	Thunder Ax7-77 balloon	W. G. Johnston & ptnrs Obelix
	G-BCDY	Cessna FRA.150L	Airwork Ltd/Perth
	G-BCEA	Sikorsky S-61N Mk II	British International Helicopters Ltd/ Aberdeen
	G-BCEB	Sikorsky S-61N Mk II	British International Helicopters Ltd/ Penzance
	G-BCEC	Cessna F.172M	United Propedent Ltd/Manchester
	G-BCEE	AA-5 Traveler	Echo Echo Ltd/Bournemouth
	G-BCEF	AA-5 Traveler	Echo Fox Ltd/Jersey
	G-BCEN	BN-2A Islander	Atlantic Air Transport Ltd/Coventry
	G-BCEO	AA-5 Traveler	Regishire Ltd/Southampton
	G-BCEP	AA-5 Traveler	Nottingham Industrial Cleaners Ltd/ Tollerton
	G-BCER	GY-201 Minicab	D. Beaumont/Sherburn
	G-BCEU	Cameron O-42 balloon	Entertainment Services Ltd Harlequin
	G-BCEX	PA-E23 Aztec 250	Weekes Bros (Welling) Ltd/Biggin Hill
	G-BCEY	D.H.C.1 Chipmunk 22	D. O. Wallis
	G-BCEZ	Cameron O-84 balloon	Anglia Aeronauts Ascension Association Stars and Bars
	G-BCFB	Cameron O-77 balloon	J. J. Harris & P. Pryce-Jones Teutonic Turkey
	G-BCFC	Cameron O-65 balloon	B. H. Mead Candy Twist
	G-BCFD	West balloon ★	British Balloon Museum Hellfire
	G-BCFF	Fuji FA-200-160	G. W. Brown & M. R. Gibbons
	G-BCFN	Cameron O-65 balloon	W. G. Johnson & H. M. Savage
	G-BCFO	PA-18-150 Super Cub	Bristol & Gloucestershire Gliding Club (Pty) Ltd/Nympsfield
	G-BCFR	Cessna FRA.150L	J. J. Baumhardt/Southend
	G-BCFW	Saab 91D Safir	D. R. Williams
	G-BCFY	Luton LA-4A Minor	R. J. Wrixon
	G-BCGB	Bensen B.8	A. Melody

Reg.	Type	Owner or Operator	Notes
G-BCGC	D.H.C.1 Chipmunk 22 (WP903)	Culdrose Gliding Club	
G-BCGG	Jodel DR.250 Srs 160	C. G. Gray (G-ATZL)	
G-BCGH	Nord NC.854S	T. J. N. H. Palmer & G. W. Oliver	
G-BCGI	PA-28 Cherokee 140	A. Dodd/Redhill	
G-BCGJ	PA-28 Cherokee 140	I. T. D. Hall & B. R. Sedgeman Tees-side	
G-BCGK	PA-28 Cherokee 140	CSE Aviation Ltd/Kidlington	
G-BCGL	Jodel D.112	J. Harris	
G-BCGM	Jodel D.120	M. Albert-Brecht/Aberdeen	
G-BCGN	PA-28 Cherokee 140	Oxford Flyers Ltd/Kidlington	
G-BCGS	PA-28R-200 Cherokee Arrow	MAP Thompson (Roofing) Ltd	
G-BCGT	PA-28 Cherokee 140	I. M. Fieldsend/Cranfield	
G-BCGW	Jodel D.11	G. H. & M. D. Chittenden	
G-BCGX	Bede BD-5A/B	R. Hodgson	
G-BCHK	Cessna F.172H	N. Yorks Aviation Ltd/Grindale	
G-BCHL	D.H.C.1 Chipmunk 22A (WP788)	Shropshire Soaring Ltd	
G-BCHM	SA.341G Gazelle	Bristol Helicopters Ltd/Yeovil	
G-BCHP	CP.1310C-3 Super Emeraude	H. Swift (G-JOSI)	
G-BCHT	Schleicher ASK.16	K. M. Barton & ptnrs/Dunstable	
G-BCHU	Dawes VP-2	G. Dawes	
G-BCHV	D.H.C.1 Chipmunk 22	N. F. Charles/Sywell	
G-BCHX	SF.23A Sperling	R. L. McClean	
G-BCID	PA-34-200-2 Seneca	Comanche Air Services Ltd/Lydd	
G-BCIE	PA-28-151 Warrior	J. A. & J. V. Bridger/Exeter	
G-BCIF	PA-28 Cherokee 140	Fryer-Robins Aviation Ltd/E. Midlands	
G-BCIH	D.H.C.1 Chipmunk 22 (WD363)	J. M. Hosey & R. A. Schofield/Stansted	
G-BCIJ	AA-5 Traveler	W. J. McCollum	
G-BCIK	AA-5 Traveler	W. Nutt & Son Ltd	
G-BCIL	AA-1B Trainer	G-Air Ltd (*stored*)/Goodwood	
G-BCIN	Thunder Ax7-77 balloon	P. G & R. A. Vale	
G-BCIR	PA-28-151 Warrior	R. J. Patton	
G-BCIT	CIT/AI Srs 1	Cranfield Institute of Technology	
G-BCIW	D.H.C.1 Chipmunk 22 (WZ868)	R. K. J. Hadlow & ptnrs/Duxford	
G-BCJF	Beagle B.206 Srs 1	A. A. Mattacks/Biggin Hill	
G-BCJH	Mooney M.20F	S. R. Cannell/Panshanger	
G-BCJM	PA-28 Cherokee 140	Paragraph Typesetting Ltd	
G-BCJN	PA-28 Cherokee 140	A. J. Steed/Goodwood	
G-BCJO	PA-28R-200 Cherokee Arrow	G. I. Cooper	
G-BCJP	PA-28 Cherokee 140	G. C. Smith/Bourn	
G-BCJS	PA-E23 Aztec 250	Woodgate Air Services (IoM) Ltd/ Ronaldsway	
G-BCKF	SA.102.5 Cavalier	K. Fairness	
G-BCKN	D.H.C.1A Chipmunk 22	RAFGSA/Bicester	
G-BCKO	PA-E23 Aztec 250	W. R. M. C. Foyle/Luton	
G-BCKP	Luton LA-5A Major	J. R. Callow	
G-BCKS	Fuji FA.200-180	J. T. Hicks/Goodwood	
G-BCKT	Fuji FA.200-180	Littlewick Green Service Station Ltd/ Booker	
G-BCKU	Cessna FRA.150L	Airwork Ltd/Perth	
G-BCKV	Cessna FRA.150L	Airwork Ltd/Perth	
G-BCLC	Sikorsky S-61N	Bristow Helicopters Ltd	
G-BCLD	Sikorsky S-61N	Bristow Helicopters Ltd	
G-BCLI	AA-5 Traveler	R. A. Williams/Panshanger	
G-BCLJ	AA-5 Traveler	M. E. Woodroffe/Shoreham	
G-BCLL	PA-28 Cherokee 180	Stu Davidson & Son Plant Hire Ltd	
G-BCLS	Cessna 170B	C. W. Proffitt-White/Shotteswell	
G-BCLU	Jodel D.117	N. A. Wallace	
G-BCLV	Bede BD-5A	R. A. Gardiner	
G-BCLW	AA-1B Trainer	R. J. Travers	
G-BCMD	PA-19 Super Cub 95	R. G. Brooks/Dunkeswell	
G-BCMJ	SA.102.5 Cavalier (tailwheel)	R. G. Sykes/Shoreham	
G-BCMT	Isaacs Fury II	M. H. Turner	
G-BCNC	GY.201 Minicab	J. R. Wraight	
G-BCNP	Cameron O-77 balloon	M. L. J. Ritchie	
G-BCNR	Thunder Ax7-77A balloon	S. J. Miliken & ptnrs	
G-BCNT	Partenavia P.68B	Welsh Airways Ltd	
G-BCNX	Piper J-3C-65 Cub	K. J. Lord/Ipswich	
G-BCNZ	Fuji FA.200-160	J. Bruton & A. Lincoln/Manchester	
G-BCOB	Piper J-3C-65 Cub	R. W. & Mrs J. W. Marjoram	
G-BCOE	H.S.748 Srs 2B	British Airways *Glen Livet*/Glasgow	
G-BCOF	H.S.748 Srs 2B	British Airways *Glen Fiddich*/Glasgow	
G-BCOG	Jodel D.112	B. A. Bower & ptnrs	
G-BCOH	Avro 683 Lancaster 10 (KB976)	Strathallan Aircraft Collection	
G-BCOI	D.H.C.1 Chipmunk 22	D. S. McGregor & A. T. Letham	

Notes	Reg.	Type	Owner or Operator
	G-BCOJ	Cameron O-56 balloon	T. J. Knott & M. J. Webber
	G-BCOL	Cessna F.172M	J. Birkett/Wickenby
	G-BCOM	Piper J-3C-65 Cub	P. M. Whitlock & J. P. Whitham/Sywell
	G-BCOO	D.H.C.1 Chipmunk 22	T. G. Fielding & M. S. Morton/Blackpool
	G-BCOP	PA-28R-200 Cherokee Arrow	E. A. Saunders/Halfpenny Green
	G-BCOR	SOCATA Rallye 100ST	H. J. Pincombe/Dunkeswell
	G-BCOU	D.H.C.1 Chipmunk 22 (WK522)	P. J. Loweth
	G-BCOX	Bede BD-5A	H. J. Cox
	G-BCOY	D.H.C.1 Chipmunk 22	Coventry Gliding Club Ltd/Husbands Bosworth
	G-BCPB	Howes radio-controlled model free balloon	R. B. & Mrs C. Howes Posbee 1
	G-BCPD	GY-201 Minicab	A. H. K. Denniss/Halfpenny Green
	G-BCPE	Cessna F.150M	E. Shipley/Jersey
	G-BCPF	PA-23 Aztec 250	M. A. Bonsall/E. Midlands
	G-BCPG	PA-28R-200 Cherokee Arrow	Echo Charlie Flying Group/Barton
	G-BCPH	Piper J-3C-65 Cub (329934)	I. R. March
	G-BCPJ	Piper J-3C-65 Cub	M. C. Barraclough
	G-BCPK	Cessna F.172M	Skegness Air Taxi Services Ltd
	G-BCPN	AA-5 Traveler	B.W. Agricultural Equipments Ltd
	G-BCPO	Partenavia P.68B	Mondiale Aviation Ltd
	G-BCPU	D.H.C.1 Chipmunk T.10	P. Waller/Booker
	G-BCPX	Szep HFC.125	A. Szep/Netherthorpe
	G-BCRA	Cessna F.150M ★	Three Counties Aero Club/Blackbushe
	G-BCRB	Cessna F.172M	Specialised Laboratory Equipment Ltd
	G-BCRE	Cameron O-77 balloon	A. R. Langton
	G-BCRH	Alaparma Baldo B.75	A. L. Scadding/(stored)
	G-BCRI	Cameron O-65 balloon	V. J. Thorne Joseph
	G-BCRJ	Taylor JT.1 Monoplane	K. J. Jarrett
	G-BCRK	SA.102.5 Cavalier	T. Barlow/Blackpool
	G-BCRL	PA-28-151 Warrior	F. N. Garland/Biggin Hill
	G-BCRN	Cessna FRA.150L	Airwork Ltd/Perth
	G-BCRP	PA-E23 Aztec 250	ReFair/Sibson
	G-BCRR	AA-5B Tiger	ReFair/Sibson
	G-BCRT	Cessna F.150M	Suffolk Aero Club Ltd/Ipswich
	G-BCRX	D.H.C.1 Chipmunk 22	J. P. V. Hunt & P. G. H. Tory/Enstone
	G-BCSA	D.H.C.1 Chipmunk 22	RAFGSA/Bicester
	G-BCSB	D.H.C.1 Chipmunk 22	RAFGSA/Bicester
	G-BCSL	D.H.C.1 Chipmunk 22	Jalawain Ltd/Barton
	G-BCSM	Bellanca 8GC BC Scout	Buckminster Gliding Club
	G-BCST	M.S.893A Rallye Commodore 180	P. J. Wilcox/Cranfield
	G-BCSX	Thunder Ax7-77 balloon	A. T. Wood Whoopski
	G-BCSY	Taylor JT.2 Titch	T. Hartwell & D. Wilkinson
	G-BCSZ	PA-28R-200 Cherokee Arrow	J. Pownall/Tollerton
	G-BCTA	PA-28-151 Warrior	T. G. Aviation Ltd/Manston
	G-BCTF	PA-28-151 Warrior	Eastern Air Executive Ltd/Sturgate
	G-BCTI	Schleicher ASK.16	R. J. Steward
	G-BCTJ	Cessna 310Q	Airwork Ltd/Perth
	G-BCTK	Cessna FR.172J	D. F. Ball
	G-BCTR	Taylor JT.2 Titch	D. H. Greenwood
	G-BCTT	Evans VP-1	B. J. Boughton
	G-BCTU	Cessna FRA.150M	Great Consall Copper Mine Co Ltd
	G-BCTV	Cessna F.150M	C. E. Derbyshire & T. L. Morris/Andrewsfield
	G-BCTW	Cessna F.150M	Woodgate Air Services Ltd/Aldergrove
	G-BCUB	Piper J-3C-65 Cub	A. L. Brown & G. Attwell/Bourn
	G-BCUF	Cessna F.172M	G. H. Kirke Ltd
	G-BCUH	Cessna F.150M	Heathgrange Ltd/Elstree
	G-BCUI	Cessna F.172M	Hillhouse Estates Ltd
	G-BCUJ	Cessna F.150M	T. Hayselden (Doncaster) Ltd
	G-BCUL	SOCATA Rallye 100ST	P. G. Hancock
	G-BCUW	Cessna F.177RG	Pageday Ltd/Cranfield
	G-BCUY	Cessna FRA.150M	S. R. Cameron
	G-BCVA	Cameron O-65 balloon	J. C. Bass & ptnrs Crepe Suzette
	G-BCVB	PA-17 Vagabond	A. T. Nowak/Popham
	G-BCVC	SOCATA Rallye 100ST	Brettshire Ltd/Southend
	G-BCVE	Evans VP-2	D. Masterson & D. B. Winstanley
	G-BCVF	Practavia Pilot Sprite	C. S. Carleton-Smith & H. C. U. Vonwiller
	G-BCVG	Cessna FRA.150L	Airwork Ltd/Perth
	G-BCVH	Cessna FRA.150L	D. A. Cockroft
	G-BCVI	Cessna FR.172J	R. M. Savage

Reg.	Type	Owner or Operator	Notes
G-BCVJ	Cessna F.172M	D. S. Newland & J. Rothwell/Blackpool	
G-BCVW	GY-80 Horizgn 180	P. M. A. Parrett/Dunkeswell	
G-BCVX	Jodel DR.1050	G. Hopkins & J. R. Heaton	
G-BCVY	PA-34-200T Seneca	C.S.E. Aviation Ltd/Kidlington	
G-BCWA	BAC One-Eleven 518	Dan-Air Services Ltd (G-AXMK)/ Gatwick	
G-BCWB	Cessna 182P	British Car Auctions (Aviation) Ltd/ Blackbushe	
G-BCWF	S.A. Twin Pioneer 1	Flight One Ltd (G-APRS)/Shobdon	
G-BCWH	Practavia Pilot Sprite	R. Tasker/Blackpool	
G-BCWI	Bensen B.8M	C. J. Blundell	
G-BCWK	Alpavia Fournier RF-3	D. I. Nickolls & ptnrs	
G-BCWL	Westland Lysander III (V9281)	Wessex Aviation & Transport Ltd	
G-BCWM	AB-206B JetRanger 2	Dollar Air Services Ltd/Coventry	
G-BCWR	BN-2A-21 Islander	Pilatus BN Ltd/Bembridge	
G-BCXB	SOCATA Rallye 100ST	A. Smails	
G-BCXE	Robin DR.400/2+2	Headcorn Flying School Ltd	
G-BCXF	H.S.125 Srs 600B	Beecham International Aviation Ltd/ Heathrow	
G-BCXH	PA-28 Cherokee 140F	C. P. Marshall	
G-BCXJ	Piper J-3C-65 Cub (413048)	W. F. Stockdale/Compton Abbas	
G-BCXN	D.H.C.1 Chipmunk 22	J. D. Featherby/Norwich	
G-BCXO	MBB Bo 105D	Bond Helicopters Ltd/Bourn	
G-BCXR	BAC One-Eleven 517	Dan-Air Services Ltd (G-BCCV)/Gatwick	
G-BCXZ	Cameron O-56 balloon	Olives from Spain Ltd *Olives from Spain*	
G-BCYH	DAW Privateer Mk. 2	D. B. Limbert	
G-BCYI	Schleicher ASK-16	J. Fox & J. Harding/Lasham	
G-BCYJ	D.H.C.1 Chipmunk 22 (WG303)	R. A. L. Falconer	
G-BCYK	Avro CF.100 Mk 4 Canuck (18393) ★	Imperial War Museum/Duxford	
G-BCYM	D.H.C.1 Chipmunk 22	C. R. R. Eagleton/Headcorn	
G-BCYR	Cessna F.172M	J. Donne	
G-BCYZ	Westland-Bell 47G-3B1	Helicrops Ltd	
G-BCZH	D.H.C.1 Chipmunk 22	A. C. Byrne & D. Featherby/Norwich	
G-BCZI	Thunder Ax7-77 balloon	R. G. Griffin & ptnrs	
G-BCZM	Cessna F.172M	Wycombe Air Centre Ltd/Booker	
G-BCZN	Cessna F.150M	Mona Aviation Ltd	
G-BCZO	Cameron O-77 balloon	W. O. T. Holmes *Leo*	
G-BDAB	SA.102.5 Cavalier	A. H. Brown	
G-BDAC	Cameron O-77 balloon	D. Fowler & J. Goody *Chocolate Ripple*	
G-BDAD	Taylor JT.1 Monoplane	A. R. & P. J. Lockie	
G-BDAE	BAC One-Eleven 518	Dan-Air Services Ltd (G-AXMI)/Gatwick	
G-BDAG	Taylor JT.1 Monoplane	R. S. Basinger	
G-BDAH	Evans VP-1	J. F. M. Barlett & F. R. Donaldson/ Biggin Hill	
G-BDAI	Cessna FRA.150M	Scotia Safari Ltd/Prestwick	
G-BDAK	R. Commander 112A	M. F. Newman/Norwich	
G-BDAL	R. 500S Shrike Commander	Quantel Ltd	
G-BDAM	AT-16 Harvard IIB (FE992)	N. A. Lees & E. C. English	
G-BDAP	AJEP Tailwind	J. Whiting	
G-BDAR	Evans VP-1	S. C. Foggin & M. T. Dugmore	
G-BDAS	BAC One-Eleven 518	Dan-Air Services Ltd (G-AXMH)/ Gatwick	
G-BDAT	BAC One-Eleven 518	Dan-Air Services Ltd (G-AYOR)/ Gatwick	
G-BDAV	PA-23 Aztec 250	Air Ipswich	
G-BDAX	PA-E23 Aztec 250	Astra Management Ltd	
G-BDAY	Thunder Ax5-42A balloon	T. M. Donnelly *Meconium*	
G-BDBD	Wittman W.8 Tailwind	J. K. Davies	
G-BDBF	FRED Srs 2	R. G. Boyton	
G-BDBH	Bellanca 7GCBC Citabria	Inkpen Gliding Club Ltd/Thruxton	
G-BDBI	Cameron O-77 balloon	C. A. Butter & J. J. Cook	
G-BDBJ	Cessna 182P	H. C. Wilson	
G-BDBL	D.H.C.1 Chipmunk 22	B. E. Simpson	
G-BDBP	D.H.C.1 Chipmunk 22	Sherwood Flying Club Ltd/Tollerton	
G-BDBR	AB-206B JetRanger 2	Westwood Engineering Ltd	
G-BDBS	Short SD3-30	Short Bros PLC/Sydenham	
G-BDBU	Cessna F.150M	E. Shipley/Jersey	
G-BDBV	Jodel D.11A	J. P. de Hevingham	
G-BDBX	Evans VP-1	Montgomeryshire Ultra-Light Flying Club	
G-BDBZ	WS.55 Whirlwind Srs 2 ★	*Ground instruction airframe*/Kidlington	
G-BDCA	SOCATA Rallye 150ST	B. W. J. Pring & ptnrs/Dunkeswell	

Notes	Reg.	Type	Owner or Operator
	G-BDCB	D.H.C.1 Chipmunk 22	R. F. Tolhurst
	G-BDCC	D.H.C.1 Chipmunk 22 (WD321)	Coventry Gliding Club Ltd/ Husbands Bosworth
	G-BDCD	Piper J-3C-65 Cub (480133)	Suzanne C. Brooks/Slinfold
	G-BDCE	Cessna F.172H	Lord Valentine William Cecil
	G-BDCI	CP.301A Emeraude	D. L. Sentance
	G-BDCK	AA-5 Traveler	Low & Duff (Developments) Ltd
	G-BDCM	Cessna F.177RG	P. R. Gunnel
	G-BDCO	B.121 Pup 1	Dr R. D. H. & Mrs K. N. Maxwell/Leeds
	G-BDCS	Cessna 421B	Mainland Car Delivery Services Ltd
	G-BDCT	PA-25 Pawnee 235C	Apple Aviation Ltd/Sibson
	G-BDCU	Cameron O-77 balloon	H. P. Carlton
	G-BDDD	D.H.C.1 Chipmunk 22	RAE Aero Club Ltd/Farnborough
	G-BDDF	Jodel D.120	Sywell Skyriders Flying Group
	G-BDDG	Jodel D.112	R. E. Snow
	G-BDDJ	Luton LA-4A Minor	D. D. Johnson
	G-BDDS	PA-25 Pawnee 235	T. J. Price
	G-BDDX	Whittaker MW.2B Excalibur ★	Cornwall Aero Park/Helston
	G-BDDZ	CP.301A Emeraude	D. L. Sentence
	G-BDEA	Boeing 707-338C	Anglo Cargo Airlines Ltd/Gatwick
	G-BDEB	SOCATA Rallye 100ST	W. G. Dunn & ptnrs/Exeter
	G-BDEC	SOCATA Rallye 100ST	Cambridge Chemical Co Ltd
	G-BDEF	PA-34-200T-2 Seneca	European Paper Sales Ltd/Biggin Hill
	G-BDEH	Jodel D.120A	D. W. Parkinson & ptnrs/Barton
	G-BDEI	Jodel D.9 Bebe	A. S. Walton
	G-BDEJ	R. Commander 112	R. W. Fairless/Goodwood
	G-BDEN	SIAI-Marchetti SF.260	Quantel Ltd/Biggin Hill
	G-BDES	Sikorsky S-61N Mk II	British International Helicopters Ltd/ Aberdeen
	G-BDEU	D.H.C.1 Chipmunk 22 (WP808)	A. Taylor
	G-BDEV	Taylor JT.1 Monoplane	D. A. Bass
	G-BDEW	Cessna FRA.150M	Compton Abbas Airfield Ltd
	G-BDEX	Cessna FRA.150M	Compton Abbas Airfield Ltd
	G-BDEY	Piper J-3C-65 Cub	Ducksworth Flying Club
	G-BDEZ	Piper J-3C-65 Cub	D. V. Wallis
	G-BDFB	Currie Wot	D. F. Faulkner-Bryant/Shoreham
	G-BDFC	R. Commander 112A	Lemrest Ltd/Denham
	G-BDFG	Cameron O-65 balloon	N. A. Robertson *Golly II*
	G-BDFH	Auster AOP.9 (XR240)	R. O. Holden/Booker
	G-BDFI	Cessna F.150M	Coventry Civil Aviation Ltd
	G-BDFJ	Cessna F.150M	T. J. Lynn/Sibson
	G-BDFM	Caudron C.270 Luciole	G. V. Gower
	G-BDFO	Hiller UH-12E	Peter Scott Agriculture Aviation Ltd
	G-BDFR	Fuji FA.200-160	C.S.E. Aviation Ltd/Kidlington
	G-BDFS	Fuji FA.200-160	R. W. Struth & A. H. Biggas
	G-BDFU	Dragonfly MPA Mk 1 ★	Museum of Flight/E. Fortune
	G-BDFW	R. Commander 112A	DTR Audio Visual Ltd/Blackbushe
	G-BDFX	Auster 5	K. E. Ballington
	G-BDFY	AA-5 Traveler	Edinburgh Flying Club Ltd
	G-BDFZ	Cessna F.150M	Skyviews & General Ltd
	G-BDGA	Bushby-Long Midget Mustang	J. R. Owen
	G-BDGB	GY-20 Minicab	D. G. Burden
	G-BDGH	Thunder Ax7-77 balloon	The London Balloon Club Ltd *London Pride III*
	G-BDGK	Beechcraft D.17S	P. M. J. Wolf/Biggin Hill
	G-BDGM	PA-28-151 Warrior	A. J. Breakspear & ptnrs
	G-BDGN	AA-5B Tiger	C. Zantow
	G-BDGO	Thunder Ax7-77 balloon	International Distillers & Vintners Ltd *J. & B. Rare*
	G-BDGP	Cameron V-65 balloon	Warwick Balloons Ltd
	G-BDGY	PA-28 Cherokee 140	R. E. Woolridge/Staverton
	G-BDHB	Isaacs Fury II	D. H. Berry
	G-BDHJ	Pazmany PL.1	C. T. Millner
	G-BDHK	Piper J-3C-65 Cub (329417)	A. Liddiard
	G-BDHL	PA-E23 Aztec 250E	Cheshire Flying Services Ltd/ Manchester
	G-BDHM	SA.102.5 Cavalier	D. H. Mitchell
	G-BDIC	D.H.C.1 Chipmunk 22	T. Bibby & D. Halliwell/Blackpool
	G-BDIE	R. Commander 112A	T. D. Saveker/Birmingham
	G-BDIG	Cessna 182P	D. P. Cranston & Bob Crowe Aircraft Sales Ltd/Cranfield
	G-BDIH	Jodel D.117	J. Chisholm/Booker
	G-BDII	Sikorsky S-61N	Bristow Helicopters Ltd
	G-BDIJ	Sikorsky S-61N	Bristow Helicopters Ltd

Reg.	Type	Owner or Operator	Notes
G-BDIM	D.H.C.1 Chipmunk 22	Protechnic Computers Ltd/Cambridge	
G-BDIW	D.H.106 Comet 4C ★	Air Classik/Dusseldorf	
G-BDIX	D.H.106 Comet 4C ★	Museum of Flight/E. Fortune	
G-BDIY	Luton LA-4A Minor	M. A. Musselwhite	
G-BDJB	Taylor JT.1 Monoplane	J. F. Barber	
G-BDJC	AJEP W.8 Tailwind	M. Risdale & S. J. Pugh	
G-BDJD	Jodel D.112	C. Davidson	
G-BDJF	Bensen B.8MV	R. P. White	
G-BDJN	Robin HR.200/100	Northampton School of Flying Co Ltd/ Sywell	
G-BDJP	Piper J-3C-65 Cub	Mrs J. M. Pothecary/Slinfold	
G-BDJR	Nord NC.858	R. F. M. Marson & ptnrs	
G-BDKC	Cessna A185F	Bridge of Tilt Co Ltd	
G-BDKD	Enstrom F-28A	D. Philp/Goodwood	
G-BDKH	CP.301A Emeraude	R. F. Bridge/Goodwood	
G-BDKJ	SA.102.5 Cavalier	H. B. Yardley	
G-BDKK	Bede BD-5B	A. W. Odell (stored)/Headcorn	
G-BDKM	SIPA 903	S. W. Markham	
G-BDKU	Taylor JT.1 Monoplane	A. C. Dove	
G-BDKV	PA-28R-200-2 Cherokee Arrow	H. Wilson/Bristol	
G-BDKW	R. Commander 112A	Denny Bros Printing Ltd	
G-BDLO	AA-5A Cheetah	S. & J. Dolan/Denham	
G-BDLR	AA-5B Tiger	McAlpine Aviation Ltd/Luton	
G-BDLS	AA-1B Trainer	M. Brown/Andrewsfield	
G-BDLT	R. Commander 112A	Wintergrain Ltd/Exeter	
G-BDLY	SA.102.5 Cavalier	J. A. Espin/Popham	
G-BDMB	Robin HR.100/210	R. J. Hitchman & Son	
G-BDMM	Jodel D.11	D. M. Metcalf	
G-BDMS	Piper J-3C-65 Cub	A. T. H. Martin & K. G. Harris	
G-BDMW	Jodel DR.100	J. T. Nixon/Blackpool	
G-BDNC	Taylor JT.1 Monoplane	C. W. Udale/Leicester	
G-BDNF	Bensen B.8M	W. F. O'Brien	
G-BDNG	Taylor JT.1 Monoplane	D. J. Phillips/Lasham	
G-BDNO	Taylor JT.1 Monoplane	W. R. Partridge	
G-BDNP	BN-2A Islander ★	Ground parachute trainer/Headcorn	
G-BDNR	Cessna FRA.150M	Cheshire Air Training School Ltd/ Liverpool	
G-BDNT	Jodel D.92	D. J. Park	
G-BDNU	Cessna F.172M	Vectaphone Manufacturing Ltd/ Sandown	
G-BDNW	AA-1B Trainer	Partlease Ltd	
G-BDNX	AA-1B Trainer	R. M. North/Manchester	
G-BDNY	AA-1B Trainer	M. R. Langford/Doncaster	
G-BDOC	Sikorsky S-61N Mk II	Bristow Helicopters Ltd	
G-BDOD	Cessna F.150M	Latharp Ltd/Booker	
G-BDOE	Cessna FR.172J	Rocket Partnership	
G-BDOF	Cameron O-56 balloon	New Holker Estates Co Fred Cavendish	
G-BDOG	SA Bullfinch Srs 2100	I. Drake/Netherthorpe	
G-BDOH	Hiller UH-12E (Soloy)	Heliwork Ltd/Thruxton	
G-BDOI	Hiller UH-12E	T. J. Clark	
G-BDOL	Piper J-3C-65 Cub	U. E. Allman & M. C. Jordan/Shoreham	
G-BDON	Thunder Ax7-77A balloon	J. R. Henderson & ptnrs	
G-BDOR	Thunder Ax6-56A balloon	M. S. Drinkwater & G. Fitzpatrick	
G-BDOS	BN-2A Mk III-2 Trislander	Kondair/Stansted	
G-BDOW	Cessna FRA.150M	P. P. D. Howard-Johnston/Edinburgh	
G-BDOY	Hughes 369HS	B. Wronski	
G-BDPA	PA-28-151 Warrior	Noon (Aircraft Leasing) Ltd/ Shoreham	
G-BDPB	Falconar F-II-3	N. M. Hitchman	
G-BDPC	Bede BD-5A	P. R. Cremer	
G-BDPF	Cessna F.172M	Huntara Ltd/Andrewsfield	
G-BDPK	Cameron O-56 balloon	R. L. Rumery	
G-BDPL	Falconar F-II	P. J. Shone	
G-BDPV	Boeing 747-136	British Airways City of Aberdeen/ Heathrow	
G-BDRB	AA-5B Tiger	D. Sharp	
G-BDRC	V.724 Viscount ★	Fire School/Manston	
G-BDRD	Cessna FRA.150M	Airwork Ltd/Perth	
G-BDRE	AA-1B Trainer	C. James/Elstree	
G-BDRF	Taylor JT.1 Monoplane	D. G. Hannam	
G-BDRG	Taylor JT.2 Titch	D. R. Gray	
G-BDRI	PA-34-200T-2 Seneca	Video Vision Air/Stapleford	
G-BDRJ	D.H.C.1 Chipmunk 22 (WP857)	J. C. Schooling	
G-BDRK	Cameron O-65 balloon	D. L. Smith Smirk	

Notes	Reg.	Type	Owner or Operator
	G-BDRL	Stitts SA-3 Playboy	D. L. MacLean
	G-BDSB	PA-28-181 Archer II	Santacane Ltd/Fairoaks
	G-BDSD	Evans VP-1	J. E. Worthington
	G-BDSE	Cameron O-77 balloon	British Airways Concorde
	G-BDSF	Cameron O-56 balloon	A. R. Greensides & B. H. Osbourne
	G-BDSH	PA-28 Cherokee 140	Bamberhurst Ltd/Tollerton
	G-BDSK	Cameron O-65 balloon	Southern Balloon Group Carousel II
	G-BDSL	Cessna F.150M	Cleveland Flying School Ltd/Tees-side
	G-BDSM	Slingsby/Kirby Cadet Mk 3	D. W. Savage
	G-BDSN	Wassmer WA.52 Europa	E. A. L. Glover & ptnrs (G-BADN)
	G-BDSO	Cameron O-31 balloon	Budget Rent-a-Car Baby Budget
	G-BDSP	Cessna U.206F Stationair	J. E. Leakey/Biggin Hill
	G-BDTB	Evans VP-1	A. Toomer
	G-BDTL	Evans VP-1	A. K. Lang
	G-BDTN	BN-2A Mk III-2 Trislander	Aurigny Air Services Ltd/Guernsey
	G-BDTU	Omega III gas balloon	Mrs K. E. Turnbull Omega II
	G-BDTV	Mooney M.20F	J. P. McDermott & ptnrs/Biggin Hill
	G-BDTW	Cassutt Racer	B. E. Smith & C. S. Thompson/Redhill
	G-BDTX	Cessna F.150M	A. A. & R. N. Croxford/Southend
	G-BDUI	Cameron V-56 balloon	D. C. Johnson
	G-BDUJ	PA-31-310 Navajo	Frantham Property Ltd
	G-BDUL	Evans VP-1	D. Beevers & ptnrs
	G-BDUM	Cessna F.150M	SFG Ltd/Shipdham
	G-BDUN	PA-34-200T-2 Seneca	Air Medical Ltd
	G-BDUO	Cessna F.150M	Sandown Aero Club
	G-BDUX	Slingsby T.31B motor glider	J. C. Anderson/Southend
	G-BDUY	Robin DR.400/140B	Waveney Flying Group/Seething
	G-BDUZ	Cameron V-56 balloon	Balloon Stable Ltd Hot Lips
	G-BDVA	PA-17 Vagabond	I. M. Callier
	G-BDVB	PA-15 (PA-17) Vagabond	B. P. Gardner
	G-BDVC	PA-17 Vagabond	A. R. Caveen
	G-BDVG	Thunder Ax6-56A balloon	R. F. Pollard Argonaut
	G-BDVS	F.27 Friendship 200	Loganair Ltd/Glasgow
	G-BDVU	Mooney M.20F	Uplands Video Ltd/Stapleford
	G-BDVW	BN-2A Islander	Loganair Ltd/Glasgow
	G-BDWA	SOCATA Rallye 150ST	H. Cowan/Newtownards
	G-BDWB	SOCATA Rallye 150ST	P. H. Johnson
	G-BDWE	Flaglor Scooter	D. W. Evernden
	G-BDWG	BN-2A Islander	Wilsons Transport Ltd
	G-BDWH	SOCATA Rallye 150ST	J. Scott/Kirkwall
	G-BDWJ	SE-5A replica (F8010)	S. M. Smith/Booker
	G-BDWK	Beech 95-B58 Baron	David Huggett Motor Factors Ltd
	G-BDWL	PA-25 Pawnee 235	J. E. F. Aviation
	G-BDWM	Mustang replica	D. C. Bonsall
	G-BDWO	Howes Ax6 balloon	R. B. & Mrs C. Howes Griffin
	G-BDWP	PA-32R-300 Cherokee Lance	Trendgreen Ltd
	G-BDWV	BN-2A Mk III-2 Trislander	Aurigny Air Services Ltd/Guernsey
	G-BDWX	Jodel D.120A	J. P. Lassey
	G-BDWY	PA-28 Cherokee 140	Cleveland Flying School/Teeside
	G-BDXA	Boeing 747-236B	British Airways City of Cardiff/Heathrow
	G-BDXB	Boeing 747-236B	British Airways City of Liverpool/Heathrow
	G-BDXC	Boeing 747-236B	British Airways City of Manchester/Heathrow
	G-BDXD	Boeing 747-236B	British Airways City of Plymouth/Heathrow
	G-BDXE	Boeing 747-236B	British Airways City of Glasgow/Heathrow
	G-BDXF	Boeing 747-236B	British Airways City of York/Heathrow
	G-BDXG	Boeing 747-236B	British Airways City of Oxford/Heathrow
	G-BDXH	Boeing 747-236B	British Airways City of Edinburgh/Heathrow
	G-BDXI	Boeing 747-236B	British Airways City of Cambridge/Heathrow
	G-BDXJ	Boeing 747-236B	British Airways City of Birmingham/Heathrow
	G-BDXK	Boeing 747-236B	British Airways City of Canterbury/Heathrow
	G-BDXL	Boeing 747-236B	British Airways City of Winchester/Heathrow
	G-BDXM	Boeing 747-236B	British Airways City of Derby/Heathrow
	G-BDXN	Boeing 747-236B	British Airways City of Stoke on Trent/Heathrow

Reg.	Type	Owner or Operator	Notes
G-BDXO	Boeing 747-236B	British Airways *City of Bath*/Heathrow	
G-BDXP	Boeing 747-236B (SCD)	British Airways	
G-BDXW	PA-28R-200 Cherokee Arrow	Directflight Ltd	
G-BDXX	Nord NC.858S	S. F. Elvins	
G-BDXY	Auster AOP.9 (XR269)	B. A. Webster	
G-BDYC	AA-1B Trainer	N. F. Whisler	
G-BDYD	R. Commander 114	SRS Aviation	
G-BDYF	Cessna 421C	Nullifire Ltd/Coventry	
G-BDYG	P.56 Provost T.1 (WV493)	Museum of Flight/E. Fortune	
G-BDYH	Cameron V-56 balloon	B. J. Godding	
G-BDYL	Beech C23 Sundowner	P. Tweedy	
G-BDYM	Skysales S-31 balloon	Miss A. I. Smith & M. J. Moore *Cheeky Devil*	
G-BDYZ	MBB Bo 105D	Bond Helicopters Ltd/Bourn	
G-BDZA	Scheibe SF.25E Super Falke	Norfolk Gliding Club Ltd/Tibenham	
G-BDZB	Cameron S-31 balloon	Kenning Motor Group Ltd *Kenning*	
G-BDZC	Cessna F.150M	Air Tows Ltd/Blackbushe	
G-BDZD	Cessna F.172M	M. T. Hodges/Blackbushe	
G-BDZF	G.164 Ag-Cat B	Miller Aerial Spraying Ltd/Wickenby	
G-BDZS	Scheibe SF.25E Super Falke	A. D. Gubbay/Panshanger	
G-BDZU	Cessna 421C	Page & Moy Ltd & ptnrs/Leicester	
G-BDZW	PA-28 Cherokee 140	Oldbus Ltd/Shoreham	
G-BDZX	PA-28-151 Warrior	E. Shipley	
G-BDZY	Phoenix LA-4A Minor	P. J. Dalby	
G-BEAA	Taylor JT.1 Monoplane	R. C. Hobbs/Bembridge	
G-BEAB	Jodel DR.1051	C. Fitton	
G-BEAC	PA-28 Cherokee 140	Eileen R. Purfield/Biggin Hill	
G-BEAD	WG.13 Lynx ★	*Instructional airframe*/Middle Wallop	
G-BEAG	PA-34-200T-2 Seneca	C.S.E. Aviation Ltd/Kidlington	
G-BEAH	J/2 Arrow	W. J. & Mrs M. D. Horler	
G-BEAK	L-1011-385 TriStar	British Airtours *Carmarthen Bay*/Gatwick	
G-BEAL	L-1011-385 TriStar	British Airtours Ltd *Cardigan Bay*/Gatwick	
G-BEAM	L-1011-385 TriStar	British Airtours Ltd *Swansea Bay*/Gatwick	
G-BEAR	Viscount V.5 balloon	B. Hargreaves & B. King	
G-BEAU	Pazmany PL.4A	B. H. R. Smith	
G-BEBC	WS.55 Whirlwind 3 (XP355) ★	Norwich Aviation Museum	
G-BEBE	AA-5A Cheetah	BLS Aviation Ltd/Elstree	
G-BEBF	Auster AOP.9	M. D. N. & Mrs A. C. Fisher	
G-BEBG	WSK-PZL SDZ-45A Ogar	The Ogar Syndicate	
G-BEBI	Cessna F.172M	Calder Equipment Ltd/Hatfield	
G-BEBL	Douglas DC-10-30	BCal/British Airways *Sir Alexander Flemming-The Scottish Challenger*/Gatwick	
G-BEBM	Douglas DC-10-30	BCal/British Airways *Robert Burns-The Scottish Bard*/Gatwick	
G-BEBN	Cessna 177B	M. A. Berriman	
G-BEBO	Turner TSW-2 Wot	The Turner Special Flying Group	
G-BEBR	GY-201 Minicab	A. S. Jones & D. R. Upston	
G-BEBS	Andreasson BA-4B	J. H. Boulton	
G-BEBU	R. Commander 112A	M. Rowland & J. K. Woodford	
G-BEBZ	PA-28-151 Warrior	Goodwood Terrena Ltd/Goodwood	
G-BECA	SOCATA Rallye 100ST	J. C. Greenslade	
G-BECB	SOCATA Rallye 100ST	A. J. Trible	
G-BECC	SOCATA Rallye 150ST	Lapwing Flying Group Ltd/Denham	
G-BECD	SOCATA Rallye 150ST	A. J. Liddle	
G-BECF	Scheibe SF.25A Falke	D. A. Wilson & ptnrs	
G-BECG	Boeing 737-204ADV	Britannia Airways Ltd *Amy Johnson*/Luton	
G-BECH	Boeing 737-204ADV	Britannia Airways Ltd *Viscount Montgomery of Alamein*/Luton	
G-BECJ	Partenavia P.68B	Hereford Parachute Club Ltd/Shobdon	
G-BECK	Cameron V-56 balloon	K. H. Greenaway	
G-BECL	C.A.S.A. C.352L (N9+AA)	Junkers Ju.52/3m Flight Ltd	
G-BECN	Piper J-3C-65 Cub (480480)	Harvest Air Ltd/Ipswich	
G-BECO	Beech A.36 Bonanza	Thorney Machinery Co Ltd	
G-BECT	C.A.S.A.1.131 Jungmann	Rendermere Ltd/Shoreham	
G-BECW	C.A.S.A.1.131 Jungmann	N. C. Jensen/Redhill	
G-BECZ	CAARP CAP.10B	Aerobatic Associates Ltd	
G-BEDA	C.A.S.A.1.131 Jungmann	M. G. Kates & D. J. Berry	

Notes	Reg.	Type	Owner or Operator
	G-BEDB	Nord 1203 Norecrin	B. F. G. Lister
	G-BEDD	Jodel D.117A	A. T. Croy/Kirkwall
	G-BEDE	Bede BD-5A	Biggin Hill BD5 Syndicate
	G-BEDF	Boeing B-17G-105-VE (485784)	B-17 Preservation Ltd/Duxford
	G-BEDG	R. Commander 112A	L. E. Blackburn
	G-BEDJ	Piper J-3C-65 Cub (44-80594)	D. J. Elliott
	G-BEDK	Hiller UH-12E	T. C. Jay
	G-BEDL	Cessna T.337D	Wilford Aviation Ltd
	G-BEDV	V.668 Varsity T.1 (WJ945) ★	D. S. Selway/Duxford
	G-BEDZ	BN-2A Islander	Loganair Ltd/Glasgow
	G-BEEE	Thunder Ax6-56A balloon	I. R. M. Jacobs Avia
	G-BEEG	BN-2A Islander	Loganair Ltd/Glasgow
	G-BEEH	Cameron V-56 balloon	B. & N. V. Moreton
	G-BEEI	Cameron N-77 balloon	Hedgehoppers Balloon Group
	G-BEEJ	Cameron O-77 balloon	DAL (Builders Merchants) Ltd Dal's Pal
	G-BEEL	Enstrom F-280C-UK-2 Shark	K. E. Wills
	G-BEEN	Cameron O-56 balloon	Swire Bottlers Ltd Coke/Hong Kong
	G-BEEO	Short SD3-30	British Air Ferries Ltd/Southend
	G-BEEP	Thunder Ax5-42 balloon	Mrs B. C. Faithful/Holland
	G-BEER	Isaacs Fury II	J. C. Lister
	G-BEEU	PA-28 Cherokee 140E	Berkshire Aviation Services Ltd
	G-BEEV	PA-28 Cherokee 140E	V. M. Lambeth/Dunkeswell
	G-BEEW	Taylor JT.1 Monoplane	K. Wigglesworth/Breighton
	G-BEFA	PA-28-151 Warrior	Firmbeam Ltd/Booker
	G-BEFC	AA-5B Tiger	A. G. McLeod/Shobdon
	G-BEFF	PA-28 Cherokee 140	Sherwood Flying Club Ltd/Tollerton
	G-BEFH	Nord 3202	William Tomkins Ltd/Sibson
	G-BEFP	BN-2A Mk III-2 Trislander	Kondair/Stansted
	G-BEFR	Fokker DR.1 Replica (1425/17)	R. A. Bowes & P. A. Crawford
	G-BEFT	Cessna 421C	Specialist Flying Training Ltd/Carlisle
	G-BEFV	Evans VP-2	Yeadon Aeroplane Group/Leeds
	G-BEFY	Hiller UH-12E	Wells (PF) Ltd
	G-BEGA	Westland Bell 47G-3Bl	Durlime Ltd/Glasgow
	G-BEGG	Scheibe SF.25E Super Falke	R. Culley & ptnrs
	G-BEGV	PA-23 Aztec 250F	Carentals Ltd/Birmingham
	G-BEHG	AB-206B JetRanger 2	Compass Helicopters/Bristol
	G-BEHH	PA-32R-300 Cherokee Lance	SMK Engineering Ltd/Leeds
	G-BEHJ	Evans VP-1	K. Heath
	G-BEHK	Agusta-Bell 47G-3B1 (Soloy)	Dollar Air Services Ltd/Coventry
	G-BEHM	Taylor JT.1 Monoplane	H. McGovern
	G-BEHN	Westland Bell 47G-3B1 (Soloy)	Dollar Air Services Ltd/Coventry
	G-BEHS	PA-25 Pawnee 260C	Farm Aviation Services Ltd/Enstone
	G-BEHU	PA-34-200T-2 Seneca	Appleby Glade Ltd
	G-BEHV	Cessna F.172N	P. P. D. Howard-Johnston/Edinburgh
	G-BEHW	Cessna F.150M	Light Planes (Lancashire) Ltd/Barton
	G-BEHX	Evans VP-2	G. S Adams
	G-BEHY	PA-28-181 Archer II	C. A. Frost/Sharjah
	G-BEIA	Cessna FRA.150M	Airwork Ltd/Perth
	G-BEIB	Cessna F.172N	R. L. Orsborn & Son Ltd/Sywell
	G-BEIC	Sikorsky S-61N	British International Helicopters Ltd/ Aberdeen
	G-BEID	Sikorsky S-61N	British International Helicopters Ltd/ Aberdeen
	G-BEIE	Evans VP-2	F. G. Morris
	G-BEIF	Cameron O-65 balloon	C. Vening
	G-BEIH	PA-25 Pawnee 235D	MPW Aviation Ltd
	G-BEII	PA-25 Pawnee 235D	Burn Gliding Club Ltd
	G-BEIK	Beech A.36 Bonanza	Hawk Aviation Ltd/Aberdeen
	G-BEIL	SOCATA Rallye 150T	The Rallye Flying Group
	G-BEIP	PA-28-181 Archer II	M. Ferguson Ltd/Newtownards
	G-BEIS	Evans VP-1	G. G. Bigwood
	G-BEIZ	Cessna 500 Citation	Solid State Logic Ltd
	G-BEJA	Thunder Ax6-56A balloon	P. A. Hutchins Jackson
	G-BEJB	Thunder Ax6-56A balloon	International Distillers & Vinters Ltd
	G-BEJD	H.S.748 Srs 1	Dan-Air Services Ltd/Gatwick
	G-BEJE	H.S.748 Srs 1	Dan-Air Services Ltd/Gatwick
	G-BEJK	Cameron S-31 balloon	Esso Petroleum Ltd
	G-BEJL	Sikorsky S-61N	British International Helicopters Ltd/ Aberdeen
	G-BEJM	BAC One-Eleven 423	Ford Motor Co Ltd/Stansted
	G-BEJP	D.H.C.6 Twin Otter 310	Loganair Ltd/Glasgow
	G-BEJV	PA-34-200T-2 Seneca	C.S.E. Aviation Ltd/Kidlington

Reg.	Type	Owner or Operator	Notes
G-BEJW	BAC One-Eleven 423	Ford Motor Co Ltd/Stansted	
G-BEKA	BAC One-Eleven 520	Dan-Air Services Ltd/Gatwick	
G-BEKC	H.S.748 Srs 1	Dan-Air Services Ltd/Gatwick	
G-BEKE	H.S.748 Srs 1	Dan-Air Services Ltd/Gatwick	
G-BEKG	H.S.748 Srs 1	Euroair Transport/Brymon Airways (G-VAJK)	
G-BEKL	Bede BD-4E	G. A. Hodges	
G-BEKM	Evans VP-1	G. J. McDill	
G-BEKN	Cessna FRA.150M	RFC (Bourn) Ltd	
G-BEKO	Cessna F.182Q	Tyler International	
G-BEKR	Rand KR-2	A. N. Purchase	
G-BELF	BN-2A Islander	Atlantic Air Transport Ltd/Coventry	
G-BELP	PA-28-151 Warrior	Coventry Civil Aviation Ltd	
G-BELR	PA-28 Cherokee 140	H. M. Clarke	
G-BELT	Cessna F.150J	Yorkshire Light Aircraft Ltd (G-AWUV)/Leeds	
G-BELX	Cameron V-56 balloon	R. J. O. Evans	
G-BEMB	Cessna F.172M	P. B. Hollands Associates Ltd	
G-BEMD	Beech 95-B55 Baron	Vaux (Aviation) Ltd/Newcastle	
G-BEMF	Taylor JT.1 Monoplane	P. J. Pratt	
G-BEMM	Slingsby T.31B Motor Cadet	M. N. Martin	
G-BEMR	BN-2A-26 Islander	Pilatus BN Ltd/Bembridge	
G-BEMU	Thunder Ax5-42 balloon	P. W. Limpus & ptnrs	
G-BEMW	PA-28-181 Archer II	Charta Furniture Ltd/Goodwood	
G-BEMY	Cessna FRA.150M	L. G. Sawyer/Blackbushe	
G-BEND	Cameron V-56 balloon	Dante Balloon Group Le Billet	
G-BENE	Cessna 402B	East-West Air Trading Ltd	
G-BENJ	R. Commander 112B	F. T. Arnold	
G-BENK	Cessna F.172M	Capeston Aviation Ltd	
G-BENN	Cameron V-56 balloon	S. H. Budd	
G-BENO	Enstrom F-280C Shark	Red Baron Property Ltd/Shoreham	
G-BENS	Saffrey S.330 balloon	D. Whitlock Hot Plastic	
G-BENT	Cameron N-77 balloon	N. Tasker	
G-BEOD	Cessna 180	Flying Tigers Ltd/Goodwood	
G-BEOE	Cessna FRA.150M	J. R. Nicholls/Sibson	
G-BEOH	PA-28R-201T Turbo Arrow III	Pratt Bedford Ltd/Bristol	
G-BEOI	PA-18 Super Cub 150	Southdown Gliding Club Ltd	
G-BEOK	Cessna F.150M	Gordon King (Aviation) Ltd/Biggin Hill	
G-BEOO	Sikorsky S-61N Mk. II	British International Helicopters Ltd	
G-BEOT	PA-25 Pawnee 235D	Moonraker Aviation Ltd/Thruxton	
G-BEOX	L-414 Hudson IV (A16-199) ★	RAF Museum/Hendon	
G-BEOY	Cessna FRA.150M	SM Reprographics Ltd/Elstree	
G-BEOZ	A.W.650 Argosy 101 ★	Elan International/E. Midlands	
G-BEPB	Pereira Osprey II	J. J. & A. J. C. Zwetsloot	
G-BEPC	SNCAN SV-4C	M. Harbron/Bodmin	
G-BEPD	SA.102.5 Cavalier	P. & Mrs E. A. Donaldson	
G-BEPE	SC.5 Belfast	HeavyLift Cargo Airlines Ltd (G-ASKE)/Southend	
G-BEPF	SNCAN SV-4A	L. J. Rice	
G-BEPH	BN-2A Mk III-2 Trislander	Aurigny Air Services Ltd/Guernsey	
G-BEPI	BN-2A Mk III-2 Trislander	Aurigny Air Services Ltd/Guernsey	
G-BEPO	Cameron N-77 balloon	G. Camplin & V. Aitken	
G-BEPS	SC.5 Belfast	HeavyLift Cargo Airlines Ltd/Stansted	
G-BEPV	Fokker S.11-I Instructor	Strathallan Aircraft Collection	
G-BEPY	R. Commander 112B	W. M. Ewington & Co Ltd	
G-BEPZ	Cameron D-96 hot-air airship	IAZ International (UK) Ltd	
G-BERA	SOCATA Rallye 150ST	Surrey & Kent Flying Club (1982) Ltd/Biggin Hill	
G-BERC	SOCATA Rallye 150ST	Severn Valley Aero Group	
G-BERD	Thunder Ax6-56A balloon	M. J. Betts	
G-BERF	Bell 212	Bristow Helicopters Ltd	
G-BERI	R. Commander 114	K. B. Harper/Blackbushe	
G-BERN	Saffrey S-330 balloon	B. Martin Beeze	
G-BERT	Cameron V-56 balloon	Southern Balloon Group Bert	
G-BERW	R. Commander 114	C. D. Allison	
G-BERY	AA-1B Trainer	R. H. J. Levi	
G-BESO	BN-2A Islander	Cranfield Aeronautical Services Ltd	
G-BESS	Hughes 369D	Flourishbest Ltd/Booker	
G-BETD	Robin HR.200/100	R. A. Parsons/Bourn	
G-BETE	Rollason B.2A Beta	T. M. Jones/Tollerton	
G-BETF	Cameron 'Champion' balloon	Balloon Stable Ltd Champion	
G-BETG	Cessna 180K Skywagon	T. P. A. Norman/Panshanger	
G-BETH	Thunder Ax6-56A balloon	Debenhams Ltd Debenhams I	
G-BETI	Pitts S-1D Special	P. Metcalfe/Tees-side	

Notes	Reg.	Type	Owner or Operator
	G-BETL	PA-25 Pawnee 235D	Crop Aviation (UK) Ltd/Wyberton
	G-BETM	PA-25 Pawnee 235D	Crop Aviation (UK) Ltd/Wyberton
	G-BETO	M.S.885 Super Rallye	R. Andrews
	G-BETP	Cameron O-65 balloon	J. R. Rix & Sons Ltd
	G-BETS	Cessna A.188B Ag Truck	J. H. Farrar
	G-BETT	PA-34-200-2 Seneca	Andrews Professional Colour Laboratories Ltd/Headcorn
	G-BETV	HS.125 Srs 600B	Rolls-Royce PLC/Filton
	G-BETW	Rand KR-2	T. A. Wiffen
	G-BEUA	PA-18 Super Cub 150	London Gliding Club (Pty) Ltd/ Dunstable
	G-BEUC	PA-28-161 Warrior II	Bailey Aviation Ltd/Fairoaks
	G-BEUD	Robin HR.100/285R	E. A. & L. M. C. Payton/Cranfield
	G-BEUI	Piper J-3C-65 Cub	M. J. Whatley
	G-BEUK	Fuji FA.200-160	C.S.E Aviation Ltd/Kidlington
	G-BEUL	Beech 95-58 Baron	Basic Metal Co Ltd/Leavesden
	G-BEUM	Taylor JT.1 Monoplane	M. T. Taylor
	G-BEUN	Cassutt Racer IIIm	R. S. Voice/Redhill
	G-BEUP	Robin DR.400/180	A. V. Pound & Co Ltd
	G-BEUR	Cessna F.172M	B. V. Ruckstuhl
	G-BEUS	SNCAN SV-4C	J. C. Tempest
	G-BEUU	PA-19 Super Cub 95	F. Sharples/Sandown
	G-BEUV	Thunder Ax6-56A balloon	P. Buxton
	G-BEUX	Cessna F.172N	Light Planes (Lancashire) Ltd/Barton
	G-BEUY	Cameron N-31 balloon	Southern Balloon Group
	G-BEVA	SOCATA Rallye 150ST	The Rallye Group
	G-BEVB	SOCATA Rallye 150ST	T. R. Sinclair
	G-BEVC	SOCATA Rallye 150ST	B. W. Walpole
	G-BEVG	PA-34-200T-2 Seneca	Stratton Motor Co (Norfolk) Ltd & Martin J. Story Ltd
	G-BEVH	Holland D.700 balloon	D. I. Holland *Sally*
	G-BEVI	Thunder Ax7-77A balloon	The Painted Clouds Balloon Co Ltd
	G-BEVO	Sportavia-Pützer RF-5	T. Barlow
	G-BEVP	Evans VP-2	C. F. Bloyce
	G-BEVS	Taylor JT.1 Monoplane	D. Hunter
	G-BEVT	BN-2A Mk III-2 Trislander	Aurigny Air Services Ltd/Guernsey
	G-BEVW	SOCATA Rallye 150ST	P. C. Goodwin & M. G. Wiltshire
	G-BEWJ	Westland-Bell 47G-3B1	E. J. Mackelden
	G-BEWL	Sikorsky S-61N Mk II	British International Helicopters Ltd/ Aberdeen
	G-BEWM	Sikorsky S-61N Mk II	British International Helicopters Ltd
	G-BEWN	D.H.82A Tiger Moth	H. D. Labouchere
	G-BEWO	Zlin 326 Trener Master	R. C. Poolman & K. D. Ballinger/ Staverton
	G-BEWR	Cessna F.172N	Cheshire Air Training School Ltd/ Liverpool
	G-BEWX	PA-28R-201 Arrow III	A. Vickers
	G-BEWY	Bell 206B JetRanger 2	John Holborn (Farm Helicopters) Ltd
	G-BEXA	BN-2A Islander	Air Furness Ltd (G-MALI/G-DIVE)/ Walney Island
	G-BEXK	PA-25 Pawnee 235D	Howard Avis (Aviation) Ltd
	G-BEXN	AA-1C Lynx	Scotia Safari Ltd/Prestwick
	G-BEXO	PA-23 Apache 160	B. Burton/Bournemouth
	G-BEXR	Mudry/CAARP CAP-10B	R. P. Lewis/Booker
	G-BEXS	Cessna F.150M	S. J. Green
	G-BEXW	PA-28-181 Archer II	P. F. Larkins
	G-BEXX	Cameron V-56 balloon	A. Tyler & ptnrs *Rupert of Rutland*
	G-BEXY	PA-28 Cherokee 140	W. M. Coupar Ltd/Perth
	G-BEXZ	Cameron N-56 balloon	D. C. Eager & G. C. Clark
	G-BEYA	Enstrom F-280C Shark	Looporder Ltd
	G-BEYB	Fairey Flycatcher (replica) (S1287)	John S. Fairey/Yeovilton
	G-BEYD	HPR-7 Herald 401	*Stored*/Southend
	G-BEYF	HPR-7 Herald 401	Elan Air Ltd/E. Midlands
	G-BEYK	HPR-7 Herald 401	South East Air Ltd
	G-BEYL	PA-28 Cherokee 180	B. G. & G. Airlines Ltd/Jersey
	G-BEYN	Evans VP-2	C. D. Denham
	G-BEYO	PA-28 Cherokee 140	Solid State Logic Ltd/Kidlington
	G-BEYP	Fuji FA.200-180AO	A. C. Pritchard/Booker
	G-BEYV	Cessna T.210M	Valley Motors/Bournemouth
	G-BEYW	Taylor JT.1 Monoplane	R. A. Abrahams/Barton
	G-BEYY	PA-31-310 Turbo Navajo	Auxili-Air Aviation Ltd/Stansted
	G-BEYZ	Jodel DR.1051/M1	M. J. McCarthy & S. Aarons/ Biggin Hill

Reg.	Type	Owner or Operator	Notes
G-BEZA	Zlin 226T Trener	L. Bezak	
G-BEZB	HPR-7 Herald 209	Channel Express/Bournemouth	
G-BEZC	AA-5 Traveler	Ilford Business Machines Ltd	
G-BEZE	Rutan Vari-Eze	J. Berry	
G-BEZF	AA-5 Traveler	KAL Aviation/Denham	
G-BEZG	AA-5 Traveler	R. C. Mark	
G-BEZH	AA-5 Traveler	H. & L. Sims Ltd	
G-BEZI	AA-5 Traveler	D. Boyd/Cranfield	
G-BEZJ	MBB Bo 105D	Bond Helicopters Ltd/Bourn	
G-BEZK	Cessna F.172H	Zulu Kilo Flying Group	
G-BEZL	PA-31-310 Navajo	Shopfitters (Lancashire) Ltd	
G-BEZO	Cessna F.172M	Staverton Flying Services Ltd	
G-BEZP	PA-32-300D Cherokee Six	Falcon Styles Ltd/Booker	
G-BEZR	Cessna F.172M	Kirmington Aviation Ltd	
G-BEZS	Cessna FR.172J	R. E. Beeton & M. R. Cavinder	
G-BEZV	Cessna F.172M	Aberdeen Dairies Distribution Ltd	
G-BEZY	Rutan Vari-Eze	R. J. Jones	
G-BEZZ	Jodel D.112	A. J. Stevens & ptnrs/Barton	
G-BFAA	GY-80 Horizon 160	Mary Poppins Ltd	
G-BFAB	Cameron N-56 balloon	Phonogram Ltd *Phonogram* Southend	
G-BFAC	Cessna F.177RG	J. J. Baumhardt/Southend	
G-BFAF	Aeronca 7BCM (7797)	D. C. W. Harper/Finmere	
G-BFAH	Phoenix Currie Wot	J. F. Dowe	
G-BFAI	R. Commander 114	D. S. Innes/Guernsey	
G-BFAK	M.S.892A Rallye Commodore 150	R. Jennings & ptnrs/Alderney	
G-BFAM	PA-31P Navajo	Video Unlimited Motion Pictures	
G-BFAN	H.S.125 Srs 600F	British Aerospace (G-AZHS)/Hatfield	
G-BFAO	PA-20 Pacer 135	J. Day & ptnrs/Goodwood	
G-BFAP	SIAI-Marchetti S.205-20R	Miss M. A. Eccles	
G-BFAR	Cessna 500-1 Citation	Paramount Executive Ltd/Birmingham	
G-BFAS	Evans VP-1	A. I. Sutherland	
G-BFAV	Orion model free balloon	D. C. Boxall	
G-BFAW	D.H.C.1 Chipmunk 22	R. V. Bowles	
G-BFAX	D.H.C.1 Chipmunk 22 (WG422)	B. Earl	
G-BFBA	Jodel DR.100A	A. Brown & R. Wood	
G-BFBB	PA-23 Aztec 250E	J. Backhouse	
G-BFBC	Taylor JT.1 Monoplane	D. Oxenham	
G-BFBD	Partenavia P.68B	Calmsafe Ltd	
G-BFBE	Robin HR.200/100	Charles Major Ltd/Blackpool	
G-BFBF	PA-28 Cherokee 140	F. R. Montgomery/Newtownards	
G-BFBM	Saffery S.330 balloon	B. Martin *Beeze II*	
G-BFBR	PA-28-161 Warrior II	Lowery Holdings Ltd/Fairoaks	
G-BFBU	Partenavia P.68B	W. Holmes & Son Ltd	
G-BFBV	Brügger Colibri M.B.2	J. C. Lister	
G-BFBW	PA-25 Pawnee 235D	Miller Aerial Spraying Ltd/Wickenby	
G-BFBX	PA-25 Pawnee 235D	Bowker Aircraft Services Ltd/ Rush Green	
G-BFBY	Piper J-3C-65 Cub	L. W. Usherwood	
G-BFCT	Cessna TU.206F	Cecil Aviation Ltd/Cambridge	
G-BFCX	BN-2A Islander	Loganair Ltd/Glasgow	
G-BFCZ	Sopwith Camel (B7270) ★	FAA Museum/Yeovilton	
G-BFDA	PA-31-350 Navajo Chieftain	Leisure Line (UK) Ltd/Bristol	
G-BFDC	D.H.C.1 Chipmunk 22	N. F. O'Neill/Newtownards	
G-BFDE	Sopwith Tabloid (replica) (168) ★	Bomber Command Museum/Hendon	
G-BFDF	SOCATA Rallye 235E	J. H. Atkinson/Skegness	
G-BFDG	PA-28R-201T Turbo-Arrow III	Hydro Dynamics Products Ltd/ Shoreham	
G-BFDI	PA-28-181 Archer II	Reedtrend Ltd/Biggin Hill	
G-BFDL	Piper L-4J Cub (454537)	K. A. Davies & N. C. Burman	
G-BFDM	Jodel D.120	Worcestershire Gliding Ltd	
G-BFDN	PA-31-350 Navajo Chieftain	Topflight Aviation Ltd/Blackbushe	
G-BFDO	PA-28R-201T Turbo-Arrow III	Grangewood Press Ltd	
G-BFDZ	Taylor JT.1 Monoplane	D. C. Barber/Woodvale	
G-BFEB	Jodel D.150	D. Aldersea & ptnrs/Sherburn	
G-BFEC	PA-23 Aztec 250F	Techspan Aviation Ltd/Cambridge	
G-BFEE	Beech 95-E55 Baron	I. K. I. Stewart/Elstree	
G-BFEF	Agusta-Bell 47G-3B1	Dollar Air Services Ltd/Coventry	
G-BFEH	Jodel D.117A	C. V. & S. J. Philpott	
G-BFEI	Westland-Bell 47G-3B1	Trent Air Services Ltd/Cranfield	

71

Notes	Reg.	Type	Owner or Operator
	G-BFEK	Cessna F.152	Staverton Flying Services Ltd
	G-BFER	Bell 212	Bristow Helicopters Ltd
	G-BFEV	PA-25 Pawnee 235	Bowker Aircraft Services Ltd/ Rush Green
	G-BFEW	PA-25 Pawnee 235	Miller Aerial Spraying Ltd/Biggin Hill
	G-BFEX	PA-25 Pawnee 235	CKS Air Ltd/Southend
	G-BFEY	PA-25 Pawnee 235	Howard Avis Aviation Ltd
	G-BFFB	Evans VP-2	D. Bradley
	G-BFFC	Cessna F.152-II	Yorkshire Flying Services Ltd/Leeds
	G-BFFE	Cessna F.152-II	Doncaster Aero Club
	G-BFFG	Beech 95-B55 Baron	Beaucette Holdings Ltd
	G-BFFJ	Sikorsky S-61N Mk II	British International Helicopters Ltd/ Aberdeen
	G-BFFK	Sikorsky S-61N Mk II	British International Helicopters Ltd/ Aberdeen
	G-BFFP	PA-18 Super Cub 150	Airways Aero Associations Ltd/Booker
	G-BFFT	Cameron V-56 balloon	R. I. M. Kerr & D. C. Boxall
	G-BFFW	Cessna F.152	Midland Aircraft Leasing Ltd
	G-BFFY	Cessna F.150M	DJH Aviation Ltd/Biggin Hill
	G-BFFZ	Cessna FR.172 Hawk XP	Goodwood Terrena Ltd
	G-BFGD	Cessna F.172N-II	Reedtrend Ltd
	G-BFGF	Cessna F.177RG	Victree (V.M.) Ltd/Birmingham
	G-BFGG	Cessna FRA.150M	Airwork Ltd/Perth
	G-BFGH	Cessna F.337G	T. Perkins/Leeds
	G-BFGK	Jodel D.117	B. F. J. Hope
	G-BFGL	Cessna FA.152	Yorkshire Flying Services Ltd/Leeds
	G-BFGO	Fuji FA.200-160	Gt Consall Copper Mine Co Ltd
	G-BFGP	D.H.C.6 Twin Otter 310	National Airways/Southend
	G-BFGS	M.S.893E Rallye 180GT	J. R. Gore
	G-BFGW	Cessna F.150H	J. F. Morgan
	G-BFGX	Cessna FRA.150M	Airwork Ltd/Perth
	G-BFGY	Cessna F.182P ★	Oxford Aviation Co Ltd/Kidlington
	G-BFGZ	Cessna FRA.150M	Airwork Ltd/Perth
	G-BFHF	C.A.S.A. C.352L	Junkers Ju.52/3m Flight Ltd
	G-BFHG	C.A.S.A. C.352L (D2+600)	Aces High Ltd/North Weald
	G-BFHH	D.H.82A Tiger Moth	P. Harrison & M. J. Gambrell/Redhill
	G-BFHI	Piper J-3C-65 Cub	J. M. Robinson
	G-BFHK	Cessna F.177RG-II	Facet Group Holdings Ltd/Southend
	G-BFHM	Steen Skybolt	R. F. Fisher & ptnrs
	G-BFHN	Scheibe SF.25E Super Falke	Booker Gliding Club Ltd
	G-BFHP	Champion 7GCAA Citabria	Rushett Flying Group/Redhill
	G-BFHR	Jodel DR.220/2+2	R. F. Huggett/Sibson
	G-BFHS	AA-5B Tiger	P. H. Johnson
	G-BFHT	Cessna F.152-II	Riger Ltd/Luton
	G-BFHU	Cessna F.152-II	Deltair Ltd
	G-BFHV	Cessna F.152-II	Angelsword Ltd/Halfpenny Green
	G-BFHX	Evans VP-1	P. Johnson
	G-BFIB	PA-31-310 Turbo Navajo	Mann Aviation Ltd/Fairoaks
	G-BFID	Taylor JT.2 Titch Mk III	B. O. Smith
	G-BFIE	Cessna FRA.150M	RFC (Bourn) Ltd
	G-BFIF	Cessna FR.172K XPII	Michael Gardner Ltd
	G-BFIG	Cessna FR.172K XPII	Tenair Ltd
	G-BFII	PA-23 Aztec 250E	Tenza Tapes Ltd
	G-BFIJ	AA-5A Cheetah	J. H. Wise/Redhill
	G-BFIN	AA-5A Cheetah	M. F. D. Bartley
	G-BFIP	Wallbro Monoplane 1909 replica	K. H. Wallis/Swanton Morley
	G-BFIR	Avro 652A Anson 21 (WD413)	G. M. K. Fraser/Bournemouth
	G-BFIT	Thunder Ax6-56Z balloon	J. A. G. Tyson
	G-BFIU	Cessna FR.172K XP	P. Fletcher & ptnrs/Netherthorpe
	G-BFIV	Cessna F.177RG	Kingfishair Ltd/Blackbushe
	G-BFIX	Thunder Ax7-77A balloon	E. Sowden Ltd
	G-BFJA	AA-5B Tiger	Sentry Courier Ltd
	G-BFJH	SA.102-5 Cavalier	B. F. J. Hope
	G-BFJI	Robin HR.100/250	M. A. Egerton
	G-BFJJ	Evans VP-1	P. R. Pykett & B. J. Dyke/Thruxton
	G-BFJK	PA-23 Aztec 250E	Drive Petroleum Co Ltd
	G-BFJM	Cessna F.152	Pegasus Aviation Ltd/Aberdeen
	G-BFJN	Westland-Bell 47G-3B1	Howden Helicopters
	G-BFJP	G.164B Ag-Cat	E. S. Axford/Nairobi
	G-BFJR	Cessna F.337G	C. J. Harling/Cranfield
	G-BFJV	Cessna F.172H	Herefordshire Aero Club Ltd/Shobdon
	G-BFJW	AB-206B JetRanger	Autobase Rotary Ltd
	G-BFJZ	Robin DR.400/140B	Forge House Restaurant Ltd/Biggin Hill

Reg.	Type	Owner or Operator	Notes
G-BFKA	Cessna F.172N	D. J. A. Seagram	
G-BFKB	Cessna F.172N	Eastern Helicopters Ltd	
G-BFKC	Rand KR.2	K. K. Cutt	
G-BFKD	R. Commander 114B	C. W. Ford/Guernsey	
G-BFKF	Cessna FA.152	Klingair Ltd/Conington	
G-BFKG	Cessna F.152	W. R. C. Foyle/Luton	
G-BFKH	Cessna F.152	T. G. Aviation Ltd/Manston	
G-BFKL	Cameron N-56 balloon	Merrythought Toys Ltd *Merrythought*	
G-BFKV	PA-25 Pawnee 235D	Moonraker Aviation Co Ltd/Thruxton	
G-BFKY	PA-34-200 Seneca	S.L.H. Construction Ltd/Biggin Hill	
G-BFLH	PA-34-200T-2 Seneca	C.S.E. Aviation Ltd/Kidlington	
G-BFLI	PA-28R-201T Turbo Arrow III	Peter Walker (Heritage) Ltd	
G-BFLK	Cessna F.152	Falcon Flying Services/Biggin Hill	
G-BFLL	H.S.748 Srs 2A	Dan-Air Services Ltd/Gatwick	
G-BFLM	Cessna 150M	Cornwall Flying Club Ltd/Bodmin	
G-BFLN	Cessna 150M	Sherburn Aero Club Ltd	
G-BFLO	Cessna F.172M	W. A. Cook & ptnrs/Sherburn	
G-BFLP	Amethyst Ax6 balloon	K. J. Hendry *Amethyst*	
G-BFLU	Cessna F.152	Inverness Flying Services Ltd	
G-BFLV	Cessna F.172N	C. J. Williams	
G-BFLX	AA-5A Cheetah	G. T. Walsh & C. Hodkinson	
G-BFLZ	Beech 95-A55 Baron	K. K. Demel Ltd/Kidlington	
G-BFMC	BAC One-Eleven 414	Ford Motor Co Ltd/Stansted	
G-BFME	Cameron V-56 balloon	Warwick Balloons Ltd	
G-BFMF	Cassutt Racer Mk IIIM	P. H. Lewis	
G-BFMG	PA-28-161 Warrior II	Bailey Aviation Ltd	
G-BFMH	Cessna 177B	Span Aviation	
G-BFMK	Cessna FA.152	RAF Halton Aeroplane Club Ltd	
G-BFMM	PA-28-181 Archer II	Bristol & Wessex Aeroplane Club Ltd/ Bristol	
G-BFMR	PA-20 Pacer 125	B. C. & J. I. Cooper	
G-BFMX	Cessna F.172N	Colton Aviation Aero Spraying Ltd	
G-BFMY	Sikorsky S-61N	Bristow Helicopters Ltd	
G-BFMZ	Payne Ax6 balloon	G. F. Payne	
G-BFNC	AS.350B Ecureuil	Dollar Air Services Ltd/Coventry	
G-BFNG	Jodel D.112	M. Lomax	
G-BFNH	Cameron V-77 balloon	P. O. Atkins & ptnrs	
G-BFNI	PA-28-161 Warrior II	C.S.E. Aviation Ltd/Kidlington	
G-BFNJ	PA-28-161 Warrior II	C.S.E. Aviation Ltd/Kidlington	
G-BFNK	PA-28-161 Warrior II	C.S.E. Aviation Ltd/Kidlington	
G-BFNM	Globe GC.1 Swift	Nottingham Flying Group/E. Midlands	
G-BFNU	BN-2B Islander	Isle of Scilly Sky Bus Ltd/St Just	
G-BFNV	BN-2A Islander	Air Furness Ltd/Walney Island	
G-BFOD	Cessna F.182Q	Graphiking Publicity Ltd/Staverton	
G-BFOE	Cessna F.152	B. W. Wells & Burbage Farms Ltd	
G-BFOF	Cessna F.152	Staverton Flying School Ltd	
G-BFOG	Cessna 150M	D. E. Tisdale	
G-BFOJ	AA-1 Yankee	A. J. Morton/Bournemouth	
G-BFOL	Beech 200 Super King Air	Bristow Helicopters Ltd	
G-BFOM	PA-31-325 Navajo	Aviation Beauport Ltd/Jersey	
G-BFOP	Jodel D.120	H. Cope/Stapleford	
G-BFOS	Thunder Ax6-56A balloon	N. T. Petty	
G-BFOT	Thunder Ax6-56A balloon	Thunder Balloons Ltd	
G-BFOU	Taylor JT.1 Monoplane	G. Bee	
G-BFOV	Cessna F.172N	Gooda Walker Ltd/Shoreham	
G-BFOX	D.H.83 Fox Moth Replica	R. K. J. Hadlow	
G-BFOZ	Thunder Ax6-56 balloon	R. L. Harbord	
G-BFPA	Scheibe SF.25B Super Falke	Yorkshire Gliding Club (Pty) Ltd	
G-BFPB	AA-5B Tiger	Guernsey Aero Club	
G-BFPF	Sikorsky S-61N	Bristow Helicopters Ltd	
G-BFPH	Cessna F.172K	A. W. Kennedy/Andrewsfield	
G-BFPJ	Procter Petrel	S. G. Craggs	
G-BFPL	Fokker D.VII Replica (4253/18)	Coys of Kensington (Petrol Sales) Ltd	
G-BFPM	Cessna F.172M	Abbey Windows Ltd	
G-BFPO	R. Commander 112B	J. G. Hale Ltd	
G-BFPP	Bell 47J-2	D. Fordham	
G-BFPS	PA-25 Pawnee 235D	Bowker Aviation Services Ltd/ Rush Green	
G-BFPX	Taylor JT.1 Monoplane	E. A. Taylor	
G-BFPZ	Cessna F.177RG	S. R. Cherry-Downes	
G-BFRA	R. Commander 114	Sabre Engines Ltd/Bournemouth	
G-BFRD	Bowers Flybaby 1A	F. R. Donaldson	
G-BFRF	Taylor JT.1 Monoplane	E. R. Bailey	

Notes	Reg.	Type	Owner or Operator
	G-BFRI	Sikorsky S-61N	Bristow Helicopters Ltd
	G-BFRL	Cessna F.152	J. J. Baumhardt/Southend
	G-BFRM	Cessna 550 Citation II	Marshall of Cambridge (Engineering) Ltd
	G-BFRO	Cessna F.150M	Skyviews & General Ltd/Carlisle
	G-BFRR	Cessna FRA.150M	Interair Aviation Ltd/Bournemouth
	G-BFRS	Cessna F.172N	Poplar Toys Ltd
	G-BFRT	Cessna FR.172K XP II	B. J. Sharpe/Booker
	G-BFRV	Cessna FA.152	Rogers Aviation Ltd/Cranfield
	G-BFRX	PA-25 Pawnee 260	Howard Avis Aviation Ltd
	G-BFRY	PA-25 Pawnee 260	C. J. Pearce
	G-BFSA	Cessna F.182Q	Clark Masts Ltd/Sandown
	G-BFSB	Cessna F.152	Seal Executive Aircraft Ltd/E. Midlands
	G-BFSC	PA-25 Pawnee 235D	Farm Aviation Services Ltd/Enstone
	G-BFSD	PA-25 Pawnee 235D	A. W. Evans
	G-BFSK	PA-23 Apache 160 ★	Oxford Air Training School/Kidlington
	G-BFSL	Cessna U.206F Stationair	J. M. Block/Nairobi
	G-BFSR	Cessna F.150J	C. Sims
	G-BFSS	Cessna FR.172G	Minerva Services
	G-BFSY	PA-28-181 Archer II	Downland Aviation/Goodwood
	G-BFTC	PA-28R-201T Turbo Arrow II	D. Hughes/Leeds
	G-BFTF	AA-5B Tiger	F. C. Burrow Ltd/Leeds
	G-BFTG	AA-5B Tiger	Freightflow International Ltd
	G-BFTH	Cessna F.172N	Atomchoice Ltd/Cranfield
	G-BFTT	Cessna 421C	P&B Metal Components Ltd/Manston
	G-BFTX	Cessna F.172N	J. N. Collins/Manston
	G-BFTY	Cameron V-77 balloon	Regal Motors (Bilston) Ltd *Regal Motors*
	G-BFTZ	*MS.880B Rallye Club*	*R. & B. Legge Ltd*
	G-BFUB	*PA-32RT-300 Turbo Lance II*	*Jolida Holdings Ltd*
	G-BFUD	*Scheibe SF.25E Super Falke*	*S. H. Hart*
	G-BFUG	*Cameron N-77 balloon*	*Headland Services Ltd*
	G-BFUZ	*Cameron V-77 balloon*	*Skysales Ltd*
	G-BFVA	*Boeing 737-204ADV*	*Britannia Airways Ltd Sir John Alcock/ Luton*
	G-BFVB	Boeing 737-204ADV	Britannia Airways Ltd *Sir Thomas Sopwith*/Luton
	G-BFVF	PA-38-112 Tomahawk	Ipswich School of Flying
	G-BFVG	PA-28-181 Archer II	P. A. Cornah & S. Reed/Blackpool
	G-BFVH	D.H.2 Replica (5964)	Russavia Collection/Duxford
	G-BFVI	H.S.125 Srs 700B	Bristow Helicopters Ltd
	G-BFVM	Westland-Bell 47G-3B1	Pilotmoor Ltd
	G-BFVO	Partenavia P.68B	Octavia Air Ltd/Staverton
	G-BFVP	PA-23 Aztec 250F	B. J. Eastwood/Newtownards
	G-BFVS	AA-5B Tiger	S. W. Biroth & T. Chapman/Denham
	G-BFVU	Cessna 150L	Thruxton Flight Centre Ltd
	G-BFVV	SA.365 Dauphin 2	Bond Helicopters Ltd/Bourn
	G-BFVW	SA.365 Dauphin 2	Bond Helicopters Ltd/Bourn
	G-BFVY	Beech C90 King Air	Vernair Transport Services/Liverpool
	G-BFWB	PA-28-161 Warrior II	C.S.E. Aviation Ltd/Kidlington
	G-BFWD	Currie Wot	F. E. Nuthall
	G-BFWE	PA-23 Aztec 250	Air Navigation & Trading Co Ltd/ Blackpool
	G-BFWF	Cessna 421B	Alcon Oil Ltd
	G-BFWK	PA-28-161 Warrior II	Woodgate Air Services (IoM) Ltd
	G-BFWL	Cessna F.150L	J. Dolan/Eglinton
	G-BFWW	Robin HR.100/210	Willingair Ltd
	G-BFXC	Mooney M.20C	R. I. Craddock/Biggin Hill
	G-BFXD	PA-28-161 Warrior II	C.S.E. Aviation Ltd/Kidlington
	G-BFXE	PA-28-161 Warrior II	C.S.E. Aviation Ltd/Kidlington
	G-BFXF	Andreasson BA.4B	A. Brown/Sherburn
	G-BFXG	D.31 Turbulent	S. Griffin
	G-BFXH	Cessna F.152	Angelsword Ltd/Halfpenny Green
	G-BFXI	Cessna F.172M	Thanet Electronics/Manston
	G-BFXK	PA-28 Cherokee 140	G. S. & Mrs M. T. Pritchard/Southend
	G-BFXL	Albatross D.5A (D5397/17)	FAA Museum/Yeovilton
	G-BFXM	Jurca MJ.5 Sirocco	R. Bradbury & A. R. Greenfield
	G-BFXO	Taylor JT.1 Monoplane	A. S. Nixon
	G-BFXR	Jodel D.112	R. E. Walker & M. Riddin/Netherthorpe
	G-BFXS	R. Commander 114	Forest Publishing (East Anglia) Ltd/ Ipswich
	G-BFXT	H.S.125 Srs 700B	Coca Cola Export Corporation
	G-BFXW	AA-5B Tiger	Crosswind Aviation Ltd/Leeds
	G-BFXX	AA-5B Tiger	Stanton Aircraft Management Ltd/ Biggin Hill

Reg.	Type	Owner or Operator	Notes
G-BFYA	MBB Bo 105D	Veritair Ltd	
G-BFYB	PA-28-161 Warrior II	C.S.E. Aviation Ltd/Kidlington	
G-BFYC	PA-32RT-300 Lance II	Peter Lang International Ltd	
G-BFYE	Robin HR.100/285	J. Hackett/Jersey	
G-BFYI	Westland-Bell 47G-3B1	Dollar Air Services Ltd/Coventry	
G-BFYJ	Hughes 369HE	Wilford Aviation Ltd/Fairoaks	
G-BFYL	Evans VP-2	A. G. Wilford	
G-BFYM	PA-28-161 Warrior II	C.S.E. Aviation Ltd/Kidlington	
G-BFYN	Cessna FA.152	Phoenix Flying Services Ltd/Glasgow	
G-BFYO	Spad XIII replica (S3398) ★	FAA Museum/Yeovilton	
G-BFYP	Bensen B.7	A. J. Philpotts	
G-BFYU	SC.5 Belfast	HeavyLift Cargo Airlines Ltd/Stansted	
G-BFZB	Piper J-3C-85 Cub	Zebedee Flying Group/Shoreham	
G-BFZD	Cessna FR.182RG	R. B. Lewis & Co/Sleap	
G-BFZG	PA-28-161 Warrior II	C.S.E. Aviation Ltd/Kidlington	
G-BFZH	PA-28R-200 Cherokee Arrow	R. E. & U. C. Mankelow	
G-BFZL	V.836 Viscount	Manx Airlines Ltd/Ronaldsway	
G-BFZM	R. Commander 112TC	Rolls-Royce Ltd/Filton	
G-BFZN	Cessna FA.152	Falcon Flying Services/Biggin Hill	
G-BFZO	AA-5A Cheetah	Heald Air Ltd/Manchester	
G-BFZT	Cessna FA.152	One Zero One Three Ltd/Guernsey	
G-BFZU	Cessna FA.152	Reedtrend Ltd/Stapleford	
G-BFZV	Cessna F.172M	W. J. Kavanagh	
G-BGAA	Cessna 152 II	Farr (Metal Fabrications) Ltd	
G-BGAB	Cessna F.152 II	TG Aviation Ltd/Manston	
G-BGAD	Cessna F.152 II	W. J. Overhead	
G-BGAE	Cessna F.152 II	Klingair Ltd/Conington	
G-BGAF	Cessna FA.152	Suffolk Aero Club Ltd/Ipswich	
G-BGAG	Cessna F.172N	Adifer Ltd	
G-BGAH	FRED Srs 2	G. A. Harris	
G-BGAJ	Cessna F.182Q II	Ground Airport Services Ltd/Guernsey	
G-BGAK	Cessna F.182Q II	Safari World Services Ltd	
G-BGAU	Rearwin 9000L	Shipping & Airlines Ltd/Biggin Hill	
G-BGAX	PA-28 Cherokee 140	Hillvine Ltd	
G-BGAY	Cameron O-77 balloon	Dante Balloon Group Antonia	
G-BGAZ	Cameron V-77 balloon	Cameron Balloons Ltd Silicon Chip	
G-BGBA	Robin R.2100A	D. Faulkner/Redhill	
G-BGBB	L.1011-385 TriStar 200	British Airways Bridlington Bay/Heathrow	
G-BGBC	L.1011-385 TriStar 200	British Airways St Andrews Bay/Heathrow	
G-BGBE	Jodel DR.1050	J. A. Wootton & ptnrs	
G-BGBF	D.31A Turbulent	S. Haye	
G-BGBG	PA-28-181 Archer II	Harlow Printing Ltd/Newcastle	
G-BGBI	Cessna F.150L	Anglian Flight Training Ltd/Norwich	
G-BGBK	PA-38-112 Tomahawk	P. K. Pemberton	
G-BGBN	PA-38-112 Tomahawk	Leavesden Flight Centre Ltd	
G-BGBP	Cessna F.152	Stapleford Flying Club Ltd	
G-BGBR	Cessna F.172N	Stanton Aircraft Management Ltd/Biggin Hill	
G-BGBU	Auster AOP.9	P. Neilson	
G-BGBW	PA-38-112 Tomahawk	Spatial Air Brokers & Forwarders Ltd/E. Midlands	
G-BGBX	PA-38-112 Tomahawk	Ipswich School of Flying	
G-BGBY	PA-38-112 Tomahawk	Cheshire Flying Services Ltd/Manchester	
G-BGBZ	R. Commander 114	R. S. Fenwick/Biggin Hill	
G-BGCG	Douglas C-47A	Datran Holdings	
G-BGCL	AA-5A Cheetah	Holmes Rentals/Goodwood	
G-BGCM	AA-5A Cheetah	Pacific Associates Ltd/Blackbushe	
G-BGCO	PA-44-180 Seminole	J. R. Henderson	
G-BGCX	Taylor JT.1 Monoplane	G. M. R. Walters	
G-BGCY	Taylor JT.1 Monoplane	R. L. A. Davies	
G-BGDA	Boeing 737-236	British Airways River Tamar/Heathrow	
G-BGDB	Boeing 737-236	British Airways River Tweed/Heathrow	
G-BGDC	Boeing 737-236	British Airways River Humber/Heathrow	
G-BGDD	Boeing 737-236	British Airways River Tees/Heathrow	
G-BGDE	Boeing 737-236	British Airways River Avon/Heathrow	
G-BGDF	Boeing 737-236	British Airways River Thames/Heathrow	
G-BGDG	Boeing 737-236	British Airways River Medway/Heathrow	
G-BGDH	Boeing 737-236	British Airways River Clyde/Heathrow	

Notes	Reg.	Type	Owner or Operator
	G-BGDI	Boeing 737-236	British Airways *River Ouse*/Heathrow
	G-BGDJ	Boeing 737-236	British Airways *River Trent*/Heathrow
	G-BGDK	Boeing 737-236	British Airways *River Mersey*/Heathrow
	G-BGDL	Boeing 737-236	British Airways *River Don*/Heathrow
	G-BGDN	Boeing 737-236	British Airways *River Tyne*/Heathrow
	G-BGDO	Boeing 737-236	British Airways *River Usk*/Heathrow
	G-BGDP	Boeing 737-236	British Airways *River Taff*/Heathrow
	G-BGDR	Boeing 737-236	British Airways *River Bann*/Heathrow
	G-BGDS	Boeing 737-236	British Airways *River Severn*/Heathrow
	G-BGDT	Boeing 737-236	British Airways *River Forth*/Heathrow
	G-BGDU	Boeing 737-236	British Airways *River Dee*/Heathrow
	G-BGEA	Cessna F.150M	Agricultural & General Aviation Ltd
	G-BGED	Cessna U.206F	Elecwind (Clay Cross) Ltd/E. Midlands
	G-BGEE	Evans VP-1	R. A. M. Purkis
	G-BGEF	Jodel D.112	G. G. Johnson & S. J. Davies
	G-BGEH	Monnet Sonerai II	A. Dodd
	G-BGEI	Baby Great Lakes	D. J. Wright/Denham
	G-BGEK	PA-38-112 Tomahawk	Cheshire Flying Services Ltd/ Manchester
	G-BGEL	PA-38-112 Tomahawk	Cheshire Flying Services Ltd/ Manchester
	G-BGEM	Partenavia P.68B	AEW Engineering Co Ltd/Norwich
	G-BGEN	D.H.C.6 Twin Otter 310	Loganair Ltd/Glasgow
	G-BGEP	Cameron D-38 balloon	Cameron Balloons Ltd
	G-BGES	Currie Wot	K. E. Ballington
	G-BGET	PA-38-112 Tomahawk	Goodwood Terrena Ltd
	G-BGEV	PA-38-112 Tomahawk	Cheshire Flying Services Ltd/ Manchester
	G-BGEW	Nord NC.854S	A. Doughty
	G-BGEX	Brookland Mosquito 2	R. T. Gough
	G-BGFC	Evans VP-2	A. Sharma
	G-BGFF	FRED Srs 2	G. R. G. Smith
	G-BGFG	AA-5A Cheetah	Fletcher Aviation Ltd/Biggin Hill
	G-BGFH	Cessna F.182Q	Mindon Engineering (Nottingham) Ltd/ Tollerton
	G-BGFI	AA-5A Cheetah	Maston Property Holdings Ltd
	G-BGFJ	Jodel D.9 Bebe	C. M. Fitton
	G-BGFK	Evans VP-1	I. N. M. Cameron
	G-BGFN	PA-25 Pawnee 235	Scanrho Aviation
	G-BGFS	Westland-Bell 47G-3B1	G. S. Mason
	G-BGFT	PA-34-200T-2 Seneca	C.S.E. Aviation Ltd/Kidlington
	G-BGFX	Cessna F.152	A. W. Fay/Cranfield
	G-BGGA	Bellanca 7GCBC Citabria	I. N. Jennison
	G-BGGB	Bellanca 7GCBC Citabria	N. A. & M. D. Cowburn
	G-BGGC	Bellanca 7GCBC Citabria	R. P. Ashfield & B. A. Jesty
	G-BGGD	Bellanca 8GCBC Scout	Bristol & Gloucestershire Gliding Club/Nympsfield
	G-BGGE	PA-38-112 Tomahawk	C.S.E. (Aircraft Services) Ltd/Kidlington
	G-BGGF	PA-38-112 Tomahawk	C.S.E. (Aircraft Services) Ltd/Kidlington
	G-BGGG	PA-38-112 Tomahawk	C.S.E. (Aircraft Services) Ltd/Kidlington
	G-BGGI	PA-38-112 Tomahawk	C.S.E. (Aircraft Services) Ltd/Kidlington
	G-BGGJ	PA-38-112 Tomahawk	C.S.E. (Aircraft Services) Ltd/Kidlington
	G-BGGL	PA-38-112 Tomahawk	Grunwick Ltd/Elstree
	G-BGGM	PA-38-112 Tomahawk	Grunwick Ltd/Elstree
	G-BGGN	PA-38-112 Tomahawk	C.S.E. Aviation Ltd/Kidlington
	G-BGGO	Cessna F.152	E. Midlands Flying School Ltd
	G-BGGP	Cessna F.152	E. Midlands Flying School Ltd
	G-BGGT	Zenith CH.200	P. R. M. Nind
	G-BGGU	Wallis WA-116R-R	K. H. Wallis
	G-BGGV	Wallis WA-120 Srs 2	K. H. Wallis
	G-BGGW	Wallis WA-112	K. H. Wallis
	G-BGGY	AB-206B Jet Ranger ★	*Instructional airframe*/Cranfield
	G-BGHA	Cessna F.152	Stanton Aircraft Management Ltd/ Biggin Hill
	G-BGHC	Saffery Hot Pants Firefly balloon	H. C. Saffery *Petuniga*
	G-BGHE	Convair L-13A	J. Davis/USA
	G-BGHF	Westland WG.30 ★	*Instructional airframe*/Yeovil
	G-BGHI	Cessna F.152	Taxon Ltd/Shoreham
	G-BGHK	Cessna F.152	Wilson Leasing/Biggin Hill
	G-BGHM	Robin R.1180T	H. Price
	G-BGHP	Beech 76 Duchess	J. J. Baumhardt Ltd
	G-BGHS	Cameron N-31 balloon	Balloon Stable Ltd
	G-BGHT	Falconar F-12	T. Kerr-Baillie
	G-BGHU	T-6G Texan (115042)	C. E. Bellhouse

Reg.	Type	Owner or Operator	Notes
G-BGHV	Cameron V-77 balloon	E. Davies	
G-BGHW	Thunder Ax8-90 balloon	Edinburgh University Balloon Group *James Tytler*	
G-BGHX	Chasle YC-12 Tourbillon	C. Clark	
G-BGHY	Taylor JT.1 Monoplane	J. Prowse	
G-BGHZ	FRED Srs 2	A. Smith	
G-BGIB	Cessna 152 II	Mona Aviation Ltd	
G-BGIC	Cessna 172N	T. R. Sinclair	
G-BGID	Westland-Bell 47G-3B1	A. E. & B. G. Brown	
G-BGIG	PA-38-112 Tomahawk	Scotia Safari Ltd/Prestwick	
G-BGIH	Rand KR-2	G. & D. G. Park	
G-BGII	PA-32-300 Cherokee Six	Rosefair Electronics Ltd/Elstree	
G-BGIK	Taylor JT.1 Monoplane	M. C. Durand	
G-BGIM	AS.350B Ecureuil	Lord Glendyne/Hayes	
G-BGIO	Bensen B.8M	C. G. Johns	
G-BGIP	Colt 56A balloon	Capitol Balloon Club	
G-BGIU	Cessna F.172H	Metro Equipment (Chesham) Ltd/ Panshanger	
G-BGIV	Bell 47G-5	Helitech (Luton) Ltd	
G-BGIX	H.295 Super Courier	Nordic Oil Services Ltd/Edinburgh	
G-BGIY	Cessna F.172N	Cormack (Aircraft Services) Ltd/ Glasgow	
G-BGIZ	Cessna F.152	Creaton Aviation Services Ltd	
G-BGJA	Cessna FA.152	Redhill Flying Club	
G-BGJB	PA-44-180 Seminole	Cardiff Flying Club	
G-BGJE	Boeing 737-236	British Airtours *Sandpiper*/Gatwick	
G-BGJF	Boeing 737-236	British Airtours *River Axe*/Gatwick	
G-BGJG	Boeing 737-236	British Airtours *River Arun*/Gatwick	
G-BGJH	Boeing 737-236	British Airtours *River Lyne*/Gatwick	
G-BGJI	Boeing 737-236	British Airtours *River Wey*/Gatwick	
G-BGJJ	Boeing 737-236	British Airtours *River Swale*/Gatwick	
G-BGJK	Boeing 737-236	British Airtours *River Cherwell*/Gatwick	
G-BGJM	Boeing 737-236	British Airtours *River Ribble*/Gatwick	
G-BGJU	Cameron V-65 Balloon	D. T. Watkins *Spoils*	
G-BGJV	H.S.748 Srs 2B	British Airways *Glen Islay*/Glasgow	
G-BGJW	GA-7 Cougar	Lambill Ltd	
G-BGKA	P.56 Provost T.1 (XF690)	D. W. Mickleburgh	
G-BGKD	SOCATA Rallye 110ST	E. J. Morris & Son	
G-BGKE	BAC One-Eleven 539	British Airways *County of Gwynedd*/ Birmingham	
G-BGKF	BAC One-Eleven 539	British Airways *County of Warwickshire*/ Birmingham	
G-BGKG	BAC One-Eleven 539	British Airways *County of Staffordshire*/ Birmingham	
G-BGKJ	MBB Bo 105C	Bond Helicopters Ltd/Bourn	
G-BGKM	SA.365C-3 Dauphin	Bond Helicopters Ltd/Bourn	
G-BGKO	GY-20 Minicab	R. B. Webber	
G-BGKS	PA-28-161 Warrior II	Woodgate Air Services (IoM) Ltd	
G-BGKT	Auster AOP.9 (XN441)	K. H. Wallis	
G-BGKU	PA-28R-201 Arrow III	Caplane Ltd	
G-BGKV	PA-28R-201 Arrow III	G. E. Salter Industrial Enterprises Ltd	
G-BGKW	Evans VP-1	I. W. Black	
G-BGKY	PA-38-112 Tomahawk	MSF Aviation	
G-BGKZ	J/5F Aiglet Trainer	R. C. H. Hibberd	
G-BGLA	PA-38-112 Tomahawk	Scotia Safari Ltd/Prestwick	
G-BGLB	Bede BD-5B	W. Sawney	
G-BGLD	Beech 76 Duchess	Devindale Ltd	
G-BGLE	Saffrey S.330 balloon	C. J. Dodd & ptnrs	
G-BGLF	Evans VP-1	B. P. Fraser-Newstead	
G-BGLG	Cessna 152	Skyviews & General Ltd	
G-BGLH	Cessna 152	Deltair Ltd/Chester	
G-BGLI	Cessna 152	Luton Flying Club (*stored*)	
G-BGLK	Monnet Sonerai II	G. L. Kemp & J. Beck	
G-BGLN	Cessna FA.152	Bournemouth Flying Club	
G-BGLO	Cessna F.172N	A. H. Slaughter/Southend	
G-BGLR	Cessna F.152	Horizon Flying Club Ltd	
G-BGLS	Super Baby Great Lakes	J. F. Dowe	
G-BGLW	PA-34-200 Seneca	P. C. Roberts	
G-BGLX	Cameron N-56 balloon	Sara A. G. Williams	
G-BGLZ	Stits SA-3A Playboy	J. R. Wynn	
G-BGMA	D.31 Turbulent	G. C. Masterton	
G-BGMB	Taylor JT.2 Titch	E. M. Bourne	
G-BGMC	D.H.C.6 Twin Otter 310	South East Air Ltd	
G-BGMD	D.H.C.6 Twin Otter 310	Hubbardair Ltd/Brymon Airways	

Notes	Reg.	Type	Owner or Operator
	G-BGME	SIPA S.903	M. Emery (G-BCML)/Redhill
	G-BGMJ	GY-201 Minicab	P. Cawkwell
	G-BGMN	H.S.748 Srs 2A	Euroair/British Airways Glen Finnan/Glasgow
	G-BGMO	H.S.748 Srs 2A	Euroair/British Airways Glen Goyne/Glasgow
	G-BGMP	Cessna F.172G	Norvic Racing Engines Ltd/Cranfield
	G-BGMR	GY-201 Minicab	J. R. Large & ptnrs
	G-BGMS	Taylor JT.2 Titch	M. A. J. Spice
	G-BGMT	MS.894E Rallye 235GT	M. E. Taylor
	G-BGMU	Westland-Bell 47G-3B1	Carskiey Ltd
	G-BGMV	Scheibe SF.25B Falke	Wolds Gliding Club Ltd/Pocklington
	G-BGMW	Edgley EA-7 Optica	Edgley Aircraft Ltd/Old Sarum
	G-BGMX	Enstrom F-280C-UK-2 Shark	P. V. Doman
	G-BGNB	Short SD3-30 Variant 100	British Air Ferries Ltd Eastleigh/Southend
	G-BGND	Cessna F.172N	Stansted Fluid Power Products Ltd
	G-BGNM	SA.365C-1 Dauphin 2	Bond Helicopters Ltd/Bourn
	G-BGNR	Cessna F.172N	Bevan Lynch Aviation Ltd/Birmingham
	G-BGNS	Cessna F.172N	Reedtrend Ltd/Shoreham
	G-BGNT	Cessna F.152	Klingair Ltd/Conington
	G-BGNU	Beech E90 King Air	Norwich Union Fire Insurance Ltd/Norwich
	G-BGNV	GA-7 Cougar	H. Snelson/Manchester
	G-BGNW	Boeing 737-219ADV	Britannia Airways Ltd George Stephenson/Luton
	G-BGNZ	Cessna FRA.150L	P. P. D. Howard-Johnston/Edinburgh
	G-BGOA	Cessna FR.182RG	CDS Trading Co Ltd/Biggin Hill
	G-BGOC	Cessna F.152	Elliot Forbes (Kirkwall) Ltd
	G-BGOD	Colt 77A balloon	J. R. Gore
	G-BGOE	Beech 76 Duchess	Niglon Ltd/Birmingham
	G-BGOF	Cessna F.152	Falcon Flying Services/Biggin Hill
	G-BGOG	PA-28-161 Warrior II	M. J. Cowham
	G-BGOH	Cessna F.182Q	Zonex Ltd/Blackpool
	G-BGOI	Cameron O-56 balloon	Balloon Stable Ltd Skymaster
	G-BGOL	PA-28R-201T Turbo Arrow IV	Lonslow Dairy Ltd & ptnrs/Birmingham
	G-BGOM	PA-31-310 Navajo	Oxford Aero Charter Ltd/Kidlington
	G-BGON	GA-7 Cougar	Wendexim Trading Co Ltd/Denham
	G-BGOO	Colt 56 SS balloon	British Gas Corporation
	G-BGOP	Dassault Falcon 20F	Nissan (UK) Ltd/Heathrow
	G-BGOR	AT-6D Harvard III	M. L. Sargeant
	G-BGOX	PA-31-350 Navajo Chieftain	Woodgate Aviation (IoM) Ltd
	G-BGOY	PA-31-350 Navajo Chieftain	Interflight (Air Charters) Ltd/Gatwick
	G-BGPA	Cessna 182Q	R. A. Robinson
	G-BGPB	AT-16 Harvard IV (385)	A. G. Walker & R. Lamplough/Sandown
	G-BGPD	Piper L-4H Cub	P. D. Whiteman
	G-BGPE	Thunder Ax6-56 balloon	C. Wolstenholme Sergeant Pepper
	G-BGPF	Thunder Ax6-56Z balloon	Thunder Balloons Ltd Pepsi
	G-BGPG	AA-5B Tiger	Garrick Aviation & BLS Aviation Ltd/Elstree
	G-BGPH	AA-5B Tiger	A. J. Dales
	G-BGPI	Plumb BGP-1	B. G. Plumb
	G-BGPJ	PA-28-161 Warrior II	E. Green
	G-BGPK	AA-5B Tiger	Ann Green Manufacturing Co Ltd/Elstree
	G-BGPL	PA-28-161 Warrior II	T. G. Aviation Ltd/Manston
	G-BGPM	Evans VP-2	M. G. Reilly
	G-BGPN	PA-18-150 Super Cub	Roy Moore Ltd/Blackpool
	G-BGPP	PA-25 Pawnee 235	Miller Aerial Spraying Ltd/Wickenby
	G-BGPS	Aero Commander 200D	G. Jones & ptnrs/Cardiff
	G-BGPT	Parker Teenie Two	K. Atkinson
	G-BGPU	PA-28 Cherokee 140	Air Navigation & Trading Co Ltd/Blackpool
	G-BGPZ	M.S.890A Rallye Commodore	J. A. Espin/Popham
	G-BGRA	Taylor JT.2 Titch	J. R. C. Thompson
	G-BGRC	PA-28 Cherokee 140	Arrow Air Centre Ltd/Shipdham
	G-BGRE	Beech A200 Super King Air	Martin-Baker (Engineering) Ltd
	G-BGRG	Beech 76 Duchess	Arrows Ltd/Manchester
	G-BGRH	Robin DR.400/2+2	T.M.A. Associates Ltd/Headcorn
	G-BGRI	Jodel DR.1051	C. R. Warcup
	G-BGRK	PA-38-112 Tomahawk	Goodwood Terrena Ltd
	G-BGRL	PA-38-112 Tomahawk	Goodwood Terrena Ltd
	G-BGRM	PA-38-112 Tomahawk	Goodwood Terrena Ltd

Reg.	Type	Owner or Operator	Notes
G-BGRN	PA-38-112 Tomahawk	Goodwood Terrena Ltd	
G-BGRO	Cessna F.172M	Northfield Garage Ltd	
G-BGRR	PA-38-112 Tomahawk	MSF Aviation Ltd/Manchester	
G-BGRS	Thunder Ax7-77Z balloon	W. & J. Evans	
G-BGRT	Steen Skybolt	D. Callabritto	
G-BGRX	PA-38-112 Tomahawk	Leavesden Flight Centre Ltd	
G-BGSA	M.S.892E Rallye 150GT	Colin Draycott Group Ltd/Leicester	
G-BGSE	Pitts S-2A Special	P. H. Meeson	
G-BGSG	PA-44-180 Seminole	D. J. McSorley	
G-BGSH	PA-38-112 Tomahawk	Scotia Safari Ltd/Prestwick	
G-BGSI	PA-38-112 Tomahawk	Cheshire Flying Services Ltd/ Manchester	
G-BGSJ	Piper J-3C-65 Cub	W. J. Higgins/Dunkeswell	
G-BGSM	M.S.892E Rallye 150GT	G. T. Leedham & D. H. Rider	
G-BGSN	Enstrom F-28C-UK-2	Aircraft Sales International Ltd/Denham	
G-BGSO	PA-31-310 Navajo	Continental Flight Services/ Southampton	
G-BGST	Thunder Ax7-65 balloon	L. H. T. Large & ptnrs *Eclipse*	
G-BGSV	Cessna F.172N	Wickenby Flying Club Ltd	
G-BGSW	Beech F33 Debonair	L. J. Paveley/Stapleford	
G-BGSX	Cessna F.152	Midland Aircraft Leasing Ltd/ Birmingham	
G-BGSY	GA-7 Cougar	Van Allen Ltd/Guernsey	
G-BGTA	Firebird Bunce B.500 balloon	S. J. Bunce	
G-BGTB	SOCATA TB.10 Tobago ★	S. Yorks Aviation Soc	
G-BGTC	Auster AOP.9 (XP282)	A. C. Byrne	
G-BGTF	PA-44-180 Seminole	New Guarantee Trust Ltd/Jersey	
G-BGTG	PA-23 Aztec 250	R. J. Howard/Leeds	
G-BGTI	Piper J-3C-65 Cub	A. P. Broad/Aberdeen	
G-BGTJ	PA-28 Cherokee 180	Serendipity Aviation/Staverton	
G-BGTK	Cessna FR.182RG	Kestrel Air Services Ltd/Denham	
G-BGTL	GY-20 Minicab	A. K. Lang	
G-BGTP	Robin HR.100/210	E. C. & C. E. E. Walker	
G-BGTR	PA-28 Cherokee 140	Keenair Services Ltd/Liverpool	
G-BGTS	PA-28 Cherokee 140	Keenair Services Ltd/Liverpool	
G-BGTT	Cessna 310R	Aviation Beauport Ltd/Jersey	
G-BGTU	BAC One-Eleven 409	Turbo Union Ltd/Filton	
G-BGTX	Jodel D.117	Madley Flying Group/Shobdon	
G-BGTY	Boeing 737-2Q8	Orion Airways Ltd/E. Midlands	
G-BGUA	PA-38-112 Tomahawk	Truman Aviation Ltd/Tollerton	
G-BGUB	PA-32-300 Cherokee Six	J. Beckers & ptnrs	
G-BGUY	Cameron V-56 balloon	G. V. Beckwith	
G-BGVA	Cessna 414A	Royalair Services Ltd/Tollerton	
G-BGVB	Robin DR.315	Cedric P. Jones Ltd	
G-BGVE	CP.1310-C3 Super Emeraude	E. J. A. Woolnough	
G-BGVF	Colt 77A balloon	Hot Air Balloon Co Ltd	
G-BGVH	Beech 76 Duchess	Velco Marketing	
G-BGVI	Cessna F.152	Farr (Metal Fabrications) Ltd	
G-BGVK	PA-28-161 Warrior II	W. E. B. Wordsworth	
G-BGVL	PA-38-112 Tomahawk	Scotia Safari Ltd/Prestwick	
G-BGVM	Wilson Cassutt IIIM	Belgravia Aviation Promotions	
G-BGVN	PA-28RT-201 Arrow IV	Essex Aviation Ltd/Stapleford	
G-BGVP	Thunder Ax6-56Z balloon	A. Bolger	
G-BGVR	Thunder Ax6-56Z balloon	A. N. G. Howie	
G-BGVS	Cessna F.172M	P. D. A. Aviation Ltd/Tollerton	
G-BGVT	Cessna R.182RG	Barnes Plastics Group Ltd/Staverton	
G-BGVU	PA-28 Cherokee 180	Cheshire Flying Services Ltd/ Manchester	
G-BGVV	AA-5A Cheetah	R. M. Messenger	
G-BGVW	AA-5A Cheetah	BLS Aviation Ltd/Elstree	
G-BGVY	AA-5B Tiger	Porter Bell Ltd/Goodwood	
G-BGVZ	PA-28-181 Archer II	Midland Aircraft Leasing Ltd/ Birmingham	
G-BGWA	GA-7 Cougar	Lough Erne Aviation Ltd	
G-BGWC	Robin DR.400/180	E. F. Braddon & D. C. Shepherd/ Rochester	
G-BGWF	PA-18 Super Cub 150	E. D. Burke	
G-BGWH	PA-18 Super Cub 150	A. W. Kennedy/Stapleford	
G-BGWI	Cameron V-65 balloon	Army Balloon Club/W. Germany	
G-BGWJ	Sikorsky S-61N	Bristow Helicopters Ltd	

NOTE: The G-BGUx sequence will not be issued unless specifically requested

Notes	Reg.	Type	Owner or Operator
	G-BGWK	Sikorsky S-61N	Bristow Helicopters Ltd
	G-BGWM	PA-28-181 Archer II	Thames Valley Flying Club Ltd
	G-BGWN	PA-38-112 Tomahawk	Scotia Safari Ltd/Prestwick
	G-BGWO	Jodel D.112	A. J. Court
	G-BGWP	MBB Bo 105C	Rotor Aviation Ltd
	G-BGWS	Enstrom F-280C Shark	G. Firbank & N. M. Grimshaw
	G-BGWT	WS-58 Wessex 60 Srs 1	Bristow Helicopters Ltd
	G-BGWU	PA-38-112 Tomahawk	MSF Aviation Ltd/Manchester
	G-BGWV	Aeronca 7AC Champion	RFC Flying Group/Popham
	G-BGWW	PA-23 Aztec 250E	Ski Air Ltd/Biggin Hill
	G-BGWY	Thunder Ax6-56Z balloon	J. G. O'Connel
	G-BGWZ	Eclipse Super Eagle ★	FAA Museum/Yeovilton
	G-BGXA	Piper J-3C-65 Cub	E. F. Fryer & K. Nicholls
	G-BGXB	PA-38-112 Tomahawk	Signtest Ltd/Cardiff
	G-BGXC	SOCATA TB.10 Tobago	A. J. Halliday/Shoreham
	G-BGXD	SOCATA TB.10 Tobago	Selles Dispensing Chemists Ltd
	G-BGXJ	Partenavia P.68B	Cecil Aviation Ltd/Cambridge
	G-BGXK	Cessna 310R	Airwork Ltd/Bournemouth
	G-BGXL	Bensen B.8MV	B. P. Triefus
	G-BGXN	PA-38-112 Tomahawk	Panshanger School of Flying Ltd
	G-BGXO	PA-38-112 Tomahawk	C.S.E. Aviation Ltd/Kidlington
	G-BGXP	Westland-Bell 47G-3B1	B. A. Hogan & ptnrs
	G-BGXR	Robin HR.200/100	G. M. Edwards
	G-BGXS	PA-28-236 Dakota	Debian Car Hire Ltd
	G-BGXT	SOCATA TB.10 Tobago	County Aviation Ltd/Halfpenny Green
	G-BGXU	WMB-1 balloon	C. J. Dodd & ptnrs
	G-BGXX	Jodel DR.1051M1	C. Evans
	G-BGXZ	Cessna FA.152	Falcon Flying Services Ltd/Biggin Hill
	G-BGYG	PA-28-161 Warrior II	C.S.E. Aviation Ltd/Kidlington
	G-BGYH	PA-28-161 Warrior II	C.S.E. Aviation Ltd/Kidlington
	G-BGYJ	Boeing 737-204	Britannia Airways Ltd Sir Barnes Wallis/Luton
	G-BGYK	Boeing 737-204	Britannia Airways Ltd R. J. Mitchell/Luton
	G-BGYL	Boeing 737-204	Britannia Airways Ltd Jean Batten/Luton
	G-BGYN	PA-18 Super Cub 150	A. G. Walker
	G-BGYR	H.S.125 Srs 600B	British Aerospace/Warton
	G-BGYT	EMB-110P1 Bandeirante	Guide Leasing Ltd
	G-BGYV	EMB-110P1 Bandeirante	Business Air Travel
	G-BGZC	C.A.S.A. 1.131 Jungmann	J. E. Douglas
	G-BGZF	PA-38-112 Tomahawk	Cambrian Flying Club/Swansea
	G-BGZJ	PA-38-112 Tomahawk	W. R. C. Foyle
	G-BGZK	Westland-Bell 47G-3B1	Sensehover Ltd/Leeds
	G-BGZL	Eiri PIK-20E	D. I. Liddell-Grainger
	G-BGZN	WMB.2 Windtracker balloon	S. R. Woolfries
	G-BGZO	M.S.880B Rallye Club	K. J. Underwood
	G-BGZP	D.H.C.6 Twin Otter 310	Hubbardair Ltd
	G-BGZR	Meagher Model balloon Mk.1	S. C. Meagher
	G-BGZS	Keirs Heated Air Tube	M. N. J. Kirby
	G-BGZW	PA-38-112 Tomahawk	Cheshire Flying Services Ltd/Manchester
	G-BGZX	PA-32 Cherokee Six 260	M. H. Bishop
	G-BGZY	Jodel D.120	J. V. George
	G-BGZZ	Thunder Ax6-56 balloon	J. M. Robinson
	G-BHAA	Cessna 152	Herefordshire Aero Club Ltd/Shobdon
	G-BHAB	Cessna 152	Herefordshire Aero Club Ltd/Shobdon
	G-BHAC	Cessna A.152	Herefordshire Aero Club Ltd/Shobdon
	G-BHAD	Cessna A.152	Shropshire Aero Club Ltd/Sleap
	G-BHAF	PA-38-112 Tomahawk	Ravenair/Manchester
	G-BHAG	Scheibe SF.25E Super Falke	British Gliding Association/Lasham
	G-BHAI	Cessna F.152	Channel Islands Aero Holdings Ltd/Jersey
	G-BHAJ	Robin DR.400/160	Rowantask Ltd
	G-BHAL	Rango Saffery S.200 SS	A. M. Lindsay Anneky Panky
	G-BHAM	Thunder Ax6-56 balloon	D. Sampson
	G-BHAR	Westland-Bell 47G-3B1	E. A. L. Sturmer
	G-BHAT	Thunder Ax7-77 balloon	C. P. Witter Ltd Witter
	G-BHAV	Cessna F.152	Iceni Leasing
	G-BHAW	Cessna F.172N	W. Lancs Aero Club Ltd/Woodvale
	G-BHAX	Enstrom F-28C-UK-2	Southern Air Ltd/Shoreham

Reg.	Type	Owner or Operator	Notes
G-BHAY	PA-28RT-201 Arrow IV	Alpha Yankee Group/Newcastle	
G-BHBA	Campbell Cricket	S. M. Irwin	
G-BHBB	Colt 77A balloon	S. D. Bellew/USA	
G-BHBE	Westland-Bell 47G-3B1 (Soloy)	Dollar Air Services Ltd/Coventry	
G-BHBF	Sikorsky S-76A	Bristow Helicopters Ltd	
G-BHBG	PA-32R-300 Lance	D. A. Stewart/Birmingham	
G-BHBI	Mooney M.20J	B. K. Arthur/Exeter	
G-BHBK	Viscount V-5 balloon	B. Hargraves & B. King	
G-BHBL	L.1011-385 TriStar 200	British Airways *Largs Bay*/Heathrow	
G-BHBM	L.1011-385 TriStar 200	British Airways *Poole Bay*/Heathrow	
G-BHBN	L.1011-385 TriStar 200	British Airways *Bideford Bay*/Heathrow	
G-BHBO	L.1011-385 TriStar 200	British Airways *St Magnus Bay*/Heathrow	
G-BHBP	L.1011-385 TriStar 200	British Airways *Whitesand Bay*/Heathrow	
G-BHBR	L.1011-385 TriStar 200	British Airways *Bude Bay*/Heathrow	
G-BHBS	PA-28RT-201T Turbo Arrow IV	MX Euromark Ltd	
G-BHBT	Marquart MA.5 Charger	R. G. & C. J. Maidment/Shoreham	
G-BHBW	Westland-Bell 47G-3B1	Heliwork Ltd/Thruxton	
G-BHBZ	Partenavia P.68B	Alpine Press Ltd/Leavesden	
G-BHCC	Cessna 172M	T. Howard	
G-BHCE	Jodel D.112	G. F. M. Garner	
G-BHCF	WMB.2 Windtracker balloon	C. J. Dodd & ptnrs	
G-BHCM	Cessna F.172H	The English Connection Ltd/Panshanger	
G-BHCP	Cessna F.152	Sherburn Aero Club Ltd	
G-BHCT	PA-23 Aztec 250	Metronote Aviation Ltd/Biggin Hill	
G-BHCW	PA-22 Tri-Pacer 150	B. Brooks	
G-BHCX	Cessna F.152	A. S. Bamrah/Biggin Hill	
G-BHCZ	PA-38-112 Tomahawk	Sandwell Scaffold Co Ltd/Manchester	
G-BHDA	Shultz balloon	G. F. Fitzjohn	
G-BHDB	Maule M5-235 Lunar Rocket	M. D. Faiers	
G-BHDD	V.668 Varsity T.1 (WL626)	Historic Flight/E. Midlands	
G-BHDE	SOCATA TB.10 Tobago	D. J. M. Wilson/Denham	
G-BHDH	Douglas DC-10-30	BCal/British Airways *Sir Walter Scott*/Gatwick	
G-BHDI	Douglas DC-10-30	BCal/British Airways *Robert The Bruce*/Gatwick	
G-BHDJ	Douglas DC-10-30	B/Cal British Airways *James S. McDonnell*/Gatwick	
G-BHDK	Boeing B-29A-BN (461748) ★	Imperial War Museum/Duxford	
G-BHDM	Cessna F.152 II	Tayside Aviation Ltd/Dundee	
G-BHDO	Cessna F.182Q II	S. Richman & ptnrs/Plymouth	
G-BHDP	Cessna F.182Q II	Rimmer Aviation Ltd/Elstree	
G-BHDR	Cessna F.152 II	Tayside Aviation Ltd/Dundee	
G-BHDS	Cessna F.152 II	Tayside Aviation Ltd/Dundee	
G-BHDT	SOCATA TB.10 Tobago	W. R. C. Foyle/Luton	
G-BHDU	Cessna F.152 II	Falcon Flying Services/Biggin Hill	
G-BHDV	Cameron V-77 balloon	E. D. Price	
G-BHDW	Cessna F.152	Air South Flying Group/Shoreham	
G-BHDX	Cessna F.172N	J. R. Surbey/Cambridge	
G-BHDZ	Cessna F.172N	J. Bines	
G-BHEC	Cessna F.152	W. R. C. Foyle	
G-BHED	Cessna FA.152	TG Aviation Ltd/Manston	
G-BHEG	Jodel D.150	P. R. Underhill	
G-BHEH	Cessna 310G	Vidlow Ltd	
G-BHEK	CP.1315C-3 Super Emeraude	D. B. Winstanley/Barton	
G-BHEL	Jodel D.117	K. J. Cockrill/Ipswich	
G-BHEM	Bensen B.8M	A. Lumley	
G-BHEN	Cessna FA.152	Leicestershire Aero Club Ltd	
G-BHEO	Cessna FR.182RG	Cosworth Engineering Ltd/Coventry	
G-BHEP	Cessna 172 RG Cutlass	E. A. L. Sturmer/Booker	
G-BHET	SOCATA TB.10 Tobago	Claude Hooper Ltd	
G-BHEU	Thunder Ax7-65 balloon	M. H. R. Govett	
G-BHEV	PA-28R Cherokee Arrow 200	N. J. Taylor & ptnrs/Ipswich	
G-BHEX	Colt 56A balloon	A. S. Dear & ptnrs *Super Wasp*	
G-BHEY	Pterodactyl O.R.	High School of Hang Gliding Ltd	
G-BHEZ	Jodel D.150	E. J. Horsfall/Blackpool	
G-BHFA	Pterodactyl O.R.	High School of Hang Gliding Ltd	
G-BHFB	Pterodactyl O.R.	High School of Hang Gliding Ltd	
G-BHFC	Cessna F.152	T. G. Aviation Ltd/Manston	
G-BHFE	PA-44-180 Seminole	Grunwick Ltd/Elstree	
G-BHFF	Jodel D.112	P. J. Swain	

81

Notes	Reg.	Type	Owner or Operator
	G-BHFG	SNCAN SV-4C (45)	The Hon A. M. M. Lindsay/Booker
	G-BHFH	PA-34-200T-2 Seneca	Hendefern Ltd/Goodwood
	G-BHFI	Cessna F.152	The BAe (Warton) Flying Group/ Blackpool
	G-BHFJ	PA-28RT-201T Turbo Arrow IV	T. L. P. Delaney
	G-BHFK	PA-28-151 Warrior	Ilkeston Car Sales Ltd
	G-BHFL	PA-28 Cherokee 180	Grayswood Aviation Services Ltd/ Coventry
	G-BHFM	Murphy S.200 balloon	M. Murphy
	G-BHFR	Eiri PIK-20E-1	G. Mackie
	G-BHFS	Robin DR.400/180	Flair (Soft Drinks) Ltd/Shoreham
	G-BHFT	H.S.125 Srs 400B	British Aerospace PLC
	G-BHFZ	Saffery S.200 balloon	D. Morris
	G-BHGA	PA-31-310 Navajo	Heltor Ltd
	G-BHGC	PA-18 Super Cub 150	D. E. Schofield
	G-BHGF	Cameron V-56 balloon	I. T. & H. Seddon *Biggles*
	G-BHGG	Cessna F.172N	Bryan Aviation Ltd
	G-BHGJ	Jodel D.120	Q. M. B. Oswell
	G-BHGK	Sikorsky S-76	Bond Helicopters Ltd/Bourn
	G-BHGM	Beech 76 Duchess	Bolton Stirland International Ltd
	G-BHGN	Evans VP-1	A. R. Cameron
	G-BHGP	SOCATA TB.10 Tobago	P. A. Bennett/Edinburgh
	G-BHGR	Robin DR.315	Headcorn Flying School Ltd
	G-BHGU	WMB.2 Windtracker balloon	I. D. Bamber & ptnrs
	G-BHGX	Colt 56B balloon	M. N. Dixon
	G-BHGY	PA-28R Cherokee Arrow 200	Inca Marketing Ltd/Southend
	G-BHHB	Cameron V-77 balloon	N. L. Betts
	G-BHHE	Jodel DR.1051/M1	P. Bridges
	G-BHHG	Cessna F.152	Northamptonshire School of Flying Ltd/ Sywell
	G-BHHH	Thunder Ax7-65 balloon	C. A. Hendley (Essex) Ltd
	G-BHHI	Cessna F.152	Andrewsfield Flying Club Ltd
	G-BHHK	Cameron N-77 balloon	S. Bridge & ptnrs
	G-BHHN	Cameron V-77 balloon	Itchen Valley Balloon Group
	G-BHHR	Robin DR.400/180R	D. B. Meeks/Booker
	G-BHHX	Jodel D.112	C. F. Walter
	G-BHHY	G.164 Turbo AgCat D	Miller Aerial Spraying Ltd/Wickenby
	G-BHHZ	Rotorway Scorpion 133	P. A. Gunn & D. Willingham
	G-BHIA	Cessna F.152	W. H. Wilkins/Stapleford
	G-BHIB	Cessna F.182Q	Ingamells (Machinery Services) Ltd & Spittalgate Motors Ltd
	G-BHIC	Cessna F.182Q	General Building Services Ltd/Leeds
	G-BHID	SOCATA TB.10 Tobago	W. B. Pinckney & Sons Farming Co Ltd
	G-BHIH	Cessna F.172N	Watkiss Group Aviation Ltd/ Biggin Hill
	G-BHII	Cameron V-77 balloon	Starcrete Ltd
	G-BHIJ	Eiri PIK-20E-1	R. W. Hall & ptnrs/Swanton Morley
	G-BHIK	Adam RA-14 Loisirs	L. Lewis
	G-BHIN	Cessna F.152	Doncaster Aero Club Ltd
	G-BHIR	PA-28R Cherokee Arrow 200	Cheshire Flying Services Ltd/ Manchester
	G-BHIS	Thunder Ax7-65 balloon	Hedgehoppers Balloon Group
	G-BHIT	SOCATA TB.9 Tampico	EAC Components Ltd
	G-BHIY	Cessna F.150K	W. H. Cole
	G-BHJA	Cessna A.152	Cellobay Ltd
	G-BHJB	Cessna A.152	E. E. Fenning & Son
	G-BHJF	SOCATA TB.10 Tobago	D. G. Dedman/Leavesden
	G-BHJI	Mooney M.20J	T. R. Bamber & B. Refson/Elstree
	G-BHJK	Maule M5-235C Lunar Rocket	G. A. & B. J. Finch
	G-BHJN	Fournier RF-4D	B. Houghton
	G-BHJO	PA-28-161 Warrior II	Nairn Flying Services Ltd/Inverness
	G-BHJR	Saffery S.200 balloon	R. S. Sweeting
	G-BHJS	Partenavia P.68B	Tewin Aviation/Panshanger
	G-BHJU	Robin DR.400/2+2	Harlow Transport Services Ltd/ Headcorn
	G-BHJW	Cessna F.152	Leicestershire Aero Club Ltd
	G-BHJY	EMB-110P1 Bandeirante	Euroair Transport Ltd/National Airways
	G-BHJZ	EMB-110P2 Bandeirante	Jersey European Airways
	G-BHKA	Evans VP-1	M. L. Perry
	G-BHKE	Bensen B.8MV	V. C. Whitehead
	G-BHKH	Cameron O-65 balloon	D. G. Body
	G-BHKJ	Cessna 421C	United Nations/Pakistan
	G-BHKR	Colt 14A balloon	British Balloon Museum

Reg.	Type	Owner or Operator	Notes
G-BHKT	Jodel D.112	R. Featherstone & ptnrs/Old Sarum	
G-BHKV	AA-5A Cheetah	Metronote Business Machines Ltd/ Biggin Hill	
G-BHKX	Beech 76 Duchess	A.B. Plant (Aviation) Ltd/Bristol	
G-BHKY	Cessna 310R ll	Airwork Ltd/Perth	
G-BHLE	Robin DR.400/180	L. H. Mayall	
G-BHLF	H.S.125 Srs 700B	The Marconi Co Ltd/Luton	
G-BHLH	Robin DR.400/180	Trinecare Ltd/Southend	
G-BHLJ	Saffery-Rigg S.200 balloon	I. A. Rigg	
G-BHLK	GA-7 Cougar	Trent Air Services Ltd/Cranfield	
G-BHLM	Cessna 421C	Brush Electrical Co Ltd/E. Midlands	
G-BHLP	Cessna 441	Rogers Aviation Ltd/Cranfield	
G-BHLT	D.H.82A Tiger Moth	R. L. Godwin/Enstone	
G-BHLU	Fournier RF-3	G. G. Milton/Felthorpe	
G-BHLW	Cessna 120	S. M. Hannan & M. J. Cross	
G-BHLX	AA-5B Tiger	Tiger Aviation (Jersey) Ltd	
G-BHLY	Sikorsky S-76A	Bristow Helicopters Ltd	
G-BHMA	SIPA 903	H. J. Taggart	
G-BHMC	M.S.880B Rallye Club	The G-BHMC Group	
G-BHMD	Rand KR-2	W. D. Francis	
G-BHME	WMB.2 Windtracker balloon	I. R. Bell & ptnrs	
G-BHMG	Cessna FA.152	Channel Islands Aero Holdings (Jersey) Ltd	
G-BHMH	Cessna FA.152	Flairhire Ltd/Redhill	
G-BHMI	Cessna F.172N	W. Lancashire Aero Club Ltd (G-WADE)/ Blackpool	
G-BHMJ	Avenger T.200-2112 balloon	R. Light Lord Anthony 1	
G-BHMK	Avenger T.200-2112 balloon	P. Kinder Lord Anthony 2	
G-BHML	Avenger T.200-2112 balloon	L. Caulfield Lord Anthony 3	
G-BHMM	Avenger T.200-2112 balloon	M. Murphy Lord Anthony 4	
G-BHMO	PA-20M Cerpa Special (Pacer)	D. Doleac	
G-BHMR	Stinson 108-3	E. H. S. Warner	
G-BHMT	Evans VP-1	P. E. J. Sturgeon	
G-BHMU	Colt 21A balloon	J. R. Parkington & Co Ltd	
G-BHMW	F.27 Friendship Mk 200	Air UK/Norwich	
G-BHMX	F.27 Friendship Mk 200	Air UK/Norwich	
G-BHMY	F.27 Friendship Mk 200	Air UK/Norwich	
G-BHMZ	F.27 Friendship Mk 200	Air UK R. J. Mitchell/Norwich	
G-BHNA	Cessna F.152	Sheffield Aero Club Ltd	
G-BHNC	Cameron O-65 balloon	D. & C. Bareford	
G-BHND	Cameron N-65 balloon	Hunter & Sons (Wells) Ltd	
G-BHNE	Boeing 727-2J4	Dan-Air Services Ltd/Gatwick	
G-BHNF	Boeing 727-2J4	Dan-Air Services Ltd/Gatwick	
G-BHNI	Cessna 404 Titan	Interflight (Air Charters) Ltd/Gatwick	
G-BHNK	Jodel D.120A	F. G. Miskelly	
G-BHNL	Jodel D.112	P. E. Barker	
G-BHNM	PA-44-180 Seminole	Cearte Tiles Ltd/Coventry	
G-BHNN	PA-32R-301 Saratoga SP	H. Young Transport Ltd/ Southampton	
G-BHNO	PA-28-181 Archer II	Davison Plant Hire Co/Compton Abbas	
G-BHNP	Eiri PIK-20E-1	M. Astley/Husbands Bosworth	
G-BHNR	Cameron N-77 balloon	Bath University Hot-Air Balloon Club	
G-BHNT	Cessna F.172N	I. J. Boyd & D. J. McCooke	
G-BHNU	Cessna F.172N	B. Swindell (Haulage) Ltd/Barton	
G-BHNV	Westland-Bell 47G-3B1	Leyline Helicopters Ltd	
G-BHNX	Jodel D.117	R. V. Rendall	
G-BHNY	Cessna 425	Eclipsol Oil Ltd/Birmingham	
G-BHOA	Robin DR.400/160	Ferguson Aviation Ltd	
G-BHOF	Sikorsky S-61N	Bristow Helicopters Ltd	
G-BHOG	Sikorsky S-61N	Bristow Helicopters Ltd	
G-BHOH	Sikorsky S-61N	Bristow Helicopters Ltd	
G-BHOI	Westland-Bell 47G-3B1	Fisher Helicopter Spares Ltd	
G-BHOL	Jodel DR.1050	B. D. Deubelbeiss	
G-BHOM	PA-18 Super Cub 95	C. H. A. Bott	
G-BHOO	Thunder Ax7-65 balloon	D. Livesey & J. M. Purves Scraps	
G-BHOP	Thunder Ax3 balloon	B. R. & M. Boyle	
G-BHOR	PA-28-161 Warrior II.	D. P. Stringfield	
G-BHOT	Cameron V-65 balloon	Dante Balloon Group	
G-BHOU	Cameron V-65 balloon	F. W. Barnes	
G-BHOW	Beech 95-58P Baron	Anglo-African Machinery Ltd/ Coventry	
G-BHOZ	SOCATA TB.9 Tampico	Propax (UK) Ltd	
G-BHPJ	Eagle Microlite	G. Breen/Enstone	

Notes	Reg.	Type	Owner or Operator
	G-BHPK	Piper J-3C-65 Cub (479865)	H. W. Sage/Sywell
	G-BHPL	C.A.S.A. 1.131E Jungmann	M. G. Jeffries
	G-BHPM	PA-18 Super Cub 95	P. I. Morgans
	G-BHPN	Colt 14 balloon	Colt Balloons Ltd
	G-BHPO	Colt 14A balloon	C. J. Boxall
	G-BHPS	Jodel D.120A	C. J. Francis/Swansea
	G-BHPT	Piper J-3C-65 Cub	Airmiles Ltd
	G-BHPX	Cessna 152	Air South Flying Group/Shoreham
	G-BHPY	Cessna 152	Christopher Lunn & Co
	G-BHPZ	Cessna 172N	O'Brian Properties Ltd/Redhill
	G-BHRA	R. Commander 114A	M. I. Edwards/Norwich
	G-BHRB	Cessna F.152	Light Planes (Lancashire) Ltd/ Barton
	G-BHRC	PA-28-161 Warrior II	Sherwood Flying Club Ltd/Tollerton
	G-BHRD	D.H.C.1 Chipmunk 22 (WP977)	ISF Aviation Ltd/Wellesbourne
	G-BHRE	Persephone S.200 balloon	Cupro-Sapphire Ltd
	G-BHRF	Airborne Industries AB400 gas balloon	Balloon Stable Ltd
	G-BHRH	Cessna FA.150K	Merlin Flying Club Ltd/Hucknall
	G-BHRI	Saffery S.200 balloon	N. J. & H. L. Dunnington
	G-BHRM	Cessna F.152	Angelsword Ltd/Wellesbourne
	G-BHRN	Cessna F.152	Channel Islands Aero Holdings Ltd/ Jersey
	G-BHRO	R. Commander 112A	John Raymond Transport Ltd/Cardiff
	G-BHRP	PA-44-180 Seminole	A. J. Hows/Denham
	G-BHRR	CP.301A Emeraude	T. W. Offen
	G-BHRS	ICA IS-28M2	British Aerospace PLC/Woodford
	G-BHRV	Mooney M.20J	Tecnovil Equipamentos Industriales
	G-BHRW	Jodel DR.221	J. T. M. Ball/Redhill
	G-BHRY	Colt 56A balloon	A. S. Davidson
	G-BHSA	Cessna 152	Skyviews & General Ltd/Sherburn
	G-BHSB	Cessna 172N	W. R. Craddock & Son Ltd/Sturgate
	G-BHSD	Scheibe SF.25E Super Falke	Lasham Gliding Soc Ltd
	G-BHSE	R. Commander 114	604 Sqdn Flying Group Ltd
	G-BHSF	AA-5A Cheetah	D.S. Plant Hire Ltd (G-BHAS)
	G-BHSL	C.A.S.A. 1.131 Jungmann	Cotswold Flying Group/Badminton
	G-BHSM	AB-206B JetRanger 2	Dollar Air Services Ltd/Coventry
	G-BHSN	Cameron N-56 balloon	Ballooning Endeavours Ltd
	G-BHSP	Thunder Ax7-77Z balloon	Chicago Instruments Ltd
	G-BHSS	Pitts S-1C Special	Booker Pitts Syndicate
	G-BHST	Hughes 369D	Autobase Rotary Ltd
	G-BHSU	H.S.125 Srs 700B	Shell Aircraft Ltd/Heathrow
	G-BHSV	H.S.125 Srs 700B	Shell Aircraft Ltd/Heathrow
	G-BHSW	H.S.125 Srs 700B	Shell Aircraft Ltd/Heathrow
	G-BHSY	Jodel DR.1050	S. R. Orwin & T. R. Allebone
	G-BHTA	PA-28-236 Dakota	Stenloss Ltd/Sywell
	G-BHTC	Jodel DR.1050/M1	S. R. Winder
	G-BHTD	Cessna T.188C AgHusky	Dallah-ADS Ltd/Egypt
	G-BHTG	Thunder Ax6-56 balloon	F. R. & Mrs S. H. MacDonald
	G-BHTH	T-6G Texan (2807)	A. Reynard/Kidlington
	G-BHTI	SA.102.5 Cavalier	R. Cochrane
	G-BHTM	Cameron 80 Can SS balloon	BP Oil Ltd
	G-BHTP	PA-31T-500 Cheyenne I	Ugland (UK) Ltd/Stansted
	G-BHTR	Bell 206B JetRanger 3	Huktra (UK) Ltd
	G-BHTT	Cessna 500 Citation	Lucas Industries Ltd/Birmingham
	G-BHTV	Cessna 310R	Aviation Beauport Ltd/Jersey
	G-BHUB	Douglas C-47 (315509) ★	Imperial War Museum/Duxford
	G-BHUE	Jodel DR.1050	M. Cowan
	G-BHUG	Cessna 172N	McArgent Aviation Ltd
	G-BHUH	Cremer PC.14 balloon	P. A. Cremer
	G-BHUI	Cessna 152	J. MacDonald
	G-BHUJ	Cessna 172N	Three Counties Aero Club Ltd/ Blackbushe
	G-BHUM	D.H.82A Tiger Moth	S. G. Towers
	G-BHUN	PZL-104 Wilga 35	W. Radwanski/Lasham
	G-BHUO	Evans VP-2	R. A. Povall
	G-BHUP	Cessna F.152	Light Planes (Lancashire) Ltd/ Barton
	G-BHUR	Thunder Ax3 balloon	B. F. G. Ribbons
	G-BHUU	PA-25 Pawnee 235	Scanrho Aviation
	G-BHUV	PA-25 Pawnee 235	Farmwork Services (Eastern) Ltd
	G-BHVB	PA-28-161 Warrior II	R.J.S. Aviation/Halfpenny Green
	G-BHVC	Cessna 172RG Cutlass	Ian Willis Publicity Ltd/Panshanger
	G-BHVE	Saffery S.330 balloon	P. M. Randles

Reg.	Type	Owner or Operator	Notes
G-BHVF	Jodel D.150A	C. A. Parker & ptnrs/Sywell	
G-BHVH	Boeing 737-2T5	Orion Airways Ltd/E. Midlands	
G-BHVM	Cessna 152	Merrett Aviation Ltd	
G-BHVN	Cessna 152	Three Counties Aero Club Ltd/ Blackbushe	
G-BHVP	Cessna 182Q	Air Tows/Lasham	
G-BHVR	Cessna 172N	Air Tows/Blackbushe	
G-BHVT	Boeing 727-212	Dan-Air Services Ltd/Gatwick	
G-BHVV	Piper J-3C-65 Cub	A. E. Molton	
G-BHVZ	Cessna 180	R. Moore/Blackpool	
G-BHWA	Cessna F.152	Wickenby Aviation Ltd	
G-BHWB	Cessna F.152	Wickenby Aviation Ltd	
G-BHWE	Boeing 737-204ADV	Britannia Airways Ltd/ Sir Sidney Camm/Luton	
G-BHWF	Boeing 737-204ADV	Britannia Airways Ltd/ Lord Brabazon of Tara/Luton	
G-BHWG	Mahatma S.200SR balloon	H. W. Gandy Spectrum	
G-BHWH	Weedhopper JC-24A	G. A. Clephane	
G-BHWK	M.S.880B Rallye Club	J. Gibbs	
G-BHWN	WMB.3 Windtracker 200 balloon	C. J. Dodd & G. J. Luckett	
G-BHWR	AA-5A Cheetah	Denham School of Flying Ltd	
G-BHWS	Cessna F.152	Stapleford Flying Club	
G-BHWT	Short SD3-30	British Air Ferries/Southend	
G-BHWW	Cessna U.206G	Aerotime Ltd/Glenrothes	
G-BHWY	PA-28R-200 Cherokee Arrow	Rack Delta Ltd/Blackbushe	
G-BHWZ	PA-28-181 Archer II	Symtec Computer Service Ltd	
G-BHXD	Jodel D.120	R. M. White	
G-BHXE	Thunder Ax3 balloon	C. Benning/W. Germany	
G-BHXJ	Nord 1203/2 Norecrin (103)	R. E. Coates/Booker	
G-BHXK	PA-28 Cherokee 140	R. A. Bulpit & A. J. Dlae	
G-BHXL	Evans VP-2	T. W. Woolley	
G-BHXN	Van's RV.3	P. R. Hing	
G-BHXO	Colt 14A balloon	Colt Balloons Ltd/Sweden	
G-BHXS	Jodel D.120	S. Billington	
G-BHXT	Thunder Ax6-56Z balloon	Ocean Traffic Services Ltd	
G-BHXU	AB-206B JetRanger 3	Castle Air Charters Ltd	
G-BHXV	AB-206B JetRanger 3	G. Greenall (G-OWJM)	
G-BHXY	Piper J-3C-65 Cub (44-79609)	Chatteam Ltd	
G-BHYA	Cessna R.182RG II	MLP Aviation Ltd/Elstree	
G-BHYB	Sikorsky S-76A	British International Helicopters Ltd/Beccles	
G-BHYC	Cessna 172RG Cutlass	T. G. Henshall	
G-BHYD	Cessna R.172K XP II	Sylmar Aviation Services Ltd	
G-BHYE	PA-34-200T-2 Seneca	C.S.E. Aviation Ltd/Kidlington	
G-BHYF	PA-34-200T-2 Seneca	C.S.E. Aviation Ltd/Kidlington	
G-BHYG	PA-34-200T-2 Seneca	C.S.E. Aviation Ltd/Kidlington	
G-BHYI	Stampe SV-4A	P. A. Irwin & W. C. Medcalfe	
G-BHYN	Evans VP-2	A. B. Cameron	
G-BHYO	Cameron N-77 balloon	C. Sisson	
G-BHYP	Cessna F.172M	J. Burgess & ptnrs/Blackpool	
G-BHYR	Cessna F.172M	Alumvale Ltd/Stapleford	
G-BHYV	Evans VP-1	L. Chiappi	
G-BHYW	AB-206B JetRanger	Gleneagles Helicopter Services (Scotland) Ltd	
G-BHYX	Cessna 152 II	Stanton Aircraft Management Ltd	
G-BHZA	Piper J-3C-65 Cub	R. G. Warwick	
G-BHZE	PA-28-181 Archer II	E. O. Smith & Co Ltd/Tollerton	
G-BHZF	Evans VP-2	R. G. Boyes/Dunkeswell	
G-BHZG	Monnet Sonerai II	V. W. B. Davies/Shoreham	
G-BHZH	Cessna F.152	Havelet Leasing Ltd	
G-BHZJ	Hughes StratoSphere 150 balloon	P. J. Hughes	
G-BHZK	AA-5B Tiger	Achandunie Farming Co/Elstree	
G-BHZM	Jodel DR.1050	G. H. Wylde/Manchester	
G-BHZO	AA-5A Cheetah	Scotia Safari Ltd/Prestwick	
G-BHZU	Piper J-3C-65 Cub	J. K. Tomkinson	
G-BHZV	Jodel D.120A	J. G. Munro/Perth	
G-BHZX	Thunder Ax7-65A balloon	S. C. Kinsey & G. E. Harns	
G-BHZY	Monnet Sonerai II	C. A. Keech	
G-BIAA	SOCATA TB.9 Tampico	B. D. Greenwood	

Notes	Reg.	Type	Owner or Operator
	G-BIAB	SOCATA TB.9 Tampico	M. V. Male
	G-BIAC	M.S.894E Rallye Minerva	Anpal Finance Ltd & Aerial Facilities Ltd/ Biggin Hill
	G-BIAH	Jodel D.112	D. Mitchell
	G-BIAI	WMB.2 Windtracker balloon	I. Chadwick
	G-BIAK	SOCATA TB.10 Tobago	Trent Combustion Components Ltd/ Tollerton
	G-BIAL	Rango NA.8 balloon	A. M. Lindsay
	G-BIAO	Evans VP-2	G. J. Walker/Popham
	G-BIAP	PA-16 Clipper	I. M. Callier & P. J. Bish/White Waltham
	G-BIAR	Rigg Skyliner II balloon	I. A. Rigg
	G-BIAU	Sopwith Pup Replica (N6452)	FAA Museum/Yeovilton
	G-BIAV	Sikorsky S-76A	British International Helicopters Ltd
	G-BIAW	Sikorsky S-76A	British International Helicopters Ltd
	G-BIAX	Taylor JT.2 Titch	G. F. Rowley
	G-BIAY	AA-5 Traveler	M. D. Dupay & ptnrs
	G-BIBA	SOCATA TB.9 Tampico	Compak Board Ltd/Ipswich
	G-BIBB	Mooney M.20C	Gloucestershire Flying Club/ Staverton
	G-BIBC	Cessna 310R	Airwork Ltd/Perth
	G-BIBD	Rotec Rally 2B	A. Clarke
	G-BIBF	Smith A12 Sport balloon	T. J. Smith
	G-BIBG	Sikorsky S-76A	Bristow Helicopters Ltd
	G-BIBJ	Enstrom F-280C-UK Shark	W. W. Kendrick & Sons Ltd/ Halfpenny Green
	G-BIBK	Taylor JT.2 Titch	T. C. Horner
	G-BIBN	Cessna FA.150K	P. H. Lewis
	G-BIBO	Cameron V-65 balloon	Southern Balloon Group
	G-BIBP	AA-5A Cheetah	Scotia Safari Ltd/Prestwick
	G-BIBS	Cameron P-20 balloon	Cameron Balloons Ltd
	G-BIBT	AA-5B Tiger	Fergusons (Blyth) Ltd/Newcastle
	G-BIBU	Morris Ax7-77 balloon	K. Morris
	G-BIBV	WMB.3 Windtracker balloon	P. B. Street
	G-BIBW	Cessna F.172N	Deltair Ltd/Chester
	G-BIBX	WMB.2 Windtracker balloon	I. A. Rigg
	G-BIBY	Beech F33A Bonanza	M. J. H. Raymont
	G-BIBZ	Thunder Ax3 balloon	F. W. Barnes
	G-BICB	Rotec Rally 2B	J. D. Lye & A. P. Jones
	G-BICC	Vulture Tx3 balloon	C. P. Clitheroe
	G-BICD	Auster 5	J. A. S. Baldry & ptnrs
	G-BICE	AT-6C Harvard IIA (CE)	C. M. L. Edwards/Ipswich
	G-BICG	Cessna F.152	R. M. Clarke/Leicester
	G-BICI	Cameron R-833 balloon	Ballooning Endeavours Ltd
	G-BICJ	Monnet Sonerai II	D. J. Willison
	G-BICM	Colt 56A balloon	T. A. R. & S. Turner
	G-BICN	F.8L Falco	R. J. Barber
	G-BICO	Neale Mitefly balloon	T. J. Neale
	G-BICP	Robin DR.360	Bravo India Flying Group/Woodvale
	G-BICR	Jodel D.120A	S. W. C. Hall & ptnrs/Redhill
	G-BICS	Robin R.2100A	AJE Gearing Co Ltd/Popham
	G-BICT	Evans VP-1	A. S. Coombe & D. L. Tribe
	G-BICU	Cameron V-56 balloon	I. S. Clarke
	G-BICW	PA-28-161 Warrior II	Fastraven Ltd/Cranfield
	G-BICX	Maule M5-235C Lunar Rocket	Stanton Aircraft Management Ltd/ Biggin Hill
	G-BICY	PA-23 Apache 160	A. M. Lynn/Sibson
	G-BIDD	Evans VP-1	J. E. Wedgbury
	G-BIDE	CP.301A Emeraude	D. Elliott
	G-BIDF	Cessna F.172P	J. J. Baumhardt/Southend
	G-BIDG	Jodel D.150A	D. R. Gray/Barton
	G-BIDH	Cessna 152	Midland Aircraft Leasing Ltd/ Birmingham
	G-BIDI	PA-28R-201 Arrow III	M. J. Webb/Birmingham
	G-BIDJ	PA-18 Super Cub 150	Marchington Gliding Club
	G-BIDK	PA-18 Super Cub 150	Scottish Gliding Union Ltd
	G-BIDM	Cessna F.172H	D. A. Mortimore/Humberside
	G-BIDO	CP.301A Emeraude	A. R. Plumb
	G-BIDP	PA-28-181 Archer II	H. S. Elkins/Bristol
	G-BIDT	Cameron A375 balloon	Ballooning Endeavours Ltd
	G-BIDU	Cameron V-77 balloon	E. Eleazor
	G-BIDV	Colt 14A balloon	International Distillers & Vintners (House Trade) Ltd
	G-BIDW	Sopwith 1½ Strutter replica (A8226) ★	RAF Museum/Hendon

Reg.	Type	Owner or Operator	Notes
G-BIDX	Jodel D.112	H. N. Nuttall & R. P. Walley	
G-BIDY	WMB.2 Windtracker balloon	D. M. Campion	
G-BIDZ	Colt 21A balloon	Hot Air Balloon Co Ltd/S. Africa	
G-BIEC	AB-206A JetRanger 2	Autair Helicopters Ltd	
G-BIEF	Cameron V-77 balloon	D. S. Bush	
G-BIEH	Sikorsky S-76A	Bond Helicopters Ltd/Bourn	
G-BIEJ	Sikorsky S-76A	Bristow Helicopters Ltd	
G-BIEK	WMB.4 Windtracker balloon	P. B. Street	
G-BIEL	WMB.4 Windtracker balloon	A. T. Walden	
G-BIEM	D.H.C.6 Twin Otter 310	Loganair Ltd/Glasgow	
G-BIEN	Jodel D.120A	Echo November Flight/Bristol	
G-BIEO	Jodel D.112	R. G. Hallom	
G-BIEP	PA-28-181 Archer II	Bickerton Aerodromes Ltd	
G-BIER	Rutan LongEz	V. Mossor	
G-BIES	Maule M5-235C Lunar Rocket	William Proctor Farms	
G-BIET	Cameron O-77 balloon	G. M. Westley	
G-BIEV	AA-5A Cheetah	A. J. Hows	
G-BIEW	Cessna U.206G	G. D. Atkinson/Guernsey	
G-BIEX	Andreasson BA-4B	H. P. Burrill/Sherburn	
G-BIEY	PA-28-151 Warrior	J. A. Pothecary/Shoreham	
G-BIFA	Cessna 310R-II	Land & Estates Consultants Ltd/ Biggin Hill	
G-BIFB	PA-28 Cherokee 150	C. J. Reed/Elstree	
G-BIFC	Colt 14A balloon	Colt Balloons Ltd	
G-BIFD	R. Commander 114	K. E. Armstrong	
G-BIFE	Cessna A.185F	Conguess Aviation Ltd	
G-BIFN	Bensen B.8M	B. Gunn	
G-BIFO	Evans VP-1	A. N. Wells	
G-BIFP	Colt 56C balloon	J. Philp	
G-BIFT	Cessna F.150L	Phoenix Aviation (Bedford) Ltd/ Cranfield	
G-BIFU	Short Skyhawk balloon	D. K. Short	
G-BIFV	Jodel D.150	J. H. Kirkham/Barton	
G-BIFW	Scruggs BL.2 Wunda balloon	D. Morris	
G-BIFY	Cessna F.150L	Phoenix Aviation (Bedford) Ltd/ Cranfield	
G-BIFZ	Partenavia P.68C	Abbey Hill Vehicle Services	
G-BIGB	Bell 212	Adastral Aircraft (UK) Ltd	
G-BIGD	Cameron V-77 balloon	D. L. Clark *Frog*	
G-BIGE	Champion Cloudseeker balloon	A. Foster	
G-BIGF	Thunder Ax7-77 balloon	M. D. Stever & C. A. Allen	
G-BIGG	Saffery S.200 balloon	R. S. Sweeting	
G-BIGH	Piper L-4H Cub	W. McNally	
G-BIGJ	Cessna F.172M	Page Vehicle Hire (Strumpshaw) Ltd & Page Security Ltd/Norwich	
G-BIGK	Taylorcraft BC-12D	B. A. Slater	
G-BIGL	Cameron O-65 balloon	P. L. Mossman	
G-BIGM	Avenger T.200-2112 balloon	M. Murphy	
G-BIGN	Attic Srs 1 balloon	G. Nettleship	
G-BIGP	Bensen B.8M	R. H. S. Cooper	
G-BIGR	Avenger T.200-2112 balloon	R. Light	
G-BIGU	Bensen B.8M	J. R. Martin	
G-BIGX	Bensen B.8M	J. R. Martin	
G-BIGY	Cameron V-65 balloon	Dante Balloon Group	
G-BIGZ	Scheibe SF.25B Falke	K. Ballington	
G-BIHB	Scruggs BL.2 Wunda balloon	D. Morris	
G-BIHC	Scruggs BL.2 Wunda balloon	P. D. Kiddell	
G-BIHD	Robin DR.400/160	G. R. Pope & ptnrs/Biggin Hill	
G-BIHE	Cessna FA.152	Inverness Flying Services Ltd	
G-BIHF	SE-5A Replica (F943)	K. J. Garrett *Lady Di*/Booker	
G-BIHG	PA-28 Cherokee 140	T. Parmenter/Clacton	
G-BIHH	Sikorsky S-61N	Bristow Helicopters Ltd	
G-BIHI	Cessna 172M	J. H. Ashby-Rogers	
G-BIHN	Skyship 500 airship	Airship Industries Ltd/Cardington	
G-BIHO	D.H.C.6 Twin Otter 310	Brymon Aviation Ltd/Plymouth	
G-BIHP	Van Den Bemden gas balloon	J. J. Harris	
G-BIHR	WMB.2 Windtracker balloon	R. S. Sweeting	
G-BIHT	PA-17 Vagabond	G. D. Thomson/Coventry	
G-BIHU	Saffery S.200 balloon	B. L. King	
G-BIHW	Aeronca A65TAC (2-7767)	I. H. Logan	
G-BIHX	Bensen B.8M	C. C. Irvine	

Notes	Reg.	Type	Owner or Operator
	G-BIHY	Isaacs Fury	P. C. Butler
	G-BIIA	Fournier RF-3	T. M. W. Webster
	G-BIIB	Cessna F.172M	Civil Service Flying Club (Biggin Hill) Ltd
	G-BIIC	Scruggs BL.2 Wunda balloon	S. J. Hoder & D. Cockerill
	G-BIID	PA-18 Super Cub 95	L. Dickson & M. Winter/Aberdeen
	G-BIIE	Cessna F.172P	Shoreham Flight Simulation Ltd/ Bournemouth
	G-BIIF	Fournier RF-4D	A. P. Walsh (G-BVET)
	G-BIIG	Thunder Ax-6-56Z balloon	P. Rose
	G-BIIH	Scruggs BL.2T Turbo balloon	B. M. Scott
	G-BIIJ	Cessna F.152	Leicestershire Aero Club Ltd
	G-BIIK	M.S.883 Rallye 115	P. Rose
	G-BIIL	Thunder Ax6-56 balloon	G. W. Reader
	G-BIIM	Scruggs BL.2A Wunda balloon	K. D. Head
	G-BIIT	PA-28-161 Warrior II	Tayside Aviation Ltd/Dundee
	G-BIIV	PA-28-181 Archer II	Stratton Motor Co Ltd
	G-BIIW	Rango NA.10 balloon	Rango Kite Co
	G-BIIX	Rango NA.12 balloon	Rango Kite Co
	G-BIIZ	Great Lakes 2T-1A Sport Trainer	The Hon A. M. M. Lindsay/Booker
	G-BIJA	Scruggs BL.2A Wunda balloon	P. L. E. Bennett
	G-BIJB	PA-18-150 Super Cub	Essex Gliding Club/North Weald
	G-BIJC	AB-206B JetRanger	Anglia Helicopters Ltd/Southend
	G-BIJD	Bo 208C Junior	D. J. Dulborough/Headcorn
	G-BIJE	Piper L-4A Cub	K. G. & J. Wakefield
	G-BIJS	Luton LA-4A Minor	I. J. Smith
	G-BIJT	AA-5A Cheetah	Mid-Sussex Timber Co Ltd
	G-BIJU	CP.301A Emeraude	D. Brooker & ptnrs (G-BHTX)/ Southend
	G-BIJV	Cessna F.152 II	Falcon Flying Services/Biggin Hill
	G-BIJW	Cessna F.152 II	G. K. Mitchell Ltd
	G-BIJX	Cessna F.152 II	Civil Service Flying Club Ltd/ Biggin Hill
	G-BIJZ	Skyventurer Mk 1 balloon	R. Sweeting
	G-BIKA	Boeing 757-236	British Airways *Dover Castle*/ Heathrow
	G-BIKB	Boeing 757-236	British Airways *Windsor Castle*/ Heathrow
	G-BIKC	Boeing 757-236	British Airways *Edinburgh Castle*/ Heathrow
	G-BIKD	Boeing 757-236	British Airways *Caernarvon Castle*/ Heathrow
	G-BIKE	PA-28R Cherokee Arrow 200	R. V. Webb Ltd/Elstree
	G-BIKF	Boeing 757-236	British Airways *Carrikfergus Castle*/ Heathrow
	G-BIKG	Boeing 757-236	British Airways *Stirling Castle*/ Heathrow
	G-BIKH	Boeing 757-236	British Airways *Richmond Castle*/ Heathrow
	G-BIKI	Boeing 757-236	British Airways *Tintagel Castle*/ Heathrow
	G-BIKJ	Boeing 757-236	British Airways *Conway Castle*/ Heathrow
	G-BIKK	Boeing 757-236	British Airways *Eilean Donan Castle*/ Heathrow
	G-BIKL	Boeing 757-236	British Airways *Nottingham Castle*/ Heathrow
	G-BIKM	Boeing 757-236	British Airways *Glamis Castle*/ Heathrow
	G-BIKN	Boeing 757-236	British Airways *Bodiam Castle*/ Heathrow
	G-BIKO	Boeing 757-236	British Airways *Harlech Castle*/ Heathrow
	G-BIKP	Boeing 757-236	British Airways *Enniskillen Castle*/ Heathrow
	G-BIKR	Boeing 757-236	British Airways *Bamburgh Castle*/ Heathrow
	G-BIKS	Boeing 757-236	British Airways *Corfe Castle*/ Heathrow
	G-BIKT	Boeing 757-236	British Airways*Carisbrooke Castle*/ Heathrow
	G-BIKU	Boeing 757-236	British Airways *Inverrary Castle*/ Heathrow

Reg.	Type	Owner or Operator	Notes
G-BIKV	Boeing 757-236	British Airways *Raglan Castle*/Heathrow	
G-BIKW	Boeing 757-236	British Airways *Colchester Castle*/Heathrow	
G-BIKX	Boeing 757-236	British Airways *Warwick Castle*/Heathrow	
G-BIKY	Boeing 757-236	British Airways *Leeds Castle*/Heathrow	
G-BIKZ	Boeing 757-236	British Airways *Kenilworth Castle*/Heathrow	
G-BILA	Daletol DM.165L Viking	R. Lamplough (*stored*)	
G-BILB	WMB.2 Windtracker balloon	B. L. King	
G-BILE	Scruggs BL.2B balloon	P. D. Ridout	
G-BILF	Practavia Sprite 125	G. Harfield	
G-BILG	Scruggs BL.2B balloon	P. D. Ridout	
G-BILI	Piper J-3C-65 Cub	D. M. Boddy & G. R. Mills	
G-BILJ	Cessna FA.152	Shoreham Flight Simulation Ltd/Bournemouth	
G-BILK	Cessna FA.152	A. Blair/Biggin Hill	
G-BILL	PA-25 Pawnee 235	Farmair (Kent) Ltd/Headcorn	
G-BILP	Cessna 152 II	Skyviews & General Ltd	
G-BILR	Cessna 152	Skyviews & General Ltd	
G-BILS	Cessna 152	Skyviews & General Ltd	
G-BILU	Cessna 172RG	Melrose Pigs Ltd	
G-BILX	Colt 31A balloon	Hot Air Balloon Co Ltd	
G-BILZ	Taylor JT.1 Monoplane	R. A. Cooper	
G-BIMK	Tiger T.200 Srs 1 balloon	M. K. Baron	
G-BIML	Turner Super T.40A	R. T. Callow	
G-BIMM	PA-18 Super Cub 150	D. S. & I. M. Morgan	
G-BIMN	Steen Skybolt	C. R. Williamson	
G-BIMO	Stampe SV-4C	G. A. Breen	
G-BIMT	Cessna FA.152	Staverton Flying Services Ltd	
G-BIMU	Sikorsky S-61N	Bristow Helicopters Ltd	
G-BIMX	Rutan Vari-Eze	A. S. Knowles	
G-BIMZ	Beech 76 Duchess	Barrein Engineers Ltd/Lulsgate	
G-BINA	Saffery S.9 balloon	A. P. Bashford	
G-BINB	WMB.2A Windtracker balloon	S. R. Woolfries	
G-BINE	Scruggs BL.2A Wunda balloon	M. Gilbey	
G-BINF	Saffery S.200 balloon	T. Lewis	
G-BING	Cessna F.172P	J. E. M. Patrick	
G-BINH	D.H.82A Tiger Moth	Arrow Air Services (Engineering) Ltd (*stored*)/Felthorpe	
G-BINI	Scruggs BL.2C balloon	S. R. Woolfries	
G-BINJ	Rango NA.12 balloon	M. R. Haslam	
G-BINL	Scruggs BL.2B balloon	P. D. Ridout	
G-BINM	Scruggs BL.2B balloon	P. D. Ridout	
G-BINN	Unicorn UE.1A balloon	Unicorn Group	
G-BINO	Evans VP-1	J. I. Visser	
G-BINR	Unicorn UE.1A balloon	Unicorn Group	
G-BINS	Unicorn UE.2A balloon	Unicorn Group	
G-BINT	Unicorn UE.1A balloon	Unicorn Group	
G-BINU	Saffery S.200 balloon	T. Lewis	
G-BINV	Saffery S.200 balloon	R. S. Harris	
G-BINW	Scruggs BL.2B balloon	P. G. Macklin	
G-BINX	Scruggs BL.2B balloon	P. D. Ridout	
G-BINY	Oriental balloon	J. L. Morton	
G-BINZ	Rango NA.8 balloon	T. J. Sweeting & M. O. Davies	
G-BIOA	Hughes 369D	Weetabix Ltd/Sywell	
G-BIOB	Cessna F.172P	Hunting Surveys & Consultants Ltd/Luton	
G-BIOC	Cessna F.150L	Seawing Flying Club/Southend	
G-BIOJ	R. Commander 112TCA	T. D. Stronge/Newtownards	
G-BIOK	Cessna F.152	Tayside Aviation Ltd/Dundee	
G-BIOM	Cessna F.152	Falcon Flying Services/Biggin Hill	
G-BION	Cameron V-77 balloon	Elliott's Pharmacy Ltd	
G-BIOO	Unicorn UE.2B balloon	Unicorn Group	
G-BIOP	Scruggs BL.2D balloon	J. P. S. Donnellan	
G-BIOR	M.S.880B Rallye Club	Aircraft Dept. Royal Aircraft Establishment/Farnborough	
G-BIOS	Scruggs BL.2B balloon	D. Eaves	
G-BIOU	Jodel D.117A	M. S. Printing & Graphics Machinery Ltd/Booker	

Notes	Reg.	Type	Owner or Operator
	G-BIOW	Slingsby T.67A	Specialist Flying Training Ltd/ Carlisle
	G-BIOX	Potter Crompton PRO.1 balloon	G. M. Potter
	G-BIOY	PAC-14 Special Shape balloon	P. A. Cremer
	G-BIPA	AA-5B Tiger	J. Campbell/Barrow
	G-BIPB	Weedhopper JC-24B	E. H. Moroney
	G-BIPC	PAC-14 Hefferlump balloon	P. A. Cremer
	G-BIPF	Scruggs BL.2C balloon	D. Morris
	G-BIPG	Global Mini balloon	P. Globe
	G-BIPH	Scruggs BL.2B balloon	C. M. Dewsnap
	G-BIPI	Everett Blackbird Mk 1	M. P. Lhermette
	G-BIPJ	PA-36-375 Brave	G. B. Pearce/Shoreham
	G-BIPK	Saffery S.200 balloon	P. J. Kelsey
	G-BIPM	Flamboyant Ax7-65 balloon	Pepsi Cola International Ltd/S. Africa
	G-BIPN	Fournier RF-3	M. R. Shelton
	G-BIPO	Mudry/CAARP CAP.20LS-200	BIPO Aviation Ltd/Booker
	G-BIPS	SOCATA Rallye 100ST	McAully Flying Group/Little Snoring
	G-BIPT	Jodel D.112	C. R. Davies
	G-BIPU	AA-5B Tiger	Aero Group 78/Netherthorpe
	G-BIPV	AA-5B Tiger	Copyacre Ltd
	G-BIPW	Avenger T.200-2112 balloon	B. L. King
	G-BIPX	Saffery S.9 balloon	J. R. Havers
	G-BIPY	Bensen B.8	A. J. Wood
	G-BIPZ	McCandless Mk 4-4	B. McIntyre
	G-BIRA	SOCATA TB.9 Tampico	Goldangel Ltd/Swansea
	G-BIRB	M.S.880B Rallye 100T	E. Smith/Newtownards
	G-BIRD	Pitts S-1C Special	B. K. Lecomber/Booker
	G-BIRE	Colt 56 Bottle balloon	Hot Air Balloon Co Ltd
	G-BIRH	PA-18 Super Cub 135 (R-163)	I. R. F. Hammond/Lee-on-Solent
	G-BIRI	C.A.S.A. 1.131E Jungmann	M. G. & J. R. Jeffries
	G-BIRK	Avenger T.200-2112 balloon	D. Harland
	G-BIRL	Avenger T.200-2112 balloon	R. Light
	G-BIRM	Avenger T.200-2112 balloon	P. Higgins
	G-BIRN	Short SD3-30	Thurston Aviation Ltd/Stansted
	G-BIRO	Cessna 172P	M. C. Grant
	G-BIRP	Arena Mk 17 Skyship balloon	A. S. Viel
	G-BIRS	Cessna 182P	D. J. Tollafield (G-BBBS)
	G-BIRT	Robin R.1180TD	W. D'A. Hall/Booker
	G-BIRV	Bensen B.8MV	R. Hart
	G-BIRW	M.S.505 Criquet (F+IS)	Museum of Flight/E. Fortune
	G-BIRX	Scruggs RS.500 balloon	J. H. Searle
	G-BIRY	Cameron V-77 balloon	J. J. Winter
	G-BIRZ	Zenair CH.250	B. A. Arnall & M. Hanley/Biggin Hill
	G-BISA	Hase IIIT balloon	M. A. Hase
	G-BISB	Cessna F.152 II	Sheffield Aero Club Ltd/ Netherthorpe
	G-BISC	Robinson R-22	Skyline Helicopters Ltd/Booker
	G-BISF	Robinson R-22	Compuster Ltd
	G-BISG	FRED Srs 3	R. A. Coombe
	G-BISH	Cameron O-42 balloon	Zebedee Balloon Service
	G-BISI	Robinson R-22	Sloane Helicopters Ltd/Luton
	G-BISJ	Cessna 340A	Castle Aviation/Leeds
	G-BISK	R. Commander 112B ★	P. A. Warner
	G-BISL	Scruggs BL.2B balloon	P. D. Ridout
	G-BISM	Scruggs BL.2B balloon	P. D. Ridout
	G-BISN	Boeing Vertol 234LR Chinook	British International Helicopters Ltd/ Aberdeen
	G-BISP	Boeing Vertol 234LR Chinook	British International Helicopters Ltd/ Aberdeen
	G-BISR	Boeing Vertol 234LR Chinook	British International Helicopters Ltd/ Aberdeen
	G-BISS	Scruggs BL.2C balloon	P. D. Ridout
	G-BIST	Scruggs BL.2C balloon	P. D. Ridout
	G-BISU	B.170 Freighter 31M	Atlantic Air Transport/Duxford
	G-BISV	Cameron O-65 balloon	Hylyne Rabbits Ltd
	G-BISW	Cameron O-65 balloon	Hylyne Rabbits Ltd
	G-BISX	Colt 56A balloon	Long John International Ltd
	G-BISY	Scruggs BL.2C balloon	P. T. Witty
	G-BISZ	Sikorsky S-76A	Bristow Helicopters Ltd
	G-BITA	PA-18-150 Super Cub	P. M. D. Wiggins
	G-BITE	SOCATA TB.10 Tobago	M. A. Smith & R. J. Bristow/Fairoaks
	G-BITF	Cessna F.152	Bristol & Wessex Aeroplane Club/ Bristol

Reg.	Type	Owner or Operator	Notes
G-BITG	Cessna F.152	Bristol & Wessex Aeroplane Club/ Bristol	
G-BITH	Cessna F.152	Bristol & Wessex Aeroplane Club/ Bristol	
G-BITI	Scruggs RS.5000 balloon	A. E. Smith	
G-BITK	FRED Srs 2	B. J. Miles	
G-BITL	Horncastle LL-901 balloon	M. J. Worsdell	
G-BITM	Cessna F.172P	D. G. Crabtree/Barton	
G-BITN	Short Albatross balloon	D. K. Short	
G-BITO	Jodel D.112D	A. Dunbar/Barton	
G-BITR	Sikorsky S-76A	Bristow Helicopters Ltd	
G-BITS	Drayton B-56 balloon	M. J. Betts	
G-BITT	Bo 208C Junior	M. Hutchinson/Netherthorpe	
G-BITV	Short SD3-30	Connectair Ltd/Gatwick	
G-BITW	Short SD3-30	Short Bros PLC (G-EASI)/Sydenham	
G-BITX	Short SD3-30		
G-BITY	FD.31T balloon	A. J. Bell	
G-BITZ	Cremer Sandoe PACDS.14 balloon	P. A. Cremer & C. D. Sandoe	
G-BIUL	Cameron 60 SS balloon	D. C. Patrick-Brown	
G-BIUM	Cessna F.152	Sheffield Aero Club Ltd/ Netherthorpe	
G-BIUN	Cessna F.152	Sheffield Aero Club Ltd/ Netherthorpe	
G-BIUP	SNCAN NC.854C	Questair Ltd	
G-BIUT	Scruggs BL.2C balloon	N. J. Ball	
G-BIUU	PA-23 Aztec 250	Kingsmetal Ltd	
G-BIUV	H.S.748 Srs 2A	Dan-Air Services Ltd (G-AYYH)/ Gatwick	
G-BIUW	PA-28-161 Warrior II	D. R. Staley	
G-BIUX	PA-28-161 Warrior II	C.S.E. Aviation Ltd/Kidlington	
G-BIUY	PA-28-181 Archer II	Maidenhead Electrical Services Ltd/ White Waltham	
G-BIVA	Robin R.2112	Cotswold Aero Club Ltd/Staverton	
G-BIVB	Jodel D.112	R. J. Lewis/Bodmin	
G-BIVC	Jodel D.112	M. J. Barmby/Cardiff	
G-BIVF	CP.301C-3 Emeraude	J. Cosker	
G-BIVI	Cremer PAC.500 airship	P. A. Cremer	
G-BIVK	Bensen B.8	J. G. Toy	
G-BIVL	Bensen B.8	R. Gardiner	
G-BIVR	Featherlight Mk 1 balloon	A. P. Newman & N. P. Kemp	
G-BIVS	Featherlight Mk 2 balloon	J. M. J. Roberts & S. R. Rushton	
G-BIVT	Saffery S.80 balloon	L. F. Guyot	
G-BIVU	AA-5A Cheetah	Fastglow Ltd/Biggin Hill	
G-BIVV	AA-5A Cheetah	W. Dass/Shobdon	
G-BIVX	Saffery S.80 balloon	P. T. Witty	
G-BIVY	Cessna 172N	Goodwood Aircraft Management Services Ltd	
G-BIVZ	D.31A Turbulent	Tiger Club Ltd/Redhill	
G-BIWA	Stevendon Skyreacher balloon	S. D. Barnes	
G-BIWB	Scruggs RS.5000 balloon	P. D. Ridout	
G-BIWC	Scruggs RS.5000 balloon	P. D. Ridout	
G-BIWD	Scruggs RS.5000 balloon	D. Eaves	
G-BIWE	Scruggs BL.2D balloon	M. D. Saunders	
G-BIWF	Warren balloon	P. D. Ridout	
G-BIWG	Zelenski Mk 2 balloon	P. D. Ridout	
G-BIWH	Cremer Super Fliteliner balloon	L. Griffiths	
G-BIWI	Cremer WS.1 balloon	P. A. Cremer	
G-BIWJ	Unicorn UE.1A balloon	B. L. King	
G-BIWK	Cameron V-65 balloon	I. R. Williams & R. G. Bickerdike	
G-BIWL	PA-32-301 Saratoga	D. Hammant/Southampton	
G-BIWN	Jodel D.112	C. R. Coates	
G-BIWO	Scruggs RS.5000 balloon	D. Morris	
G-BIWP	Mooney M.20J	Earl of Caledon	
G-BIWR	Mooney M.20F	C. W. Yarnton & J. D. Heykoop/ Redhill	
G-BIWS	Cessna 182R	Anglian Double Glazing Ltd/ Norwich	
G-BIWU	Cameron V-65 balloon	J. T. Whicker & J. W. Unwin	
G-BIWV	Cremer PAC-550T balloon	P. A. Rutherford	
G-BIWW	AA-5 Traveler	B&K Aviation/Cranfield	
G-BIWX	AT-16 Harvard IV (FT239)	A. E. Hutton/White Waltham	

Notes	Reg.	Type	Owner or Operator
	G-BIWY	Westland WG.30	British International Helicopters Ltd/ (stored)
	G-BIXA	SOCATA TB.9 Tampico	D. T. Parfitt
	G-BIXB	SOCATA TB.9 Tampico	Kitchen Bros/Little Snoring
	G-BIXH	Cessna F.152	Cambridge Aero Club Ltd
	G-BIXI	Cessna 172RG Cutlass	J. F. P. Lewis/Sandown
	G-BIXJ	Saffery S.40 balloon	T. M. Pates
	G-BIXK	Rand KR.2	R. G. Cousins
	G-BIXL	P-51D Mustang (472216)	R. Lamplough/North Weald
	G-BIXN	Boeing A.75N1 Stearman	I. L. Craig-Wood & ptnrs
	G-BIXR	Cameron A-140 balloon	Skysales Ltd
	G-BIXS	Avenger T.200-2112 balloon	M. Stuart
	G-BIXT	Cessna 182R	W. Lipka/Panshanger
	G-BIXV	Bell 212	Bristow Helicopters Ltd
	G-BIXW	Colt 56B balloon	J. R. Birkenhead
	G-BIXX	Pearson Srs 2 balloon	D. Pearson
	G-BIXZ	Grob G-109	V. J. R. Day
	G-BIYI	Cameron V-65 balloon	Sarnia Balloon Group
	G-BIYJ	PA-19 Super Cub 95	S. Russell
	G-BIYK	Isaacs Fury	R. S. Martin/Dunkeswell
	G-BIYM	PA-32R-301 Saratoga SP	E. O. Liebert/Jersey
	G-BIYN	Pitts S-1S Special	W. H. Milner
	G-BIYO	PA-31-310 Turbo Navajo	Northern Executive Aviation Ltd/ Manchester
	G-BIYP	PA-20 Pacer 135	R. A. Lloyd-Hubbard & R. J. Whitcombe
	G-BIYR	PA-18 Super Cub 135	Delta Foxtrot Flying Group/ Dunkeswell
	G-BIYT	Colt 17A balloon	A. F. Selby
	G-BIYU	Fokker S.11.1 Instructor (E-15)	H. R. Smallwood & A. J. Lee/ Denham
	G-BIYV	Cremer 14.700-15 balloon	G. Lowther & ptnrs
	G-BIYW	Jodel D.112	W. J. Tanswell
	G-BIYX	PA-28 Cherokee 140	Telepoint Ltd/Manchester
	G-BIYY	PA-18 Super Cub 95	A. E. & W. J. Taylor/Ingoldmells
	G-BIZB	AB-206 JetRanger 3	Martin Butler Associates Ltd/ Fairoaks
	G-BIZE	SOCATA TB.9 Tampico	London Flight Centre (Headcorn) Ltd
	G-BIZF	Cessna F.172P	R. S. Bentley
	G-BIZG	Cessna F.152	Aero Group 78/Netherthorpe
	G-BIZI	Robin DR.400/120	Headcorn Flying School Ltd
	G-BIZJ	Nord 3202	Keenair Services Ltd/Liverpool
	G-BIZK	Nord 3202	Keenair Services Ltd/Liverpool
	G-BIZL	Nord 3202	Keenair Services Ltd/Liverpool
	G-BIZM	Nord 3202	Magnificent Obsession Ltd
	G-BIZN	Slingsby T.67A	Specialist Flying Training Ltd/ Carlisle
	G-BIZO	PA-28R Cherokee Arrow 200	Penny (Mechanical Services) Ltd
	G-BIZT	Bensen B.8M	J. Ferguson
	G-BIZU	Thunder Ax6-56Z balloon	S. L. Leigh
	G-BIZV	PA-19 Super Cub 95 (18-2001)	T. E. G. Buckett
	G-BIZW	Champion 7GCBC Citabria	G. Read & Son
	G-BIZY	Jodel D.112	C. R. A. Wood
	G-BJAA	Unicorn UE.1A balloon	K. H. Turner
	G-BJAD	FRED Srs 2	C. Allison
	G-BJAE	Lavadoux Starck AS.80	D. J. & S. A. E. Phillips/Coventry
	G-BJAF	Piper J-3C-65 Cub	P. J. Cottle
	G-BJAG	PA-28-181 Archer II	H. Hunter
	G-BJAH	Unicorn UE.1A balloon	A. D. Hutchings
	G-BJAJ	AA-5B Tiger	Sco-Fro Foods Ltd/Glasgow
	G-BJAK	Mooney M.20C	P. W. Skinmore/Stapleford
	G-BJAL	C.A.S.A. 1.131E Jungmann	Buccaneer Aviation Ltd/Booker
	G-BJAN	SA.102-5 Cavelier	J. Powlesland
	G-BJAO	Bensen B.8M	G. L. Stockdale
	G-BJAP	D.H.82A Tiger Moth	J. Pothecary
	G-BJAR	Unicorn UE.3A balloon	Unicorn Group
	G-BJAS	Rango NA.9 balloon	A. Lindsay
	G-BJAU	PZL-104 Wilga 35	Anglo Polish Sailplanes Ltd
	G-BJAV	GY-80 Horizon 160	R. Pickett/Leicester
	G-BJAW	Cameron V-65 balloon	G. W. McCarthy
	G-BJAX	Pilatus P2-05 (14)	C. J. Diggins & ptnrs/Redhill
	G-BJAY	Piper J-3C-65 Cub	K. L. Clarke/Ingoldmells
	G-BJBI	Cessna 414A	Borfin Ltd/Manchester

Reg.	Type	Owner or Operator	Notes
G-BJBK	PA-19 Super Cub 95	M. S. Bird/Old Sarum	
G-BJBL	Unicorn UE.1A balloon	Unicorn Group	
G-BJBM	Monnet Sonerai II	J. Pickerell & B. L. Sims/Southend	
G-BJBN	Ball JB.980 balloon	J. D. Ball	
G-BJBO	Jodel DR.250/160	T. P. Bowen/Staverton	
G-BJBP	Beech A200 Super King Air	All Charter Ltd (G-HLUB)/ Bournemouth	
G-BJBR	Robinson R-22	Stenoak Fencing & Construction Co Ltd	
G-BJBS	Robinson R-22	Cosworth Engineering Ltd/Sywell	
G-BJBV	PA-28-161 Warrior II	C.S.E. Aviation Ltd/Kidlington	
G-BJBW	PA-28-161 Warrior II	C.S.E. Aviation Ltd/Kidlington	
G-BJBX	PA-28-161 Warrior II	C.S.E. Aviation Ltd/Kidlington	
G-BJBY	PA-28-161 Warrior II	C.S.E. Aviation Ltd/Kidlington	
G-BJBZ	Rotorway 133 Executive	Rotorway (UK) Ltd	
G-BJCA	PA-28-161 Warrior II	G. E. Salter Industrial Enterprises Ltd	
G-BJCC	Unicorn UE.1A balloon	R. J. Pooley	
G-BJCD	Bede BD-5BH	Brockmoor-Bede Aircraft (UK) Ltd	
G-BJCF	CP.1310-C3 Super Emeraude	K. M. Hodson & C. G. H. Gurney	
G-BJCH	Ocset 1 balloon	B.H.M.E.D. Balloon Group	
G-BJCI	PA-18-150 Super Cub	The Borders (Milfield) Aero-Tour Club Ltd	
G-BJCJ	PA-28-181 Archer II	Coolstead Ltd/Panshanger	
G-BJCM	FRED Srs 2	J. C. Miller	
G-BJCP	Unicorn UE.2B balloon	Unicorn Group	
G-BJCR	Partenavia P.68C	Nullifire Ltd/Coventry	
G-BJCS	Meagher Mk 2 balloon	S. A. Fowler	
G-BJCT	Boeing 737-204ADV	Britannia Airways Ltd The Hon C. S. Rolls/Luton	
G-BJCU	Boeing 737-204ADV	Britannia Airways Ltd Sir Henry Royce/Luton	
G-BJCV	Boeing 737-204ADV	Britannia Airways Ltd Viscount Trenchard/Luton	
G-BJCW	PA-32R-301 Saratoga SP	Viscount Chelsea/Kidlington	
G-BJDE	Cessna F.172M	S. Lynn	
G-BJDF	M.S.880B Rallye 100T	W. R. Savin & ptnrs	
G-BJDI	Cessna FR.182RG	Spoils Kitchen Reject Shops Ltd	
G-BJDJ	H.S.125 Srs 700B	Consolidated Contractors International Ltd/Heathrow	
G-BJDK	European E.14 balloon	Aeroprint Tours	
G-BJDL	Rango NA.9 balloon	D. Lawrence	
G-BJDM	SA.102-5 Cavalier	J. D. McCracken	
G-BJDO	AA-5A Cheetah	Border Transport/Southampton	
G-BJDP	Cremer Cloudcruiser balloon	P. J. Petitt & M. J. Harper	
G-BJDS	British Bulldog balloon	A. J. Cremer	
G-BJDT	SOCATA TB.9 Tampico	Tampico Group/Old Sarum	
G-BJDU	Scruggs BL.2B-2 balloon	C. D. Ibell	
G-BJDV	Kingram balloon	T. J. King & S. Ingram	
G-BJDW	Cessna F.172M	Suffolk Aero Club Ltd/Ipswich	
G-BJDX	Scruggs BL.2D-2 balloon	A. R. Maple	
G-BJDZ	Unicorn UE.1A balloon	A. P. & K. E. Chown	
G-BJEI	PA-18 Super Cub 95	H. J. Cox	
G-BJEL	Nord NC.854	N. F. & S. G. Hunter	
G-BJEM	Cube balloon	A. J. Cremer	
G-BJEN	Scruggs RS.5000 balloon	N. J. Richardson	
G-BJEO	PA-34-220T Seneca III	D. W. Clark Land Drainage Ltd (G-TOMF)	
G-BJES	Scruggs RS.5000 balloon	J. E. Christopher	
G-BJEU	Scruggs BL.2D-2 balloon	G. G. Kneller	
G-BJEV	Aeronca 11AC Chief	R. D. Willcox	
G-BJEW	Cremer balloon	C. D. Sandoe	
G-BJEX	Bo 208C Junior	G. D. H. Crawford/Thruxton	
G-BJEY	BHMED Srs 1 balloon	D. R. Meades & J. S. Edwards	
G-BJFB	Mk 1A balloon	Aeroprint Tours	
G-BJFC	European E.8 balloon	P. D. Ridout	
G-BJFD	BHMED Srs 1 balloon	D. G. Dance & I. R. Bell	
G-BJFE	PA-19 Super Cub 95 (L-18C)	C. E. & W. B. Cooper	
G-BJFH	Boeing 737-2S3	Air Europe Ltd Sandie/Gatwick	
G-BJFI	Bell 47G-2A1	Helicopter Supplies & Engineering Ltd/ Bournemouth	
G-BJFK	Short SD3-30	National Airways/Southend	
G-BJFL	Sikorsky S-76A	Bristow Helicopters Ltd	
G-BJFM	Jodel D.120	M. L. Smith & ptnrs/Popham	
G-BJFN	Mk IV balloon	Windsor Balloon Group	

Notes	Reg.	Type	Owner or Operator
	G-BJFO	Mk II balloon	Windsor Balloon Group
	G-BJFP	Mk III balloon	Windsor Balloon Group
	G-BJFR	Mk IV balloon	Windsor Balloon Group
	G-BJFS	Mk IV balloon	Windsor Balloon Group
	G-BJFT	Mk IV balloon	Windsor Balloon Group
	G-BJFU	Mk IV balloon	Windsor Balloon Group
	G-BJFV	Mk V balloon	Windsor Balloon Group
	G-BJFW	Mk V balloon	Windsor Balloon Group
	G-BJFX	Mk V balloon	Windsor Balloon Group
	G-BJFY	Mk I balloon	Windsor Balloon Group
	G-BJFZ	Mk II balloon	Windsor Balloon Group
	G-BJGA	Mk IV balloon	Windsor Balloon Group
	G-BJGB	Mk I balloon	Windsor Balloon Group
	G-BJGC	Mk IV balloon	Windsor Balloon Group
	G-BJGD	Mk IV balloon	Windsor Balloon Group
	G-BJGE	Thunder Ax3 balloon	K. A. Williams
	G-BJGF	Mk 1 balloon	D. & D. Eaves
	G-BJGG	Mk 2 balloon	D. & D. Eaves
	G-BJGK	Cameron V-77 balloon	A. Simpson & R. Bailey
	G-BJGL	Cremer balloon	G. Lowther
	G-BJGM	Unicorn UE.1A balloon	D. Eaves & P. D. Ridout
	G-BJGN	Scruggs RS.5000 balloon	K. H. Turner
	G-BJGO	Cessna 172N	Stratair Ltd
	G-BJGS	Cremer balloon	C. A. Larkins
	G-BJGT	Mooney M.20K	C. & K. Software Ltd
	G-BJGW	M.H.1521M Broussard (92)	G. A. Warner/Duxford
	G-BJGX	Sikorsky S-76A	Bristow Helicopters Ltd
	G-BJGY	Cessna F.172P	D. C. H. Crouch
	G-BJHA	Cremer balloon	G. Cape
	G-BJHB	Mooney M.20J	Zitair Flying Club Ltd/Redhill
	G-BJHC	Swan 1 balloon	C. A. Swan
	G-BJHD	Mk 3B balloon	S. Meagher
	G-BJHE	Osprey 1B balloon	R. B. Symonds & J. M. Hopkins
	G-BJHG	Cremer balloon	P. A. Cremer & H. J. A. Green
	G-BJHJ	Osprey 1C balloon	D. Eaves
	G-BJHK	EAA Acro Sport	J. H. Kimber
	G-BJHL	Osprey 1C balloon	E. Bartlett
	G-BJHM	Osprey 1B balloon	W. P. Fulford
	G-BJHN	Osprey 1B balloon	J. E. Christopher
	G-BJHO	Osprey 1C balloon	G. G. Kneller
	G-BJHP	Osprey 1C balloon	N. J. Richardson
	G-BJHR	Osprey 1B balloon	J. E. Christopher
	G-BJHS	S.25 Sunderland V	Sunderland Ltd/Chatham
	G-BJHT	Thunder Ax7-65 balloon	A. H. & L. Symonds
	G-BJHU	Osprey 1C balloon	G. G. Kneller
	G-BJHV	Voisin Replica	M. P. Sayer/O. Warden
	G-BJHW	Osprey 1C balloon	N. J. Richardson
	G-BJHX	Osprey 1C balloon	A. B. Gulliford
	G-BJHY	Osprey 1C balloon	T. J. King & S. Ingram
	G-BJHZ	Osprey 1C balloon	M. Christopher
	G-BJIA	Allport balloon	D. J. Allport
	G-BJIB	D.31 Turbulent	N. H. Lemon
	G-BJIC	Dodo 1A balloon	P. D. Ridout
	G-BJID	Osprey 1B balloon	P. D. Ridout
	G-BJIE	Sphinx balloon	P. T. Witty
	G-BJIF	Bensen B.8M	H. Redwin
	G-BJIG	Slingsby T.67A	B. R. Chapman/Redhill
	G-BJII	Sphinx balloon	I. French
	G-BJIJ	Osprey 1B balloon	R. Hownsell
	G-BJIR	Cessna 550 Citation II	Tower House Consultants Ltd
	G-BJIS	Mk 1 balloon	P. Paine
	G-BJIU	Bell 212	Bristow Helicopters Ltd
	G-BJIV	PA-18-150 Super Cub	Yorkshire Gliding Club (Pty) Ltd
	G-BJIW	T-1 balloon	S. Holland & G. Watmore
	G-BJIX	T-1 balloon	S. Holland & G. Watmore
	G-BJIY	Cessna T337D	Woodside Kincora Ltd
	G-BJJE	Dodo Mk 3 balloon	D. Eaves
	G-BJJF	Dodo Mk 4 balloon	D. Eaves
	G-BJJG	Dodo Mk 5 balloon	D. Eaves
	G-BJJI	SAS balloon	R. Hounsell & M. R. Rooke
	G-BJJJ	Bitterne balloon	R. Hounsell & M. R. Rooke
	G-BJJK	Bitterne balloon	R. Hounsell & M. R. Rooke

Reg.	Type	Owner or Operator	Notes
G-BJJL	SAS balloon	M. R. Rooke	
G-BJJN	Cessna F.172M	Ospreystar Ltd (*stored*)/Stapleford	
G-BJJO	Bell 212	Bristow Helicopters Ltd	
G-BJJP	Bell 212	Bristow Helicopters Ltd	
G-BJJS	Sphinx balloon	C. N. Childs	
G-BJJT	Mabey balloon	M. W. Mabey	
G-BJJU	Sphinx balloon	T. M. Bates	
G-BJJW	Mk B balloon	S. Meagher	
G-BJJX	Mk B balloon	S. Meagher	
G-BJJY	Mk B balloon	S. Meagher	
G-BJJZ	Unicorn UE.1A balloon	R. Woodley	
G-BJKA	SA.365C Dauphin 2	Bond Helicopters Ltd/Bourn	
G-BJKB	SA.365C Dauphin 2	Bond Helicopters Ltd/Bourn	
G-BJKC	Mk B balloon	S. Meagher	
G-BJKD	Mk B balloon	S. Meagher	
G-BJKE	Mk A balloon	D. Addison	
G-BJKF	SOCATA TB.9 Tampico	H. Bollman Ltd	
G-BJKG	Mk A balloon	D. Addison	
G-BJKH	Mk A balloon	D. Addison	
G-BJKI	Mk A balloon	D. Addison	
G-BJKJ	Mk A balloon	D. Addison	
G-BJKK	Mk A balloon	D. Addison	
G-BJKL	Mk A balloon	D. Addison	
G-BJKM	Mk II balloon	S. Meagher	
G-BJKN	Mk 1 balloon	D. Addison	
G-BJKO	Mk 1 balloon	D. Addison	
G-BJKP	Mk 7 balloon	D. Addison	
G-BJKR	Mk 1 balloon	D. Addison	
G-BJKS	Mk 1 balloon	D. Addison	
G-BJKT	Mk B balloon	S. Meagher	
G-BJKU	Osprey 1B balloon	S. A. Dalmas & P. G. Tarr	
G-BJKV	Opsrey 1F balloon	B. Diggle	
G-BJKW	Wills Aera II	J. K. S. Wills	
G-BJKX	Cessna F.152	Eglinton Flying Club	
G-BJKY	Cessna F.152	Westair Flying Services Ltd/Blackpool	
G-BJKZ	Osprey 1F balloon	M. J. N. Kirby	
G-BJLA	Osprey 1B balloon	D. Lawrence	
G-BJLC	Monnet Sonerai IIL	J. P. Whitham	
G-BJLD	Eagle 8 Mk 2 balloon	R. M. Richards	
G-BJLE	Osprey 1B balloon	I. Chadwick	
G-BJLF	Unicorn UE.1C balloon	I. Chadwick	
G-BJLG	Unicorn UE.1B balloon	I. Chadwick	
G-BJLH	PA-18 Super Cub 95 (K-33)	D. S. Kirkham	
G-BJLJ	Cameron D-50 balloon	Cameron Balloons Ltd	
G-BJLK	Short SD3-30	Gill Air/Newcastle	
G-BJLN	Featherlight Mk 3 balloon	A. P. Newman & T. J. Sweeting	
G-BJLO	PA-31-310 Navajo	Linco (Poultry Machinery) Ltd/ Biggin Hill	
G-BJLP	Featherlight Mk 3 balloon	N. P. Kemp & M. O. Davies	
G-BJLR	Featherlight Mk 3 balloon	M. O. Davies & S. R. Roberts	
G-BJLT	Featherlight Mk 3 balloon	J. M. J. Roberts & C. C. Marshall	
G-BJLU	Featherlight Mk 3 balloon	T. J. Sweeting & N. P. Kemp	
G-BJLV	Sphinx balloon	L. F. Guyot	
G-BJLW	Gleave CJ-I balloon	C. J. Gleave	
G-BJLX	Cremer balloon	P. W. May	
G-BJLY	Cremer balloon	P. Cannon	
G-BJLZ	Cremer balloon	S. K. McLean	
G-BJMA	Colt 21A balloon	Colt Balloons Ltd	
G-BJMB	Osprey 1B balloon	S. Meagher	
G-BJMG	European E.26C balloon	D. Eaves & A. P. Chown	
G-BJMH	Osprey Mk 3A balloon	D. Eaves	
G-BJMI	European E.84 balloon	D. Eaves	
G-BJMJ	Bensen B.8M	J. I. Hewlett	
G-BJMK	Cremer balloon	B. J. Larkins	
G-BJML	Cessna 120	D. F. Lawlor/Panshanger	
G-BJMO	Taylor JT.1 Monoplane	R. C. Mark	
G-BJMR	Cessna 310R	A-One Transport (Leeds) Ltd/Sherburn	
G-BJMT	Osprey Mk 1E balloon	M. J. Sheather	
G-BJMU	European E.157 balloon	A. C. Mitchell	
G-BJMV	BAC One-Eleven 531FS	Dan-Air Services Ltd/Gatwick	
G-BJMW	Thunder Ax8-105 balloon	G. M. Westley	
G-BJMX	Jarre JR.3 balloon	P. D. Ridout	

Notes	Reg.	Type	Owner or Operator
	G-BJMZ	European EA.8A balloon	P. D. Ridout
	G-BJNA	Arena Mk 117P balloon	P. D. Ridout
	G-BJNB	WAR F4U Corsair	A. V. Francis
	G-BJNC	Osprey Mk 1E balloon	G. Whitehead
	G-BJND	Osprey Mk 1E balloon	A. Billington & D. Whitmore
	G-BJNE	Osprey Mk 1E balloon	D. R. Sheldon
	G-BJNF	Cessna F.152	Exeter Flying Club Ltd
	G-BJNG	Slingsby T.67A	Specialist Flying Training Ltd
	G-BJNH	Osprey Mk 1E balloon	D. A. Kirk
	G-BJNI	Osprey Mk 1C balloon	M. J. Sheather
	G-BJNL	Evans VP-2	K. Morris
	G-BJNN	PA-38-112 Tomahawk	Scotia Safari Ltd/Prestwick
	G-BJNP	Rango NA.32 balloon	N. H. Ponsford
	G-BJNX	Cameron O-65 balloon	B. J. Petteford
	G-BJNY	Aeronca 11CC Super Chief	P. I. & D. M. Morgans
	G-BJNZ	PA-23 Aztec 250	Distance No Object Ltd (G-FANZ)/ Stansted
	G-BJOA	PA-28-181 Archer II	Channel Islands Aero Holdings (Jersey) Ltd
	G-BJOB	Jodel D.140C	T. W. M. Beck & M. J. Smith
	G-BJOD	Hollman HA-2M Sportster	W. O'Riordan
	G-BJOE	Jodel D.120A	Jodair Flying Group/Fenland
	G-BJOI	Isaacs Special	J. O. Isaacs
	G-BJOP	BN-2B Islander	Loganair Ltd/Glasgow
	G-BJOT	Jodel D.117	R. L. A. Davies
	G-BJOV	Cessna F.150K	R. J. Lock
	G-BJOZ	Scheibe SF.25B Falke	P. W. Hextall
	G-BJPA	Osprey Mk 3A balloon	N. D. Brabham
	G-BJPB	Osprey Mk 4A balloon	C. B. Rundle
	G-BJPC	Cremer 1 gyroplane	P. A. Cremer
	G-BJPD	Osprey Mk 4D balloon	E. L. Fuller
	G-BJPE	Osprey Mk 1E balloon	M. A. Hase
	G-BJPI	Bede BD-5G	M. D. McQueen
	G-BJPJ	Osprey Mk 3A	K. R. Bundy
	G-BJPK	Osprey Mk 1B balloon	G. M. Hocquard
	G-BJPL	Osprey Mk 4A balloon	M. Vincent
	G-BJPM	Bursell PW.1 balloon	I. M. Holdsworth
	G-BJPN	JK Mk 1 balloon	A. Kaye & J. Corcoran
	G-BJPO	B&C balloon	S. Browne & J. Cheetham
	G-BJPU	Osprey Mk 4B balloon	P. Globe
	G-BJPV	Haigh balloon	M. J. Haigh
	G-BJPW	Osprey Mk 1C balloon	P. J. Cooper & M. Draper
	G-BJPX	Phoenix balloon	Cupro Sapphire Ltd
	G-BJPY	Cremer balloon	P. A. Cremer & P. V. M. Green
	G-BJPZ	Osprey Mk 1C balloon	C. E. Newman
	G-BJRA	Osprey Mk 4B balloon	E. Osborn
	G-BJRB	European E.254 balloon	D. Eaves
	G-BJRC	European E.84R balloon	D. Eaves
	G-BJRD	European E.84R balloon	D. Eaves
	G-BJRF	Saffery S.80 balloon	C. F. Chipping
	G-BJRG	Osprey Mk 4B balloon	A. de Gruchy
	G-BJRH	Rango NA.36 balloon	N. H. Ponsford
	G-BJRI	Osprey Mk 4D balloon	G. G. Kneller
	G-BJRJ	Osprey Mk 4D balloon	G. G. Kneller
	G-BJRK	Osprey Mk 1E balloon	G. G. Kneller
	G-BJRL	Osprey Mk 4B balloon	G. G. Kneller
	G-BJRO	Osprey Mk 4D balloon	M. Christopher
	G-BJRP	Cremer balloon	M. Williams
	G-BJRR	Cremer balloon	M. Wallbank
	G-BJRS	Cremer balloon	P. Wallbank
	G-BJRT	BAC One-Eleven 528	BCal/British Airways *New Town of East Kilbride*/Gatwick
	G-BJRU	BAC One-Eleven 528	BCal/British Airways *City of Edinburgh*/Gatwick
	G-BJRV	Cremer balloon	M. D. Williams
	G-BJRW	Cessna U.206G	A. I. Walgate & Son Ltd
	G-BJRX	RMB Mk 1 balloon	R. J. MacNeil
	G-BJRY	PA-28-151 Warrior	Eastern Counties Aero Club Ltd/ Southend
	G-BJRZ	Partenavia P.68C	Gledhill Water Storage Ltd & M. F. J. Watson/Blackpool
	G-BJSA	BN-2A Islander	Harvest Air Ltd/Southend

Reg.	Type	Owner or Operator	Notes
G-BJSC	Osprey Mk 4D balloon	N. J. Richardson	
G-BJSD	Osprey Mk 4D balloon	N. J. Richardson	
G-BJSE	Osprey Mk 1E balloon	J. E. Christopher	
G-BJSF	Osprey Mk 4B balloon	N. J. Richardson	
G-BJSG	V.S.361 Spitfire LF.IXE (ML417)	B. J. S. Grey/Duxford	
G-BJSI	Osprey Mk 1E balloon	N. J. Richardson	
G-BJSJ	Osprey Mk 1E balloon	M. Christopher	
G-BJSK	Osprey Mk 4B balloon	J. E. Christopher	
G-BJSL	Flamboyant Ax7-65 balloon	Pepsi Cola International Ltd	
G-BJSM	Bursell Mk 1 balloon	M. C. Bursell	
G-BJSP	Guido 1A Srs 61 balloon	G. A. Newsome	
G-BJSR	Osprey Mk 4B balloon	C. F. Chipping	
G-BJSS	Allport balloon	D. J. Allport	
G-BJST	CCF Harvard 4	V. Norman & M. Lawrence	
G-BJSU	Bensen B.8M	J. D. Newlyn	
G-BJSV	PA-28-161 Warrior II	A. F. Aviation Ltd/Stansted	
G-BJSW	Thunder Ax7-65 balloon	Sandcliffe Garage Ltd	
G-BJSX	Unicorn UE-1C balloon	N. J. Richardson	
G-BJSY	Beech C90 King Air	Aircharter Ltd/Bournemouth	
G-BJSZ	Piper J-3C-65 Cub	H. Gilbert	
G-BJTA	Osprey Mk 4B balloon	C. F. Chipping	
G-BJTB	Cessna A.150M	Leisure Lease Aviation/Andrewsfield	
G-BJTF	Skyrider Mk 1 balloon	D. A. Kirk	
G-BJTG	Osprey Mk 4B balloon	M. Millen	
G-BJTH	Kestrel AC Mk 1 balloon	R. P. Waller	
G-BJTI	Woodie K2400J-2 balloon	M. J. Woodward	
G-BJTJ	Osprey Mk 4B balloon	G. Hocquard	
G-BJTK	Taylor JT.1 Monoplane	E. N. Simmons (G-BEUM)	
G-BJTN	Osprey Mk 4B balloon	M. Vincent	
G-BJTO	Piper L-4H Cub	K. R. Nunn	
G-BJTP	PA-19 Super Cub 95	J. T. Parkins	
G-BJTS	Osprey Mk 4B balloon	G. Hocquard	
G-BJTT	Sphinx SP.2 balloon	N. J. Godfrey	
G-BJTU	Cremer Cracker balloon	D. R. Green	
G-BJTV	M.S.880B Rallye Club	E. C. Hender	
G-BJTW	European E.107 balloon	C. J. Brealey	
G-BJTY	Osprey Mk 4B balloon	A. E. de Gruchy	
G-BJTZ	Osprey Mk 4A balloon	M. J. Sheather	
G-BJUA	Sphinx SP.12 balloon	T. M. Pates	
G-BJUB	BVS Special 01 balloon	P. G. Wild	
G-BJUC	Robinson R-22	Jones & Brooks Ltd	
G-BJUD	Robin DR.400/180R	Southern Sailplanes Ltd	
G-BJUE	Osprey Mk 4B balloon	M. Vincent	
G-BJUG	SOCATA TB.9 Tampico	R. Howton & B. P. Waites/Biggin Hill	
G-BJUI	Osprey Mk 4B balloon	B. A. de Gruchy	
G-BJUK	Short SD3-30	Jersey European Airways (G-OCAS)	
G-BJUP	Osprey Mk 4B balloon	W. J. Pill	
G-BJUR	PA-38-112 Tomahawk	Truman Aviation Ltd/Tollerton	
G-BJUS	PA-38-112 Tomahawk	Panshanger School of Flying	
G-BJUU	Osprey Mk 4B balloon	M. Vincent	
G-BJUV	Cameron V-20 balloon	Cameron Balloons Ltd	
G-BJUW	Osprey Mk 4B balloon	C. F. Chipping	
G-BJUX	Bursell balloon	I. M. Holdsworth	
G-BJUY	Colt Ax-77 balloon	Colt Balloons Ltd	
G-BJUZ	BAT Mk II balloon	A. R. Thompson	
G-BJVA	BAT Mk I balloon	B. L. Thompson	
G-BJVB	Cremcorn Ax1.4 balloon	P. A. Cremer & I. Chadwick	
G-BJVC	Evans VP-2	R. G. Fenn/Leicester	
G-BJVF	Thunder Ax3 balloon	A. G. R. Calder & F. J. Spite	
G-BJVH	Cessna F.182Q	A. R. G. Brooker Engineering Ltd/ Wellesbourne	
G-BJVI	Osprey Mk 4D balloon	S. M. Colville	
G-BJVJ	Cessna F.152	Cambridge Aero Club Ltd	
G-BJVK	Grob G-109	B. Kimberley/Enstone	
G-BJVL	Saffery Hermes balloon	Cupro Sapphire Ltd	
G-BJVM	Cessna 172M	Angelsword Ltd/Wellesbourne	
G-BJVO	Cameron D-50 airship	Cameron Balloons Ltd	
G-BJVS	CP.1315C-3 Super Emeraude	M. W. Wooldridge & A. E. Futter/ Norwich	
G-BJVT	Cessna F.152	Cambridge Aero Club Ltd	
G-BJVU	Thunder Ax6-56 balloon	G. V. Beckwith	
G-BJVV	Robin R.1180	Medway Flying Group Ltd/Rochester	

Notes	Reg.	Type	Owner or Operator
	G-BJVX	Sikorsky S-76A	Bristow Helicopters Ltd
	G-BJVZ	Sikorsky S-76A	Bristow Helicopters Ltd
	G-BJWC	Saro Skeeter AOP.12 ★	J. E. Wilkie
	G-BJWD	Zenith CH.300	D. Winton
	G-BJWH	Cessna F.152	Metronote Aviation Ltd/Biggin Hill
	G-BJWI	Cessna F.172P	Shoreham Flight Simulation Ltd/ Bournemouth
	G-BJWJ	Cameron V-65 balloon	R. G. Turnbull & S. G. Forse
	G-BJWL	BN-2A-8 Islander	Region Airways Ltd (G-BBMC)/ Southend
	G-BJWM	BN-2A-26 Islander	Harvest Air Ltd (G-BCAE)/Southend
	G-BJWN	BN-2A-8 Islander	Harvest Air Ltd (G-BALO)/Southend
	G-BJWO	BN-2A-8 Islander	Harvest Air Ltd (G-BAXC)/Southend
	G-BJWP	BN-2A-26 Islander	Harvest Air Ltd (G-BCEJ)/Southend
	G-BJWR	D.H.82A Tiger Moth	D. R. Whitby & ptnrs
	G-BJWT	Wittman W.10 Tailwind	J. F. Bakewell & R. A. Shelley
	G-BJWV	Colt 17A balloon	Lighter-Than-Air Ltd
	G-BJWW	Cessna F.172N	Westair Flying Services Ltd/Blackpool
	G-BJWX	PA-19 Super Cub 95	D. E. Lamb
	G-BJWY	Sikorsky S-55 Whirlwind 21 (WV198)	J. E. Wilkie
	G-BJWZ	PA-19 Super Cub 95	G. V. Harfield/Thruxton
	G-BJXA	Slingsby T.67A	Specialist Flying Training Ltd/Carlisle
	G-BJXB	Slingsby T.67A	Light Planes (Lancs) Ltd/Barton
	G-BJXD	Colt 17A balloon	Hot Air Balloon Co Ltd
	G-BJXJ	Boeing 737-219	Britannia Airways Ltd/Luton
	G-BJXK	Fournier RF-5	P. Storey & ptnrs
	G-BJXL	Boeing 737-2T4	Dan-Air Services Ltd/Gatwick
	G-BJXN	Boeing 747-230B	BCal/British Airways *Mungo Park — The Scottish Explorer*/Gatwick
	G-BJXO	Cessna 441	Hatfield Executive Aviation Ltd
	G-BJXP	Colt 56B balloon	Birmingham Broadcasting Ltd
	G-BJXR	Auster AOP.9 (XR267)	Cotswold Aircraft Restoration Group
	G-BJXU	Thunder Ax7-77 balloon	Perdix Ltd
	G-BJXX	PA-23 Aztec 250E	Creative Conferences Aviation Ltd
	G-BJXZ	Cessna 172N	T. M. Jones
	G-BJYC	Cessna 425	Carters Aviation Ltd/E. Midlands
	G-BJYD	Cessna F.152 II	Cleveland Flying School Ltd/ Tees-side
	G-BJYF	Colt 56A balloon	Hot Air Balloon Co Ltd
	G-BJYG	PA-28-161 Warrior II	Channel Aviation Ltd/Guernsey
	G-BJYK	Jodel D.120A	T. Fox & D. A. Thorpe
	G-BJYL	BAC One-Eleven 515FB	Dan-Air Services Ltd (G-AZPE)/Gatwick
	G-BJYM	BAC One-Eleven 531FS	Dan-Air Services Ltd/Gatwick
	G-BJYN	PA-38-112 Tomahawk	Panshanger School of Flying Ltd (G-BJTE)
	G-BJZA	Cameron N-65 balloon	A. D. Pinner
	G-BJZB	Evans VP-2	A. Graham
	G-BJZC	Thunder Ax7-65Z balloon	Greenpeace (UK) Ltd/S. Africa
	G-BJZD	Douglas DC-10-10	Cal Air Ltd (G-GFAL)/Gatwick
	G-BJZE	Douglas DC-10-10	Cal Air Ltd (G-GSKY)/Gatwick
	G-BJZF	D.H.82A Tiger Moth	C. A. Parker/Sywell
	G-BJZK	Cessna T.303	Standard Aviation Ltd/Newcastle
	G-BJZL	Cameron V-65 balloon	S. L. G. Williams
	G-BJZN	Slingsby T.67A	Light Planes (Lancs) Ltd/Barton
	G-BJZR	Colt 42A balloon	C. F. Sisson
	G-BJZT	Cessna FA.152	Metronote Aviation Ltd/Biggin Hill
	G-BJZX	Grob G.109	Oxfordshire Sport Flying Ltd/Enstone
	G-BJZY	Bensen B.8MV	D. E. & M. A. Cooke
	G-BKAA	H.S.125 Srs 700B	Aravco Ltd/Heathrow
	G-BKAC	Cessna F.150L	Andrewsfield Flying Club Ltd (G-BAIO)
	G-BKAE	Jodel D.120	M. P. Wakem
	G-BKAF	FRED Srs 2	L. G. Millen
	G-BKAG	Boeing 727-217	Dan-Air Services Ltd/Gatwick
	G-BKAK	Beech C90 King Air	National Airways Ltd/Southend
	G-BKAM	Slingsby T.67M Firefly	A. J. Daley & R. K. Warren
	G-BKAN	Cessna 340A	Manchester Air Charter Ltd
	G-BKAO	Jodel D.112	E. Carter & G. Higgins
	G-BKAR	PA-38-112 Tomahawk	C.S.E. Aviation Ltd/Kidlington
	G-BKAS	PA-38-112 Tomahawk	C.S.E. Aviation Ltd/Kidlington
	G-BKAT	Pitts S-1C Special	I. M. G. Senior & J. G. Harper

Reg.	Type	Owner or Operator	Notes
G-BKAY	R. Commander 114	Costello Gears Ltd/Biggin Hill	
G-BKAZ	Cessna 152	Skyviews & General Ltd	
G-BKBB	Hawker Fury replica (K1930)	The Hon A. M. M. Lindsay	
G-BKBD	Thunder Ax3 balloon	D. L. Clark *Tow-Rite*	
G-BKBE	AA-5A Cheetah	G. W. Plowman & Sons Ltd/Elstree	
G-BKBF	M.S.894A Rallye Minerva 220	Callow Aviation/Shobdon	
G-BKBI	Quickie Q.2	R. H. Gibbs	
G-BKBK	Stampe SV-4A	B. M. O'Brien/Redhill	
G-BKBM	H.S.125 Srs 600B	Twinjet Aircraft Sales Ltd	
G-BKBN	SOCATA TB.10 Tobago	Cross Bros Ltd/Andrewsfield	
G-BKBO	Colt 17A balloon	J. Armstrong	
G-BKBP	Bellanca 7GCBC Scout	L. B. Jefferies	
G-BKBR	Cameron Chateau 84 balloon	Forbes Europe Ltd/France	
G-BKBS	Bensen B.8MV	Construction & Site Administration Ltd	
G-BKBV	SOCATA TB.10 Tobago	M. E. O'Brien	
G-BKBW	SOCATA TB.10 Tobago	P. Murphy/Blackbushe	
G-BKCB	PA-28R Cherokee Arrow 200	P. S. Miller/Blackbushe	
G-BKCC	PA-28 Cherokee 180	K. C. Boreland & Creative Logistics Enterprises/Staverton	
G-BKCE	Cessna F.172PII	M. Askanoglu	
G-BKCF	Rutan Long Ez	I. C. Fallows	
G-BKCH	Thompson Cassutt	S. C. Thompson/Redhill	
G-BKCI	Brugger MB.2 Colibri	E. R. Newall	
G-BKCJ	Oldfield Baby Great Lakes	S. V. Roberts/Sleap	
G-BKCL	PA-30 Twin Comanche 160	Jubilee Airways Ltd (G-AXSP)/ Conington	
G-BKCM	Bell 206B JetRanger 3	Patgrove Ltd	
G-BKCN	Currie Wot	S. E. Tomlinson	
G-BKCR	SOCATA TB.9 Tampico	Surrey & Kent Flying Club (1982) Ltd/ Biggin Hill	
G-BKCT	Cameron V-77 balloon	Quality Products General Engineering (Wickwat) Ltd	
G-BKCU	Sequoia F.8L Falco	J. J. Anziani & D. F. Simpson	
G-BKCV	EAA Acro Sport II	M. J. Clark	
G-BKCW	Jodel D.120A	A. Greene & G. Kerr/Dundee	
G-BKCX	Mudry CAARP CAP.10	Mahon & Associates/Booker	
G-BKCY	PA-38-112 Tomahawk II	Wellesbourne Aviation Ltd	
G-BKCZ	Jodel D.120A	P. Penn-Sayers Model Services Ltd/ Shoreham	
G-BKDA	AB-206B JetRanger	Dollar Air Services Ltd/Coventry	
G-BKDC	Monnet Sonerai II	J. Boobyer	
G-BKDD	Bell 206B JetRanger	Dollar Air Services Ltd/Coventry	
G-BKDE	Kendrick I Motorglider	J. K. Rushton	
G-BKDF	Kendrick II Motorglider	J. K. Rushton	
G-BKDH	Robin DR.400/120	W. R. C. Foyle/Thruxton	
G-BKDI	Robin DR.400/120	Cotswold Aero Club Ltd/Staverton	
G-BKDJ	Robin DR.400/120	W. R. C. Foyle/Thruxton	
G-BKDK	Thunder Ax7-77Z balloon	A. J. Byrne	
G-BKDP	FRED Srs 3	M. Whittaker	
G-BKDR	Pitts S.1S Special	T. R. G. Barnby & ptnrs/Redhill	
G-BKDT	S.E.5A replica (F943)	J. H. Tetley & W. A. Sneesby/Sherburn	
G-BKDW	K.1260/3 Stu gas balloon	P. C. Carlton	
G-BKDX	Jodel DR.1050	F. A. L. Castleden & ptnrs	
G-BKDY	Jodel D.120A	B. Kaldenberg/Redhill	
G-BKEK	PA-32 Cherokee Six 300	Cruspane Ltd/Stapleford	
G-BKEM	SOCATA TB.9 Tampico	D. V. D. Reed/Dunkeswell	
G-BKEN	SOCATA TB.10 Tobago	D. A. Williamson	
G-BKEP	Cessna F.172M	Reedtrend Ltd/Biggin Hill	
G-BKER	S.E.5A replica (F5447)	N. K. Geddes	
G-BKES	Cameron SS bottle balloon	Lighter-Than-Air Ltd	
G-BKET	PA-19 Super Cub 95	J. A. Wills	
G-BKEU	Taylor JT.1 Monoplane	R. J. Whybrow & J. M. Springham	
G-BKEV	Cessna F.172M	One Zero One Three Ltd	
G-BKEW	Bell 206B JetRanger 3	N. R. Foster	
G-BKEX	Rich Prototype glider	D. B. Rich	
G-BKEY	FRED Srs 3	G. S. Taylor	
G-BKEZ	PA-18 Super Cub 95	A. N. G. Gardiner	
G-BKFA	Monnet Sonerai IIL	R. F. Bridge	
G-BKFC	Cessna F.152II	D. W. Walton/Husbands Bosworth	
G-BKFG	Thunder Ax3 balloon	P. Ray	
G-BKFI	Evans VP-1	F. A. R. de Lavergne	
G-BKFK	Isaacs Fury II	G. C. Jones	

Notes	Reg.	Type	Owner or Operator
	G-BKFM	QAC Quickie	R. I. Davidson & P. J. Cheyney
	G-BKFN	Bell 214ST	Bristow Helicopters Ltd
	G-BKFP	Bell 214ST	Bristow Helicopters Ltd
	G-BKFR	CP.301C Emeraude	A. J. Stevens/Barton
	G-BKFV	Rand KR-2	F. H. French/Swansea
	G-BKFW	P.56 Provost T.1	M. Howson
	G-BKFX	Colt 17A balloon	Colt Balloons Ltd
	G-BKFY	Beech C90 King Air	Omega Consultants Ltd/Guernsey
	G-BKFZ	PA-28R Cherokee Arrow 200	Shacklewell Flying Group/Leicester
	G-BKGA	M.S.892E Rallye 150GT	Harwoods of Essex Ltd
	G-BKGB	Jodel D.120	R. W. Greenwood
	G-BKGC	Maule M.6-235	Stol-Air Ltd/Sibson
	G-BKGD	Westland WG.30 Srs 100	British International Helicopters Ltd (G-BKBJ)/Beccles
	G-BKGL	Beech 18 (164)	G. A. Warner/Duxford
	G-BKGO	Piper J-3C-65 Cub	J. A. S. & I. K. Baldry
	G-BKGR	Cameron O-65 balloon	S. R. Bridge
	G-BKGT	SOCATA Rallye 110ST	Long Marston Flying Group
	G-BKGW	Cessna F.152-II	Leicestershire Aero Club Ltd
	G-BKGX	Isaacs Fury	I. L. McMahon
	G-BKGZ	Bensen B.8	C. F. Simpson
	G-BKHA	WS.55 Whirlwind HAR.10 (XJ763)	D. Wilson/Biggin Hill
	G-BKHB	WS.55 Whirlwind HAR.10 (XJ407)	R. Windley
	G-BKHC	WS.55 Whirlwind HAR.10 (XP328)	Flight C Helicopters Ltd
	G-BKHD	Oldfield Baby Great Lakes	P. J. Tanulak
	G-BKHE	Boeing 737-204	Britannia Airways Ltd Sir Francis Chichester/Luton
	G-BKHF	Boeing 737-204	Britannia Airways Ltd Sir Alliot Verdon Roe/Luton
	G-BKHG	Piper J-3C-65 Cub (479766)	K. G. Wakefield
	G-BKHH	Thunder Ax10-160Z balloon	R. Carr/France
	G-BKHL	Thunder Ax9-140 balloon	R. Carr/France
	G-BKHO	Boeing 737-2T4	Orion Airways Ltd/E. Midlands
	G-BKHP	P.56 Provost T.1 (WW397)	M. J. Crymble/Lyneham
	G-BKHR	Luton LA-4 Minor	R. J. Parkhouse
	G-BKHT	BAe 146-100	Dan-Air Services Ltd/Gatwick
	G-BKHV	Taylor JT.2 Titch	P. D. Holt
	G-BKHW	Stoddard-Hamilton Glasair SH.2RG	N. Clayton
	G-BKHX	Bensen B.8M	D. H. Greenwood
	G-BKHY	Taylor JT.1 Monoplane	J. Hall
	G-BKHZ	Cessna F.172P	Birmingham Aerocentre Ltd
	G-BKIA	SOCATA TB.10 Tobago	Redhill Flying School
	G-BKIB	SOCATA TB.9 Tampico	A. J. Baggerley & F. D. J. Simmons/ Goodwood
	G-BKIC	Cameron V-77 balloon	C. A. Butler
	G-BKIF	Fournier RF-6B	G. G. Milton
	G-BKII	Cessna F.172N	M. S. Knight/Goodwood
	G-BKIJ	Cessna F.172M	V. Speck
	G-BKIK	Cameron DG-10 airship	Cameron Balloons Ltd
	G-BKIM	Unicorn UE.5A balloon	I. Chadwick & K. H. Turner
	G-BKIN	Alon A.2A Aircoupe	P. A. Williams
	G-BKIR	Jodel D.117	R. Shaw & D. M. Hardaker/ Crosland Moor
	G-BKIS	SOCATA TB.10 Tobago	Ospreystar Ltd
	G-BKIT	SOCATA TB.9 Tampico	D. G. Bligh/Ipswich
	G-BKIU	Colt 17A balloon	Robert Pooley Ltd
	G-BKIV	Colt 21A balloon	Colt Balloons Ltd
	G-BKIX	Cameron V-31 balloon	M. N. J. Kirby
	G-BKIY	Thunder Ax3 balloon	A. Hornak
	G-BKIZ	Cameron V-31 balloon	A. P. Greathead
	G-BKJB	PA-18 Super Cub 135	Cormack (Aircraft Services) Ltd/ Glasgow
	G-BKJD	Bell 214ST	Bristow Helicopters Ltd
	G-BKJE	Cessna 172N	The G-BKJE Group/E. Midlands
	G-BKJF	M.S.880B Rallye 100T	G. F. Black
	G-BKJR	Hughes 269C	March Helicopters Ltd
	G-BKJS	Jodel D.120A	S. Walmsley
	G-BKJT	Cameron O-65 balloon	K. A. Ward
	G-BKJW	PA-23 Aztec 250	Alan Williams Entertainments Ltd
	G-BKJZ	G.159 Gulfstream 1	Rolls-Royce PLC/Filton

Reg.	Type	Owner or Operator	Notes
G-BKKI	Westland WG.30 Srs 100	Westland Helicopters Ltd/Yeovil	
G-BKKM	Aeronca 7AC Champion	M. McChesney	
G-BKKN	Cessna 182R	Marvagraphic Ltd/Panshanger	
G-BKKO	Cessna 182R	B. & G. Jebson Ltd/Leeds	
G-BKKP	Cessna 182R	ISF Aviation Ltd/Leicester	
G-BKKR	Rand KR-2	D. R. Trouse	
G-BKKS	Mercury Dart Srs 1	B. A. Mills	
G-BKKY	BAe Jetstream 3102	British Aerospace PLC/Prestwick	
G-BKKZ	Pitts S-1D Special	G. C. Masterton	
G-BKLB	S2R Thrush Commander	Ag-Air	
G-BKLC	Cameron V-56 balloon	M. A. & J. R. H. Ashworth	
G-BKLJ	Westland Scout AH.1 ★	J. E. Wilkie	
G-BKLM	Thunder Ax9-140 balloon	Balloon & Airship Co Ltd	
G-BKLO	Cessna F.172M	Reedtrend Ltd	
G-BKLP	Cessna F.172N	Reedtrend Ltd	
G-BKLS	SA.341G Gazelle	Helicopter Services Ltd	
G-BKLT	SA.341G Gazelle	Blades Helicopters Ltd	
G-BKLU	SA.341G Gazelle	Blades Helicopters Ltd	
G-BKLZ	Vinten-Wallis WA-116MC	W. Vinten Ltd	
G-BKMA	Mooney M.20J Srs 201	Clement Garage Ltd/Stapleford	
G-BKMB	Mooney M.20J Srs 201	W. A. Cook & ptnrs	
G-BKMD	SC.7 Skyvan Srs 3	Aviation Investments (G-BAHK)	
G-BKME	SC.7 Skyvan Srs 3	Flightspares PLC (G-AYJN)/Southend	
G-BKMF	SC.7 Skyvan Srs 3	Flightspares PLC (G-AYJO)/Southend	
G-BKMG	Handley Page O/400 replica	M. G. King	
G-BKMH	Flamboyant Ax7-65 balloon	Pepsi-Cola International Ltd/S. Africa	
G-BKMI	V.S.359 Spitfire HF VIII (MV154)	Aerial Museum (North Weald) Ltd	
G-BKMK	PA-38-112 Tomahawk	Cormack (Aircraft Services) Ltd/ Glasgow	
G-BKMM	Cessna 180K	G. Cormack	
G-BKMN	BAe 146-100	Dan-Air Services Ltd (G-ODAN)/ Gatwick	
G-BKMR	Thunder Ax3 balloon	B. F. G. Ribbons	
G-BKMT	PA-32R-301 Saratoga SP	Hillary Investments Ltd	
G-BKMX	Short SD3-60	Loganair Ltd/Glasgow	
G-BKNA	Cessna 421	Star Paper Ltd/Blackpool	
G-BKNB	Cameron V-42 balloon	S. A. Burnett	
G-BKND	Colt 56A balloon	Flying Colours Balloon Group	
G-BKNE	PA-28-161 Warrior II	J. R. Coughlan/Andrewsfield	
G-BKNH	Boeing 737-210	Dan-Air Services Ltd/Gatwick	
G-BKNI	GY-80 Horizon 160D	A. Hartigan & ptnrs/Fenland	
G-BKNJ	Grob G.109	Oxfordshire Sport Flying Ltd/Enstone	
G-BKNL	Cameron D-96 airship	Drawarm Ltd	
G-BKNN	Cameron Minar E Pakistan balloon	Forbes Europe Ltd/France	
G-BKNO	Monnet Sonerai IIL	S. Tattersfield & K. Bailey/Netherthorpe	
G-BKNX	SA.102.5 Cavalier	G. D. Horn	
G-BKNY	Bensen B.8M-P-VW	D. A. C. MacCormack	
G-BKNZ	CP.301A Emeraude	R. Evernden/Barton	
G-BKOA	M.S.893E Rallye 180GT	Cheshire Flying Services Ltd/ Manchester	
G-BKOB	Z.326 Trener Master	W. G. V. Hall	
G-BKOR	Barnes 77 balloon	Robert Pooley Ltd	
G-BKOS	P.56 Provost T.51 (178)	J. G. Cassidy/Woodvale	
G-BKOT	Wassmer WA.81 Piranha	B. D. Deubelbeiss	
G-BKOU	P.84 Jet Provost T.3 (XN637)	A. Topen/Cranfield	
G-BKOV	Jodel DR.220A	E. H. Ellis & G. C. Winter	
G-BKOW	Cameron 77A balloon	Hot Air Ballon Co Ltd	
G-BKPA	Hoffman H-36 Dimona	Airmark Aviation Ltd/Booker	
G-BKPB	Aerosport Scamp	R. Scroby	
G-BKPC	Cessna A.185F	Black Knights Parachute Centre	
G-BKPD	Viking Dragonfly	P. E. J. Sturgeon	
G-BKPE	Jodel DR.250/160	J. S. & J. D. Lewer	
G-BKPG	Luscombe Rattler Strike	Luscombe Aircraft Ltd/Lympne	
G-BKPH	Luscombe Valiant	Luscombe Aircraft Ltd/Lympne	
G-BKPK	John McHugh Gyrocopter	J. C. McHugh	
G-BKPM	Schempp-Hirth HS.5 Nimbus 2	J. L. Rolls	
G-BKPN	Cameron N-77 balloon	P. S. H. Frewer	
G-BKPS	AA-5B Tiger	Eyewitness Ltd/Southampton	
G-BKPT	M.H.1521M Broussard	Wessex Aviation & Transport Ltd	
G-BKPU	M.H.1521M Broussard	M. R. Keen/Liverpool	
G-BKPV	Stevex 250.1	A. F. Stevens	
G-BKPW	Boeing 767-204	Britannia Airways Ltd The Earl Mountbatten of Burma/Luton	

Notes	Reg.	Type	Owner or Operator
	G-BKPX	Jodel D.120A	C. G. Richardson
	G-BKPY	Saab 91B/2 Safir (56321)★	Newark Air Museum Ltd
	G-BKPZ	Pitts S-1T Special	B. Maggs/Redhill
	G-BKRA	T-6G Texan (51-15227)	M. D. Faiers
	G-BKRB	Cessna 172N	Saunders Caravans Ltd
	G-BKRD	Cessna 320E	Thackwell Motorsports Ltd/Fairoaks
	G-BKRF	PA-18 Super Cub 95	K. M. Bishop
	G-BKRG	Beechcraft C-45G	Aces High Ltd/North Weald
	G-BKRH	Brugger MB.2 Colibri	M. R. Benwell
	G-BKRI	Cameron V-77 balloon	J. R. Lowe & R. J. Fuller
	G-BKRJ	Colt 105A balloon	Owners Abroad Group PLC
	G-BKRK	SNCAN Stampe SV-4C	J. M. Alexander & ptnrs/Aberdeen
	G-BKRL	Designability Leopard	Chichester-Miles Consultants Ltd
	G-BKRM	Boeing 757-236	Air Europe Ltd/Air Europa
	G-BKRN	Beechcraft D.18S ★	Scottish Aircraft Collection/Perth
	G-BKRR	Cameron N-56 balloon	S. L. G. Williams
	G-BKRS	Cameron V-56 balloon	D. N. & L. J. Close
	G-BKRT	PA-34-220T-3 Seneca	Paucristar Ltd
	G-BKRU	Ensign Crossley Racer	M. Crossley
	G-BKRV	Hovey Beta Bird	A. V. Francis
	G-BKRW	Cameron O-160 balloon	Bondbaste Ltd
	G-BKRX	Cameron O-160 balloon	Bondbaste Ltd
	G-BKRZ	Dragon 77 balloon	Anglia Balloon School Ltd
	G-BKSB	Cessna T.310Q	P. S. King
	G-BKSC	Saro Skeeter AOP.12 (XN351)	R. A. L. Falconer
	G-BKSD	Colt 56A balloon	M. J. & G. C. Casson
	G-BKSE	QAC Quickie Q-2	M. D. Burns
	G-BKSG	Hoffman H-36 Dimona	F. C. Y. Cheung/H. Kong
	G-BKSH	Colt 21A balloon	T. A. Gilmour
	G-BKSJ	Cameron N-108 balloon	Cameron Balloons Ltd
	G-BKSO	Cessna 421C	Anglian Double Glazing Co Ltd/Norwich
	G-BKSP	Schleicher ASK.14	M. R. Shelton
	G-BKSR	Cessna 550 Citation II	Osiwell Ltd/Biggin Hill
	G-BKSS	Jodel D.150	D. H. Wilson-Spratt/Ronaldsway
	G-BKST	Rutan Vari-Eze	R. Towle
	G-BKSX	SNCAN Stampe SV-4C	A. J. Hall-Carpenter
	G-BKSZ	Cessna P.210N	Clark Masts Ltd/Sandown
	G-BKTA	PA-18 Super Cub 95	A. W. Chapman/Southend
	G-BKTH	CCF Hawker Sea Hurricane IB (Z7015)	Shuttleworth Trust/Duxford
	G-BKTM	PZL SZD-45A Ogar	Repclif Aviation Ltd/Liverpool
	G-BKTO	Beech 58P Baron	Gold Key Trust Ltd
	G-BKTR	Cameron V-77 balloon	G. F. & D. D. Bouten
	G-BKTS	Cameron O-65 balloon	C. H. Pearce & Sons (Contractors) Ltd
	G-BKTT	Cessna F.152	Stapleford Flying Club Ltd
	G-BKTU	Colt 56A balloon	E. Ten Houten
	G-BKTV	Cessna F.152	London Flight Centre Ltd/Stansted
	G-BKTW	Cessna 404 Titan II	Hawk Aviation Ltd (G-WTVE)/ E. Midlands
	G-BKTY	SOCATA TB.10 Tobago	F. J. Lingham/Biggin Hill
	G-BKTZ	Slingsby T.67M Firefly	Slingsby Aviation Ltd (G-SFTV)/ Kirkbymoorside
	G-BKUE	SOCATA TB.9 Tampico	W. J. Moore/Carlisle
	G-BKUI	D.31 Turbulent	R. F. Smith
	G-BKUJ	Thunder Ax6-56 balloon	R. J. Bent
	G-BKUM	AS.350B Ecureuil	T. W. Walker Ltd
	G-BKUR	CP.301A Emeraude	P. Gilmour/Perth
	G-BKUS	Bensen B.80	I. J. Lawson
	G-BKUT	M.S.880B Rallye Club	J. J. Hustwitt/Bodmin
	G-BKUU	Thunder Ax7-77-1 balloon	City of London Balloon Group
	G-BKUX	Beech C90 King Air	Alfred McAlpine Ltd/Luton
	G-BKUY	BAe Jetstream 3102	British Aerospace PLC/Prestwick
	G-BKUZ	Zenair CH.250	K. Morris
	G-BKVA	SOCATA Rallye 180T	R. Evans
	G-BKVB	SOCATA Rallye 110ST	Martin Ltd/Biggin Hill
	G-BKVC	SOCATA TB.9 Tampico	Martin Ltd/Biggin Hill
	G-BKVE	Rutan Vari-Eze	H. R. Rowley (G-EZLT)
	G-BKVF	FRED Srs 3	N. E. Johnson
	G-BKVG	Scheibe SF.25E Super Falke	Westland Flying Club Ltd/Yeovil
	G-BKVJ	Colt 21A balloon	Colt Balloons Ltd
	G-BKVK	Auster AOP.9 (WZ662)	R. J. Starling & C. W. Monsell/Norwich
	G-BKVL	Robin DR.400/160	The Cotswold Aero Club Ltd/Staverton
	G-BKVM	PA-18 Super Cub 150	W. R. C. Foyle/Southampton
	G-BKVN	PA-23 Aztec 250F	B. A. Eastwell/Shoreham

Reg.	Type	Owner or Operator	Notes
G-BKVO	Pietenpol Aircamper	M. J. Honeychurch	
G-BKVP	Pitts S-1D Special	P. J. Leggo	
G-BKVR	PA-28 Cherokee 140	Page Aviation Ltd/Andrewsfield	
G-BKVS	Bensen B.8M	V. Scott	
G-BKVT	PA-23 Aztec 250E	Crane Investments Ltd (G-HARV)	
G-BKVV	Beech 95-B55 Baron	L. Mc. G. Tulloch	
G-BKVW	Airtour 56 balloon	G. Fitzpatrick	
G-BKVX	Airtour 56 balloon	E. G. Woolnough	
G-BKVY	Airtour 31 balloon	Airtour Balloon Co Ltd	
G-BKVZ	Boeing 767-204	Britannia Airways Ltd *Sir Winston Churchill*/Luton	
G-BKWA	Cessna 404 Titan	Hawk Aviation Ltd (G-BELV)/ E. Midlands	
G-BKWB	EMB-110P2 Bandeirante	Nessatone Ltd (G-CHEV)	
G-BKWD	Taylor JT.2 Titch	E. Shouler	
G-BKWE	Colt 17A balloon	Hot-Air Balloon Co Ltd	
G-BKWG	PZL-104 Wilga 35A	Anglo-Polish Sailplanes Ltd	
G-BKWI	Pitts S-2A	R. A. Seeley/Denham	
G-BKWR	Cameron V-65 balloon	April & Gilbert Games Photographers	
G-BKWW	Cameron O-77 balloon	A. M. Marten	
G-BKWY	Cessna F.152	Cambridge Aero Club	
G-BKXA	Robin R.2100	G. J. Anderson & ptnrs	
G-BKXC	Cameron V-77 balloon	P. Sarretti	
G-BKXD	SA.365N Dauphin 2	Bond Helicopters Ltd/Bourn	
G-BKXE	SA.365N Dauphin 2	Bond Helicopters Ltd/Bourn	
G-BKXF	PA-28R Cherokee Arrow 200	P. L. Brunton	
G-BKXG	Cessna T.303	Sutton Windows Ltd	
G-BKXI	Cessna T.303	Repclif Aviation Ltd	
G-BKXK	SA.365N Dauphin 2	The Marconi Co Ltd	
G-BKXL	Cameron Bottle 70 balloon	Cameron Balloons Ltd	
G-BKXM	Colt 17A balloon	R. G. Turnbull	
G-BKXN	ICA IS-28M2A	British Aerospace PLC/Filton	
G-BKXO	Rutan LongEz	P. J. Wareham	
G-BKXP	Auster AOP.6	R. Skingley	
G-BKXR	D.31A Turbulent	S. B. Churchill	
G-BKXS	Colt 56A balloon	Hot-Air Balloon Co Ltd	
G-BKXT	Cameron D-50 airship	Cameron Balloons Ltd	
G-BKXU	Cameron Dairy Queen Cone balloon	Cameron Balloons Ltd	
G-BKXX	Cameron V-65 balloon	A. J. Legg & C. H. Harbord	
G-BKXY	Westland WG.30 Srs 100-60	Westland Helicopters Ltd/Yeovil	
G-BKYA	Boeing 737-236	British Airways *River Derwent*/ Heathrow	
G-BKYB	Boeing 737-236	British Airways *River Stour*/Heathrow	
G-BKYC	Boeing 737-236	British Airways *River Wye*/Heathrow	
G-BKYD	Boeing 737-236	British Airways *River Conway*/ Heathrow	
G-BKYE	Boeing 737-236	British Airways *River Lagan*/Heathrow	
G-BKYF	Boeing 737-236	British Airways *River Spey*/Heathrow	
G-BKYG	Boeing 737-236	British Airways *River Exe*/Heathrow	
G-BKYH	Boeing 737-236	British Airways *River Dart*/Heathrow	
G-BKYI	Boeing 737-236	British Airways *River Waveney*/ Heathrow	
G-BKYJ	Boeing 737-236	British Airways *River Neath*/Heathrow	
G-BKYK	Boeing 737-236	British Airways *River Foyle*/Heathrow	
G-BKYL	Boeing 737-236	British Airways *River Isis*/Heathrow	
G-BKYM	Boeing 737-236	British Airways *River Cam*/Heathrow	
G-BKYN	Boeing 737-236	British Airways *River Ayr*/Heathrow	
G-BKYO	Boeing 737-236	British Airways *River Kennet*/ Heathrow	
G-BKYP	Boeing 737-236	British Airways *River Ystwyth*/ Heathrow	
G-BKYR	—	British Airways/Heathrow	
G-BKYS	—	British Airways/Heathrow	
G-BKYT	—	British Airways/Heathrow	
G-BKYU	—	British Airways/Heathrow	
G-BKYV	—	British Airways/Heathrow	
G-BKYW	—	British Airways/Heathrow	
G-BKYX	—	British Airways/Heathrow	
G-BKYY	—	British Airways/Heathrow	
G-BKYZ	—	British Airways/Heathrow	
G-BKZA	Cameron N-77 balloon	University of Bath Students Union	
G-BKZB	Cameron V-77 balloon	A. J. Montgomery	
G-BKZC	Cessna A.152	Montaguis Ltd/Kuwait	

Notes	Reg.	Type	Owner or Operator
	G-BKZD	Cessna A.152	Montaguis Ltd/Kuwait
	G-BKZE	AS.332L Super Puma	British International Helicopters/ Aberdeen
	G-BKZF	Cameron V-56 balloon	G. M. Hobster
	G-BKZG	AS.332L Super Puma	British International Helicopters/ Aberdeen
	G-BKZH	AS.332L Super Puma	British International Helicopters/ Aberdeen
	G-BKZI	Bell 206B JetRanger 2	Heliwork Ltd/Thruxton
	G-BKZJ	Bensen B.8MV	S. H. Kirkby
	G-BKZL	Colt AS-42 airship	Colt Balloons Ltd
	G-BKZM	Isaacs Fury II (K2060)	J. Evans
	G-BKZT	FRED Srs 2	A. E. Morris
	G-BKZV	Bede BD-4A	A. L. Bergamasco/Headcorn
	G-BKZW	Beech C90 King Air	National Airways/Southend
	G-BKZY	Cameron N-77 balloon	W. Counties Automobile Co Ltd
	G-BLAA	Fournier RF-5	A. D. Wren/Southend
	G-BLAC	Cessna FA.152	Lancashire Aero Club/Barton
	G-BLAD	Thunder Ax7-77-1 balloon	V. P. Gardiner
	G-BLAF	Stolp V-Star SA.900	J. E. Malloy
	G-BLAG	Pitts S-1D Special	S. A. W. Becker
	G-BLAH	Thunder Ax7-77-1 balloon	T. Donnelly
	G-BLAI	Monnet Sonerai IIL	T. Simpson
	G-BLAJ	Pazmany PL.4A	J. D. LePine
	G-BLAM	Jodel DR.360	B. F. Baldock
	G-BLAS	V.S.361 Spitfire F.IX (MJ730)	Aero Vintage Ltd
	G-BLAT	Jodel D.150	R. Tyler
	G-BLAW	PA-28-181 Archer II	David Martin Couriers Ltd/Booker
	G-BLAX	Cessna FA.152	Shoreham Flight Simulation Ltd/ Bournemouth
	G-BLAY	Robin HR.100/200B	B. A. Mills
	G-BLCA	Bell 206B JetRanger 3	R.M.H. Stainless Ltd
	G-BLCC	Thunder Ax7-77Z balloon	P. Hassell Ltd
	G-BLCF	EAA AcroSport 2	M. J. Watkins & ptnrs
	G-BLCG	SOCATA TB.10 Tobago	J. A. & D. I. Hope (G-BHES)/Shoreham
	G-BLCH	Colt 56D balloon	A. D. McCutcheon
	G-BLCI	EAA Acrosport	P. A. Falter/Biggin Hill
	G-BLCK	V.S.361 Spitfire F.IX (TE566)	Historic Aircraft Collection Ltd
	G-BLCM	SOCATA TB.9 Tampico	Repclif Aviation Ltd/Liverpool
	G-BLCT	Jodel DR.220 2+2	H. W. Jemmett
	G-BLCU	Scheibe SF.25B Falke	B. Lumb & ptnrs/Rufforth
	G-BLCV	Hoffman H-36 Dimona	Economic Insulations Ltd
	G-BLCW	Evans VP-1	K. D. Pearce
	G-BLCX	Glaser-Dirks DG.400	B. A. Eastwell
	G-BLCY	Thunder Ax7-65Z balloon	Thunder Balloons Ltd
	G-BLCZ	Cessna 441	Northair Aviation Ltd/Leeds
	G-BLDA	SOCATA Rallye 110ST	Martin Ltd/Biggin Hill
	G-BLDB	Taylor JT.1 Monoplane	C. J. Bush
	G-BLDC	K&S Jungster 1	C. A. Laycock
	G-BLDD	WAG-Aero CUBy AcroTrainer	C. A. Laycock
	G-BLDE	Boeing 737-2E7	Dan-Air Services Ltd/Gatwick
	G-BLDG	PA-25 Pawnee 260C	L. G. & M. Appelbeck
	G-BLDH	BAC One-Eleven 475EZ	McAlpine Aviation Ltd/Luton
	G-BLDJ	PA-28-161 Warrior II	SFT Aviation Ltd/Bournemouth
	G-BLDK	Robinson R-22	William Towns Ltd
	G-BLDL	Cameron Truck 56 balloon	Cameron Balloons Ltd
	G-BLDM	Hiller UH-12E	G. & S. G. Neal (Helicopters) Ltd
	G-BLDN	Rand KR-2	R. Y. Kendal
	G-BLDP	Slingsby T.67M Firefly	Cavendish Aviation Ltd/Netherthorpe
	G-BLDT	BN-2B Islander	Pilatus BN Ltd/Bembridge
	G-BLDU	BN-2B Islander	Pilatus BN Ltd/Bembridge
	G-BLDX	BN-2B Islander	Air Furness Ltd/Walney Island
	G-BLDY	Bell 212	Bristow Helicopters Ltd
	G-BLEB	Colt 69A balloon	I. R. M. Jacobs
	G-BLEC	BN-2B-27 Islander	LEC Refrigeration PLC (G-BJBG)
	G-BLEI	BN-2B-26 Islander	Pilatus BN Ltd/Bembridge
	G-BLEJ	PA-28-161 Warrior II	Eglinton Flying Group
	G-BLEL	Ax7-77-245 balloon	T. S. Price
	G-BLEP	Cameron V-65 balloon	D. Chapman

The G-BLBA-BZ batch has been reserved for British Airways.

Reg.	Type	Owner or Operator	Notes
G-BLES	SA.750 Acroduster Too	R. W. L. Breckell	
G-BLET	Thunder Ax7-77-1 balloon	Servatruc Ltd	
G-BLEV	AS.355F Twin Squirrel	Haydon-Baillie Naval & Aircraft Museum/Southampton	
G-BLEW	Cessna F.182Q	Interair Aviation Ltd/Bournemouth	
G-BLEY	SA.365N Dauphin 2	Bond Helicopters Ltd/Bourn	
G-BLEZ	SA.365N Dauphin 2	Bond Helicopters Ltd/Bourn	
G-BLFE	Cameron Sphinx SS balloon	Forbes Europe Inc	
G-BLFF	Cessna F.172M	Air Advertising UK Ltd	
G-BLFJ	F.27 Friendship Mk 100	Air UK Ltd (G-OMAN/G-SPUD)/Norwich	
G-BLFT	P.56 Provost T.1	B. W. H. Parkhouse	
G-BLFV	Cessna 182R	Goddard Kay Rogers & Associates Ltd/Booker	
G-BLFW	AA-5 Traveler	M. Swanborough	
G-BLFY	Cameron V-77 balloon	A. N. F. Pertwee	
G-BLFZ	PA-31-310C Turbo Navajo	Huktra UK Ltd	
G-BLGB	Short SD3-60	Loganair Ltd/Glasgow	
G-BLGH	Robin DR.300/180R	Booker Gliding Club Ltd	
G-BLGI	McCullogh J.2	R. J. Everett	
G-BLGM	Cessna 425	J. Hanson	
G-BLGN	Skyhawk Gyroplane	S. M. Hawkins	
G-BLGO	Bensen B.8M	F. Vernon	
G-BLGP	WAG-Aero Super CUBy	International School of Choveifat	
G-BLGR	Bell 47G-4A	Land Air Ltd	
G-BLGS	SOCATA Rallye 180T	Lasham Gliding Society Ltd	
G-BLGT	PA-18 Super Cub 95	T. A. Reed/Dunkeswell	
G-BLGV	Bell 206B JetRanger	Land Air Ltd	
G-BLGW	F.27 Friendship Mk 200	Air UK Ltd/Norwich	
G-BLGX	Thunder Ax7-65 balloon	Harper & Co (Glasgow) Ltd	
G-BLGY	Grob G.109B	T. I. Dale-Harris & K.N.C. (One) Ltd	
G-BLHA	Thunder Ax10-160 balloon	Thunder Balloons Ltd	
G-BLHB	Thunder Ax10-160 balloon	Thunder Balloons Ltd	
G-BLHD	BAC One-Eleven 492GM	McAlpine Aviation Ltd/Luton	
G-BLHE	Pitts S-1E Special	W. R. Penaluna	
G-BLHF	Nott/Cameron ULD.2 balloon	J. R. P. Nott	
G-BLHG	Hoffman H-36 Dimona	C. H. Dobson	
G-BLHH	Jodel DR.315	G. G. Milton	
G-BLHI	Colt 17A balloon	Thunder & Colt Ltd	
G-BLHJ	Cessna F.172P	P. P. D. Howard-Johnston/Edinburgh	
G-BLHK	Colt 105A balloon	Hale Hot-Air Balloon Club	
G-BLHM	PA-18 Super Cub 95	J. S. Simmonds/Kidlington	
G-BLHN	Robin HR.100/285	H. M. Bouquiere/Biggin Hill	
G-BLHO	AA-5A Cheetah	Andreason Racing & Tuning Ltd	
G-BLHR	GA-7 Cougar	Fotex Aviation Ltd	
G-BLHS	Bellanca 7ECA Citabria	J. W. Platten & E. J. Timmins	
G-BLHW	Varga 2150A Kachina	Willoughby Farms Ltd	
G-BLHZ	Varga 2150A Kachina	MLP Aviation Ltd/Elstree	
G-BLID	D.H.112 Venom FB.50	P. F. A. Hoar/Cranfield	
G-BLIE	D.H.112 Venom FB.50	Air Charter (Scotland) Ltd/Glasgow	
G-BLIG	Cameron V-65 balloon	W. Davison	
G-BLIH	PA-18 Super Cub 135	I. R. F. Hammond	
G-BLIK	Wallis WA-116/F/S	K. H. Wallis	
G-BLIO	Cameron R-42 gas balloon	Cameron Balloons Ltd	
G-BLIP	Cameron N-77 balloon	Systems 80 Group Ltd	
G-BLIT	Thorp T-18 CW	A. J. Waller	
G-BLIV	Cameron O-105 balloon	A. M. Thompson	
G-BLIW	P.56 Provost T.51	Pulsegrove Ltd (stored)/Shoreham	
G-BLIX	Saro Skeeter Mk 12 (XL809)	A. P. Nowicki	
G-BLIY	M.S.892A Rallye Commodore	L. Everex & Sons Ltd	
G-BLIZ	PA-46-310P Malibu	Malibu Flying Services Ltd	
G-BLJD	Glaser-Dirks DG.400	P. A. Hearne & ptnrs	
G-BLJE	AB-206B JetRanger	Transit Support Services Ltd/Humberside	
G-BLJF	Cameron O-65 balloon	D. Fowler	
G-BLJG	Cameron N-105 balloon	New DFS Furniture Ltd	
G-BLJH	Cameron N-77 balloon	A. J. Clarke & J. M. Hallam	
G-BLJI	Colt 105A balloon	Colt Balloons Ltd	
G-BLJJ	Cessna 305 Bird Dog	P. Dawe	
G-BLJK	Evans VP-2	R. R. Pierce	
G-BLJM	Beech 95-B55 Baron	Elstree Aircraft Hire Ltd	
G-BLJN	Nott-Cameron ULD-1 balloon	J. R. P. Nott	
G-BLJO	Cessna F.152	M. J. Endacott	
G-BLJP	Cessna F.150L	F. & S. E. Horridge/Lasham	
G-BLJX	Bensen B.8M	R. Snow	

Notes	Reg.	Type	Owner or Operator
	G-BLJY	Sequoia F.8L Falco	K. Morris
	G-BLKA	D.H.112 Venom FB.54 (WR410)	A. Topen/Cranfield
	G-BLKB	Boeing 737-3T5	Orion Airways Ltd/E. Midlands
	G-BLKC	Boeing 737-3T5	Orion Airways Ltd *Ciudad de Mojocar*/ E. Midlands
	G-BLKD	Boeing 737-3T5	Orion Airways Ltd/E. Midlands
	G-BLKE	Boeing 737-3T5	Orion Airways Ltd/E. Midlands
	G-BLKF	Thunder Ax10-160 balloon	Thunder Balloons Ltd
	G-BLKG	Thunder Ax10-160 balloon	Thunder Balloons Ltd
	G-BLKH	Thunder Ax10-160 balloon	Thunder Balloons Ltd
	G-BLKI	Thunder Ax10-160 balloon	Thunder Balloons Ltd
	G-BLKJ	Thunder Ax7-65 balloon	D. T. Watkins
	G-BLKK	Evans VP-1	R. W. Burrows
	G-BLKL	D.31 Turbulent	D. L. Ripley
	G-BLKM	Jodel DR.1051	T. C. Humphreys
	G-BLKP	BAe Jetstream 3102	British Aerospace Ltd/Prestwick
	G-BLKU	Colt 56 SS balloon	Hot-Air Balloon Co Ltd
	G-BLKV	Boeing 767-204	Britannia Airways Ltd/Luton
	G-BLKW	Boeing 767-204	Britannia Airways Ltd *Sir Frank Whittle*/ Luton
	G-BLKY	Beech 95-58	Kebbell Holdings Ltd/Leavesden
	G-BLKZ	Pilatus P2-05	Autokraft Ltd
	G-BLLA	Bensen B.8M	K. T. Donaghey
	G-BLLB	Bensen B.8M	D. H. Moss
	G-BLLC	Beech 200 Super King Air	British Airways (G-LKOW)/Booker
	G-BLLD	Cameron O-77 balloon	J. P. Edge
	G-BLLE	Cameron 60 Burger King SS balloon	Burger King UK Ltd
	G-BLLH	Jodel DR.220A 2+2	D. R. Scott-Songhurst/Booker
	G-BLLM	PA-23 Aztec 250E	C. & M. Thomas (G-BBNM)/Cardiff
	G-BLLN	PA-18 Super Cub 95	W. H. Henry & A. T. Jeans
	G-BLLO	PA-18 Super Cub 95	D. G. & M. G. Marketts/Shobdon
	G-BLLP	Slingsby T.67B	Biggin Hill School of Flying
	G-BLLR	Slingsby T.67B	Trent Air Services Ltd/Cranfield
	G-BLLS	Slingsby T.67B	Trent Air Services Ltd/Cranfield
	G-BLLT	AA-5B Tiger	Alpha Welding & Engineering Ltd
	G-BLLU	Cessna 421C	J. Rowe/Manchester
	G-BLLV	Slingsby T.67B	BLS Aviation Ltd/Elstree
	G-BLLW	Colt 56B balloon	J. C. Stupples
	G-BLLY	Cessna 340A	Thunder & Colt Ltd
	G-BLLZ	Rutan LongEz	G. E. Relf & ptnrs
	G-BLMA	Zlin 326 Trener Master	G. P. Northcott/Shoreham
	G-BLMC	Avro 698 Vulcan B.2A (XM575) ★	Aeropark/E. Midlands
	G-BLMD	Robinson R-22	Sloane Helicopters Ltd/Luton
	G-BLME	Robinson R-22	Kindell Motors
	G-BLMG	Grob G.109B	K. & A. Barton
	G-BLMI	PA-18 Super Cub 95	B. J. Borsberry
	G-BLMN	Rutan LongEz	D. J. Bowie
	G-BLMO	Cameron 60 Demistica Bottle SS balloon	Cameron Balloons Ltd
	G-BLMP	PA-17 Vagabond	M. Austin/Popham
	G-BLMR	PA-18 Super Cub 150	Skyfever Aviation Enterprises/ Biggin Hill
	G-BLMT	PA-18 Super Cub 135	I. S. Runnalls
	G-BLMV	Jodel DR.1051	S. Windsor
	G-BLMW	Nipper T.66 RA45/3	S. L. Millar
	G-BLMX	Cessna FR.172H	A. J. Fuller & ptnrs/Felthorpe
	G-BLMZ	Colt 105A balloon	M. J. Hutchins
	G-BLNA	Beech B90 King Air	National Airways (G-BHGT/G-AWWK)/ Southend
	G-BLNB	V.802 Viscount	British Air Ferries (G-AOHV)/Southend
	G-BLNC	BN-2B Islander	Pilatus BN Ltd/Bembridge
	G-BLNJ	BN-2B Islander	Loganair Ltd/Glasgow
	G-BLNK	BN-2B Islander	Pilatus BN Ltd/Bembridge
	G-BLNL	BN-2B Islander	Pilatus BN Ltd/Bembridge
	G-BLNM	BN-2B Islander	Pilatus BN Ltd/Bembridge
	G-BLNN	PA-38-112 Tomahawk	Nalson Aviation Ltd (G-CGFC)/ Biggin Hill
	G-BLNO	FRED Srs 3	L. W. Smith
	G-BLNS	BN-2B Islander	Pilatus BN Ltd/Bembridge
	G-BLNT	BN-2B Islander	Pilatus BN Ltd/Bembridge
	G-BLNU	BN-2B Islander	Pilatus BN Ltd/Bembridge
	G-BLNV	BN-2B Islander	Pilatus BN Ltd/Bembridge

Reg.	Type	Owner or Operator	Notes
G-BLNW	BN-2B Islander	Pilatus BN Ltd/Bembridge	
G-BLNX	BN-2B Islander	Pilatus BN Ltd/Bembridge	
G-BLNY	BN-2B Islander	Pilatus BN Ltd/Bembridge	
G-BLNZ	BN-2B Islander	Pilatus BN Ltd/Bembridge	
G-BLOA	V.806 Viscount	British Air Ferries Ltd (G-AOYJ)/ Southend	
G-BLOB	Colt 31A balloon	Jacques W. Soukup Ltd	
G-BLOC	Rand KR-2	F. Woodhouse	
G-BLOE	PA-31-350 Navajo Chieftain	PW Cleaning Services Ltd (G-NITE)	
G-BLOG	Cameron O-77 balloon	Britannia Balloon Group	
G-BLOJ	Thunder Ax7-77 Srs 1 balloon	J. W. Cato	
G-BLOK	Colt 77A balloon	D. L. Clark *Spritsa*	
G-BLOL	SNCAN Stampe SV-4A	Skysport Engineering	
G-BLOO	Sopwith Dove Replica	Skysport Engineering	
G-BLOR	PA-30 Twin Comanche 160	S. B. McIntyre & K. W. Felton	
G-BLOS	Cessna 185A (also flown with floats)	E. Brun	
G-BLOT	Colt Ax6-56B balloon	Thunder & Colt Ltd	
G-BLOU	Rand KR-2	D. Cole	
G-BLOV	Colt Ax5-42 Srs 1 balloon	Thunder & Colt Ltd	
G-BLPA	Piper J-3C-65 Cub	G. A. Card	
G-BLPB	Turner TSW Hot Two Wot	J. R. Woolford & K. M. Thomas	
G-BLPE	PA-18 Super Cub 95	A. Haig-Thomas	
G-BLPF	Cessna FR.172G	E. J. McMillan/Perth	
G-BLPG	J/1N Alpha	P. G. & A. Valentine (G-AZIH)	
G-BLPH	Cessna FRA.150L	S. Moss & B. Salter/Shoreham	
G-BLPI	Slingsby T.67B	W. F. Hall	
G-BLPK	Cameron V-65 balloon	A. J. & C. P. Nicholls	
G-BLPM	AS.332L Super Puma	Bristow Helicopters Ltd	
G-BLPN	M.S.894E Rallye 220GT	Midair Services Ltd	
G-BLPP	Cameron V-77 balloon	L. P. Purfield	
G-BLPV	Short SD3-60	Air UK Ltd/Norwich	
G-BLPY	Short SD3-60	Air UK Ltd/Norwich	
G-BLRB	D.H.104 Devon C.2 (VP962)	V. S. E. Norman/Kemble	
G-BLRC	PA.18 Super Cub 135	R. A. L. Hubbard	
G-BLRD	MBB Bo.209 Monsun 150FV	M. D. Ward	
G-BLRE	Slingsby T.67D	Slingsby Aviation Ltd/Kirkbymoorside	
G-BLRF	Slingsby T.67C	Slingsby Aviation Ltd/Kirkbymoorside	
G-BLRG	Slingsby T.67B	Denham School of Flying	
G-BLRH	Rutan Long Ez	G. L. Thompson	
G-BLRJ	Jodel DR.1051	M. P. Hallam	
G-BLRL	CP.301C-1 Emeraude	R. A. Abrahams/Barton	
G-BLRM	Glaser-Dirks DG.400	R. L. McLean & J. N. Ellis	
G-BLRN	D.H.104 Devon C.2	C. W. Simpson	
G-BLRP	FMA IA.58-A Pucara	Grampian Helicopters International Ltd	
G-BLRS			
G-BLRT	Short SD3-60	Guernsey Airlines Ltd	
G-BLRW	Cameron 77 Elephant balloon	Forbes Europe Inc	
G-BLRX	SOCATA TB.9 Tampico	Wiselock Ltd/Elstree	
G-BLRY	AS.332L Super Puma	Bristow Helicopters Ltd	
G-BLRZ	SOCATA TB.9 Tampico	Aldred Associates Ltd	
G-BLSC	Consolidated PBY-5A Catalina (JV928)	J. N. Watts & J. P. W. Wilson/ Barkston Heath	
G-BLSF	AA-5A Cheetah	J. P. E. Walsh (G-BGCK)	
G-BLSH	Cameron V-77 balloon	Property Six	
G-BLSI	Colt AS-56 airship	Hot-Air Balloon Co Ltd	
G-BLSJ	Thunder Ax8-90 balloon	Thunder Balloons Ltd	
G-BLSK	Colt 77A balloon	HR & H. Marketing Research International Ltd	
G-BLSM	H.S.125 Srs 700B	Dravidian Air Services Ltd/Heathrow	
G-BLSN	Colt AS-56 airship	Colt Balloons Ltd	
G-BLSO	Colt AS-42 airship	K. L. C. M. Busemeyer	
G-BLSR	Everett autogyro	R. J. Everett	
G-BLST	Cessna 421C	Cecil Aviation Ltd/Cambridge	
G-BLSU	Cameron A-210 balloon	Skysales Ltd	
G-BLSX	Cameron O-105 balloon	B. J. Petteford	
G-BLSY	Bell 222A	Glen International PLC	
G-BLTA	Thunder Ax7-77A	M. J. Forster & K. A. Schlussler	
G-BLTB	PA-42-720 Cheyenne IIIA	McAlpine Aviation Ltd/Luton	
G-BLTC	D.31 Turbulent	G. P. Smith & A. W. Burton	
G-BLTE	Cessna F.182G	Western Automobile Ltd/Edinburgh	
G-BLTF	Robinson R-22A	Forest Dale Hotels Ltd	
G-BLTG	WAR Sea Fury (WJ237)	P. J. Collins	
G-BLTH	Cessna 404	Casair Aviation Ltd (G-BKVH/G-WTVA)/ Teesside	

Notes	Reg.	Type	Owner or Operator
	G-BLTK	R. Commander 112TC	B. Rogalewski/Denham
	G-BLTM	Robin HR.200/100	P. D. Wheatland/Barton
	G-BLTN	Thunder Ax7-65 balloon	J. A. Liddle
	G-BLTO	Short SD3-60	Guernsey Airlines Ltd
	G-BLTP	H.S.125 Srs 700B	Dravidian Air Services Ltd/Heathrow
	G-BLTR	Scheibe SF.25B Falke	V. Mallon/W. Germany
	G-BLTS	Rutan Long Ez	R. W. Cutler
	G-BLTT	Slingsby T.67B	Denham School of Flying
	G-BLTU	Slingsby T.67B	W. F. Hall
	G-BLTV	Slingsby T.67B	Slingsby Aviation PLC/Kirkbymoorside
	G-BLTW	Slingsby T.67B	Slingsby Aviation PLC/Kirkbymoorside
	G-BLTX	—	—
	G-BLTZ	SOCATA TB.10 Tobago	Martin Hill/Biggin Hill
	G-BLUA	Robinson R-22	Kanestar Ltd
	G-BLUB	—	—
	G-BLUE	Colting Ax7-77A balloon	M. R. & C. Cumpston
	G-BLUF	Thunder Ax10-180 balloon	Thunder & Colt Ltd
	G-BLUG	Thunder Ax10-180 balloon	Thunder & Colt Ltd
	G-BLUH	Thunder Ax10-180 balloon	Thunder & Colt Ltd
	G-BLUI	Thunder Ax7-65 balloon	A. Stace
	G-BLUJ	Cameron V-56 balloon	J. N. W. West
	G-BLUK	Bond Sky Dancer	J. Owen
	G-BLUL	Jodel DR.1051/M1	J. Owen
	G-BLUM	SA.365N Dauphin 2	Bond Helicopters Ltd
	G-BLUN	SA.365N Dauphin 2	Bond Helicopters Ltd
	G-BLUO	SA.365N Dauphin 2	Bond Helicopters Ltd
	G-BLUP	SA.365N Dauphin 2	Bond Helicopters Ltd
	G-BLUS	L.1011 TriStar 500	British Airways Laggan Bay/Heathrow
	G-BLUT	L.1011 TriStar 500	British Airways Dunnet Bay/Heathrow
	G-BLUV	Grob G.109B	Go-Grob Ltd
	G-BLUX	Slingsby T.67M	Slingsby Aviation Ltd/Kirkbymoorside
	G-BLUY	Colt 69A balloon	The Balloon Goes Up Ltd
	G-BLUZ	D.H.82B Queen Bee (LF858)	B. Bayes
	G-BLVA	Airtour AH-56 balloon	Airtour Balloon Co Ltd
	G-BLVB	Airtour AH-56 balloon	Airtour Balloon Co Ltd
	G-BLVC	Airtour AH-31 balloon	Airtour Balloon Co Ltd
	G-BLVE	Boeing 747-2B4B	British Airtours City of Lincoln/Gatwick
	G-BLVF	Boeing 747-2B4B	British Airtours City of Lancaster/Gatwick
	G-BLVG	EMB-110P1 Bandeirante	Business Air Centre Ltd (G-RLAY)
	G-BLVH	Boeing 757-236	Air Europe Ltd Jackie/Gatwick
	G-BLVI	Slingsby T.67M	Slingsby Aviation Ltd/Kirkbymoorside
	G-BLVK	CAARP CAP-10B	BAC Aviation Ltd/Southend
	G-BLVL	PA-28-161 Warrior II	C.S.E. Aviation Ltd/Kidlington
	G-BLVN	Cameron N-77 balloon	B. Hodge
	G-BLVR	—	—
	G-BLVS	Cessna 150M	W. Lancashire Aero Club Ltd/Woodvale
	G-BLVT	Cessna FR.172J	T. R. Scorer & J. J. Booth/Cambridge
	G-BLVU	Pitts S-2A	A. J. E. Ditheridge
	G-BLVV	Bell 206B JetRanger	Bristow Helicopters Ltd
	G-BLVW	Cessna F.172H	G. S. Evans
	G-BLVY	Colt 21A balloon	Colt Balloons Ltd
	G-BLVZ	R. Commander 114	Adrian Seal Textiles Ltd
	G-BLWB	Thunder Ax6-56 balloon	G. G. Bacon
	G-BLWD	PA-34-200T Seneca	C.S.E. Aviation Ltd/Kidlington
	G-BLWE	Colt 90A balloon	Thunder & Colt Ltd
	G-BLWF	Robin HR.100/210	Hill Leigh Group Ltd
	G-BLWG	Varga 2150A Kachina	MLP Aviation Ltd/Elstree
	G-BLWH	Fournier RF-6B-100	Gloster Aero Club Ltd/Staverton
	G-BLWL	Colt 31A balloon	Hot Air Balloon Co Ltd
	G-BLWM	Bristol M.1C replica (C4912)	D. M. Cashmore
	G-BLWO	Cameron N-77 balloon	A. B. Williams
	G-BLWP	PA-38-112 Tomahawk	A. Dodd/Booker
	G-BLWR	—	—
	G-BLWT	Evans VP-1	G. B. O'Neill
	G-BLWV	Cessna F.152	Redhill Flying Club
	G-BLWW	Taylor Mini Imp Model C	M. K. Field
	G-BLWX	Cameron N-56 balloon	Skipton Building Soc
	G-BLWY	Robin 2161D	A. Walton
	G-BLWZ	M.S.883 Rallye 115	J. H. Betton
	G-BLXA	SOCATA TB.20 Trinidad	Street Construction (Wigan) Ltd
	G-BLXB	Colt 240A balloon	Colt Balloons Ltd

Reg.	Type	Owner or Operator	Notes
G-BLXC	Colt 240A balloon	Colt Balloons Ltd	
G-BLXF	Cameron V-77 balloon	D. I. Gray-Fisk	
G-BLXG	Colt 21A balloon	Balloon & Airship Co Ltd	
G-BLXH	Fournier RF-3	D. T. Kaberry/Blackpool	
G-BLXI	CP.1310-C3 Super Emeraude	M. I. Ingamells	
G-BLXJ	SA.315B Lama	Autair Ltd/Cranfield	
G-BLXK	Agusta-Bell 205	Autair Helicopters Ltd/Cranfield	
G-BLXL	Colt AS-105 airship	Thunder & Colt Ltd	
G-BLXM	—	—	
G-BLXO	Jodel D.150	P. R. Powell	
G-BLXP	PA-28R Cherokee Arrow 200	London Flight Centre (Stansted) Ltd	
G-BLXR	AS.332L Super Puma	Bristow Helicopters Ltd	
G-BLXS	AS.332L Super Puma	Bristow Helicopters Ltd	
G-BLXT	RAF SE-5A (B4863)	The Hon A. M. M. Lindsay/Booker	
G-BLXX	PA-23 Aztec 250	Hockstar Ltd (G-PIED)	
G-BLXY	Cameron V-65 balloon	Gone With The Wind Ltd	
G-BLYB	Beech B200 Super King Air	Alfred McAlpine Aviation Ltd	
G-BLYC	PA-38-112 Tomahawk	D. R. Gliddon	
G-BLYD	SOCATA TB.20 Trinidad	R. J. Crocker	
G-BLYE	SOCATA TB.10 Tobago	Presspart Manufacturing Ltd	
G-BLYJ	Cameron V-77 balloon	E. E. Clark & J. A. Lomas	
G-BLYK	PA-34-220T Seneca 2	G. E. Walker/Jersey	
G-BLYM	B.121 Pup 2	D. J. Sage	
G-BLYP	Robin 3000/120	Lydd Air Training Centre Ltd	
G-BLYR	Airtour AH-77B balloon	Airtour Balloon Co Ltd	
G-BLYT	Airtour AH-77 balloon	Airtour Balloon Co Ltd	
G-BLYU	Airtour AH-31 balloon	Airtour Balloon Co Ltd	
G-BLYV	Airtour AH-56 balloon	Airtour Balloon Co Ltd	
G-BLYY	PA-28-181 Archer II	Fairway Graphics Ltd	
G-BLZA	Scheibe SF.25B Falke	P. Downes & D. Gardner	
G-BLZB	Cameron N-65 balloon	D. Bareford	
G-BLZC	Flamboyant Ax7-65 balloon	T. A. Adams	
G-BLZD	Robin R.1180T	A. D. Russell/Cambridge	
G-BLZE	Cessna F.152	Flairhire Ltd (G-CSSC)/Redhill	
G-BLZF	Thunder Ax7-77 balloon	J. A. Snowball & ptnrs	
G-BLZH	Cessna F.152	Metronote Aviation Ltd/Biggin Hill	
G-BLZM	Rutan Long Ez	B. C. Barton	
G-BLZN	Bell 206B JetRanger	J. P. Millward	
G-BLZP	Cessna F.152	W. H. & J. Rogers Group Ltd/Cranfield	
G-BLZR	Cameron A-140 balloon	Clipper Worldwide Trading Ltd	
G-BLZS	Cameron O-77 balloon	M. M. Cobbold	
G-BLZT	Short SD3-60	Air UK Ltd/Norwich	
G-BLZZ	CAARP CAP.21	D. M. Britten	
G-BMAA	Douglas DC-9-15	British Midland Airways Ltd *The Shah Diamond*/(G-BFIH)/E. Midlands	
G-BMAB	Douglas DC-9-15	British Midland Airways Ltd *The Great Mogul Diamond*/E. Midlands	
G-BMAC	Douglas DC-9-15	British Midland Airways Ltd *The Eugenie Diamond*/E. Midlands	
G-BMAD	Cameron V-77 balloon	F. J. J. Fielder	
G-BMAE	F-27 Friendship Mk 200	British Midland Airways Ltd/E. Midlands	
G-BMAF	Cessna 180F	P. Scales (G-BDVR)	
G-BMAG	Douglas DC-9-15	British Midland Airways Ltd *The Nassau Diamond*/E. Midlands	
G-BMAH	Douglas DC-9-14	British Midland Airways Ltd *The Florentine Diamond*/E. Midlands	
G-BMAI	Douglas DC-9-14	British Midland Airways Ltd *The Star of Este Diamond*/E. Midlands	
G-BMAK	Douglas DC-9-30	British Midland Airways Ltd *The Stewart Diamond*/E. Midlands	
G-BMAL	Sikorsky S-76A	Bond Helicopters Ltd/Bourn	
G-BMAM	Douglas DC-9-30	British Midland Airways Ltd *The Cullinan Diamond*/E. Midlands	
G-BMAO	Taylor JT.1 Monoplane	V. A. Wordsworth	
G-BMAP	F-27 Friendship Mk 200	Manx Airlines/Loganair Ltd	
G-BMAR	Short SD3-60	Loganair Ltd (G-BLCR)/Glasgow	
G-BMAT	V.813 Viscount	Sean T. Hully (Sales) Ltd (G-AZLT)	
G-BMAV	AS.350B Ecureuil	Scotia Investments Ltd	
G-BMAW	F-27 Friendship Mk 200	British Midland Airways Ltd/E. Midlands	
G-BMAX	FRED Srs 2	P. Cawkwell	
G-BMAY	PA-18 Super Cub 135	G. V. Harfield/Popham	
G-BMBB	Cessna F.150L	Telepoint Ltd	
G-BMBC	PA-31-350 Navajo Chieftain	Casair Aviation Ltd/Teesside	

Notes	Reg.	Type	Owner or Operator
	G-BMBD	—	—
	G-BMBE	PA-46-310P Malibu	Artix Ltd
	G-BMBF	Nord 3202B	F. & H. Aircraft Ltd/Sibson
	G-BMBI	PA-31-350 Navajo Chieftain	Streamline Aviation Ltd/E. Midlands
	G-BMBJ	Schempp-Hirth Janus CM	Oxfordshire Sportflying Ltd/Enstone
	G-BMBP	Colt Whisky Bottle balloon	Thunder & Colt Ltd
	G-BMBR	Issoire D77-M Motor Iris	G. R. Horner
	G-BMBS	Colt 105A balloon	A. P. Hardiman & H. G. Davies
	G-BMBT	Thunder Ax8-90 balloon	Capital Balloon Club Ltd
	G-BMBW	Bensen B.80	M. Vahdat
	G-BMBY	Beech A36 Bonanza	Shadow Photographic Ltd
	G-BMBZ	Scheibe SF.25E Falke	Cairngorm Gliding Club
	G-BMCB	Partenavia P.68B	Air Kilroe Ltd/Manchester
	G-BMCC	Thunder Ax7-77 balloon	H. N. Harben Ltd
	G-BMCD	Cameron V-65 balloon	M. C. Drye
	G-BMCE	Bensen B.8M	J. Lee
	G-BMCG	Grob G.109B	Soaring (Oxford) Ltd/Enstone
	G-BMCH	AB-206B JetRanger	Trent Air Services Ltd/Cranfield
	G-BMCI	Cessna F.172H	P. P. D. Howard-Johnston/Edinburgh
	G-BMCJ	PA-31-350 Navajo Chieftain	Chelsea Land (Finance) Ltd
	G-BMCK	Cameron O-77 balloon	D. L. Smith
	G-BMCM	Grob G.109B	Sonardyne Ltd/Blackbushe
	G-BMCN	Cessna F.152	Lincoln Aero Club Ltd/Sturgate
	G-BMCO	Colomban MC.15 Cri-Cri	G. P. Clarke
	G-BMCS	PA-22 Tri-Pacer 135	W. A. P. Darbishire
	G-BMCT	Cameron D-50 airship	Cameron Balloons Ltd
	G-BMCV	Cessna F.152	Leicester Aero Club Ltd
	G-BMCW	AS.332L Super Puma	Bristow Helicopters Ltd
	G-BMCX	AS.332L Super Puma	Bristow Helicopters Ltd
	G-BMCZ	Colt 69A balloon	Thunder & Colt Ltd
	G-BMDB	SE-5A replica	D. Biggs
	G-BMDC	PA-32-301 Saratoga	Maclaren Aviation/Newcastle
	G-BMDD	Slingsby T.29	D. I. H. Johnstone & L. Ward
	G-BMDE	Pientenpol Aircamper	D. Silsbury & B. P. Irish
	G-BMDF	Boeing 737-2E7	Dan-Air Services Ltd/Gatwick
	G-BMDG	Cameron O-105 balloon	Buddy Bombard Balloons Ltd
	G-BMDH	Cameron O-105 balloon	Buddy Bombard Balloons Ltd
	G-BMDI	Thunder Ax8-105Z balloon	Buddy Bombard Balloons Ltd
	G-BMDJ	Price Ax7-77S balloon	T. S. Price
	G-BMDK	PA-34-220T Seneca 3	Skyline Helicopters Ltd/Booker
	G-BMDM	Cessna 340A	Comsup Ltd
	G-BMDO	ARV Super 2	H. L. Wensley
	G-BMDP	Partenavia P.64B Oscar 200	D. Foey
	G-BMDR	—	—
	G-BMDS	Jodel D.120	D. Stansfield & M. Smith
	G-BMDU	Bell 214ST	Bristow Helicopters Ltd
	G-BMDV	Bell 47G-5	Trent Air Services Ltd/Cranfield
	G-BMDW	Dangerous Sports Club/Colt Hoppalong 1 balloon	D. A. C. Kirke
	G-BMDY	GA-7 Cougar	Eastern Air Taxis/Elstree
	G-BMDZ	Cessna 310Q	Computaplane Ltd/Glasgow
	G-BMEA	PA-18 Super Cub 95	I. M. Callier
	G-BMEB	Rotorway Scorpion 145	I. M. Bartlett
	G-BMEF	Beech C90 King Air	National Airways/Southend
	G-BMEG	SOCATA TB.10 Tobago	G. H. N. & R. V. Chamberlain
	G-BMEH	Jodel Super Special Mascaret	E. J. Horsfall/Blackpool
	G-BMEJ	PA-28R Cherokee Arrow 200	London Flight Centre (Stansted) Ltd
	G-BMEM	Fournier RF-4D	A. M. Witt
	G-BMET	Taylor JT.1 Monoplane	M. K. A. Blyth
	G-BMEU	Isaacs Fury II	A. W. Austin
	G-BMEV	PA-32RT-300T Lance	M. F. Calvert
	G-BMEX	Cessna A.150K	R. Kirkham & N. Brain/Netherthorpe
	G-BMEZ	Cameron D-50 airship	Cameron Balloons Ltd
	G-BMFB	Douglas AD-4W Skyraider	Coys of Kensington (Petrol Sales) Ltd
	G-BMFC	Douglas AD-4W Skyraider	Coys of Kensington (Petrol Sales) Ltd
	G-BMFD	PA-23 Aztec 250	Bomford & Evershed Ltd (G-BGYY)/ Coventry
	G-BMFG	Dornier Do.27A-4	Onderstar Aviation Ltd/Booker
	G-BMFH	Dornier Do.27A-4	Onderstar Aviation Ltd/Booker
	G-BMFI	PZL SZD-45A Ogar	Marrix Ltd/Redhill
	G-BMFJ	Thunder Ax7-77 balloon	Thunder & Colt Ltd
	G-BMFK	PA-28-236 Dakota	C. C. Butt
	G-BMFL	Rand KR-2	E. W. B. Comber & M. F. Leusby
	G-BMFN	QAC Quickie 200	W. Blair-Hickman

Reg.	Type	Owner or Operator	Notes
G-BMFP	PA-28-161 Warrior II	T. J. Froggatt & ptnrs/Blackbushe	
G-BMFT	H.S.748 Srs 2A	Euroair/British Airways	
G-BMFU	Cameron N-90 balloon	Cameron Balloons Ltd	
G-BMFW	Hughes 369E	Ford Helicopters Ltd	
G-BMFY	Grob G.109B	P. J. Shearer	
G-BMFZ	Cessna F.152	Cornwall Flying Club Ltd	
G-BMGB	PA-28 Cherokee Arrow 200	Malmesbury Specialist Cars	
G-BMGC	Fairey Swordfish Mk II	Strathallan Aircraft Collection	
G-BMGD	Colt 17A balloon	Airbureau Ltd	
G-BMGG	Cessna 152	A. S. Bamrah/Biggin Hill	
G-BMGH	PA-31-325 Navajo	Chaseside Holdings Ltd/Exeter	
G-BMGJ	—	—	
G-BMGK	—	—	
G-BMGL	—	—	
G-BMGM	—	—	
G-BMGN	—	—	
G-BMGO	—	—	
G-BMGP	Hughes 269C	A. H. Canvin	
G-BMGR	Grob G.109B	M. E. Garvey	
G-BMGS	Boeing 747-283B	British Airways *City of Swansea*/Heathrow	
G-BMGT	Cessna 310R	Airwork Ltd/Bournemouth	
G-BMGV	Robinson R-22	Foreman Hart Ltd	
G-BMGY	Lake LA-4-200 Buccaneer	M. A. Ashmole (G-BWKS/G-BDDI)	
G-BMHA	Rutan Long Ez	S. F. Elvins	
G-BMHF	Mooney M.20J	J. H. Cross/Biggin Hill	
G-BMHI	Cessna F.152	Skyviews & General Ltd/Leeds	
G-BMHJ	Thunder Ax7-65 balloon	D. Cole	
G-BMHK	Cameron V-77 balloon	B. J. Workman	
G-BMHL	Wittman W.8 Tailwind	T. G. Hoult	
G-BMHN	Robinson R-22A	Cross Lane Properties (Builders) Ltd	
G-BMHR	Grob G.109B	HRN Aviation Ltd	
G-BMHS	Cessna F.172M	C. H. Ludar-Smith	
G-BMHT	PA-28RT-201T Turbo Arrow	Vehicle Fleet Management Ltd	
G-BMHU	Viking Dragonfly	H. A. Bancroft-Wilson	
G-BMHX	Short SD3-60	Loganair Ltd/Manx Airlines	
G-BMHY	Short SD3-60	British Midland Airways Ltd/E. Midlands	
G-BMHZ	PA-28RT-201T Turbo Arrow	Bioeve Ltd	
G-BMIA	Thunder Ax8-90 balloon	A. G. R. Calder	
G-BMIB	Bell 206B JetRanger	Lee Aviation Ltd/Booker	
G-BMID	Jodel D.120	A. W. Cooke	
G-BMIF	AS.350B Ecureuil	Colt Car Co Ltd/Staverton	
G-BMIG	Cessna 172N	J. R. Nicholls/Conington	
G-BMIK	Dornier Do.27-A4	Wessex Aviation & Transport Ltd	
G-BMIL	—	—	
G-BMIM	Rutan Long Ez	R. M. Smith	
G-BMIO	Stoddard-Hamilton Glasair RG	A. H. Carrington	
G-BMIP	Jodel D.112	M. T. Kinch	
G-BMIR	Westland Wasp HAS.1	R. Windley	
G-BMIS	—	—	
G-BMIU	Enstrom F-28A	Rotor Enterprises Ltd	
G-BMIV	PA-28R-201T Turbo Arrow	Trindon Ltd/Little Snoring	
G-BMIW	PA-28-181 Archer II	J. R. Massey	
G-BMIY	Oldfield Baby Great Lakes	J. B. Scott (G-NOME)	
G-BMJA	PA-32R-301 Saratoga SP	Continental Cars (Stansted) Ltd	
G-BMJB	Cessna 152	RJS Aviation Ltd	
G-BMJC	Cessna 152	Cambridge Aero Club Ltd	
G-BMJD	Cessna 152	Fife Airport Management Ltd/Glenrothes	
G-BMJG	PA-28R Cherokee Arrow 200	D. J. D. Ritchie & ptnrs/Elstree	
G-BMJL	R. Commander 114	Air Charter Scotland Ltd/Glasgow	
G-BMJM	Evans VP-1	J. A. Mawby	
G-BMJN	Cameron O-65 balloon	E. J. A. Machole	
G-BMJO	PA-34-220T Seneca	Richard Arnold & Co Ltd	
G-BMJP	Colt AS-56 airship	Thunder & Colt Ltd	
G-BMJR	Cessna T.337H	John Roberts Services Ltd (G-NOVA)	
G-BMJS	Thunder Ax7-77 balloon	Anglia Balloon School Ltd	
G-BMJT	Beech 76 Duchess	Mike Osborne Insurance Services Ltd	
G-BMJV	Hughes 369D	Bristol Estates Ltd	
G-BMJW	AT-6D Harvard III	J. Woods	
G-BMJX	Wallis WA-116X	K. H. Wallis	
G-BMJY	Yakolev C18M	R. Lamplough/North Weald	
G-BMJZ	Cameron N-90 balloon	Windsor Pharmaceuticals Ltd	
G-BMKA	Robin 3000/120	Lydd Air Training Centre Ltd	

Notes	Reg.	Type	Owner or Operator
	G-BMKB	PA-18 Super Cub 135	C. Marsh
	G-BMKC	Piper J-3C-65 Cub	J. J. Anziani
	G-BMKD	Beech C90A King Air	Saipur Investments Ltd
	G-BMKE	PA-28-201 Arrow IV	P. A. Lancaster/Booker
	G-BMKF	Jodel DR.221	B. M. R. Clavel & J. M. A. Lassauze
	G-BMKG	PA-38-112 Tomahawk	R. J. Hickson
	G-BMKH	Colt 105A balloon	Thunder & Colt Ltd
	G-BMKI	Colt 21A balloon	Thunder & Colt Ltd
	G-BMKJ	Cameron V-77 balloon	R. C. Thursby
	G-BMKK	PA-28R Cherokee Arrow 200	J. D. Poole & S. J. Green
	G-BMKM	AB-206B JetRanger 3	Fizzle Ltd
	G-BMKN	Colt 31A balloon	Thunder & Colt Ltd
	G-BMKO	PA-28-181 Archer II	CP Aviation Ltd
	G-BMKP	Cameron V-77 balloon	Jacques W. Soukup Enterprises Ltd
	G-BMKR	PA-28-161 Warrior II	Field Flying Group (G-BGKR)/ Goodwood
	G-BMKS	Aerosport Scamp	J. N. Hamlen
	G-BMKV	Thunder Ax7-77 balloon	A. Hornak & M. J. Nadel
	G-BMKW	Cameron V-77 balloon	A. C. Garnett
	G-BMKX	Cameron 77 Elephant balloon	Cameron Balloons Ltd
	G-BMKY	Cameron O-65 balloon	First Reflex Ltd
	G-BMLA	Bell UH-1H ★	Grampian Helicopters International Ltd
	G-BMLB	Jodel D.120A	W. O. Brown
	G-BMLC	Short SD3-60	Loganair Ltd/Glasgow
	G-BMLH	Mooney M.20C	Fairprime Ltd/Blackbushe
	G-BMLJ	Cameron N-77 balloon	J. Money-Kyrle
	G-BMLK	Grob G.109B	A. Batters
	G-BMLL	Grob G.109B	A. H. R. Stansfield
	G-BMLP	Boeing 727-264	Dan-Air Services Ltd/Gatwick
	G-BMLS	PA-28R-201 Arrow III	Michael Gardner Ltd
	G-BMLT	Pietenpol Aircamper	R. A. & F. A. Hawke/Redhill
	G-BMLU	Colt 90A balloon	Danish Catering Services Ltd
	G-BMLV	Robinson R-22A	Skyline Helicopters Ltd/Booker
	G-BMLW	Cameron V-65 balloon	M. L. & L. P. Willoughby
	G-BMLX	Cessna F.150L	K. Gallo
	G-BMLY	Grob G.109B	P. H. Yarrow & D. G. Margetts
	G-BMLZ	Cessna 421C	Chaseside Holdings Ltd (G-OTAD/ G-BEVL)
	G-BMMC	Cessna T310Q	W. H. G. Nunn/Elstree
	G-BMMD	Rand KR-2	K. R. Wheatley
	G-BMME	Hoffman H-36 Dimona	D. D. Booker
	G-BMMF	FRED Srs 2	J. M. Jones
	G-BMMG	Thunder Ax7-77A balloon	Thunder & Colt Ltd
	G-BMMI	Pazmany PL.4	M. L. Martin
	G-BMMJ	Siren PIK-30	J. D. S. Thorne
	G-BMMK	Cessna 182P	M. S. Knight/Goodwood
	G-BMML	PA-38-112 Tomahawk	Atlantic Aviation Ltd
	G-BMMM	Cessna 152	A. S. Bamrah/Biggin Hill
	G-BMMN	Thunder Ax8-105 balloon	R. C. Weyda
	G-BMMP	Grob G.109B	B. F. Fraser-Smith & B. F. Pearson
	G-BMMR	Dornier Do.228-200	Suckling Airways Ltd/Ipswich
	G-BMMU	Thunder Ax8-105 balloon	H. C. Wright
	G-BMMV	ICA-Brasov IS-28M2A	T. Cust
	G-BMMW	Thunder Ax7-77 balloon	P. A. Georges
	G-BMMX	ICA-Brasov IS-28M2A	The Burn Gliding Club Ltd
	G-BMMY	Thunder Ax7-77 balloon	Double Glazing Components Ltd
	G-BMMZ	Boeing 737-2D6	Britannia Airways Ltd/Luton
	G-BMNB	Airbus A.300B4-203	Dan-Air Services Ltd/Gatwick
	G-BMNC	Airbus A.300B4-203	Dan-Air Services Ltd/Gatwick
	G-BMNE	—	—
	G-BMNF	Beech B200 Super King Air	Bernard Matthews PLC/Norwich
	G-BMNL	PA-28R Cherokee Arrow 200	Airways Aero Associations Ltd/Booker
	G-BMNO	PA-38-112 Tomahawk	J. A. Barlow/Staverton
	G-BMNP	PA-38-112 Tomahawk	Seal Executive Aircraft Ltd
	G-BMNT	PA-34-220T Seneca	R. J. Alford
	G-BMNU	Cameron V-77 balloon	V. Westerman
	G-BMNV	SNCAN Stampe SV-4D	Wessex Aviation & Transport Ltd
	G-BMNW	PA-31-350 Navajo Chieftain	Fletcher Rentals Ltd/Coventry
	G-BMNX	Colt 56A balloon	A. D. Pinner
	G-BMNY	Everett gyroplane	J. D. Colvin
	G-BMNZ	Cessna U206F	Macpara Ltd/Shobdon
	G-BMOA	Cessna 441	Automobile Association Developments Ltd
	G-BMOE	PA-28R Cherokee Arrow 200	P. S. Jessop

Reg.	Type	Owner or Operator	Notes
G-BMOF	Cessna U206G	Integrated Hydraulics Ltd	
G-BMOG	Thunder Ax7-77A balloon	Anglia Balloon School Ltd	
G-BMOH	Cameron N-77 balloon	Legal & General PLC	
G-BMOI	Partenavia P.68B	Simmette Ltd	
G-BMOJ	Cameron V-56 balloon	S. R. Bridge	
G-BMOK	ARV Super 2	Nik Coates Ltd	
G-BMOL	PA-23 Aztec 250	LDL Enterprises (G-BBSR)/Elstree	
G-BMOM	ICA-Brasov IS-28M2A	R. E. Todd	
G-BMON	Boeing 737-2K9	Monarch Airlines Ltd/Luton	
G-BMOO	FRED Srs 2	N. Purllant	
G-BMOP	PA-28R-201T Turbo Arrow III	Coleridge Self Service/Cardiff	
G-BMOT	Bensen B.8M	R. S. W. Jones	
G-BMOV	Cameron O-105 balloon	I. M. Hughes	
G-BMOW	G.159 Gulfstream 1	Birmingham Executive Airways PLC	
G-BMOX	Hovey Beta Bird	A. D. Tatton	
G-BMOY	Cameron A-250 balloon	Gone With The Wind Ltd	
G-BMOZ	Cameron O-160 balloon	R. M. Bishop	
G-BMPA	G.159 Gulfstream 1	Peregrine Air Services Ltd/Aberdeen	
G-BMPC	PA-28-181 Archer II	Charles Setton Trading Co Ltd	
G-BMPD	Cameron V-65 balloon	Cameron Balloons Ltd	
G-BMPF	OA.7 Optica	Brooklands Aircraft Co Ltd/Old Sarum	
G-BMPI	OA.7 Optica	Optica Industries Ltd/Old Sarum	
G-BMPL	OA.7 Optica	Optica Industries Ltd/Old Sarum	
G-BMPM	OA.7 Optica	Optica Industries Ltd/Old Sarum	
G-BMPN	OA.7 Optica	Optica Industries Ltd/Old Sarum	
G-BMPO	Cessna 182Q	John Lloyd & Sons Car Sales Ltd	
G-BMPP	Cameron N-77 balloon	Sarnia Balloon Group	
G-BMPR	PA-28R-200 Arrow III	J. Lloyd	
G-BMPS	Strojnik S-2A	T. J. Gardiner	
G-BMPU	Robinson R-22	Sloane Helicopters Ltd/Luton	
G-BMPV	PA-31-325 Navajo	L & M Food Group Ltd	
G-BMPY	D.H.82A Tiger Moth	S. M. F. Eisenstein	
G-BMRA	Boeing 757-236	British Airways *Beaumaris Castle*/Heathrow	
G-BMRB	Boeing 757-236	British Airways *Colchester Castle*/Heathrow	
G-BMRC	Boeing 757-236	British Airways *Rochester Castle*	
G-BMRD	Boeing 757-236	British Airways *Bothwell Castle*	
G-BMRE	Boeing 757-236	British Airways *Killyleagh Castle*	
G-BMRF	Boeing 757-236	British Airways *Hever Castle*	
G-BMRG	Boeing 757-236	British Airways *Caerphilly Castle*	
G-BMRH	Boeing 757-236	British Airways *Norwich Castle*	
G-BMRI	Boeing 757-236	British Airways *Tonbridge Castle*	
G-BMRJ	Boeing 757-236	British Airways *Old Wardour Castle*	
G-BMRK	—	British Airways	
G-BMRL	—	British Airways	
G-BMSA	Stinson HW.75 Voyager	P. F. Bennison (G-BCUM)/Barton	
G-BMSB	V.S.509 Spitfire IX	M. S. Bayliss (G-ASOZ)	
G-BMSC	Evans VP-2	F. R. Donaldson	
G-BMSD	PA-28-181 Archer II	Fairprime Ltd/Bournemouth	
G-BMSE	Valentin Taifun 17E	K. P. O'Sullivan	
G-BMSF	PA-38-112 Tomahawk	N. Bradley/Leeds	
G-BMSG	Saab 32A Lansen	Aces High Ltd/North Weald	
G-BMSH	Cessna 425	RCR Aviation Ltd	
G-BMSI	Cameron N-105 balloon	Direction Air Conditioning Ltd	
G-BMSK	Hoffman H-36 Dimona	J. P. Kovacs	
G-BMSL	FRED Srs 3	A. C. Coombe	
G-BMSO	—	—	
G-BMSP	Hughes 369HS	R. Windley	
G-BMSR	G.159 Gulfstream 1	Peregrine Air Services Ltd/Aberdeen	
G-BMSS	—	—	
G-BMST	Cameron N-31 balloon	Hot Air Balloon Co Ltd	
G-BMSU	Cessna 152	D. M. Leonard/Tees-side	
G-BMSV	PA-31-350 Navajo Chieftain	Regency Aviation Services Ltd	
G-BMSW	Cessna T.210M	Foxgrove Construction Ltd	
G-BMSX	PA-30 Twin Comanche 160	M. Sparks/Bristol	
G-BMSY	Cameron A-140 balloon	Duskytone Ltd	
G-BMSZ	Cessna 152	D. M. Leonard/Tees-side	
G-BMTA	Cessna 152	Basic Vale Ltd/Netherthorpe	
G-BMTB	Cessna 152	J. A. Pothecary/Shoreham	
G-BMTE	Boeing 737-3S3	Air Europe Ltd/Gatwick	
G-BMTF	Boeing 737-3S3	Air Europe Ltd/Gatwick	
G-BMTG	Boeing 737-3S3	Air Europe Ltd/Gatwick	
G-BMTH	Boeing 737-3S3	Air Europe Ltd/Gatwick	

Notes	Reg.	Type	Owner or Operator
	G-BMTI	Robin 3000/120	Air Touring Services Ltd/Biggin Hill
	G-BMTJ	Cessna 152	Creaton Aviation Services Ltd
	G-BMTK	Cessna 152	Cloudshire Ltd/Wellesbourne
	G-BMTL	Cessna 152	Agricultural & General Aviation/ Bournemouth
	G-BMTN	Cameron O-77 balloon	Industrial Services (MH) Ltd
	G-BMTO	PA-38-112 Tomahawk	K. J. Baron
	G-BMTP	PA-38-112 Tomahawk	London Flight Centre (Stansted) Ltd
	G-BMTR	PA-28-161 Warrior II	London Flight Centre (Stansted) Ltd
	G-BMTS	Cessna 172N	DJH Aviation Ltd/Biggin Hill
	G-BMTU	Pitts S-1E Special	O. R. Howe
	G-BMTW	PA-31-350 Navajo Chieftain	Air Northwest Ltd
	G-BMTX	Cameron V-77 balloon	J. A. Langley
	G-BMTY	Colt 77A balloon	L. D. Ormerod
	G-BMUB	SA.315B Lama	Dollar Air Services Ltd/Coventry
	G-BMUD	Cessna 182P	Ingham Aviation Ltd
	G-BMUF	Cessna R182RG	Wilsons Feeds Ltd
	G-BMUG	Rutan LongEz	P. Richardson & J. Shanley
	G-BMUH	Bensen B.8M-R	J. M. Montgomerie
	G-BMUI	Brugger MB.2 Colibri	Carlton Flying Group/Netherthorpe
	G-BMUN	Cameron Harley 78 balloon	Forbes Europe Inc/France
	G-BMUO	Cessna A.152	Redhill Flying Club
	G-BMUP	PA-31-350 Navajo Chieftain	National Airways/Southend
	G-BMUR	Cameron gas airship	Cameron Balloons Ltd
	G-BMUT	PA-34-200T Seneca 2	BI Aviation Services
	G-BMUU	Thunder Ax7-77 balloon	Thunder & Colt Ltd
	G-BMUZ	PA-28-161 Warrior II	Newcastle-upon-Tyne Aero Club Ltd
	G-BMVA	Schiebe SF.25B Falke	R. Brown
	G-BMVB	Cessna 152	Light Planes (Lancashire) Ltd/Barton
	G-BMVC	Beech 95-B55A Baron	T. N. Ellefson/Newcastle
	G-BMVE	PA-28RT-201 Arrow IV	F. E. Gooding/Biggin Hill
	G-BMVF	Bell 212	Bristow Helicopters Ltd
	G-BMVG	QAC Quickie Q.1	P. M. Wright
	G-BMVI	Cameron O-105 balloon	W. O. T. Holmes
	G-BMVJ	Cessna 172N	Crystal Air Ltd
	G-BMVK	PA-38-112 Tomahawk	Airways Aero Associations Ltd/Booker
	G-BMVL	PA-38-112 Tomahawk	Airways Aero Associations Ltd/Booker
	G-BMVM	PA-38-112 Tomahawk	Airways Aero Associations Ltd/Booker
	G-BMVO	Cameron O-77 balloon	Warners Motors (Leasing) Ltd
	G-BMVR	Bensen B.80R	A. O. Smith
	G-BMVS	Cameron 77 SS balloon	Shellrise Ltd
	G-BMVT	Thunder Ax7-77A balloon	M. L. & L. P. Willoughby
	G-BMVU	Monnet Moni	S. R. Jee
	G-BMVV	Rutan Vari-Viggen	G. B. Roberts
	G-BMVW	Cameron O-65 balloon	S. P. Richards
	G-BMVX	M.S.733 Alycon Srs 1	J. D. Read
	G-BMVY	Beech B200 Super King Air	Colin Draycott Group Ltd
	G-BMVZ	Cameron 65 Cornetto balloon	Cameron Balloons Ltd
	G-BMWA	Hughes 269C	March Helicopters Ltd/Sywell
	G-BMWB	Cessna 421C	Capital Trading Aviation Ltd/Cardiff
	G-BMWD	Douglas DC-9-32	British Midland Airways Ltd *The Orloff Diamond*/E. Midlands (*until 4/88*)
	G-BMWE	ARV Super 2	Interair (Aviation) Ltd/Bournemouth
	G-BMWF	ARV Super 2	ARV Aviation Ltd/Sandown
	G-BMWG	ARV Super 2	Airspeed Aviation Ltd/Burnaston
	G-BMWH	ARV Super 2	Colton Aviation International Ltd
	G-BMWJ	ARV Super 2	ARV Aviation Ltd/Sandown
	G-BMWM	ARV Super 2	ARV Aviation Ltd/Sandown
	G-BMWN	Cameron 80 Temple balloon	Forbes Europe Inc
	G-BMWO	BN-2A-26 Islander	Pilatus BN Ltd/Bembridge
	G-BMWP	PA-34-200T-2 Seneca	G-Air Ltd/Goodwood
	G-BMWR	R. Commander 112A	M. Edwards & B. Fields
	G-BMWU	—	—
	G-BMWV	Putzer Elster B	E. A. J. Hibberd
	G-BMWY	Bell 206B JetRanger	Northern Helicopter Services Ltd/ Leeds
	G-BMWZ	AS.350B Ecureuil	McAlpine Helicopters Ltd/Hayes
	G-BMXA	Cessna 152	Chamberlain Leasing
	G-BMXB	Cessna 152	Andrewsfield Flying Club Ltd
	G-BMXC	Cessna 152	Armstrong-Whitworth Flying Group/ Coventry
	G-BMXD	F.27 Friendship Mk 500	Air UK Ltd *Victor Hugo*/Norwich
	G-BMXE	—	—
	G-BMXF	Valentin Taifun 17E	Zone Contracts Ltd

Reg.	Type	Owner or Operator	Notes
G-BMXG	—	—	
G-BMXH	Robinson R-22HP	KF Inns Ltd	
G-BMXI	—	—	
G-BMXJ	Cessna F.150L	J. W. G. Ellis	
G-BMXL	PA-38-112 Tomahawk	Airways Aero Associations Ltd/Booker	
G-BMXM	Colt 180A balloon	Thunder & Colt Ltd	
G-BMXN	Lake LA.4-200 Buccaneer	Cold Storage (Jersey) Ltd	
G-BMXO	Beech C90 King Air	National Airways/Southend	
G-BMXV	—	—	
G-BMXW	D.H.C.6 Twin Otter 310	Loganair Ltd/Glasgow	
G-BMXX	Cessna 152	Midland Aircraft Leasing Ltd	
G-BMXY	Scheibe SF.25B Falke	Marrix Ltd	
G-BMYA	Colt 56A balloon	Thunder & Colt Ltd	
G-BMYB	—	—	
G-BMYC	SOCATA TB.10 Tobago	Drake Organic Chemicals Ltd	
G-BMYD	Beech A36 Bonanza	F. B. Gibbons & Sons Ltd	
G-BMYE	BAe 146-200	British Aerospace PLC (G-WAUS/ G-WISC)/Hatfield	
G-BMYF	Bensen B.8M	P. Entwhistle	
G-BMYG	Cessna F.152	Rolim Ltd/Aberdeen	
G-BMYH	Rotorway 133 Executive	J. Netherwood	
G-BMYI	AA-5 Traveler	C. B. Dew	
G-BMYJ	Cameron V-65 balloon	C. R. W. & E. K. Morrell	
G-BMYK	BAe 748ATP	British Midland Airways Ltd/E. Midlands	
G-BMYL	BAe 748ATP	British Midland Airways Ltd/E. Midlands	
G-BMYM	BAe 748ATP	British Midland Airways Ltd/E. Midlands	
G-BMYN	Colt 77A balloon	Nationwide Building Soc	
G-BMYO	Cameron V-65 balloon	N. V. Moreton	
G-BMYP	Fairey Gannet AEW.3 (XL502)	N. G. R. Moffatt & R. King	
G-BMYR	Robinson R-22	B. Warrington	
G-BMYS	Thunder Ax7-77Z balloon	J. E. Weidema	
G-BMYU	Jodel D.120	G. Davies	
G-BMYV	Bensen B.8M	R. G. Cotman	
G-BMYW	Hughes 269C	March Helicopters Ltd/Sywell	
G-BMYY	—	—	
G-BMZA	Air Command 503 Commander	R. W. Husband	
G-BMZB	Cameron N-77 balloon	D. C. Eager	
G-BMZC	Cessna 421C	Octavious Hunt Ltd	
G-BMZD	Beech C90 King Air	Colt International Ltd	
G-BMZE	SOCATA TB.9 Tampico	Air Touring Services Ltd/Biggin Hill	
G-BMZF	Mikoyan Gurevich MiG-15	FAA Museum/Yeovilton	
G-BMZG	QAC Quickie Q.2	K. W. Brooker	
G-BMZH	Cameron A-140 balloon	The Balloon Stable Ltd	
G-BMZJ	—	—	
G-BMZK	Airbus A.300B4-203	Orion Airways Ltd/E. Midlands	
G-BMZL	Airbus A.300B4-203	Orion Airways Ltd/E. Midlands	
G-BMZM	Rand KR-2	K. McNaughton	
G-BMZN	Everett gyroplane	R. J. Brown	
G-BMZO	—	—	
G-BMZP	Everett gyroplane	B. C. Norris	
G-BMZR	—	—	
G-BMZS	Everett gyroplane	C. W. Cload	
G-BMZT	—	—	
G-BMZV	Cessna 172P	TEL (75) Ltd	
G-BMZW	Bensen B.8	P. D. Widdicombe	
G-BMZX	Wolf W-II Boredom Fighter	J. J. Penney	
G-BMZY	Cameron 77 Elephant balloon	Cameron Balloons Ltd	
G-BMZZ	Stephens Akro Z	P. G. Kynsey & J. Harper	
G-BNAA	V.806 Viscount	British Air Ferries (G-AOYH)/Southend	
G-BNAB	GA-7 Cougar	Brod Gallery (G-BGYP)/Elstree	
G-BNAC	Jurca MJ-100 Spitfire	S. E. Richards	
G-BNAD	Rand KR-2	M. J. Field	
G-BNAG	Colt 105A balloon	R. W. Batcholer	
G-BNAH	Colt Paper Bag SS balloon	Thunder & Colt Ltd	
G-BNAI	Wolf W-II Boredom Fighter	P. J. D. Gronow	
G-BNAJ	Cessna 152	G. Duncan	
G-BNAL	F.27 Friendship Mk 600	Air UK Ltd/Norwich	
G-BNAM	Colt 8A balloon	Thunder & Colt Ltd	
G-BNAN	Cameron V-65 balloon	A. M. Lindsay	
G-BNAO	Colt AS-105 airship	Thunder & Colt Ltd	
G-BNAP	Colt 240A balloon	Thunder & Colt Ltd	
G-BNAR	Taylor JT.1 Monoplane	C. J. Smith	
G-BNAS	AS.350B Ecureuil	McAlpine Helicopters Ltd/Hayes	

Notes	Reg.	Type	Owner or Operator
	G-BNAT	Beech C90 King Air	National Airways (G-OMET/G-COTE/ G-BBKN)/Southend
	G-BNAU	Cameron V-65 balloon	J. Buckle
	G-BNAV	Rutan Cozy	G. E. Broome
	G-BNAW	Cameron V-65 balloon	A. Walker
	G-BNAY	Grob G.109B	Microperm Ltd
	G-BNAZ	SOCATA TB.20 Trinidad	Air Touring Services Ltd/Biggin Hill
	G-BNBD	Short SD3-60	Connectair Ltd/Gatwick
	G-BNBJ	AS.355F-1 Twin Squirrel	McAlpine Helicopters Ltd/Hayes
	G-BNBL	Thunder Ax7-77 balloon	J. R. Henderson
	G-BNBM	Colt 90A balloon	Thunder & Colt Ltd
	G-BNBN	Replica P-38 Lightning	R. C. Cummings
	G-BNBP	Colt Snowflake balloon	Thunder & Colt Ltd
	G-BNBR	Cameron N-90 balloon	Morning Star Motors Ltd
	G-BNBS	Enstrom F-28C	John Battleday at Kirtons Farm Ltd
	G-BNBT	Robinson R-22B	E. Wooton
	G-BNBU	Bensen B.8MV	D. T. Murchie
	G-BNBV	Thunder Ax7-77 balloon	J. M. Robinson
	G-BNBW	Thunder Ax7-77 balloon	Reeds Rains Prudential
	G-BNBY	Beech 95-B55A Baron	Jubilee Airways Ltd (G-AXXR)
	G-BNBZ	LET L-200D Morava	T. F. Thornton & ptnrs/Elstree
	G-BNCA	Lightning F.2A ★	P. Hoar
	G-BNCB	Cameron V-77 balloon	Phoenix Tyre & Battery Co Ltd
	G-BNCC	Thunder Ax7-77 balloon	D. C. Chipping
	G-BNCD	SOCATA TB.20 Trinidad	TKS (Aircraft De-Icing) Ltd
	G-BNCE	G.159 Gulfstream 1	Peregrine Air Services Ltd/Aberdeen
	G-BNCG	QAC Quickie Q.2	T. F. Francis
	G-BNCH	Cameron V-77 balloon	Royal Engineers Balloon Club
	G-BNCJ	Cameron N-77 balloon	I. S. Bridge
	G-BNCK	Cameron V-77 balloon	G. W. G. C. Sudlow
	G-BNCL	—	—
	G-BNCM	Cameron N-77 balloon	S. & A. Stone Ltd
	G-BNCN	Glaser-Dirks DG.400	M. C. Costin
	G-BNCO	PA-38-112 Tomahawk	Nultree Ltd/Denham
	G-BNCR	PA-28-161 Warrior II	Airpart Supply Ltd
	G-BNCS	Cessna 180	Michael Gardner Ltd
	G-BNCT	Boeing 737-3Q8	Airways International Cymru/Cardiff
	G-BNCU	Thunder Ax7-77 balloon	Thunder & Colt Ltd
	G-BNCV	Bensen B.8	L. W. Cload
	G-BNCW	Boeing 767-204	Britannia Airways Ltd/Luton
	G-BNCX	Hunter T.7	Lovaux Ltd
	G-BNCY	F.27 Friendship Mk 500	Air UK Ltd/Norwich
	G-BNCZ	Rutan LongEz	R. M. Bainbridge
	G-BNDC	D.H.C.7-110 Dash Seven	Eurocity Express/London City
	G-BNDD	PA-31-310 Turbo Navajo	W. F. Turnbull
	G-BNDG	Wallis WA-201/R Srs1	K. H. Wallis
	G-BNDH	Colt 21A balloon	Hot-Air Balloon Co Ltd
	G-BNDM	Short SD3-60 Srs 300	Capital Airlines Ltd/Leeds
	G-BNDN	Cameron V-77 balloon	J. A. Smith
	G-BNDO	Cessna 152 II	Grumman Travel (Surrey) Ltd
	G-BNDP	Brugger MB.2 Colibri	M. Black
	G-BNDR	SOCATA TB.10 Tobago	Air Touring Services Ltd/Biggin Hill
	G-BNDS	PA-31-350 Navajo Chieftain	Havilland Air Ltd
	G-BNDT	Brugger MB.2 Colibri	A. Szep
	G-BNDV	Cameron V-77 balloon	R. Jones
	G-BNDW	D.H.82A Tiger Moth	N. D. Welch
	G-BNDX	H.S.125 Srs 600B	Genavco Air Ltd (G-BAYT)/Heathrow
	G-BNDY	Cessna 425-1	Standard Aviation Ltd/Newcastle
	G-BNED	PA-22 Tri-Pacer 135	P. Storey
	G-BNEE	PA-28R-201 Arrow III	Britannic Management (Aviation) Ltd
	G-BNEF	PA-31-310 Turbo Navajo	C. A. Breeze
	G-BNEH	H.S. 125 Srs 800B	Genavco Air Ltd/Heathrow
	G-BNEI	PA-34-200T Seneca II	A. Bucknole
	G-BNEJ	PA-38-112 Tomahawk	G. K. Swindell
	G-BNEK	PA-38-112 Tomahawk	Seal Executive Aircraft Ltd/E. Midlands
	G-BNEL	PA-28-161 Warrior II	J. A. Pothecary/Shoreham
	G-BNEM	Robinson R-22	Rassler Aero Services/Booker
	G-BNEN	PA-34-200T Seneca II	Willall Ltd
	G-BNEO	Cameron V-77 balloon	Graham Tatum & Sons Ltd
	G-BNEP	PA-34-220T Seneca III	D. W. Clark Land Drainage Ltd
	G-BNER	PA-34-200T Seneca	P. Wills & ptnrs/Southampton
	G-BNES	Cameron V-77 balloon	G. Wells
	G-BNET	Cameron O-84 balloon	J. Bennett & Son (Insurance Brokers) Ltd

Reg.	Type	Owner or Operator	Notes
G-BNEU	Colt 105A balloon	Thunder & Colt Ltd	
G-BNEV	Viking Dragonfly	N. W. Eyre	
G-BNEW	Cessna 421C	World Carriers (London) Ltd	
G-BNEX	Cameron O-120 balloon	The Balloon Club Ltd	
G-BNEZ	Cessna 421C	P. Mitchell	
G-BNFF	—	—	
G-BNFG	Cameron O-77 balloon	Capital Balloon Club Ltd	
G-BNFI	Cessna 150J	M. Jackson	
G-BNFJ	Cameron 70 Pump SS balloon	Cameron Balloons Ltd	
G-BNFK	Cameron 89 Egg SS balloon	Cameron Balloons Ltd	
G-BNFL	WHE Airbuggy	Roger Savage (Photography) (G-AXXN)	
G-BNFM	Colt 21A balloon	M. E. Dworksi	
G-BNFN	Cameron N-105 balloon	Western Counties Automobile Co Ltd	
G-BNFO	Cameron V-77 balloon	D. C. Patrick-Brown	
G-BNFP	Cameron O-84 balloon	A. J. & E. J. Clarke	
G-BNFR	Cessna 152 II	London Flight Centre (Stansted) Ltd	
G-BNFS	Cessna 152 II	London Flight Centre (Stansted) Ltd	
G-BNFV	Robin DR.400/120	Aeromarine Ltd/Southampton	
G-BNFW	H.S.125 Srs 700B	British Aerospace PLC	
G-BNFX	Colt 21A balloon	Thunder & Colt Ltd	
G-BNFY	Cameron N-77 balloon	Holker Estates Ltd	
G-BNGB	PA-34-200 Seneca	Aces High Ltd/North Weald	
G-BNGC	Robinson R-22	Rassler Aero Services/Booker	
G-BNGD	Cessna 152	AV Aviation Ltd	
G-BNGE	Auster AOP.6	R. W. W. Eastman	
G-BNGF	D.H.C.7-102 Dash Seven	Eurocity Express/London City	
G-BNGG	—	—	
G-BNGH	Boeing 707-321C	Tradewinds Airways Ltd (G-BFZF)/ Stansted	
G-BNGJ	Cameron V-77 balloon	Latham Timber Centres (Holdings) Ltd	
G-BNGL	—	—	
G-BNGM	—	—	
G-BNGN	Cameron V-77 balloon	E. N. Preece	
G-BNGO	Thunder Ax7-77 balloon	J. S. Finlan	
G-BNGP	Colt 77A balloon	Headland Services Ltd	
G-BNGR	PA-38-112 Tomahawk	Frontline Aviation Ltd/Teesside	
G-BNGS	PA-38-112 Tomahawk	Frontline Aviation Ltd/Teesside	
G-BNGT	PA-28-181 Archer II	Aviation Development & Management Ltd	
G-BNGU	Cameron 76 Golf SS balloon	Cameron Balloons Ltd	
G-BNGV	ARV Super 2	Golf Victor Ltd/Guernsey	
G-BNGW	ARV Super 2	Southern Aero Club (Shoreham) Ltd	
G-BNGX	ARV Super 2	Southern Aero Club (Shoreham) Ltd	
G-BNGY	ARV Super 2	Southern Aero Club (Shoreham) Ltd	
G-BNHB	ARV Super 2	ARV Aviation Ltd/Sandown	
G-BNHC	ARV Super 2	ARV Aviation Ltd/Sandown	
G-BNHD	ARV Super 2	ARV Aviation Ltd/Sandown	
G-BNHE	ARV Super 2	ARV Aviation Ltd/Sandown	
G-BNHF	Cameron N-31 balloon	P. G. Dunnington	
G-BNHG	PA-38-112 Tomahawk	Cheltenham & Gloucester School of Flying Ltd	
G-BNHH	Thunder Ax7-77 balloon	Gee-Tee Signs Ltd	
G-BNHI	Cameron V-77 balloon	Cameron Balloons Ltd	
G-BNHJ	Cessna 152	Antler Enterprises Ltd	
G-BNHK	Cessna 152	Antler Enterprises Ltd	
G-BNHL	Colt 90 Beer Glass SS balloon	Thunder & Colt Ltd	
G-BNHM	Thunder Ax8-105 balloon	Thunder & Colt Ltd	
G-BNHN	Colt Aerial Bottle SS balloon	The Balloon Stable Ltd	
G-BNHO	Thunder Ax7-77 balloon	M. J. Forster	
G-BNHP	Saffrey S.330 balloon	N. H. Ponsford *Alpha II*	
G-BNHR	Cameron V-77 balloon	R. L. Rummery	
G-BNHS	Thunder Ax7-77 balloon	R. A. Jaffe	
G-BNHT	Fournier RF-3	D. Harker	
G-BNHU	Thunder Ax10-180 balloon	Thunder & Colt Ltd	
G-BNHV	Thunder Ax10-180 balloon	Thunder & Colt Ltd	
G-BNHW	Thunder Ax10-180 balloon	Thunder & Colt Ltd	
G-BNHX	Thunder Ax10-180 balloon	Thunder & Colt Ltd	
G-BNHY	AMF Chevvron 232	J. Hatswell	
G-BNIB	Cameron A-105 balloon	A. G. E. Faulkner	
G-BNID	Cessna 152	Midland Aircraft Leasing Ltd	
G-BNIE	Cameron O-160 balloon	The Balloon Club Ltd	
G-BNIF	Cameron O-56 balloon	D. V. Fowler	
G-BNIH	RomBac One-Eleven 561RC	London European Airways PLC/Luton	
G-BNII	Cameron N-90 balloon	DW (Direct Wholesale) PLC	

Notes	Reg.	Type	Owner or Operator
	G-BNIJ	SOCATA TB.10 Tobago	Air Touring Services Ltd/Biggin Hill
	G-BNIK	Robin HR.200/120	W. C. Smeaton/Popham
	G-BNIL	—	
	G-BNIM	PA-38-112 Tomahawk	P. Q. Owen
	G-BNIN	Cameron V-77 balloon	Cloud Nine Balloon Group
	G-BNIO	Luscombe 8A Silvaire	D. Collyer
	G-BNIP	Luscombe 8A Silvaire	P. J. Penn-Sayers/Shoreham
	G-BNIR	Bell 206B JetRanger	Dollar Air Services Ltd/Coventry
	G-BNIS	Bell 206B JetRanger	Dollar Air Services Ltd/Coventry
	G-BNIT	Bell 206B JetRanger	Dollar Air Services Ltd/Coventry
	G-BNIU	Cameron O-77 balloon	A. J. Matthews & D. S. Dunlop
	G-BNIV	Cessna 152	Cloudshire Ltd/Wellesbourne
	G-BNIW	Boeing Stearman PT-17	AJD Engineering Ltd/Ipswich
	G-BNIX	EMB-110P1 Bandeirante	National Airways/Southend
	G-BNIY	F.27 Friendship Mk 600	Air UK Ltd/Norwich
	G-BNIZ	F.27 Friendship Mk 600 (cargo)	Air UK Ltd/Norwich
	G-BNJA	Wag-Aero Wag-a-Bond	G. K. Hare
	G-BNJB	Cessna 152	Samka Ltd/Shoreham
	G-BNJC	Cessna 152	Samka Ltd/Shoreham
	G-BNJD	Cessna 152	R. S. Lambert
	G-BNJE	Cessna A.152	Seawing Flying Club Ltd/Southend
	G-BNJF	PA-32RT-300 Turbo Lance II	Mike Mansfield Enterprises Ltd
	G-BNJG	—	
	G-BNJH	Cessna 152	Basic Vale Ltd
	G-BNJJ	Cessna 152	Merrett Aviation Ltd
	G-BNJK	Macavia BAe 748 Turbine Tanker	Macavia International Ltd
	G-BNJL	Bensen B.8	M. W. Joynes
	G-BNJM	PA-28-161 Warrior II	Frontline Aviation Ltd/Teesside
	G-BNJN	—	
	G-BNJO	QAC Quickie Q.2	J. D. Crymble
	G-BNJP	PA-28-161 Warrior II	P. A. Lancaster
	G-BNJR	PA-28RT-201T Turbo Arrow IV	MM & G Aviation
	G-BNJS	PA-32R-301T Turbo Saratoga SP	K. G. Wood
	G-BNJT	PA-28-161 Warrior II	Airways Aero Associations Ltd/Booker
	G-BNJU	Cameron 80 Bust SS balloon	Forbes Europe Inc
	G-BNJV	Cessna 152	London Flight Centre (Headcorn) Ltd
	G-BNJW	Rutan Cozy	J. Whiting
	G-BNJX	Cameron N-90 balloon	Mars UK Ltd
	G-BNJY	PA-38-112 Tomahawk	Merrett Aviation Ltd
	G-BNJZ	Cassutt IIIM	R. J. Lake
	G-BNKA	—	
	G-BNKB	Robinson R-22A	Willow Vale Electronics Ltd
	G-BNKC	Cessna 152	Royal Air Services Ltd
	G-BNKD	Cessna 172N	Royal Air Services Ltd
	G-BNKE	Cessna 172N	Royal Air Services Ltd
	G-BNKF	Colt AS-56 airship	Thunder & Colt Ltd
	G-BNKG	Alexander Todd Steen Skybolt	Cavendish Aviation Ltd (G-RATS/ G-RHFI)
	G-BNKH	PA-38-112 Tomahawk	T. Miller
	G-BNKI	Cessna 152	RAF Halton Aeroplane Club Ltd
	G-BNKL	Beech 58P Baron	E. L. Klinge/Fairoaks
	G-BNKM	Cessna 152	Halsmith (Aircraft Sales) Ltd
	G-BNKN	G.159 Gulfstream 1	Birmingham Executive Airways PLC
	G-BNKO	G.159 Gulfstream 1	Birmingham Executive Airways PLC
	G-BNKP	Cessna 152	AV Aviation Ltd/Newcastle
	G-BNKR	Cessna 152	AV Aviation Ltd/Newcastle
	G-BNKS	Cessna 152	AV Aviation Ltd/Newcastle
	G-BNKT	Cameron O-77 balloon	British Airtours Ltd
	G-BNKU	SOCATA TB.20 Trinidad	Air Touring Services Ltd/Biggin Hill
	G-BNKV	Cessna 152	I. C. Adams & Vectair Aviation Ltd
	G-BNKW	PA-38-112 Tomahawk	P. G. Greenslade
	G-BNKX	Robinson R-22	H. R. Cayzer
	G-BNKZ	Hughes 369HS	March Helicopters Ltd/Sywell
	G-BNLA	Boeing 747-436	British Airways/Heathrow
	G-BNLB	Boeing 747-436	British Airways/Heathrow
	G-BNLC	Boeing 747-436	British Airways/Heathrow
	G-BNLD	Boeing 747-436	British Airways/Heathrow
	G-BNLE	Boeing 747-436	British Airways/Heathrow
	G-BNLF	Boeing 747-436	British Airways/Heathrow
	G-BNLG	Boeing 747-436	British Airways/Heathrow
	G-BNLH	Boeing 747-436	British Airways/Heathrow
	G-BNLI	Boeing 747-436	British Airways/Heathrow
	G-BNLJ	Boeing 747-436	British Airways/Heathrow
	G-BNLK	Boeing 747-436	British Airways/Heathrow

Reg.	Type	Owner or Operator	Notes
G-BNLL	Boeing 747-436	British Airways/Heathrow	
G-BNLM	Boeing 747-436	British Airways/Heathrow	
G-BNLN	Boeing 747-436	British Airways/Heathrow	
G-BNLO	Boeing 747-436	British Airways/Heathrow	
G-BNLP	Boeing 747-436	British Airways/Heathrow	
G-BNLR	—	—	
G-BNLS	—	—	
G-BNLT	—	—	
G-BNLU	—	—	
G-BNLV	—	—	
G-BNLW	—	—	
G-BNLX	—	—	
G-BNLY	—	—	
G-BNLZ	—	—	
G-BNMA	Cameron O-77 balloon	H. R. Evans	
G-BNMB	PA-28-151 Warrior	D. M. Leonard/Teesside	
G-BNMC	Cessna 152	D. M. Leonard/Teesside	
G-BNMD	Cessna 152	D. M. Leonard/Teesside	
G-BNME	Cessna 152	D. M. Leonard/Teesside	
G-BNMF	Cessna 152	D. M. Leonard/Teesside	
G-BNMG	Cameron V-77 balloon	Windsor Life Assurance Co Ltd	
G-BNMH	Pietenpol Aircamper	N. M. Hitchman	
G-BNMI	Colt Flying Fantasy SS balloon	Thunder & Colt Ltd	
G-BNMK	Dornier Do.27A-1	G. Machie	
G-BNML	Rand KR-2	R. J. Smyth	
G-BNMM	Bell 206B JetRanger	Veritair Ltd	
G-BNMN	PA-28R-201 Arrow III	S. A. Tikriti	
G-BNMO	Cessna R.182RG	Avionics Research Ltd/Cambridge	
G-BNMP	Cessna R.182RG	Avionics Research Ltd/Cambridge	
G-BNMR	Beech 200 Super King Air	Havilland Air Ltd/Guernsey	
G-BNMX	Thunder Ax7-77 balloon	S. A. D. Beard	
G-BNMZ	Isaacs Fury II	T. E. G. Buckett	
G-BNNA	Stolp SA.300 Starduster Too	D. F. Simpson & M. A. P. Thompson	
G-BNNC	Cameron N-77 balloon	West Country Business Machines Ltd	
G-BNNE	Cameron N-77 balloon	The Balloon Stable Ltd	
G-BNNF	SA.315B Lama	Dollar Air Services Ltd/Coventry	
G-BNNG	Cessna T.337D	Somet Ltd (G-COLD)	
G-BNNH	—	—	
G-BNNI	Boeing 727-276	Dan-Air Services Ltd/Gatwick	
G-BNNJ	Boeing 737-3Q8	Dan-Air Services Ltd/Gatwick	
G-BNNK	Boeing 737-4Q8	Dan-Air Services Ltd/Gatwick	
G-BNNL	Boeing 737-4Q8	Dan-Air Services Ltd/Gatwick	
G-BNNM	Colt 77A balloon	Thunder & Colt Ltd	
G-BNNN	AS.355F-2 Twin Squirrel	McAlpine Helicopters Ltd/Hayes	
G-BNNO	PA-28-161 Warrior II	W. Lancs Aero Club Ltd/Woodvale	
G-BNNP	PA-28-181 Archer II	Flairhire Ltd/Redhill	
G-BNNR	Cessna 152	B. W. Wells & Burbage Farms Ltd	
G-BNNS	PA-28-161 Warrior II	Seal Executive Aircraft Ltd	
G-BNNT	PA-28-151 Warrior	D. J. Kirkwood	
G-BNNU	PA-38-112 Tomahawk	Seal Executive Aircraft Ltd	
G-BNNV	Enstrom F-280C-UK	Southern Air Ltd/Shoreham	
G-BNNW	Cessna P.210N	A. H. & R. S. Crawley	
G-BNNX	PA-28RT-201T Turbo Arrow III	C. Dugard Ltd/Shoreham	
G-BNNY	PA-28-161 Warrior II	C. Dugard Ltd/Shoreham	
G-BNNZ	PA-28-161 Warrior II	C. Dugard Ltd/Shoreham	
G-BNOA	PA-38-112 Tomahawk	Halsmith (Aircraft Sales) Ltd	
G-BNOB	Wittman W.8 Tailwind	M. Robson-Robinson	
G-BNOC	EMB-110P1 Bandeirante	Connectair Ltd/Gatwick	
G-BNOD	PA-28-161 Warrior II	BAe Flying College/Prestwick	
G-BNOE	PA-28-161 Warrior II	BAe Flying College/Prestwick	
G-BNOF	PA-28-161 Warrior II	BAe Flying College/Prestwick	
G-BNOG	PA-28-161 Warrior II	BAe Flying College/Prestwick	
G-BNOH	PA-28-161 Warrior II	BAe Flying College/Prestwick	
G-BNOI	PA-28-161 Warrior II	BAe Flying College/Prestwick	
G-BNOJ	PA-28-161 Warrior II	BAe Flying College/Prestwick	
G-BNOK	PA-28-161 Warrior II	BAe Flying College/Prestwick	
G-BNOL	PA-28-161 Warrior II	BAe Flying College/Prestwick	
G-BNOM	PA-28-161 Warrior II	BAe Flying College/Prestwick	
G-BNON	PA-28-161 Warrior II	BAe Flying College/Prestwick	
G-BNOO	PA-28-161 Warrior II	BAe Flying College/Prestwick	
G-BNOP	PA-28-161 Warrior II	BAe Flying College/Prestwick	
G-BNOR	PA-28-161 Warrior II	BAe Flying College/Prestwick	
G-BNOS	PA-28-161 Warrior II	BAe Flying College/Prestwick	
G-BNOT	PA-28-161 Warrior II	BAe Flying College/Prestwick	

Notes	Reg.	Type	Owner or Operator
	G-BNOU	PA-28-161 Warrior II	BAe Flying College/Prestwick
	G-BNOV	PA-28-161 Warrior II	BAe Flying College/Prestwick
	G-BNOW	PA-28-161 Warrior II	BAe Flying College/Prestwick
	G-BNOX	Cessna R.182	Avionics Research Ltd/Cambridge
	G-BNOY	Colt 90A balloon	Thunder & Colt Ltd
	G-BNOZ	Cessna 152	B. W. Wells & Burbage Farms Ltd
	G-BNPA	Boeing 737-3S3	Air Europe Ltd/Gatwick
	G-BNPB	Boeing 737-3S3	Air Europe Ltd/Gatwick
	G-BNPC	Boeing 737-3S3	Air Europe Ltd/Gatwick
	G-BNPD	PA-23 Aztec 250	Lion Air Lease/Glasgow
	G-BNPE	Cameron N-77 balloon	Kent Garden Centres Ltd
	G-BNPF	Slingsby T.31M	S. Luck & ptnrs
	G-BNPG	P.66 Pembroke C.1	J. S. Allison
	G-BNPH	P.66 Pembroke C.1	J. S. Allison
	G-BNPI	Colt 21A balloon	Virgin Atlantic Airways Ltd
	G-BNPK	Cameron DP-70 airship	Cameron Balloons Ltd
	G-BNPL	PA-38-112 Tomahawk	Leavesden Flight Centre Ltd
	G-BNPM	PA-38-112 Tomahawk	Leavesden Flight Centre Ltd
	G-BNPN	PA-28-181 Archer II	Archer Aviation Ltd
	G-BNPO	PA-28-181 Archer II	Leavesden Flight Centre Ltd
	G-BNPP	Colt 90A balloon	Thunder & Colt Ltd
	G-BNPR	Colt 90A balloon	Thunder & Colt Ltd
	G-BNPS	MBB Bo105CBS/4	Helicopters UK Ltd
	G-BNPT	PA-38-112 Tomahawk II	Cormack (Aircraft Services) Ltd/ Glasgow
	G-BNPU	P.66 Pembroke C.1	T. S. Warren
	G-BNPV	Bowers Flybaby 1A	J. G. Day
	G-BNPY	Cessna 152	Halsmith (Aircraft Sales) Ltd
	G-BNPZ	Cessna 152	Halsmith (Aircraft Sales) Ltd
	G-BNRA	SOCATA TB.10 Tobago	Air Touring Services Ltd/Biggin Hill
	G-BNRB	Robin DR.400/180R	Soaring (Oxford) Ltd/Booker
	G-BNRC	AB-206A JetRanger	Coventry Helicopters
	G-BNRD	AB-206A JetRanger	Coventry Helicopters
	G-BNRE	AB-206A JetRanger	Coventry Helicopters
	G-BNRF	PA-28-181 Archer II	G-Air Ltd/Goodwood
	G-BNRG	PA-28-161 Warrior II	B. E. Simpson/Booker
	G-BNRH	Beech 95-E55 Baron	National Airways/Southend
	G-BNRI	Cessna U.206G	Flying Tigers Ltd
	G-BNRJ	Cessna U.206G	B. W. Wells & Burbage Farms Ltd
	G-BNRK	Cessna 152	South Eastern Aviation Ltd/Ipswich
	G-BNRL	Cessna 152	South Eastern Aviation Ltd/Ipswich
	G-BNRM	—	
	G-BNRN	PA-28R-201T Turbo Arrow III	G-Air Ltd/Goodwood
	G-BNRP	PA-28-181 Archer II	G-Air Ltd/Goodwood
	G-BNRR	Cessna 172P	J. M. Hoblyn
	G-BNRS	MBB Bo 105DBS	Helicopters UK Ltd
	G-BNRT	Boeing 737-3T5	Orion Airways Ltd/E. Midlands
	G-BNRU	Cameron V-77 balloon	M. A. Mueller
	G-BNRV	Thunder Ax7-77 balloon	R. & R. Edgar-Dimmack
	G-BNRW	Colt 69A balloon	Callers Pegasus Travel Service Ltd
	G-BNRX	PA-34-200T Seneca 2	B. E. Simpson/Booker
	G-BNRY	Cessna 182Q	Reefly Ltd
	G-BNRZ	Robinson R-22B	W. Jorden-Millers Ltd
	G-BNSA	Douglas DC-9-83	British Island Airways Ltd/Gatwick
	G-BNSB	Douglas DC-9-83	British Island Airways Ltd/Gatwick
	G-BNSC	Cessna 550 Citation II	Oceanair (CI) Ltd
	G-BNSD	Boeing 757-236	Air Europe Ltd/Gatwick
	G-BNSE	Boeing 757-236	Air Europe Ltd/Gatwick
	G-BNSF	Boeing 757-236	Air Europe Ltd/Gatwick
	G-BNSG	PA-28-201 Arrow III	P. Marlow & M. Lindfield
	G-BNSH	Sikorsky S-76A	Bond Helicopters Ltd/Bourn
	G-BNSI	Cessna 152	Erafan Ltd/Bournemouth
	G-BNSJ	Cessna 152	D. A. Williamson
	G-BNSK	Cessna 172N	Channel Aviation Ltd
	G-BNSL	PA-38-112 Tomahawk II	Halsmith (Aircraft Sales) Ltd
	G-BNSM	Cessna 152	Halsmith (Aircraft Sales) Ltd
	G-BNSN	Cessna 152	Halsmith (Aircraft Sales) Ltd
	G-BNSO	Slingsby T.67M Mk II	Slingsby Aviation Ltd/Kirkbymoorside
	G-BNSP	Slingsby T.67M	Slingsby Aviation Ltd/Kirkbymoorside
	G-BNSR	Slingsby T.67M	Slingsby Aviation Ltd/Kirkbymoorside
	G-BNSS	Cessna 150M	Erafan Ltd/Bournemouth
	G-BNST	Cessna 172N	C. M. Vlieland-Boddy
	G-BNSU	Cessna 152	Channel Aviation Ltd
	G-BNSV	Cessna 152	Channel Aviation Ltd

Reg.	Type	Owner or Operator	Notes
G-BNSW	Cessna 152	S. V. R. Williamson	
G-BNSX	AS.355F-2 Twin Squirrel	McAlpine Helicopters Ltd/Hayes	
G-BNSY	PA-28-161 Warrior II	E. P. C. Rabson	
G-BNSZ	PA-28-161 Warrior II	Carill Aviation Ltd	
G-BNTA	F.27 Friendship Mk 600	Air UK Ltd/Norwich	
G-BNTB	—		
G-BNTC	PA-28RT-201T Turbo Arrow IV	Techspan Aviation Ltd	
G-BNTD	PA-28-161 Warrior II	Handley (Poole) Ltd	
G-BNTE	FFA AS.202/184A Wren	BAe Flying College Ltd/Prestwick	
G-BNTF	FFA AS.202/184A Wren	BAe Flying College Ltd/Prestwick	
G-BNTG	FFA AS.202/184A Wren	BAe Flying College Ltd/Prestwick	
G-BNTH	FFA AS.202/184A Wren	BAe Flying College Ltd/Prestwick	
G-BNTI	FFA AS.202/184A Wren	BAe Flying College Ltd/Prestwick	
G-BNTJ	FFA AS.202/184A Wren	BAe Flying College Ltd/Prestwick	
G-BNTK	FFA AS.202/184A Wren	BAe Flying College Ltd/Prestwick	
G-BNTL	FFA AS.202/184A Wren	BAe Flying College Ltd/Prestwick	
G-BNTM	FFA AS.202/184A Wren	BAe Flying College Ltd/Prestwick	
G-BNTN	FFA AS.202/184A Wren	BAe Flying College Ltd/Prestwick	
G-BNTO	FFA AS.202/184A Wren	BAe Flying College Ltd/Prestwick	
G-BNTP	Cessna 172N	Aerojet Ltd/Barton	
G-BNTR	Cessna 172N	Aerojet Ltd/Barton	
G-BNTS	PA-28RT-201T Turbo Arrow IV	G-Air Ltd/Goodwood	
G-BNTT	Beech 76 Duchess	Sunny Sky Aviation Ltd	
G-BNTU	Cessna 152	Seal Executive Aviation Ltd	
G-BNTV	Cessna 172N	M. O. O'Nions	
G-BNTW	Cameron V-77 balloon	P. R. S. Briault	
G-BNTX	Short SD3-30 Variant 100	Fairflight Ltd (G-BKDN)/Biggin Hill	
G-BNTY	Short SD3-30 Variant 100	Fairflight Ltd (G-BKDO)/Biggin Hill	
G-BNTZ	Cameron N-77 balloon	Nationwide Anglia Building Soc	
G-BNUB	—	—	
G-BNUC	Cameron O-77 balloon	Bridges Van Hire Ltd	
G-BNUD	Cameron A-250 balloon	Cameron Balloons Ltd	
G-BNUE	Thunder Ax8-105Z balloon	Thunder & Colt Ltd	
G-BNUF	Thunder Ax8-105Z balloon	Thunder & Colt Ltd	
G-BNUG	Cameron O-105 balloon	Thunder & Colt Ltd	
G-BNUH	Cameron O-105 balloon	Thunder & Colt Ltd	
G-BNUI	Rutan Vari-Eze	T. N. F. Skead	
G-BNUJ	Thunder Ax8-105Z balloon	Thunder & Colt Ltd	
G-BNUK	Cameron O-84 balloon	Thunder & Colt Ltd	
G-BNUL	Cessna 152	Osprey Air Services Ltd	
G-BNUM	Stinson L-5C-VW Sentinal	M. R. Keen/Liverpool	
G-BNUN	Beech 95-58P Baron	British Midland Airways Ltd/E. Midlands	
G-BNUO	Beech 76 Duchess	B. & W. Aircraft Ltd	
G-BNUP	PA-28-161 Warrior II	Lydd Airport Group Ltd	
G-BNUR	Cessna 172E	J. A. Chetta	
G-BNUS	Cessna 152	Stapleford Flying Club Ltd	
G-BNUT	Cessna 152	Stapleford Flying Club Ltd	
G-BNUU	PA-44-180T Seminole	MM & G Aviation	
G-BNUV	PA-23 Aztec 250	J. Williams	
G-BNUW	Bell 206B JetRanger	Hewitts of Cranleigh Ltd	
G-BNUX	Hoffmann H-36 Dimona	Soaring (Oxford) Ltd/Booker	
G-BNUY	PA-38-112 Tomahawk II	P. A. Lancaster/Booker	
G-BNUZ	Robinson R-22B	J. L. E. Smith	
G-BNVA	Cameron DP-70 airship	Cameron Balloons Ltd	
G-BNVB	AA-5A Cheetah	E. P. C. Rabson	
G-BNVD	PA-38-112 Tomahawk	A. S. Bamrah/Biggin Hill	
G-BNVE	PA-28-181 Archer II	Janair Services Ltd/Stapleford	
G-BNVF	Robinson R-22B	Jetbury Ltd	
G-BNVG	ARV Super 2	ARV Aviation Ltd/Sandown	
G-BNVH	ARV Super 2	ARV Aviation Ltd/Sandown	
G-BNVI	ARV Super 2	ARV Aviation Ltd/Sandown	
G-BNVJ	ARV Super 2	ARV Aviation Ltd/Sandown	
G-BNVK	—	—	
G-BNVL	—	—	
G-BNVM	—	—	
G-BNVN	—	—	
G-BNVO	—	—	
G-BNVP	—	—	
G-BNVR	—	—	
G-BNVT	—	—	
G-BNVU	H.S.125 Srs 700B	Civil Aviation Authority (G-CCAA/ G-DBBI)/Luton	
G-BNVV	—	—	
G-BNVW	Dornier Do.28A-1	Wessex Aviation & Transport Ltd	

Notes	Reg.	Type	Owner or Operator
	G-BNVX	Dornier Do.27A-4	Wessex Aviation & Transport Ltd
	G-BNVY	Cessna 500 Citation	Gill Aviation Ltd/Newcastle
	G-BNVZ	Beech 95-B55 Baron	C. A. Breeze/Barton
	G-BNWA	—	—
	G-BNWB	—	—
	G-BNWC	—	—
	G-BNWD	—	—
	G-BNWE	—	—
	G-BNWF	—	—
	G-BNWG	—	—
	G-BNWH	—	—
	G-BNWI	—	—
	G-BNWJ	—	—
	G-BNWK	—	—
	G-BNWL	—	—
	G-BNWM	—	—
	G-BNWN	—	—
	G-BNWO	—	—
	G-BNWP	—	—
	G-BNWR	—	—
	G-BNWS	—	—
	G-BNWT	—	—
	G-BNWU	—	—
	G-BNWV	—	—
	G-BNWW	—	—
	G-BNWX	—	—
	G-BNWY	—	—
	G-BNWZ	—	—
	G-BNXA	BN-2A Islander	Atlantic Air Transport Ltd/Coventry
	G-BNXB	BN-2A Islander	Atlantic Air Transport Ltd/Coventry
	G-BNXC	Cessna 152	B. W. Wells & Burbage Farms Ltd
	G-BNXD	Cessna 172N	B. W. Wells & Burbage Farms Ltd
	G-BNXE	PA-28-161 Warrior II	B. W. Wells & Burbage Farms Ltd
	G-BNXF	Bell 206B JetRanger	P. Pilkington & K. M. Armitage
	G-BNXG	Cameron DP-70 airship	Cameron Balloons Ltd
	G-BNXH	Cessna T.210N	Wilson Feeds Ltd
	G-BNXI	Robin DR.400-180R	London Gliding Club Ltd/Dunstable
	G-BNXJ	Robinson R-22B	J. D. Marsh
	G-BNXK	Nott-Cameron ULD-3 balloon	J. R. P. Nott
	G-BNXL	Glaser-Dirks DG.400	B. A. Eastwell
	G-BNXM	PA-19 Super Cub 95	D. M. Jagger
	G-BNXN	Partenavia P.68B	Connector Technology Ltd
	G-BNXO	Colt 21A balloon	Thunder & Colt Ltd
	G-BNXP	Boeing 737-3QA	Air Europe/Air Europa EC-EDM
	G-BNXR	Cameron O-84 balloon	J. A. & N. J. Ballard Gray
	G-BNXS	Cessna 404	BCal/British Airways/Gatwick
	G-BNXT	PA-28-161 Warrior II	S. P. Donoghue/Leavesden
	G-BNXU	PA-28-161 Warrior II	S. P. Donoghue/Leavesden
	G-BNXX	SOCATA TB.20 Trinidad	Air Touring Services Ltd/Biggin Hill
	G-BNXY	Cessna 172M	South Coast Aviation Ltd
	G-BNXZ	Thunder Ax7-77 balloon	Hale Hot Air Balloon Group
	G-BNYA	Short SD3-30	Fairflight Ltd/Gill Air (G-BKSU)
	G-BNYB	—	—
	G-BNYD	Bell 206B JetRanger	Dollar Air Services Ltd/Coventry
	G-BNYE	Short SD3-60	Short Bros PLC/Sydenham
	G-BNYJ	Cessna 421B	Charles Robertson (Developments) Ltd
	G-BNYK	PA-38-112 Tomahawk	Seal Executive Aircraft Ltd
	G-BNYL	Cessna 152	Seal Executive Aircraft Ltd
	G-BNYM	Cessna 172N	Decoy Engineering Projects Ltd
	G-BNYN	Cessna 152	Redhill Flying Club
	G-BNYO	Beech 76 Duchess	Skyhawk Ltd
	G-BNYP	PA-28-181 Archer II	Janair Services Ltd
	G-BNYR	Cameron N-105 balloon	Cameron Balloons Ltd
	G-BNYS	Boeing 767-204	Britannia Airways Ltd/Luton
	G-BNYT	Boeing 737-2E1	Britannia Airways Ltd/Luton
	G-BNYU	Faithfull Ax7-61A balloon	M. L. Faithfull
	G-BNYV	PA-38-112 Tomahawk	A. S. Bamrah/Biggin Hill
	G-BNYW	Cessna 172P	C. Wright
	G-BNYX	Kitfox	R. W. Husband
	G-BNYY	PA-28RT-201T Turbo Arrow IV	K. G. Ward
	G-BNYZ	Stampe SV-4E	Tapestry Colour Ltd
	G-BNZA	Beech 300LW Super King Air	British Airways/Heathrow
	G-BNZB	PA-28-161 Warrior II	Swallow Cruisers Ltd
	G-BNZC	D.H.C.1 Chipmunk 22	British Aerial Museum (G-ROYS)/ Duxford

Reg.	Type	Owner or Operator	Notes
G-BNZD	BN-2A Mk III-2 Trislander	Regency Airways Ltd (G-BEVV)	
G-BNZE	F.27 Friendship Mk 500	Federal Express Aviation Services Ltd	
G-BNZF	Grob G.109B	N. Adam	
G-BNZG	PA-28RT-201T Turbo Arrow IV	Trinity Garage (Gainsborough) Ltd	
G-BNZH	Beech 200 Super King Air	Leacock & Creed Ltd	
G-BNZI	PA-31-350 Navjo Chieftain	Airstar (Air Transport) Ltd	
G-BNZJ	Colt 21A balloon	Thunder & Colt Ltd	
G-BNZK	Thunder Ax7-77 balloon	Wye Valley Aviation Ltd	
G-BNZL	Rotorway Scorpion 133	G. Snook	
G-BNZM	Cessna T.210N	Malcomair Ltd	
G-BNZN	Cameron N-56 balloon	Cameron Balloons Ltd	
G-BNZO	Rotorway Executive	M. G. Wiltshire	
G-BNZP	Cessna 500 Citation	World Carrier Aviation Ltd	
G-BNZR	FRED Srs 2	R. M. Waugh	
G-BNZS	Mooney M.20K	Pathrace Ltd	
G-BNZT	Boeing 737-2E3	Air UK Leisure Ltd/Stansted	
G-BNZU	—	—	
G-BNZV	—	—	
G-BNZW	H.S.125 Srs 800A	British Aerospace PLC	
G-BNZX	—	—	
G-BNZY	SA.365N Dauphin 2	McAlpine Helicopters Ltd/Hayes	
G-BNZZ	PA-28-161 Warrior II	J. P. Alexander	
G-BOAA	Concorde 102	British Airways (G-N94AA)/Heathrow	
G-BOAB	Concorde 102	British Airways (G-N94AB)/Heathrow	
G-BOAC	Concorde 102	British Airways (G-N81AC)/Heathrow	
G-BOAD	Concorde 102	British Airways (G-N94AD)/Heathrow	
G-BOAE	Concorde 102	British Airways (G-N94AE)/Heathrow	
G-BOAF	Concorde 102	British Airways (G-N94AF/G-BFKX)/ Heathrow	
G-BOAG	Concorde 102	British Airways (G-BFKW)/Heathrow	
G-BOAH	PA-28-161 Warrior II	Garrick Aviation	
G-BOAI	Cessna 152	G. Duncan	
G-BOAJ	—	—	
G-BOAK	PA-22 Caribbean 150	I. B. Grace	
G-BOAL	Cameron V-65 balloon	A. Lindsay	
G-BOAM	Robinson R-22B	Willow Vale Electronics Ltd	
G-BOAN	PA-30 Twin Comanche 160	MPW Aviation Ltd/Booker	
G-BOAO	Thunder Ax7-77 balloon	D. V. Fowler	
G-BOAP	Colt 160A balloon	Thunder & Colt Ltd	
G-BOAR	—	—	
G-BOAS	Air Command 503 Commander	R. Robinson	
G-BOAU	Cameron V-77 balloon	J. Smallwood	
G-BOAV	Cameron DP-70 airship	Cameron Balloons Ltd	
G-BOAW	—	—	
G-BOAX	—	—	
G-BOAY	—	—	
G-BOAZ	—	—	
G-BOBA	PA-28R-201 Arrow III	Lyndon Scaffolding Hire Ltd	
G-BOBB	Cameron O-120 balloon	J. M. Albury	
G-BOBC	BN-2T Islander	Rhine Army Parachute Association (G-BJYZ)	
G-BOBD	Cameron O-160 balloon	G. Tatum	
G-BOBE	Cameron O-160 balloon	G. Tatum	
G-BOBF	Brugger MB.2 Colibri	R. Bennett	
G-BOBG	Jodel D.140	C. A. Laycock	
G-BOBH	Airtour AH-77 balloon	Airtour Balloon Co Ltd	
G-BOBI	Cessna 152	R. M. Seath (G-BHJD)/Sherburn	
G-BOBJ	PA-38-112 Tomahawk	Surrey & Kent Flying Club (1982) Ltd/ Biggin Hill	
G-BOBK	PA-38-112 Tomahawk	Surrey & Kent Flying Club (1982) Ltd/ Biggin Hill	
G-BOBL	PA-38-112 Tomahawk	Surrey & Kent Flying Club (1982) Ltd/ Biggin Hill	
G-BOBM	Beech 200 Super King Air	Leacock & Creed Ltd	
G-BOBN	—	—	
G-BOBO	Robinson R-22	R. E. Todd	
G-BOBP	Cameron A-250 balloon	W. A. Q. McGill	
G-BOBR	Cameron N-77 balloon	Loganair Ltd	
G-BOBS	Quickie Q.2	R. R. Stevens/Denham	
G-BOBT	Stolp SA.300 Starduster Too	K. E. Armstrong	
G-BOBU	Colt 90A balloon	Thunder & Colt Ltd	
G-BOBV	Cessna F. 1509M	L. E. Usher	
G-BOBW	Air & Space 18A gyroplane	M. A. Schumann	
G-BOBX	G.159 Gulfstream 1	Birmingham Executive Airways PLC	
G-BOBY	Monnet Sonerai II	R. G. Hallam (stored)/Sleap	
G-BOBZ	PA-28-181 Archer II	Trustcomms International Ltd	
G-BOCA	PA-38-112 Tomahawk	B. E. Simpson	

Notes	Reg.	Type	Owner or Operator
	G-BOCB	H.S.125 Srs 1B/522	McAlpine Aviation Ltd (G-OMCA/ G-DJMJ/G-AWUE)/Luton
	G-BOCC	PA-38-112 Tomahawk	B. E. Simpson
	G-BOCD	Grob G.115	Soaring (Oxford) Ltd
	G-BOCE	F.27 Friendship Mk 500	Federal Express Aviation Services Ltd
	G-BOCF	Colt 77A balloon	P. S. J. Mason
	G-BOCG	PA-34-200T Seneca	Preston Contractors Ltd
	G-BOCH	PA-32 Cherokee Six 300	Basicvale Ltd
	G-BOCI	Cessna 140A	D. Nieman
	G-BOCJ	Cameron 90 Watch SS balloon	Cameron Balloons Ltd
	G-BOCK	Sopwith Triplane replica	Shuttleworth Trust/O. Warden
	G-BOCL	Slingsby T.67C	C.S.E. Aviaton Ltd/Kidlington
	G-BOCM	Slingsby T.67C	C.S.E. Aviation Ltd/Kidlington
	G-BOCN	Robinson R-22B	J. Bignall
	G-BOCO	Schweizer 269C	C.S.E. Aviation Ltd/Kidlington
	G-BOCP	PA-34-220T Seneca	BAe Flying College Ltd/Prestwick
	G-BOCR	—	—
	G-BOCS	—	—
	G-BOCT	—	—
	G-BOCU	—	—
	G-BOCV	—	—
	G-BOCW	—	—
	G-BOCX	—	—
	G-BOCY	—	—
	G-BOCZ	—	—
	G-BODA	PA-28-161 Warrior II	C.S.E. Aviation Ltd/Kidlington
	G-BODB	PA-28-161 Warrior II	C.S.E. Aviation Ltd/Kidlington
	G-BODC	—	—
	G-BODD	—	—
	G-BODE	—	—
	G-BODF	—	—
	G-BODG	—	—
	G-BODH	Slingsby T.31 Cadet III	C. D. Denham
	G-BODI	—	—
	G-BODJ	Slingsby T.67J	S. J. Donkin
	G-BODK	Rotorway Scorpion 133	J. Brannigan
	G-BODL	Steen Skybolt	K. E. Armstrong
	G-BODM	PA-28 Cherokee 180	Bristol & Wessex Aeroplane Club Ltd
	G-BODN	PA-28R-201 Arrow III	P. A. Lancaster
	G-BODO	Cessna 152	P. A. Lancaster
	G-BODP	PA-38-112 Tomahawk	N. C. Gray
	G-BODR	PA-28-161 Warrior II	Airways Aero Associations Ltd/Booker
	G-BODS	PA-38-112 Tomahawk	B. E. Simpson
	G-BODT	Jodel D.18	R. A. Jarvis
	G-BODU	—	—
	G-BODV	Cameron 90 Penta balloon	Cameron Balloons Ltd
	G-BODW	Bell 206B JetRanger	Heli-Flair Ltd
	G-BODX	—	—
	G-BODY	Cessna 310R	Atlantic Air Transport Ltd/Coventry
	G-BODZ	Robinson R-22B	Rassler Aero Services/Booker
	G-BOEA	BAe 146-100	British Aerospace PLC
	G-BOEB	PA-38-112 Tomahawk	Botsford & Willard Ltd/Panshanger
	G-BOEC	PA-38-112 Tomahawk	Botsford & Willard Ltd/Panshanger
	G-BOED	Cameron Opera House SS balloon	Cameron Balloons Ltd
	G-BOEE	PA-28-181 Archer II	T. B. Parmenter
	G-BOEF	Short SD3-60	Short Bros PLC/Sydenham
	G-BOEG	Short SD3-60	Short Bros PLC/Sydenham
	G-BOEH	Jodel DR.340	E. J. Horsfall
	G-BOEI	Short SD3-60	Short Bros PLC/Sydenham
	G-BOEJ	Short SD3-60	Short Bros PLC/Sydenham
	G-BOEK	Cameron V-77 balloon	A. J. E. Jones
	G-BOEL	Short SD3-60	Short Bros PLC/Sydenham
	G-BOEM	—	—
	G-BOEN	—	—
	G-BOEP	Bell 212	Bristow Helicopters Ltd
	G-BOER	PA-28-161 Warrior II	South Coast Aviation Ltd
	G-BOES	—	—
	G-BOET	PA-28RT-201 Arrow IV	K. Phillips Ltd
	G-BOEU	Cameron N-90 balloon	Cameron Balloons Ltd
	G-BOEV	Robinson R-22B	Bristow Helicopters Ltd
	G-BOEW	Robinson R-22B	Bristow Helicopters Ltd
	G-BOEX	Robinson R-22B	Bristow Helicopters Ltd
	G-BOEY	Robinson R-22B	Bristow Helicopters Ltd

Reg.	Type	Owner or Operator	Notes
G-BOEZ	Robinson R-22B	Bristow Helicopters Ltd	
G-BOFA	—	—	
G-BOFB	Sikorsky S-76A	Bond Helicopters Ltd/Bourn	
G-BOFC	Beech 76 Duchess	Wickenby Aviation Ltd	
G-BOIS	PA-31 Turbo Navajo	G. Grenall (G-AYNB)/Bristol	
G-BOKW	Bo208C Junior	R. A. Farrington (G-BITT)	
G-BOLT	R. Commander 114	Hooper & Jones Ltd/Kidlington	
G-BOMB	Cassutt Racer	R. W. L. Breckell	
G-BOND	Sikorsky S-76A	Bond Helicopters Ltd/Bourn	
G-BONE	Pilatus P2-06 (U-142)	Aeromech Ltd	
G-BONK	Colt 180A balloon	Wye Valley Aviation Ltd	
G-BOOB	Cameron N-56 balloon	I. J. Sadler	
G-BOOK	Pitts S-1S Special	A. N. R. Houghton	
G-BOOZ	Cameron N-77 balloon	J. A. F. Croft	
G-BOTL	Colt 42R balloon	Colt Balloons Ltd	
G-BOVA	PA-31-310 Turbo Navajo	Air Bristol Ltd (G-BECP)	

Out-of-Sequence Registrations

Reg.	Type	Owner or Operator	Notes
G-BPAH	Colt 69A balloon	International Distillers & Vintners Ltd	
G-BPAJ	D.H.82A Tiger Moth	P. A. Jackson (G-AOIX)	
G-BPAL	D.H.C.1 Chipmunk 22 (WG350)	Parker Airways Ltd (G-BCYE)/Denham	
G-BPAM	Jodel D.150A	A. J. Symes-Bullen	
G-BPAV	FRED Srs 2	P. A. Valentine	
G-BPBP	Brugger Colibri Mk II	M. F. Collett	
G-BPCH	Beech 300 Super King Air	Harris Queensway Aviation Ltd/ Biggin Hill	
G-BPEG	Currie Wot	D. M. Harrington	
G-BPFA	Knight GK-2 Swallow	G. Knight & D. G. Pridham	
G-BPGW	Boeing 757-236	Air Europe Ltd *Anna-Marie*/Gatwick	
G-BPJH	PA-19 Super Cub 95	P. J. Heron	
G-BPLC	Beech 200 Super King Air	Bass PLC	
G-BPMB	Maule M5-235C Lunar Rocket	P. M. Breton	
G-BPMN	Super Coot Model A	P. Napp	
G-BPND	Boeing 727-2D3	Dan-Air Services Ltd/Gatwick	
G-BPNO	Z.326 Trener Master	I. Mansfield & F. M. Fiore	
G-BPOG	PA-23 Aztec 250	Air Charter Scotland Ltd/Glasgow	
G-BPOP	Aircraft Designs Sheriff	Sheriff Aerospace Ltd (*stored*)/Sandown	
G-BPPN	Cessna F.182Q	Hunt Norris Ltd	
G-BPPS	CAARP CAP.21	Nullmint Ltd/Booker	
G-BPUF	Thunder Ax6-56Z balloon	Buf-Puf Balloon Group *Buf-Puf*	
G-BPYN	Piper J-3C-65 Cub	D. W. Stubbs & ptnrs/White Waltham	
G-BPZD	Nord NC.858S	A. Richards & ptnrs	
G-BRAD	Beech 95-B55 Baron	C. Walker/Perth	
G-BRAF	V. S. Spitfire XVIII (SM969)	D. W. Arnold	
G-BRAG	Taylor JT.2 Titch	A. R. Greenfield	
G-BRAL	G.159 Gulfstream 1	Ford Motor Co Ltd/Stansted	
G-BRDI	H.S.125 Srs 700B	Aravco Ltd (G-HHOI/G-BHTJ)/Heathrow	
G-BREW	PA-31-350 Navajo Chieftain	Whitbread & Co Ltd/Biggin Hill	
G-BRFC	P.57 Sea Prince T.1 (WP321)	Rural Naval Air Service/Bourn	
G-BRGH	FRED Srs 2	F. G. Hallam	
G-BRGN	BAe Jetstream 3102	Berlin Regional UK Ltd (G-BLHC)	
G-BRGW	GY-201 Minicab	R. G. White	
G-BRID	Cessna U.206A	Emair Bridlington Ltd	

Notes	Reg.	Type	Owner or Operator
	G-BRIK	Tipsy Nipper 3	C. W. R. Piper
	G-BRIT	Cessna 421C	Chaseside Holdings Ltd/Exeter
	G-BRIX	PA-32-301 Saratoga SP	Taylor Maxwell & Co Ltd/Bristol
	G-BRJW	Bellanca 7GCBC Citabria	Cleanacres Ltd/Staverton
	G-BRMA	WS-51 Dragonfly Mk 5 (WG719) ★	British Rotorcraft Museum
	G-BRMB	B.192 Belvedere Mk 1 (XG452) ★	British Rotorcraft Museum
	G-BRMC	Stampe SV-4B	A. Cullen/Andrewsfield
	G-BRMH	Bell 206B JetRanger 2	R. M. H. Stainless Ltd (G-BBUX)
	G-BROM	ICA IS-28M2	Kent Motor Gliding & Soaring Centre
	G-BRPM	Nipper T.66 Srs 3	M. M. H. J. Omar
	G-BRSA	Airbus A.320-110	BCal/British Airways/Gatwick
	G-BRSB	Airbus A.320-110	BCal/British Airways/Gatwick
	G-BRSC	Airbus A.320-110	BCal/British Airways/Gatwick
	G-BRSD	Airbus A.320-110	BCal/British Airways/Gatwick
	G-BRSE	Airbus A.320-110	BCal/British Airways/Gatwick
	G-BRSF	Airbus A.320-110	BCal/British Airways/Gatwick
	G-BRSG	Airbus A.320-110	BCal/British Airways/Gatwick
	G-BRSH	Airbus A.320-110	BCal/British Airways/Gatwick
	G-BRSI	Airbus A.320-110	BCal/British Airways/Gatwick
	G-BRSJ	Airbus A.320-110	BCal/British Airways/Gatwick
	G-BRSL	Cameron N-56 balloon	S. Budd
	G-BRUM	Cessna A.152	Warwickshire Flying Training Centre Ltd
	G-BRUX	PA-44-180 Seminole	Hambrair Ltd/Tollerton
	G-BRWN	G.159 Gulfstream 1	Capital Airlines Ltd/Leeds
	G-BRYA	D.H.C. 7-110 Dash Seven	Brymon Aviation Ltd/Plymouth
	G-BRYB	D.H.C. 7-110 Dash Seven	Brymon Aviation Ltd/Plymouth
	G-BRYC	D.H.C. 7-110 Dash Seven	Brymon Aviation Ltd/Plymouth
	G-BRYL	Agusta A.109A	Castle Air Charters Ltd (G-ROPE/G-OAMH)
	G-BSAN	G.1159A Gulfstream 3	Shell Aviation Ltd/Heathrow
	G-BSBH	Short SD3-30	Short Bros Ltd/Sydenham
	G-BSDL	SOCATA TB.10 Tobago	Consort Aviation Ltd
	G-BSEC	SOCATA TB.9 Tampico	GB Security (London) Ltd (G-BIZR)
	G-BSEL	Slingsby T-61G	RAFGSA/Bicester
	G-BSET	B.206 Srs 1 Basset	J. S. Flavell/Shoreham
	G-BSFC	PA-38-112 Tomahawk	Sherwood Flying Club Ltd/Tollerton
	G-BSFL	PA-23 Aztec 250	T. Kilroe & Sons Ltd/Manchester
	G-BSFT	PA-31-300 Navajo	SFT Aviation Ltd (G-AXYC)/Bournemouth
	G-BSGA	Beech C90 King Air	Anglian Windows Ltd/Norwich
	G-BSHL	H.S.125 Srs 600B	S. H. Services Ltd (G-BBMD)/Luton
	G-BSHR	Cessna F.172N	H. Rothwell (G-BFGE)/Dundee
	G-BSIS	Pitts S-1S Special	P. J. Bolderson
	G-BSOL	PA-32R-301 Saratoga SP	B. A. Soloman
	G-BSPC	Jodel D.140C	B. E. Cotton/Headcorn
	G-BSPE	Cessna F.172P	P. & M. Jones/Denham
	G-BSSL	Beech B80 Queen Air	Parker & Heard Ltd (G-BFEP)/Biggin Hill
	G-BSSM	AS.355F-1 Twin Squirrel	Blue Star Ship Management Ltd (G-BMTC/G-BKUK)
	G-BSSS	Cessna 421C	Westair Flying Services Ltd/Blackpool
	G-BSST	Concorde 002 ★	Fleet Air Arm Museum
	G-BSUS	Taylor JT.1 Monoplane	R. Parker
	G-BSVP	PA-23 Aztec 250F	Time Electronics Ltd
	G-BTAL	Cessna F.152	TG Aviation Ltd
	G-BTAN	Thunder Ax7-65Z balloon	The BTAN Balloon Group
	G-BTAX	PA-31-350 Navajo Chieftain	Chaseside Holdings Ltd
	G-BTBT	PA-32R-301 Saratoga SP	B. Taylor
	G-BTCG	PA-23 Aztec 250	Eagle Tugs Ltd (G-AVRX)/Mombasa
	G-BTCM	Cameron N-90 balloon	Chesterfield Cold Storage Co Ltd
	G-BTDK	Cessna 421B	RK Technologies Ltd/Manchester
	G-BTEA	Cameron N-105 balloon	Southern Balloon Group
	G-BTFC	Cessna F.152 II	Tayside Aviation Ltd/Dundee
	G-BTGS	Stolp SA.300 Starduster Too	T. G. Soloman (G-AYMA)
	G-BTIE	SOCATA TB.10 Tobago	Rotaters Ltd/Manchester
	G-BTJM	Taylor JT.2 Titch	T. J. Miller/Dunkeswell
	G-BTLE	PA-31-350 Navajo Chieftain	Andwell Mill Trout Farm Ltd
	G-BTOM	PA-38-112 Tomahawk	C. R. Timber Ltd
	G-BTOW	SOCATA Rallye 180T	Mixamate Ltd/Biggin Hill
	G-BTPB	Cameron N-105 balloon	British Telecom PLC
	G-BTSC	Evans VP-2	B. P. Irish
	G-BTSG	Cessna 414A	T. S. Grimshaw Ltd (G-BTFH)
	G-BTUC	EMB-312 Tucano	Short Bros PLC/Sydenham

Reg.	Type	Owner or Operator	Notes
G-BTUG	SOCATA Rallye 180T	Lasham Gliding Soc Ltd	
G-BTWW	AB-206B JetRanger	Dollar Air Services Ltd/Coventry	
G-BTXL	BAe Jetstream 3102	Berlin Regional UK Ltd (G-BLDO)	
G-BUBL	Thunder Ax8-105 balloon	Moet & Chandon (London) Ltd	
G-BUBU	PA-34-220T Seneca 3	Brinor (Holdings) Ltd	
G-BUCC	C.A.S.A. 1.131E Jungmann	E. J. McEntee/White Waltham	
G-BUCK	C.A.S.A. 1.131E Jungmann (BU+CK)	W. G. V. Hall	
G-BUDG	Cessna 421C	A. F. Budge Ltd (G-BKWX)/E. Midlands	
G-BUDS	Rand KR-2	D. W. Munday	
G-BUDY	Colt 17A balloon	Bondbaste Ltd	
G-BUFF	Jodel D.112	D. J. Buffham/Fenland	
G-BUMF	Robinson R-22	J. Bignall (G-BMBU)	
G-BUMP	PA-28-181 Archer II	H. McC. Clarke	
G-BUNY	Beech 95-B55 Baron	Gama Aviation Ltd	
G-BURD	Cessna F.172N	RJS Aviation Ltd/Halfpenny Green	
G-BURT	PA-28-161 Warrior II	A. T. Howarth/Biggin Hill	
G-BUSY	Thunder Ax6-56A balloon	B. R. & Mrs M. Boyle Busy Bodies	
G-BUTL	PA-24 Comanche 250	D. Buttle (G-ARLB)/Blackbushe	
G-BUTT	Cessna FA.150K	M. Buttery (G-AXSJ)	
G-BUZZ	AB-206B JetRanger 2	ICS Worldwide Courier Ltd	
G-BVMM	Robin HR.200/100	M. G. Owen	
G-BVMZ	Robin HR.100/210	Chiltern Handbags (London) Ltd	
G-BVPI	Evans VP-1	C. M. Gibson	
G-BVPM	Evans VP-2	P. Marigold	
G-BWDJ	Jurca MJ.5 Sirocco	B. W. Davies	
G-BWEC	Cassutt-Colson Variant	N. R. Thomason & M. P. J. Hill	
G-BWFJ	Evans VP-1	W. F. Jones	
G-BWHY	Robinson R-22	Specialist Heat Exchangers Ltd	
G-BWIG	G.17S replica	K. Wigglesworth	
G-BWJB	Thunder Ax8-105 balloon	Justerini & Brooks Ltd Whiskey J. & B.	
G-BWKK	Auster AOP.9 (XP279)	Sussex Spraying Services Ltd/Shoreham	
G-BWMB	Jodel D.119	K. Jarman	
G-BWMP	Gulfstream 695A	R. B. Tyler (Plant) Ltd	
G-BWOC	PA-31-350 Navajo Chieftain	BWOC Ltd	
G-BWRB	D.H.C.6 Twin Otter 310	Brymon Aviation Ltd/Plymouth	
G-BWSI	K&S SA.102.5 Cavalier	B. W. Shaw	
G-BWTX	PA-42-720 Cheyenne	Broome & Wellington (Aviation) Ltd	
G-BWWJ	Hughes 269C	B. W. W. Jones (G-BMYZ)	
G-BWWW	BAe Jetstream 3102	British Aerospace PLC/Dunsfold	
G-BXVI	V.S.361 Spitfire F.XVI	D. Arnold	
G-BXYZ	R. Turbo Commander 690C	British Airports Authority/Gatwick	
G-BYLL	F.8L Falco	N. J. Langrick	
G-BYRD	Mooney M.20K	V. J. Holden/Teesside	
G-BYSE	AB-206B JetRanger 2	Bewise Ltd (G-BFND)	
G-BYSL	Cameron O-56 balloon	Charles of the Ritz Ltd	
G-BZAC	Sikorsky S-76A	British International Helicopters Ltd/Aberdeen	
G-BZBH	Thunder Ax6-65 balloon	R. S. Whittaker & P. E. Sadler	
G-BZBY	Colt 56 Buzby balloon	British Telecom	
G-BZFE	PA-23 Aztec 250	City Flight Ltd (G-AZFE)	
G-BZKK	Cameron V-56 balloon	P. J. Green & C. Bosley Gemini II	
G-BZZZ	Enstrom F-28C-UK	Owners Abroad Aviation Ltd (G-BBBZ)	
G-CALL	PA-23 Aztec 250F	Woodgate Aviation Ltd/Ronaldsway	
G-CAXF	Cameron O-77 balloon	R. D. & S. J. Sarjeant	
G-CBEA	BAe Jetstream 3102-01	Birmingham Executive Airways Ltd	
G-CBIA	BAC One-Eleven 416	British Island Airways PLC (G-AWXJ) Island Ensign/Gatwick	
G-CBIL	Cessna 182K	N. Law/Manchester	
G-CBOR	Cessna F.172N	L. Belet	
G-CCAR	Cameron N-77 balloon	A. G. E. Faulkner	
G-CCCC	Cessna 172H	B. J. Crow/Elstree	
G-CCIX	V.S.361 Spitfire LF.IX	Charles Church (Spitfires) Ltd (G-BIXP)	
G-CCOZ	Monnet Sonerai II	P. R. Cozens	
G-CCUB	Piper J-3C-65 Cub	Cormack (Aircraft Services) Ltd	
G-CDAH	Taylor Sooper Coot A	D. A. Hood	
G-CDET	Culver LCA Cadet	H. B. Fox/Booker	
G-CDGA	Taylor JT.1 Monoplane	R. M. Larimore	
G-CDGL	Saffery S.330 balloon	C. J. Dodd & G. J. Luckett Penny	
G-CEAS	HPR-7 Herald 214	Channel Express Freight (UK) Ltd (G-BEBB)/Bournemouth	
G-CEGA	PA-34-200T-2 Seneca	Hendefern Ltd	

Notes	Reg.	Type	Owner or Operator
	G-CEGB	AS.355F1 Twin Squirrel	Central Electricity Generating Board (G-BLJL)
	G-CELL	PA-32R-301 Saratoga SP	CEL Electronics Ltd
	G-CERT	Mooney M.20K	N. Jagger
	G-CETA	Cessna E.310Q	CETA Video Ltd (G-BBIM)/Fairoaks
	G-CETC	Aeronca 15AC Sedan	G. Churchill/Finmere
	G-CEXP	HPR-7 Herald 209	Channel Express Air Services Ltd (G-BFRJ)/Bournemouth
	G-CEZY	Thunder Ax9-140 balloon	R. Carr/France
	G-CFBI	Colt 56A balloon	G. H. Dorrell
	G-CFLY	Cessna 172F	Cee-Fly
	G-CGHM	PA-28 Cherokee 140	CGH Managements Ltd/Elstree
	G-CHAR	Grob G.109B	RAFGSA/Bicester
	G-CHDI	Cessna 414A	Northair Aviation Ltd/Leeds
	G-CHEM	PA-34-200T Seneca 2	Mega Yield Ltd
	G-CHIK	Cessna F.152	Stapleford Flying Club Ltd (G-BHAZ)
	G-CHIL	Robinson R-22HP	L. M. Dresher
	G-CHIP	PA-28-181 Archer II	Forward Vision Ltd
	G-CHOP	Westland Bell 47G-3B1	Time Choppers Ltd/Chilbolton
	G-CHSR	BAe 146-200	Air UK Ltd/Norwich
	G-CHTA	AA-5A Cheetah	London Aviation Ltd (G-BFRC)/ Biggin Hill
	G-CHTT	Varga 2150A Kachina	C.H.T. Trace
	G-CINE	Bell 206L-1 LongRanger	PLM Helicopters Ltd
	G-CIPI	AJEP Wittman W.8 Tailwind	G. J. Z. Cipirski (G-AYDU)/Biggin Hill
	G-CITB	Boeing 747-2D3B	BCal/British Airways/Gatwick
	G-CITI	Cessna 501 Citation	Consultant Services Ltd
	G-CITY	PA-31-350 Navajo Chieftain	Woodgate Aviation Ltd/Ronaldsway
	G-CJBC	PA-28 Cherokee 180	J. B. Cave/Halfpenny Green
	G-CJCB	Bell 206L LongRanger	J. C. Bamford (Excavators) Ltd (G-LIII)/ E. Midlands
	G-CJCI	Pilatus P2-06	C. Church
	G-CJET	Learjet 35A	Manx Helicopters Ltd (G-SEBE/G-ZIPS/ G-ZONE)
	G-CJHI	Bell 206B JetRanger	Tudorbury (Air Services) Ltd (G-BBFB)
	G-CJIM	Taylor JT.1 Monoplane	J. Crawford
	G-CLAC	PA-28-161 Warrior II	J. D. Moonie
	G-CLEA	PA-28-161 Warrior II	Creative Logistics Enterprises & Aviation Ltd
	G-CLEM	Bo 208A2 Junior	G. Clements (G-ASWE)/Netherthorpe
	G-CLIK	PA-18 Super Cub 95	N. J. R. Empson/Ipswich
	G-CLNT	Bell 206L LongRanger	Air Hanson Ltd (G-BFTR)
	G-CLOS	PA-34-200-2 Seneca	Green Close Ltd
	G-CLUB	Cessna FRA.150M	R. C. Button
	G-CLUX	Cessna F.172N	D. Bardsley/Manchester
	G-CMAL	Auster 5	C. Malcolm (G-APAF)
	G-CNIS	Partenavia P.68B	Wyndley Nurseries Ltd (G-BJOF/ G-PAUL)
	G-CNMF	BAe 146-200	Air UK Ltd/Norwich
	G-COCO	Cessna F.172M	SEH (Ipswich) Ltd
	G-COIN	Bell 206B JetRanger 2	P. Woodward
	G-COKE	Cameron O-65 balloon	M. C. Bradley
	G-COLL	Enstrom F-280C	Decoy Engineering Projects Ltd
	G-COLN	AS.350B Ecureuil	C. M. Meade (G-BHIV)
	G-COLR	Colt 69A balloon	Graeme Scaife Productions Ltd
	G-COMB	PA-30 Twin Comanche 160	Airman Aviation Ltd (G-AVBL)
	G-COMM	PA-23 Aztec 250	Commair Aviation Ltd (G-AZMG)/ E. Midlands
	G-COMP	Cameron N-90 balloon	Computacenter Ltd
	G-CONI	L.749A Constellation (N7777G) ★	Science Museum/Wroughton
	G-COOK	Cameron N-77 balloon	IAZ (International) Ltd
	G-COOP	Cameron N-31 balloon	Balloon Stable Ltd Co-op
	G-COPE	Enstrom F-280C-UK-2 Shark	A. Cope
	G-COPS	Piper J-3C-65 Cub	W. T. Sproat
	G-COPY	AA-5A Cheetah	Emberden Ltd (G-BIEU)/Biggin Hill
	G-COTT	Cameron 60 SS balloon	Nottingham Hot-Air Balloon Club
	G-COWI	Cessna 414A	Cowie Aviation Ltd (G-MLCS/G-MHGI/ G-BHKK)
	G-COZY	Rutan Cozy	J. F. Mackay
	G-CPFC	Cessna F.152	Osprey Air Services Ltd/Cranfield
	G-CPTS	AB-206B JetRanger 2	A. R. B. Aspinall
	G-CRAN	Robin R.1180T	Slea Aviation Ltd/Cranwell
	G-CRIC	Colomban Cri-Cri MC-15	A. J. Maxwell
	G-CRIL	R. Commander 112B	Rockwell Aviation Group/Cardiff

G-AANF D.H.60GM Moth. *Alan J. Wright (AJW)*

G-ABWP Spartan Arrow.　Peter R. March (PRM)

G-BBMW D.H.C.1 Chipmunk 22. *PRM*

G-BCEB Sikorsky S-61N Mk II of British International Helicopters. *AJW*

G-BEJP D.H.C.6 Twin Otter 310 of Loganair.   AJW

G-BITV Short SD3-30 of Connectair   AJW

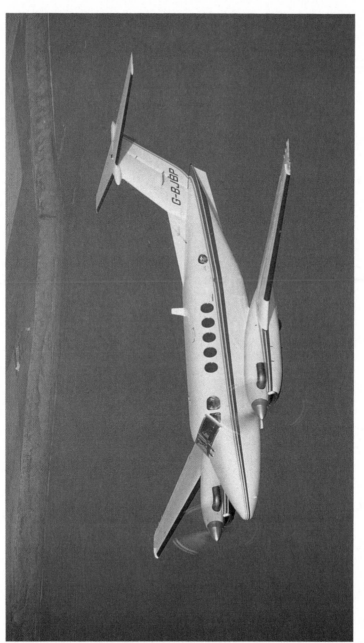

G-BJBP Beech 200 Super King Air. *PRM*

G-BLDD WAG-Aero CUBy AcroTrainer. AJW

G-KARI Fuji FA.200-160.   *PRM*

G-ORED BN-2T Islander. *AJW*

14+ ★ Pilatus P2-05, civil identity G-BJAX. AJW

HB-IPA Airbus A.310-221 of Swissair. *PRM*

LN-SUJ Boeing 737-205 of Braathens. AJW

N185AT L-1011-385 TriStar 1 of American Trans Air. *AJW*

YI-ALT Ilyushin Il-76MD of Iraqi Airways. *PRM*

G-TIRE Colt Flying Tyre SS balloon. *PRM*

Reg.	Type	Owner or Operator	Notes
G-CRIS	Taylor JT.1 Monoplane	C. J. Bragg	
G-CRZY	Thunder Ax8-105 balloon	R. Carr (G-BDLP)/France	
G-CSBM	Cessna F.150M	Coventry (Civil) Aviation Ltd	
G-CSCS	Cessna F.172N	Conegate Ltd	
G-CSFC	Cessna 150L	Shropshire Aero Club Ltd	
G-CSFT	PA-23 Aztec 250	SFT Aviation Ltd (G-AYKU)/ Bournemouth	
G-CSNA	Cessna 421C	Knightway Air Charter Ltd/Leeds	
G-CSZB	V.807B Viscount	British Air Ferries Viscount Scotland (G-AOXU)/Southend	
G-CTIX	V.S.509 Spitfire T.IX	Charles Church (Spitfires) Ltd	
G-CTKL	CCF Harvard IV (54136)	J. A. Carr	
G-CTRN	Enstrom F-28C-UK	W. E. Taylor & Son Ltd	
G-CTRX	H.P.137 Jetstream 200	Centrax Ltd (G-BCWW/G-AXUN)/Exeter	
G-CTSI	Enstrom F-280C Shark	Sullivan Management Control Ltd (G-BKIO)	
G-CUBB	PA-18-150 Super Cub	Booker Gliding Club Ltd	
G-CUBI	PA-18-135 Super Cub	Hambletons Gliding Club Ltd	
G-CUBJ	PA-18 Super Cub 150	A. K. Leasing (Jersey) Ltd	
G-CUGA	GA-7 Cougar	Frontline Aviation Ltd	
G-CUKL	Beech 200 Super King Air	Conoco (UK) Ltd (G-CNSI/G-OSKA)	
G-CWOT	Currie Wot	D. A. Lord	
G-CXCX	Cameron N-90 balloon	Cathay Pacific Airways (London) Ltd	
G-CYMA	GA-7 Cougar	Cyma Petroleum Ltd (G-BKOM)/Elstree	
G-DAAH	PA-28R-201T Turbo Arrow IV	A. A. Hunter	
G-DACA	P.57 Sea Prince T.1	Atlantic & Caribbean Aviation Ltd/ Staverton	
G-DACC	Cessna 401B	Pressband Ltd (G-AYOU)	
G-DAFS	Cessna 404 Titan	Dept. of Agriculture & Fisheries for Scotland (G-BHNH)/Edinburgh	
G-DAJB	Boeing 757-2T7	Monarch Airlines Ltd/Luton	
G-DAJW	K & S Jungster 1	A. J. Walters	
G-DAKS	Dakota 3 (KG874)	Aces High Ltd/North Weald	
G-DAND	SOCATA TB.10 Tobago	Whitemoor Engineering Co Ltd	
G-DANN	Stampe SV-4B	I. M. White	
G-DART	Rollason Beta B2	M. G. Ollis	
G-DASH	R. Commander 112A	Josef D. J. Jons & Co Ltd (G-BDAJ)	
G-DASI	Short SD3-60	Air UK Ltd (G-BKKW)/Norwich	
G-DATA	EMB-110P2 Bandeirante	National Airways/Business Air Travel (G-BGNK)	
G-DAVE	Jodel D.112	D. A. Porter/Sturgate	
G-DAVY	Evans VP-2	D. Morris	
G-DBAL	H.S.125 Srs 3B	Falcon Jet Centre Ltd (G-BSAA)	
G-DBAR	Beech 200 Super King Air	Brown & Root (UK) Ltd	
G-DCAN	PA-38-112 Tomahawk	Airways Aero Associations Ltd/Booker	
G-DCCH	MBB Bo 105D	Devon & Cornwall Police Authority	
G-DCIO	Douglas DC-10-30	BCal/British Airways Flora McDonald — The Scottish Heroine	
G-DCKK	Cessna F.172N	C. R. Timber Ltd/Andrewsfield	
G-DDCD	D.H.104 Dove 8	C. Daniel (G-ARUM)/Biggin Hill	
G-DDDV	Boeing 737-2S3	Air Europe Ltd Peggy/Gatwick	
G-DEBS	Colt AA-150 gas balloon	Hot-Air Balloon Co Ltd	
G-DEDE	Cessna 421C	Dick McNeil Associates Ltd	
G-DELI	Thunder Ax7-77 balloon	Thunder & Colt Ltd	
G-DEMO	BN-2T Islander	Pilatus BN Ltd (G-BKEA)/Bembridge	
G-DENS	CP.301S Smaragd	D. Russell	
G-DESS	Mooney M.20J	D. Russell	
G-DEVN	D.H.104 Devon C.2 (WB533)	T. P. Luscombe & P. Gaston/Lympne	
G-DEVS	PA.28 Cherokee 180	H. C. Devenish (G-BGVJ)/Southend	
G-DEXI	Cessna 340A	Barons (UK) Ltd	
G-DEXP	ARV Super 2	ARV Aviation Ltd	
G-DFLY	PA-38-112 Tomahawk	Airways Aero Associations Ltd/Booker	
G-DFTS	Cessna FA.152	Tayside Aviation Ltd/Dundee	
G-DFUB	Boeing 737-2K9	Monarch Airlines Ltd/Luton	
G-DFVA	Cessna R.172K	R. A. Plowright	
G-DGDG	Glaser-Dirks DG.400/17	DG400 Flying Group/Lasham	
G-DHSW	Boeing 737-3Y0	Monarch Airlines Ltd/Luton	
G-DHTM	D.H.82A Tiger Moth replica	C. R. Hardiman	
G-DIAN	Extra EA.230	D. M. Britten	
G-DICK	Thunder Ax6-56Z balloon	Bandag Tyre Co	
G-DIDI	PA-31-310 Navajo	Airstar (Air Transport) Ltd/Luton	
G-DINA	AA-5B Tiger	Simon Deverall Print Ltd/ Compton Abbas	

Notes	Reg.	Type	Owner or Operator
	G-DIPS	Taylor JT.1 Monoplane	B. J. Halls
	G-DIRK	Glaser-Dirks DG.400	D. M. Chalmers
	G-DISC	Cessna U.206A	I. A. Louttit (G-BGWR)/Exeter
	G-DISO	Jodel D.150	P. F. Craven & J. H. Shearer
	G-DIVA	Cessna R.172K XPII	R. A. Plowright & J. A. Kaye/ Biggin Hill
	G-DIXI	PA-31-350 Navajo Chieftain	Birmingham Aerocentre Ltd
	G-DJBE	Cessna 550 Citation II	Fisons PLC/E. Midlands
	G-DJHB	Beech A23-19 Musketeer	R. A. Young (G-AZZE)
	G-DJIM	MHCA-I	J. Crawford
	G-DJJA	PA-28-181 Archer II	Astro Technology Ltd
	G-DKDP	Grob G.109B	Diss Aviation Ltd
	G-DKGF	Viking Dragonfly	K. G. Fathers
	G-DLRA	BN-2T Islander	Pilatus BN Ltd (G-BJYU)/Bembridge
	G-DLTI	Robinson R-22B	Springfield Aviation Ltd
	G-DMAF	Bell 222A	Genavco Air Ltd (G-BLSZ)
	G-DMCH	Hiller UH-12E	D. McK. Carnegie & ptnrs
	G-DMCS	PA-28R Cherokee Arrow 200-2	Carriage Communications Consultancy Ltd (G-CPAC)
	G-DNLD	Cameron 97 Donald SS balloon	The Walt Disney Co Ltd
	G-DODD	Cessna F.172P-II	K. Watts/Elstree
	G-DODS	PA-46-310P Malibu	Abersoch Land & Sea Ltd
	G-DOFY	Bell 206B JetRanger	Air Hanson Sales Ltd
	G-DOGS	Cessna R.182RG	Usoland Ltd
	G-DOOK	Beech 60 Duke	Pan Gulf Construction (UK) Ltd (G-AXEN)
	G-DOVE	Cessna 182Q	P. J. Contracting
	G-DRAY	Taylor JT.1 Monoplane	L. J. Dray
	G-DRJC	Boeing 757-2T7	Monarch Airlines Ltd/Luton
	G-DROP	Cessna U.206C	A. A. Louttit (G-UKNO-G-BAMN)
	G-DSAM	AS.350B Ecureuil	Samworth Brothers Ltd
	G-DTOO	PA-38-112 Tomahawk	A. Todd
	G-DUCH	Beech 76 Duchess	Ralph Anderson Ltd
	G-DUET	Wood Duet	C. Wood
	G-DUNN	Zenair CH.250	A. Dunn
	G-DUVL	Cessna F.172N	Duval Studios Ltd/Denham
	G-DVON	D.H.104 Devon C.2 (VP955)	C. L. Thatcher
	G-DWHH	Boeing 737-2T7	Monarch Airlines Ltd/Luton
	G-DWMI	Bell 206L-1 LongRanger	Glenwood Helicopters Ltd/Fairoaks
	G-DYNE	Cessna 414	Commair Aviation Ltd/E. Midlands
	G-DYOU	PA-38-112 Tomahawk	Airways Aero Associations Ltd/Booker
	G-EAGL	Cessna 421C	Associated Dairies Ltd/Leeds
	G-EBJI	Hawker Cygnet Replica	A. V. Francis
	G-ECAV	Beech 200 Super King Air	GEC Avionics Ltd/Rochester
	G-ECBH	Cessna F.150K	Air Fenland Ltd
	G-ECGC	Cessna F.172N-II	Leicestershire Aero Club Ltd
	G-ECHO	Enstrom F-280C-UK-2 Shark	ALP Electrical (Maidenhead) Ltd (G-LONS/G-BDIB)/White Waltham
	G-ECMA	PA-31-310 Turbo Navajo	Elliot Bros (London) Ltd/Rochester
	G-ECOX	Grega GN.1 Air Camper	H. C. Cox
	G-EDEN	SOCATA TB.10 Tobago	N. I. Mandell & J. D. Wittich/ Elstree
	G-EDIF	Evans VP-2	R. Simpson
	G-EDIN	H.S.748 Srs 2A	—
	G-EDIT	Beech B95 Travel Air	P. Tweedy (G-AXUX)
	G-EDNA	PA-38-112 Tomahawk	MSF Aviation Ltd
	G-EDRY	Cessna T.303	Pat Eddery Ltd
	G-EEEE	Slingsby T.31 Motor Glider	R. F. Selby
	G-EEGE	Robinson R-22A	C. J. Elvidge (G-BKZK)
	G-EENY	GA-7 Cougar	Charles Henry Leasing/Elstree
	G-EESE	Cessna U.206G	D. Penny
	G-EEUP	SNCAN SV-4C	Minrealm Ltd
	G-EEZE	Rutan Vari-Eze	A. J. Nurse
	G-EGAP	Sequoia F.8L Falco	E. G. A. Prance
	G-EGEE	Cessna 310Q	A. J. Fuller & ptnrs (G-AZVY)
	G-EGGS	Robin DR.400/180	R. Foot
	G-EGLE	Christen Eagle II	Myrick Aviation Services Ltd
	G-EHAP	Sportavia-Pützer RF.7	M. J. Revill/Exeter
	G-EHIL	Westland-Agusta EH.101	Westland Helicopters Ltd/Yeovil
	G-EHMM	Robin DR.400/180R	Booker Gliding Club Ltd
	G-EIIR	Cameron N-77 balloon	Major C. J. T. Davey *Silver Jubilee*
	G-EIWT	Cessna FR.182RG	P. P. D. Howard-Johnston/Edinburgh
	G-EJCB	Agusta A.109A Mk2	J. C. Bamford Excavators Ltd

Reg.	Type	Owner or Operator	Notes
G-EJGO	Z.226HE Trener	N. J. Radford	
G-ELEC	Westland WG.30 Srs 200	Westland Helicopters Ltd (G-BKNV)/ Yeovil	
G-EMAK	PA-28R-201 Cherokee Arrow II	Arrow Aircraft Group/E. Midlands	
G-EMKM	Jodel D.120A	Cawdor Flying Group/Inverness	
G-EMMA	Cessna F.182Q	Watkiss Group Aviation	
G-EMMS	PA-38-112 Tomahawk	G. C. J. Moffatt & Co Ltd/Cardiff	
G-EMMY	Rutan Vari-Eze	M. J. Tooze	
G-ENAM	Cessna 340A	Malcolm Enamellers (Midlands) Ltd	
G-ENCE	Partenavia P.68B	P. A. de Courcy-Swoffe & D. S. Innes (G-OROY/G-BFSU)	
G-ENIE	Nipper T.66 Srs 3	G. Weale/Shoreham	
G-ENII	Cessna F.172M	MRK Aviation Ltd	
G-ENIU	PA-24 Comanche 260	A. F. Warnell (G-AVJU)/Stapleford	
G-ENNY	Cameron V-77 balloon	B. G. Jones	
G-ENOA	Cessna F.172F	M. Konstantinovic (G-ASZW)/ Stapleford	
G-ENSI	Beech F33A Bonanza	F. B. Gibbons & Sons Ltd	
G-EOFF	Taylor JT.2 Titch	G. H. Wylde	
G-EORG	PA-38-112 Tomahawc	Airways Aero Association/Booker	
G-EPDI	Cameron N-77 balloon	R. Moss & Pegasus Aviation Ltd	
G-ERIC	R. Commander 112TC	P. P. Patterson/Newcastle	
G-ERMO	ARV Super 2	M. J. Holdsworth Ltd (G-BMWK)	
G-ERRY	AA-5B Tiger	Swingdale Ltd (G-BFMJ)	
G-ERTY	D.H.82A Tiger Moth	J. A. Thomas & R. F. Tolhurst (G-ANDC)	
G-ESSX	PA-28-161 Warrior II	S. Harcourt (G-BHYY)/Shoreham	
G-ESTE	AA-5A Cheetah	McGeoghan Plant Hire & Excavations Ltd (G-GHNC)	
G-ETCD	Colt 77A balloon	Philips Electronics Ltd	
G-EURA	Agusta-Bell 47J-2	E. W. Schnedlitz (G-ASNV)	
G-EVAN	Taylor JT.2 Titch	E. Evans	
G-EWBJ	SOCATA TB.10 Tobago	Lydd Air Training Centre Ltd	
G-EWIZ	Pitts S-2E Special	R. H. Jago	
G-EWUD	Cessna F.172F	Viewmoor Ltd (G-ATBK)	
G-EXEC	PA-34-200 Seneca	C. R. Lord/Coventry	
G-EXEX	Cessna 404	Hubbard Air Ltd/Norwich	
G-EXIT	SOCATA Rallye 180GT	G-Exit Ltd/Rochester	
G-EXPR	Colt 90A balloon	Air Canada Ltd	
G-EYEI	Bell 206A JetRanger	Clyde Helicopters Ltd	
G-EZEE	Rutan Vari-Eze	M. G. E. Hutton	
G-EZOS	Rutan Vari-Eze	O. Smith/Tees-side	
G-FACA	Cessna 172P	P. Malcolm	
G-FACB	Cessna 172P	P. M. Green	
G-FAGN	Robinson R-22B	Fagins Toys Ltd	
G-FAIR	SOCATA TB.10 Tobago	Sally Marine Ltd/Guernsey	
G-FALC	Aeromere F.8L Falco	P. W. Hunter (G-AROT)/Elstree	
G-FALK	Sequoia F.8L Falco 4	I. Chancellor	
G-FALL	Cessna 182L	D. M. Penny	
G-FANG	AA-5A Cheetah	Reedtrend Ltd/Blackbushe	
G-FANL	Cessna FR.172K XP-II	J. Woodhouse & Co/Staverton	
G-FARM	SOCATA Rallye 235GT	M. J. Jardine-Paterson	
G-FARR	Jodel D.150	G. H. Farr	
G-FAST	Cessna 337G	Acorn Computers Ltd/Cambridge	
G-FAYE	Cessna F.150M	Cheshire Air Training School Ltd/ Liverpool	
G-FBWH	PA-28R Cherokee Arrow 180	Servicecentre Systems (Cambs) Ltd	
G-FCHJ	Cessna 340A	P. L. & M. J. E. Builder (G-BJLS)	
G-FDGM	Beech B60 Duke	Parissi Air Ltd/Perth	
G-FELT	Cameron N-77 balloon	Allan Industries Ltd	
G-FERY	Cessna 550 Citation II	Moseley Group (PSV) Ltd (G-DJBI)/ E. Midlands	
G-FFEN	Cessna F.150M	Suffolk Aero Club Ltd/Ipswich	
G-FFLT	H.S.125 Srs 600B	Fairflight Ltd/Biggin Hill	
G-FFOR	Cessna 310R	Fountain Forestry Ltd (G-BMGF)	
G-FFTN	Bell 206B JetRanger	Fountain Forestry Ltd	
G-FHAS	Scheibe SF.25E Super Falke	A. R. Dearden	
G-FIFI	SOCATA TB.20 Trinidad	D. J. & M. Gower (G-BMWS)	
G-FIGA	Cessna 152	Relstage Trading Ltd	
G-FIGB	Cessna 152	Fujair Flight (UK) Ltd	
G-FILE	PA-34-200T Seneca	Filemart Ltd	
G-FIMI	Bell 206L-1 LongRanger	Lynton Aviation Ltd	
G-FINS	AB-206B JetRanger	Willow Vale Electronics Ltd (G-BFCL)	
G-FIRE	V.S.379 Spitfire XIVc	Classic Air Displays Ltd/Kidlington	

Notes	Reg.	Type	Owner or Operator
	G-FISH	Cessna 310R-II	Boston Deep Sea Fisheries Ltd/ Humberside
	G-FIST	Fieseler Fi.156C Storch	Spoils Kitchen Reject Shops Ltd
	G-FIZZ	PA-28-161 Warrior II	N. C. L. & J. E. Wright
	G-FKKM	PA-28RT-201 Turbo Arrow IV	Hubert C. Leach (Overseas) Ltd
	G-FLCH	AB-206B JetRanger 3	Fletchair (G-BGGX)/Leeds
	G-FLCO	Sequoia F.8L Falco	J. B. Mowforth
	G-FLEA	SOCATA TB.10 Tobago	Fleair Trading Co/Biggin Hill
	G-FLIC	Cessna FA.152	Stanton Aircraft Management Ltd (G-BILV)/Biggin Hill
	G-FLIK	Pitts S.1S Special	R. P. Millinship
	G-FLIP	Cessna FA.152	Brailsford Aviation Ltd/Netherthorpe
	G-FLIX	Cessna E.310P	C Air Ltd (G-AZFL)
	G-FLPI	R. Commander 112A	Tuscany Ltd/Leicester
	G-FLYI	PA-34-200 Seneca	BLS Aviation Ltd (G-BHVO)/Elstree
	G-FMUS	Robinson R-22	C. W. Cayzer (G-BJBT)
	G-FOCK	WAR Focke-Wulf Fw.190-A	P. R. Underhill
	G-FOGG	Cameron N-90 balloon	Derwent Valley Foods Ltd
	G-FONE	Colt Cityman SS balloon	Thunder & Colt Ltd
	G-FOOD	Beech B200 Super King Air	Specbridge Ltd/Gamston
	G-FORC	SNCAN Stampe SV-4A	J. A. Sykes
	G-FORD	SNCAN SV-4B	P. Meeson
	G-FOTO	PA-23 Aztec 250	Davis Gibson Advertising Ltd (G-BJDH/ G-BDXV)/Denham
	G-FOUX	AA-5A Cheetah	Baryn Finance Ltd/Elstree
	G-FRAA	Dassault Falcon 20F	FR Finances Ltd/Bournemouth
	G-FRAB	Dassault Falcon 20F	FR Finances Ltd/Bournemouth
	G-FRAC	Dassault Falcon 20F	FR Finances Ltd/Bournemouth
	G-FRAD	Dassault Falcon 20E	FR Finances Ltd (G-BYCF)/Bournemouth
	G-FRAE	Dassault Falcon 20E	FR Finances Ltd/Bournemouth
	G-FRAF	Dassault Falcon 20E	FR Finances Ltd/Bournemouth
	G-FRAG	PA-32-300 Cherokee Six	R. Goodwin & Co Ltd/Southend
	G-FRAN	Piper J-3C-65 Cub (480321)	D. E. Blaxford & ptnrs (G-BIXY)
	G-FRAX	Cessna 441	FR Finances Ltd (G-BMTZ)/ Bournemouth
	G-FRAZ	Cessna 441	FR Finances Ltd/Bournemouth
	G-FRED	FRED Srs 2	R. Cox
	G-FREE	Pitts S-2A Special	Pegasus Flying Group/Fairoaks
	G-FRJB	Britten Sheriff SA-1 ★	Aeropark/E. Midlands
	G-FROZ	Cessna 421C	Beavergrain Ltd
	G-FRST	PA-44T Turbo Seminole 180	Frost & Frost/Kidlington
	G-FSDA	AB-206B JetRanger 2	Heli-Flair Ltd (G-AWJW)
	G-FSDC	Enstrom F-280C-UK	Heli-Flair Ltd (G-BKTG)
	G-FSDG	AB-206B JetRanger	Flair (Soft Drinks) Ltd (G-ROOT/G-JETR)
	G-FSPL	PA-32R-300 Lance	P. J. Withinshaw/Conington
	G-FTAX	Cessna 421C	Chaseside Holdings Ltd/Exeter
	G-FTWO	AS.355F-2 Twin Squirrel	McAlpine Helicopters Ltd (G-BMUS)/ Hayes
	G-FUEL	Robin DR.400/180	R. Darch/Compton Abbas
	G-FUJI	Fuji FA.200-180	G. H. Willson & ptnrs
	G-FULL	PA-28R-200-2 Cherokee Arrow	Fuller Aviation (G-HWAY/G-JULI)
	G-FUND	Thunder Ax7-65Z balloon	Schroder Life Assurance Ltd
	G-FUZZ	PA-19 Super Cub 95	G. W. Cline
	G-FVEE	Monnet Sonerai I	D. R. Sparke
	G-FWRP	Cessna 421C	Vange Scaffolding & Engineering Co Ltd
	G-FXIV	V.S.379 Spitfire FR.XIV (MV370)	R. Lamplough
	G-FZZY	Colt 69A balloon	Hot-Air Balloon Co Ltd
	G-FZZZ	Colt 56A balloon	Hot-Air Balloon Co Ltd
	G-GABD	GA-7 Cougar	J. Bett/Glasgow
	G-GACA	P.57 Sea Prince T.1	Atlantic & Caribbean Aviation Ltd/ Staverton
	G-GAIR	PA-60 Aerostar 601P	G-Air Ltd/Goodwood
	G-GAJB	AA-5B Tiger	G. A. J. Bowles (G-BHZN)
	G-GALE	PA-34-200T-2 Seneca	Gale Construction Co Ltd/Norwich
	G-GAMA	Beech B58 Baron	Gama Aviation Ltd (G-BBSD)/Fairoaks
	G-GAME	Cessna T.303	Ripley Aviation Ltd
	G-GANE	Sequoia F.8L Falco	S. J. Gane
	G-GANJ	Fournier RF-6B-100	Soaring Equipment Ltd/Coventry
	G-GASA	Hughes 369HS	Black Isle Helicopters Ltd
	G-GASC	Hughes 369HS	Charles Clowes (Estates) Co Ltd (G-WELD/G-FROG)

Reg.	Type	Owner or Operator	Notes
G-GAYL	Learjet 35A	Automobile Association Developments Ltd (G-ZING)/Coventry	
G-GAZE	Robinson R-22A	G. Clarke/Stapleford	
G-GBAO	Robin R.1180TD	J. Kay-Movat	
G-GBLP	Cessna F.172M	B. L. Pratt	
G-GBLR	Cessna F.150L	Peter Collier Aviation Ltd	
G-GBSL	Beech 76 Duchess	George Barlow & Sons Ltd (G-BGVG)	
G-GCAA	PA-28R Cherokee Arrow 200	Southern Air Ltd/Shoreham	
G-GCAB	PA-30 Twin Comanche 180	Southern Air Ltd/Shoreham	
G-GCAL	Douglas DC-10-10	Cal Air Ltd (G-BELO)/Gatwick	
G-GCAT	PA-28 Cherokee 140B	G. S. B. Large (G-BFRH)/Denham	
G-GCCL	Beech 76 Duchess	Golden Castle Caravans Ltd	
G-GCKI	Mooney M.20K	G. C. Kent/Tollerton	
G-GDAM	PA-18 Super Cub 135	G. D. A. Martin	
G-GDAY	Robinson R-22B	G. A. Watchorn	
G-GEAR	Cessna FR.182Q	Ashcombe Distributors/Sywell	
G-GEEP	Robin R.1180T	Organic Concentrates Ltd/Booker	
G-GEES	Cameron N-77 balloon	Mark Jarvis Ltd *Mark Jarvis*	
G-GEEZ	Cameron N-77 balloon	Charnwood Forest Turf Accountants Ltd	
G-GEIL	H.S.125 Srs 800B	Heron Management Ltd	
G-GEOF	Pereira Osprey 2	G. Crossley	
G-GEUP	Cameron N-77 balloon	D. P. & B. O. Turner	
G-GFLY	Cessna F.150L	W. Lancashire Aero Club Ltd/Woodvale	
G-GGGG	Thunder Ax7-77A balloon	T. A. Gilmour	
G-GHRW	PA-28RT-201 Arrow IV	Distance No Object Ltd (G-ONAB/G-BHAK)/Stansted	
G-GIGI	M.S.893A Rallye Commodore	P. J. C. Phillips (G-AYVX)	
G-GILY	Robinson R-22B	Reynard Racing Cars Ltd	
G-GINA	AS.350B Ecureuil	Endeavour Aviation Ltd	
G-GJCB	H.S.125 Srs 800B	J. C. Bamford Excavators Ltd	
G-GLAS	H.S.748 Srs 2A		
G-GLEN	Bell 212	Autair International Ltd/Panshanger	
G-GLOS	H.P.137 Jetstream 200	British Aerospace (G-BCGU/G-AXRI)	
G-GLUE	Cameron N-65 balloon	L. J. M. Muir & G. D. Hallett	
G-GLYN	Boeing 747-211B	BCal/British Airways/Gatwick	
G-GMAX	SNCAN Stampe SV-4C	Glidegold Ltd (G-BXNW)	
G-GMSI	SOCATA TB.9 Tampico	Subtec Aviation Ltd	
G-GNAT	H.S. Gnat T.1 (XS101)	Ruanil Investments Ltd/Cranfield	
G-GNSY	HPR-7 Herald 209	Channel Express Air Services Ltd (G-BFRK)/Bournemouth	
G-GOGO	Hughes 369D	A. W. Alloys Ltd	
G-GOLD	Thunder Ax6-56A balloon	Joseph Terry & Sons Ltd	
G-GOLF	SOCATA TB.10 Tobago	K. Piggott/Fairoaks	
G-GOMM	PA-32R-300 Lance	A. Kazaz/Leicester	
G-GONE	D.H.112 Venom FB.50	P. Meeson/Bournemouth	
G-GOOS	Cessna F.182Q	Roger Clark (Air Transport) Ltd	
G-GOSS	Jodel DR.221	M. I. Goss	
G-GOZO	Cessna R.182	Transmatic Fyllan Ltd (G-BJZO)/Cranfield	
G-GRAC	GA-7 Cougar	B. W. Wells & Burbage Farms Ltd	
G-GRAY	Cessna 172N	Truman Aviation Ltd/Tollerton	
G-GREG	Jodel DR.220 2+2	G. Long	
G-GRIF	R. Commander 112TCA	International Motors Ltd (G-BHXC)	
G-GROB	Grob G.109	G-GROB Ltd	
G-GROW	Cameron N-77 balloon	Derbyshire Building Society	
G-GRUB	PA-28 Cherokee 180	M. Woodley (G-AYAS)	
G-GSFC	Robinson R-22B	Stenoak Fencing & Construction Co Ltd	
G-GTHM	PA-38-112 Tomahawk	T. Miller	
G-GTPL	Mooney M.20K	Air Charter Scotland Ltd (G-BHOS)/Glasgow	
G-GUNN	Cessna F.172H	J. G. Gunn (G-AWGC)	
G-GUYI	PA-28-181 Archer II	B. Butler	
G-GUYS	PA-34-200T Seneca	H. Jowett & Co Ltd (G-BMWT)	
G-GWEA	PA-31-350 Navajo Chieftain	G-Air Ltd/Goodwood	
G-GWHH	AS.355F Twin Squirrel	Wimpey Homes Holdings Ltd (G-BKUL)	
G-GWIL	AS.350B Ecureuil	Talan Ltd	
G-GWIT	Cameron O-84 balloon	M. Pearce & V. J. Thorne	
G-GWYN	Cessna F.172M	C. Bosher	
G-GYAV	Cessna 172N	Fletcher Bros (Car Hire) Ltd	
G-GYRO	Bensen B.8	N. A. Pitcher & A. L. Howell	
G-HAEC	Commonwealth Mustang 22	R. G. Hanna/Duxford	
G-HAGS	Bensen B.8	R. H. Harry	

Notes	Reg.	Type	Owner or Operator
	G-HAIG	Rutan LongEz	P. N. Haigh
	G-HALK	H.S.125 Srs 600B	Halkin Estates Ltd (G-PJWB/G-DMAN)
	G-HALL	PA-22 Tri-Pacer 160	F P. Hall (G-ARAH)
	G-HALP	SOCATA TB.10 Tobago	D. Halpera (G-BITD)/Elstree
	G-HAMA	Beech 200 Super King Air	Gama Aviation Ltd/Fairoaks
	G-HANK	Cessna FR.172H	H. Hunt (G-AYTH)
	G-HANS	Robin DR.400 2+2	Headcorn Flying School Ltd
	G-HAPR	B.171 Sycamore HR.14 (XG547) ★	British Rotorcraft Museum
	G-HARE	Cameron N-77 balloon	M. F. Glue
	G-HASL	AA-5A Cheetah	D.B.G. Ltd (G-BGSL)/(stored)
	G-HAUL	Westland WG.30 Srs 300	Westland Helicopters PLC/Yeovil
	G-HAWK	H.S.1182 Hawk	British Aerospace/Dunsfold
	G-HBCA	Agusta A.109A-II	British Car Auctions (Aviation) Ltd
	G-HBCO	PA-31-325 Turbo Navajo	Holding & Barnes Ltd
	G-HBUS	Bell 206L-1 LongRanger	Toleman Delivery Service Ltd
	G-HDBA	H.S.748 Srs 2B	British Airways Glen Esk/Glasgow
	G-HDBB	H.S.748 Srs 2B	British Airways Glen Clova/Glasgow
	G-HEAD	Colt 56 balloon	Colt Balloons Ltd
	G-HELI	Saro Skeeter Mk 12 (XM556) ★	British Rotorcraft Museum
	G-HELN	PA-18 Super Cub 95	J. J. Anziani (G-BKDG)/Booker
	G-HELO	Bell 206B JetRanger 2	Surrey Helicopter Hire Ltd (G-BAZN)
	G-HELP	Colt 17A balloon	Ligher-Than-Air Ltd
	G-HELX	Cameron N-31 balloon	Hot-Air Balloon Co Ltd
	G-HELY	Agusta 109A	Castle Air Charters Ltd
	G-HENS	Cameron N-65 balloon	Horrells Dairies Ltd
	G-HERB	PA-28R-201 Arrow III	Woodgate Aviation Services Ltd
	G-HEWI	Piper J-3C-65 Cub	Parker Airways Ltd (G-BLEN)/Denham
	G-HEWS	Hughes 369D	Apex Tubulars Ltd
	G-HEWT	Hughes 369D	Hewitts of Cranleigh Ltd
	G-HEYY	Cameron 77 Bear SS balloon	Hot-Air Balloon Co Ltd George
	G-HFCB	Cessna F.150L	Horizon Flying Club Ltd (G-AZVR)/Ipswich
	G-HFCI	Cessna F.150L	Horizon Flying Club Ltd/Ipswich
	G-HFCT	Cessna F.152	P. Ratcliffe
	G-HFGP	Beech 200 Super King Air	Hughes Food Group PLC
	G-HFTG	PA-23 Aztec 250	Field Aircraft Services (Heathrow) Ltd (G-BSOB/G-BCJR)
	G-HGPC	BN-2A-27 Islander	Para-Freight Ltd (G-FANS)/Halfpenny Green
	G-HIGG	Beech 200 Super King Air	National Airways (G-BLKN)/Southend
	G-HIGS	Cessna 404 Titan	Hubbardair Ltd (G-ODAS)/Norwich
	G-HIHO	Boeing 747-123	Highland Express Airways Ltd Highlander/Prestwick
	G-HILR	Hiller UH-12E	G. & S. G. Neal (Helicopters) Ltd
	G-HILT	SOCATA TB.10 Tobago	A. Castell
	G-HIRE	GA-7 Cougar	London Aerial Tours Ltd (G-BGSZ)/Biggin Hill
	G-HIRO	Robin HR.100/120	
	G-HIVE	Cessna F.150M	M. P. Lynn (G-BCXT)/Sibson
	G-HJET	AS.355F-1 Twin Squirrel	Corporate Aviation Ltd
	G-HLFT	SC.5 Belfast 2	HeavyLift Cargo Airlines Ltd/Stansted
	G-HLIX	Cameron 80 Oil Can balloon	Hot-Air Balloon Co Ltd
	G-HMAN	AS.305B Ecureuil	Direct Produce Supplies Ltd (G-SKIM/G-BIVP)
	G-HMMM	Cameron N-65 balloon	S. Moss
	G-HOCK	PA-28 Cherokee 180	C. Hampshire & B. Allan (G-AVSH)
	G-HOFM	Cameron N-56 balloon	Hot-Air Balloon Co Ltd
	G-HOLL	Cessna 500 Citation	Albion Aviation Ltd
	G-HOLT	Taylor JT.1 Monoplane	K. D. Holt
	G-HOME	Colt 77A balloon	Anglia Balloon School Tardis
	G-HOOV	Cameron N-56 balloon	H. R. Evans
	G-HOPE	Beech F33A Bonanza	Eurohaul Ltd/Southampton
	G-HORN	Cameron V-77 balloon	Travel Gas (Midlands) Ltd
	G-HOST	Cameron N-77 balloon	D. Grimshaw
	G-HOTI	Colt 77A balloon	R. Ollier
	G-HOTS	Thunder Colt AS-80 airship	Island Airship Ltd
	G-HOUL	FRED Srs 2	D. M. M. Richardson
	G-HOUS	Colt 31A balloon	Anglia Balloons Ltd
	G-HOVA	Enstrom F-280C-UK Shark	Nelson Helicopter Services Ltd (G-BEYR)/Shoreham
	G-HPVC	Partenavia P.68B	Airtime (Hampshire) Ltd
	G-HRAY	AB-206B JetRanger 3	Hecray Co Ltd (G-VANG/G-BIZA)
	G-HRIO	Robin HR.100/120	Moto Baldet (Northampton) Ltd/Sywell

Reg.	Type	Owner or Operator	Notes
G-HRIS	Cessna P210N	Warwickshire Flying Training Centre Ltd/Birmingham	
G-HRLM	Brugger MB.2 Colibri	R. A. Harris	
G-HRZN	Colt 77A balloon	D. Gaze	
G-HSDW	Bell 206B JetRanger	Winfield Shoe Co Ltd	
G-HUBB	Partenavia P.68B	Hubbardair Ltd/Norwich	
G-HUEY	Bell UH-1H	RAF Benevolent Fund/Odiham	
G-HUFF	Cessna 182P	J. R. W. Keates/Biggin Hill	
G-HUGE	Boeing 747-2D3B	BCal/British Airways Andrew Carnegie — The Scottish American Philanthropist/Gatwick	
G-HULL	Cessna F.150M	Oldment Ltd/Grindale	
G-HUMF	Robinson R-22B	Hands Technical Services Ltd	
G-HUMP	Beech 95-B55 Baron	J. H. Humphreys (G-BAMI)/Guernsey	
G-HUMT	Bell 206B JetRanger	H. J. Walters	
G-HUNN	Hispano HA.1112MIL	C. Church (G-BJZZ)	
G-HUNY	Cessna F.150G	T. J. Lynn (G-AVGL)	
G-HURI	CCF Hawker Hurricane IIB	B. J. S. Grey	
G-HVRD	PA-31-350 Navajo Chieftain	Biggin Hill Executive Aviation Ltd (G-BEZU)	
G-HWBK	Agusta A.109A	Camlet Helicopters Ltd	
G-HYGA	H.S.125 Srs 800B	York Aviation Ltd	
G-HYLT	PA-32R-301 Saratoga	G-Air Ltd/Goodwood	
G-IBAC	Beech 95-58 Baron	BAC Aviation Ltd/Southend	
G-IBAK	Cessna 421C	Middle East Business Club Ltd	
G-IBCA	Beech 200 Super King Air	British Car Auctions (Aviation) Ltd (G-BCMA)	
G-IBFW	PA-28R-201 Arrow III	B. Walker & Co (Dursley) Ltd & J. & C. Ward (Holdings) Ltd/ Staverton	
G-ICED	Cessna 501 Citation	Iceland Frozen Foods PLC	
G-IDDY	D.H.C.1 Super Chipmunk	A. J. E. Ditheridge (G-BBMS)	
G-IDEA	AA.5A Cheetah	Autohover Ltd (G-BGNO)	
G-IDJB	Cessna 150L	Michael Gardner Ltd	
G-IDWR	Hughes 369HS	Ryburn Air Ltd (G-AXEJ)	
G-IEPF	Robinson R-28B	Airmarch Ltd	
G-IESA	Cessna 421C	Grapestar Components Ltd	
G-IESH	D.H.82A Tiger Moth	I. E. S. Huddleston (G-ANPE)	
G-IFIT	PA-31-350 Navajo Chieftain	Noortman & Brod Ltd (G-NABI/ G-MARG)/Elstree	
G-IFLI	AA-5A Cheetah	Archpoint Ltd/Elstree	
G-IFTA	PA-31-350 Navajo Chieftain	Interflight (Air Charters) Ltd (G-BAVM)/ Gatwick	
G-IFTD	Cessna 404	Interflight (Air Charters) Ltd (G-BKUN)/ Gatwick	
G-IGAR	PA-31-310C Turbo Navajo	BWOC Ltd	
G-IGON	PA-31-310 Turbo Navajo	Air Charter (Scotland) Ltd/Glasgow	
G-IIRR	G.1159 Gulfstream 2	Rolls-Royce PLC/Filton	
G-IJET	H.S.125 Srs 700B	Yeates of Leicester Ltd (G-RACL)	
G-IKIS	Cessna 210M	A. C. Davison	
G-ILEG	Robin HR.100/200B	S. V. Swallow (G-AZHK)	
G-ILFC	Boeing 737-2U4	Dan-Air Services Ltd (G-BOSL)/Gatwick	
G-ILLY	PA-28-181 Archer II	A. G. & K. M. Spiers	
G-ILSE	Corby CJ-1 Starlet	S. Stride	
G-IMBE	PA-31 Turbo Navajo	Ambrion Aviation Ltd (G-BXYB/ G-AXYB)/Leavesden	
G-IMLH	Bell 206A JetRanger 3	Subaru (UK) Ltd	
G-IMLI	Cessna 310Q	Michael Leonard Interiors Ltd (G-AZYK)/ Blackbushe	
G-IMPW	PA-32R-301 Saratoga SP	MPW Aviation Ltd/Booker	
G-INAV	Aviation Composites Mercury	Aviation Composites Co Ltd	
G-INCA	Glaser-Dirks DG.400	H. W. Ober	
G-INDC	Cessna T.303	Biograft Medical Group Ltd (G-BKFH)	
G-INMO	PA-31-310 Turbo Navajo	Subaru (UK) Ltd/Coventry	
G-INNY	SE-5A Replica (F5459)	R. M. Ordish/Old Sarum	
G-INOW	Monnet Moni	T. W. Clark	
G-IOOI	Robin DR.400/160	Moto Baldet (Northampton) Ltd/ Sywell	
G-IOOO	Gulfstream Commander 1000	Falcon Jet Centre Ltd/Heathrow	
G-IOSI	Jodel DR.1051	R. G. E. Simpson & A. M. Alexander	
G-IPEC	SIAI-Marchetti S.205-18F	P. J. Annard & G. Hunter (G-AVEG)	
G-IPPM	SA.102-5 Cavalier	I. D. Perry & P. S. Murfitt	
G-IPRA	Beech A200 Super King Air	J. H. Ritblat (G-BGRD)/Stansted	

Notes	Reg.	Type	Owner or Operator
	G-IPSI	Grob G.109B	J. Statham (G-BMLO)
	G-IPSY	Rutan Vari-Eze	R. A. Fairclough/Biggin Hill
	G-IRIS	AA-5B Tiger	E. I. Bett (G-BIXU)
	G-IRLS	Cessna FR.172J	Starvillas Ltd/Luton
	G-ISIS	D.H.82A Tiger Moth	D. R. & M. Wood (G-AODR)
	G-ISLE	Short SD3-60	Manx Airlines Ltd/Loganair Ltd (G-BLEG)
	G-ITTU	PA-23 Aztec 250	London Flight Centre (Stansted) Ltd & A. F. Aviation Ltd (G-BCSW)
	G-IVAN	Shaw TwinEze	I. Shaw
	G-IVOR	Aeronca 11AC Chief	E. T. Wicks
	G-IWPL	Cessna F.172M	Reedy Supplies Ltd/Exeter
	G-IZMO	Thunder Ax8-90 balloon	Landrell Fabric Engineering Ltd
	G-JACT	Partenavia P.68C	JCT 600 Ltd (G-NVIA)/Leeds
	G-JADE	Beech 95-58 Baron	Myrick Aviation Services Ltd
	G-JAJV	Partenavia P.68C	Octavia Air Ltd/Staverton
	G-JAKE	D.H.C.1 Chipmunk 22	J. M. W. Henstock (G-BBMY)/ Netherthorpe
	G-JAKY	PA-31-325 Navajo	Ace Aviation Ltd/Glasgow
	G-JANA	PA-28-181 Archer II	Janair Services Ltd/Stapleford
	G-JANE	Cessna 340A	Bumbles Ltd/Jersey
	G-JANS	Cessna FR.172J	I. G. Aizlewood/Luton
	G-JANT	PA-28-181 Archer II	Janair Services Ltd/Stapleford
	G-JASM	Robinson R-22A	J. L. Lawrence & ptnrs
	G-JASP	PA-23 Aztec 250	Landsurcon (Air Survey) Ltd/Staverton
	G-JAZZ	AA-5A Cheetah	Biggin Hill School of Flying
	G-JBUS	FRED Srs 2	R. V. Joyce
	G-JCUB	PA-18 Super Cub 135	Piper Cub Consortium Ltd/Jersey
	G-JDEE	SOCATA TB.20 Trinidad	John Dee Transport Ltd (G-BKLA)
	G-JDHI	Enstrom F-28C-UK	Valiant Press Ltd (G-BCOT)
	G-JDIX	Mooney M.20B	J. E. Dixon (G-ARTB)
	G-JDTI	Cessna 421C	Eastfield Air Ltd/Sturgate
	G-JEAN	Cessna 500 Citation	Foster Associates Ltd
	G-JEET	Cessna FA.152	A. S. Bamrah (G-BHMF)
	G-JEFF	PA-38-112 Tomahawk	Channel Aviation Ltd/Guernsey
	G-JELY	PA-18A Super Cub 150	W. R. M. C. Foyle
	G-JENA	Mooney M.20K	P. Leverkuehn/Biggin Hill
	G-JENI	Cessna R.182	Datamart (Scotland) Ltd/Edinburgh
	G-JENN	AA-5B Tiger	R. P. Coyle & R. Shearwood
	G-JENS	SOCATA Rallye 100ST	Palmer Pastoral Co Ltd (G-BDEG)
	G-JENY	Baby Great Lakes	J. M. C. Pothecary
	G-JEST	PA-22 Tri-Pacer 160	Saltair Ltd (G-ARGY)
	G-JETA	Cessna 550 Citation II	IDS Aircraft Ltd/Heathrow
	G-JETB	Cessna 550 Citation II	IDS Aircraft Ltd/Heathrow
	G-JETC	Cessna 550 Citation II	IDS Aircraft Ltd/Heathrow
	G-JETD	Cessna 550 Citation II	Bermuda Jet Ltd
	G-JETE	Cessna 500 Citation	IDS Aircraft Ltd (G-BCKM)/Heathrow
	G-JETH	Hawker Sea Hawk FGA.6	—
	G-JETI	H.S.125 Srs 800B	Yeates of Leicester Ltd
	G-JETM	Gloster Meteor T.7	Aces High Ltd/North Weald
	G-JETP	Hunting Jet Provost T.54A	D. & I. Craig-Wood
	G-JETS	A.61 Terrier 2	J. E. Tootell (G-ASOM)
	G-JFWI	Cessna F.172N	R. J. Scott
	G-JGAL	Beech E90 King Air	J. Gulliver
	G-JGCL	Cessna 414A	Johnson Group Management Services Ltd/Blackpool
	G-JGFF	AB-206B JetRanger 3	S.W. Electricity Board/Lulsgate
	G-JHEW	Robinson R-22B	Burbage Farms Ltd
	G-JILL	R. Commander 112TCA	Hanover Aviation/Elstree
	G-JIMS	Cessna 340A-II	Granpack Ltd (G-PETE)/Leavesden
	G-JJSG	Learjet 35A	Smurfit Ltd
	G-JLBZ	Bell 222	Air Hanson Sales Ltd (G-BNDB)
	G-JLRW	Beech 76 Duchess	B. Walker & Co (Dursley) Ltd
	G-JLTB	Varga 2150A Kachina	Acorn Ltd/Elstree
	G-JMCC	Beech 95-58 Baron	Ibis Enterprises Ltd/Jersey
	G-JMFW	Taylor JT.1 Monoplane	G. J. M. F. Winder
	G-JMTT	PA-28R-201T Turbo Arrow II	Thoroughbred Technology Ltd (G-BMHM)
	G-JMVB	AB-206B JetRanger 3	Heathlands Charter Co Ltd (G-OIML)
	G-JMWT	SOCATA TB.10 Tobago	Halton Communications Ltd/Liverpool
	G-JODL	Jodel DR.1050M	S. R. Winder
	G-JOES	Cessna 421B	Sipson Coachworks Ltd (G-BLOH/ G-NAIR/G-KACT)
	G-JOEY	BN-2A Mk III-2 Trislander	Auragny Air Services (G-BDGG)/ Guernsey

Reg.	Type	Owner or Operator	Notes
G-JOIN	Cameron V-65 balloon	Derbyshire Building Society	
G-JOKE	AB-206B JetRanger 3	Jokeman Ltd (G-CSKY/G-TALY)	
G-JOLY	Cessna 120	J. D. Tarrant	
G-JONE	Cessna 172M	A. Pierce	
G-JONI	Cessna FA.152	Luton Flight Training Ltd (G-BFTU)	
G-JONO	Colt 77A balloon	The Sandcliffe Motor Group	
G-JONS	PA-31-350 Navajo Chieftain	Topflight Aviation Ltd/Fairoaks	
G-JORR	AS.350B Ecureuil	Helicopters UK Ltd (G-BJMY)	
G-JOSH	Cameron N-105 balloon	Duskytone Ltd	
G-JRBI	AS.350B Ecureuil	Berkeley Leisure Group Ltd (G-BKJY)	
G-JSSD	SA. Jetstream 3001	British Aerospace (G-AXJZ)/Prestwick	
G-JTCA	PA-23 Aztec 250	J. D. Tighe (G-BBCU)/Sturgate	
G-JUDI	AT-6D Harvard III (FX301)	A. Haig-Thomas	
G-JUDY	AA-5A Cheetah	World Business Publications Ltd	
G-JULY	AA-5A Cheetah	Sentry Courier Ltd (G-BHTZ)	
G-JURG	R. Commander 114A	Jurgair Ltd	
G-JVJA	Partenavia P.68C	Leacock & Creed Ltd (G-BMEI)	
G-JVMR	Partenavia P.68B	Sonardyne Ltd (G-JCTI/G-OJOE)/ Blackbushe	
G-JWIV	Jodel DR.1051	R. A. Bragger	
G-KADY	Rutan Long Ez	M. W. Caddy	
G-KAFC	Cessna 152	Seal Executive Aircraft Ltd	
G-KAFE	Cameron N-65 balloon	Hot-Air Balloon Co Ltd	
G-KAIR	PA-28-181 Archer II	Academy Lithoplates Ltd/Aldergrove	
G-KARI	Fuji FA.200-160	C. J. Zetter (G-BBRE)	
G-KATE	Westland WG.30 Srs 100	Helicopter Hire Ltd/Southend	
G-KATH	Cessna P.210N	Avionics Research Ltd	
G-KATS	PA-28 Cherokee 140	ALP Electrical (Maidenhead) Ltd (G-BIRC)/White Waltham	
G-KBCA	Beech 200 Super King Air	British Car Auctions (Aviation) Ltd	
G-KBPI	PA-28-161 Warrior II	K. B. Page (Aviation) Ltd (G-BFSZ)/ Shoreham	
G-KCAS	Beech 95-B55 Baron	KC Air Services Ltd	
G-KCIG	Sportavia RF-5B	K. A. Nicholls	
G-KDFF	Scheibe SF.25E Super Falke	Deeside Super Falke Group	
G-KDIX	Jodel D.9 Bebe	D. J. Wells	
G-KEAN	PA-28 Cherokee 140	M. J. Tew (G-AWTM)	
G-KEEN	Stolp SA.300 Starduster Too	L. V. B. van Groenou	
G-KEMC	Grob G.109B	Eye-Fly Ltd	
G-KENN	Robinson R-22B	Thetford Compactors Finance Ltd	
G-KERC	Nord NC.854S	Kirk Aviation	
G-KERR	Cessna FR.172K-XP	A. G. Chrismas Ltd/Shoreham	
G-KERY	PA-28 Cherokee 180	Kerrytype Ltd (G-ATWO)/Goodwood	
G-KEYS	PA-23 Aztec 250	Wards Aviation Ltd	
G-KFIT	Beech F90 King Air	Kwik Fit Euro Ltd (G-BHUS)/Edinburgh	
G-KHRE	M.S.893E Rallye 150SV	Kenlyn Enterprises Ltd/Shoreham	
G-KIAM	Grob G.109B	D. T. Hulme	
G-KIDS	PA-34-220T-3 Seneca	BWOC Ltd	
G-KINE	AA-5A Cheetah	G. W. Plowman Ltd	
G-KING	PA-38-112 Tomahawk	M. Hunter	
G-KIRK	Piper J-3C-65 Cub	M. J. Kirk	
G-KISS	Rand KR-2	A. J. Barthwick	
G-KLAY	Enstrom F-280C Shark	Daron Motors Ltd (G-BGZD)	
G-KMAC	Bell 206B JetRanger	Specbridge Ltd	
G-KODA	Cameron O-77 balloon	United Photofinishers Ltd	
G-KOOL	D.H.104 Devon C.2 ★	E. Surrey Technical College/nr Redhill	
G-KRIS	Maule M5-235C Lunar Rocket	Lord Howard de Walden	
G-KSBF	Hughes 369D	Ken Stokes (Business Forms) Ltd (G-BMJH)	
G-KUKU	Pfalzkuku (BS676)	A. D. Lawrence	
G-KUTU	Quickie Q2	J. Parkinson & ptnrs	
G-KWAX	Cessna 182E Skylane	A. R. Carrillo/Bournemouth	
G-KWIK	Partenavia P.68B	Birchwood Aviation Ltd	
G-KYAK	Yakolev C-11 (00)	R. Lamplough/Duxford	
G-LADE	PA-32 Cherokee Six 300E	Freshcode Ltd/White Waltham	
G-LAKI	Jodel DR.1050	V. Panteli	
G-LAMB	Beech C90 King Air	Lambson Group Ltd	
G-LANA	SOCATA TB.10 Tobago	Pektron Ltd	
G-LANC	Avro 683 Lancaster X ★	Imperial War Museum/Duxford	
G-LAND	Robinson R-22B	Charter Group PLC	
G-LANE	Cessna F.172N	Michael Newman Aviation/Denham	

Notes	Reg.	Type	Owner or Operator
	G-LARK	Helton Lark 95	J. Fox
	G-LASH	Monnet Sonerai II	A. Lawson
	G-LASS	Rutan Vari-Eze	G. Lewis/Liverpool
	G-LATC	EMB-110P1 Bandeirante	National Airways/Southend
	G-LAZE	Jodel DR.1050	N. B. Holmes
	G-LCOK	Colt 69A balloon	Hot-Air Balloon Co Ltd (G-BLWI)
	G-LDYS	Colt 56A balloon	A. Green
	G-LEAM	PA-28-236 Dakota	Ritair Ltd (G-BHLS)
	G-LEAN	Cessna FR.182	J. G. Hogg (G-BGAP)
	G-LEAP	BN-2B Islander	Pilatus BN Ltd (G-BLND)/Bembridge
	G-LEAR	Learjet 35A	Northern Executive Aviation Ltd/ Manchester
	G-LEAU	Cameron N-31 balloon	Balloon Stable Ltd
	G-LECA	AS.355F-1 Twin Squirrel	S. W. Electricity Board (G-BNBK)
	G-LEEM	PA-28R-200-2 Cherokee Arrow	B. J. Mounce (G-BJXW)
	G-LEGS	Short SD3-60	Manx Airlines Ltd (G-BLEF)/Ronaldsway
	G-LEIC	Cessna FA.152	Leicestershire Aero Club Ltd
	G-LENS	Thunder Ax7-77Z balloon	Big Yellow Balloon Group
	G-LEON	PA-31-350 Navajo Chieftain	Chauffair Ltd/Blackbushe
	G-LEPF	Fairchild 24R-46A Argus III	J. M. Greenland
	G-LEPI	Colt 16A balloon	Thunder & Colt Ltd
	G-LEXI	Cameron N-77 balloon	R. H. Welch
	G-LEZE	Rutan Long Ez	K. G. M. Loyal & ptnrs
	G-LFCA	Cessna F.152	Midland Aircraft Leasing Ltd
	G-LFIX	V.S.509 Spitfire LF.IX (ML407)	C. P. B. Horsley & E. N. Grace/ Middle Wallop
	G-LIBS	Hughes 369HS	Satinclass Ltd
	G-LIDE	PA-31-350 Navajo Chieftain	Oxford Aero Charter Ltd/Kidlington
	G-LIFE	Thunder Ax6-56Z balloon	Schroder Life Assurance Ltd
	G-LIMA	R. Commander 114	P. E. Williams
	G-LIME	Schempp-Hirth Janus CM	Limecall Ltd/Booker
	G-LINC	Hughes 369HS	John Holborn (Helicopters) Ltd
	G-LING	Thunder Ax7-65 balloon	Bridges Van Hire Ltd
	G-LIOA	Lockheed 10A Electra ★ (NC5171N)	Science Museum/Wroughton
	G-LION	PA-18 Super Cub 135 (542457)	A. W. Kennedy
	G-LIPP	BN-2T Turbine Islander	Rhine Army Parachute Association (G-BKJG)
	G-LISA	Steen Skybolt	T. C. Humphreys
	G-LITE	R. Commander 112A	Rhoburt Ltd/Manchester
	G-LIZY	Westland Lysander III	G. A. Warner/Duxford
	G-LLAI	Colt 21A balloon	Lighter-Than-Air Ltd
	G-LOAG	Cameron N-77 balloon	Matthew Gloag & Son Ltd
	G-LOAN	Cameron N-77 balloon	Newbury Building Soc
	G-LOCH	Piper J-3C-90 Cub	J. M. Greenland
	G-LOND	V.806 Viscount	Calcos International Airways Ltd (G-AOYI)
	G-LONG	Bell 206L LongRanger	Air Hanson Ltd/Brooklands
	G-LOOP	Pitts S-1C Special	J. N. Carter/Swanton Morley
	G-LORI	H.S.125 Srs 403B	Re-Enforce Trading Co Ltd (G-AYOJ)
	G-LORY	Thunder Ax4-31Z balloon	A. J. Moore
	G-LOSM	Gloster Meteor NF.11 (WM167)	Berowell Management Ltd/ Bournemouth
	G-LOSS	Cameron N-77 balloon	J. A. Kershaw
	G-LOTI	Bleriot XI (replica)	M. L. Beach
	G-LOVX	Cessna 441 Conquest	Lovaux Ltd (G-BLCJ)
	G-LOWE	Monnet Sonerai II	P. Fabish
	G-LOYD	SA.341G Gazelle Srs 1	Appollo Manufacturing (Derby) Ltd (G-SFTC)
	G-LRII	Bell 206L LongRanger	Carroll Industries Leasing Ltd
	G-LSFI	AA-5A Cheetah	G. W. Plowman & Son Ltd (G-BGSK)/ Elstree
	G-LSMI	Cessna F.152	Andrewsfield Flying Club Ltd
	G-LUAR	SOCATA TB.10 Tobago	L. R. & L. M. Marks/Southampton
	G-LUBE	Cameron N-77 balloon	A. C. K. Rawson
	G-LUCA	Thunder Ax7-77Z balloon	Lucas Aerospace Ltd
	G-LUCK	Cessna F.150M	A. M. Dobson & M. J. Carrigan
	G-LUKE	Rutan Long-Ez	S. G. Busby
	G-LULU	Grob G.109	Strathtay Flying Group
	G-LUNA	PA-32RT-300T Turbo Lance II	W. Surrey Engineering Ltd
	G-LUSC	Luscombe 8E Silvaire	M. Fowler
	G-LUXE	BAe 146-300	British Aerospace PLC (G-SSSH)/ Hatfield
	G-LYNN	PA-32RT-300 Lance II	Neilson Leisure Group Ltd (G-BGNY)/ Leeds

Reg.	Type	Owner or Operator	Notes
G-LYNX	Westland WG.13 Lynx	Westland Helicopters Ltd/Yeovil	
G-LYTE	Thunder Ax7-77 balloon	A. S. Morton	
G-MABI	Cessna F.150L	Anglian Flight Training Ltd (G-BGOJ)/ Norwich	
G-MACH	SIAI-Marchetti SF.260	Cheyne Motors Ltd/Popham	
G-MACK	PA-28R Cherokee Arrow 200	Grumman Travel (Surrey) Ltd	
G-MADI	Cessna 310R	Birchwood Boat International Ltd	
G-MAFF	BN-2T Islander	FR Aviation Ltd/(G-BJEO)/Bournemouth	
G-MAFI	Dornier Do.228-200	FR Finances Ltd/Bournemouth	
G-MAGG	Pitts S-1SE Special	R. J. Pickin	
G-MAGS	Cessna 340A	Tunstall Group PLC	
G-MAGY	AS.350B Ecureuil	Quantel Ltd (G-BIYC)	
G-MALA	PA-28-181 Archer II	H. Burtwhistle & Son	
G-MALB	BN-2A-26 Islander	Pilatus BN Ltd (G-BIUG)/Bembridge	
G-MALC	AA-5 Traveler	Elmred Ltd (G-BCPM)	
G-MALK	Cessna F.172N	R. R. & M. Mackay/Liverpool	
G-MALS	Mooney M.20K-231	C & D Extended Warranties Ltd	
G-MAMO	Cameron V-77 balloon	The Marble Mosaic Co Ltd	
G-MANN	SA.341G Gazelle	Helicopters UK Ltd (G-BKLW)	
G-MANT	Cessna 210L	B. W. Wells & Burbage Farms Ltd (G-MAXY)	
G-MANX	FRED Srs 2	T. A. Timms	
G-MARC	AS.350B Ecureuil	Denis Ferranti Hoverknights Ltd (G-BKHU)	
G-MARR	Cessna 421C	Jacmil Ltd (G-JTIE/G-RBBE)	
G-MARY	Cassutt Special 1	J. Chadwick/Redhill	
G-MATI	Stolp SA.200 Starduster Too	M. R. Clarke	
G-MATP	BAe 748ATP	British Aerospace PLC/Woodford	
G-MATS	Colt GA-42 balloon	Thunder & Colt Ltd	
G-MATT	Robin R.2160	Sierra Flying Group (G-BKRC)/ Newcastle	
G-MAUK	Colt 77A balloon	Lighter-Than-Air Ltd	
G-MAWL	Maule M4-210C Rocket	D. Group	
G-MAXI	PA-34-200T-2 Seneca	C. W. Middlemass	
G-MAYO	PA-28-161 Warrior II	Jermyk Engineering/Fairoaks	
G-MCAR	PA-32 Cherokee Six 300D	Miller Aerial Spraying Ltd (G-LADA/G-AYWK)/Wickenby	
G-MCOX	Fuji FA.200-180AO	W. Surrey Engineering (Shepperton) Ltd	
G-MDAC	PA-28-181 Archer II	Chalkfarm Productions Ltd	
G-MDAS	PA-31-310 Navajo	Warwickshire Flying Training Centre Ltd (G-BCJZ)/Birmingham	
G-MEBC	Cessna 310-1	Westhighland Aviation Ltd (G-ROGA/ G-ASVV)	
G-MEGA	PA-28R-201T Arrow III	Travelworth Ltd	
G-MELD	AA-5A Cheetah	Judgeshire Ltd (G-BHCB)/Biggin Hill	
G-MELT	Cessna F.172H	Alvair Aviation (Sales) Ltd (G-AWTI)/ Coventry	
G-MELV	SOCATA Rallye 235E	M. G. Sanders Co Ltd (G-BIND)/Sywell	
G-MERC	Colt 56A balloon	Castles Northgate Ltd	
G-MERI	PA-28-181 Archer II	J. Bett/Glasgow	
G-MERL	PA-28RT-201 Arrow IV	M. Giles	
G-META	Bell 222	The Metropolitan Police/Lippitts Hill	
G-METB	Bell 222	The Metropolitan Police/Lippitts Hill	
G-METC	Bell 222	The Metropolitan Police (G-JAMC)/ Lippitts Hill	
G-METP	Short SD3-30	National Airways (G-METO/G-BKIE)	
G-MFMN	Bell 206B JetRanger 3	S.W. Electricity Board (G-BJNJ)	
G-MFMM	Scheibe SF-25C Falke	S. Telfer-Evans & ptnrs	
G-MHBD	Cameron O-105 balloon	P. C. C. Clark	
G-MICH	Robinson R-22B	T. D. Mitchell	
G-MICK	Cessna F.172N	S. Grant & ptnrs	
G-MIKE	Hornet Gyroplane	M. H. J. Goldring	
G-MIKY	Cameron 90 Mickey SS balloon	The Walt Disney Co Ltd	
G-MILK	SOCATA TB.10 Tobago	G. Whincup	
G-MINI	Currie Wot	D. Collinson	
G-MINT	Pitts S-1S Special	T. G. Anderson/Tollerton	
G-MIOO	Miles GM.100 Student 2	M. Woodley (G-APLK)/(stored) N. Weald	
G-MISS	Taylor JT.2 Titch	A. Brennan	
G-MIST	Cessna T.210K	Allzones Travel Ltd (G-AYGM)/ Biggin Hill	
G-MITS	Cameron N-77 balloon	Colt Car Co Ltd	
G-MKAY	Cessna 172N	Limbros Demolition Ltd	

Notes	Reg.	Type	Owner or Operator
	G-MKEE	EAA Acro Sport	G. M. McKee
	G-MKIX	V.S.361 Spitfire F.IX (NH238)	D. W. Arnold
	G-MLAS	Cessna 182E	Mark Luton Aviation Services (stored)
	G-MLBU	PA-46-310P Malibu	Northern Scaffold Group Ltd
	G-MLDO	Dornier Do.228-200	—/Glasgow
	G-MLGL	Colt 21A balloon	Colt Balloons Ltd
	G-MLNR	Dornier Do.228-200	—/Glasgow
	G-MLWI	Thunder Ax7-77 balloon	M. L. & L. P. Willoughby
	G-MOAT	Beech 200 Super King Air	Queens Moat Houses PLC
	G-MOBL	EMB-110P2 Bandeirante	Tal-Air Ltd/National Airways
	G-MOGG	Cessna F.172N	J. G. James (G-BHDY)
	G-MOGI	AA-5A Cheetah	BLS Aviation Ltd (G-BFMU)/Elstree
	G-MOLE	Taylor JT.2 Titch	S. R. Mowle
	G-MOLY	PA-23 Apache 160	A. H. Hunt & ptnrs (G-APFV)/ St Just
	G-MONA	M.S.880B Rallye Club	G. L. Thomas
	G-MONB	Boeing 757-2T7	Monarch Airlines Ltd/Luton
	G-MONC	Boeing 757-2T7	Monarch Airlines Ltd/Luton
	G-MOND	Boeing 757-2T7	Monarch Airlines Ltd/Luton
	G-MONE	Boeing 757-2T7	Monarch Airlines Ltd/Luton
	G-MONF	Boeing 737-3YO	Monarch Airlines Ltd/Luton
	G-MONG	Boeing 737-3YO	Monarch Airlines Ltd/Luton
	G-MONH	Boeing 737-3YO	Monarch Airlines Ltd/Luton
	G-MONI	Monnet Moni	R. Towle
	G-MONO	Taylor JT.1 Monoplane	A. J. Holmes
	G-MOTH	D.H.82A Tiger Moth (K2567)	M. C. Russell/Duxford
	G-MOTO	PA-24 Comanche 160	Moto Baldet (Northampton) Ltd (G-EDHE/G-ASFH)/Sywell
	G-MOUS	Cameron 90 Mickey SS balloon	The Walt Disney Co Ltd
	G-MOVE	Aerostar 601P	Red Dragon Travel Ltd/Cardiff
	G-MOZY	D.H.98 (replica)	J. Beck & G. L. Kemp
	G-MPWI	Robin HR.100/210	The AT Group/Bristol
	G-MRFB	H.S.125 Srs 3B	Food Brokers (Holdings) Ltd (G-AZVS)/Gatwick
	G-MRST	PA-28-RT-201 Arrow IV	Winchfield Enterprises Ltd
	G-MRTY	Cameron N-77 balloon	R. A. & P. G. Vale
	G-MSFY	H.S.125 Srs 700B	Mohamed Said Fakhry/Heathrow
	G-MTLE	Cessna 501 Citation	Mountleigh Air Services Ltd (G-GENE)
	G-MUFF	AS.355-1 Twin Squirrel	Lynton Aviation Ltd (G-CORR)
	G-MULL	Douglas DC-10-30	BCal/British Airways/Gatwick
	G-MURF	AA-5B Tiger	D. Murphy (G-JOAN/G-BFML)
	G-MUSO	Rutan Long-Ez	M. Moran
	G-NACA	Norman NAC.2 Freelance 180	The Norman Aeroplane Co Ltd/Cardiff
	G-NACI	Norman NAC.1 Srs 100	The Norman Aeroplane Co Ltd/Cardiff
	G-NACL	Norman NAC.6 Fieldmaster	The Norman Aeroplane Co Ltd (G-BNEG)/Cardiff
	G-NACO	Norman NAC.6 Fieldmaster	The Norman Aeroplane Co Ltd
	G-NACP	Norman NAC.6 Fieldmaster	The Norman Aeroplane Co Ltd
	G-NASH	AA-5A Cheetah	Sky Rambler Ltd/Southampton
	G-NATT	R. Commander 114A	Northgleam Ltd
	G-NAVY	D.H.104 Sea Devon C.20	J. S. Flavell & K. Fehrenbach (stored) (XJ348) (G-AMXX)/Shoreham
	G-NBSI	Cameron N-77 balloon	Nottingham Hot-Air Balloon Club
	G-NCMT	Cessna 500 Citation	Numerically Controlled Machine Tools (G-BIZZ)
	G-NCUB	Piper J-3C-65 Cub	N. Thomson (G-BGXV)/Norwich
	G-NDGC	Grob G.109	Soaring Southwest
	G-NDNI	NDN-1 Firecracker	Norman Marsh Aircraft Ltd
	G-NEAL	PA-32 Cherokee Six 260	Midland Aircraft Maintenance Ltd (G-BFPY)
	G-NEGS	Thunder Ax7-77 balloon	R. Holden
	G-NEIL	Thunder Ax3 balloon	Islington Motors (Trowbridge) Ltd
	G-NELL	R. Commander 112A	M. J. Scott/E. Midlands
	G-NEPB	Cameron N-77 balloon	The Post Office
	G-NEUS	Brugger MB.2 Colibri	G. E. Smeaton
	G-NEWR	PA-31-350 Navajo Chieftain	Eastern Air Executive Ltd/Sturgate
	G-NEWS	Bell 206B JetRanger 3	Peter Press Ltd
	G-NEXT	AS.355F-1 Twin Squirrel	Next PLC (G-OAMV)
	G-NGBI	AA-5B Tiger	Filemart Ltd (G-JAKK/G-BHWI)/ Biggin Hill
	G-NHRH	PA-28 Cherokee 140	H. Dodd
	G-NHVH	Maule M5-235C Lunar Rocket	Commercial Go-Karts Ltd/Exeter
	G-NIAL	AS.350B Ecureuil	Hope Sixteen (No 107) Ltd

Reg.	Type	Owner or Operator	Notes
G-NICK	PA-19 Super Cub 95	J. G. O'Donnell & I. Woolacott	
G-NIGB	Boeing 747-211B	BCal/British Airways/Gatwick	
G-NIKY	PA-31-350 Navajo Chieftain	Stanton Aircraft Management Ltd G-BPAR)/Biggin Hill	
G-NILE	Colt 77A balloon	Zebedee Balloon Services	
G-NISR	R. Commander 690A	Z. I. Bilbeisi	
G-NITA	PA-28 Cherokee 180	J. Staite (G-AVVG)/Coventry	
G-NIUK	Douglas DC-10-30	BCal/British Airways/Gatwick	
G-NJAG	Cessna 207	G. H. Nolan Ltd	
G-NNAC	PA-18 Super Cub 135	P. A. Wilde	
G-NOBY	Rand KR-2	N. P. Rieser	
G-NODE	AA-5B Tiger	Curd & Green Ltd/Elstree	
G-NORD	Nord NC.854	R. G. E. Simpson & A. M. Alexander/ (stored)	
G-NORS	Cessna 425	Norcross Transport PLC/Blackbushe	
G-NOTT	Nott ULD-2 balloon	J. R. P. Nott	
G-NOVO	Colt AS-56 airship	Rowntree Mackintosh Confectionery Ltd	
G-NRDC	NDN-6 Fieldmaster	The Norman Aeroplane Co Ltd/Cardiff	
G-NROA	Boeing 727-217	Dan-Air Services Ltd (G-BKNG)/Gatwick	
G-NTMN	Gulfstream Commander 690D	Noortman (London) Ltd (G-IBLL)	
G-NUIG	Beech C90-1 King Air	Norwich Union Fire Insurance Soc (G-BKIP)	
G-NUTS	Cameron 35SS balloon	The Balloon Stable Ltd	
G-NUTZ	AS.355F-1 Twin Squirrel	Powersense Ltd (G-BLRI)	
G-NWPB	Thunder Ax7-77Z balloon	Lighter-Than-Air Ltd	
G-NWPR	Cameron N-77 balloon	Post Office N.W. Postal Board	
G-NYTE	Cessna F.337G	Nite Signs Ltd (G-BATH)	
G-NZGL	Cameron O-105 balloon	P. G. & P. M. Vale	
G-OABC	Colt 69A balloon	Airship & Balloon Co Ltd	
G-OABG	Hughes 369E	A. B. Gee of Ripley	
G-OABI	Cessna 421C	Blue Star Ship Management Ltd	
G-OACE	Valentin Taifun 17E	Aero Club Enstone	
G-OACS	Bell 206B JetRanger 3	Atlantic Computer Systems PLC (G-OCAP)	
G-OADE	Cessna F.177RG	Vehicle Fleet Management Ltd (G-AZKH)/Coventry	
G-OADS	Cessna 401	Automated Data Systems Ltd (G-OROG/ G-ZEUS/G-ODJS/G-BSIX/G-CAFE/ G-AWXM)	
G-OADY	Beech B76 Duchess	Adcliffe Engineers Ltd	
G-OAFB	Beech 200 Super King Air	A. F. Budge Ltd	
G-OAIM	Hughes 369HS	J. E. Clarke (G-BDFP)/Bournemouth	
G-OAJH	AA-5A Cheetah	Garrick Aviation (G-KILT/G-BJFA)/ Elstree	
G-OAKL	Beech 200 Super King Air	Air Kilroe Ltd (G-BJZG)/Manchester	
G-OAKM	Beech 200 Super King Air	Air Kilroe Ltd (G-BCUZ)/Manchester	
G-OAKS	Cessna 421C	Barratt Developments Ltd/Newcastle	
G-OAMG	Bell 206B JetRanger 3	Camlet Helicopters Ltd (G-COAL)	
G-OAMY	Cessna 152	Warwickshire Flying Training Centre Ltd/Birmingham	
G-OANC	PA-28-161 Warrior II	ANC (Tyne & Wear) Ltd (G-BFAD)	
G-OAPA	Pilatus PC-6/B2-H2 Turbo Porter	Army Parachute Association/ Netheravon	
G-OARV	ARV.1 Prototype	ARV Aviation Ltd/Sandown	
G-OATS	PA-38-112 Tomahawk	Truman Aviation Ltd/Tollerton	
G-OAUS	Sikorsky S-76A	Ashton Upthorpe Stud & Farms Ltd	
G-OBAL	Mooney M.20J	Britannia Airways Ltd/Luton	
G-OBAT	Cessna F.152	J. J. Baumhardt	
G-OBEA	BAe Jetstream 3102-01	Birmingham Executive Airways Ltd	
G-OBED	PA-34-200T-2 Seneca	V. J. Holden/Newcastle	
G-OBEY	PA-23 Aztec 250	Creaton Aircraft Services (G-BAAJ)	
G-OBHD	Short SD3-60	Jersey European Airways (G-BNDK)	
G-OBHX	Cessna F.172H	Jones Aviation Sales Ltd (G-AWMU)	
G-OBLC	Beech 76 Duchess	Auxili-Air Ltd/Stansted	
G-OBLK	Short SD3-60	Jersey European Airways (G-BNDI)	
G-OBMA	Boeing 737-33A	British Midland Airways Ltd/E. Midlands	
G-OBMB	Boeing 737-33A	British Midland Airways Ltd/E. Midlands	
G-OBMC	Boeing 737-33A	British Midland Airways Ltd/E. Midlands	
G-OBMD	Boeing 737-33A	British Midland Airways Ltd/E. Midlands	
G-OBME	Boeing 737-33A	British Midland Airways Ltd/E. Midlands	
G-OBMF	Boeing 737-33A	British Midland Airways Ltd/E. Midlands	
G-OBMS	Cessna F.172N	BMS Electrical Services Ltd/ Birmingham	

Notes	Reg.	Type	Owner or Operator
	G-OBMW	AA-5 Traveler	Fretcourt Ltd (G-BDPV)
	G-OBOH	Short SD3-60	Jersey European Airways (G-BNDJ)
	G-OBPG	Brantly B.2B	A. C. Dent (G-AWIO)
	G-OBSV	Partenavia P.68B Observer	Octavia Air Ltd/Staverton
	G-OBUD	Colt 69A balloon	Hot-Air Balloon Co Ltd
	G-OBUS	PA-28-181 Archer II	Oldbus Ltd (G-BMTT)
	G-OCAB	GA-7 Cougar	BLS Aviation Ltd (G-BICF)/Elstree
	G-OCAL	Partenavia P.68B	Grosvenor Aviation Services Ltd (G-BGMY)/Manchester
	G-OCAR	Colt 77A balloon	Toyota (UK) Ltd
	G-OCAT	Eiri PIK-20E	W. A. D. Thorp/Doncaster
	G-OCCC	H.S.125 Srs 800B	Consolidated Contractors International
	G-OCDS	Aviamilano F.8L Falco II	D. I. Simpson & Computer Diskdrive Services ltd (G-VEGL)
	G-OCFS	PA-23 Aztec 250	Continental Flight Services (G-BBFU)/Southampton
	G-OCHD	Beech 300 Super King Air	Cameron Hall Developments Ltd
	G-OCJK	Schweizer 269C	Oxford Helicopters Ltd
	G-OCME	BN-2A Mk III-1 Trislander	Avon Aviation Services Ltd (G-AYWI)
	G-OCND	Cameron O-77 balloon	D. P. H. Smith & Dalby
	G-OCPC	Cessna FA.152	Westward Airways (Lands End) Ltd/St Just
	G-OCTA	BN-2A Mk III-2 Trislander	Octavia Air Ltd (G-BCXW)/Staverton
	G-OCUB	Piper J-3C-90 Cub	C. A. Foss
	G-OCWC	AA-5A Cheetah	Canonbury Wine Ltd (G-WULL)
	G-ODAH	Aerotek-Pitts S.2A Special	PDQ Computer Graphics Ltd (G-BDKS)
	G-ODAY	Cameron N-56 balloon	C. O. Day (Estate Agents)
	G-ODEL	Falconar F-II-3	A. Brinkley & R. H. Ford
	G-ODER	Cameron O-77 balloon	W. H. Morgan
	G-ODJP	Robinson R-22	D. J. Powell
	G-ODMM	PA-31-350 Navajo Chieftain	DMM Ltd
	G-ODON	AA-5B Tiger	Moynihan Motor Engineering Ltd/Elstree
	G-ODSF	AA-5A Cheetah	Holmes Rentals (G-BEUW)
	G-OEMS	Beech 200 Super King Air	National Airways Ltd/Southend
	G-OESX	PA-23 Aztec 250	J. J. Baumhardt (G-BAJX)
	G-OEZE	Rutan Vari-Eze	S. Stride & ptnrs
	G-OFAS	Robinson R-22B	J. L. Leonard
	G-OFBL	Beech C90 King Air	Thurston Aviation Ltd (G-MEDI)/Stansted
	G-OFCM	Cessna F172L	F. C. M Aviation Ltd (G-AZUN)/Guernsey
	G-OFHJ	Cessna 441	Tilling Associates Ltd (G-HSON)
	G-OFLI	Colt 105A balloon	Virgin Atlantic Airways Ltd
	G-OFLY	Cessna 210L	A. P. Mothew/Stapleford
	G-OFOR	Thunder Ax3 balloon	T. Donnelly
	G-OFRB	Everett gyroplane	F. R. Blennerhassett
	G-OFRH	Cessna 421C	Rogers Aviation Sales Ltd (G-NORX)/Cranfield
	G-OFUN	Valentin Taifun 17E	J. A. Sangster/Booker
	G-OGAS	Westland WG.30 Srs 100	Bristol Helicopters Ltd (G-BKNW)
	G-OGDN	Beech A200 Super King Air	A. Ogden & Sons Ltd/Leeds
	G-OGET	PA-39 Twin Comanche 160 C/R	Northern Aviation Ltd (G-AYXY)/Tees-side
	G-OGRV	PA-31-350 Navajo Chieftain	Grosvenor Aviation Services Ltd (G-BMPX)
	G-OHBD	Beech 200 Super King Air	Hubbardair Ltd (G-UBHL)/Southend
	G-OHCA	SC.5 Belfast (XR363)	HeavyLift Cargo Airlines Ltd/Southend
	G-OHEA	H.S.125 Srs 3B/RA	Rogers Aviation Sales Ltd (G-AVRG)/Cranfield
	G-OHTL	Sikorsky S-76A	Air Hanson Ltd/Brooklands
	G-OHUB	Cessna 404 Titan	Hubbardair Ltd/Norwich
	G-OIAN	M.S.880B Rallye Club	Ian Richard Transport Services Ltd
	G-OIAS	PA-31-350 Navajo Chieftain	Air Charter (Scotland) Ltd/Glasgow
	G-OICI	Quickie Q.2	Quickie Aircraft (Europe) Ltd (G-OGKN)
	G-OIFR	Cessna 172RG	J. J. Baumhardt (G-BHJG) (stored)
	G-OIMC	Cessna 152	E. Midlands Flying School Ltd
	G-OING	AA-5A Cheetah ★	Abraxas Aviation Ltd (G-BFPD)/Denham
	G-OINK	Piper J-3C-65 Cub	A. R. Harding (G-BILD/G-KERK)
	G-OIOM	Bell 206L-3 LongRanger	Nigel Mansell Racing Ltd
	G-OIOO	PA-23 Aztec 250	A. A. Kelly (G-AVLV)
	G-OJCB	AB-206B JetRanger 2	Air Hanson Ltd/Weybridge
	G-OJCT	Partenavia P.68C	Save the Children Fund (G-BHOV)
	G-OJCW	PA-32RT-300 Lance II	M. J. Metham/Blackbushe
	G-OJEE	Bede BD-4	G. Hodges

Reg.	Type	Owner or Operator	Notes
G-OJET	BAe 146-100	Manx Airlines Ltd (G-BRJS/G-OBAF/ G-SCHH)/Ronaldsway	
G-OJFR	Bell 206B JetRanger	Daniel Martin Plant Ltd	
G-OJIM	PA-28R-201T Turbo Arrow III	J. J. McVey	
G-OJON	Taylor JT.2 Titch	J. H. Fell	
G-OJOR	AS.355-2 Twin Squirrel	Daniel Martin Plant Ltd (G-FTWO/ G-BMUS)	
G-OJPW	PA-31-310 Turbo Navajo	Walsh Aviation (G-BGCC)	
G-OJRS	Cessna F.152	Stanton Aircraft Management Ltd (G-BFFD)	
G-OJSY	Short SD3-60	Jersey European Airways Ltd (G-BKKT)	
G-OJVC	J/1N Alpha	R. W. J. Holland (G-AHCL)/Sywell	
G-OJVH	Cessna F.150H	Yorkshire Light Aircraft Ltd (G-AWJZ)/ Leeds	
G-OKAY	Pitts S-1E Special	Aerial & Aerobatic Service/Booker	
G-OKEN	PA-28R-201T Turbo Arrow III	K. Hassall	
G-OKIT	Rotorway Executive	C. W. Thomas	
G-OKSP	Cessna 500 Citation	Osiwel Ltd/Leavesden	
G-OKYA	Cameron V-77 balloon	J. Howard	
G-OLAF	Beech C90 King Air	Marak Aviation Ltd (G-BFVX)	
G-OLDN	Bell 206L LongRanger	Autoklenz (UK) Ltd (G-TBCA/G-BFAL)	
G-OLDS	Colt AS-105 airship	Hot-Air Balloon Co Ltd	
G-OLDY	Luton LA-5 Major	M. P. & A. P. Sargent	
G-OLEE	Cessna F.152	Warwickshire Flying Training Centre Ltd/Birmingham	
G-OLFC	PA-38-112 Tomahawk	Leavesden Flight Centre (G-BGZG)	
G-OLFT	R. Commander 114	W. R. M. C. Foyle (G-WJMN)/Luton	
G-OLIN	PA-30 Twin Comanche 160	Skyhawk Ltd (G-AWMB)/Stapleford	
G-OLLE	Cameron O-84 balloon	N. A. Robertson	
G-OLLI	Cameron O-31 SS balloon	N. A. Robertson	
G-OLLY	PA-31-350 Navajo Chieftain	Robertson Foods Ltd (G-BCES)/Bristol	
G-OLMA	Partenavia P.68B	Landell Mills Associates Ltd (G-BGBT)	
G-OLSC	Cessna 182A	London Skydiving Centre Ltd (G-ATNU)/Cranfield	
G-OLVR	FRED Srs 2	A. R. Oliver	
G-OMAC	Cessna FR.172E	R. G. & M. W. Warwick	
G-OMAD	Cessna 210	Mantime Magic Services (Greenwich) Ltd (G-BMDN)	
G-OMAF	Dornier Do.228-200	FR Aviation Ltd/Bournemouth	
G-OMAT	PA-28 Cherokee 140	Midland Air Training School (G-JIMY/ G-AYUG)/Coventry	
G-OMAX	Brantly B.2B	P. D. Benmax (G-AVJN)	
G-OMCL	Cessna 550 Citation II	Quantel Ltd/Biggin Hill	
G-OMCP	Enstrom F-280C	Midland City Partnership PLC (G-KENY/ G-BJFG)	
G-OMED	AA-5B Tiger	Caslon Ltd (G-BERL)/Elstree	
G-OMEG	PA-31-325 Navajo	AEW Engineering Ltd (G-BFBH)	
G-OMHC	PA-28RT-201 Arrow IV	M. H. Cundley/Redhill	
G-OMMC	Mooney M.20J	G. Brown	
G-OMNI	PA-28R Cherokee Arrow 200D	A. Somerville (G-BAWA)/Blackbushe	
G-ONAD	Cessna 421C	Gatebar Ltd	
G-ONOR	Cessna 425	Mont Arthur Finance Ltd (G-BKSA)	
G-ONTA	Hughes 369D	Cosworth Engineering Ltd/Sywell	
G-ONZO	Cameron N-77 balloon	J. A. Kershaw	
G-OOAG	Beech E90 King Air	Owners Abroad Group PLC (G-BAVG)	
G-OODE	SNCAN SV-4B	Rookwood Estates Ltd (G-AZNN)	
G-OODI	Pitts S-1D Special	R. N. Goode (G-BBBU)/White Waltham	
G-OODS	Extra EA.230	R. N. Goode	
G-OODW	PA-28-181 Archer II	Goodwood Terrena Ltd	
G-OOFI	Cameron N-77 balloon	I. Fishwick	
G-OOFY	Rollason Beta	G. Staples	
G-OOGA	GA-7 Cougar	C. Henry/Elstree	
G-OOLY	Everett Gyroplane	N. A. Brandish/Southend	
G-OONE	Mooney M.20J	Creedair International Ltd	
G-OOOA	Boeing 757-28A	Air 2000 Ltd/Manchester	
G-OOOB	Boeing 757-28A	Air 2000 Ltd/Manchester	
G-OOOC	Boeing 757-28A	Air 2000 Ltd/Manchester	
G-OOSE	Rutan Vari-Eze	J. A. Towers	
G-OPAL	Robinson R-22B	Property Associates Ltd	
G-OPAM	Cessna F.152	Stapleford Flying Club Ltd (G-BFZS)	
G-OPAT	Beech 76 Duchess	Ray Holt (Land Drainage) Ltd/(G-BHAO)	
G-OPED	Partenavia P.68B	Pedley Woodwork Ltd/(G-BFKP)	
G-OPEE	Cessna 421C	Activewear Ltd (G-OSSH)	
G-OPIG	ARV Super 2	Airtime (Hampshire) Ltd (G-BMSJ)	

Notes	Reg.	Type	Owner or Operator
	G-OPIK	Eiri PIK-20E	K. & S. C. A. Dudley
	G-OPOL	H.S.125 Srs F3B/RA	McAlpine Aviation Ltd (G-BXPU/ G-IBIS/G-AXPU)
	G-OPOP	Enstrom F-280C-UK-2 Shark	J. C. Elmer (G-OFED)/Shoreham
	G-OPPL	AA-5A Cheetah	London School of Flying Ltd (G-BGNN)/ Elstree
	G-OPSF	PA-38-112 Tomahawk	Panshanger School of Flying (G-BGZI)
	G-OPUP	B.121 Pup 2	P. W. Hunter (G-AXEU)
	G-ORAY	Cessna F.182Q II	C. Robinson (G-BHDN)/Blackpool
	G-ORCL	Cessna 421C	Oracle Corporation UK Ltd
	G-ORED	BN-2T Islander	The Red Devils (G-BJYW)/Farnborough
	G-OREG	BN-2A Mk III-1 Trislander	Regency Aviation Services Ltd (G-OAVW/G-AZLJ)
	G-ORFC	Jurca MJ.5 Sirocco	RFC Flying Group/Popham
	G-ORGE	SA.341G Gazelle Srs 1	Xanadu Aviation Ltd (G-BBHU)
	G-ORTM	Glaser-Dirks DG.400	Morgan Laboratories Ltd
	G-OSAL	Cessna 421C	Ultraseal International Ltd
	G-OSCC	PA-32 Cherokee Six 300	Plant Aviation Ltd (G-BGFD)/Elstree
	G-OSDI	Beech 95-58 Baron	Systems Designers Aviation Ltd (G-BHFY)
	G-OSEA	BN-2B-26 Islander	Pilatus BN/Loganair (G-BKOL)
	G-OSEB	Bell 222	Air Hanson Sales Ltd (G-BNDA)
	G-OSFC	Cessna F.152	Stapleford Flying Club (G-BIVJ)
	G-OSIX	PA-32 Cherokee Six 260	J. F. M. McGrath (G-AZMO)
	G-OSKY	Cessna 172M	Waygrand Ltd
	G-OSND	Cessna FRA.150M	J. J. Baumhardt (G-BDOU)/Southend
	G-OSRF	Cessna 421C	Marginslot Ltd/Elstree
	G-OSST	Colt 77A balloon	British Airways PLC
	G-OSSY	PA-28-181 Archer II	Bryan Goss Motorcycles Ltd/ Bournemouth
	G-OSUE	Bell 206B JetRanger 3	British Car Auctions (Aviation) Ltd (G-BKBY)
	G-OTAL	ARV Super 2	ARV Aviation Ltd (G-BNGZ)/Sandown
	G-OTAX	PA-31-350 Navajo Chieftain	Chaseside Holdings Ltd
	G-OTHE	Enstrom F-280C-UK	The Engineering Co Ltd (G-OPJT/ G-BKCO)
	G-OTOW	Cessna 175BX	Sywell Air Services (G-AROC)
	G-OTRG	Cessna TR.182RG	A. Hopper
	G-OTSB	BN-2A Mk III-2 Trislander	Aurigny Air Services Ltd (G-BDTO)
	G-OTSL	Agusta A.109A Srs 11	Direct Smooth Ltd
	G-OTTA	Colt 1.5 MCB balloon	Colt Balloons Ltd
	G-OTUG	PA-18 Super Cub 150	B. Walker & Co (Dursley) Ltd
	G-OTUX	PA-28R-201T Turbo Arrow III	M. A. M. Quadrini/Newcastle
	G-OTVS	BN-2T Islander	M. E. Mortlock & London Parachuting Ltd (G-BPNG/G-BCMY)/Pampisford
	G-OTWO	Rutan Defiant	D. G. Foreman
	G-OULD	Gould Mk I balloon	C. A. Gould
	G-OUPP	Bell 206B JetRanger 3	Exclusive Helicopters
	G-OUSA	Colt 105A balloon	Continental Airlines Inc
	G-OVAN	SC.7 Skyvan 3 Variant 100	Peterborough Parachute Centre (G-AYZA)/Sibson
	G-OVFR	Cessna F.172N	Sunningdale Aviation Services Ltd
	G-OVIP	G.1159 Gulfstream 2	VIP Marine & Aviation Ltd (G-AYMI)
	G-OVMC	Cessna F.152 II	Staverton Flying Services Ltd
	G-OWAC	Cessna F.152	Stanton Aircraft Management Ltd (G-BHEB)
	G-OWAK	Cessna F.152	Stanton Aircraft Management Ltd (G-BHEA)
	G-OWEB	H.S.125 Srs 700B	Rapid 3451 Ltd/Luton
	G-OWEN	K & S Jungster	R. C. Owen
	G-OWIN	BN-2A-8 Islander	UK Parachute Services Ltd (G-AYXE)
	G-OWNR	Beech 200 Super King Air	Owners Abroad Group PLC/Luton
	G-OWVA	PA-28 Cherokee 140	Woodvale Aviation Co Ltd
	G-OWYN	Aviamilano F.14 Nibbio	J. R. Wynn
	G-OZOI	Cessna R.182	Velcourt (East) Ltd (G-ROBK)
	G-OZUP	Colt 77A balloon	Yanin International Ltd
	G-PACE	Robin R.1180T	Millicron Instruments Ltd/Coventry
	G-PACY	Rutan Vari-Viggen	E. Pace
	G-PAGE	Cessna F.150L	E. Shipley/Clacton
	G-PALS	Enstrom F-280C-UK-2 Shark	Acme Jewellery Ltd
	G-PAMI	AS.355F-1 Twin Squirrel	Airzed Ltd (G-BUSA)/Southampton
	G-PAPA	AS.355F-1 Twin Squirrel	McCarthy & Stone (Group Services) Ltd
	G-PARA	Cessna 207	Paraski/Swansea

Reg.	Type	Owner or Operator	Notes
G-PARI	Cessna 172RG Cutlass	Fairline Boats Ltd	
G-PARS	Evans VP-2	A. Parsfield	
G-PART	Partenavia P.68B	Highway Windscreens Ltd/Stapleford	
G-PATA	Douglas DC-9-83	Paramount Airways Ltd	
G-PATB	Douglas DC-9-83	Paramount Airways Ltd	
G-PATC	Douglas DC-9-83	Paramount Airways Ltd	
G-PATT	Cessna 404 Titan	Casair Aviation Ltd (G-BHGL)/ Teesside	
G-PATY	Colt Flying Sausage balloon	Colt Balloons Ltd	
G-PAWL	PA-28 Cherokee 140	Halton Taxis Ltd (G-AWEU)	
G-PAWS	AA-5A Cheetah	Reedtrend Ltd/Biggin Hill	
G-PAXX	PA-20 Pacer 135	D. W. & M. R. Grace	
G-PBBT	Cameron N-56 balloon	British Telecom PLC	
G-PCUB	PA-18 Super Cub 135 (L-21B) (54-2474)	M. J. Wilson/Redhill	
G-PDHJ	Cessna T.182R	G. P. Grant-Suttie	
G-PDOC	PA-44-180 Seminole	Medicare (G-PVAF)	
G-PDON	WMB.2 Windtracker balloon	P. Donnellan	
G-PEAT	Cessna 421B	Forest Aviation Ltd (G-BBIJ)/ Manchester	
G-PEET	Cessna 401A	Villotel Ltd	
G-PENN	AA-5B Tiger	Compair	
G-PENY	Sopwith LC-IT Triplane	J. S. Penny	
G-PERR	Cameron 60 bottle balloon	The Balloon Stable Ltd	
G-PERS	Colt Soapbox SS balloon	Thunder & Colt Ltd	
G-PFAA	EAA Model P biplane	P. E. Barker	
G-PFAB	Colomban MC.15 Cri-Cri	P. Fabish	
G-PFAC	FRED Srs 2	J. H. H. Turner	
G-PFAD	Wittman W.8 Tailwind	M. R. Stamp	
G-PFAE	Taylor JT.1 Monoplane	G. Johnson	
G-PFAF	FRED Srs 2	M. S. Perkins	
G-PFAG	Evans VP-1	N. S. Giles-Townsend	
G-PFAH	Evans VP-1	J. A. Scott	
G-PFAI	Clutton EC.2 Easy Too	G. W. Cartledge	
G-PFAL	FRED Srs 2	J. McCullough	
G-PFAM	FRED Srs 2	W. C. Rigby	
G-PFAN	Avro 558 (replica)	N. P. Harrison	
G-PFAO	Evans VP-1	P. W. Price	
G-PFAP	Currie Wot/SE-5A (C1904)	P. G. Abbey	
G-PFAR	Isaacs Fury II (K2059)	C. J. Repik	
G-PFAS	GY-20 Minicab	J. Sproston & F. W. Speed	
G-PFAT	Monnet Sonerai II	H. B. Carter	
G-PFAU	Rand KR-2	D. E. Peace	
G-PFAV	D.31 Turbulent	B. A. Luckins	
G-PFAW	Evans VP-1	R. F. Shingler	
G-PFAX	FRED Srs 2	A. J. Dunston	
G-PFAY	EAA Biplane	A. K. Lang & A. L. Young	
G-PFAZ	Evans VP-1	B. Kylo	
G-PHIL	Hornet Gyroplane	A. J. Philpotts	
G-PICS	Cessna 182F	Astral Aerial Surveys Ltd (G-ASHO)	
G-PIES	Thunder Ax7-77Z balloon	Pork Farms Ltd	
G-PIGN	Bolmet Paloma Mk 1	T. P. Metson & J. A. Bollen	
G-PINT	Cameron 65 SS balloon	Charles Wells Ltd	
G-PIPE	Cameron N-56 SS balloon	Carreras Rothmans Ltd	
G-PITS	Pitts S-2AE	D. Rolfe	
G-PITZ	Pitts S.2A Special	Swift 1673 Ltd	
G-PJET	Learjet 35A	Corporate Aviation Ltd	
G-PJWB	H.S.125 Srs 600B	Aravia (CI) Ltd (G-DMAN)	
G-PKBM	Douglas DC-9-32	British Midland Airways Ltd *The Tiffany Diamond*/E. Midlands	
G-PLAN	Cessna F.150L	Phoenix Aviation (Bedford) Ltd/ Cranfield	
G-PLAS	GA-7 Cougar	S. J. A. Smith (G-BGHL)/Biggin Hill	
G-PLAY	Robin R.2100A	Cotswold Aero Club Ltd/Staverton	
G-PLEE	Cessna 182Q	Sunderland Parachute Centre Ltd	
G-PLEV	Cessna 340	KJ Bill Aviation Ltd/Halfpenny Green	
G-PLIV	Pazmany PL.4	B. P. North	
G-PLMA	AS.350B Ecureuil	PLM Helicopters Ltd (G-BMMA)	
G-PLMB	AS.350B Ecureuil	PLM Helicopters Ltd (G-BMMB)	
G-PLOW	Hughes 269B	March Helicopters Ltd (G-AVUM)/ Sywell	
G-PLUS	PA-34-200T-2 Seneca	C. G. Strasser/Jersey	
G-PMAM	Cameron V-65 balloon	P. A. Meecham	
G-PMCN	Monnet Sonerai II	P. J. McNamee	

Notes	Reg.	Type	Owner or Operator
	G-PMNL	Extra EA.230	Aerobatic Displays Ltd
	G-PNAV	PA-31P Pressurised Navajo	D. Parker & A. Smith
	G-POLE	Rutan LongEz	A. M. Dutton
	G-POLO	PA-31-350 Navajo Chieftain	Grosvenor Aviation Services Ltd/ Manchester
	G-POLY	Cameron N-77 balloon	Empty Wallets Balloon Group
	G-PONY	Colt 31A balloon	Advertising Balloon Co Ltd
	G-POOH	Piper J-3C-65 Cub	P. & H. Robinson
	G-POOL	ARV Super 2	ARV Aviation Ltd (G-BNHA)/Sandown
	G-POON	AS.355F-2 Twin Squirrel	Lynton Aviation Ltd (G-MCAL)
	G-POPE	Eiri PIK-20E-1	C. J. Hadley
	G-PORK	AA-5B Tiger	P. H. Johnson (G-BFHS)
	G-POSH	Colt 56A balloon	Thunder & Colt Ltd (G-BMPT)
	G-POST	EMB-110P1 Bandeirante	Fairflight/National Airways
	G-POWL	Cessna 182R	J. & B. Powell (Printers) Ltd
	G-PPLI	Pazmany PL.1	G. Anderson
	G-PRAG	Brugger MB.2 Colibri	R. J. Hodder & ptnrs
	G-PRIM	PA-38-112 Tomahawk	Nultree Ltd
	G-PRIT	Cameron N-90 balloon	Henkel Chemicals Ltd
	G-PRMC	H.S.125 Srs 700B	RMC Group Services Ltd (G-BFSP)/ Biggin Hill
	G-PROP	AA-5A Cheetah	Falcon Flying Services Ltd (G-BHKU)/ Biggin Hill
	G-PROV	Hunting Jet Provost T.54A	D. & I. Craig-Wood
	G-PRTT	Cameron N-31 balloon	Henkel Chemicals Ltd
	G-PRUE	Cameron O-84 balloon	Lalondes Residential Ltd
	G-PRXI	V.S.365 Spitfire PR.XI (PL983)	D. W. Arnold
	G-PSID	P-51D-20-NA Mustang	Fighter Collection/Duxford
	G-PSVS	Beech 58 Baron	Astra Aviation Ltd/Guernsey
	G-PTER	Beech C90 King Air	Moseley Group (PSV) Ltd (G-BIEE)
	G-PTWB	Cessna T.303 Crusader	Numerically Controlled Machine Tools
	G-PTWO	Pilatus P2-05 (RF+16)	AJD Engineering Ltd
	G-PUBS	Colt 56 SS balloon	The Balloonatics
	G-PUFF	Thunder Ax7-77A balloon	Intervarsity Balloon Club *Puffin II*
	G-PULL	PA-18 Super Cub 150 ★	G. R. Janney/Lympne
	G-PUMA	AS.332L Super Puma	Bond Helicopters Ltd/Bourn
	G-PUMB	AS.332L Super Puma	Bond Helicopters Ltd/Bourn
	G-PUMD	AS.332L Super Puma	Bond Helicopters Ltd/Bourn
	G-PUME	AS.332L Super Puma	Bond Helicopters Ltd/Bourn
	G-PUMG	AS.332L Super Puma	Bond Helicopters Ltd/Bourn
	G-PUMH	AS.332L Super Puma	Bond Helicopters Ltd/Bourn
	G-PUMI	AS.332L Super Puma	Bond Helicopters Ltd/Bourn
	G-PURR	AA-5A Cheetah	Blackbushe School of Flying Ltd (G-BJDN)
	G-PUSH	Rutan LongEz	E. G. Peterson
	G-PUSS	Cameron N-77 balloon	London Life Association Ltd
	G-PVAM	Port Victoria 7 Grain Kitten replica	A. J. Manning
	G-PYRO	Cameron N-65 balloon	P. S. Wheeler
	G-RACA	P.57 Sea Prince T.1	Atlantic & Caribbean Aviation Ltd/ Staverton
	G-RACH	Robinson R-22B	T. C. Barry
	G-RADE	Cessna 210L	R. J. Herbert (G-CENT)
	G-RAEM	Rutan LongEz	G. F. H. Singleton
	G-RAFC	Robin R.2112	RAF Cranwell Flying Club
	G-RAFE	Thunder Ax7-77 balloon	A. J. W. Rose
	G-RAFF	Learjet 35A	Graff Aviation Ltd/Heathrow
	G-RAFT	Rutan LongEz	D. G. Foreman
	G-RAFW	Mooney M.20E	G. C. Smith (G-ATHW)/Southend
	G-RAIN	Maule M5-235C Lunar Rocket	J. S. Mehew
	G-RALE	SA.341G Gazelle Srs 1	Malcolm Wilson (Motorsport) Ltd (G-SFTG)
	G-RALI	Hughes 369HS	David Richards Autosport Ltd (G-BLKO)
	G-RALY	Robinson R-22	Malcolm Wilson (Motorsport) Ltd
	G-RAMS	PA-32R-301 Saratoga SP	Peacock & Archer Ltd/Manchester
	G-RAND	Rand KR-2	R. L. Wharmby
	G-RANY	Cessna 421C	McCarthy & Stone (Developments) Ltd (G-BHLA)
	G-RAPA	BN-2T Islander	Joint Services Parachute Centre
	G-RARE	Thunder Ax5-42 SS balloon	International Distillers & Vintners Ltd
	G-RASC	Evans VP-2	R. A. Codling
	G-RASS	Bell 206L-1 LongRanger 1	Arlington Securities Ltd (G-JLBI)
	G-RATE	AA-5A Cheetah	J. P. Alexander (G-BIFF)/Denham
	G-RAVL	H.P.137 Jetstream Srs 200	Racal Avionics Ltd (G-AWVK)

Reg.	Type	Owner or Operator	Notes
G-RAYS	Zenair CH.250	R. E. Delves	
G-RBIN	Robin DR.400/2+2	Headcorn Flying School Ltd	
G-RBOS	Colt AS-105 airship	Royal Bank of Scotland	
G-RCMF	Cameron V-77 balloon	Mouldform Ltd	
G-RCPW	AA-5A Cheetah	Walsh Aviation (G-BERM)	
G-RDCI	R. Commander 112A	A. C. Hendriksen	
G-RDON	WMB.2 Windtracker balloon	P. J. Donnellan (G-BICH)	
G-READ	Colt 77A balloon	CB Helicopters Ltd	
G-REAT	GA-7 Cougar	Hadley Green Garage Ltd/Elstree	
G-REEK	AA-5A Cheetah	Velopend Ltd	
G-REEN	Cessna 340	Ernest Green International Ltd (G-AZYR)	
G-REES	Jodel D.140C	M. D. S. Hood/Redhill	
G-REID	Rotorway Scorpion 133	J. Reid (G-BGAW)	
G-REIS	PA-28R-201T Turbo Arrow III	H. Reis (Hard Chrome) Ltd/ Halfpenny Green	
G-RENO	SOCATA TB.10 Tobago	Lascar Electronics Ltd/Old Sarum	
G-REPM	PA-38-112 Tomahawk	Nultree Ltd	
G-REST	Beech P35 Bonanza	C. R. Taylor (G-ASFJ)	
G-RETA	C.A.S.A. 1.131 Jungmann	D. L. Plumridge	
G-REXP	Beech 65-70 Queen Air	Parker & Heard Ltd (G-AYPC)/Biggin Hill	
G-REXS	PA-28-181 Archer II	Channel Islands Aero Holdings (Jersey) Ltd	
G-REXY	Beech 65-A80 Queen Air	Parker & Heard Ltd (G-AVNG)/Biggin Hill	
G-RGUS	Fairchild 24R-46A Argus 3	A. E. Poulson	
G-RHCC	PA-31-350 Navajo Chieftain	Delta Commerical Ltd	
G-RHCN	Cessna FR.182RG	R. H. C. Neville	
G-RHHT	PA-32RT-300 Lance II	Hart Poultry Ltd	
G-RIAN	AB-206A JetRanger	Autoklass (South Shields) Ltd (G-BHSG)	
G-RICH	Cessna F.152	Stanton Aircraft Management Ltd	
G-RICK	Beech 95-B55 Baron	R. M. S. Holland (G-BAAG)	
G-RIDE	Stephens Akro	R. Mitchell/Coventry	
G-RIFF	SA.341G Gazelle 1	Sarpendon Ltd (G-BLAN)	
G-RIGS	Aerostar 601P	Rigs Design Services Ltd/Fairoaks	
G-RILL	Cessna 421C	Maxwell Restaurants Ltd (G-BGZM)/ Elstree	
G-RILY	Monnet Sonerai II	K. D. Riley	
G-RIND	Cessna 335	ATA Grinding Processes/Leavesden	
G-RING	Cessna FR.182RG	Oxford Aviation Co Ltd	
G-RINO	Thunder Ax7-77 balloon	S. P. Davis	
G-RIST	Cessna 310R-II	Velcourt (East) Ltd & ptnrs (G-DATS)/ Staverton	
G-RJMI	AA-5A Cheetah	R. J. Mole	
G-RJWW	Maule M5-235C Lunar Rocket	R. J. W. Wood (G-BRWG)	
G-RMAE	PA-31 Turbo Navajo	Logbirch Ltd (G-BAEG)	
G-RMAM	Musselwhite MAM.1	M. A. Musselwhite	
G-RMGN	AS.355F-1 Twin Squirrel	VIP Marine & Aviation Ltd (G-BMCY)	
G-RMSS	Short SD3-60	Fairflight Ltd/Biggin Hill	
G-RNAS	D.H.104 Sea Devon C.20 (XK896)	D. W. Hermiston-Hooper/Sandown	
G-RNCO	R. Commander 690C	Ranco Europe Ltd/Plymouth	
G-RNMO	Short SD3-30	Fairflight Ltd/Gill Air (G-BFZW)/ Newcastle	
G-RNRM	Cessna A.185F	G-Air Ltd/Goodwood	
G-RNTV	PA-30 Twin Comanche 160	Amcan Electronic Developments Ltd (G-AXDL)	
G-ROAN	Boeing E.75N-1 Stearman ★	R. Windley (stored)	
G-ROAR	Cessna 401	Cleanacres Ltd (G-BZFL/G-AWSF)/ Staverton	
G-ROBB	Grob G.109B	Grobb-Air	
G-ROBE	Grob G.109B	Corbett Farms Ltd/Shobdon	
G-ROBI	Grob G.109B	A. W. McGarrigle/Cardiff	
G-ROBN	Robin R.1180T	J. G. Beaumont	
G-ROBO	Robinson R-22B	A. J. Jessel	
G-ROBY	Colt 17A balloon	Lighter-Than-Air Ltd	
G-ROCK	Thunder Ax7-77 balloon	The Long Rake Spar Co Ltd	
G-RODI	Isaacs Fury (K3731)	D. C. J. Summerfield	
G-RODS	A-Bell 206B JetRanger 2	Crook & Son (G-NOEL/G-BCWN)	
G-ROGR	Bell 206A JetRanger	Crook & Son (G-AXMM(	
G-ROLA	PA-34-200T Seneca	Highsteeple Ltd	
G-ROLF	PA-32R-301 Saratoga SP	R. W. Burchardt	
G-ROLL	Pitts S-2A Special	RPM Aviation Ltd/Guernsey	
G-RONT	Enstrom F-28A	R. Thomas (G-BDAW)	
G-RONW	Fred Srs 2	P. J. D. Granow	

147

Notes	Reg.	Type	Owner or Operator
	G-ROOF	Brantly B.2B	S. Lee (G-AXSR)
	G-ROOK	Cessna F.172P	Cejam Electronics Ltd/Biggin Hill
	G-ROOM	Short SD3-60	Short Bros Ltd (G-BSBL)/Sydenham
	G-ROPI	Hughes 369HS	C. J. M. Greenwood (G-ROMA/G-ONPP)
	G-RORO	Cessna 337B	Barston Ltd (G-AVIX)/Ronaldsway
	G-ROSE	Evans VP-1	W. K. Rose
	G-ROSS	Practavia Pilot Sprite	F. M. T. Ross
	G-ROTA	Bensen B.8	D. Ellerton
	G-ROUP	Cessna F.172M	Stanton Aircraft Management Ltd (G-BDPH)/Biggin Hill
	G-ROUS	PA-34-200T-2 Seneca	C.S.E. Aviation Ltd/Kidlington
	G-ROVE	PA-18 Super Cub 135	Computaplane Ltd/Glasgow
	G-ROWL	AA-5B Tiger	Rengade Artists Management Ltd/ Elstree
	G-ROWN	Beech 200 Super King Air	Gatebar Ltd (G-BHLC)
	G-ROWS	PA-28-151 Warrior	P. G. Lee
	G-ROYI	PA-32R-301 Saratoga	R. L. West (G-BMEY)
	G-ROYL	Taylor JT.1 Monoplane	R. L. Wharmby
	G-ROYW	PA-28RT-201 Arrow IV	R. L. West (G-CRTI)
	G-ROZY	Cameron R.36 balloon	Jacques W. Soukup Ltd
	G-RPAH	Rutan Vari-Eze	B. Hanson
	G-RPEZ	Rutan LongEz	B. A. Fairston & D. Richardson
	G-RRRR	Privateer Motor Glider	R. F. Selby
	G-RRSG	Thunder Ax7-77 balloon	J. N. Harley
	G-RRTM	Sikorsky S-70C	Rolls-Royce PLC/Filton
	G-RSUL	Cessna T.303	Sulair Services Ltd/Gamston
	G-RTHL	Leivers Special	R. Leivers
	G-RUBB	AA-5B Tiger	J. M. Summerfield/Elstree
	G-RUBI	Thunder Ax7-77 balloon	Anglia Balloon School Ltd
	G-RUDD	Cameron V-65 balloon	N. A. Apsey
	G-RUIA	Cessna F.172M	F. Daly
	G-RUMN	AA-1A Trainer	L. J. Smith
	G-RUNT	Cassutt IIIM	N. A. Brendish/Southend
	G-RUSH	Cessna 404	Kondair (G-BEMX)/Stansted
	G-RUSS	Cessna 172N	Leisure Lease/Southend
	G-RYAN	PA-28R-201T Turbo Arrow III	M. Collins & P. J. Tallant (G-BFMN)
	G-RYOB	Bell 206 JetRanger 2	Oastdane Ltd (G-BLWU)
	G-SAAB	R. Commander 112TC	S. Richmen (G-BEFS)
	G-SAAM	Cessna T.182R	Hopstop Ltd (G-TAGL)/Elstree
	G-SABA	PA-28R-201T Turbo Arrow III	Barlow Tyrie Ltd (G-BFEN)
	G-SACA	Cessna 152 II	Graham Cook Aviation Ltd (G-HOSE)/ Shoreham
	G-SACB	Cessna F.152 II	Graham Cook Aviation Ltd (G-BFRB)/ Shoreham
	G-SACD	Cessna F.172H	Graham Cook Aviation Ltd (G-AVCD)/ Shoreham
	G-SACE	Cessna F.150L	Graham Cook Aviation Ltd (G-AZLK)/ Shoreham
	G-SACF	Cessna 152 II	Graham Cook Aviation Ltd (G-BHSZ)/ Shoreham
	G-SAFE	Cameron N-77 balloon	Nottingham Hot Air Balloon Club
	G-SAHI	Trago Mills SAH-1	Trago Mills Ltd/Bodmin
	G-SAIR	Cessna 421C	Essair Ltd (G-OBCA)
	G-SALA	PA-32-300 Cherokee Six	Golf-Sala Ltd/Elstree
	G-SALL	Cessna F.150L (Tailwheel)	Lubair (Transport Services) Ltd/ E. Midlands
	G-SALT	PA-23 Aztec 250	Peacock Salt Ltd (G-BGTH)/Glasgow
	G-SALU	Short SD3-60	Short Bros PLC (G-BKZR)/Sydenham
	G-SALV	Beech C90 King Air	Christian Salvensen Ltd (G-BIXM)/ Edinburgh
	G-SALY	Hawker Sea Fury FB.11 (WJ288)	T. P. Luscombe & ptnrs/Lympne
	G-SAMA	PA-31-350 Navajo Chieftain	Asseman Ltd (N27897)
	G-SAMG	Grob G.109B	RAFGSA/Bicester
	G-SAMS	M.S.880B Rallye Club	D. L. Johns/Sibson
	G-SAMZ	Cessna 150D	N. E. Sames (G-ASSO)
	G-SARA	PA-28-181 Archer II	R. H. Ford/Elstree
	G-SARO	Saro Skeeter Mk 12	F. F. Chamberlain/Inverness
	G-SATO	PA-23 Aztec 250	J. J. Baumhardt (G-BCXP)/Southend
	G-SAVE	PA-31-350 Navajo Chieftain	Skyguard Ltd/Birmingham
	G-SBUS	BN-2A-26 Islander	Isles of Scilly Skybus Ltd (G-BMMH)/St Just
	G-SCAH	Cameron V-77 balloon	S. C. A. Howarth
	G-SCAN	Vinten-Wallis WA-116/100	W. Vinten Ltd

Reg.	Type	Owner or Operator	Notes
G-SCAT	Cessna F.150F	Cheshire Air Training School (G-ATRN)/ Liverpool	
G-SCFO	Cameron O-77 balloon	D. V. Fowler	
G-SCHH	BAe 146-100	Dan-Air Services Ltd/Gatwick	
G-SCOT	PA-31-350 Navajo Chieftain	Hubbardair Ltd/Southend	
G-SCUB	PA-18 Super Cub 135 (542447)	N. D. Needham Farms	
G-SCUH	Boeing 737-3Q8	Dan-Air Services Ltd/Gatwick	
G-SEAH	Hawker Sea Hawk FB.3	Berowell Management Ltd/ Bournemouth	
G-SEAR	Pazmany PL.4	A. J. Sear	
G-SEAT	Colt 42 balloon	Virgin Atlantic Airways	
G-SEBB	Brugger MB.2 Colibri	M. Riddin	
G-SEED	Piper J-3C-65 Cub	J. H. Seed	
G-SEEK	Cessna T.210N	3M United Kingdom PLC	
G-SEJW	PA-28-161 Warrior II	Truman Aviation Ltd/Tollerton	
G-SELL	Robin DR.400/180	Sellair	
G-SEVA	SE-5A replica	I. D. Gregory	
G-SEWL	PA-28-151 Warrior	A. R. Sewell & Sons/Andrewsfield	
G-SEXY	AA-1 Yankee	W. Davies (G-AYLM)/Cardiff	
G-SFHR	PA-23 Aztec 250	E. L. Becker & J. Harper (G-BHSO)	
G-SFTD	SA.341G Gazelle Srs 1	Blades Helicopters Ltd/Goodwood	
G-SFTH	SA.341G Gazelle	Specialist Flying Training Ltd (G-BLAP)/Carlisle	
G-SFTR	NDN-1T Turbo Firecracker	Specialist Flying Training Ltd/Carlisle	
G-SFTS	NDN-1T Turbo Firecracker	Specialist Flying Training Ltd/Carlisle	
G-SFTX	Slingsby T.67M Firefly	Specialist Flying Training Ltd/Carlisle	
G-SFTZ	Slingsby T.67M Firefly	Specialist Flying Training Ltd/Carlisle	
G-SHAW	PA-30 Twin Comanche 160	Micro Metalsmiths Ltd	
G-SHEL	Cameron O-56 balloon	The Shell Company of Hong Kong Ltd	
G-SHIP	PA-23 Aztec 250 ★	Midland Air Museum/Coventry	
G-SHIV	GA-7 Cougar	G. L. Cailes & Robin Hood Aviation Ltd/ Southampton	
G-SHOT	Cameron V-77 balloon	Bucks Hot-Air Balloon Group	
G-SHOW	M.S.733 Alycon	Vintage Aircraft Team/Cranfield	
G-SIGN	PA-39 Twin Comanche C/R	Liontravel Ltd/Elstree	
G-SILV	Cessna 340A	Middle East Business Club/Guernsey	
G-SING	Beech B60 Duke	Sasha Fashions International Ltd/ Leavesden	
G-SIPA	SIPA 903	M. Collins (G-BGBM)	
G-SITU	Partenavia P.68C	Insituform Holdings Ltd (G-NEWU/ G-BHJX)	
G-SIXC	Douglas DC-6B	Atlantic Air Transport Ltd/Coventry	
G-SJAB	PA-39 Twin Comanche 160 C/R	Foyle Flyers Ltd	
G-SKAN	Cessna F.172M	Aircraft Rentals Humberside Ltd (G-BFKT)	
G-SKIP	Cameron N-77 balloon	Skipton Building Soc	
G-SKSA	Airship Industries SKS.500	Airship Industries Ltd/Cardington	
G-SKSB	Airship Industries SKS.500	Airship Industries Ltd/Cardington	
G-SKSC	Airship Industries SKS.600	Airship Industries Ltd/Cardington	
G-SKSF	Airship Industries SKS.600	Airship Industries Ltd/Cardington	
G-SKSG	Airship Industries SKS.600/03	Airship Industries Ltd/Cardington	
G-SKSH	Airship Industries SKS.500/06	Airship Industries Ltd/Cardington	
G-SKSJ	Airship Industries SKS.600/05	Airship Industries Ltd/Cardington	
G-SKSL	Airship Industries SKS.600	Airship Industries (UK) Ltd	
G-SKSM	Airship Industries SKS.600	Airship Industries (UK) Ltd	
G-SKYE	Cessna TU.206G	RAF Sport Parachute Association	
G-SKYH	Cessna 172N	Elgor Hire Purchase & Credit Ltd/ Southend	
G-SKYM	Cessna F.337E	Bencray Ltd (G-AYHW) (stored)/ Blackpool	
G-SKYS	Cameron O-84 balloon	J. R. Christopher	
G-SLEA	Mudry/CAARP CAP.10B	P. D. Southerington/Sturgate	
G-SLIK	Taylor JT.2 Titch	J. Jennings	
G-SLIM	Colt 56A balloon	Hot-Air Balloon Co Ltd	
G-SLOT	Cessna 340A	Ace Coin Equipment Ltd	
G-SMHK	Cameron D-38 airship	San Miguel Brewery Ltd	
G-SMIG	Cameron O-65 balloon	Hong Kong Balloon & Airship Club	
G-SMJJ	Cessna 414A	Gull Air Ltd/Guernsey	
G-SMUJ	Enstrom F-28C-UK	Rotorchamp Ltd (G-BHTF)	
G-SNAP	Cameron V-77 balloon	N. A. Apsey	
G-SNIP	Cessna F.172H	Anglian Flight Training Ltd (G-AXSI)/ Norwich	
G-SNOW	Cameron V-77 balloon	M. J. Snow	

Notes	Reg.	Type	Owner or Operator
	G-SOAR	Eiri PIK-20E	P. Rees
	G-SOFA	Cameron N-65 balloon	Northern Upholstery Ltd
	G-SOFE	Cessna 441	Imbergem Ltd/Goodwood
	G-SOFI	PA-60 Aerostar 601P (Machen Superstar II)	Imbergem Ltd/Goodwood
	G-SOFS	F.27 Friendship Mk 200	Secretary of State for Scotland & Department of Agriculture and Fisheries (G-BLML)/Edinburgh
	G-SOLD	Robinson R-22A	Travel Management Ltd
	G-SOLO	Pitts S-2S Special	Fyat Ltd/Booker
	G-SONA	SOCATA TB.10 Tobago	J. Greenwood (G-BIBI)
	G-SOOE	Hughes 369E	Manchester Air Charter Ltd
	G-SPAR	Cameron N-77 balloon	Nicholas Sanders Ltd
	G-SPEY	AB-206B JetRanger 3	Castle Air Charters Ltd (G-BIGO)
	G-SPIN	Pitts S-2A Special	R. N. Goode/White Waltham
	G-SPIT	V.S.379 Spitfire XIV (MV293)	B. J. S. Grey (G-BGHB)/Duxford
	G-SRES	Beech 300 Super King Air	Vernair Transport Services Ltd Liverpool
	G-SSBS	Colting Ax77 balloon	P. C. Marriott
	G-SSFT	PA-28-161 Warrior II	SFT Aviation Ltd (G-BHIL)/Bournemouth
	G-STAG	Cameron O-65 balloon	Holker Estates Ltd
	G-STAN	F.27 Friendship Mk.200	Air UK/Norwich
	G-STAP	Cessna FA.152	Stapleford Flying Club Ltd
	G-STAT	Cessna U.206F	SMK Engineers Ltd
	G-STEF	Hughes 369HS	D. J. L. Wood (G-BKTK)
	G-STEV	Jodel DR.221	S. W. Talbot/Long Marston
	G-STMP	SNCAN Stampe SV-4A	W. Partridge
	G-STOY	Robinson R-22B	Tickstop Ltd
	G-STST	Bell 206B JetRanger 3	Petrochemical Supplies Ltd
	G-STWO	ARV Super 2	ARV Aviation Ltd
	G-SULL	PA-32R-301 Saratoga SP	G-Air Ltd/Goodwood
	G-SULY	Monnet Moni	M. J. Sullivan
	G-SUPA	PA-18 Super Cub 135	Yorkshire Gliding Club (Pty) Ltd
	G-SUSI	Cameron V-77 balloon	H. S. & C. J. Dryden
	G-SUSY	P-51D-25-NA Mustang	C. Church
	G-SUTT	Hughes 369E	Southern Air Ltd (G-OEPF/G-OMJH)/ Shoreham
	G-SUZI	Beech 95-B55 Baron	M. Joy (G-BAXR)
	G-SUZY	Taylor JT.1 Monoplane	E. J. Blackoe
	G-SVHA	Partenavia P.68B	D. Martin Couriers Ltd
	G-SWFT	Beech 200 Super King Air	Airswift Ltd (G-SIBE/G-MCEO/G-BILY)
	G-SWOT	Currie Super Wot	R. A. Bowes
	G-SWPR	Cameron N-56 balloon	Balloon Stable Ltd
	G-SXVI	V.S.361 Spitfire F.XVI	D. Arnold
	G-SYFW	Focke-Wulf Fw.190 replica (7334)	M. R. Parr
	G-TACA	P.57 Sea Prince T.1	Atlantic & Caribbean Aviation Ltd/ Staverton
	G-TACE	H.S.125 Srs 403B	Lynx Aviation Ltd (G-AYIZ)/Cranfield
	G-TACK	Grob G.109B	Oval (275) Ltd/Bristol
	G-TAFF	CASA 1.131 Jungmann	Custompac Ltd (G-BFNE)
	G-TAIR	PA-34-200T Seneca	GT Aviation
	G-TALI	AS.355F-1 Twin Squirrel	The Duke of Westminster
	G-TAMY	Cessna 421B	Abbergail Ltd/Luton
	G-TAPE	PA-23 Aztec 250D	Edair Ltd (G-AWVW)/Fairoaks
	G-TARA	Christen Eagle II	F. E. P. Holmes
	G-TATT	GY-20 Minicab	L. Tattershall
	G-TAXI	PA-23 Aztec 250	Northern Executive Aviation Ltd/ Manchester
	G-TBIO	SOCATA TB.10 Tobago	B. R. Rayward
	G-TBXX	SOCATA TB.20 Trinidad	JDM Electrical & Mechanical Services Ltd/Denham
	G-TBZO	SOCATA TB.20 Trinidad	M. Barnett/Elstree
	G-TCAR	Robin HR.100/210	Gibad Aviation Ltd
	G-TCUB	Piper J-3C-65 Cub	M. & J. McGachy
	G-TDFS	IMCO Callair A.9	Dollarhigh Ltd (G-AVZA)
	G-TEAC	AT-6C Harvard IIA (EX280)	E. C. English/Bourn
	G-TECH	R. Commander 114	P. A. Reed (G-BEDH)/Denham
	G-TECK	Cameron V-77 balloon	G. M. N. Spencer
	G-TEDS	SOCATA TB.10 Tobago	Redhill Flying Club (G-BHCO)
	G-TEES	Cessna F.152	Cleveland Flying School Ltd (G-BIUI)/ Tees-side
	G-TEFC	PA-28 Cherokee 140	A. J. Perry & A. Strachan/Southend
	G-TEFH	Cessna 500 Citation	Donington Aviation Ltd (G-BCII)/ E. Midlands

Reg.	Type	Owner or Operator	Notes
G-TELE	Partenavia P.68C	Aerocharter (Midlands) Ltd (G-DORE)	
G-TEMI	BN-2T Islander	Pilatus BN Ltd (G-BJYX)/Bembridge	
G-TESS	Quickie Q.2	D. Evans	
G-TFCI	Cessna FA.152	Tayside Aviation Ltd/Dundee	
G-TFUN	Valentin Taifun 17E	P. J. Evans/Biggin Hill	
G-TGAS	Cameron O-160 balloon	Travel Gas (Midlands) Ltd	
G-TGER	AA-5B Tiger	Fullfile Ltd (G-BFZP)/Elstree	
G-THAM	Cessna F.182Q	German Tourist Facilities Ltd/Luton	
G-THCL	Cessna 550 Citation II	Tower House Consultants Ltd	
G-THEA	Boeing E75 Stearman	L. M. Walton	
G-THOM	Thunder Ax6-56 balloon	T. H. Wilson	
G-THOR	Thunder Ax8-105 balloon	N. C. Faithful *Turncoat*	
G-THOS	Thunder Ax7-77 balloon	Thos Wood & Son (Builders) Ltd	
G-THSL	PA-28R-201 Arrow II	G. Fearnley/Southend	
G-TICK	Cameron V-77 balloon	T. J. Tickler	
G-TIDS	Jodel D.150	R. A. Locke	
G-TIFF	Cessna 550 Citation	Haslemere Aviation Services Ltd (G-DJHH)/Gatwick	
G-TIGA	D.H.82A Tiger Moth	Truman Aviation Ltd (G-AOEG)	
G-TIGB	AS.332L Super Puma	Bristow Helicopters Ltd (G-BJXC)	
G-TIGC	AS.332L Super Puma	Bristow Helicopters Ltd (G-BJYH)	
G-TIGE	AS.332L Super Puma	Bristow Helicopters Ltd (G-BJYJ)	
G-TIGF	AS.332L Super Puma	Bristow Helicopters Ltd	
G-TIGG	AS.332L Super Puma	Bristow Helicopters Ltd	
G-TIGH	AS.332L Super Puma	Bristow Helicopters Ltd	
G-TIGI	AS.332L Super Puma	Bristow Helicopters Ltd	
G-TIGJ	AS.332L Super Puma	Bristow Helicopters Ltd	
G-TIGK	AS.332L Super Puma	Bristow Helicopters Ltd	
G-TIGL	AS.332L Super Puma	Bristow Helicopters Ltd	
G-TIGM	AS.332L Super Puma	Bristow Helicopters Ltd	
G-TIGN	AS.332L Super Puma	Bristow Helicopters Ltd	
G-TIGO	AS.332L Super Puma	Bristow Helicopters Ltd	
G-TIGP	AS.332L Super Puma	Bristow Helicopters Ltd	
G-TIGR	AS.332L Super Puma	Bristow Helicopters Ltd	
G-TIGS	AS.332L Super Puma	Bristow Helicopters Ltd	
G-TIGT	AS.332L Super Puma	Bristow Helicopters Ltd	
G-TIGU	AS.332L Super Puma	Bristow Helicopters Ltd	
G-TIGV	AS.332L Super Puma	Bristow Helicopters Ltd	
G-TIGW	AS.332L Super Puma	Bristow Helicopters Ltd	
G-TIKI	Colt 105A balloon	Lighter-Than-Air Ltd (G-BKWV)	
G-TIMB	Rutan Vari-Eze	T. M. Bailey (G-BKXJ)	
G-TIME	Aerostar 601P	J. J. Donn	
G-TIMJ	Rand KR-2	T. M. Justice	
G-TIMK	PA-28-181 Archer II	RJS Aviation Ltd/Halfpenny Green	
G-TIMW	PA-28 Cherokee 140C	D. Smith (G-AXSH)/Bristol	
G-TINA	SOCATA TB.10 Tobago	A. Lister	
G-TIRE	Colt Flying Tyre balloon	Colt Balloons Ltd	
G-TISH	PA-31-310 Turbo Navajo	Casair Aviation Ltd (G-BFKJ)/Teesside	
G-TJET	Lockheed T-33A-1-LO	Aces High Ltd/North Weald	
G-TLOL	Cessna 421C	Littlewoods Organisation Ltd/Liverpool	
G-TMAS	H.S.125 Srs 600B	Jetlease Ltd (G-MFEU)	
G-TMJH	Hughes 369E	Rassler Aero Services/Booker	
G-TMMC	AS.355F-1 Twin Squirrel	The Colt Car Co Ltd (G-JLCO)	
G-TNTA	BAe 146-200QT	TNT Roadfreight (UK) Ltd/Birmingham	
G-TNTB	BAe 146-200QT	TNT Roadfreight (UK) Ltd/Birmingham	
G-TOBE	PA-28R Cherokee Arrow 200	J. Bradley & Barry Ltd (G-BNRO)	
G-TOBI	Cessna F.172K	John Bradley & Barry Ltd (G-AYVB)/Sandown	
G-TOBY	Cessna 172B	J. A. Kelman (G-ARCM)/Elstree	
G-TODD	ICA IS-28M2A	C. I. Roberts	
G-TOFF	AS.355F Twin Squirrel	Atlantic Computer Leasing PLC (G-BKJX)	
G-TOGA	PA-32-301 Saratoga	W. H. Carson/Elstree	
G-TOMI	H.S.125 Srs 600B	Falcon Jet Centre Ltd G-BBEP/G-BJOY)/Heathrow	
G-TOMO	BAC One-Eleven 487GK	Anglo Cargo Airlines Ltd/Manston	
G-TOMS	PA-38-112 Tomahawk	Channel Aviation Ltd/Guernsey	
G-TONE	Pazmany PL.4	J. A. Walmsley	
G-TONI	Cessna 421C	Schalwill Ltd/Jersey	
G-TOUR	Robin R.2112	Barnes Martin Ltd	
G-TOWN	Piaggio FWP.149D	J. Townhill	
G-TOYS	Enstrom F-280C-UK-2	Southern Air Ltd (G-BISE)/Shoreham	

Notes	Reg.	Type	Owner or Operator
	G-TPPH	AB-206B JetRanger 2	Winterbourne Construction Ltd (G-BCYP)
	G-TPTR	AB-206B JetRanger 3	Mann Aviation Ltd (G-LOCK)/Fairoaks
	G-TRAF	SA.365N Dauphin 2	Trans World Leasing Ltd (G-BLDR)
	G-TRAK	OA.7 Optica	Brooklands Aircraft Co Ltd (G-BLFC)
	G-TREE	Bell 206B JetRanger	Alan Mann Helicopters Ltd
	G-TREV	Saffery S.330 balloon	T. W. Gurd
	G-TRFM	PA-23 Aztec 250	R. E. Coldham/Biggin Hill
	G-TRIM	Monnet Moni	J. E. Bennell
	G-TRIP	PA-32R-301 Saratoga SP	A. P. J. Lavelle & I. Fabini (G-HOSK)
	G-TRIX	V.S.509 Spitfire T.IX	S. Atkins
	G-TROP	Cessna 310R	Tropair Cooling and Heating Ltd
	G-TRUK	Stoddard Hamilton Glassair RG	Archer Engineering (Leeds) Ltd
	G-TSAM	H.S.125 Srs 800B	BSM Holdings Ltd/Heathrow
	G-TSIX	AT-6C Harvard IIA	D. Taylor/E. Midlands
	G-TTAM	Taylor JT.2 Titch	A. J. Manning
	G-TTWO	Colt 56A balloon	P. N. Tilney
	G-TUBS	Beech 65-80 Queen Air	A. H. Bowers (G-ASKM)/Staverton
	G-TUBY	Cessna 310J	G. S. Taylor & A. M. R. Middleton (G-ASZZ)
	G-TUDR	Cameron V-77 balloon	Jacques W. Soukup Ltd
	G-TUGG	PA-18 Super Cub 150	Ulster Gliding Club Ltd
	G-TUKE	Robin DR.400/160	Tukair/Headcorn
	G-TURB	D.31 Turbulent	A. Ryan-Fecitt
	G-TVKE	Cessna 310R	Ewart & Co (Studio) Ltd (G-EURO)/ Elstree
	G-TVSA	R. Commander 690B	Air Manser Ltd (G-JRMM)/Southampton
	G-TVSI	Campbell Cricket	W. H. Beevers (G-AYHH)
	G-TWEL	PA-28-181 Archer II	Universal Salvage (Holdings) Ltd
	G-TWEY	Colt 69A balloon	British Telecom Thameswey
	G-TWIN	PA-44-180 Seminole	Leavesden Flight Centre Ltd
	G-TWOB	BN-2B-26 Islander	Pilatus BN Ltd (G-BKJJ)/Bembridge
	G-TYGA	AA-5B Tiger	Autohover Ltd (G-BHNZ)/Biggin Hill
	G-TYME	R. Commander 690B	Marlborough (London) Ltd
	G-TYRE	Cessna F.172M	Staverton Flying Services Ltd
	G-UARD	Sequoia F.8L Falco	A. J. Baggarley
	G-UBSH	Beech 300 Super King Air	United Biscuits (UK) Ltd/Denham
	G-UERN	BN-2B-26 Islander	Air Sarnia Ltd (G-BHXI)/Guernsey
	G-UIDE	Jodel D.120	S. T. Gilbert/Popham
	G-UILD	Grob G.109B	Runnymede Consultants Ltd
	G-UKCA	H.S.125 Srs 700B	McAlpine Aviation Ltd/Luton
	G-UMBO	Thunder Ax7-77A balloon	Virgin Atlantic Airways Ltd
	G-UPDN	Cameron V-65 balloon	R. J. O. Evans
	G-UPPP	Colt 77A balloon	M. Williams
	G-USAF	T-28C Trojan	M. B. Walker
	G-USAM	Cameron Uncle Sam balloon	Jacques W. Soukup Ltd
	G-USGB	Colt 105A balloon	Thunder & Colt Ltd
	G-USTY	FRED Srs 2	K. Jones
	G-UTSY	PA-28R-201 Arrow II	D. G. Perry/Stapleford
	G-UTZY	SA.341G Gazelle 1	Davinci Aviation Ltd (G-BKLV)
	G-VAGA	PA-15 Vagabond	Pyrochem Ltd/White Waltham
	G-VARG	Varga 2150A Kachina	J. Hannibal/Halfpenny Green
	G-VAUN	Cessna 340	F. E. Peacock & Son (Thorney) Ltd
	G-VENI	D.H.112 Venom FB.50	Source Premium & Promotional Consultants Ltd
	G-VEZE	Rutan Vari-Eze	P. J. Henderson
	G-VGIN	Boeing 747-243B	Virgin Atlantic Airways Ltd Scarlet Lady/ Gatwick
	G-VICK	PA-31 Turbo Navajo	Howard Richard & Co Ltd (G-AWED)/ Elstree
	G-VIDI	D.H.112 Venom FB.50	Source Premium & Promotional Consultants Ltd
	G-VIEW	Vinten-Wallis WA-116/100	W. Vinten Ltd
	G-VIKE	Bellanca 1730A Viking	Modular Business Computers Ltd/ Elstree
	G-VIRG	Boeing 747-287B	Virgin Atlantic Airways Ltd Maiden Voyager/Gatwick
	G-VIST	PA-30 Twin Comanche 160	S. H. Robinson & ptnrs (G-AVHZ)/Elstree
	G-VITE	Robin R.1180T	Trans Global Aviation Supply Co Ltd/ Booker
	G-VIVA	Thunder Ax7-65 balloon	J. G. Spearing
	G-VIXN	D.H.110 Sea Vixen FAW.2	Brencham Historic Aircraft Ltd/ Bournemouth

Reg.	Type	Owner or Operator	Notes
G-VIZZ	Sportavia RS.180 Sportsman	Executive Air Sport Ltd/Exeter	
G-VJAI	GA-7 Cougar	United Breweries (International) Ltd (G-BICF)	
G-VJCT	Partenavia P.68C	JCT 600 Ltd/Leeds	
G-VJET	Avro 698 Vulcan B.2 (XL426)	R. E. Jacobsen	
G-VKRS	Cessna 550 Citation 2	Vickers PLC	
G-VMAX	Mooney M.20K	Glidegold Ltd	
G-VMDE	Cessna P.210N	V. S. Evans & Horne & Sutton Ltd/Cranfield	
G-VNOM	D.H.112 Venom FB.50	A. Topen/Cranfield	
G-VOID	PA-28RT-201 Arrow IV	R. B. H. Vetch	
G-VPLC	Beech 200 Super King Air	Vickers Shipbuilding & Engineering Ltd	
G-VPTO	Evans VP-2	J. Cater	
G-VRES	Beech A200 Super King Air	Northern Executive Aviation Ltd/Manchester	
G-VSEL	Beech 200 Super King Air	Vickers Shipbuilding & Engineering Ltd (G-SONG/G-BKTI)/Barrow	
G-VSOP	Cameron SS balloon	J. R. Parkington & Co Ltd	
G-VTAX	PA-31-350 Navajo Chieftain	Chaseside Holdings Ltd	
G-VTEN	Vinten-Wallis WA-117	W. Vinten Ltd	
G-VTII	D.H.115 Vampire T.11 (WZ507)	J. Turnbull & ptnrs/Cranfield	
G-VTOL	H.S. Harrier T52	British Aerospace/Dunsfold	
G-VULC	Avro 698 Vulcan B.2	R. E. Jacobsen	
G-WAAC	Cameron N-56 balloon	Advertising Balloon Co	
G-WACA	Cessna F.152	Wycombe Air Centre Ltd	
G-WACB	Cessna F.152	Wycombe Air Centre Ltd	
G-WACC	Cessna F.152	Wycombe Air Centre Ltd	
G-WACD	Cessna F.152	Wycombe Air Centre Ltd	
G-WACE	Cessna F.152	Wycombe Air Centre Ltd	
G-WACF	Cessna 152	Wycombe Air Centre Ltd	
G-WACG	Cessna F.152	Wycombe Air Centre Ltd	
G-WACH	Cessna FA.152	Wycombe Air Centre Ltd	
G-WACK	Short SD3-60 Variant 100	Manx Airlines Ltd (G-BMAJ)	
G-WACO	Waco UPF.7	Ray Holt (Land Drainage) Ltd	
G-WACR	PA-28 Cherokee 180	Wycombe Air Centre Ltd (G-BCZF)	
G-WACS	Cessna F.152	Hartmann Ltd/Booker	
G-WACT	Cessna F.152 II	Hartmann Ltd (G-BKFT)/Booker	
G-WACU	Cessna FA.152	Hartmann Ltd (G-BJZU)/Booker	
G-WACV	Cessna 182N	Hartmann Ltd (G-AZEA)/Booker	
G-WACX	Cessna F.172M	Wycombe Air Centre Ltd (G-BAEX)	
G-WACY	Cessna F.172P	Wycombe Air Centre Ltd	
G-WACZ	Cessna F.172M	Wycombe Air Centre Ltd (G-BCUK)	
G-WAGY	Cessna F.172N	J. B. Wagstaff/E. Midlands	
G-WALK	Cessna F.182Q	Walk-Air Ltd (G-BEZM)/Leeds	
G-WALL	Beech 95-58P Baron	C. D. Weiswall/Elstree	
G-WARD	Taylor JT.1 Monoplane	G. & G. D. Ward	
G-WASH	Noble 1250 balloon	Noble Adventures Ltd	
G-WASP	Brantly B.2B	W. C. Evans & M. L. Morris (G-ASXE)	
G-WBPR	H.S.125 Srs 800B	Trusthouse Forte PLC/Heathrow	
G-WCEI	M.S.894 Rallye 220GT	G-WCEI Flying Group (G-BAOC)	
G-WEBB	PA-23 Aztec 250	Brands Hatch Circuit Ltd (G-BJBU)	
G-WELI	Cameron N-77 balloon	London Life Assurance Ltd	
G-WELL	Beech E90 King Air	CEGA Aviation Ltd/Goodwood	
G-WELS	Cameron N-65 balloon	Charles Wells Ltd	
G-WEND	PA-28RT-201 Arrow IV	Trent Insulations Ltd/Birmingham	
G-WERY	SOCATA TB.20 Trinidad	G. J. Werry/Manston	
G-WEST	Agusta A.109A	Westland Helicopters Ltd/Yeovil	
G-WETI	Cameron N-31 balloon	Zebedee Balloon Service	
G-WGCS	PA-19 Super Cub 95	T. M. Storey/Shoreham	
G-WHIZ	Pitts S-1 Special	K. M. McLeod	
G-WHIZ	V.732 Viscount (fuselage only) ★	Wales Aircraft Museum (G-ANRS)/Cardiff	
G-WICH	FRED Srs 2	R. H. Hearn	
G-WICK	Partenavia P.68B	Fortune Services Ltd (G-BGFZ)/Manchester	
G-WILD	Pitts S-1T Special	B. K. Lecomber	
G-WILO	Bell 206B JetRanger	Candyfleet Ltd	
G-WILY	Rutan Long-Ez	W. S. Allen	
G-WIMP	Colt 56A balloon	C. Wolstenholme	
G-WINE	Thunder Ax7-77Z balloon	R. Brooker	
G-WIRL	Robinson R-22B	A. P. J. Lavelle & ptnrs	
G-WITE	Cessna 414A	Essair Ltd (G-LOVO/G-KENT)	

Notes	Reg.	Type	Owner or Operator
	G-WIZO	PA-34-220T Seneca 3	Partipak Ltd
	G-WIZZ	AB-206B JetRanger 2	Willow Vale Electronics Ltd
	G-WLAD	BAC One-Eleven 304AX	Airways Cymru International (G-ATPI)
	G-WMCC	BAe Jetstream 3102-01	Birmingham Executive Airways PLC (G-TALL)
	G-WOLF	PA-28 Cherokee 140	E. Ford
	G-WOOD	Beech 95-B55 Baron	Gama Aviation Ltd (G-AYID)/Fairoaks
	G-WOSP	Bell 206B JetRanger 3	Gleneagles Helicopter Services (Scotland) Ltd
	G-WOTG	BN-2T Islander	Secretary of State for Defence (G-BJYT)/Bicester
	G-WREN	Pitts S-2A Special	P. Meeson/Booker
	G-WRMN	Glaser-Dirks DG-400	W. R. McNair
	G-WSFT	PA-23 Aztec 250	SFT Aviation Ltd (G-BTHS)/ Bournemouth
	G-WSKY	Enstrom F-280C Shark	Pulsegrove Ltd (G-BEEK)/Shoreham
	G-WSSC	PA-31-350 Navajo Chieftain	Air Kilroe Ltd/Manchester
	G-WSSL	PA-31-350 Navajo Chieftain	Foster Yeoman Ltd
	G-WTFA	Cessna F.182P	WTFA Ltd
	G-WTVB	Cessna 404 Titan	Casair Aviation Ltd/Teesside
	G-WULF	WAR Focke-Wulf Fw.190 (08)	R. C. Dean & ptnrs
	G-WWHL	Beech 200 Super King Air	Sark International Airways Ltd (G-BLAE)/Guernsey
	G-WWII	V.S. Spitfire 18 (SM832)	D. W. Arnold & ptnrs
	G-WWUK	Enstrom F-28A-UK	Shimfoam Ltd (G-BFFN)
	G-WWWW	AS.355F-2 Twin Squirrel	Chivas Bros Ltd
	G-WYCH	Cameron 90 Witch balloon	Jacques W. Soukup Enterprises Ltd
	G-WYNN	Rand KR-2	W. Thomas
	G-WYNT	Cameron N-56 balloon	Jacques W. Soukup Enterprises Ltd
	G-WYRL	Robinson R-22A	B. E. Pond
	G-WYTE	Bell 47G-2A-1	CKS Air Ltd/Southend
	G-WZZZ	Colt AS-42 airship	Hot-Air Balloon Co Ltd
	G-XCUB	PA-18-150 Super Cub	W. G. Fisher/Sandown
	G-XITD	Cessna 310G	ITD Aviation Ltd (G-ASYV)
	G-XMAF	G.1159A Gulfstream 3	Fayair (Jersey) 1984 Ltd
	G-XRAY	Rand KR-2	R. S. Smith
	G-XSFT	PA-23 Aztec 250	SFT Aviation Ltd (G-CPPC/G-BGBH)/ Bournemouth
	G-XTRA	Extra EA.230	B. K. Lecomber
	G-XTWO	EMB-121A Xingu II	C.S.E. Aviation Ltd (G-XING)/Kidlington
	G-YBAA	Cessna FR.172J	J. Blackburn
	G-YIII	Cessna F.150L	Sherburn Aero Club Ltd
	G-YMRU	BAC One-Eleven 304AX	Airways Cymru International (G-ATPH)
	G-YNOT	D.62B Condor	T. Littlefair (G-AYFH)
	G-YOGI	Robin DR.400/140B	R. M. Gosling (G-BDME)
	G-YORK	Cessna F.172M	Sherburn Aero Club Ltd
	G-YPSY	Andreasson BA-4B	H. P. Burrill
	G-YROI	Air Command Commander 532	W. B. Lumb
	G-YROS	Bensen B.80-D	J. M. Montgomerie
	G-YSFT	PA-23 Aztec 250	SFT Aviation Ltd (G-BEJT)
	G-YTWO	Cessna F.172M	Sherburn Aero Club Ltd
	G-YULL	PA-28 Cherokee 180E	Lansdowne Chemical Co (G-BEAJ)/ Kidlington
	G-ZARI	AA-5B Tiger	Zarina Husein-Ellis (G-BHVY)
	G-ZAZA	PA-18 Super Cub 95	M. C. Barraclough
	G-ZBAC	AS.350B Écureuil	BAC Ltd (G-SEBI/G-BMCU)
	G-ZBCA	Colt 77A balloon	British Car Auctions Ltd
	G-ZERO	AA-5B Tiger	Snowadem Ltd/Luton
	G-ZIPI	Robin DR.400/180	Stahl Engineering Co Ltd/Headcorn
	G-ZIPP	Cessna E.310Q	Bank Farm Ltd (G-BAYU)
	G-ZLIN	Z.526 Trener Master	V. S. E. Norman
	G-ZSOL	Zlin Z.50L	V. S. E. Norman/Kemble
	G-ZUMP	Cameron N-77 balloon	M. J. Allen *Gazump*
	G-ZZIM	Rutan Laser 200	J. G. M. Heathcote

Toy Balloons

Reg.	Type	Owner or Operator	Notes
G-FYAA	Osprey Mk 4D	C. Wilson	
G-FYAB	Osprey Mk 4B	M. R. Wilson	
G-FYAC	Portswood Mk XVI	J. D. Hall	
G-FYAD	Portswood Mk XVI	J. D. Hall	
G-FYAE	Portswood Mk XVI	J. D. Hall	
G-FYAF	Portswood Mk XVI	J. D. Hall	
G-FYAG	Portswood Mk XVI	J. D. Hall	
G-FYAH	Portswood Mk XVI	J. D. Hall	
G-FYAI	Portswood Mk XVI	J. D. Hall	
G-FYAJ	Kelsey	P. J. Kelsey	
G-FYAK	European E.21	J. E. Christopher	
G-FYAL	Osprey Mk 4E2	J. Goodman	
G-FYAM	Osprey Mk 4E2	P. Goodman	
G-FYAN	Williams	M. D. Williams	
G-FYAO	Williams	M. D. Williams	
G-FYAP	Williams Mk 2	G. E. Clarke	
G-FYAR	Williams Mk 2	S. T. Wallbank	
G-FYAS	Osprey Mk 4H2	K. B. Miles	
G-FYAT	Osprey Mk 4D	S. D. Templeman	
G-FYAU	Williams MK 2	P. Bowater	
G-FYAV	Osprey Mk 4E2	C. D. Egan & C. Stiles	
G-FYAW	Portswood Mk XVI	R. S. Joste	
G-FYAX	Osprey Mk 4B	S. A. Dalmas & P. G. Tarr	
G-FYAY	Osprey Mk 1E	M. K. Levenson	
G-FYAZ	Osprey Mk 4D2	M. A. Roblett	
G-FYBA	Portswood Mk XVI	C. R. Rundle	
G-FYBD	Osprey Mk 1E	M. Vincent	
G-FYBE	Osprey Mk 4D	M. Vincent	
G-FYBF	Osprey Mk V	M. Vincent	
G-FYBG	Osprey Mk 4G2	M. Vincent	
G-FYBH	Osprey Mk 4G	M. Vincent	
G-FYBI	Osprey Mk 4H	M. Vincent	
G-FYBK	Osprey Mk 4G2	A. G. Coe & S. R. Burgess	
G-FYBM	Osprey Mk 4G	P. C. Anderson	
G-FYBN	Osprey Mk 4G2	M. Ford	
G-FYBO	Osprey Mk 4B	D. Eaves	
G-FYBP	European E.84PW	D. Eaves	
G-FYBR	Osprey Mk 4G2	N. A. Partridge	
G-FYBT	Portswood Mk XVI	M. Hazelwood	
G-FYBU	Portswood Mk XVI	M. A. Roblett	
G-FYBV	Osprey Mk 4D2	D. I. Garrod	
G-FYBW	Osprey Mk 4D	N. I. McAllen	
G-FYBX	Portswood Mk XVI	I. Chadwick	
G-FYBY	Osprey Mk 4D	K. H. Turner	
G-FYBZ	Osprey Mk 1E	S. J. Showbridge	
G-FYCA	Osprey Mk 4D	R. G. Crewe	
G-FYCB	Osprey Mk 4B	I. R. Hemsley	
G-FYCC	Osprey Mk 4G2	A. Russell	
G-FYCD	BHMED Gulfstream Three	D. Meades & ptnrs	
G-FYCE	Portswood Mk XVI	R. S. Joste	
G-FYCF	Portswood Mk XVI	R. S. Joste	
G-FYCG	Portswood Mk XVI	R. S. Joste	
G-FYCH	Swan Mk 1	R. S. Joste	
G-FYCI	Portswood Mk XVI	R. S. Joste	
G-FYCJ	Osprey Mk 4H2	A. G. Coe & S. R. Burgess	
G-FYCK	Lovell Supaliner Mk 1	G. P. Lovell	
G-FYCL	Osprey Mk 4G	P. J. Rogers	
G-FYCN	Osprey Mk 4D	C. F. Chipping	
G-FYCO	Osprey Mk 4B	C. F. Chipping	
G-FYCP	Osprey Mk 1E	C. F. Chipping	
G-FYCR	Osprey MK 4D	C. F. Chipping	
G-FYCS	Portswood Mk XVI	S. McDonald	
G-FYCT	Osprey Mk 4D	S. T. Wallbank	
G-FYCU	Osprey Mk 4D	G. M. Smith	
G-FYCV	Osprey Mk 4D	M. Thomson	
G-FYCW	Osprey Mk 4D	M. L. Partridge	
G-FYCX	Sumner Jefferson Mk IV	J. R. Sumner	
G-FYCZ	Osprey Mk 4D2	P. Middleton	
G-FYDA	Saffery SB.1000 Firefly Atom	H. C. Saffrey	

Notes	Reg.	Type	Owner or Operator
	G-FYDB	European E.84EL	D. Eaves
	G-FYDC	European EDH-1	D. Eaves & H. Goddard
	G-FYDD	Osprey Mk 4D	A. C. Mitchell
	G-FYDE	Osprey Mk 4D	P. F. Mitchell
	G-FYDF	Osprey Mk 4D	K. A. Jones
	G-FYDG	Osprey Mk 4D	M. D. Williams
	G-FYDI	Williams Westwind Two	M. D. Williams
	G-FYDK	Williams Westwind Two	M. D. Williams
	G-FYDM	Williams Westwind Four	M. D. Williams
	G-FYDN	European 8C	P. D. Ridout
	G-FYDO	Osprey Mk 4D	N. L. Scallan
	G-FYDP	Williams Westwind Three	M. D. Williams
	G-FYDR	European 118	P. F. Mitchell
	G-FYDS	Osprey Mk 4D	N. L. Scallan
	G-FYDT	Viking Warrior Mk 1	D. G. Tomlin
	G-FYDU	Osprey Mk 4D	J. R. Moody
	G-FYDV	Osprey Mk 4D	A. J. Jackson
	G-FYDW	Osprey Mk 4B	R. A. Balfre
	G-FYDX	Osprey Mk 4B	G. T. Young
	G-FYDY	Osprey Mk 4B	P. S. Flanagan
	G-FYDZ	Portswood Mk XVI	S. M. Chance
	G-FYEA	Osprey Mk 4B	S. M. Chance
	G-FYEB	Rango Rega	N. H. Ponsford
	G-FYEC	Osprey Mk 4B	T. R. Spruce
	G-FYED	Osprey Mk 1C	T. P. Pusey
	G-FYEE	Osprey Mk 4B	T. R. Spruce
	G-FYEF	Portswood Mk XVI	T. R. Spruce
	G-FYEG	Osprey Mk 1C	P. E. Prime
	G-FYEI	Portswood Mk XVI	A. Russell
	G-FYEJ	Rango NA.24	N. H. Ponsford
	G-FYEK	Unicorn UE.1C	D. & D. Eaves
	G-FYEL	European E.84Z	D. Eaves
	G-FYEO	Eagle Mk 1	M. E. Scallon
	G-FYEP	Boing 746-200A	S. M. Colville & D. J. Hall
	G-FYER	Osprey Mk 4B	S. J. Menges
	G-FYES	Osprey Mk 2 SJM	S. J. Menges
	G-FYET	Markmite Mk 2	M. W. Mabey & M. Davies
	G-FYEV	Osprey Mk 1C	M. E. Scallen
	G-FYEW	Saturn Mk 2A	M. J. Sheather
	G-FYEY	Largess Binbagbubble MK 1A	S. J. Menges
	G-FYEZ	Firefly Mk 1	M. E. & N. L. Scallan
	G-FYFA	European E.84LD	D. Goddard & D. Eaves
	G-FYFB	Osprey Mk 1E	K. Marsh
	G-FYFC	European E.84NZ	R. MacPherson
	G-FYFD	Osprey Mk 2CM	M. Carp
	G-FYFE	Osprey Mk 2GB	G. Bone
	G-FYFF	Osprey Mk 2SW	S. Willis
	G-FYFG	European E.84DE	D. Eaves
	G-FYFH	European E.84DS	D. Eaves
	G-FYFI	European E.84DS	M. Stelling
	G-FYFJ	Williams Westland 2	P. Feasey
	G-FYFK	Williams Westland 2	D. Feasey
	G-FYFL	Osprey Mk 2CL	C. Kennedy
	G-FYFM	Trojan Mk IV	G. M. Rose
	G-FYFN	Osprey Saturn 2	J. & M. Woods
	G-FYFS	Rango NA-55	Sir Ian MacTaggart
	G-FYFT	Rango NA-32BC	Rango Kite & Balloon Co
	G-FYFU	Rango NA-39	Rango Kite & Balloon Co
	G-FYFV	Saffrey Grand Edinburgh	I. G. & G. M. McIntosh
	G-FYFW	Rango NA-55	Rango Kite & Balloon Co
	G-FYFX	Rango NA-42	Woods Garden Centre
	G-FYFY	Rango NA-55RC	A. M. Lindsay
	G-FYFZ	Booth C-141D	N. R. Booth
	G-FYGA	Rango NA-50RC	Rango Kite & Balloon Co
	G-FYGB	Rango NA-105RC	Rango Kite & Balloon Co
	G-FYGC	Rango NA-42B	L. J. Wardle
	G-FYGE	Rango NA-42B	G. Ewbank
	G-FYGG	Buz-B20	D. P. Busby & S. Spink
	G-FYNC	Rango NA-555RC	Sir Ian MacTaggart

Microlights

Reg.	Type	Owner or Operator	Notes
G-MBAA	Hiway Skytrike Mk 2	Hiway Hang Gliders Ltd	
G-MBAB	Hovey Whing-Ding II	R. F. Morton	
G-MBAD	Weedhopper JC-24A	M. Stott	
G-MBAE	Lazair	H. A. Leek	
G-MBAF	R. J. Swift 3	C. G. Wrzesien	
G-MBAG	Skycraft Scout	B. D. Jones	
G-MBAH	Harker D. H.	D. Harker	
G-MBAI	Typhoon Tripacer 250	C. J. & K. Yarrow	
G-MBAJ	Chargus T.250	V. F. Potter	
G-MBAK	Eurowing Spirit	J. S. Potts	
G-MBAL	Hiway Demon	D. J. Smith	
G-MBAM	Skycraft Scout 2	J. P. & C. J. Carney	
G-MBAN	American Aerolights Eagle	R. W. Millward	
G-MBAP	Rotec Rally 2B	P. D. Lucas	
G-MBAR	Skycraft Scout	L. Chiappi	
G-MBAS	Typhoon Tripacer 250	T. J. Birkbeck	
G-MBAU	Hiway Skytrike	R. E. Tallack	
G-MBAV	Weedhopper	L. F. Smith	
G-MBAW	Pterodactyl Ptraveller	J. C. K. Soardifield	
G-MBAX	Hiway Skytrike	D. Clarke	
G-MBAZ	Rotec Rally 2B	Western Skysports Ltd	
G-MBBA	Ultraflight Lazair	P. Roberts	
G-MBBB	Skycraft Scout 2	A. J. & B. Chalkley	
G-MBBC	Chargus T.250	R. R. G. Close-Smith	
G-MBBD	Pterodactyl Ptraveller	R. N. Greenshields	
G-MBBE	Striplin Skyranger	A. S. Coombes	
G-MBBF	Chargus Titan 38	Chargus Gliding Co	
G-MBBG	Weedhopper JC-24B	A. J. Plumbridge & G. E. Kershaw	
G-MBBH	Flexiform Sealander 160	D. A. Campbell	
G-MBBI	Ultraflight Mirage	G. A. Squires	
G-MBBJ	Hiway Demon Trike	E. B. Jones	
G-MBBL	Lightning Microlight	I. M. Grayland	
G-MBBM	Eipper Quicksilver MX	J. Brown	
G-MBBN	Eagle Microlight	S. Taylor & D. Williams	
G-MBBO	Rotec Rally 2B	P. T. Dawson	
G-MBBP	Chotia Weedhopper	G. L. Moon	
G-MBBR	Weedhopper JC-24B	J. G. Wallers	
G-MBBS	Chargus T.250	P. R. De Fraine	
G-MBBT	Ultrasports Tripacer 330	The Post Office	
G-MBBU	Southdown Savage	D. Ward & B. J. Holloway	
G-MBBV	Rotec Rally 2B	Blois Aviation Ltd	
G-MBBW	Flexiform Hilander	R. J. Hamilton & W. J. Shaw	
G-MBBX	Chargus Skytrike	M. J. Ashley-Rogers	
G-MBBY	Flexiform Sealander	P. M. Fidell & H. M. Johnson	
G-MBBZ	Volmer Jensen VJ-24W	D. G. Cook	
G-MBCA	Chargus Cyclone T.250	E. M. Jelonek	
G-MBCD	La Mouette Atlas	M. G. Dean	
G-MBCE	American Aerolights Eagle	I. H. Lewis	
G-MBCF	Pterodactyl Ptraveler	T. C. N. Carroll	
G-MBCG	Ultrasports Tripacer T.250	A. G. Parkinson	
G-MBCI	Hiway Skytrike	J. R. Bridge	
G-MBCJ	Mainair Sports Tri-Flyer	R. A. Smith	
G-MBCK	Eipper Quicksilver MX	G. W. Rowbotham	
G-MBCL	Hiway Demon Triflyer	B. R. Underwood & P. J. Challis	
G-MBCM	Hiway Demon 175	G. M. R. & D. M. Walters	
G-MBCN	Hiway Super Scorpion	M. J. Hadland	
G-MBCO	Flexiform Sealander Buggy	P. G. Kavanagh	
G-MBCP	Mainair Tri-Flyer 250	J. B. Wincott	
G-MBCR	Ultraflight Mirage	B. N. Bower	
G-MBCS	American Aerolights Eagle	Pleasurecraft Ltd	
G-MBCT	American Aerolights Eagle	Pleasurecraft Ltd	
G-MBCU	American Aerolights Eagle	J. L. May	
G-MBCV	Hiway Skytrike	C. J. Greasley	
G-MBCW	Hiway Demon 175	C. Foster & S. B. Elwis	
G-MBCX	Airwave Nimrod 165	M. J. Ashley-Rogers	
G-MBCY	American Aerolights Eagle	C. J. Blundell	
G-MBCZ	Chargus Skytrike 160	R. M. Sheppard	
G-MBDA	Rotec Rally 2B	Blois Aviation Ltd	
G-MBDB	Solar Wings Typhoon	D. J. Smith	
G-MBDC	Skyhook Cutlass	R. M. Tunstall	
G-MBDD	Skyhook Skytrike	D. Hancock	
G-MBDE	Flexiform Skytrike	R. W. Chatterton	
G-MBDF	Rotec Rally 2B	J. R. & B. T. Jordan	
G-MBDG	Eurowing Goldwing	N. W. Beadle & ptnrs	

Notes	Reg.	Type	Owner or Operator
	G-MBDH	Hiway Demon Triflyer	A. T. Delaney
	G-MBDI	Flexiform Sealander	K. Bryan
	G-MBDJ	Flexiform Sealander Triflyer	J. W. F. Hargrave
	G-MBDK	Solar Wings Typhoon	A. O'Brien
	G-MBDL	Lone Ranger Microlight	Aero & Engineering Services Ltd
	G-MBDM	Southdown Sigma Trike	A. R. Prentice
	G-MBDN	Hornet Atlas	P. J. Kidson
	G-MBDO	Flexiform Sealander Trike	K. Kerr
	G-MBDP	Flexiform Sealander Skytrike	D. Mackillop
	G-MBDR	U.A.S. Stormbuggy	R. V. Hoss
	G-MBDT	American Aerolights Eagle	I. D. Stokes
	G-MBDU	Chargus Titan 38	Property Associates Ltd
	G-MBDW	Ultrasports Tripacer Skytrike A	J. T. Meager
	G-MBDX	Electraflyer Eagle	Ardenco Ltd
	G-MBDY	Weedhopper 2	G. N. Mayes
	G-MBDZ	Eipper Quicksilver MX	H. Glover
	G-MBEA	Hornet Nimrod	M. Holling
	G-MBEB	Hiway Skytrike 250 Mk II	K. D. Napier & ptnrs
	G-MBEC	Hiway Super Scorpion	C. S. Wates
	G-MBED	Chargus Titan 38	G. G. Foster
	G-MBEE	Hiway Super Scorpion Skytrike 160	C. D. Wills
	G-MBEG	Eipper Quicksilver MX	M. S. Walker
	G-MBEJ	Electraflyer Eagle	D. J. Royce & C. R. Gale
	G-MBEL	Electraflyer Eagle	J. R. Fairweather
	G-MBEN	Eipper Quicksilver MX	A. A. McKenzie
	G-MBEO	Flexiform Sealander	H. W. Williams
	G-MBEP	American Aerolights Eagle	R. W. Lavender
	G-MBER	Skyhook Sailwings TR-1	Skyhook Sailwings Ltd
	G-MBES	Skyhook Cutlass	Skyhook Sailwings Ltd
	G-MBET	MEA Mistral Trainer	J. W. V. Edmunds
	G-MBEU	Hiway Demon T.250	R. C. Smith
	G-MBEV	Chargus Titan 38	N. Hooper
	G-MBEW	UAS Solar Buggy	A. G. Davies
	G-MBEZ	Pterodactyl Ptraveller II	M. P. Bywater
	G-MBFA	Hiway Skytrike 250	P. S. Jones
	G-MBFD	Gemini Hummingbird	Micro Aviation Ltd
	G-MBFE	American Aerolights Eagle	P. W. Cole
	G-MBFF	Southern Aerosports Scorpion	H. Redwin
	G-MBFG	Skyhook Sabre	M. Williamson
	G-MBFH	Hiway Skytrike	P. Baldwin
	G-MBFI	Hiway Skytrike II	J. R. Brabbs
	G-MBFJ	Chargus Typhoon T.250	R. J. B. Perry
	G-MBFK	Hiway Demon	D. W. Stamp
	G-MBFL	Hiway Demon	J. C. Houghton
	G-MBFM	Hiway Hang Glider	G. P. Kimmons & T. V. O. Mahony
	G-MBFN	Hiway Skytrike II	R. Williamson
	G-MBFO	Eipper Quicksilver MX	F. G. Shepherd
	G-MBFR	American Aerolights Eagle	W. G. Bradley
	G-MBFS	American Aerolights Eagle	R. Fox
	G-MBFT	Southdown Sigma 12 Meter	D. P. Watts
	G-MBFU	Ultrasports Tripacer	T. H. J. Prowse
	G-MBFV	Comet Skytrike	R. Willis
	G-MBFX	Hiway Skytrike 250	D. A. Robinson
	G-MBFY	Mirage II	J. P. Metcalf
	G-MBFZ	M. S. S. Goldwing	I. T. Barr
	G-MBGA	Solar Wings Typhoon	A. D. Fennell
	G-MBGB	American Aerolights Eagle	J. C. Miles
	G-MBGD	Pterodactyl 430C Replica	C. Wilkinson
	G-MBGE	Hiway Scorpion Trike	J. A. Rudd
	G-MBGF	Twamley Trike	T. B. Woolley
	G-MBGG	Chargus Titan 38	Solar Wings Ltd
	G-MBGH	Chargus T.250	A. G. Doubtfire
	G-MBGI	Chargus T.250	A. G. Doubtfire
	G-MBGJ	Hiway Skytrike Mk 2	B. C. Norris & J. R. Edwards
	G-MBGK	Electra Flyer Eagle	R. J. Osbourne
	G-MBGL	Flexiform Sealander Skytrike	H. Field
	G-MBGM	Eipper Quicksilver MX	G. G. Johnson
	G-MBGN	Weedhopper Model A	D. Roberts
	G-MBGO	American Aerolights Eagle	J. E. Bennison
	G-MBGP	Solar Wings Typhoon Skytrike	C. A. Mitchell
	G-MBGR	Eurowing Goldwing	G. A. J. Salter
	G-MBGS	Rotec Rally 2B	P. C. Bell
	G-MBGT	American Aerolights Eagle	D. C. Lloyd

Reg.	Type	Owner or Operator	Notes
G-MBGV	Skyhook Cutlass	D. M. Parsons	
G-MBGW	Hiway Skytrike	G. W. R. Cooke	
G-MBGX	Southdown Lightning	T. Knight	
G-MBGY	Hiway Demon Skytrike	W. Hopkins	
G-MBGZ	American Aerolights Eagle	Flying Machine (Circa 1910) Ltd	
G-MBHA	Trident Trike	P. Jackson	
G-MBHB	Cenrair Moto Delta G-11	Moto Baldet (Northampton) Ltd	
G-MBHC	Chargus Lightning T.250	R. E. Worth	
G-MBHD	Hiway Vulcan Trike	D. Kiddy	
G-MBHE	American Aerolights Eagle	D. J. Lewis	
G-MBHF	Pterodactyl Ptraveller	D. B. Girry	
G-MBHH	Flexiform Sealander Skytrike	G. G. & G. J. Norris	
G-MBHI	Ultrasports Tripacer 250	P. T. Anstey	
G-MBHJ	Hornet Skyhook Cutlass	D. Shakelton	
G-MBHK	Flexiform Skytrike	E. Barfoot	
G-MBHL	Skyhook Skytrike	C. R. Brewitt	
G-MBHM	Weedhopper	J. Hopkinson	
G-MBHN	Weedhopper	S. Hopkinson	
G-MBHO	Skyhook Super Sabre Trike	E. Smith	
G-MBHP	American Aerolights Eagle II	P. V. Trollope & H. Caldwell	
G-MBHR	Flexiform Skytrike	Y. P. Osbourne	
G-MBHT	Chargus T.250	S. F. Dawe	
G-MBHU	Flexiform Hilander Skytrike	R. Bridgstock	
G-MBHV	Pterodactyl Ptraveller	H. Partridge	
G-MBHW	American Aerolights Eagle	P. D. Lloyd-Davies	
G-MBHX	Pterodactyl Ptraveller	P. Samal	
G-MBHZ	Pterodactyl Ptraveller	T. Deeming	
G-MBIA	Flexiform Sealander Skytrike	I. P. Cook	
G-MBIB	Mainair Flexiform Sealander	A. D. Pearson	
G-MBIC	Maxair Hummer	G. C. Calow	
G-MBID	American Aerolights Eagle	D. A. Campbell	
G-MBIE	Flexiform Striker	Flying Machine (Circa 1910) Ltd	
G-MBIF	American Aerolights Eagle	Flying Machine (Circa 1910) Ltd	
G-MBIG	American Aerolights Eagle	H. G. I. Goodheart	
G-MBIH	Flexiform Skytrike	M. Hurtley	
G-MBII	Hiway Skytrike	K. D. Beeton	
G-MBIK	Wheeler Scout	J. R. Keen	
G-MBIM	American Aerolights Sea Eagle	A. J. Sheardown	
G-MBIN	Wheeler Sea Scout	I. F. Kerr	
G-MBIO	American Aerolights Eagle Z Drive	B. J. C. Hill	
G-MBIP	Gemini Hummingbird	Micro Aviation Ltd	
G-MBIR	Gemini Hummingbird	Micro Aviation Ltd	
G-MBIS	American Aerolights Eagle	I. R. Bendall	
G-MBIT	Hiway Demon Skytrike	Kuernaland (UK) Ltd	
G-MBIU	Hiway Super Scorpion	M. E. Wills	
G-MBIV	Flexiform Skytrike	C. D. Weaver & ptnrs	
G-MBIW	Hiway Demon Tri-Flyer Skytrike	Computer Mart Ltd	
G-MBIX	Ultra Sports	S. A. V. Smith	
G-MBIY	Ultra Sports	J. C. Beatham	
G-MBIZ	Mainair Tri-Flyer	E. F. Clapham & ptnrs	
G-MBJA	Eurowing Goldwing	J. L. Gaunt	
G-MBJB	Hiway Skytrike Mk II	P. Cooper	
G-MBJC	American Aerolights Eagle	R. Jenkins	
G-MBJD	American Aerolights Eagle	R. W. F. Boarder	
G-MBJE	Airwave Nimrod	M. E. Glanvill	
G-MBJF	Hiway Skytrike Mk II	C. H. Bestwick	
G-MBJG	Airwave Nimrod	D. H. George	
G-MBJH	Chargus Titan	IOW Microlight Club Training Centre	
G-MBJI	Southern Aerosports Scorpion	Robert Montgomery Ltd	
G-MBJJ	Mirage Mk II	H. Glover	
G-MBJK	American Aerolights Eagle	B. W. Olley	
G-MBJL	Airwave Nimrod	A. G. Lowe	
G-MBJM	Striplin Lone Ranger	C. K. Brown	
G-MBJN	Electraflyer Eagle	C. N. Carin	
G-MBJO	Birdman Cherokee	T. A. Hinton	
G-MBJP	Hiway Skytrike	R. C. Crowley	
G-MBJR	American Aerolights Eagle	M. P. Skelding	
G-MBJS	Mainair Tri-Flyer	T. W. Taylor	
G-MBJT	Hiway Skytrike II	R. A. Kennedy	
G-MBJU	American Aerolights Eagle	J. Basford	
G-MBJV	Rotec Rally 2B	C. J. G. Welch	
G-MBJW	Hiway Demon Mk II	M. J. Grace	
G-MBJX	Hiway Super Scorpion	D. G. Hughes	

Notes	Reg.	Type	Owner or Operator
	G-MBJY	Rotec Rally 2B	C. R. V. Hitch
	G-MBJZ	Eurowing Catto CP.16	Neville Chamberlain Ltd
	G-MBKA	Mistral Trainer	G. H. Liddle
	G-MBKB	Pterodactyl Ptraveller	W. H. Foddy
	G-MBKC	Southdown Lightning	D. Bradbury
	G-MBKD	Chargus T.250	T. Knight
	G-MBKE	Eurowing Catto CP.16	R. S. Tuberville
	G-MBKF	Striplin Skyranger	R. Towle
	G-MBKG	Batchelor-Hunt Skytrike	M. J. Batchelor & ptnrs
	G-MBKH	Southdown Skytrike	S. T. D. Hands
	G-MBKI	Solar Wings Typhoon	S. T. Jones
	G-MBKJ	Chargus TS.440 Titan 38	Westair Microlights
	G-MBKK	Pterodactyl Ascender	T. D. Baker
	G-MBKL	Hiway Demon Skytrike	D. C. Bedding
	G-MBKN	Chargus TS.440 Titan	Solar Wings Ltd
	G-MBKO	Chargus TS.440 Titan	Solar Wings Ltd
	G-MBKP	Hiway Skytrike 160	R. A. Davies
	G-MBKR	Hiway Skytrike	C. J. Macey
	G-MBKS	Hiway Skytrike 160	J. Dilks
	G-MBKT	Mitchell Wing B.10	T. Beckett
	G-MBKU	Hiway Demon Skytrike	P. W. Twizell
	G-MBKV	Eurowing Goldwing	J. Yates
	G-MBKW	Pterodactyl Ptraveller	R. C. H. Russell
	G-MBKY	American Aerolights Eagle	B. Fussell
	G-MBKZ	Hiway Skytrike	S. I. Harding
	G-MBLA	Flexiform Skytrike	R. Wilding
	G-MBLB	Eipper Quicksilver MX	Southern Microlight Centre Ltd
	G-MBLD	Flexiform Striker	K. Akister
	G-MBLE	Hiway Demon Skytrike II	R. E. Harvey
	G-MBLF	Hiway Demon 195 Tri Pacer	A. P. Rostron
	G-MBLG	Chargus Titan T.38	P. R. F. Glenville
	G-MBLH	Flexwing Tri-Flyer 330	S. G. A. Heward
	G-MBLJ	Eipper Quicksilver MX	Flylight South East
	G-MBLK	Southdown Puma	P. Davies
	G-MBLM	Hiway Skytrike	W. N. Natson
	G-MBLN	Pterodactyl Ptraveller	W. F. Tremayne
	G-MBLO	Sealander Skytrike	A. R. Fawkes
	G-MBLP	Pterodactyl Ptraveller	R. N. Greenshields
	G-MBLR	Ultrasports Tripacer	M. N. Asquith
	G-MBLS	MEA Mistral	I. D. Stokes
	G-MBLT	Chargus TS.440 Titan	P. J. Harvey
	G-MBLU	Southdown Lightning L.195	C. R. Franklin
	G-MBLV	Ultrasports Hybrid	M. A. Gosden
	G-MBLX	Eurowing Goldwing	W. B. Thomas
	G-MBLY	Flexiform Sealander Trike	J. Clithero
	G-MBLZ	Southern Aerosports Scorpion	J. P. Bennett-Snewin
	G-MBMA	Eipper Quicksilver MX	M. Maxwell
	G-MBMC	Waspair Tomcat	F. D. Buckle
	G-MBMD	Eurowing CP.16	S. Dorrance
	G-MBME	American Aerolights Eagle Z Drive	Perme Westcott Flying Club
	G-MBMF	Rotec Rally 2B	J. G. Woods
	G-MBMG	Rotec Rally 2B	J. R. Pyper
	G-MBMH	American Aerolights Eagle	M. S. Scott
	G-MBMI	Chargus T.440	G. Durbin
	G-MBMJ	Mainair Tri-Flyer	P. A. Gardner
	G-MBMK	Weedhopper Model B	P. W. Grange
	G-MBML	American Aerolights Zenoah Eagle	R. C. Jones
	G-MBMN	Skyhook Silhouette	A. D. F. Clifford
	G-MBMO	Hiway Skytrike 160	L. D. Carter
	G-MBMP	Mitchell Wing B.10	J. Pavelin
	G-MBMR	Ultrasports Tripacer Typhoon	L. Mills
	G-MBMS	Hornet	R. L. Smith
	G-MBMT	Mainair Tri-Flyer	T. R. Yeomans
	G-MBMU	Eurowing Goldwing	P. R. Wason
	G-MBMV	Chargus TS.440 Titan 38	K. Brogden
	G-MBMW	Solar Wings Typhoon	R. Harrison
	G-MBMY	Pterodactyl Fledge	C. J. Blundell
	G-MBMZ	Sealander Tripacer	T. D. Otho-Briggs
	G-MBNA	American Aerolights Eagle	N. D. Hall
	G-MBNC	Southdown Sailwings Puma	Southern Airsports Ltd
	G-MBND	Skyhook Sailwings SK TR.2	Eastern Microlight Aircraft Centre Ltd
	G-MBNF	American Aerolights Eagle	D. Read

Reg.	Type	Owner or Operator	Notes
G-MBNG	Hiway Demon Skytrike	C. J. Clayson	
G-MBNH	Southern Airsports Scorpion	R. F. Thomas	
G-MBNJ	Eipper Quicksilver MX	C. Lamb	
G-MBNK	American Aerolights Eagle	R. Moss	
G-MBNL	Hiway Skytrike C.2	K. V. Shail & H. W. Preston	
G-MBNM	American Aerolights Eagle	D. W. J. Orchard	
G-MBNN	Southern Microlight Gazelle P.160N	N. A. Pitcher	
G-MBNP	Eurowing Catto CP.16	M. H. C. Bishop	
G-MBNS	Chargus Titan 38	P. N. Lynch	
G-MBNT	American Aerolights Eagle	M. D. O'Brien	
G-MBNU	Hilander/Hiway Skytrike	D. Wilson & I. Williams	
G-MBNV	Sheffield Aircraft Skytrike	D. L. Buckley	
G-MBNW	Meagher Flexwing	P. R. Collier	
G-MBNX	Solar Storm	F. Kratky	
G-MBNY	Steer Terror Fledge II	M. J. Steer	
G-MBNZ	Hiway Skytrike Demon	J. E. Brown	
G-MBOA	Flexiform Hilander	A. F. Stafford	
G-MBOB	American Aerolights Eagle	K. A. C. Black	
G-MBOD	American Aerolights Eagle	M. A. Ford & ptnrs	
G-MBOE	Solar Wing Typhoon Trike	W. Turner & C. Ferrie	
G-MBOF	Pakes Jackdaw	L. G. Pakes	
G-MBOG	Flexiform Sealander	M. J. B. Knapp	
G-MBOH	Microlight Engineering Mistral	N. A. Bell	
G-MBOI	Ultralight Flight Mirage II	H. I. Jones	
G-MBOJ	Pterodactyl Pfledgling	S. P. Dewhurst	
G-MBOK	Dunstable Microlight	W. E. Brooks	
G-MBOL	Pterodactyl Pfledgling 360	W. J. Neath	
G-MBOM	Hiway Hilander	P. H. Beaumont	
G-MBON	Eurowing Goldwing Canard	A. H. Dunlop	
G-MBOP	Hiway Demon Skytrike	R. E. Holden	
G-MBOR	Chotia 460B Weedhopper	D. J. Whysall	
G-MBOS	Hiway Super Scorpion	C. Montgomery	
G-MBOT	Hiway 250 Skytrike	I. C. Campbell	
G-MBOU	Wheeler Scout	P. Stark	
G-MBOV	Southdown Lightning Trike	J. Messenger	
G-MBOW	Solar Wing Typhoon	R. Luke	
G-MBOX	American Aerolights Eagle	J. S. Paine	
G-MBPA	Weedhopper Srs 2	C. H. & P. B. Smith	
G-MBPB	Pterodactyl Ptraveller	P. E. Bailey	
G-MBPC	American Aerolights Eagle	Aerial Imaging Systems Ltd	
G-MBPD	American Aerolights Eagle	R. G. Harris & K. Hall	
G-MBPE	Ultrasports Trike	K. L. Turner	
G-MBPG	Hunt Skytrike	W. Shaw	
G-MBPI	MEA Mistral Trainer	M. J. Kenniston	
G-MBPJ	Moto-Delta	J. B. Jackson	
G-MBPL	Hiway Demon	B. J. Merrett	
G-MBPM	Eurowing Goldwing	F. W. McCann	
G-MBPN	American Aerolights Eagle	N. O. G. & P. C. Wooler	
G-MBPO	Volnik Arrow	N. A. Seymour	
G-MBPP	American Aerolights Eagle	R. C. Colbeck	
G-MBPR	American Aerolights Eagle	P. Kift	
G-MBPS	Gryphon Willpower	J. T. Meager	
G-MBPT	Hiway Demon	K. M. Simpson	
G-MBPU	Hiway Demon	N. Shaw	
G-MBPW	Weedhopper	P. G. Walton	
G-MBPX	Eurowing Goldwing	W. R. Haworth & V. C. Cannon	
G-MBPY	Ultrasports Tripacer 330	P. A. Joyce	
G-MBPZ	Flexiform Striker	C. Harris	
G-MBRA	Eurowing Catto CP.16	J. Brown	
G-MBRB	Electraflyer Eagle 1	R. C. Bott	
G-MBRC	Wheeler Scout Mk 3A	Skycraft (UK) Ltd	
G-MBRD	American Aerolights Eagle	D. G. Fisher	
G-MBRE	Wheeler Scout	R. G. Buck	
G-MBRF	Weedhopper 460C	L. R. Smith	
G-MBRH	Ultraflight Mirage Mk II	R. A. L. Hubbard	
G-MBRK	Huntair Pathfinder	F. M. Sharland	
G-MBRM	Hiway Demon	T. M. Clarke	
G-MBRN	Hiway Demon 175	G. J. Dunn	
G-MBRO	Hiway Skytrike 160	M. A. Saunders	
G-MBRP	American Aerolights Eagle	F. G. Rainbow	
G-MBRS	American Aerolights Eagle	R. W. Chatterton	
G-MBRU	Skyhook Cutlass	T. J. McLauchlan	
G-MBRV	Eurowing Goldwing	J. H. G. Lywood & A. A. Boyle	

Notes	Reg.	Type	Owner or Operator
	G-MBRZ	Hiway Vulcan 250	D. J. Jackson
	G-MBSA	Ultraflight Mirage II	M. J. Laxton
	G-MBSB	Ultraflight Mirage II	Windsports Centre
	G-MBSC	Ultraflight Mirage II	R. P. Warren
	G-MBSD	Southdown Puma DS	D. J. Whysall
	G-MBSF	Ultraflight Mirage II	A. J. Horne
	G-MBSG	Ultraflight Mirage II	P. E. Owen
	G-MBSI	American Aerolights Eagle	M. Day
	G-MBSN	American Aerolights Eagle	D. Duckworth
	G-MBSR	Southdown Puma DS	J. G. H. Featherstone
	G-MBSS	Ultrasports Puma 2	Swancar
	G-MBSU	Ultraflight Mirage II	R. Lynn
	G-MBSW	Ultraflight Mirage II	G. Clare
	G-MBTA	UAS Storm Buggy 5 Mk 2	N. & D. McEwan
	G-MBTB	Davies Tri-Flyer S	R. J. Wilson
	G-MBTC	Weedhopper	P. C. Lovegrove
	G-MBTD	Solar Wings Cherokee 250 Trike	R. D. Yaxley
	G-MBTE	Hornet Dual Trainer Trike	A. R. Glenn
	G-MBTF	Mainair Tri-Flyer Skytrike	C. Fox
	G-MBTG	Mainair Gemini	A. J. Smith
	G-MBTH	Whittaker MW.4	MWA Flying Group
	G-MBTI	Hovey Whing Ding	A. Carr & R. Saddington
	G-MBTJ	Solar Wings Microlight	J. Swingler
	G-MBTL	Hiway Super Scorpion	C. S. Beer
	G-MBTN	Mitchell Wing B.10	N. F. James
	G-MBTO	Mainair Tri-Flyer 250	W. H. Sherlock
	G-MBTP	Hiway Demon	E. M. Jelonek
	G-MBTR	Skyhook Sailwings	R. Smith
	G-MBTS	Hovey WD-II Whing-Ding	T. G. Solomon
	G-MBTU	Cloudhopper Mk II	P. C. Lovegrove
	G-MBTV	Ultraflight Tomcat	M. C. Latham
	G-MBTW	Raven Vector 600	J. Spavins & A. L. Coleman
	G-MBTY	American Aerolights Eagle	Southall College of Technology
	G-MBTZ	Huntair Pathfinder	G. M. Hayden
	G-MBUA	Hiway Demon	R. J. Nicholson
	G-MBUB	Horne Sigma Skytrike	L. G. Horne
	G-MBUC	Huntair Pathfinder	Huntair Ltd
	G-MBUD	Wheeler Scout Mk III	R. J. Adams
	G-MBUE	MBA Tiger Cub 440	N. M. Cuthbertson
	G-MBUH	Hiway Skytrike	G. T. Cairns
	G-MBUI	Wheeler Scout Mk I	G. C. Martin
	G-MBUJ	Rotec Rally 2B	L. T. Swallham
	G-MBUK	Mainair 330 Tri Pacer	R. G. Withey
	G-MBUL	American Aerolights Eagle	Nottingham Offshore Marine
	G-MBUO	Southern Aerosports Scorpion	I. C. Vanner
	G-MBUP	Hiway Skytrike	P. Hamilton
	G-MBUS	MEA Mistral	G. W. Hockey
	G-MBUT	UAS Storm Buggy	J. N. Wrigley
	G-MBUU	Mainair Triflyer	G. E. Edwards
	G-MBUV	Huntair Pathfinder	G. H. Cork
	G-MBUW	Skyhook Sabre Trike	D. F. Soul
	G-MBUX	Pterodactyl Ptraveller	J. J. Harris
	G-MBUY	American Aerolights Eagle	Nottingham Offshore Marine
	G-MBUZ	Wheeler Scout Mk II	A. B. Cameron
	G-MBVA	Volmer Jensen VJ-23E	D. P. Eichorn
	G-MBVC	American Aerolights Eagle	E. M. Salt
	G-MBVE	Hiway 160 Valmet	T. J. Daly
	G-MBVF	Hornet	P. D. Hopkins
	G-MBVG	American Aerolights Eagle	Cipher Systems Ltd
	G-MBVH	Mainair Triflyer Striker	S. Wigham
	G-MBVI	Hiway 250 Skytrike	D. L. B. Holliday
	G-MBVJ	Skyhook Trike	A. H. Milne
	G-MBVK	Ultraflight Mirage II	C. W. Grant
	G-MBVL	Southern Aerosports Scorpion	R. H. Wentham
	G-MBVM	Ultraflight Mirage II	Normalair Garrett Ltd
	G-MBVP	Mainair Triflyer 330 Striker	S. M. C. Kenton
	G-MBVR	Rotec Rally 2B	A. C. W. Day
	G-MBVS	Hiway Skytrike	M. A. Brown
	G-MBVT	American Aerolights Eagle	D. Cracknell
	G-MBVU	Flexiform Sealander Triflyer	D. Laverick
	G-MBVV	Hiway Skytrike	G. Hayton
	G-MBVW	Skyhook TR.2	C. Churchyard
	G-MBVX	Tigair Power Fledge	D. G. Tigwell
	G-MBVY	Eipper Quicksilver MX	J. Moss

Reg.	Type	Owner or Operator	Notes
G-MBVZ	Hornet Trike 250	R. F. Southcott	
G-MBWA	American Aerolights Eagle	S. Pizzey	
G-MBWB	Hiway Skytrike	C. K. Board	
G-MBWD	Rotec Rally 2B	A. Craw	
G-MBWE	American Aerolights Eagle	R. H. Tombs	
G-MBWF	Mainair Triflyer Striker	C. Smith	
G-MBWG	Huntair Pathfinder	S. M. Pascoe	
G-MBWH	Designability Duet I	Designability Ltd	
G-MBWI	Microlight Lafayette Mk 1	F. W. Harrington	
G-MBWK	Mainair Triflyer	G. C. Weighwell	
G-MBWL	Huntair Pathfinder	D. A. Izod & R. C. Wright	
G-MBWM	American Aerolights Eagle	J. N. B. Mourant	
G-MBWN	American Aerolights Eagle	J. N. B. Mourant	
G-MBWO	Hiway Demon Skytrike	J. T. W. J. Edwards	
G-MBWP	Ultrasports Trike	C. Riley	
G-MBWR	Hornet	G. Edwards	
G-MBWT	Huntair Pathfinder	D. G. Gibson	
G-MBWU	Hiway Demon Skytrike	R. M. Lister	
G-MBWW	Southern Aerosports Scorpion	Twinflight Ltd	
G-MBWX	Southern Aerosports Scorpion	Twinflight Ltd	
G-MBWY	American Aerolights Eagle	J. P. Donovan	
G-MBWZ	American Aerolights Eagle	B. Busby	
G-MBXB	Southdown Sailwings Puma	P. R. Snowden	
G-MBXC	Eurowing Goldwing	A. J. J. Bartak	
G-MBXD	Huntair Pathfinder	Border Aviation Ltd	
G-MBXE	Hiway Skytrike	T. A. Harlow	
G-MBXF	Hiway Skytrike	J. Robinson	
G-MBXG	Mainair Triflyer	R. Bailey	
G-MBXH	Southdown Sailwings Puma	M. Sorbie	
G-MBXI	Hiway Skytrike	R. K. Parry	
G-MBXJ	Hiway Demon Skytrike	D. C. & J. M. Read	
G-MBXK	Ultrasports Puma	P. J. Brookman	
G-MBXL	Eipper Quicksilver MX2	Flying Machines (Circa 1910) Ltd	
G-MBXM	American Aerolights Eagle	P. D. Schramm	
G-MBXN	Southdown Sailwings Lighting	T. W. Robinson	
G-MBXO	Sheffield Trident	M. I. Watson	
G-MBXP	Hornet Skytrike	G. Little	
G-MBXR	Hiway Skytrike 150	C. Shutt	
G-MBXT	Eipper Quicksilver MX2	B. J. Gordon	
G-MBXW	Hiway Skytrike	R. M. Hydes	
G-MBXX	Ultraflight Mirage II	Westward Airways (Lands End) Ltd	
G-MBXY	Hornet	C. Leach	
G-MBXZ	Skyhook TR2	Dennar Engineering Ltd	
G-MBYD	American Aerolights Eagle	J. M. Hutchinson	
G-MBYE	Eipper Quicksilver MX	M. J. Beeby	
G-MBYF	Skyhook TR2	E. J. Larnder	
G-MBYH	Maxair Hummer	A. Edwards	
G-MBYI	Ultraflight Lazair	A. M. Fleming	
G-MBYJ	Hiway Super Scorpion IIC	R. Flaum	
G-MBYK	Huntair Pathfinder	W. E. Lambert	
G-MBYL	Huntair Pathfinder 330	J. S. S. Calder & R. Tyler	
G-MBYM	Eipper Quicksilver MX	J. Wibberley	
G-MBYN	Livesey Super-Fly	D. M. Livesey	
G-MBYO	American Aerolights Eagle	B. J. & M. G. Ferguson	
G-MBYP	Hornet 440cc Flexwing Cutlass	T. J. B. Daly	
G-MBYR	American Aerolights Eagle	F. Green & G. McCready	
G-MBYT	Ultraflight Mirage II	L. J. Perring	
G-MBYU	American Aerolights Eagle	F. L. Wiseman	
G-MBYV	Mainair Tri-Flyer 330	I. T. Ferguson	
G-MBYW	Levi Magpie	R. Levi	
G-MBYX	American Aerolights Eagle	N. P. Austen	
G-MBYY	Southern Aerosports Scorpion	D. J. Lovell	
G-MBZA	Ultrasports Tripacer 330	C. R. Thorne	
G-MBZB	Hiway Skytrike	M. W. Hurst & B. Emery	
G-MBZD	Hiway Volmet 160cc	G. G. Williams	
G-MBZF	American Aerolights Eagle	G. Calder & A. C. Bernard	
G-MBZG	Twinflight Scorpion 2 seat	H. T. Edwards	
G-MBZH	Eurowing Goldwing	P. Samal	
G-MBZI	Eurowing Goldwing	G. M. Hayden	
G-MBZJ	Ultrasports Puma	G. A. Burridge	
G-MBZK	Ultrasports Tripacer 250	M. T. Pearce	
G-MBZL	Weedhopper	A. R. Prior	
G-MBZM	UAS Storm Buggy	S. Comber & A. Crabtree	
G-MBZN	Ultrasports Puma	D. J. Cole	

Notes	Reg.	Type	Owner or Operator
	G-MBZO	Mainair Triflyer 330	J. Baxendale
	G-MBZP	Skyhook TR2	Army Hang Gliding School
	G-MBZR	Eipper Quicksilver MX	R. Gill
	G-MBZS	Ultrasports Puma	T. Coughlan
	G-MBZT	Solarwings Skytrike	S. Hetherton
	G-MBZU	Skyhook Sabre C	G. N. Beyer-Kay
	G-MBZV	American Aerolights Eagle	M. H. & G. C. Davies
	G-MBZW	American Aerolights Eagle	M. J. Pugh
	G-MBZX	American Aerolights Eagle	D. W. Roberts
	G-MBZY	Waspair Tom Cat HM.81	A. C. Wendelken
	G-MBZZ	Southern Aerosports Scorpion	P. J. Harlow
	G-MGUY	CFM Shadow Srs BD	CFM Metal-Fax Ltd
	G-MJAA	Ultrasports Tripacer	D. Bolton
	G-MJAB	Ultrasports Skytrike	I. W. Kemsley
	G-MJAC	American Aerolights Eagle 3	P. R. Fellden
	G-MJAD	Eipper Quicksilver MX	J. McCullough
	G-MJAE	American Aerolights Eagle	T. B. Wooley
	G-MJAF	Ultrasports Puma 440	A. B. Greenbank
	G-MJAG	Skyhook TR1	D. J. Wright & L. Florence
	G-MJAH	American Aerolights Eagle	R. L. Arscott
	G-MJAI	American Aerolights Eagle	D. J. Gardner
	G-MJAJ	Eurowing Goldwing	J. S. R. Moodie
	G-MJAK	Hiway Demon	F. C. Potter
	G-MJAL	Wheeler Scout 3	D. Howe
	G-MJAM	Eipper Quicksilver MX	J. C. Larkin
	G-MJAN	Hiway Skytrike	G. M. Sutcliffe
	G-MJAO	Hiway Skytrike	T. Le Gassicke
	G-MJAP	Hiway 160	N. A. Bray
	G-MJAR	Chargus Titan	Quest Air Ltd
	G-MJAT	Hiway Demon Skytrike	P. H. Howell
	G-MJAU	Hiway Skytrike 244cc	A. P. Cross
	G-MJAV	Hiway Demon Skytrike 244cc	M. P. Bloomfield
	G-MJAW	Solar Wings Typhoon	M. R. Nicholls
	G-MJAX	American Aerolights Eagle	J. P. Simpson & C. W. Mellard
	G-MJAY	Eurowing Goldwing	J. F. White
	G-MJBA	Raven Vector 610	Raven Leisure Industries Ltd
	G-MJBB	Raven Vector 610	Raven Leisure Industries Ltd
	G-MJBC	Raven Vector 610	Raven Leisure Industries Ltd
	G-MJBD	Raven Vector 610	Raven Leisure Industries Ltd
	G-MJBE	Wheeler Scout X	Newell Aircraft & Tool Co Ltd
	G-MJBF	Southdown Puma 330	C. Jacobs
	G-MJBG	Mainair Solarwings Typhoon	N. J. Mackay
	G-MJBH	American Aerolights Eagle	P. Smith
	G-MJBI	Eipper Quicksilver MX	J. I. Visser
	G-MJBK	Swallow AeroPlane Swallow B	B. J. Towers
	G-MJBL	American Aerolights Eagle	B. W. Olley
	G-MJBM	Eurowing CP.16	A. H. Milne
	G-MJBN	American Aerolights Eagle	D. Darke
	G-MJBO	Bell Microlight Type A	G. Bell
	G-MJBP	Eurowing Catto CP.16	I. Wilson
	G-MJBS	Ultralight Stormbuggy	G. I. Sargeant
	G-MJBT	Eipper Quicksilver MX	G. A. Barclay
	G-MJBV	American Aerolights Eagle	B. H. Stephens
	G-MJBW	American Aerolights Eagle	J. D. Penman
	G-MJBX	Pterodactyl Ptraveller	R. E. Hawkes
	G-MJBY	Rotec Rally 2B	B. Eastwood
	G-MJBZ	Huntair Pathfinder	J. C. Rose
	G-MJCA	Skyhook Sabre	B. G. Axworthy
	G-MJCB	Hornet 330	A. C. Aspden & ptnrs
	G-MJCC	Ultrasports Puma	S. Hudson
	G-MJCD	Sigma Tetley Skytrike	N. L. Betts & B. Tetley
	G-MJCE	Ultrasports Tripacer	Charter Systems
	G-MJCF	Maxair Hummer	J. G. Bussell
	G-MJCG	S.M.C. Flyer Mk 1	E. N. Skinner
	G-MJCH	Ultraflight Mirage II	R. Sherwin
	G-MJCI	Kruchek Firefly 440	E. Kepka
	G-MJCJ	Hiway Spectrum	J. F. Mayes
	G-MJCK	Southern Aerosports Scorpion	S. L. Moss
	G-MJCL	Eipper Quicksilver MX	R. F. Witt
	G-MJCM	S.M.C. Flyer Mk 1	P. L. Gooch
	G-MJCN	S.M.C. Flyer Mk 1	C. W. Merriam
	G-MJCO	Striplin Lone Ranger	J. G. Wellans
	G-MJCP	Huntair Pathfinder	R. C. Wright
	G-MJCR	American Aerolights Eagle	R. F. Hinton

Reg.	Type	Owner or Operator	Notes
G-MJCS	EFS Pterodactyl	D. W. Evans	
G-MJCT	Hiway Skytrike	E. W. Barker	
G-MJCU	Tarjani	T. A. Sayer	
G-MJCV	Southern Flyer Mk 1	G. N. Harris	
G-MJCW	Hiway Super Scorpion	M. G. Sheppard	
G-MJCX	American Aerolights Eagle	S. C. Weston	
G-MJCY	Eurowing Goldwing	A. E. Dewdeswell	
G-MJCZ	Southern Aerosports Scorpion 2	C. Baldwin	
G-MJDA	Hornet Trike Executive	J. Hainsworth	
G-MJDB	Birdman Cherokee	W. G. Farr	
G-MJDC	Mainair Tri-Flyer Dual	A. C. Dommett	
G-MJDE	Huntair Pathfinder	E. H. Gould	
G-MJDF	Tripacer 250cc Striker	F. R. Loft	
G-MJDG	Hornet Supertrike	I. Roy	
G-MJDH	Huntair Pathfinder	I. K. Ratcliffe	
G-MJDI	Southern Flyer Mk 1	N. P. Day	
G-MJDJ	Hiway Skytrike Demon	A. J. Cowan	
G-MJDK	American Aerolights Eagle	P. A. McPherson & ptnrs	
G-MJDL	American Aerolights Eagle	M. T. Edwards	
G-MJDM	Wheeler Scout Mk III	Skycraft (UK) Ltd	
G-MJDN	Skyhook Single Seat	G. Morgan	
G-MJDO	Southdown Puma 440	C. S. Beer	
G-MJDP	Eurowing Goldwing	A. E. Armstrong	
G-MJDR	Hiway Demon Skytrike	P. J. Bullock	
G-MJDU	Eipper Quicksilver MX2	Microlight Airsport Services Ltd	
G-MJDV	Skyhook TR-1	R. Mason	
G-MJDW	Eipper Quicksilver MX	Remus International Ltd	
G-MJDX	Moyes Mega II	P. H. Davies	
G-MJDY	Ultrasports Solarwings	S. A. Barnes	
G-MJEA	Flexiform Striker	S. J. O'Neill	
G-MJEC	Ultrasports Puma	F. W. Hartshorn	
G-MJED	Eipper Quicksilver MX	R. Haslam	
G-MJEE	Mainair Triflyer Trike	M. F. Eddington	
G-MJEF	Gryphon 180	F. C. Coulson	
G-MJEG	Eurowing Goldwing	G. J. Stamper	
G-MJEH	Rotec Rally 2B	J. G. Lindley	
G-MJEI	American Aerolights Eagle	A. Moss	
G-MJEJ	American Aerolights Eagle	J. Cole	
G-MJEK	Hiway Demon 330 Skytrike	J. Grant	
G-MJEL	GMD-01 Trike	G. M. Drinkell	
G-MJEM	Griffon 440 Trike	R. G. Griffin	
G-MJEN	Eurowing Catto CP.16	A. D. G. Wright	
G-MJEO	American Aerolights Eagle	A. M. Shaw	
G-MJEP	Pterodactyl Ptraveller	G. H. Liddle	
G-MJER	Flexiform Striker	D. S. Simpson	
G-MJES	Stratos Prototype 3 Axis 1	Stratos Aviation Ltd	
G-MJET	Stratos Prototype 3 Axis 1	Stratos Aviation Ltd	
G-MJEU	Hiway Skytrike	P. Best	
G-MJEV	Flexiform Striker	C. Scoble	
G-MJEX	Eipper Quicksilver MX	M. J. Sundaram	
G-MJEY	Southdown Lightning	P. M. Coppola	
G-MJEZ	Raven Vector 600	D. H. Handley	
G-MJFB	Flexiform Striker	B. Tetley	
G-MJFD	Ultrasports Tripacer	R. N. O. Kingsbury	
G-MJFE	Hiway Scorpion	N. A. Fisher	
G-MJFF	Huntair Pathfinder	S. R. L. Eversfield & ptnrs	
G-MJFG	Eurowing Goldwing	J. G. Aspinall & H. R. Marsden	
G-MJFH	Eipper Quicksilver MX	I. Waldram	
G-MJFI	Flexiform Striker	A. L. Virgoe	
G-MJFJ	Hiway Skytrike 250	A. D. Stewart	
G-MJFK	Flexiform Skytrike Dual	J. Hollings	
G-MJFL	Mainair Tri-Flyer 440	J. Phillips	
G-MJFM	Huntair Pathfinder	R. W. Sage	
G-MJFN	Huntair Pathfinder	Times Newspapers Ltd	
G-MJFP	American Aerolights Eagle	R. C. Colbeck	
G-MJFR	American Aerolights Eagle	Southall College of Technology	
G-MJFS	American Aerolights Eagle	P. R. A. Elliston	
G-MJFT	American Aerolights Eagle	D. S. McMullen	
G-MJFV	Ultrasports Tripacer	Hatfield Polytechnic Students Union	
G-MJFW	Ultrasports Puma	J. McCarthy	
G-MJFX	Skyhook TR-1	M. R. Dean	
G-MJFY	Hornet 250	H. Lang	
G-MJFZ	Hiway Demon Skytrike	J. A. Lowie	
G-MJGA	Hiway Skytrike 160	J. H. Wadsworth	

Notes	Reg.	Type	Owner or Operator
	G-MJGB	American Aerolights Eagle	N. P. Day
	G-MJGC	Hornet	P. C. & S. J. Turnbull
	G-MJGD	Huntair Pathfinder	A. Carling
	G-MJGE	Eipper Quicksilver MX	D. Brown
	G-MJGF	Poisestar Aeolus Mk 1	Poisestar Ltd
	G-MJGG	Skyhook TR-1	R. Pritchard
	G-MJGH	Flexiform Skytrike	P. Newman
	G-MJGI	Eipper Quicksilver MX	J. M. Hayer & J. R. Wilman
	G-MJGJ	American Aerolights Eagle	B. J. Houlihan
	G-MJGK	Eurowing Goldwing	P. E. P. Shephard
	G-MJGL	Chargus Titan 38	J. Houston & J. R. Appleton
	G-MJGM	Hiway Demon 195 Skytrike	J. M. Creasey
	G-MJGN	Greenslade Monotrike	P. G. Greenslade
	G-MJGO	Barnes Avon Skytrike	B. R. Barnes
	G-MJGP	Hiway Demon Skytrike	G. I. J. Thompson
	G-MJGR	Hiway Demon Skytrike	L. V. Strickland & P. H. Howell
	G-MJGS	American Aerolights Eagle	P. D. Griffiths
	G-MJGT	Skyhook Cutlass Trike	T. Silvester
	G-MJGU	Pterodactyl Mk 1	J. Pemberton
	G-MJGV	Eipper Quicksilver MX2	D. Beer
	G-MJGW	Solar Wings Trike	D. J. D. Beck
	G-MJGX	Ultrasports Puma 330	TDJ Flying Club
	G-MJGZ	Mainair Triflyer 330	A. Holt
	G-MJHA	Hiway Skytrike 250 Mk II	R. J. Perry
	G-MJHB	AES Sky Ranger	J. H. L. B. Wijsmuller
	G-MJHC	Ultrasports Tripacer 330	S. J. Baker
	G-MJHD	Campbell-Jones Ladybird	M. A. Campbell-Jones
	G-MJHE	Hiway Demon Skytrike	T. R. Grief
	G-MJHF	Skyhook Sailwing Trike	R. A. Watering
	G-MJHG	Huntair Pathfinder 330	A. Nice
	G-MJHH	Soleair Dactyl	C. N. Giddings
	G-MJHI	Soleair Dactyl	S. B. Giddings
	G-MJHJ	Redwing G.W.W.1	N. J. Mackay
	G-MJHK	Hiway Demon 195	J. C. Bowden
	G-MJHL	Mainair Triflyer Mk II	D. G. Jones
	G-MJHM	Ultrasports Trike	J. Richardson
	G-MJHN	American Aerolights Eagle	P. K. Ewens
	G-MJHO	Shilling Bumble Bee Srs 1	C. R. Shilling
	G-MJHP	American Aerolights Eagle	B. A. G. Scott & ptnrs
	G-MJHR	Southdown Lightning	G. N. Sugg
	G-MJHS	American Aerolights Eagle	R. M. Bacon
	G-MJHT	Eurowing Goldwing	J. D. Penman
	G-MJHU	Eipper Quicksilver MX	P. J. Hawcock & ptnrs
	G-MJHV	Hiway Demon 250	A. G. Griffiths
	G-MJHW	Ultrasports Puma 1	R. C. Barnett
	G-MJHX	Eipper Quicksilver MX	P. D. Lucas
	G-MJHY	American Aerolights Eagle	J. T. H. McAlpine
	G-MJHZ	Southdown Sailwings	D. Corke
	G-MJIA	Flexiform Striker	N. R. Beale
	G-MJIB	Hornet 250	S. H. Williams
	G-MJIC	Ultrasports Puma 330	C. R. Marriott
	G-MJID	Southdown Sailwings Puma DS	P. Jarman
	G-MJIE	Hornet 330	C. J. Dalby
	G-MJIF	Mainair Triflyer	R. J. Payne
	G-MJIG	Hiway Demon Skytrike	E. Dauncey
	G-MJIH	Ultrasports Tripacer	J. L. Bakewell
	G-MJII	American Aerolights Eagle	M. Flitman
	G-MJIJ	Ultrasports Tripacer 250	D. H. Targett
	G-MJIK	Southdown Sailwings Lightning	J. F. Chithalan
	G-MJIL	Bremner Mitchell B.10	D. S. & R. M. Bremner
	G-MJIM	Skyhook Cutlass	P. Rayner
	G-MJIN	Hiway Skytrike	P. W. Harding
	G-MJIO	American Aerolights Eagle	R. Apps & J. Marshall
	G-MJIP	Wheeler Scout Mk 33A	A. V. Wilson
	G-MJIR	Eipper Quicksilver MX	H. Feeney
	G-MJIS	American Aerolights Eagle	E. Gee
	G-MJIT	Hiway Skytrike	F. A. Mileham & D. W. B. Hatch
	G-MJIU	Eipper Quicksilver MX	O. W. A. Church
	G-MJIV	Pterodactyl Ptraveller	G. E. Fowles
	G-MJIX	Flexiform Hilander	D. Beer
	G-MJIY	Flexiform Voyage	R. J. Sims
	G-MJIZ	Southdown Lightning	J. J. Crudington
	G-MJJA	Huntair Pathfinder	J. B. & J. M. Watkins
	G-MJJB	Eipper Quicksilver MX	S. P. Pinn

Reg.	Type	Owner or Operator	Notes
G-MJJC	Eipper Quicksilver MX2	R. G. Pickard	
G-MJJD	Birdman Cherokee	B. J. Sanderson	
G-MJJE	Douglas Type 1	R. A. Douglas	
G-MJJF	Sealey	L. G. Thomas & R. D. Thomasson	
G-MJJI	Mackinder Skyrider	R. H. Mackinder	
G-MJJJ	Moyes Knight	R. J. Broomfield	
G-MJJK	Eipper Quicksilver MX2	M. J. O'Malley	
G-MJJL	Solar Wings Storm	P. Wharton	
G-MJJM	Birdman Cherokee Mk 1	R. J. Wilson	
G-MJJN	Ultrasports Puma	J. E. Gooch	
G-MJJO	Flexiform Skytrike Dual	Kington Mead Flying Group	
G-MJJP	American Aerolights Eagle	Flying Machines (Circa 1910) Ltd	
G-MJJR	Huntair Pathfinder 330	R. D. Beavan	
G-MJJS	Swallow AeroPlane Swallow B	D. Corrigan	
G-MJJT	Huntair Pathfinder	Macpara Ltd	
G-MJJU	Hiway Demon	I. C. Willetts	
G-MJJV	Wheeler Scout	C. G. Johes	
G-MJJW	Chargus Kilmarnock	J. S. Potts	
G-MJJX	Hiway Skytrike	P. C. Millward	
G-MJJY	Tirith Firefly	Tirith Microplane Ltd	
G-MJJZ	Hiway Demon 175 Skytrike	B. C. Williams	
G-MJKA	Skyhook Sabre Trike	J. Petter & J. Armstrong	
G-MJKB	Striplin Skyranger	A. P. Booth	
G-MJKC	Mainair Triflyer 330 Striker	W. H. Prince	
G-MJKE	Mainair Triflyer 330	R. E. D. Bailey	
G-MJKF	Hiway Demon	S. D. Hill	
G-MJKG	John Ivor Skytrike	R. C. Wright	
G-MJKH	Eipper Quicksilver MX II	E. H. E. Nunn	
G-MJKI	Eipper Quicksilver MX	D. R. Gibbons	
G-MJKJ	Eipper Quicksilver MX	Aerolite Aviation Co Ltd	
G-MJKL	Ultrasports Puma	D. P. McHenry	
G-MJKM	Chargus Titan TS.440/38	Hiway Flight Services Ltd	
G-MJKN	Hiway Demon	Hiway Flight Services Ltd	
G-MJKO	Goldmarque 250 Skytrike	M. J. Barry	
G-MJKP	Hiway Super Scorpion	M. Horsfall	
G-MJKR	Rotec Rally 2B	J. R. Darlow & J. D. Whitcock	
G-MJKS	Mainair Triflyer	P. Sutton	
G-MJKT	Hiway Super Scorpion	K. J. Morris	
G-MJKU	Hiway Demon 175	B. G. Staniscia & M. J. McCarthy	
G-MJKV	Hornet	C. Parkinson	
G-MJKW	Maxair Hummer TX	D. Roberts	
G-MJKX	Ultralight Skyrider Phantom	L. K. Fowler	
G-MJKY	Hiway Skytrike	J. P. Wild	
G-MJLA	Ultrasports Puma 2	G. F. Cutler	
G-MJLB	Ultrasports Puma 2	Breen Aviation Ltd	
G-MJLC	American Aerolights Double Eagle	Ardenco Ltd	
G-MJLD	Wheeler Scout Mk III	M. Buchanan-Jones	
G-MJLE	Lightwing Rooster 2 Type 5	J. Lee	
G-MJLF	Southern Microlight Trike	P. A. Grimes	
G-MJLG	Hiway Skytrike Mk II	R. E. Neilson	
G-MJLH	American Aerolights Eagle 2	A. Cussins	
G-MJLI	Hiway Demon Skytrike	A. J. P. Farmer	
G-MJLJ	Flexiform Sealander	Questair Ltd	
G-MJLK	Dragonfly 250-II	G. Carter	
G-MJLL	Hiway Demon Skytrike	D. Hines	
G-MJLM	Mainair Triflyer 250	I. D. Evans	
G-MJLN	Southern Microlight Gazelle	R. Rossiter	
G-MJLO	Goldmarque Skytrike	K. G. Steer	
G-MJLR	Skyhook SK-1	T. Moore	
G-MJLS	Rotec Rally 2B	G. Messenger	
G-MJLT	American Aerolights Eagle	P. de Vere Hunt	
G-MJLU	Skyhook	C. A. Shayes	
G-MJLV	Eipper Quicksilver MX	W. Wade-Gery	
G-MJLW	Chargus Titan	C. Ellison	
G-MJLX	Rotec Rally 2B	J. Houldenshaw	
G-MJLY	American Aerolights Eagle	A. H. Read	
G-MJLZ	Hiway Demon Skytrike	K. Pickering	
G-MJMA	Hiway Demon	R. I. Simpson	
G-MJMB	Weedhopper	J. E. Brown	
G-MJMC	Huntair Pathfinder	R. Griffiths	
G-MJMD	Hiway Demon Skytrike	D. Cussen	
G-MJME	Ultrasports Tripacer Mega II	A. D. Cranfield	
G-MJMG	Weedhopper	S. Reynolds	

Notes	Reg.	Type	Owner or Operator
	G-MJMH	American Aerolights Eagle	D. Crowson
	G-MJMI	Skyhook Sabre	W. P. Klotz
	G-MJMJ	Wheeler Scout III	R. Mitchell
	G-MJMK	Ultrasports Tripacer	M. F. J. Shipp
	G-MJML	Weedhopper D	V. Dixon
	G-MJMM	Chargus Vortex	D. Gwenin
	G-MJMN	Mainair Trike	D. Harrison
	G-MJMO	Lancashire Microlight Striker	N. Heap
	G-MJMP	Eipper Quicksilver MX	D. R. Peppercorn
	G-MJMR	Mainair Trike	T. Anderson
	G-MJMS	Hiway Skytrike	G. J. Foard
	G-MJMT	Hiway Demon Skytrike	N. J. Brunskill
	G-MJMU	Hiway Demon	J. Hall
	G-MJMV	Vulcan 2	R. Rawcliffe
	G-MJMW	Eipper Quicksilver MX2	S. E. Borrow
	G-MJMX	Ultrasports Tripacer	M. A. H. Milne
	G-MJMZ	Robertson Ultralight B1-RD	Southwest Aviation
	G-MJNA	Mainair Triflyer	M. T. Byrne
	G-MJNB	Hiway Skytrike	G. Hammond
	G-MJNC	Hiway Demon Skytrike	T. Gdaniec
	G-MJNE	Hornet Supreme Dual Trike	Hornet Microlights
	G-MJNG	Eipper Quicksilver MX	R. Briggs-Price
	G-MJNH	Skyhook Cutlass Trike	M. E. James
	G-MJNI	Hornet Sabre	T. M. Carter
	G-MJNJ	Gregory Typhoon	M. R. Gregory
	G-MJNK	Hiway Skytrike	S. J. Beecroft
	G-MJNL	American Aerolights Eagle	W. A. H. Vick
	G-MJNM	American Aerolights Double Eagle	E. G. Cullen
	G-MJNN	Ultraflight Mirage II	Breen Aviation Ltd
	G-MJNO	American Aerolights Double Eagle	R. S. Martin & J. L. May
	G-MJNP	American Aerolights Eagle	M. P. Harper & P. A. George
	G-MJNR	Ultralight Solar Buggy	D. J. Smith
	G-MJNS	Swallow AeroPlane Swallow B	D. G. Hey
	G-MJNT	Hiway Skytrike	A. W. Abraham
	G-MJNU	Skyhook Cutlass	D. M. Camm
	G-MJNV	Eipper Quicksilver MX	W. Toulmin
	G-MJNW	Skyhook Silhouette	R. Hamilton
	G-MJNX	Eipper Quicksilver MX	R. Hurley
	G-MJNY	Skyhook Sabre Trike	P. Ratcliffe
	G-MJNZ	Skyhook Sabre Trike	R. Huthison
	G-MJOA	Chargus T.250 Vortex	R. J. Ridgway
	G-MJOB	Skyhook Cutlass CD Trike	J. M. Oliver
	G-MJOC	Huntair Pathfinder	R. Bowring
	G-MJOD	Rotec Rally 2B	A. J. Capel & K. D. Halsey
	G-MJOE	Eurowing Goldwing	R. J. Osbourne
	G-MJOF	Eipper Quicksilver MX	S. M. Wellband
	G-MJOG	American Aerolights Eagle	J. B. Rush
	G-MJOH	Flexiform Striker	P. Hobson
	G-MJOI	Hiway Demon	S. J. Walker
	G-MJOJ	Flexiform Skytrike	D. Haynes
	G-MJOK	Mainair Triflyer 250	S. Pike & K. Fagan
	G-MJOL	Skyhook Cutlass	G. Singh
	G-MJOM	Southdown Puma 40F	J. G. Crawford
	G-MJON	Southdown Puma 40F	Peninsula Flight Ltd
	G-MJOO	Southdown Puma 40F	D. J. England
	G-MJOP	Southdown Puma 40F	Peninsula Flight Ltd
	G-MJOR	Solair Phoenix	T. V. Wood
	G-MJOS	Southdown Lightning 170	A. Faiers
	G-MJOT	Airwave Nimrod	W. G. Lamyman
	G-MJOU	Hiway Demon 175	H. Phipps
	G-MJOV	Solar Wings Typhoon	I. R. Hoad
	G-MJOW	Eipper Quicksilver MX	P. N. Haigh
	G-MJOX	Solar Wings Typhoon	L. Johnston
	G-MJOY	Eurowing CP.16	J. P. B. Chilton
	G-MJPA	Rotec Rally 2B	G. S. Adams
	G-MJPB	Manuel Ladybird	W. L. Manuel
	G-MJPC	American Aerolights Double Eagle	D. M. Jackson
	G-MJPD	Hiway Demon Skytrike	K. A. Stewart
	G-MJPE	Hiway Demon Skytrike	D. Hill
	G-MJPF	American Aerolights Eagle 430R	A. E. F. McClintock

Reg.	Type	Owner or Operator	Notes
G-MJPG	American Aerolights Eagle 430R	C. J. W. Marriott	
G-MJPH	Huntair Pathfinder	A. J. Lambert	
G-MJPI	Flexiform Striker	D. A. Watkins	
G-MJPJ	Flexiform Dual Trike 440	M. D. Phillips & ptnrs	
G-MJPK	Hiway Vulcan	R. G. Darcy	
G-MJPL	Birdman Cherokee	P. A. Leach	
G-MJPM	Huntair Pathfinder	Swift Systems Ltd	
G-MJPN	Mitchell B10	T. Willford	
G-MJPO	Eurowing Goldwing	M. Merryman	
G-MJPP	Hiway Super Scorpion	K. L. Mercer	
G-MJPR	Birdman Cherokee 250	G. A. Webb	
G-MJPS	American Aerolights Eagle 430R	Peter Symonds & Co	
G-MJPT	Dragon	Fly-In Ltd	
G-MJPU	Solar Wings Typhoon	K. N. Dickinson	
G-MJPV	Eipper Quicksilver MX	J. B. Walker	
G-MJPW	Mainair Merlin	G. Deegan	
G-MJPX	Hiway Demon	R. Todd	
G-MJPY	American Aerolights Eagle	N. G. Jagger	
G-MJPZ	American Aerolights Eagle	A. T. Croy	
G-MJRA	Hiway Demon	P. Richardson & J. Martin	
G-MJRC	Eipper Quicksilver MX	R. W. Bunting	
G-MJRE	Hiway Demon	P. A. Smith	
G-MJRG	Ultrasports Puma	J. Lakin	
G-MJRH	Hiway Skytrike	A. J. Wood	
G-MJRI	American Aerolights Eagle	N. N. Brown	
G-MJRJ	Hiway Demon 175 Skytrike	M. Tomlinson	
G-MJRK	Flexiform Striker	P. J. & G. Long	
G-MJRL	Eurowing Goldwing	L. S. Nicholson	
G-MJRM	Dragon 150	Fly-In Ltd	
G-MJRN	Flexiform Striker	K. Handley	
G-MJRO	Eurowing Goldwing	G. A. J. Salter	
G-MJRP	Mainair Triflyer 330	A. Hulme	
G-MJRR	Striplin Skyranger Srs 1	J. R. Reece	
G-MJRS	Eurowing Goldwing	R. V. Hogg	
G-MJRT	Southdown Lightning DS	R. G. Padfield	
G-MJRU	MBA Tiger Cub 440	D. V. Short	
G-MJRV	Eurowing Goldwing	D. N. Williams	
G-MJRX	Ultrasports Puma II	E. M. Woods	
G-MJRY	MBA Super Tiger Cub 440	Vintage Displays & Training Services Ltd	
G-MJRZ	MBA Super Tiger Cub 440	Vintage Displays & Training Services Ltd	
G-MJSA	Mainair 2-Seat Trike	M. K. W. Hughes	
G-MJSB	Eurowing Catto CP.16	Independent Business Forms (Scotland) Ltd	
G-MJSC	American Aerolights Eagle	E. McGuiness	
G-MJSD	Rotec Rally 2B Srs 1	K. J. Dickson	
G-MJSE	Skyrider Airsports Phantom	S. Montandon	
G-MJSF	Skyrider Airsports Phantom	Skyrider Airsports	
G-MJSH	American Aerolights Eagle	J. Walsom	
G-MJSI	Huntair Pathfinder	Huntair Ltd	
G-MJSK	Skyhook Sabre	G. E. Coole	
G-MJSL	Dragon 200	S. C. Weston	
G-MJSM	Weedhopper B	J. R. Bancroft	
G-MJSO	Hiway Skytrike	G. A. Ede	
G-MJSP	MBA Super Tiger Cub 440	J. W. E. Romain	
G-MJSR	Flexiform Micro-Trike II	R. J. S. Galley	
G-MJSS	American Aerolights Eagle	G. N. S. Farrant	
G-MJST	Pterodactyl Ptraveler	C. H. J. Goodwin	
G-MJSU	MBA Tiger Cub	R. J. Adams	
G-MJSV	MBA Tiger Cub	D. A. Izod	
G-MJSX	Simplicity Microlight	N. Smith	
G-MJSY	Eurowing Goldwing	A. J. Rex	
G-MJSZ	D.H. Wasp	D. Harker	
G-MJTA	Flexiform Striker	K. J. Regan	
G-MJTB	Eipper Quicksilver MX	R. F. G. King	
G-MJTC	Solar Wings Typhoon	D. W. Foreman & J. A. Iszard	
G-MJTD	Gardner T-M Scout	D. Gardner	
G-MJTE	Skyrider Airsports Phantom	A. L. Hastings	
G-MJTF	Gryphon Wing	A. T. Armstrong	
G-MJTG	AES Sky Ranger	Aero & Engineering Services Ltd	
G-MJTH	S.M.D. Gazelle	D. Marsh	

Notes	Reg.	Type	Owner or Operator
	G-MJTI	Huntair Pathfinder II	B. Gunn
	G-MJTJ	Weedhopper	M. J. Blanchard
	G-MJTK	American Aerolights Eagle	N. R. MacRae
	G-MJTL	Aerostructure Pipistrelle 2B	J. McD. Robinson & C. G. McCrae
	G-MJTM	Aerostructure Pipistrelle 2B	Southdown Aero Services Ltd
	G-MJTN	Eipper Quicksilver MX	N. F. Cuthbert
	G-MJTO	Jordan Duet Srs 1	J. R. Jordan
	G-MJTP	Flexiform Striker	M. R. Clucas
	G-MJTR	Southdown Puma DS Mk 1	P. Soanes
	G-MJTU	Skyhook Cutlass 185	P. D. Wade
	G-MJTV	Chargus Titan 38	D. L. Harrison
	G-MJTW	Eurowing Trike	W. G. Lindsay
	G-MJTX	Skyrider Phantom	Haywood Design
	G-MJTY	Huntair Pathfinder	C. H. Smith
	G-MJTZ	Skyrider Airsports Phantom	A. I. Stott
	G-MJUA	MBA Super Tiger Cub	M. Ward
	G-MJUB	MBA Tiger Cub 440	C. C. Butt
	G-MJUC	MBA Tiger Cub 440	R. R. Hawkes
	G-MJUD	Southdown Puma 440	T. W. Jennings & R. A. H. Falla
	G-MJUE	Southdown Wild Cat II	W. M. A. Alladin
	G-MJUF	MBA Super Tiger Cub 440	J. A. Robinson
	G-MJUH	MBA Tiger Cub 440	J. E. Johnes
	G-MJUI	Flexiform Striker	L. M. & R. E. Bailey
	G-MJUJ	Eipper Quicksilver MX II	P. J. McEvoy
	G-MJUK	Eipper Quicksilver MX II	J. C. M. Haigh
	G-MJUL	Southdown Puma Sprint	S. M. Cook
	G-MJUM	Flexiform Striker	M. J. W. Holding
	G-MJUN	Hiway Skytrike	A. Donohue
	G-MJUO	Eipper Quicksilver MX II	Border Aviation Ltd
	G-MJUP	Weedhopper B	R. A. P. Cox
	G-MJUR	Skyrider Airsports Phantom	J. Hannibal
	G-MJUS	MBA Tiger Cub 440	B. Jenks
	G-MJUT	Eurowing Goldwing	D. L. Eite
	G-MJUU	Eurowing Goldwing	B. Brown
	G-MJUV	Huntair Pathfinder	B. E. Francis
	G-MJUW	MBA Tiger Cub 440	H. F. Robertson & R. J. Anderson
	G-MJUX	Skyrider Airsports Phantom	C. M. Tomkins
	G-MJUY	Eurowing Goldwing	J. E. M. Barnatt-Millns
	G-MJUZ	Dragon Srs 150	J. R. Fairweather
	G-MJVA	Skyrider Airsports Phantom	Skyrider Airsports
	G-MJVB	Skyhook TR-2	Skyhook Sailwings Ltd
	G-MJVC	Hiway Skytrike	J. H. Stage
	G-MJVE	Hybred Skytrike	S. F. Carey
	G-MJVF	CFM Shadow	D. G. Cook
	G-MJVG	Hiway Skytrike	D. Bridges
	G-MJVH	American Aerolights Eagle	R. G. Glenister
	G-MJVI	Lightwing Rooster 1 Srs 4	J. M. Lee
	G-MJVJ	Flexiform Striker	Hornet Microlights
	G-MJVL	Flexiform Striker	H. Phipps
	G-MJVM	Dragon 150	A. Fairweather
	G-MJVN	Ultrasports Puma 440	O. R. Pluck
	G-MJVP	Eipper Quicksilver MX II	R. F. Witt
	G-MJVR	Flexiform Striker	S. J. Wistance
	G-MJVS	Hiway Super Scorpion	T. C. Harrold
	G-MJVT	Eipper Quicksilver MX	A. M. Reid
	G-MJVU	Eipper Quicksilver MX	B. J. Gordon
	G-MJVV	Hornet Supreme Dual	C. C. Watts
	G-MJVW	Airwave Nimrod	T. P. Mason
	G-MJVX	Skyrider Airsports Phantom	J. A. Grindley
	G-MJVY	Dragon Srs 150	M. J. Postlewaite
	G-MJVZ	Hiway Demon Tripacer	M. G. & M. L. Sadler
	G-MJWA	Birdman Cherokee	R. Jakeway
	G-MJWB	Eurowing Goldwing	R. A. Davies
	G-MJWC	Paraglide Fabric Self Inflating Wing	O. W. Neumark
	G-MJWD	Solar Wings Typhoon XL	I. Cummins
	G-MJWE	Hiway Demon	S. R. Loomes
	G-MJWF	MBA Tiger Cub 440	B. R. Hunter
	G-MJWG	MBA Tiger Cub 440	D. H. Carter
	G-MJWI	Flexiform Striker	R. W. Twamley
	G-MJWJ	MBA Tiger Cub 440	H. A. Bromiley
	G-MJWK	Huntair Pathfinder	M. R. Swaffield & J. E. Bogart
	G-MJWL	Chargus Vortex T250	Solar Wings Ltd
	G-MJWM	Chargus Vortex T250	Solar Wings Ltd

Reg.	Type	Owner or Operator	Notes
G-MJWN	Flexiform Striker	A. L. Flude	
G-MJWO	Hiway Skytrike	P. Wright	
G-MJWR	MBA Tiger Cub 440	M. G. &. M. W. Sadler	
G-MJWS	Eurowing Goldwing	J. W. Salter & R. J. Bell	
G-MJWT	American Aerolights Eagle	D. S. Baber	
G-MJWU	Maxair Hummer TX	J. Bagnall	
G-MJWV	Southdown Puma MS	D. E. Gwehih	
G-MJWW	MBA Super Tiger Cub 440	P. R. Colyer	
G-MJWX	Flexiform Striker	W. A. Bibby	
G-MJWY	Flexiform Striker	M. B. Horan	
G-MJWZ	Ultrasports Panther XL	T. V. Ward	
G-MJXA	Flexiform Striker	C. A. Palmer	
G-MJXB	Eurowing Goldwing	A. W. Odell	
G-MJXD	MBA Tiger Cub 440	W. L. Rogers	
G-MJXE	Hiway Demon	H. Sykes	
G-MJXF	MBA Tiger Cub 440	N. P. Day	
G-MJXG	Flexiform Striker	D. W. Barnes	
G-MJXH	Mitchell Wing B10	M. M. Ruck	
G-MJXI	Flexiform Striker	A. P. Pearson	
G-MJXJ	MBA Tiger Cub 440	J. L. E. Griffiths	
G-MJXL	MBA Tiger Cub 440	M. J. Lister	
G-MJXM	Hiway Skytrike	G. S. & P. W. G. Carter	
G-MJXN	American Aerolights Eagle	C. H. Middleton	
G-MJXO	Middleton CM.5	C. H. Middleton	
G-MJXR	Huntair Pathfinder II	J. F. H. James	
G-MJXS	Huntair Pathfinder II	A. E. Sawyer	
G-MJXT	Phoenix Falcon 1	Phoenix Aircraft Co	
G-MJXU	MBA Tiger Cub 440	Radio West Ltd	
G-MJXV	Flexiform Striker	E. T. Mapes	
G-MJXW	Southdown Sigma	C. J. Tansley	
G-MJXX	Flexiform Striker	R. T. Lancaster	
G-MJXY	Hiway Demon Skytrike	N. Jackson & A. Dring	
G-MJXZ	Hiway Demon	O. Wood	
G-MJYA	Huntair Pathfinder	Ultrasports Ltd	
G-MJYB	Eurowing Goldwing	D. A. Farnworth	
G-MJYC	Ultrasports Panther XL Dual 440	P. G. Woodcock	
G-MJYD	MBA Tiger Cub 440	R. Lumb	
G-MJYE	Southdown Lightning Trike	J. A. Hindley	
G-MJYF	Mainair Gemini Flash	E. R. Ellis	
G-MJYG	Skyhook Orion Canard	Skyhook Sailwings Ltd	
G-MJYI	Mainair Triflyer	R. A. Rawes	
G-MJYJ	MBA Tiger Cub 440	M. F. Collett	
G-MJYL	Airwave Nimrod	R. Bull	
G-MJYM	Southdown Puma Sprint	Breen Aviation Ltd	
G-MJYN	Mainair Triflyer 440	A. J. Girling	
G-MJYO	Mainair Triflyer 330	P. Best	
G-MJYP	Mainair Triflyer 440	Mainair Sports Ltd	
G-MJYR	Catto CP.16	M. Hindley	
G-MJYS	Southdown Puma Sprint	G. Breen	
G-MJYT	Southdown Puma Sprint	G. Breen	
G-MJYV	Mainair Triflyer 2 Seat	D. A. McFadyean	
G-MJYW	Wasp Gryphon III	P. D. Lawrence	
G-MJYX	Mainair Triflyer	R. K. Birlison	
G-MJYY	Hiway Demon	N. Smith	
G-MJYZ	Flexiform Striker	S. C. Beesley	
G-MJZA	MBA Tiger Cub	P. D. Annison	
G-MJZB	Flexiform Striker Dual	A. Faiers	
G-MJZC	MBA Tiger Cub 440	P. G. Walton	
G-MJZD	Mainair Gemini Flash	A. R. Gaivoto	
G-MJZE	MBA Tiger Cub 440	D. Ridley & ptnrs	
G-MJZF	La Mouette Atlas 16	W. R. Crew	
G-MJZG	Mainair Triflyer 440	K. C. Bennett	
G-MJZH	Southdown Lightning 195	P. H. Risdale	
G-MJZI	Eurowing Goldwing	A. J. Sharpe	
G-MJZJ	Hiway Cutlass Skytrike	G. D. H. Sandlin	
G-MJZK	Southdown Puma Sprint 440	K. B. Tolley	
G-MJZL	Eipper Quicksilver MX II	E. E. White	
G-MJZM	MBA Tiger Cub 440	F. M. Ward	
G-MJZN	Pterodactyl	C. J. Blundell	
G-MJZO	Flexiform Striker	M. G. Rawsthorne	
G-MJZP	MBA Tiger Cub 440	Herts & Cambs Biplanes Ltd	
G-MJZR	Eurowing Zephyr 1	I. M. Vass	
G-MJZS	MMT Scorpion	C. Mowat	
G-MJZT	Flexiform Striker	J. Whitehouse	

Notes	Reg.	Type	Owner or Operator
	G-MJZU	Flexiform Striker	G. J. Foard
	G-MJZV	Livesey Micro 5	D. M. Livesey
	G-MJZW	Eipper Quicksilver MX II	W. Smith & ptnrs
	G-MJZX	Maxair Hummer TX	R. J. Folwell
	G-MJZZ	Skyhook Cutlass	P. E. Penrose
	G-MMAC	Dragon Srs 150	R. W. Sage
	G-MMAE	Dragon Srs 150	I. Fleming
	G-MMAG	MBA Tiger Cub 440	W. R. Tull
	G-MMAH	Eipper Quicksilver MX II	J. C. Larkin
	G-MMAI	Dragon Srs 150	T. W. Dukes
	G-MMAJ	Mainair Tri-Flyer 440	D. A. Frank & M. J. Moon
	G-MMAK	MBA Tiger Cub 440	G. E. Heritage
	G-MMAL	Flexiform Striker Dual	D. J. Hand
	G-MMAM	MBA Tiger Cub 440	I. M. Bartlett
	G-MMAN	Flexiform Striker	E. Dean
	G-MMAO	Southdown Puma Sprint	R. A. Downham
	G-MMAP	Hummer TX	J. S. Millard
	G-MMAR	Southdown Puma Sprint MS	J. R. North
	G-MMAS	Southdown Sprint	Mainair Sports Ltd
	G-MMAT	Southdown Puma Sprint MS	Mainair Sports Ltd
	G-MMAU	Flexiform Rapier	R. Hemsworth
	G-MMAV	American Aerolights Eagle	Aeri-Visual Ltd
	G-MMAW	Mainair Rapier	T. Green
	G-MMAX	Flexiform Striker	G. P. Jones
	G-MMAY	Airwave Magic Nimrod	R. E. Patterson
	G-MMAZ	Southdown Puma Sprint	A. R. Smith
	G-MMBA	Hiway Super Scorpion	P. Dook
	G-MMBB	American Aerolights Eagle	M. R. Starling
	G-MMBC	Hiway Super Scorpion	A. T. Grain
	G-MMBD	Spectrum 330	J. Hollings
	G-MMBE	MBA Tiger Cub 440	R. J. B. Jordan & R. W. Pearce
	G-MMBF	American Aerolights Eagle	N. V. Middleton
	G-MMBG	Chargus Cyclone	P. N. Long
	G-MMBH	MBA Super Tiger Cub 440	C. H. Jennings & J. F. Howesman
	G-MMBJ	Solar Wings Typhoon	R. J. Ridgway
	G-MMBK	American Aerolights Eagle	B. M. Quinn
	G-MMBL	Southdown Puma	A. J. M. Berry
	G-MMBM	La Mouette Azure	A. Christian
	G-MMBN	Eurowing Goldwing	M. R. Grunwell
	G-MMBR	Hiway Demon 175	S. S. M. Turner
	G-MMBS	Flexiform Striker	P. Thompson
	G-MMBT	MBA Tiger Cub 440	F. F. Chamberlain
	G-MMBU	Eipper Quicksilver MX II	R. Barrow
	G-MMBV	Huntair Pathfinder	M. P. Phillippe
	G-MMBW	MBA Tiger Cub 440	J. C. Miles
	G-MMBX	MBA Tiger Cub 440	Fox Brothers Blackpool Ltd
	G-MMBY	Solar Wings Typhoon	R. M. Clarke
	G-MMCA	Solar Wings Storm	P. B. Currell
	G-MMCB	Huntair Pathfinder	S. Pizzey
	G-MMCC	American Aerolights Eagle	Microlight Aviation (UK) Ltd
	G-MMCD	Southdown Lightning DS	I. K. Wilson
	G-MMCE	MBA Tiger Cub 440	M. K. Dring
	G-MMCF	Solar Wings Panther 330	N. Birkin
	G-MMCG	Eipper Quicksilver MX I	R. W. Payne
	G-MMCH	Southdown Lightning Phase II	R. S. Andrew
	G-MMCI	Southdown Puma Sprint	D. M. Parsons
	G-MMCJ	Flexiform Striker	P. Hayes
	G-MMCK	Stewkie Aer-O-Ship LTA	K. Stewart
	G-MMCL	Stewkie Aer-O-Ship HAA	K. Stewart
	G-MMCM	Southdown Puma Sprint	J. G. Kane
	G-MMCN	Solar Wings Storm	A. P. S. Presland
	G-MMCO	Southdown Sprint	R. J. O. Walker
	G-MMCP	Southdown Lightning	J. McAlpine
	G-MMCR	Eipper Quicksilver MX	T. L. & B. L. Holland
	G-MMCS	Southdown Puma Sprint	R. G. Calvert
	G-MMCT	Hiway Demon	R. G. Gray
	G-MMCV	Solar Wings Typhoon III	G. W. Doswell
	G-MMCW	Southdown Puma Sprint	M. R. Wilson
	G-MMCX	MBA Super Tiger Cub 440	D. Harkin
	G-MMCY	Flexiform Striker	K. E. Preston
	G-MMCZ	Flexiform Striker	T. D. Adamson
	G-MMDA	Mitchell Wing B-10	H. F. French
	G-MMDB	La Mouette Atlas	K. A. Martin

Reg.	Type	Owner or Operator	Notes
G-MMDC	Eipper Quicksilver MXII	M. Risdale & C. Lamb	
G-MMDD	Huntair Pathfinder	M. R. Starling	
G-MMDE	Solar Wings Typhoon	D. E. Smith	
G-MMDF	Southdown Lightning Phase II	P. Kelly	
G-MMDG	Eurowing Goldwing	Edgim Ltd	
G-MMDH	Manta Fledge 2B	R. G. Hooker	
G-MMDI	Hiway Super Scorpion	R. E. Hodge	
G-MMDJ	Solar Wings Typhoon	D. Johnson	
G-MMDK	Flexiform Striker	P. D. Blyth	
G-MMDL	Dragon Srs 150	Dragon Light Aircraft Co Ltd	
G-MMDM	MBA Tiger Cub 440	D. Marsh	
G-MMDN	Flexiform Striker	M. G. Griffiths	
G-MMDO	Southdown Sprint	S. Stevens	
G-MMDP	Southdown Sprint	R. M. Strange	
G-MMDR	Huntair Pathfinder II	M. Shapland	
G-MMDS	Ultrasports Panther XLS	K. N. Dickinson	
G-MMDT	Flexiform Striker	A. Pauline	
G-MMDU	MBA Tiger Cub 440	P. Flynn	
G-MMDV	Ultrasports Panther	S. J. M. Morling	
G-MMDW	Pterodactyl Pfledgling	J. Fletcher	
G-MMDX	Solar Wings Typhoon	E. J. Lloyd	
G-MMDY	Southdown Puma Sprint	A. J. Perry	
G-MMDZ	Flexiform Dual Strike	D. C. Seager-Thomas	
G-MMEA	MBA Tiger Cub 440	Border Aviation Ltd	
G-MMEB	Hiway Super Scorpion	A. A. Ridgway	
G-MMEC	Southdown Puma DS	A. E. Wilson	
G-MMED	Aeolus Mk 1	Aeolus Aviation	
G-MMEE	American Aerolights Eagle	G. R. Bell & J. D. Bailey	
G-MMEF	Hiway Super Scorpion	J. H. Cooling	
G-MMEG	Eipper Quicksilver MX	W. K. Harris	
G-MMEH	Ultrasports Panther	P. A. Harris	
G-MMEI	Hiway Demon	W. H. Shakeshaft	
G-MMEJ	Flexiform Striker	R. A. Bates	
G-MMEK	Solar Wings Typhoon XL2	T. A. Baker	
G-MMEL	Solar Wings Typhoon XL2	D. Rigden	
G-MMEM	Solar Wings Typhoon XL2	Wyndham Wade Ltd	
G-MMEN	Solar Wings Typhoon XL2	I. M. Rapley	
G-MMEP	MBA Tiger Cub 440	P. M. Yeoman & D. Freestone-Barks	
G-MMES	Southdown Puma Sprint	B. J. Sanderson	
G-MMET	Skyhook Sabre TR-1 Mk II	A. B. Greenbank	
G-MMEU	MBS Tiger Cub 440	R. Taylor	
G-MMEV	American Aerolights Eagle	J. G. Jennings	
G-MMEW	MBA Tiger Cub 440	V. N. Baker	
G-MMEX	Solar Wings Sprint	E. Bayliss	
G-MMEY	MBA Tiger Cub 440	M. G. Selley	
G-MMEZ	Southdown Puma Sprint	Southdown Sailwings	
G-MMFB	Flexiform Striker	G. R. Wragg	
G-MMFC	Flexiform Striker	D. Haynes	
G-MMFD	Flexiform Striker	M. E. & W. L. Chapman	
G-MMFE	Flexiform Striker	J. Ljustina	
G-MMFF	Flexiform Striker	D. S. Simpson	
G-MMFG	Flexiform Striker	D. L. Aspinall	
G-MMFH	Flexiform Striker	Flexiform Sky Sails	
G-MMFI	Flexiform Striker	Viscount Lowther	
G-MMFJ	Flexiform Striker	A. W. Abraham	
G-MMFK	Flexiform Striker	S. W. England	
G-MMFL	Flexiform Striker	P. A. Windsor-Stevens	
G-MMFM	Piranha Srs 200	A. Howarth	
G-MMFN	MBA Tiger Cub 440	R. L. Barnett	
G-MMFP	MBA Tiger Cub 440	R. J. Adams	
G-MMFR	MBA Tiger Cub 440	R. J. Adams	
G-MMFS	MBA Tiger Cub 440	P. J. Hodgkinson	
G-MMFT	MBA Tiger Cub 440	E. Barfoot	
G-MMFV	Flexiform Dual Striker	R. A. Walton	
G-MMFW	Skyhook Cutlass	W. Chapel	
G-MMFX	MBA Tiger Cub 440	J. W. E. Romain	
G-MMFY	Flexiform Dual Striker	J. V. Meikle	
G-MMFZ	AES Sky Ranger	H. A. Ward	
G-MMGA	Bass Gosling	G. J. Bass	
G-MMGB	Southdown Puma Sprint	G. Breen	
G-MMGC	Southdown Puma Sprint	Innovative Air Services Ltd	
G-MMGD	Southdown Puma Sprint	I. Hughes	
G-MMGE	Hiway Super Scorpion	P. Gregory	
G-MMGF	MBA Tiger Cub 440	L. P. Durrant	

Notes	Reg.	Type	Owner or Operator
	G-MMGG	Southdown Puma	J. D. Penman
	G-MMGH	Flexiform Dual Striker	J. Whitehouse
	G-MMGI	Flexiform Dual Striker	M. Hurtley
	G-MMGJ	MBA Tiger Cub 440	J. Laidler
	G-MMGK	Skyhook Silhouette	N. E. Smith
	G-MMGL	MBA Tiger Cub 440	A. R. Cornelius
	G-MMGN	Southdown Puma Sprint	H. Stieker
	G-MMGO	MBA Tiger Cub 440	T. J. Court
	G-MMGP	Southdown Puma Sprint	R. Coar
	G-MMGR	Flexiform Dual Striker	E. J. Richards
	G-MMGS	Solar Wings Panther Dual	C. J. H. Weeks
	G-MMGT	Solar Wings Typhoon	J. A. Hunt
	G-MMGU	Flexiform Sealander	C. J. Meadows
	G-MMGV	Sorcerer MW.5 Srs A	Microknight Aviation Ltd
	G-MMGW	Sorcerer MW.5 Srs B	Microknight Aviation Ltd
	G-MMGX	Southdown Puma	G. S. Mitchell
	G-MMGY	Dean Piranha 1000	M. G. Dean
	G-MMGZ	Mitchell U2 Super Wing	R. A. Caudron
	G-MMHA	Skyhook TR-1 Pixie	Skyhook Sailwings Ltd
	G-MMHB	Skyhook TR-1 Pixie	Skyhook Sailwings Ltd
	G-MMHC	American Aerolights Eagle	G. Davies
	G-MMHD	Hiway Demon 175	F. L. Allatt
	G-MMHE	Southdown Puma Sprint MS	I. D. Baxter
	G-MMHF	Southdown Puma Sprint	B. R. Claughton
	G-MMHG	Solar Wings Storm	W. T. Price
	G-MMHH	Solar Wings Panther Dual	D. R. Beaumont
	G-MMHI	MBA Tiger Cub 440	R. W. Iddon
	G-MMHJ	Flexiform Hilander	A. N. Baggaley
	G-MMHK	Hiway Super Scorpion	R. Pearson
	G-MMHL	Hiway Super Scorpion	G. Ross
	G-MMHM	Goldmarque Gyr	G. J. Foard
	G-MMHN	MBA Tiger Cub 440	Gt Consall Copper Mines Co Ltd
	G-MMHO	MBA Tiger Cub 440	C. R. Perfect
	G-MMHP	Hiway Demon	P. Bedford
	G-MMHR	Southdown Puma Sprint DS	C. A. Eagles
	G-MMHS	SMD Viper	C. Scoble
	G-MMHT	Flexiform Striker	T. G. F. Trenchard
	G-MMHU	Flexiform Striker	P. R. Farnell
	G-MMHV	Chargus Vortex 120/T225	P. D. Larkin
	G-MMHW	Chargus Vortex 120/T225	P. D. Larkin
	G-MMHX	Hornet Invader 440	Hornet Microlights
	G-MMHY	Hornet Invader 440	W. Finlay
	G-MMHZ	Solar Wings Typhoon XL	S. J. Pain
	G-MMIA	Westwind Phoenix XP-3	Westwind Corporation Ltd
	G-MMIB	MEA Mistral	D. Hines
	G-MMIC	Luscombe Vitality	Luscombe Aircraft Ltd
	G-MMID	Flexiform Dual Striker	D. C. North
	G-MMIE	MBA Tiger Cub 440	M. L. Philpott
	G-MMIF	Wasp Gryphon	F. Coulson
	G-MMIG	MBA Tiger Cub 440	R. F. Witt
	G-MMIH	MBA Tiger Cub 440	W. A. Taylor
	G-MMII	Southdown Puma Sprint 440	T. C. Harrold
	G-MMIJ	Ultrasports Tripacer	R. W. Evans
	G-MMIK	Eipper Quicksilver MX II	Microlight Airsport Services Ltd
	G-MMIL	Eipper Quicksilver MX II	C. K. Brown
	G-MMIM	MBA Tiger Cub 440	D. A. Small
	G-MMIN	Luscombe Vitality	Luscombe Aircraft Ltd
	G-MMIO	Huntair Pathfinder II	C. Slater
	G-MMIP	Hiway Vulcan	A. A. Cale
	G-MMIR	Mainair Tri-Flyer 440	F. A. Prescott
	G-MMIS	Hiway Demon	M. P. Wing
	G-MMIT	Hiway Demon	D. M. Lyall
	G-MMIU	Southdown Puma Sprint	P. J. Bullock
	G-MMIV	Southdown Puma Sprint	J. S. Walton
	G-MMIW	Southdown Puma Sprint	A. Twedell
	G-MMIX	MBA Tiger Cub 440	M. J. Butler & C. Bell
	G-MMIY	Eurowing Goldwing	R. J. Wood
	G-MMIZ	Southdown Lightning II	G. A. Martin
	G-MMJA	Mitchell Wing B.10	J. Abbott
	G-MMJC	Southdown Sprint	P. G. Marshall
	G-MMJD	Southdown Puma Sprint	N. G. Tibbenham
	G-MMJE	Southdown Puma Sprint	F. N. M. Sergeant
	G-MMJF	Ultrasports Panther Dual 440	D. H. Stokes
	G-MMJG	Mainair Tri-Flyer 440	A. R. Rhodes

Reg.	Type	Owner or Operator	Notes
G-MMJH	Southdown Puma Sprint	A. R. Lawrence & T. J. Weston	
G-MMJI	Southdown Puma Sprint	W. H. J. Knowles	
G-MMJJ	Solar Wings Typhoon	R. J. Wood	
G-MMJK	Hiway Demon	J. B. C. Brown & M. L. Jones	
G-MMJL	Flexiform 1+1 Sealander	R. Whitby	
G-MMJM	Southdown Puma Sprint	R. J. Sanger	
G-MMJN	Eipper Quicksilver MX II	R. M. Gunn	
G-MMJO	MBA Tiger Cub 440	R. J. Adams	
G-MMJP	Southdown Lightning II	A. Slaghekke	
G-MMJR	MBA Tiger Cub 440	J. F. Ratcliffe	
G-MMJS	MBA Tiger Cub	Woodgate Air Services Ltd	
G-MMJT	Southdown Puma Sprint MS	G. E. Jewitt	
G-MMJU	Hiway Demon	D. Whiteside	
G-MMJV	MBA Tiger Cub 440	K. Bannister	
G-MMJW	Southdown Puma Sprint	C. L. S. Boswell	
G-MMJX	Teman Mono-Fly	B. F. J. Hope	
G-MMJY	MBA Tiger Cub 440	Peterson Clarke Sports Ltd	
G-MMJZ	Skyhook Pixie	P. J. McNamee	
G-MMKA	Ultrasports Panther Dual	R. S. Wood	
G-MMKB	Ultralight Flight Mirage II	K. G. Wigley	
G-MMKC	Southdown Puma Sprint MS	J. Potts	
G-MMKD	Southdown Puma Sprint	L. W. Cload	
G-MMKE	Birdman Chinook WT-11	C. R. Gale & D. J. Royce	
G-MMKF	Ultrasports Panther Dual 440	G. H. Cork	
G-MMKG	Solar Wings Typhoon XL	P. G. Valentine	
G-MMKH	Solar Wings Typhoon XL	D. E. Home & M. Baylis	
G-MMKI	Ultasports Panther 330	Lightflight Aviation	
G-MMKJ	Ultrasports Panther 330	P. Kinsella	
G-MMKK	Mainair Flash	J. R. Brabbs	
G-MMKL	Mainair Flash	Mainair Sports Ltd	
G-MMKM	Flexiform Dual Striker	M. R. Starling	
G-MMKN	Mitchell Wing B-10	R. A. Rumney	
G-MMKO	Southdown Puma Sprint	G. Breen	
G-MMKP	MBA Tiger Cub 440	A. L. Burton	
G-MMKR	Southdown Lightning DS	R. I. Lowe	
G-MMKS	Southdown Lightning 195	B. J. Marshall	
G-MMKT	MBA Tiger Cub 440	K. N. Townsend	
G-MMKU	Southdown Puma Sprint MS	G. J. Latham & R. A. Morris	
G-MMKV	Southdown Puma Sprint	J. Walsom	
G-MMKW	Solar Wings Storm	P. M. & R. Dewhurst	
G-MMKY	Jordan Duet	C. H. Smith	
G-MMKZ	Ultrasports Puma 440	M. G. Edwards	
G-MMLA	American Aerolights Eagle	Ardenco Ltd	
G-MMLB	MBA Tiger Cub 440	C. D. Denham	
G-MMLC	Scaled Composites 97M	Group Lotus Car Co Ltd	
G-MMLD	Solar Wings Typhoon S	N. P. Moran	
G-MMLE	Eurowing Goldwing SP	D. Lamberty	
G-MMLF	MBA Tiger Cub 440	J. R. Chichester-Constable	
G-MMLG	Solar Wings Typhoon S4 XL	M. G. Welsh	
G-MMLH	Hiway Demon	P. M. Hendry & D. J. Lukery	
G-MMLI	Solar Wings Typhoon S	J. D. Grey	
G-MMLJ	—		
G-MMLK	MBA Tiger Cub 440	P. Flynn	
G-MMLL	Midland Ultralights Sirocco	Midland Ultralights Ltd	
G-MMLM	MBA Tiger Cub 440	L. M. Campbell	
G-MMLN	Skyhook Pixie	P. G. G. Taylor	
G-MMLO	Skyhook Pixie	T. G. Hilton	
G-MMLP	Southdown Sprint	Aactron Equipment Co Ltd	
G-MMLR	Ultrasports Panther 330	Lightflight Aviation	
G-MMLU	—		
G-MMLV	Southdown Puma 330	P. K. Dean	
G-MMLW	—		
G-MMLX	Ultrasports Panther	R. Almond	
G-MMLY	—		
G-MMLZ	Mainair Tri-Flyer	A. Farnworth	
G-MMMA	Flexiform Dual Striker	N. P. Heap	
G-MMMB	Mainair Tri-Flyer	D. M. Rusbridge	
G-MMMC	Southdown Puma SS	M. E. Hollis	
G-MMMD	Flexiform Dual Striker	K. P. Southwell & ptnr	
G-MMME	American Aerolights Eagle	G. Davies	
G-MMMF	American Aerolights Eagle	Aeronautical Logistics Ltd	
G-MMMG	Eipper Quicksilver MXL	W. Murphy	
G-MMMH	Hadland Willow	M. J. Hadland	
G-MMMI	Southdown Lightning	J. N. Whelan	

Notes	Reg.	Type	Owner or Operator
	G-MMMJ	Southdown Sprint	R. R. Wolfenden
	G-MMMK	Hornet Invader	R. R. Wolfenden
	G-MMML	Dragon 150	R. G. Huntley
	G-MMMN	Ultrasports Panther Dual 440	T. L. Travis
	G-MMMO	Solar Wings Typhoon	B. R. Underwood
	G-MMMP	Flexiform Dual Striker	K. P. Southwell
	G-MMMR	Flexiform Striker	M. A. Rigler
	G-MMMS	MBA Tiger Cub 440	M. H. D. Soltau
	G-MMMT	Hornet Sigma	R. Nay
	G-MMMU	Skyhook Cutlass CD	F. J. Lightburn
	G-MMMV	Skyhook Cutlass Dual	R. R. Wolfenden
	G-MMMW	Flexiform Striker	K. & M. Spedding
	G-MMMX	Hornet Nimrod	R. Patrick
	G-MMMY	Hornet Nimrod	Bradford Motorcycle Ltd
	G-MMMZ	Southdown Puma Sprint MS	J. S. Potts
	G-MMNA	Eipper Quicksilver MX II	R. W. Payne
	G-MMNB	Eipper Quicksilver MX	N. J. Williams
	G-MMNC	Eipper Quicksilver MX	K. R. Daly
	G-MMND	Eipper Quicksilver MX II-Q2	J. E. Holloway
	G-MMNF	Hornet	C. Hudson
	G-MMNG	Solar Wings Typhoon XL	R. Simpson
	G-MMNH	Dragon 150	H. & P. Neil Ltd
	G-MMNI	Solar Wings Typhoon S	S. Galley
	G-MMNJ	Hiway Skytrike	A. Helliwell
	G-MMNK	Solar Wings Typhoon S4	P. Jackson
	G-MMNL	Solar Wings Typhoon S4	P. Jackson
	G-MMNM	Hornet 330	J. M. Elvy
	G-MMNN	Buzzard	E. W. Sherry
	G-MMNO	American Aerolights Eagle	P. J. Pentreath
	G-MMNP	Ultrasports Panther 250	R. Richardson
	G-MMNR	Dove	A. D. Wright
	G-MMNS	Mitchell U-2 Super Wing	D. J. Baldwin
	G-MMNT	Flexiform Striker	D. G. Chambers
	G-MMNU	Ultrasports Panther	S. J. Baker
	G-MMNV	Weedhopper	N. L. Rice
	G-MMNW	Mainair Tri-Flyer 330	T. Jackson
	G-MMNX	Solar Wings Panther XL	B. Montsern
	G-MMNY	Skyhook TR-1	N. H. Morley
	G-MMNZ	—	—
	G-MMOA	—	—
	G-MMOB	Southdown Sprint	N. J. Ackers
	G-MMOC	Huntair Pathfinder II	E. H. Gould
	G-MMOD	MBA Tiger Cub 440	G. W. de Lancey Aitchison
	G-MMOE	Mitchell Wing B-10	T. Boyd
	G-MMOF	MBA Tiger Cub 440	Sunderland Microlights
	G-MMOG	Huntair Pathfinder	R. G. Maguire
	G-MMOH	Solar Wings Typhoon XL	T. H. Scott
	G-MMOI	MBA Tiger Cub 440	J. S. Smith & P. R. Talbot
	G-MMOJ	—	—
	G-MMOK	Solar Wings Panther XL	R. F. Foster
	G-MMOL	Skycraft Scout R3	P. D. G. Weller
	G-MMOM	Flexiform Striker	D. Haynes
	G-MMON	Microflight Monarch	Microflight
	G-MMOO	Southdown Storm	S. Hudson
	G-MMOP	Solar Wings Panther Dual 440	J. Murphy
	G-MMOR	American Aerolights Eagle Cuyana	Southwest Air Sports Ltd
	G-MMOT	Solar Wings Typhoon XL	R. E. D. Bailey
	G-MMOU	American Aerolights Eagle	T. Crispin
	G-MMOV	Mainair Gemini Flash	R. C. Coles
	G-MMOW	Mainair Gemini Flash	T. Rankin
	G-MMOX	Mainair Gemini Flash	K. Handley
	G-MMOY	Mainair Gemini Sprint	Mainair Sports Ltd
	G-MMPB	Solar Wings Typhoon S	P. T. F. Bowden
	G-MMPC	Skyhook TR-1	J. S. Garvey
	G-MMPD	Mainair Tri-Flyer	A. R. J. Dorling
	G-MMPE	Eurowing Goldwing	J. Cuff
	G-MMPF	Eurowing Goldwing	J. Cuff
	G-MMPG	Southdown Puma	N. E. Asplin
	G-MMPH	Southdown Puma Sprint	M. T. Hill
	G-MMPI	Pterodactyl Ptraveller	Goodwins of Hanley Ltd
	G-MMPJ	Mainair Tri-Flyer 440	H. L. Pye
	G-MMPK	Solar Wings Typhoon 1	P. J. D. Kerr
	G-MMPL	Flexiform Dual Striker	P. D. Lawrence

Reg.	Type	Owner or Operator	Notes
G-MMPM	Ultrasports Puma 330	C. G. Veitch	
G-MMPN	Chargus T250	S. M. Powrie	
G-MMPO	Mainair Gemini Flash	H. B. Baker	
G-MMPP	ParaPlane	GQ Defence Equipment Ltd	
G-MMPR	Dragon 150	P. N. B. Rosenfeld	
G-MMPS	American Aerolights Eagle	J. M. Tingle	
G-MMPT	SMD Gazelle	E. C. Poole	
G-MMPU	Ultrasports Tripacer 250	A. P. Skipper	
G-MMPV	MBA Tiger Cub 440	R. Felton	
G-MMPW	Airwave Nimrod	D. A. Smith	
G-MMPX	Ultrasports Panther Dual 440	M. T. Jones	
G-MMPY	Solar Wings Typhoon	A. W. Read	
G-MMPZ	Teman Mono-Fly	J. W. Highton	
G-MMRA	Mainair Tri-Flyer 250	S. R. Criddle	
G-MMRB	Hiway Skytrike 250	E. Garbutt	
G-MMRC	Southdown Lightning	R. T. Curant	
G-MMRD	Skyhook Cutlass CD	B. Barry	
G-MMRE	Maxair Hummer	N. P. Thompson	
G-MMRF	MBA Tiger Cub 440	R. Gardner	
G-MMRG	Eipper Quicksilver MX	L. P. Diede	
G-MMRH	Hiway Demon	J. S. McCaig	
G-MMRI	Skyhook Sabre	G. M. Wrigley	
G-MMRJ	Solar Wings Panther XL	D. T. James	
G-MMRK	Ultrasports Panther XL	Enstone Microlight Centre	
G-MMRL	Solar Wings Panther XL	C. Smith	
G-MMRM	—	—	
G-MMRN	Southdown Puma Sprint	C. F. Bloyce	
G-MMRO	Mainair Gemini 440	P. Power	
G-MMRP	Mainair Gemini	M. A. Pugh	
G-MMRR	Southdown Panther 250	D. D. & A. R. Young	
G-MMRS	Dragon 150	R. H. W. Strange	
G-MMRT	Southdown Puma Sprint	V. Brierley	
G-MMRU	Tirith Firebird FB-2	Tirith Microplane Ltd	
G-MMRV	MBA Tiger Cub 440	C. J. R. V. Baker	
G-MMRW	Flexiform Dual Striker	M. D. Hinge	
G-MMRX	Willmot J.W.1	N. J. Willmot	
G-MMRY	Chargus T.250	D. L. Edwards 1/8 ptnrs	
G-MMRZ	Ultrasports Panther Dual 440	Lancaster Partners (Holdings) Ltd	
G-MMSA	Ultrasports Panther XL	D. W. Taylor	
G-MMSB	Huntair Pathfinder II	S. R. Baugh	
G-MMSC	Mainair Gemini	A. B. Jones	
G-MMSD	—	—	
G-MMSE	Eipper Quicksilver MX	S. Bateman	
G-MMSF	—	—	
G-MMSG	Solar Wings Typhoon XL	R. Simpson	
G-MMSH	Solar Wings Panther XL	C. Stallard	
G-MMSI	ParaPlane	International Fund for Animal Welfare	
G-MMSJ	ParaPlane	International Fund for Animal Welfare	
G-MMSK	—	—	
G-MMSL	Ultrasports Panther XLS	G. J. Slater	
G-MMSM	Mainair Gemini Flash	C. J. Sanson	
G-MMSN	Mainair Gemini	P. M. Feasey	
G-MMSO	Mainair Tri-Flyer 440	D. Morley	
G-MMSP	Mainair Gemini Flash	D. Medley	
G-MMSR	MBA Tiger Cub 440	G. Quarendon	
G-MMSS	Solar Wings Panther 330	S. J. Baker	
G-MMST	Southdown Puma Sprint	I. Davis	
G-MMSU	American Aerolights Eagle B	C. Bilham	
G-MMSV	Southdown Puma Sprint	A. P. Trumper	
G-MMSW	MBA Tiger Cub 440	D. R. Hemmings	
G-MMSX	Ultrasports Panther	M. J. Linford	
G-MMSY	Ultrasports Panther	R. W. Davies	
G-MMSZ	Medway Half Pint	Lancaster Partners (Holdings) Ltd	
G-MMTA	Ultrasports Panther XL	J. W. Wall	
G-MMTB	—	—	
G-MMTC	Ultrasports Panther Dual	J. M. Butler	
G-MMTD	Mainair Tri-Flyer 330	E. I. Armstrong	
G-MMTE	Mainair Gemini	B. F. Crick	
G-MMTF	Southdown Puma Sprint	P. J. K. Scriven	
G-MMTG	Mainair Gemini	R. P. W. Johnstone	
G-MMTH	Southdown Puma Sprint	R. G. Tomlinson	
G-MMTI	Southdown Puma Sprint	M. A. Baldwin	
G-MMTJ	Southdown Puma Sprint	M. R. Pearce	
G-MMTK	Medway Hybred	J. F. Nicholls	

Notes	Reg.	Type	Owner or Operator
	G-MMTL	Mainair Gemini	M. R. Bailey
	G-MMTM	Mainair Tri-Flyer 440	Medi-Cine Productions Ltd
	G-MMTN	Hiway Skytrike	A. J. Blake
	G-MMTO	Mainair Tri-Flyer	R. G. Swales
	G-MMTP	Eurowing Goldwing	T. Crispin
	G-MMTR	Ultrasports Panther	R. A. Youngs
	G-MMTS	Solar Wings Panther XL	J. D. Webb
	G-MMTT	Ultrasports Panther XL	W. Levinson
	G-MMTU	Flylite Super Scout	M. C. Drew
	G-MMTV	American Aerolights Eagle	P. J. Scott
	G-MMTW	American Aerolights Eagle	K. R. Gillett
	G-MMTX	Mainair Gemini 440	R. L. Mann
	G-MMTY	Fisher FP.202U	B. E. Maggs
	G-MMTZ	Eurowing Goldwing	R. K. Young
	G-MMUA	Southdown Puma Sprint	J. T. Houghton
	G-MMUB	Ultrasports Tripacer 250	P. G. Thompson
	G-MMUC	Mainair Gemini 440	R. E. D. Bailey
	G-MMUD	Willmot Junior Cub	N. J. Willmot
	G-MMUE	Mainair Gemini Flash	Motor Services (Manchester) Ltd
	G-MMUF	Mainair Gemini	C. J. Ellison
	G-MMUG	Mainair Tri-Flyer	P. A. Leach
	G-MMUH	Mainair Tri-Flyer	J. P. Nicklin
	G-MMUI	—	—
	G-MMUJ	Southdown Puma Sprint 440	T. A. Hinton
	G-MMUK	Mainair Tri-Flyer	B. R. Kirk
	G-MMUL	Ward Elf E.47	M. Ward
	G-MMUM	MBA Tiger Cub 440	N. C. Butcher
	G-MMUN	Ultrasports Panther Dual XL	K. S. Smith
	G-MMUO	Mainair Gemini Flash	Cloudbase
	G-MMUP	Airwave Nimrod 140	R. J. Bickham
	G-MMUR	Hiway Skytrike 250	W. J. Clayton
	G-MMUS	Mainair Gemini	R. M. Findlay
	G-MMUT	Mainair Tri-Flyer 440	A. Anderson
	G-MMUU	ParaPlane PM-1	Colt Balloons Ltd
	G-MMUV	Southdown Puma Sprint	D. C. Read
	G-MMUW	Mainair Gemini Flash	J. C. K. Scardifield
	G-MMUX	Mainair Gemini	S. E. Dollery
	G-MMUY	Mainair Gemini Flash	K. A. Fagan
	G-MMUZ	American Aerolights Eagle	A. C. Lowings
	G-MMVA	Southdown Puma Sprint	P. Johnson
	G-MMVB	Skyhook Pixie	G. A. Breen
	G-MMVC	Ultrasports Panther XL	E. R. Holton
	G-MMVE	—	—
	G-MMVF	Ultrasports Panther XL	Microlight Tuition & Sales Ltd
	G-MMVG	MBA Tiger Cub 440	C. W. Grant
	G-MMVH	Southdown Raven	A. Reynolds
	G-MMVI	Southdown Puma Sprint	Enstone Microlight Centre
	G-MMVJ	Southdown Puma Sprint	S. L. Robbins
	G-MMVK	Sigh Wing ParaPlane	M. T. Byrne
	G-MMVL	Ultrasports Panther XL-S	B. Milton
	G-MMVM	Whiteley Orion 1	P. N. Whiteley
	G-MMVN	Solar Wings Typhoon	D. C. Davies
	G-MMVO	Southdown Puma Sprint	A. M. Shepherd & F. Brownshill
	G-MMVP	Mainair Gemini Flash	G. P. Shepherd
	G-MMVR	Hiway Skytrike 1	F. Naylor
	G-MMVS	Skyhook Pixie	G. Bilham
	G-MMVT	Mainair Gemini Flash	Aircraft Microlight Services
	G-MMVU	Mainair Gemini Flash	R. Wheeler
	G-MMVW	Skyhook Pixie	R. Keighley
	G-MMVX	Southdown Puma Sprint	D. J. Reynolds
	G-MMVY	American Aerolights Eagle	R. Savva
	G-MMVZ	Southdown Puma Sprint	M. R. Bayliss
	G-MMWA	Mainair Gemini Flash	K. Akister
	G-MMWB	Huntair Pathfinder II	Brinhan Ltd
	G-MMWC	Eipper Quicksilver MXII	P. W. Cole & L. R. Mudge
	G-MMWE	Hiway Skytrike 250	R. Bailey
	G-MMWF	Hiway Skytrike 250	J. R. Du Plessis
	G-MMWG	Greenslade Mono-Trike	P. G. Greenslade
	G-MMWH	Southdown Puma Sprint 440	G. Nightingale
	G-MMWI	Southdown Lightning	C. A. Crick
	G-MMWJ	Pterodactyl Ptraveler	P. Careless
	G-MMWK	Hiway Demon	L. Bennett
	G-MMWL	Eurowing Goldwing	D. J. White
	G-MMWM	—	—

Reg.	Type	Owner or Operator	Notes
G-MMWN	Ultrasports Tripacer	I. M. Wilsher	
G-MMWO	Ultrasports Panther XL	P. F. J. Rogers	
G-MMWP	American Aerolights Eagle	C. E. Tait	
G-MMWR	—	—	
G-MMWS	Mainair Tri-Flyer	S. E. Huxtable	
G-MMWT	CFM Shadow	K. H. Abel	
G-MMWU	Ultrasports Tripacer 250	J. A. Clare	
G-MMWV	Flight Research Nomad 425F	R. J. B. S. Escott	
G-MMWX	Southdown Puma Sprint	D. O. Lewis & ptnrs	
G-MMWY	Skyhook Pixie	N. M. Cuthbertson	
G-MMWZ	Southdown Puma Sprint	C. G. Hoy	
G-MMXA	Mainair Gemini Flash	J. W. Broadhead	
G-MMXB	—	—	
G-MMXC	Mainair Gemini Flash	Aircraft Microlight Services	
G-MMXD	Mainair Gemini Flash	Aircraft Microlight Services	
G-MMXE	Mainair Gemini Flash	Aircraft Microlight Services	
G-MMXF	Mainair Gemini Flash	D. Hughes	
G-MMXG	Mainair Gemini Flash	Allied Electrical	
G-MMXH	Mainair Gemini Flash	M. J. Starling	
G-MMXI	Horizon Prototype	Horizon Aerosails Ltd	
G-MMXJ	Mainair Gemini Flash	R. Meredith-Hardy	
G-MMXK	Mainair Gemini Flash	N. S. Brown	
G-MMXL	Mainair Gemini Flash	S. M. Cawthra	
G-MMXM	Mainair Gemini Flash	R. Perrett	
G-MMXN	Southdown Puma Sprint	R. J. Grainger	
G-MMXO	Southdown Puma Sprint	D. J. Tasker	
G-MMXP	Southdown Puma Sprint	D. M. Humphreys	
G-MMXR	Southdown Puma DS	J. S. Freestone	
G-MMXS	Southdown Puma Sprint	G. Breen	
G-MMXT	Mainair Gemini Flash	S. J. Basey-Fisher	
G-MMXU	Mainair Gemini Flash	T. J. Franklin	
G-MMXV	Mainair Gemini Flash	A. V. Szolin	
G-MMXW	Mainair Gemini	A. Hodgson	
G-MMXX	Mainair Gemini	S. & S. Warburton-Pitt	
G-MMXY	—	—	
G-MMXZ	Eipper Quicksilver MXII	Mangreen Holdings Ltd	
G-MMYA	Solar Wings Pegasus XL	Solar Wings Ltd	
G-MMYB	Solar Wings Pegasus XL	Solar Wings Ltd	
G-MMYC	Gryphon Cheetah	B. C. Norris	
G-MMYD	CFM Shadow Srs B	CFM Metal-Fax Ltd	
G-MMYE	—	—	
G-MMYF	Southdown Puma Sprint	D. O. Crane	
G-MMYG	—	—	
G-MMYH	—	—	
G-MMYI	Southdown Puma Sprint	L. A. J. Parren	
G-MMYJ	Southdown Puma Sprint	C. A. Crick	
G-MMYK	Southdown Puma Sprint	I. Hawes	
G-MMYL	Cyclone 70	J. T. Halford	
G-MMYM	—	—	
G-MMYN	Ultrasports Panther XL	G. M. R. Walters & H. Clarke	
G-MMYO	Southdown Puma Sprint	K. J. Taylor	
G-MMYP	—	—	
G-MMYR	Eipper Quicksilver MXII	M. Reed	
G-MMYS	Southdown Puma Sprint	Enstone Microlight Centre	
G-MMYT	Southdown Puma Sprint	I. A. Stamp & T. P. Daniels	
G-MMYU	Southdown Puma Sprint	I. Parr	
G-MMYV	Webb Trike	A. P. Fenn	
G-MMYW	Hiway Demon 115	J. Mayer	
G-MMYX	Mitchell U-2	R. A. Codling	
G-MMYY	Southdown Puma Sprint	J. C. & A. M. Rose	
G-MMYZ	Southdown Puma Sprint	N. Crisp	
G-MMZA	Mainair Gemini Flash	G. W. Peacock	
G-MMZB	Mainair Gemini Flash	R. A. Guntrip	
G-MMZC	Mainair Gemini Flash	G. T. Johnston	
G-MMZD	Mainair Gemini Flash	R. Clegg	
G-MMZE	Mainair Gemini Flash	S. Saul	
G-MMZF	Mainair Gemini Flash	W. Myers	
G-MMZG	Ultrasports Panther XL-S	G. D. Fogg	
G-MMZH	Ultrasports Tripacer	R. Bacon	
G-MMZI	Medway 130SX	P. M. Lang	
G-MMZJ	Mainair Gemini Flash	D. J. Griffiths	
G-MMZK	Mainair Gemini Flash	J. D. O. Gill	
G-MMZL	Mainair Gemini Flash	P. R. Sexton	
G-MMZM	Mainair Gemini Flash	J. D. Hall	

Notes	Reg.	Type	Owner or Operator
	G-MMZN	Mainair Gemini Flash	A. J. Cooper
	G-MMZO	Microflight Spectrum	Microflight Aircraft Ltd
	G-MMZP	Ultrasports Panther XL	H. Phipps
	G-MMZR	Southdown Puea Sprint	P. M. & R. Dewhurst
	G-MMZS	Eipper Quicksilver MX1	N. W. O'Brien
	G-MMZT	Ultrasports Tripacer	J. Bell
	G-MMZU	Southdown Puma DS	E. Clark
	G-MMZV	Mainair Gemini Flash	J. F. Bishop
	G-MMZW	Southdown Puma Sprint	T. & M. Bowyer
	G-MMZX	Southdown Puma Sprint	T. A. Saunderson
	G-MMZY	Ultrasports Tripacer 330	B. Lomax
	G-MMZZ	Maxair Hummer	Microflight Ltd
	G-MNAA	Striplin Sky Ranger	Ingleby Microlight Flying Club
	G-MNAB	Ultrasports Panther XL	Scottish Microlights
	G-MNAC	Mainair Gemini Flash	D. Holliday
	G-MNAD	Mainair Gemini Flash	P. G. Moore
	G-MNAE	Mainair Gemini Flash	P. Henry
	G-MNAF	Solar Wings Panther XL	A. C. Gordon
	G-MNAG	Hiway Skytrike 1	R. J. Grogan
	G-MNAH	Solar Wings Panther XL	P. W. Miller & K. D. Calvert
	G-MNAI	Ultrasports Panther XL-S	J. C. Johnson
	G-MNAJ	Solar Wings Panther XL-S	C. Laverty
	G-MNAK	Solar Wings Panther XL-S	Windsports Centre Ltd
	G-MNAL	MBA Tiger Cub 440	Ace Aero Ltd
	G-MNAM	Solar Wings Panther XL-S	A. Seymour
	G-MNAN	Solar Wings Panther XL-S	B. Clough
	G-MNAO	Solar Wings Panther XL-S	A. H. Richardson
	G-MNAP	—	
	G-MNAR	Solar Wings Panther XL-S	B. Curtis
	G-MNAS	Solar Wings Pegasus XL-R	N. S. Payne
	G-MNAT	—	—
	G-MNAU	Solar Wings Pegasus XL-R	D. Corke
	G-MNAV	Southdown Puma Sprint	M. Ward
	G-MNAW	Solar Wings Pegasus XL-R	A. W. Kowles
	G-MNAX	Solar Wings Pegasus XL-R	D. R. Gazey
	G-MNAY	Ultrasports Panther XL-S	N. Baumber
	G-MNAZ	Solar Wings Pegasus XL-R	D. Rogers
	G-MNBA	Solar Wings Pegasus XL-R	S. F. Buckingham-Smart
	G-MNBB	Solar Wings Pegasus XL-R	M. Sims
	G-MNBC	Solar Wings Pegasus XL-R	M. N. Hudson
	G-MNBD	Mainair Gemini Flash	G. J. & G. G. Norris
	G-MNBE	Southdown Puma Sprint	J. P. Bleakley & J. M. Travers
	G-MNBF	Mainair Gemini Flash	J. C. Duncan
	G-MNBG	Mainair Gemini Flash	D. A. Riggs & A. B. Shepherd
	G-MNBH	Southdown Puma Sprint	J. H. Button
	G-MNBI	Ultrasports Panther XL	Microflight Tuition & Sales Ltd
	G-MNBJ	Skyhook Pixie	G. M. Mansfield
	G-MNBK	Hiway Skytrike	J. D. Swinbank
	G-MNBL	American Aerolights Z Eagle	J. H. Telford
	G-MNBM	Southdown Puma Sprint	M. W. Hurst
	G-MNBN	Mainair Gemini Flash	D. Adams
	G-MNBP	Mainair Gemini Flash	L. R. H. D'eath
	G-MNBR	Mainair Gemini Flash	M. R. Haines
	G-MNBS	Mainair Gemini Flash	J. G. Crawford
	G-MNBT	Mainair Gemini Flash	H. Grindred & K. Wedl
	G-MNBU	Mainair Gemini Flash	K. L. Turner
	G-MNBV	Mainair Gemini Flash	R. D. Chiles
	G-MNBW	Mainair Gemini Flash	J. A. C. Terry
	G-MNBX	—	
	G-MNBY	Mainair Gemini	G. Popplewell
	G-MNBZ	Medway Half Pint	C. J. Draper
	G-MNCA	Adams Trike	D. Adams
	G-MNCB	Mainair Gemini Flash	K. B. O'Regan
	G-MNCC	Mainair Gemini	P. Browne
	G-MNCD	Harmsworth Trike	A. D. Cranfield
	G-MNCE	Skyhook Pixie	C. F. Corke
	G-MNCF	Mainair Gemini Flash	M. Greene
	G-MNCG	Mainair Gemini Flash	J. K. Cross
	G-MNCH	Lancashire Micro Trike 330	C. F. Horsall
	G-MNCI	Southdown Puma Sprint	D. S. Anker
	G-MNCJ	Mainair Gemini Flash	J. M. & P. J. Bridge
	G-MNCK	Southdown Puma Sprint	D. J. Gibbs
	G-MNCL	Southdown Puma Sprint	N. M. Lassman

Reg.	Type	Owner or Operator	Notes
G-MNCM	CFM Shadow Srs B	P. B. Merritt	
G-MNCN	Hiway Skytrike 250	N. J. Clemens	
G-MNCO	Eipper Quicksilver MXII	S. Lawton	
G-MNCP	Southdown Puma Sprint	J. G. Sealey	
G-MNCR	Flexiform Striker	I. M. Stamp	
G-MNCS	Skyrider Airsports	E. A. Matty	
G-MNCT	—	—	
G-MNCU	Medway Hybred	K. L. Fenn	
G-MNCV	Medway Typhoon XL	M. Pryke	
G-MNCW	Hornet Dual Trainer	D. L. Bowtell & J. B. Harper	
G-MNCX	Mainair Gemini Flash	Oban Divers Ltd	
G-MNCY	Skyhook Pixie	B. F. Johnson	
G-MNCZ	Solar Wings Pegasus XL-T	Solar Wings Ltd	
G-MNDA	Thruster TST	Thruster Aircraft (UK) Ltd	
G-MNDB	Southdown Puma Sprint	J. C. Neale	
G-MNDC	Mainair Gemini Flash	P. J. Hepburn	
G-MNDD	Mainair Scorcher Solo	J. Cunliffe	
G-MNDE	Medway Half Pint	D. Thorpe	
G-MNDF	Mainair Gemini Flash	R. Meredith-Hardy	
G-MNDG	Southdown Puma Sprint	F. D. Bennett	
G-MNDH	Hiway Skytrike	N. R. Holloway	
G-MNDI	MBA Tiger Cub 440	F. Clarke	
G-MNDJ	—	—	
G-MNDK	Mainair Tri-Flyer 440	D. Kerr	
G-MNDM	Mainair Gemini Flash	J. P. McGuinness	
G-MNDN	Southdown Puma Sprint	C. H. Middleton	
G-MNDO	Mainair Flash	Solar Wings Ltd	
G-MNDP	Southdown Puma Sprint	K. O'Connell	
G-MNDR	NIB II Vertigo	S. J. Sharley	
G-MNDS	—	—	
G-MNDT	—	—	
G-MNDU	Midland Sirocco 377GB	R. F. Bridgeland	
G-MNDV	Midland Sirocco 377GB	V. H. Spencer	
G-MNDW	Midland Sirocco 377GB	G. van der Gaag	
G-MNDX	—	—	
G-MNDY	Southdown Puma Sprint	M. A. Ford	
G-MNDZ	Southdown Puma Sprint	M. F. Belbin	
G-MNEA	Southern Airwolf	Southdown International Ltd	
G-MNEB	Southern Airwolf	Southdown International Ltd	
G-MNEC	Southern Airwolf	Southdown International Ltd	
G-MNED	Skyhook Pixie	O. McCullogh	
G-MNEE	—	—	
G-MNEF	Mainair Gemini Flash	S. Meadowcroft	
G-MNEG	Mainair Gemini Flash	D. P. Moxon	
G-MNEH	Mainair Gemini Flash	I. Rawson	
G-MNEI	Medway Hybred 440	R. F. Miller	
G-MNEK	Medway Half Pint	R. S. Peaks	
G-MNEL	Medway Half Pint	D. R. Young	
G-MNEM	Solar Wings Pegasus Dual	C. Smith	
G-MNEN	Southdown Puma Sprint	A. J. Mann	
G-MNEO	Southdown Raven	A. B. Jones	
G-MNEP	Aerostructure Pipstrelle P.2B	M. R. Guerard	
G-MNER	CFM Shadow Srs B	D. Roberts	
G-MNET	Mainair Gemini Flash	N. H. Martin	
G-MNEU	—	—	
G-MNEV	Mainair Gemini Flash	Alfasound Ltd	
G-MNEW	Mainair Tri-Flyer	M. A. Reeve	
G-MNEX	Mainair Gemini Flash	Airecraft Microlight Services Ltd	
G-MNEY	Mainair Gemini Flash	T. S. Elmhirst	
G-MNEZ	Skyhook TR1 Mk 2	H. Lang	
G-MNFA	Solar Wings Typhoon	D. R. Joint	
G-MNFB	Southdown Puma Sprint	C. Lawrence	
G-MNFC	Midland Ultralights Sirocco 377GB	Bach Air Ltd	
G-MNFD	Southdown Raven	F. Dorsett	
G-MNFE	Mainair Gemini Flash	C. H. Spencer	
G-MNFF	Mainair Gemini Flash	C. H. Spencer	
G-MNFG	Southdown Puma Sprint	K. D. Beeton	
G-MNFH	Mainair Gemini Flash	W. D. Holmes	
G-MNFI	Medway Half Pint	C. Grainger	
G-MNFJ	Mainair Gemini Flash	L. A. Humphreys	
G-MNFK	Mainair Gemini Flash	A. Konieczek	
G-MNFL	AMF Chevron	P. W. Wright	
G-MNFM	Mainair Gemini Flash	R. Blenkey	

Notes	Reg.	Type	Owner or Operator
	G-MNFN	Mainair Gemini Flash	J. R. Martin
	G-MNFP	Mainair Gemini Flash	S. Farnsworth & P. Howarth
	G-MNFR	Wright Tri-Flyer	R. L. Arscott
	G-MNFS	Ikarus Sherpa Dopplesitzer	U. Silvan
	G-MNFT	Mainair Gemini Flash	Meridian Microlight Centre
	G-MNFU	—	
	G-MNFV	Ultrasports Trike	R. G. Grundy
	G-MNFW	Medway Hybred 44XL	R. L. Wadley
	G-MNFX	Southdown Puma Sprint	A. M. Shaw
	G-MNFY	Hornet 250	M. O'Hearne
	G-MNFZ	Southdown Puma Sprint	I. G. Cole
	G-MNGA	Aerial Arts Chaser 110SX	J. F. Chitalan
	G-MNGB	Mainair Gemini Flash	R. Harrison
	G-MNGC	CFM Shadow Srs B	C. R. Garner
	G-MNGD	Quest Air Services	P. R. Davey
	G-MNGE	Solar Wings Photon	Solar Wings Ltd
	G-MNGF	Solar Wings Pegasus	E. A. Wrathall
	G-MNGG	Solar Wings Pegasus XL-R	F. C. Claydon
	G-MNGH	Skyhook Pixie	A. R. Smith
	G-MNGI	—	
	G-MNGJ	Skyhook Zipper	Skyhook Sailwings Ltd
	G-MNGK	Mainair Gemini Flash	S. N. Hall
	G-MNGL	Mainair Gemini Flash	C. C. Mercer
	G-MNGM	Mainair Gemini Flash	M. A. Hayward
	G-MNGN	Mainair Gemini Flash	M. A. Dobson
	G-MNGO	Solar Wings Storm	S. Adams
	G-MNGP	—	
	G-MNGR	Southdown Puma Sprint	H. L. Dyson
	G-MNGS	Southdown Puma 330	C. R. Mortlock & B. P. Cooke
	G-MNGT	Mainair Gemini Flash	G. A. Brown
	G-MNGU	Mainair Gemini Flash	C. S. Purdy
	G-MNGV	—	
	G-MNGW	Mainair Gemini Flash	S. A. F. Nesbitt
	G-MNGX	Southdown Puma Sprint	R. J. Morris
	G-MNGY	Hiway Skytrike 160	A. J. Wood
	G-MNGZ	Mainair Gemini Flash	G. T. Snoddon
	G-MNHA	Noble Hardman Snowbird	Noble Hardman Aviation Ltd
	G-MNHB	Solar Wings Pegasus XL-R	P. Jarman
	G-MNHC	Solar Wings Pegasus XL-R	W. R. Pryce
	G-MNHD	Solar Wings Pegasus XL-R	P. D. Stiles
	G-MNHE	Solar Wings Pegasus XL-R	C. Kay
	G-MNHF	Solar Wings Pegasus XL-R	J. Cox
	G-MNHG	Solar Wings Pegasus XL-R	Sure Chemicals Ltd
	G-MNHH	Solar Wings Panther XL-S	D. J. Hampson
	G-MNHI	Solar Wings Pegasus XL-R	P. G. Pickett
	G-MNHJ	Solar Wings Pegasus XL-R	R. F. Evans
	G-MNHK	Solar Wings Pegasus XL-R	Dartsprint Ltd
	G-MNHL	Solar Wings Pegasus XL-R	Agro Exports Ltd
	G-MNHM	Solar Wings Pegasus XL-R	Solar Wings Ltd
	G-MNHN	Solar Wings Pegasus XL-R	G. W. Scarborough
	G-MNHO	—	
	G-MNHP	Solar Wings Pegasus XL-R	A. D. & G. P. Leslie
	G-MNHR	Solar Wings Pegasus XL-R	M. F. Eddington
	G-MNHS	Solar Wings Pegasus XL-R	M. S. Henson
	G-MNHT	Solar Wings Pegasus XL-R	P. E. England
	G-MNHU	Solar Wings Pegasus XL-R	J. P. Clifford & P. P. Tolfree
	G-MNHV	Solar Wings Pegasus XL-R	P. R. Gapper
	G-MNHW	Medway Half Pint	J. S. Murray
	G-MNHX	Solar Wings Typhoon S4	R. Blackwell
	G-MNHY	Mainair Tri-Flyer 440	K. Wright
	G-MNHZ	Mainair Gemini Flash	R. J. Evans
	G-MNIA	Mainair Gemini Flash	A. E. Dix
	G-MNIB	American Aerolights Eagle 215B	C. R. Cattell
	G-MNIC	MBA Tiger Cub 440	N. B. Kirby
	G-MNID	Mainair Gemini Flash	G. Penson
	G-MNIE	Mainair Gemini Flash	P. Eden & B. Weinrabe
	G-MNIF	Mainair Gemini Flash	D. Yarr
	G-MNIG	Mainair Gemini Flash	R. D. Noble
	G-MNIH	Mainair Gemini Flash	I. C. Lomax
	G-MNII	Mainair Gemini Flash	R. F. Finnis
	G-MNIK	Solar Wings Pegasus Photon	Solar Wings Ltd
	G-MNIL	Southdown Puma Sprint	C. D. West
	G-MNIM	Maxair Hummer	P. J. Brookman
	G-MNIN	Designability Duet	S. Osmond

Reg.	Type	Owner or Operator	Notes
G-MNIO	Mainair Gemini Flash	M. A. Hayward	
G-MNIP	Mainair Gemini Flash	G. S. Bulpitt	
G-MNIR	Skyhook Pixie 130	I. G. Cole	
G-MNIS	CFM Shadow Srs B	R. W. Payne	
G-MNIT	Aerial Arts 130SX	G. R. Baker	
G-MNIU	Solar Wings Pegasus Photon	K. Roberts	
G-MNIV	Solar Wings Typhoon	D. Tipping	
G-MNIW	Airwave Nimrod 165	J. A. McIntosh & R. W. Mitchell	
G-MNIX	Mainair Gemini Flash	B. J. Bishop	
G-MNIY	Skyhook Pixie Zipper	Skyhook Sailwings Ltd	
G-MNIZ	Mainair Gemini Flash	B. Cowburn	
G-MNJA	Southdown Lightning Skytrike	D. Guest	
G-MNJB	Southdown Raven	D. Millar	
G-MNJC	MBA Tiger Cub 440	J. G. Carpenter	
G-MNJD	Southdown Puma Sprint	J. B. Duffus	
G-MNJE	Southdown Puma Sprint	T. Powell	
G-MNJF	Dragon 150	L. R. Jillings	
G-MNJG	Mainair Tri-Flyer	C. R. Read	
G-MNJH	Solar Wings Pegasus Flash	D. Gandle	
G-MNJI	Solar Wings Pegasus Flash	M. J. O'Connor	
G-MNJJ	Solar Wings Pegasus Flash	B. P. Peissel	
G-MNJK	Solar Wings Pegasus Flash	C. Green	
G-MNJL	Solar Wings Pegasus Flash	G. H. Cork	
G-MNJM	Solar Wings Pegasus Flash	N. Jefferson	
G-MNJN	Solar Wings Pegasus Flash	D. J. Pay	
G-MNJO	Solar Wings Pegasus Flash	S. J. Farrant & Sons Ltd	
G-MNJP	Solar Wings Pegasus Flash	R. J. Butler	
G-MNJR	Solar Wings Pegasus Flash	J. Stokes	
G-MNJS	Southdown Puma Sprint	C. E. Bates	
G-MNJT	Southdown Raven	W. G. Reynolds	
G-MNJU	Mainair Gemini Flash	N. V. Wnekowski	
G-MNJV	Medway Half Pint	C. C. W. Mates	
G-MNJW	Mitchell Wing B10	J. D. Webb	
G-MNJX	Medway Hybred 44XL	H. A. Stewart	
G-MNJY	Medway Half Pint	P. M. Stoney	
G-MNJZ	Aerial Arts Alpha 130SX	I. M. Grayland	
G-MNKA	Solar Wings Pegasus Photon	T. E. Edmond	
G-MNKB	Solar Wings Pegasus Photon	M. E. Gilbert	
G-MNKC	Solar Wings Pegasus Photon	H. C. Mowthorpe	
G-MNKD	Solar Wings Pegasus Photon	R. Colquhoun	
G-MNKE	Solar Wings Pegasus Photon	T. M. Edmond	
G-MNKF	Solar Wings Pegasus Photon	H. C. Mowthorpe	
G-MNKG	Solar Wings Pegasus Photon	P. D. Atkinson	
G-MNKH	Solar Wings Pegasus Photon	A. G. Drury	
G-MNKI	Solar Wings Pegasus Photon	J. E. Halsall	
G-MNKJ	Solar Wings Pegasus Photon	D. D. Robertson	
G-MNKK	Solar Wings Pegasus Photon	K. Hann	
G-MNKL	Mainair Gemini Flash	J. R. Booth	
G-MNKM	MBA Tiger Cub 440	L. J. Forinton	
G-MNKN	Skycraft Scout Mk III	E. A. Diamond	
G-MNKO	Solar Wings Pegasus XL-O	P. D. Atkinson	
G-MNKP	Solar Wings Pegasus Flash	M. West	
G-MNKR	Solar Wings Pegasus Flash	C. Broadley	
G-MNKS	Solar Wings Pegasus Flash	A. D. Langtree	
G-MNKT	Solar Wings Typhoon S4	C. R. Sykes	
G-MNKU	Southdown Puma Sprint	R. W. Jones	
G-MNKV	Solar Wings Pegasus Flash	J. F. Mallinson	
G-MNKW	Solar Wings Pegasus Flash	P. Ridout	
G-MNKX	Solar Wings Pegasus Flash	J. Spavin	
G-MNKY	Southdown Raven	A. L. Coleman	
G-MNKZ	Southdown Raven	A. E. Silvey	
G-MNLA	Solar Wings Typhoon	J. A. Havers	
G-MNLB	Southdown Raven X	N. E. Smith	
G-MNLC	Southdown Raven	P. M. Coppola	
G-MNLD	Solar Wings Pegasus Photon	Solar Wings Ltd	
G-MNLE	Southdown Raven X	B. Bayley	
G-MNLF	Southdown Puma	K. Brunnekant	
G-MNLG	Southdown Lightning	D. J. Edwards	
G-MNLH	Romain Cobra Biplane	J. W. E. Romain	
G-MNLI	Mainair Gemini Flash	J. I. Greenshields	
G-MNLJ	—	—	
G-MNLK	Southdown Raven	G. C. Weighell	
G-MNLL	Southdown Raven	W. P. Woodcock	
G-MNLM	Southdown Raven	A. P. White	

Notes	Reg.	Type	Owner or Operator
	G-MNLN	Southdown Raven	R. J. Garland
	G-MNLO	Southdown Raven	D. Kiddy
	G-MNLP	Southdown Raven	G. M. Mansfield
	G-MNLR	Solar Wings Typhoon	B. J. Farrell
	G-MNLS	Southdown Raven	L. P. Geer
	G-MNLU	Southdown Raven	Southdown International Ltd
	G-MNLV	Southdown Raven	J. Murphy
	G-MNLW	Medway Halt Pint	C. F. Medgett
	G-MNLX	Mainair Gemini Flash	B. J. Cook
	G-MNLY	Mainair Gemini Flash	P. Orritt & ptnrs
	G-MNLZ	Southdown Raven	D. M. Punnett
	G-MNMA	Solar Wings Pegasus Flash	J. C. B. Halford
	G-MNMB	Solar Wings Pegasus Flash	M. Wells
	G-MNMC	Southdown Puma MS	T. M. Clark
	G-MNMD	Southdown Raven	E. M. Woods & D. Little
	G-MNME	Hiway Skytrike	W. T. Church
	G-MNMF	Maxair Hummer TX	M. I. Smith
	G-MNMG	Mainair Gemini Flash	N. A. M. Beyer-Kay
	G-MNMH	Mainair Gemini Flash	R. St John Harrison
	G-MNMI	Mainair Gemini Flash	T. E. McDonald
	G-MNMJ	Mainair Gemini Flash	P. A. Mercer
	G-MNMK	Solar Wings Pegasus XL-R	Knowles Transport Ltd
	G-MNML	Southdown Puma Sprint	M. J. Hammond
	G-MNMM	Aerotech MW.5 Sorcerer	Aerotech International Ltd
	G-MNMN	Medway Microlights Hybred 44	R. Skene
	G-MNMO	Mainair Gemini Flash	M. W. Walsh
	G-MNMP	Pritchard Experimental Mk 1	M. H. Pritchard
	G-MNMR	Solar Wings Typhoon 180	B. D. Jackson
	G-MNMS	Wheeler Scout	M. I. Smith
	G-MNMT	Southdown Raven	Hornet Microlights
	G-MNMU	Southdown Raven	W. B. Cardew
	G-MNMV	Mainair Gemini Flash	C. Foster
	G-MNMW	Aerotech MW.6 Merlin	E. F. Clapham & ptnrs
	G-MNMX	Sigh-Wing Paraplane	Sigh-Wing Ltd
	G-MNMY	Cyclone 70	Cyclone Hovercraft Ltd
	G-MNMZ	—	—
	G-MNNA	Southdown Raven	D. & G. D. Palfrey
	G-MNNB	Southdown Raven	M. J. Linford
	G-MNNC	Southdown Raven	J. G. Beesley
	G-MNND	Solar Wings Pegasus Flash	G. C. Baird
	G-MNNE	Mainair Gemini Flash	B. Kirkland
	G-MNNF	Mainair Gemini Flash	P. J. Jenson
	G-MNNG	Squires Lightfly	P. G. Angus
	G-MNNH	Medway 130SX Export	Chris Taylor Racing Preparations
	G-MNNI	Mainair Gemini Flash	A. Anderson
	G-MNNJ	Mainair Gemini Flash	The Eagle Group
	G-MNNK	Mainair Gemini Flash	S. B. Hodgson
	G-MNNL	Mainair Gemini Flash	D. Wilson & A. Bielawski
	G-MNNM	Mainair Scorcher Solo	M. R. Parr
	G-MNNN	Southdown Raven	F. Byford & S. Hooker
	G-MNNO	Southdown Raven	J. R. Poolman
	G-MNNP	Mainair Gemini Flash	K. J. Regan
	G-MNNR	Mainair Gemini Flash	Milequip Computer Systems
	G-MNNS	Eurowing Goldwing	D. Johnstone & R. J. Wood
	G-MNNT	Medway Microlights Hybred	J. R. A. Dickinson & D. J. Cropper
	G-MNNU	Mainair Gemini Flash	Jabot
	G-MNNV	Mainair Gemini Flash	Ardrossan Auto Spares
	G-MNNX	—	—
	G-MNNY	Solar Wings Pegasus Flash	C. M. Blanchard
	G-MNNZ	Solar Wings Pegasus Flash	P. A. R. Hicks
	G-MNPA	Solar Wings Pegasus Flash	E. J. Blyth
	G-MNPB	Solar Wings Pegasus Flash	E. J. Blyth
	G-MNPC	Mainair Gemini Flash	J. R. North
	G-MNPD	Midland Ultralights 130SX	L. T. Ryder
	G-MNPF	Mainair Gemini Flash	M. G. A. Wood
	G-MNPG	Mainair Gemini Flash	P. Kirton
	G-MNPH	Flexiform Dual Striker	D. L. Aspinall
	G-MNPI	Southdown Pipistrelle 2C	Southdown Aerostructure Ltd
	G-MNPJ	Southdown Pipistrelle 2C	D. A. Gleason
	G-MNPK	Southdown Pipistrelle 2C	Southdown Aerostructure Ltd
	G-MNPL	Ultrasports Panther 330	P. N. Long
	G-MNPM	Southdown Pipistrelle 2C	Southdown Aerostructure Ltd
	G-MNPN	Southdown Pipistrelle 2C	Southdown Aerostructure Ltd
	G-MNPO	Romain Cobra Biplane	D. Stott

Reg.	Type	Owner or Operator	Notes
G-MNPP	Romain Cobra Biplane	J. W. E. Romain	
G-MNPR	Hiway Demon 175	R. M. Clarke	
G-MNPS	Skyhook Pixie	Skyhook Sailwings Ltd	
G-MNPT	Skyhook Pixie	Skyhook Sailwings Ltd	
G-MNPU	Skyhook Pixie	Skyhook Sailwings Ltd	
G-MNPV	Mainair Scorcher Solo	G. Naylor	
G-MNPW	AMF Chevron	AMF Microlight Ltd	
G-MNPX	Mainair Gemini Flash	T. A. Cockerell	
G-MNPY	Mainair Scorcher Solo	R. N. O. Kingsbury	
G-MNPZ	Mainair Scorcher Solo	Mainair Sports Ltd	
G-MNRA	CFM Shadow Srs B	CFM Metal-Fax Ltd	
G-MNRB	Southdown Puma	Aerotech Africa Ltd	
G-MNRC	Skyhook TR1	Skyhook Sailwings Ltd	
G-MNRD	Ultraflight Lazair	D. W. & M. F. Briggs	
G-MNRE	Mainair Scorcher Solo	G. A. Archer	
G-MNRF	Mainair Scorcher Solo	W. C. Yates	
G-MNRG	Mainair Scorcher Solo	Mainair Sports Ltd	
G-MNRH	Mainair Scorcher Solo	Mainair Sports Ltd	
G-MNRI	Hornet Dual Trainer	R. L. Manby	
G-MNRJ	Hornet Dual Trainer	K. W. E. Brunnenkant	
G-MNRK	Hornet Dual Trainer	D. J. Walter	
G-MNRL	Hornet Dual Trainer	Hornet Microlights	
G-MNRM	Hornet Dual Trainer	R. I. Cannon	
G-MNRN	Hornet Dual Trainer	Hornet Microlights	
G-MNRO	Southdown Raven	Mosaic King (UK) Ltd	
G-MNRP	Southdown Raven	C. Moore	
G-MNRR	Southdown Raven X	J. G. Jennings	
G-MNRS	Southdown Raven	P. Roberts	
G-MNRT	Midland Ultralights Sirocco	R. F. Hinton	
G-MNRU	Midland Ultralights Sirocco	Midland Ultralights Ltd	
G-MNRV	American Aerolights Eagle	P. J. Buckner	
G-MNRW	Mainair Gemini Flash II	L. A. Maynard	
G-MNRX	Mainair Gemini Flash II	S. J. Shelley	
G-MNRY	Mainair Gemini Flash	M. A. Lomas	
G-MNRZ	Mainair Scorcher Solo	S. J. Tate	
G-MNSA	Mainair Gemini Flash	N. P. A. & W. R. J. Wallis	
G-MNSB	Southdown Puma Sprint	C. J. Whittaker	
G-MNSC	Flexiform Hi-Line	J. F. Holdsworth	
G-MNSD	Solar Wings Typhoon	W. Read & A. J. Lloyd	
G-MNSE	Mainair Gemini Flash	A. C. Dommett	
G-MNSF	Hornet Dual Trainer	R. Pattrick	
G-MNSG	Hornet Dual Trainer	R. R. Wolfenden	
G-MNSH	Solar Wings Pegasus Flash II	P. A. Lee	
G-MNSI	Mainair Gemini Flash	G. C. Hobson	
G-MNSJ	Mainair Gemini Flash	M. L. Plant Insulations Ltd	
G-MNSK	Hiway Skytrike	E. B. Jones	
G-MNSL	Southdown Raven X	P. B. Robinson	
G-MNSM	Hornet Demon	A. R. Glenn	
G-MNSN	Solar Wings Pegasus Flash II	Pegasus Flight Training Ltd	
G-MNSO	Solar Wings Pegasus Flash II	P. W. Giesler	
G-MNSP	Aerial Arts 130SX	C. J. Upton-Taylor	
G-MNSR	Mainair Gemini Flash	J. Brown	
G-MNSS	American Aerolights Eagle	G. P. Jones	
G-MNST	Vector 600	M. Quigley	
G-MNSU	Aerial Arts 130SX	I. M. Grayland & ptnrs	
G-MNSV	CFM Shadown Srs B	P. J. W. Rowell	
G-MNSW	Southdown Raven X	P. J. Barton	
G-MNSX	Southdown Raven X	R. Dainty	
G-MNSY	Southdown Raven X	R. Stoner	
G-MNSZ	Noble Hardman Snowbird	Noble Hardman Aviation Ltd	
G-MNTA	—	—	
G-MNTB	Solar Wings Typhoon S4	A. H. Trapp	
G-MNTC	Southdown Raven X	R. B. D. Baker	
G-MNTD	Aerial Arts Chaser 110SX	H. Phipps	
G-MNTE	Southdown Raven X	D. Kiddy	
G-MNTF	Southdown Raven X	J. S. Long	
G-MNTG	Southdown Raven X	D. Thorpe	
G-MNTH	Mainair Gemini Flash	B. A. Phillips	
G-MNTI	Mainair Gemini Flash	R. T. Strathie	
G-MNTJ	American Aerolights Eagle	D. S. J. Boston	
G-MNTK	CFM Shadow Srs B	M. I. M. Smith	
G-MNTL	Arbee Wasp Gryphon	D. K. Liddard	
G-MNTM	Southdown Raven X	M. W. Hurst	
G-MNTN	Southdown Raven X	J. Hall	

Notes	Reg.	Type	Owner or Operator
	G-MNTO	Southdown Raven X	J. T. Nunn
	G-MNTP	CFM Shadow Srs B	G. E. Gould
	G-MNTR	—	
	G-MNTS	Mainair Gemini Flash II	K. J. & G. E. Cole
	G-MNTT	Medway Half Pint	Lancaster Partners (Holdings) Ltd
	G-MNTU	Mainair Gemini Flash II	M. A. E. Harris
	G-MNTV	Mainair Gemini Flash II	E. M. Lamb
	G-MNTW	Mainair Gemini Flash II	A. Dix & S. Clarke
	G-MNTX	Mainair Gemini Flash II	C. W. Thomas
	G-MNTY	Southdown Raven X	T. E. Baxter
	G-MNTZ	Mainair Gemini Flash II	Weston Furnishers
	G-MNUA	Mainair Gemini Flash II	E. R. Fisher
	G-MNUB	Mainair Gemini Flash II	R. V. Emerson
	G-MNUC	Solar Wings Pegasus Flash II	V. E. J. Smith
	G-MNUD	Solar Wings Pegasus Flash II	J. D. R. Broadbent
	G-MNUE	Solar Wings Pegasus Flash II	S. Rands
	G-MNUF	Mainair Gemini Flash II	E. Marsh
	G-MNUG	Mainair Gemini Flash II	A. F. Stafford
	G-MNUH	Southdown Raven X	L. H. Phillips
	G-MNUI	Skyhook Cutlass Dual	M. Holling
	G-MNUJ	Solar Wings Pegasus Photon	W. G. Farr
	G-MNUK	Midland Ultralights SX130	J. F. Sheridan
	G-MNUL	Midland Ultralights SX130	M. A. Cooper
	G-MNUM	Southdown Puma Sprint MS	B. Rawlance
	G-MNUN	—	
	G-MNUO	Mainair Gemini Flash II	P. Cooper
	G-MNUP	Mainair Gemini Flash II	S. Fairweather
	G-MNUR	Mainair Gemini Flash II	Airbourne Aviation Ltd
	G-MNUS	Mainair Gemini Flash II	Containerway Ltd
	G-MNUT	Southdown Raven X	G. S. Mitchell
	G-MNUU	Southdown Raven X	Ardenco Ltd
	G-MNUV	Southdown Raven X	D. Houghton
	G-MNUW	Southdown Raven X	Southdown International Ltd
	G-MNUX	Solar Wings Pegasus XL-R	H. J. Johnson
	G-MNUY	Mainair Gemini Flash II	W. J. Dufour & P. S. Pontin
	G-MNUZ	Mainair Gemini Flash II	N. Redpath
	G-MNVA	Solar Wings Pegasus XL-R	M. Bird
	G-MNVB	Solar Wings Pegasus XL-R	K. Garnett
	G-MNVC	Solar Wings Pegasus XL-R	T. Davies
	G-MNVE	Solar Wings Pegasus XL-R	M. Aris
	G-MNVF	Solar Wings Pegasus Flash II	A. Rooker
	G-MNVG	Solar Wings Pegasus Flash II	M. A. Farr
	G-MNVH	Solar Wings Pegasus Flash II	S. G. Murray
	G-MNVI	CFM Shadow Srs B	D. R. C. Pugh
	G-MNVJ	CFM Shadow Srs B	B. F. Hill
	G-MNVK	CFM Shadow Srs B	G. W. Sisson
	G-MNVL	Medway Half Pint	J. H. Cooling
	G-MNVM	Southdown Raven X	R. Turnbull
	G-MNVN	Southdown Raven X	J. E. Glendinning
	G-MNVO	Hovey Whing-Ding II	C. Wilson
	G-MNVP	Southdown Raven X	R. A. Keene
	G-MNVR	Mainair Gemini Flash II	Multiscope Ltd
	G-MNVS	Mainair Gemini Flash II	D. P. Ballard
	G-MNVT	Mainair Gemini Flash II	ACB Hydraulics
	G-MNVU	Mainair Gemini Flash II	W. R. Marsh
	G-MNVV	Mainair Gemini Flash II	P. T. Stamer
	G-MNVW	Mainair Gemini Flash II	L. M. Westwood
	G-MNVX	Solar Wings Pegasus Flash II	Pegasus Flight Training Ltd
	G-MNVY	Solar Wings Pegasus Photon	J. R. Charlton
	G-MNVZ	Solar Wings Pegasus Photon	J. J. Russ
	G-MNWA	Southdown Raven X	A. Reynolds
	G-MNWB	Thruster TST	Thruster Aircraft (UK) Ltd
	G-MNWC	Mainair Gemini Flash II	J. V. Thompson
	G-MNWD	Mainair Gemini Flash	P. Crossman
	G-MNWE	—	
	G-MNWF	Southdown Raven X	Southdown International Ltd
	G-MNWG	Southdown Raven X	B. R. Underwood
	G-MNWH	Aerial Arts 130SX	P. N. & A. M. Keohane
	G-MNWI	Mainair Gemini Flash II	B. Bennison
	G-MNWJ	Mainair Gemini Flash II	A. J. Brown
	G-MNWK	CFM Shadow Srs B	T. Green
	G-MNWL	Aerial Arts 130SX	Arbiter Services Ltd
	G-MNWM	CFM Shadow Srs B	J. E. Laidler
	G-MNWN	Mainair Gemini Flash II	Airbourne Aviation Ltd

Reg.	Type	Owner or Operator	Notes
G-MNWO	Mainair Gemini Flash II	I. C. Terry	
G-MNWP	Solar Wings Pegasus Flash II	M. M. Mason	
G-MNWR	Medway Hybred 44LR	C. J. Draper	
G-MNWS	Airwave Magic III	A. W. Buchan	
G-MNWT	Southdown Raven	M. T. Tongne	
G-MNWU	Solar Wings Pegasus Flash II	Cyclone Hovercraft Ltd	
G-MNWV	Solar Wings Pegasus Flash II	Southwest Airsports Ltd	
G-MNWW	Solar Wings Pegasus XL-R	P. J. D. Kerr	
G-MNWX	Solar Wings Pegasus XL-R	B. N. Thresher	
G-MNWY	CFM Shadow Srs B	M. H. Player	
G-MNWZ	Mainair Gemini Flash II	J. McDowall	
G-MNXA	Southdown Raven X	D. Coging	
G-MNXB	Solar Wings Photon	F. S. Ogden	
G-MNXC	Aerial Arts 110SX	J. E. Sweetingham	
G-MNXD	Southdown Raven	J. C. O'Donnell	
G-MNXE	Southdown Raven X	A. K. Pomroy	
G-MNXF	Southdown Raven	D. R. Cox	
G-MNXG	Southdown Raven X	S. J. Galloway	
G-MNXH	La Mouette Azure	D. S. Bremner	
G-MNXI	Southdown Raven X	I. R. & A. J. Lilburne	
G-MNXJ	Medway Half Pint	M. Dougall	
G-MNXK	Medway Half Pint	E. W. P. van Zeller	
G-MNXL	Medway Half Pint	M. Evanson	
G-MNXM	Medway Hybred 44XLR	C. J. Draper	
G-MNXN	Medway Hybred 44XLR	J. Rodger & J. Dinwoodey	
G-MNXO	Medway Hybred 44XLR	S. R. Grant	
G-MNXP	Solar Wings Pegasus Flash II	T. J. Walsh	
G-MNXR	Mainair Gemini Flash II	B. J. Crockett	
G-MNXS	Mainair Gemini Flash II	F. T. Rawlings	
G-MNXT	Mainair Gemini Flash II	N. W. Barnett	
G-MNXU	Mainair Gemini Flash II	F. R. Curtis	
G-MNXV	—	—	
G-MNXW	Mainair Gemini Flash II	P. B. McNicholas	
G-MNXX	CFM Shadow Srs BD	F. J. Luckhurst	
G-MNXY	Whittaker MW.5 Sorcerer	R. K. Willcox	
G-MNXZ	Whittaker MW.5 Sorcerer	M. N. Gauntlett	
G-MNYA	Solar Wings Pegasus Flash II	B. O. Dowsett	
G-MNYB	Solar Wings Pegasus XL-R	J. G. Robinson	
G-MNYC	Solar Wings Pegasus XL-R	E. G. Astin	
G-MNYD	Aerial Arts 110SX	H. Phipps	
G-MNYE	Aerial Arts 110SX	J. N. Bell	
G-MNYF	Aerial Arts 110SX	B. Richardson	
G-MNYG	Southdown Raven	D. V. Brunt	
G-MNYH	Southdown Puma Sprint	E. K. Battersea	
G-MNYI	Southdown Raven X	Industrial Foam Systems Ltd	
G-MNYJ	Mainair Gemini Flash II	J. G. Jones	
G-MNYK	Mainair Gemini Flash II	Mainair Sports Ltd	
G-MNYL	Southdown Raven X	R. W. Tompkins	
G-MNYM	Southdown Raven X	M. Timwey	
G-MNYN	Southdown Raven X	Aerotech International Ltd	
G-MNYO	Southdown Raven X	Aerotech International Ltd	
G-MNYP	Southdown Raven X	C. L. Betts	
G-MNYR	—	—	
G-MNYS	Southdown Raven X	M. R. Dickens	
G-MNYT	Solar Wings Pegasus XL-R	P. D. Bloom	
G-MNYU	Solar Wings Pegasus XL-R	P. D. Bethal & R. M. Lusty	
G-MNYV	Solar Wings Pegasus XL-R	G. R. Oscroft	
G-MNYW	Solar Wings Pegasus XL-R	M. P. Waldock	
G-MNYX	Solar Wings Pegasus XL-R	Dartsprint Ltd	
G-MNYY	Solar Wings Pegasus Flash II	S. A. Jaques	
G-MNYZ	Solar Wings Pegasus Flash	Howe Green Ltd	
G-MNZA	Solar Wings Pegasus Flash II	P. F. Cosgrove	
G-MNZB	Mainair Gemini Flash II	C. J. Millership	
G-MNZC	Mainair Gemini Flash II	A. R. Lawrence	
G-MNZD	Mainair Gemini Flash II	G. R. Maclean	
G-MNZE	Mainair Gemini Flash II	A. I. Grant	
G-MNZF	Mainair Gemini Flash II	Airbourne Aviation Ltd	
G-MNZG	Aerial Arts 110SX	C. F. Grainger	
G-MNZH	AMF Chevron 2-32	AMF Microlight Ltd	
G-MNZI	Prone Power Typhoon 2	R. J. Folwell	
G-MNZJ	CFM Shadow Srs BD	B. D. Godden	
G-MNZK	Solar Wings Pegasus XL-R	G. Twomlow	
G-MNZL	Solar Wings Pegasus XL-R	M. A. Concannon	
G-MNZM	Solar Wings Pegasus XL-R	Solar Wings Ltd	

Notes	Reg.	Type	Owner or Operator
	G-MNZN	Solar Wings Pegasus Flash II	Solar Wings Ltd
	G-MNZO	Solar Wings Pegasus Flash II	K. B. Woods
	G-MNZP	CFM Shadow Srs B	S. N. Freestone & J. G. Wakefield
	G-MNZR	CFM Shadown Srs BD	CFM Metal-Fax Ltd
	G-MNZS	Aerial Arts 130SX	T. J. Acton
	G-MNZU	Eurowing Goldwing	H. B. Baker
	G-MNZV	Southdown Raven X	J. Riley
	G-MNZW	Southdown Raven X	P. G. Greenslade
	G-MNZX	Southdown Raven X	M. D. Phillips
	G-MNZY	Striker Tri-Flyer 330	P. W. Fieldman
	G-MNZZ	CFM Shadow Srs B	Lancaster Partners (Holdings) Ltd
	G-MTAA	Solar Wings Pegasus XL-R	G. N. Carew
	G-MTAB	Mainair Gemini Flash II	J. P. Leigh
	G-MTAC	Mainair Gemini Flash II	F. Credland
	G-MTAD	Mainair Gemini Skyflash	Mainair Sports Ltd
	G-MTAE	Mainair Gemini Flash II	B. J. Scott
	G-MTAF	Mainair Gemini Flash II	C. Johnson
	G-MTAG	Mainair Gemini Flash II	R. G. Verdon-Roe
	G-MTAH	Mainair Gemini Flash II	E. K. Fleming
	G-MTAI	Solar Wings Pegasus XL-R	M. E. Bates Engineering
	G-MTAJ	Solar Wings Pegasus XL-R	N. R. Holloway
	G-MTAK	Solar Wings Pegasus XL-R	T. A. Sayer
	G-MTAL	Solar Wings Photon	I. Munro
	G-MTAM	Solar Wings Pegasus Flash	J. P. Scales
	G-MTAN	Bragg Dual Seat	I. Ellithorn
	G-MTAO	Solar Wings Pegasus XL-R	B. Bond
	G-MTAP	Southdown Raven X	J. B. Rutland
	G-MTAR	Mainair Gemini Flash II	J. Sharman
	G-MTAS	Whittaker MW.5 Sorcerer	E. A. Henman
	G-MTAT	Solar Wings Pegasus XL-R	M. J. Kimber
	G-MTAU	Solar Wings Pegasus XL-R	R. K. Parry
	G-MTAV	Solar Wings Pegasus XL-R	D. B. Ash
	G-MTAW	Solar Wings Pegasus XL-R	T. Cameron
	G-MTAX	Solar Wings Pegasus XL-R	M. D. Haynes
	G-MTAY	Solar Wings Pegasus XL-R	C. A. Booth
	G-MTAZ	Solar Wings Pegasus XL-R	H. W. Banham
	G-MTBA	Solar Wings Pegasus XL-R	J. Kinson
	G-MTBB	Southdown Raven X	C. M. Raven
	G-MTBC	Mainair Gemini Flash II	M. J. Coomber
	G-MTBD	Mainair Gemini Flash II	A. M. Smyth
	G-MTBE	CFM Shadow Srs BD	S. Delia
	G-MTBF	Mirage Mk II	I. M. Willeher
	G-MTBG	Mainair Gemini Flash II	N. Spencer-Baryn
	G-MTBH	Mainair Gemini Flash II	R. Holt
	G-MTBI	Mainair Gemini Flash II	D. J. Bowie
	G-MTBJ	Mainair Gemini Flash II	P. K. Bishop
	G-MTBK	Southdown Raven X	R. C. Barnett
	G-MTBL	Solar Wings Pegasus XL-R	R. N. Whiting
	G-MTBM	Airwave Nimrod	B. R. Beer
	G-MTBN	Southdown Raven X	S. P. Allen
	G-MTBO	Southdown Raven X	A. Miller
	G-MTBP	Aerotech MW.5 Sorcerer	A. A. Heseldine
	G-MTBR	Aerotech MW.5 Sorcerer	D. Stott
	G-MTBS	Aerotech MW.5 Sorcerer	S. Solley
	G-MTBT	—	—
	G-MTBU	Solar Wings Pegasus XL-R	Building Profiles Ltd
	G-MTBV	Solar Wings Pegasus XL-R	G. E. Etheridge
	G-MTBW	Mainair Gemini Flash II	I. J. Drewett
	G-MTBX	Mainair Gemini Flash II	R. H. Bambury
	G-MTBY	Mainair Gemini Flash II	THA Heating Supplies Ltd
	G-MTBZ	Southdown Raven X	R. J. Henney
	G-MTCA	CFM Shadow Srs B	J. B. T. Christie
	G-MTCB	Snowbird Mk III	Noble Hardman Aviation Ltd
	G-MTCC	Mainair Gemini Flash II	N. Redpath
	G-MTCD	Southdown Raven X	P. Whitney
	G-MTCE	Mainair Gemini Flash II	Konfax Ltd
	G-MTCF	Farnell Flexwing	P. R. Farnell
	G-MTCG	Solar Wings Pegasus XL-R	R. W. Allen
	G-MTCH	Solar Wings Pegasus XL-R	R. E. H. Harris
	G-MTCI	Aerial Arts Chaser S	I. M. Grayland
	G-MTCJ	Aerial Arts Avenger	I. M. Grayland
	G-MTCK	Solar Wings Pegasus Flash	Richard Daniels Homes Ltd
	G-MTCL	—	—

Reg.	Type	Owner or Operator	Notes
G-MTCM	Southdown Raven X	J. J. Lancaster	
G-MTCN	Solar Wings Pegasus XL-R	R. W. H. de Serville	
G-MTCO	Solar Wings Pegasus XL-R	D. M. Savage	
G-MTCP	Aerial Arts Chaser 110SX	D. Cannon	
G-MTCR	Solar Wings Pegasus XL-R	K. Pratt	
G-MTCS	CFM Shadow Srs BD	J. S. Crewe	
G-MTCT	CFM Shadow Srs BD	J. W. Lang	
G-MTCU	Mainair Gemini Flash II	Mainair Sports Ltd	
G-MTCV	Microflight Spectrum	Microflight Aircraft Ltd	
G-MTCW	Mainair Gemini Flash	M. R. Starling	
G-MTCX	Solar Wings Pegasus XL-R	D. Shackleton	
G-MTCY	Southdown Raven X	Airbourne Aviation Ltd	
G-MTCZ	Ultrasports Tripacer 250	R. Parkin	
G-MTDA	Hornet Dual Trainer	R. Nay	
G-MTDB	Owen Pola Mk 1	P. E. Owen	
G-MTDC	Owen Pola Mk 1	P. E. Owen	
G-MTDD	Aerial Arts Chaser 110SX	R. Bacon	
G-MTDE	American Aerolights 110SX	E. K. Jupp	
G-MTDF	Mainair Gemini Flash II	K. M. Pinkard	
G-MTDG	Solar Wings Pegasus XL-R	S. A. Jagnes	
G-MTDH	Solar Wings Pegasus XL-R	D. B. Casley-Smith	
G-MTDI	Solar Wings Pegasus XL-R	P. M. Wisniewski	
G-MTDJ	Medway Hybred 44XL	J. A. Slocombe & C. D. Gates	
G-MTDK	Aerotech MW.5 Sorcerer	A. J. Edwards	
G-MTDL	Solar Wings Pegasus XL-R	Solar Wings Ltd	
G-MTDM	Mainair Gemini Flash II	J. F. Cawley	
G-MTDN	Ultraflight Lazair IIIE	R. D. Good	
G-MTDO	Eipper Quicksilver MXII	D. L. Ham	
G-MTDP	Solar Wings Pegasus XL-R	S. P. Mcandy	
G-MTDR	Mainair Gemini Flash II	K. Dale	
G-MTDS	Solar Wings Photon	A. J. Macfie	
G-MTDT	Solar Wings Pegasus XL-R	M. T. Jones	
G-MTDU	CFM Shadow Srs BD	M. Jones	
G-MTDV	Solar Wings Pegasus XL-R	B. Curtis	
G-MTDW	Mainair Gemini Flash II	S. R. Leeper	
G-MTDX	CFM Shadow Srs BD	M. P. Chetwynd-Talbot	
G-MTDY	Mainair Gemini Flash II	S. Penoyre	
G-MTDZ	Eipper Quicksilver MXII	Survival Anglia Ltd	
G-MTEA	Solar Wings Pegasus XL-R	F. H. Shaw	
G-MTEB	Solar Wings Pegasus XL-R	R. A. Barnett	
G-MTEC	Solar Wings Pegasus XL-R	J. Wohl	
G-MTED	Solar Wings Pegasus XL-R	W. S. Smith	
G-MTEE	Solar Wings Pegasus XL-R	D. K. Ross	
G-MTEF	Solar Wings Pegasus XL-R	B. D. Waller	
G-MTEG	Mainair Gemini Flash II	HRH Sheikh Omar Bin Saqr Al Qassimi Ras Al Khaimah	
G-MTEH	Mainair Gemini Flash II	D. Clarke	
G-MTEJ	Mainair Gemini Flash II	C. H. Booth	
G-MTEK	Mainair Gemini Flash II	P. J. Craven	
G-MTEL	Mainair Gemini Flash II	J. W. Townsend	
G-MTEM	Mainair Gemini Flash II	S. J. Pullan	
G-MTEN	Mainair Gemini Flash II	S. Mersay	
G-MTEO	Midland Ultralight Sirocco 337	J. D. Hall	
G-MTER	Solar Wings Pegasus XL-R	W. G. Bond	
G-MTES	Solar Wings Pegasus XL-R	I. Callaghan	
G-MTET	Solar Wings Pegasus XL-R	R. C. Crowley	
G-MTEU	Solar Wings Pegasus XL-R	G. Revill	
G-MTEV	Solar Wings Pegasus XL-R	J. S. & M. R. Fuller	
G-MTEW	Solar Wings Pegasus XL-R	M. J. Lancey & B. Bott	
G-MTEX	Solar Wings Pegasus XL-R	G. D. Reed	
G-MTEY	Mainair Gemini Flash II	F. D. Bennett	
G-MTEZ	Ultraflight Lazair IIIE	M. J. Ford	
G-MTFA	Solar Wings Pegasus XL-R	C. Montgomery	
G-MTFB	Solar Wings Pegasus XL-R	A. A. Craig	
G-MTFC	Medway Hybred 44XLR	Speed Couriers Ltd	
G-MTFD	Hiway Demon	M. A. Hodgson	
G-MTFE	Solar Wings Pegasus XL-R	M. P. Lewis	
G-MTFF	Mainair Gemini Flash II	T. N. Taylor	
G-MTFG	AMF Chevvron 232	AMF Microflight Ltd	
G-MTFH	Aerotech MW.5B Sorcerer	R. C. H. Russell	
G-MTFI	Mainair Gemini Flash II	R. A. P. Swainston	
G-MTFJ	Mainair Gemini Flash II	G. Souch & M. D. Peacock	
G-MTFK	Flexiform Striker	D. I. Moult	
G-MTFL	AMF Lazair IIIE	P. J. Turrell	

Notes	Reg.	Type	Owner or Operator
	G-MTFM	Solar Wings Pegasus XL-R	Pegasus Flight Training Ltd
	G-MTFN	Aerotech MW.5 Sorcerer	S. J. Smith
	G-MTFO	Solar Wings Pegasus XL-R	E. Findley
	G-MTFP	Solar Wings Pegasus XL-R	F. R. Hart
	G-MTFR	Solar Wings Pegasus XL-R	A. W. Buchan
	G-MTFS	Solar Wings Pegasus XL-R	C. Vandenberge
	G-MTFT	Solar Wings Pegasus XL-R	C. Woodhouse
	G-MTFU	CFM Shadow Series BD	G. R. Eastwood
	G-MTFW	Mainair Gemini Flash	M. T. G. Pope
	G-MTFX	Mainair Gemini Flash	R. E. D. Bailey
	G-MTFY	CFM Shadow Srs BD	T. W. Dukes
	G-MTFZ	CFM Shadow Srs BD	Target Technology Ltd
	G-MTGA	Mainair Gemini Flash	H. R. Bethune & S. P. Watkins
	G-MTGB	Thruster TST Mk 1	G. Arthur
	G-MTGC	Thruster TST Mk 1	Thruster Aircraft (UK) Ltd
	G-MTGD	Thruster TST Mk 1	Cumbria Microlights
	G-MTGE	Thruster TST Mk 1	R. Gowles
	G-MTGF	Thruster TST Mk 1	Sure Computers Ltd
	G-MTGG	Solar Wings Pegasus Photon	Solar Wings Ltd
	G-MTGI	Solar Wings Pegasus XL-R	P. D. Myer & T. P. Bee
	G-MTGJ	Solar Wings Pegasus XL-R	C. M. Council
	G-MTGK	Solar Wings Pegasus XL-R	I. A. Smith
	G-MTGL	Solar Wings Pegasus XL-R	R. T. Curant
	G-MTGM	Solar Wings Pegasus XL-R	B. M. Marsh
	G-MTGO	Mainair Gemini Flash	S. M. C. Kenyon
	G-MTGP	Thruster TST Mk 1	G. J. Pill
	G-MTGR	Thruster TST Mk 1	S. A. Wood
	G-MTGS	Thruster TST Mk 1	G. & G. E. F. Warren
	G-MTGT	Thruster TST Mk 1	James Ladd & Sons Ltd
	G-MTGU	Thruster TST Mk 1	AV Aviation Ltd
	G-MTGV	CFM Shadow Srs BD	S. A. Wood
	G-MTGW	CFM Shadow Srs BD	CFM Metal-Fax Ltd
	G-MTGX	Hornet Dual Trainer	A. R. Wells
	G-MTGY	Southdown Lightning	P. J. S. Ritchie
	G-MTGZ	Solar Wings Pegasus Photon	Solar Wings Ltd
	G-MTHA	Solar Wings Pegasus Photon	Solar Wings Ltd
	G-MTHB	Aerotech MW.5B Sorcerer	D. B. White
	G-MTHC	Raven X	N. G. Souter
	G-MTHD	Hiway Demon 195	J. M. Spatchert
	G-MTHE	Solar Wings Pegasus XL-Q	Solar Wings Ltd
	G-MTHG	Solar Wings Pegasus XL-R	P. M. Gosney
	G-MTHH	Solar Wings Pegasus XL-R	A. J. Noble
	G-MTHI	Solar Wings Pegasus XL-R	J. F. Walker
	G-MTHJ	Solar Wings Pegasus XL-R	B. R. Ward & P. A. Simpson
	G-MTHK	Solar Wings Pegasus XL-R	B. P. Somerville-Large
	G-MTHL	Solar Wings Pegasus XL-R	B. H. Ashman
	G-MTHM	Solar Wings Pegasus XL-R	D. Cameron
	G-MTHN	Solar Wings Pegasus XL-R	M. J. Mawle
	G-MTHO	Solar Wings Pegasus XL-R	P. Cotton
	G-MTHP	Solar Wings Pegasus XL-R	J. S. Wright
	G-MTHS	CFM Shadow Srs BD	R. Clegg
	G-MTHT	CFM Shadow Srs BD	CFM Metal-Fax Ltd
	G-MTHU	Hornet Dual Trainer	D. M. Couling
	G-MTHV	CFM Shadow Srs BD	P. Walker
	G-MTHW	Mainair Gemini Flash II	I. Todd
	G-MTHX	Mainair Gemini Flash IIA	Microflight Sales Ltd
	G-MTHY	Mainair Gemini Flash IIA	M. Stevenson
	G-MTHZ	Mainair Gemini Flash IIA	G. J. Stallard
	G-MTIA	Mainair Gemini Flash IIA	Airbourne Aviation Ltd
	G-MTIB	Mainair Gemini Flash IIA	G. C. Hobson
	G-MTIC	Mainair Gemini Flash IIA	Mainair Sports Ltd
	G-MTID	Southdown Raven X	R. G. Feathersby
	G-MTIE	Solar Wings Pegasus XL-R	A. G. Sayers
	G-MTIF	Solar Wings Pegasus XL-R	D. J. Gardner
	G-MTIG	Solar Wings Pegasus XL-R	R. Riley
	G-MTIH	Solar Wings Pegasus XL-R	J. A. Iszard
	G-MTII	Solar Wings Pegasus XL-R	W. G. McKinnon
	G-MTIJ	Solar Wings Pegasus XL-R	D. O'Gorman
	G-MTIK	Southdown Raven X	B. W. Atkinson
	G-MTIL	Mainair Gemini Flash IIA	J. L. Hamer
	G-MTIM	Mainair Gemini Flash IIA	C. E. D. Smith
	G-MTIN	Mainair Gemini Flash IIA	B. J. Avery
	G-MTIO	Solar Wings Pegasus XL-R	M. A. Coe
	G-MTIP	Solar Wings Pegasus XL-R	L. F. Banham

Reg.	Type	Owner or Operator	Notes
G-MTIR	Solar Wings Pegasus XL-R	Solar Wings Ltd	
G-MTIS	Solar Wings Pegasus XL-R	D. C. M. Wilson	
G-MTIT	Solar Wings Pegasus XL-R	Solar Wings Ltd	
G-MTIU	Solar Wings Pegasus XL-R	J. W. Teesdale	
G-MTIV	Solar Wings Pegasus XL-R	K. S. Kelso	
G-MTIW	Solar Wings Pegasus XL-R	A. Holmes	
G-MTIX	Solar Wings Pegasus XL-R	Solar Wings Ltd	
G-MTIY	Solar Wings Pegasus XL-R	I. R. Banbury	
G-MTIZ	Solar Wings Pegasus XL-R	H. R. Block	
G-MTJA	Mainair Gemini Flash IIA	J. A. Cuthbertson	
G-MTJB	Mainair Gemini Flash IIA	J. K. Cross	
G-MTJC	Mainair Gemini Flash IIA	D. J. Sagar	
G-MTJD	Mainair Gemini Flash IIA	Vinmar Holdings Ltd	
G-MTJE	Mainair Gemini Flash IIA	D. S. Worman	
G-MTJF	Mainair Gemini Flash IIA	J. H. Hambleton	
G-MTJG	Medway Hybred 44XLR	M. J. Kate	
G-MTJH	Solar Wings Pegasus Flash	C. L. Parker	
G-MTJI	Raven X	L. E. Frank	
G-MTJJ	Solar Wings Pegasus XL-Q	Solar Wings Ltd	
G-MTJK	Mainair Gemini Flash IIA	R. C. White	
G-MTJL	Mainair Gemini Flash IIA	C. Foster	
G-MTJM	Mainair Gemini Flash IIA	J. Wilson	
G-MTJN	Midland Ultralights Sirocco 377GB	R. Harris	
G-MTJO	Mainair Gemini Flash II	G. Dalgarno	
G-MTJP	Medway Hybred 44XLR	J. R. Wells	
G-MTJR	Solar Wings Pegasus XL-R	Pegasus Skylink Ltd	
G-MTJS	Solar Wings Pegasus XL-Q	J. C. W. Smith	
G-MTJT	Mainair Gemini Flash IIA	R. G. Morris	
G-MTJU	MBA Tiger Cub	N. P. Thomson	
G-MTJV	Mainair Gemini Flash IIA	N. Charles & J. Richards	
G-MTJW	Mainair Gemini Flash IIA	J. D. Smith	
G-MTJX	—	—	
G-MTJY	Mainair Gemini Flash IIA	G. Hoult	
G-MTJZ	Mainair Gemini Flash IIA	A. R. Max	
G-MTKA	Thruster TST Mk 1	S. McKenzie & S. Cordova	
G-MTKB	Thruster TST Mk 1	A. Troughton	
G-MTKD	Thruster TST Mk 1	Southwest Airsports Ltd	
G-MTKE	Thruster TST Mk 1	M. P. Allinson	
G-MTKG	Solar Wings Pegasus XL-R	S. J. Beecroft	
G-MTKH	Solar Wings Pegasus XL-R	R. J. Kelly	
G-MTKI	Solar Wings Pegasus XL-R	M. G. McMurray	
G-MTKJ	Solar Wings Pegasus XL-R	S. L. Cropley	
G-MTKK	Solar Wings Pegasus XL-R	J. L. Rawlings	
G-MTKL	—	—	
G-MTKM	Gardner T-M Scout S.2	D. Gardner	
G-MTKN	Mainair Gemini Flash IIA	A. J. Taylor	
G-MTKO	Mainair Gemini Flash IIA	Microflight Sales Ltd	
G-MTKP	Solar Wings Pegasus XL-R	E. J. Blyth	
G-MTKR	CFM Shadow Srs BD	CFM Metal-Fax Ltd	
G-MTKS	CFM Shadow Srs BD	R. B. Milton	
G-MTKU	CFM Shadow Srs BD	CFM Metal-Fax Ltd	
G-MTKV	Mainair Gemini Flash	R. E. D. Bailey	
G-MTKW	Mainair Gemini Flash IIA	K. E. Wedl	
G-MTKX	Mainair Gemini Flash IIA	C. Foster	
G-MTKY	Mainair Gemini Flash IIA	A. J. Haworth	
G-MTKZ	Mainair Gemini Flash IIA	D. Naylor	
G-MTLA	Mainair Gemini Flash IIA	J. M. Thornton	
G-MTLB	Mainair Gemini Flash IIA	H. W. Cullen	
G-MTLC	Mainair Gemini Flash IIA	R. J. Alston	
G-MTLD	Mainair Gemini Flash IIA	D. J. Wood	
G-MTLE	—	—	
G-MTLF	Solar Wings Pegasus XL-R	G. A. Harman	
G-MTLG	Solar Wings Pegasus XL-R	C. J. Dodwell	
G-MTLH	Solar Wings Pegasus XL-R	B. S. Waite	
G-MTLI	Solar Wings Pegasus XL-R	Metropolitan Ambulance Services Co Ltd	
G-MTLJ	Solar Wings Pegasus XL-R	T. D. P. Gates	
G-MTLK	Raven X	Raven Aircraft International Ltd	
G-MTLL	Mainair Gemini Flash IIA	M. F. Shaw & M. J. Bird	
G-MTLM	Thruster TST Mk 1	R. E. Derbyshire	
G-MTLN	Thruster TST Mk 1	Bode Laboratories (UK)	
G-MTLO	Thruster TST Mk 1	M. Rudd	
G-MTLP	Thruster TST Mk 1	N. A. Lobel	

Notes	Reg.	Type	Owner or Operator
	G-MTLR	Thruster TST Mk 1	I. Bartlett
	G-MTLS	Solar Wings Pegasus XL-R	K. M. Simmons
	G-MTLT	Solar Wings Pegasus XL-R	J. C. W. Smith
	G-MTLU	Solar Wings Pegasus XL-R	S. M. Hall
	G-MTLV	Solar Wings Pegasus XL-R	Solar Wings Ltd
	G-MTLW	Solar Wings Pegasus XL-R	S. R. Sutch
	G-MTLX	Medway Hybred 44XLR	Medway Microlights
	G-MTLY	Solar Wings Pegasus XL-R	G. P. Wilkins
	G-MTLZ	Whittaker MW.5 Sorceror	E. H. Gould
	G-MTMA	Mainair Gemini Flash IIA	H. Grindrod
	G-MTMB	Mainair Gemini Flash IIA	E. A. Archer
	G-MTMC	Mainair Gemini Flash IIA	Microflight Sales Ltd
	G-MTMD	Whittaker MW.6 Merlin	F. A. Letcher & J. G. Beesley
	G-MTME	Solar Wings Pegasus XL-R	D. L. Clark
	G-MTMF	Solar Wings Pegasus XL-R	V. J. Wilton
	G-MTMG	Solar Wings Pegasus XL-R	C. W. & P. E. F. Suckling
	G-MTMH	Solar Wings Pegasus XL-R	V. E. J. Smith
	G-MTMI	Solar Wings Pegasus XL-R	T. D. Barrass
	G-MTMJ	Maxair Hummer	M. J. Makin
	G-MTMK	Raven X	P. J. D. Kerr
	G-MTML	Mainair Gemini Flash IIA	I. Walton
	G-MTMM	CFM Shadow Srs BD	W. Friend
	G-MTMO	Raven X	T. A. Saunderson
	G-MTMP	Hornet Dual Trainer/Raven	A. R. Wellsorth
	G-MTMR	Hornet Dual Trainer/Raven	J. G. Teague
	G-MTMS	Hornet Dual Trainer/Raven	A. R. Hogg
	G-MTMT	Mainair Gemini Flash IIA	C. Briggs
	G-MTMU	Mainair Gemini Flash IIA	B. Kirkland
	G-MTMV	Mainair Gemini Flash IIA	J. Clarke
	G-MTMW	Mainair Gemini Flash IIA	D. M. Law
	G-MTMX	CFM Shadow Srs BD	CFM Metal-Fax Ltd
	G-MTMY	CFM Shadow Srs BD	P. A. James
	G-MTMZ	CFM Shadow Srs BD	C. A. Keens
	G-MTNA	CFM Shadow Srs BD	CFM Metal-Fax Ltd
	G-MTNB	Raven X	R. Coar
	G-MTNC	Mainair Gemini Flash IIA	R. Handley
	G-MNTD	Medway Hybred 44XLR	R. A. Clarke
	G-MTNE	Medway Hybred 44XLR	P. Sawday
	G-MTNF	Medway Hybred 44XLR	A. Lupin
	G-MTNG	Mainair Gemini Flash IIA	S. Lichtenstein
	G-MTNH	Mainair Gemini Flash IIA	Airbourne Aviation Ltd
	G-MTNI	Mainair Gemini Flash IIA	K. P. Widdowson
	G-MTNJ	Mainair Gemini Flash IIA	D. C. Mant
	G-MTNK	Weedhopper JC-24B	K. J. Tomlinson
	G-MTNL	Mainair Gemini Flash IIA	Microflight Sales Ltd
	G-MTNM	Mainair Gemini Flash IIA	Microflight Sales Ltd
	G-MTNN	Mainair Gemini Flash IIA	M. Byl
	G-MTNO	Solar Wings Pegasus XL-Q	Solar Wings Ltd
	G-MTNP	Solar Wings Pegasus XL-Q	Solar Wings Ltd
	G-MTNR	Thruster TST Mk 1	Thruster Aircraft (UK) Ltd
	G-MTNS	Thruster TST Mk 1	Thruster Aircraft (UK) Ltd
	G-MTNT	Thruster TST Mk 1	Thruster Aircraft (UK) Ltd
	G-MTNU	Thruster TST Mk 1	Thruster Aircraft (UK) Ltd
	G-MTNV	Thruster TST Mk 1	Thruster Aircraft (UK) Ltd
	G-MTNW	Thruster TST Mk 1	Thruster Aircraft (UK) Ltd
	G-MTNX	Mainair Gemini Flash II	P. J. Corker
	G-MTNY	Mainair Gemini Flash IIA	S. J. Ives
	G-MTNZ	Solar Wings Pegasus XL-Q	Solar Wings Ltd
	G-MTOA	Solar Wings Pegasus XL-R	J. E. Glendinning
	G-MTOB	Solar Wings Pegasus XL-R	R. F. Walbank
	G-MTOC	Solar Wings Pegasus XL-R	D. Jordan
	G-MTOD	Solar Wings Pegasus XL-R	G. G. Clayton
	G-MTOE	Solar Wings Pegasus XL-R	Solar Wings Ltd
	G-MTOF	Solar Wings Pegasus XL-R	Solar Wings Ltd
	G-MTOG	Solar Wings Pegasus XL-R	Solar Wings Ltd
	G-MTOH	Solar Wings Pegasus XL-R	H. Cook
	G-MTOI	Solar Wings Pegasus XL-R	J. Grotian
	G-MTOJ	Solar Wings Pegasus XL-R	T. J. Bax
	G-MTOK	Solar Wings Pegasus XL-R	R. B. Randall
	G-MTOL	Solar Wings Pegasus XL-R	Solar Wings Ltd
	G-MTOM	Solar Wings Pegasus XL-R	A. J. Macfie
	G-MTON	Solar Wings Pegasus XL-R	Solar Wings Ltd
	G-MTOO	Solar Wings Pegasus XL-R	Solar Wings Ltd
	G-MTOP	Solar Wings Pegasus XL-R	Solar Wings Ltd

Reg.	Type	Owner or Operator	Notes
G-MTOR	Solar Wings Pegasus XL-R	Solar Wings Ltd	
G-MTOS	Solar Wings Pegasus XL-R	N. A. Summerbell	
G-MTOT	Solar Wings Pegasus XL-R	Solar Wings Ltd	
G-MTOU	Solar Wings Pegasus XL-R	W. A. Emmerson	
G-MTOV	Solar Wings Pegasus XL-R	Solar Wings Ltd	
G-MTOW	Solar Wings Pegasus XL-R	Solar Wings Ltd	
G-MTOX	Solar Wings Pegasus XL-R	Solar Wings Ltd	
G-MTOY	Solar Wings Pegasus XL-R	Solar Wings Ltd	
G-MTOZ	Solar Wings Pegasus XL-R	Solar Wings Ltd	
G-MTPA	Mainair Gemini Flash IIA	W. H. Smith	
G-MTPB	Mainair Gemini Flash IIA	M. T. Lequip Ltd	
G-MTPC	Raven X	R. L. Cross	
G-MTPD	—	—	
G-MTPE	Solar Wings Pegasus XL-R	Solar Wings Ltd	
G-MTPF	Solar Wings Pegasus XL-R	Solar Wings Ltd	
G-MTPG	Solar Wings Pegasus XL-R	Solar Wings Ltd	
G-MTPH	Solar Wings Pegasus XL-R	Solar Wings Ltd	
G-MTPI	Solar Wings Pegasus XL-R	Solar Wings Ltd	
G-MTPJ	Solar Wings Pegasus XL-R	Solar Wings Ltd	
G-MTPK	Solar Wings Pegasus XL-R	Solar Wings Ltd	
G-MTPL	Solar Wings Pegasus XL-R	Solar Wings Ltd	
G-MTPM	Solar Wings Pegasus XL-R	Solar Wings Ltd	
G-MTPN	Solar Wings Pegasus XL-Q	Solar Wings Ltd	
G-MTPO	Solar Wings Pegasus XL-Q	Solar Wings Ltd	
G-MTPP	Solar Wings Pegasus XL-R	Solar Wings Ltd	
G-MTPR	Solar Wings Pegasus XL-R	Solar Wings Ltd	
G-MTPS	Solar Wings Pegasus XL-Q	Solar Wings Ltd	
G-MTPT	Thruster TST Mk 1	Thruster Aircraft (UK) Ltd	
G-MTPU	Thruster TST Mk 1	Thruster Aircraft (UK) Ltd	
G-MTPV	Thruster TST Mk 1	Thruster Aircraft (UK) Ltd	
G-MTPW	Thruster TST Mk 1	Thruster Aircraft (UK) Ltd	
G-MTPX	Thruster TST Mk 1	Thruster Aircraft (UK) Ltd	
G-MTPY	Thruster TST Mk 1	A. N. Wicks	
G-MTPZ	Solar Wings Pegasus XL-R	M. R. P. McCarthy	
G-MTRA	Mainair Gemini Flash IIA	A. Bulling	
G-MTRB	Mainair Gemini Flash IIA	Microflight Sales Ltd	
G-MTRC	Midlands Ultralights Sirocco 377GB	W. B. Cardew	
G-MTRD	Midlands Ultralights Sirocco 377GB	J. R. North	
G-MTRE	Whittaker MW.6 Merlin	M. J. Batchelor	
G-MTRF	Mainair Gemini Flash IIA	J. McGaughran	
G-MTRG	Mainair Gemini Flash IIA	D. C. Harrison	
G-MTRH	Hiway Demon	D. C. P. Cardey	
G-MTRI	Hiway Demon	S. D. Pain	
G-MTRJ	AMF Chevvron 232	Chartersteps Ltd	
G-MTRK	Hornet Dual Trainer	Templeward Ltd	
G-MTRL	Hornet Dual Trainer	M. J. Sinnett	
G-MTRM	Solar Wings Pegasus XL-R	Solar Wings Ltd	
G-MTRN	Solar Wings Pegasus XL-R	Solar Wings Ltd	
G-MTRO	Solar Wings Pegasus XL-R	Solar Wings Ltd	
G-MTRP	Solar Wings Pegasus XL-R	Solar Wings Ltd	
G-MTRR	Solar Wings Pegasus XL-R	Solar Wings Ltd	
G-MTRS	Solar Wings Pegasus XL-R	Solar Wings Ltd	
G-MTRT	Raven X	G. C. Weighell	
G-MTRU	Solar Wings Pegasus XL-Q	Solar Wings Ltd	
G-MTRV	Solar Wings Pegasus XL-Q	Solar Wings Ltd	
G-MTRW	Raven X	R. J. Lumb	
G-MTRX	Whittaker MW.5 Sorceror	W. Turner	
G-MTRY	Noble Hardman Snowbird IV	Noble Hardman Aviation Ltd	
G-MTRZ	Mainair Gemini Flash IIA	G. C. Hobson	
G-MTSA	Mainair Gemini Flash IIA	Microflight Sales Ltd	
G-MTSB	Mainair Gemini Flash IIA	Microflight Sales Ltd	
G-MTSC	Mainair Gemini Flash IIA	B. D. Godden	
G-MTSD	Raven X	H. J. Aldridge	
G-MTSE	Flexiform Striker	D. Dixon	
G-MTSF	Aerial Arts Chaser 110SX	D. Dixon	
G-MTSG	CFM Shadow Srs BD	CFM Metal-Fax Ltd	
G-MTSH	Thruster TST Mk 1	Thruster Aircraft (UK) Ltd	
G-MTSI	Thruster TST Mk 1	Thruster Aircraft (UK) Ltd	
G-MTSJ	Thruster TST Mk 1	Thruster Aircraft (UK) Ltd	
G-MTSK	Thruster TST Mk 1	Thruster Aircraft (UK) Ltd	
G-MTSL	Thruster TST Mk 1	Thruster Aircraft (UK) Ltd	
G-MTSM	Thruster TST Mk 1	Thruster Aircraft (UK) Ltd	

Notes	Reg.	Type	Owner or Operator
	G-MTSN	Solar Wings Pegasus XL-R	Solar Wings Ltd
	G-MTSO	Solar Wings Pegasus XL-R	Solar Wings Ltd
	G-MTSP	Solar Wings Pegasus XL-R	Solar Wings Ltd
	G-MTSR	Solar Wings Pegasus XL-R	Solar Wings Ltd
	G-MTSS	Solar Wings Pegasus XL-R	Solar Wings Ltd
	G-MTST	Thruster TST Mk 1	Thruster Aircraft (UK) Ltd
	G-MTSU	—	—
	G-MTSV	—	—
	G-MTSW	—	—
	G-MTSX	—	—
	G-MTSY	—	—
	G-MTSZ	—	—
	G-MTTA	—	—
	G-MTTB	—	—
	G-MTTC	—	—
	G-MTTD	—	—
	G-MTTE	—	—
	G-MTTF	Whittaker MW.6 Merlin	V. E. Booth
	G-MTTG	Excalibur TriPacer 250	S. C. Goozee
	G-MTTH	CFM Shadow Srs BD	C. T. H. Pattinson
	G-MTTI	Mainair Gemini Flash IIA	D. Houghton
	G-MTTJ	CFM Shadow Srs BD	CFM Metal-Fax Ltd
	G-MTTK	Southdown Lightning DS	D. E. Oakley
	G-MTTL	—	—
	G-MTTM	—	—
	G-MVAF	Southdown Puma Sprint	P. N. Cruise
	G-MWCR	Southdown Puma Sprint	C. R. Read
	G-MWFT	MBA Tiger Cub 440	W. F. Tremayne
	G-MWOW	CFM Shadow Srs B	Global Aviation Projects Ltd
	G-MWPL	MBA Tiger Cub 440	P. A. Lee
	G-MWRS	Ultravia Super Pelican	Embermere Ltd
	G-MWTF	Mainair Gemini	G. D. C. Buyers

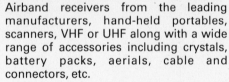

Military to Civil Cross-Reference

Serial carried	Civil identity	Serial carried	Civil identity
08 (Luftwaffe)	G-WULF	B6401	G-AWYY
14 (Luftwaffe)	G-BJAX	B7270	G-BFCZ
17 (Luftwaffe)	G-ATBG	C4912	G-BLWM
26 (US)	G-BAVO	D88	G-AWXZ
45 (Aeronavale)	G-BHFG	D5397/17	G-BFXL
75	G-AFDX	C1904	G-PFAP
88 (USN)	G-BKCK	D7889	G-AANM
92 (31-GW FrAF)	G-BJGW	D8096 (D)	G-AEPH
103 (Aeronavale)	G-BHXJ	E-15 (RNethAF)	G-BIYU
120 (Fr AF)	G-AZGC	E449	G-EBJE
152/17	G-ATJM	EM-01 (Spanish AF)	G-AAOR
164 (USN)	G-BKGL	F904	G-EBIA
168	G-BFDE	F938	G-EBIC
178 (Irish AC)	G-BKOS	F939 (6)	G-EBIB
385 (RCAF)	G-BGPB	F943	G-BIHF
422-15	G-AVJO	F943	G-BKDT
1076	G-AVEB	F1425 (17)	G-BEFR
2345	G-ATVP	F5447 (N)	G-BKER
2807 (VE-111 USN)	G-BHTH	F5459	G-INNY
3066	G-AETA	F8010	G-BDWJ
4253/18	G-BFPL	F8614	G-AWAU
5964	G-BFVH	G-48-1 (Class B)	G-ALSX
7198/18	G-AANJ	H2311	G-ABAA
7334 (2+1 Luftwaffe)	G-SYFW	H5199	G-ADEV
7797 (USAAF)	G-BFAF	J9941 (57)	G-ABMR
8449M	G-ASWJ	— (K-33 USAAF)	G-BJLH
18393 (C.A.F.)	G-BCYK	K1786	G-AFTA
2-7767	G-BIHW	K1930	G-BKBB
30210	N9455Z	K2050	G-ASCM
54136 (USN)	G-CTKL	K2059	G-PFAR
56321 (U-AB RNorAF)	G-BKPY	K2060	G-BKZM
88297	N8297	K2567	G-MOTH
115042 (TA-042 USAF)	G-BGHU	K2568	G-APMM
18-2001 (USAAF)	G-BIZV	K2572	G-AOZH
226671 (USAAF)	N47DD	K3215	G-AHSA
231983 (USAAF)	F-BDRS	K3731	G-RODI
315509 (USAAF)	G-BHUB	K4235	G-AHMJ
329417 (USAAF)	G-BDHK	K5414	G-AENP
329601 (D-44 USAAF)	G-AXHR	L2301	G-AIZG
329934 (72-B USAAF)	G-BCPH	L8032	G-AMRK
330485 (C-44 USAAF)	G-AJES	N1854	G-AIBE
413048 (39-E USAAF)	G-BCXJ	N3788	G-AKPF
429366 (USAAF)	N9115Z	N4877 (VX-F)	G-AMDA
454537 (04-J)	G-BFDL	N5180	G-EBKY
461748	G-BHDK	N5182	G-APUP
463221 (G4-5 USAAF)	N51JJ	N5195	G-ABOX
472216	G-BIXL	N6452	G-BIAU
479766 (USAAF)	G-BKHG	N6466	G-ANKZ
479865 (A-44)	G-BHPK	N6532	G-ANTS
480015 (USAAF)	G-AKIB	N6847	G-APAL
480133 (44-B USAAF)	G-BDCD	N6848	G-BALX
480321 (44-H USAAF)	G-FRAN	N6985	G-AHMN
480480 (USAAF)	G-BECN	N9191	G-ALND
485784 (YB-E)	G-BEDF	N9238	G-ANEL
44-79609 (USAAF)	G-BHXY	N9389	G-ANJA
44-80594 (USAAF)	G-BEDJ	N9508	G-APCU
511371 (USAAF VF-S)	NL1051S	N9510	G-AOEL
542447	G-SCUB	P6382	G-AJRS
542457	G-LION	R-163 (RNethAF)	G-BIRH
542474 (R-184)	G-PCUB	R1914	G-AHUJ
51-15227 (USN)	G-BKRA	R4907	G-ANCS
A16-199 (SF-R RAAF)	G-BEOX	R4959	G-ARAZ
A8226	G-BIDW	R5086	G-APIH
B1807	G-EAVX	S1287	G-BEYB
B4863	G-BLXT	S3398 (2)	G-BFYO

Serial carried	Civil identity	Serial carried	Civil identity
T5424	G-AJOA	NJ703	G-AKPI
T5493	G-ANEF	NP181	G-AOAR
T5672	G-ALRI	NP184	G-ANYP
T5854	G-ANKK	NP303	G-ANZJ
T5879	G-AXBW	NX611	G-ASXX
T6313	G-AHVU	PG617	G-AYVY
T6645	G-AIIZ	PG651	G-AYUX
T6818	G-ANKT	PL983	G-PRXI
T7281	G-ARTL	RG333	G-AIEK
T7404	G-ANMV	RG333	G-AKEZ
T7997	G-AOBH	RH377	G-ALAH
T7909	G-ANON	RL962	G-AHED
T9707	G-AKKR	RM221	G-ANXR
T9738	G-AKAT	RM689 (MN-E)	G-ALGT
U-0247	G-AGOY	RR299 (HT-E)	G-ASKH
U-142 (Swiss AF)	G-BONE	RT486	G-AJGJ
V3388	G-AHTW	SM832	G-WWII
V9281 (RU-M)	G-BCWL	SM969	G-BRAF
V9441 (AR-A)	G-AZWT	TA634	G-AWJV
Z2033	G-ASTL	TA719	G-ASKC
Z7015	G-BKTH	TE566	G-BLCK
Z7197	G-AKZN	TJ569	G-AKOW
Z7258	G-AHGD	TW439	G-ANRP
AP507 (KX-P)	G-ACWP	TW467	G-ANIE
AR213 (PR-D)	G-AIST	TW591	G-ARIH
AR501 (NN-D)	G-AWII	TW641	G-ATDN
BS676 (K-U)	G-KUKU	VF516	G-ASMZ
DE208	G-AGYU	VI-3 (Finnish AF)	G-BAAY
DE363	G-ANFC	VL348	G-AVVO
DE623	G-ANFI	VL349	G-AWSA
DE992	G-AXXV	VM360	G-APHV
DF128 (RCO-U)	G-AOJJ	VP955	G-DVON
DF155	G-ANFV	VP962	G-BLRB
DF198	G-BBRB	VR192	G-APIT
DG590	G-ADMW	VR249	G-APIY
DR613	G-AFJB	VS356	G-AOLU
EM720	G-AXAN	VS610	G-AOKL
EM903	G-APBI	VS623	G-AOKZ
EX280	G-TEAC	VX118	G-ASNB
FE992	G-BDAM	VZ728	G-AGOS
FR870	NL1009N	WA576	G-ALSS
FS728	G-BAFM	WA577	G-ALST
FT239	G-BIWX	WB533	G-DEVN
FT391	G-AZBN	WB588	G-AOTD
FX301 (FD-NQ)	G-JUDI	WB660	G-ARMB
HB275	N5063N	WB763	G-BBMR
HB751	G-BCBL	WD363 (5)	G-BCIH
HD368 (VO-A)	G-BKXW	WD379 (K)	G-APLO
JV928 (Y)	G-BLSC	WD413	G-BFIR
KB976 (LQ-K)	G-BCOH	WE569	G-ASAJ
KG874 (YS-L)	G-DAKS	WG307	G-BCYJ
KL161	N88972	WG316	G-BCAH
LB312	G-AHXE	WG348	G-BBMV
LB375	G-AHGW	WG350	G-BPAL
LF858	G-BLUZ	WG422 (16)	G-BFAX
LZ766	G-ALCK	WG719	G-BRMA
MD497	G-ANLW	WJ288 (029)	G-SALY
MH434 (ZD-B)	G-ASJV	WJ237 (113/O)	G-BLTG
MJ730	G-BLAS	WJ358	G-ARYD
ML407 (OU-L)	G-LFIX	WJ945	G-BEDV
ML417 (2I-T)	G-BJSG	WK522	G-BCOU
MP425	G-AITB	WL626	G-BHDD
MT360	G-AKWT	WM167	G-LOSM
MT438	G-AREI	WP321 (750/CU)	G-BRFC
MT818 (G-M)	G-AIDN	WP788	G-BCHL
MV154	G-BKMI	WP790	G-BBNC
MV293	G-SPIT	WP808	G-BDEU
MV370 (AV-L)	G-FXIV	WP857	G-BDRJ
MW100	G-AGNV	WP903	G-BCGC
NF875 (603/CH)	G-AGTM	WP977	G-BHRD
NH238 (D-A)	G-MKIX	WR410	G-BLKA
NJ695	G-AJXV	WT933	G-ALSW

Serial carried	Civil identity	Serial carried	Civil identity
WV198	G-BJWY	XM655	N655AV
WV493	G-BDYG	XM685	G-AYZJ
WV783	G-ALSP	XN351	G-BKSC
WW397 (N-E)	G-BKHP	XN437	G-AXWA
WZ507	G-VTII	XN441	G-BGKT
WZ662	G-BKVK	XN637	G-BKOU
WZ711	G-AVHT	XP279	G-BWKK
WZ868	G-BCIW	XP282	G-BGTC
XB733	G-ATBF	XP328	G-BKHC
XF690	G-BGKA	XP355	G-BEBC
XF785	G-ALBN	XR240	G-BDFH
XF836 (J-G)	G-AWRY	XR241	G-AXRR
XF877 (JX)	G-AWVF	XR267	G-BJXR
XG452	G-BRMB	XR269	G-BDXY
XG547	G-HAPR	XR363	G-OHCA
XJ348	G-NAVY	XR944	G-ATTB
XJ389	G-AJJP	XS101	G-GNAT
XJ407	G-BKHB	A1+BT	G-APRR
XJ763	G-BKHA	F+IS (Luftwaffe)	G-BIRW
XK417	G-AVXY	BA+AY (Luftwaffe)	G-BAAY
XK896	G-RNAS	BU+CK (Luftwaffe)	G-BUCK
XL426	G-VJET	D2+600 (Luftwaffe)	G-BFHG
XL502	G-BMYP	1Z+EK (Luftwaffe)	N9012P
XL717	G-AOXG	RF+16 (Luftwaffe)	G-PTWO
XL809	G-BLIX	N9+AA (Luftwaffe)	G-BECL
XM553	G-AWSV	ZA+WN (Luftwaffe)	G-AZMH
XM556	G-HELI	① (Russian AF)	G-KYAK
XM575	G-BLMC	CE (USAAF)	G-BICE

Overseas Airliner Registrations

(Aircraft included in this section are those most likely to be seen at UK and major European airports on scheduled or charter services.)

A6 (United Arab Emirates)

Notes	Reg.	Type	Owner or Operator
	A6-EKA	Airbus A.310-304	Emirate Airlines
	A6-EKB	Airbus A.310-304	Emirate Airlines
	A6	Airbus A.300-603R	Emirate Airlines

A40 (Oman)

	A40-TP	L-1011-385 TriStar 100 (110)	Gulf Air
	A40-TR	L-1011-385 TriStar 100 (111)	Gulf Air
	A40-TS	L-1011-385 TriStar 100 (109)	Gulf Air
	A40-TT	L-1011-385 TriStar 200 (107)	Gulf Air
	A40-TV	L-1011-385 TriStar 200 (108)	Gulf Air
	A40-TW	L-1011-385 TriStar 200 (101)	Gulf Air
	A40-TX	L-1011-385 TriStar 200 (102)	Gulf Air
	A40-TY	L-1011-385 TriStar 200 (103)	Gulf Air
	A40-TZ	L-1011-385 TriStar 200 (104)	Gulf Air
	A40-	Boeing 767-300ER	Gulf Air
	A40-	Boeing 767-300ER	Gulf Air

Note: Gulf Air also operates TriStar 200s N92TA (105) and N92TB (106).

AP (Pakistan)

	AP-AXA	Boeing 707-340C	Pakistan International Airlines
	AP-AXG	Boeing 707-340C	Pakistan International Airlines
	AP-AYV	Boeing 747-282B	Pakistan International Airlines
	AP-AYW	Boeing 747-282B	Pakistan International Airlines
	AP-AZW	Boeing 707-351B	Pakistan International Airlines
	AP-BAA	Boeing 707-351B	Pakistan International Airlines
	AP-BAK	Boeing 747-240B (SCD)	Pakistan International Airlines
	AP-BAT	Boeing 747-240B (SCD)	Pakistan International Airlines
	AP-BBK	Boeing 707-323C	Pakistan International Airlines
	AP-BCL	Boeing 747-217B	Pakistan International Airlines
	AP-BCM	Boeing 747-217B	Pakistan International Airlines
	AP-BCN	Boeing 747-217B	Pakistan International Airlines
	AP-BCO	Boeing 747-217B	Pakistan International Airlines

B (China/Taiwan)

	B-198	Boeing 747-2R7F (SCD)	China Airlines
	B-1862	Boeing 747SP-09	China Airlines
	B-1864	Boeing 747-209B (SCD)	China Airlines
	B-1866	Boeing 747-209B	China Airlines
	B-1880	Boeing 747SP-09	China Airlines
	B-1886	Boeing 747-209B	China Airlines
	B-1888	Boeing 747-209B	China Airlines
	B-1894	Boeing 747-209F (SCD)	China Airlines
	B-2402	Boeing 707-3J6B	CAAC
	B-2404	Boeing 707-3J6B	CAAC
	B-2406	Boeing 707-3J6B	CAAC
	B-2408	Boeing 707-3J6B	CAAC
	B-2410	Boeing 707-3J6C	CAAC
	B-2412	Boeing 707-3J6C	CAAC
	B-2414	Boeing 707-3J6C	CAAC
	B-2416	Boeing 707-3J6C	CAAC
	B-2418	Boeing 707-3J6C	CAAC
	B-2420	Boeing 707-3J6C	CAAC

Reg.	Type	Owner or Operator	Notes
B-2442	Boeing 747SP-J6	CAAC	
B-2444	Boeing 747SP-J6	CAAC	
B-2446	Boeing 747-2J6B (SCD)	CAAC	
B-2448	Boeing 747-2J6B (SCD)	CAAC	
B-2450	Boeing 747-2J6B	CAAC	

Note: CAAC also operates Boeing 747SPs N1301E and N1304E. China Airlines operates N4508H and N4522V, both Boeing 747SP-09s.

C5 (Gambia)

Note: Gambia Airways operates one Boeing 707 on lease.

C9 (Mozambique)

Note: Lineas Aereas de Mocambique (LAM) operates DC-10-30 F-GDJK on lease from UTA.

C-F and C-G (Canada)

Reg.	Type	Owner or Operator	Notes
C-FCPO	Douglas DC-8-63 (801)	Worldways Canada	
C-FCPP	Douglas DC-8-63 (802)	Worldways Canada	
C-FCPQ	Douglas DC-8-63 (803)	Worldways Canada	
C-FCPS	Douglas DC-8-63 (804)	Worldways Canada	
C-FCRA	Douglas DC-10-30 (909)	Canadian Airlines International *Empress of Hong Kong*	
C-FCRB	Douglas DC-10-30 (910)	Canadian Airlines International *Empress of Tokyo*	
C-FCRD	Douglas DC-10-30 (912)	Canadian Airlines International *Empress of Lisbon*	
C-FCRE	Douglas DC-10-30 (911)	Canadian Airlines International *Empress of Canada*	
C-FDJC	Boeing 747-1D1 (399)	Wardair Canada *Phil Garrett*	
C-FFUN	Boeing 747-1D1 (398)	Wardair Canada *Romeo Vachan*	
C-FGWD	Airbus A.310-304 (803)	Wardair Canada *G. Levine Leigh*	
C-FHWD	Airbus A.310-304 (804)	Wardair Canada *S. R. Stan McMillan*	
C-FNWD	Airbus A.310-304 (805)	Wardair Canada *Don C. Braun*	
C-FSWD	Airbus A.310-304	Wardair Canada	
C-FTIK	Douglas DC-8-73AF (867)	Air Canada	
C-FTIO	Douglas DC-8-73AF (871)	Air Canada	
C-FTIP	Douglas DC-8-73AF (872)	Air Canada	
C-FTIQ	Douglas DC-8-73CF (873)	Air Canada	
C-FTIR	Douglas DC-8-73AF (874)	Air Canada	
C-FTIS	Douglas DC-8-73AF (875)	Air Canada	
C-FTIU	Douglas DC-8-73AF (876)	Air Canada	
C-FTIV	Douglas DC-8-73AF (877)	Air Canada	
C-FTNH	L.1011-385 TriStar 100 (508)	Air Canada	
C-FTNI	L.1011-385 TriStar 100 (509)	Air Canada	
C-FTNJ	L.1011-385 TriStar 100 (510)	Air Canada	
C-FTNK	L.1011-385 TriStar 100 (511)	Air Canada	
C-FTNL	L.1011-385 TriStar 100 (512)	Air Canada	
C-FTOB	Boeing 747-133 (302)	Wardair Canada *H. A. Doc Oakes*	
C-FTOC	Boeing 747-133 (303)	Air Canada	
C-FTOD	Boeing 747-133 (304)	Air Canada	
C-FTOE	Boeing 747-133 (305)	Air Canada	
C-GAGA	Boeing 747-233B (306)	Air Canada	
C-GAGB	Boeing 747-233B (307)	Air Canada	
C-GAGC	Boeing 747-238B	Air Canada	
C-GAGF	L.1011-385 TriStar 500 (551)	Air Canada	
C-GAGG	L.1011-385 TriStar 500 (552)	Air Canada	
C-GAGH	L.1011-385 TriStar 500 (553)	Air Canada	
C-GAGI	L.1011-385 TriStar 500 (554)	Air Canada	
C-GAGJ	L.1011-385 TriStar 500 (555)	Air Canada	
C-GAGK	L.1011-385 TriStar 500 (556)	Air Canada	
C-GAUY	Boeing 767-233 (609)	Air Canada	
C-GAVC	Boeing 767-233ER (611)	Air Canada	
C-GAVF	Boeing 767-233ER (612)	Air Canada	
C-GCPC	Douglas DC-10-30 (901)	Canadian Airlines International *Empress of Amsterdam*	

Notes	Reg.	Type	Owner or Operator
	C-GCPD	Douglas DC-10-30 (902)	Canadian Airlines International *Empress of British Colombia*
	C-GCPE	Douglas DC-10-30 (903)	Canadian Airlines International *Empress of Buenos Aires*
	C-GCPF	Douglas DC-10-30 (904)	Canadian Airlines International *Empress of Santiago*
	C-GCPG	Douglas DC-10-30 (905)	Canadian Airlines International *Empress of Fiji*
	C-GCPH	Douglas DC-10-30 (906)	Canadian Airlines International *Empress of Lima*
	C-GCPI	Douglas DC-10-30 (907)	Canadian Airlines International *Empress of Auckland*
	C-GCPJ	Douglas DC-10-30 (908)	Canadian Airlines International *Empress of Rome*
	C-GDSP	Boeing 767-233ER	Air Canada
	C-GDSS	Boeing 767-233ER	Air Canada
	C-GDSU	Boeing 767-233ER	Air Canada
	C-GDSY	Boeing 767-233ER	Air Canada
	C-GFHX	Douglas DC-10-30 (103)	Wardair Canada *S. R. McMilland*
	C-GIES	L.1011-385 TriStar 50 (101)	Worldways Canada
	C-GIFE	L.1011-385 TriStar 50 (102)	Worldways Canada
	C-GMXB	Douglas DC-8-61 (801)	Nationair
	C-GMXD	Douglas DC-8-61 (805)	Nationair
	C-GMXQ	Douglas DC-8-61 (802)	Nationair
	C-GMXR	Douglas DC-8-62 (803)	Nationair
	C-GMXY	Douglas DC-8-62 (804)	Nationair
	C-GQBA	Douglas DC-8-63	Nationair
	C-GQBF	Douglas DC-8-63	Nationair
	C-GXRB	Douglas DC-10-30 (101)	Wardair Canada *C. H. Punch Dickens*
	C-GXRC	Douglas DC-10-30 (102)	Wardair Canada *W. R. Wop May*

Note: Airline fleet number carried on aircraft is shown in parenthesis. All Wardair's DC-10s will leave the airline during 1988.

CCCP (Russia)

All aircraft listed are operated by Aeroflot. The registrations are prefixed by CCCP in each case.

Notes	Reg.	Type	Notes	Reg.	Type
	65020	Tu-134A		65610	Tu-134
	65024	Tu-134A		65611	Tu-134
	65027	Tu-134A		65612	Tu-134
	65028	Tu-134A		65613	Tu-134
	65035	Tu-134A		65614	Tu-134
	65036	Tu-134A		65615	Tu-134
	65038	Tu-134A		65616	Tu-134
	65040	Tu-134A		65617	Tu-134
	65042	Tu-134A		65618	Tu-134
	65044	Tu-134A		65619	Tu-134
	65048	Tu-134A		65620	Tu-134
	65050	Tu-134A		65621	Tu-134
	65051	Tu-134A		65625	Tu-134
	65076	Tu-134A		65627	Tu-134
	65077	Tu-134A		65628	Tu-134
	65087	Tu-134A		65629	Tu-134
	65089	Tu-134A		65630	Tu-134
	65107	Tu-134A		65631	Tu-134
	65119	Tu-134A		65632	Tu-134
	65134	Tu-134A		65633	Tu-134
	65135	Tu-134A		65634	Tu-134
	65145	Tu-134A		65635	Tu-134
	65550	Tu-134A		65636	Tu-134
	65551	Tu-134A		65637	Tu-134
	65601	Tu-134		65639	Tu-134
	65602	Tu-134		65642	Tu-134
	65603	Tu-134		65643	Tu-134
	65604	Tu-134		65644	Tu-134A
	65605	Tu-134		65645	Tu-134A
	65606	Tu-134		65646	Tu-134A
	65607	Tu-134		65647	Tu-134A
	65608	Tu-134		65648	Tu-134A
	65609	Tu-134		65649	Tu-134A

Reg.	Type	Notes	Reg.	Type	Notes
65650	Tu-134A		85003	Tu-154	
65651	Tu-134A		85004	Tu-154	
65652	Tu-134A		85005	Tu-154	
65653	Tu-134A		85006	Tu-154	
65654	Tu-134A		85007	Tu-154	
65655	Tu-134A		85008	Tu-154	
65656	Tu-134A		85009	Tu-154	
65657	Tu-134A		85010	Tu-154	
65658	Tu-134A		85011	Tu-154	
65659	Tu-134A		85012	Tu-154	
65660	Tu-134A		85013	Tu-154	
65661	Tu-134A		85014	Tu-154	
65662	Tu-134A		85015	Tu-154	
65663	Tu-134A		85016	Tu-154	
65664	Tu-134A		85017	Tu-154	
65665	Tu-134A		85018	Tu-154	
65666	Tu-134A		85019	Tu-154	
65667	Tu-134A		85020	Tu-154	
65669	Tu-134A		85021	Tu-154	
65681	Tu-134A		85022	Tu-154	
65697	Tu-134A		85024	Tu-154	
65717	Tu-134A		85025	Tu-154	
65739	Tu-134A		85028	Tu-154	
65757	Tu-134A		85029	Tu-154	
65758	Tu-134A		85030	Tu-154	
65765	Tu-134A		85031	Tu-154	
65769	Tu-134A-3		85032	Tu-154	
65770	Tu-134A-3		85033	Tu-154	
65772	Tu-134A		85034	Tu-154	
65777	Tu-134A-3		85035	Tu-154	
65780	Tu-134A		85037	Tu-154	
65781	Tu-134A-3		85038	Tu-154	
65782	Tu-134A		85039	Tu-154	
65783	Tu-134A-3		85040	Tu-154	
65784	Tu-134A-3		85041	Tu-154	
65785	Tu-134A-3		85042	Tu-154	
65786	Tu-134A-3		85043	Tu-154	
65790	Tu-134A-3		85044	Tu-154	
65791	Tu-134A		85049	Tu-154	
65794	Tu-134A		85050	Tu-154	
65795	Tu-134A		85051	Tu-154	
65801	Tu-134A		85052	Tu-154	
65802	Tu-134A		85055	Tu-154	
65815	Tu-134A		85056	Tu-154	
65837	Tu-134A		85057	Tu-154	
65838	Tu-134A		85059	Tu-154A	
65851	Tu-134A		85060	Tu-154A	
65854	Tu-134A		85061	Tu-154A	
65862	Tu-134A		85062	Tu-154C	
65864	Tu-134A		85063	Tu-154C	
65872	Tu-134A		85064	Tu-154A	
65886	Tu-134A		85065	Tu-154A	
65888	Tu-134A		85066	Tu-154A	
65892	Tu-134A		85067	Tu-154C	
65894	Tu-134A		85068	Tu-154A	
65904	Tu-134A		85069	Tu-154A	
65912	Tu-134A-3		85070	Tu-154A	
65915	Tu-134A		85071	Tu-154A	
65916	Tu-134A		85072	Tu-154A	
65919	Tu-134A		85074	Tu-154A	
65950	Tu-134A		85075	Tu-154A	
65951	Tu-134A		85076	Tu-154A	
65953	Tu-134A		85078	Tu-154A	
65954	Tu-134A		85079	Tu-154A	
65955	Tu-134A		85080	Tu-154A	
65965	Tu-134A		85081	Tu-154A	
65967	Tu-134A		85082	Tu-154A	
65971	Tu-134A		85083	Tu-154A	
65972	Tu-134A		85084	Tu-154A	
65973	Tu-134A		85085	Tu-154A	
65974	Tu-134A		85086	Tu-154A	
65976	Tu-134A		85087	Tu-154A	
85001	Tu-154		85088	Tu-154A	
85002	Tu-154		85089	Tu-154A	

Notes	Reg.	Type	Notes	Reg.	Type
	85090	Tu-154A		85170	Tu-154B
	85091	Tu-154A		85171	Tu-154B
	85092	Tu-154B-1		85172	Tu-154B
	85093	Tu-154A		85173	Tu-154B
	85094	Tu-154A		85174	Tu-154B
	85095	Tu-154A		85176	Tu-154B
	85096	Tu-154B-2		85177	Tu-154B
	85097	Tu-154B-1		85178	Tu-154B
	85098	Tu-154A		85179	Tu-154B
	85099	Tu-154A		85180	Tu-154B
	85100	Tu-154A		85181	Tu-154B
	85101	Tu-154A		85182	Tu-154B
	85102	Tu-154A		85183	Tu-154B
	85103	Tu-154A		85184	Tu-154B
	85104	Tu-154A		85185	Tu-154B
	85105	Tu-154A		85186	Tu-154B
	85106	Tu-154B-2		85187	Tu-154B
	85107	Tu-154A		85188	Tu-154B
	85108	Tu-154A		85189	Tu-154B
	85109	Tu-154B-1		85190	Tu-154B
	85110	Tu-154A		85191	Tu-154B
	85111	Tu-154A		85192	Tu-154B
	85112	Tu-154A		85193	Tu-154B
	85113	Tu-154A		85194	Tu-154B
	85114	Tu-154A		85195	Tu-154B
	85115	Tu-154A		85196	Tu-154B
	85116	Tu-154A		85197	Tu-154B
	85117	Tu-154A		85198	Tu-154B
	85118	Tu-154B		85199	Tu-154B
	85119	Tu-154A		85200	Tu-154B
	85120	Tu-154B		85201	Tu-154B
	85121	Tu-154B		85202	Tu-154B
	85122	Tu-154B		85203	Tu-154B
	85123	Tu-154B		85204	Tu-154B
	85124	Tu-154B		85205	Tu-154B
	85125	Tu-154B		85206	Tu-154B
	85129	Tu-154B		85207	Tu-154B
	85130	Tu-154B		85210	Tu-154B
	85131	Tu-154B		85211	Tu-154B
	85132	Tu-154B		85212	Tu-154B
	85133	Tu-154B		85213	Tu-154B
	85134	Tu-154B		85214	Tu-154B
	85135	Tu-154B		85215	Tu-154B
	85136	Tu-154B		85216	Tu-154B
	85137	Tu-154B		85217	Tu-154B
	85138	Tu-154B		85218	Tu-154B
	85139	Tu-154B		85219	Tu-154B
	85140	Tu-154B		85220	Tu-154B
	85141	Tu-154B		85221	Tu-154B
	85142	Tu-154B		85222	Tu-154B
	85143	Tu-154B		85223	Tu-154B
	85145	Tu-154B		85226	Tu-154B
	85146	Tu-154B		85227	Tu-154B
	85147	Tu-154B		85228	Tu-154B
	85148	Tu-154B		85229	Tu-154B-1
	85149	Tu-154B		85230	Tu-154B-1
	85150	Tu-154B		85231	Tu-154B-1
	85151	Tu-154B		85232	Tu-154B-1
	85152	Tu-154B		85233	Tu-154B-1
	85153	Tu-154B		85234	Tu-154B-1
	85154	Tu-154B		85235	Tu-154B-1
	85155	Tu-154B		85236	Tu-154B-1
	85156	Tu-154B		85237	Tu-154B-1
	85157	Tu-154B		85238	Tu-154B-1
	85158	Tu-154B		85240	Tu-154B-1
	85160	Tu-154B		85241	Tu-154B-1
	85162	Tu-154B		85242	Tu-154B-1
	85163	Tu-154B		85243	Tu-154B-1
	85164	Tu-154B		85244	Tu-154B-1
	85165	Tu-154B		85245	Tu-154B-1
	85166	Tu-154B		85246	Tu-154B-1
	85167	Tu-154B		85247	Tu-154B-1
	85168	Tu-154B		85248	Tu-154B-1
	85169	Tu-154B		85249	Tu-154B-1

Reg.	Type	Notes	Reg.	Type	Notes
85250	Tu-154B-1		85329	Tu-154B-2	
85251	Tu-154B-1		85330	Tu-154B-2	
85252	Tu-154B-1		85331	Tu-154B-2	
85253	Tu-154B-1		85332	Tu-154B-2	
85254	Tu-154B-1		85333	Tu-154B-2	
85255	Tu-154B-1		85334	Tu-154B-2	
85256	Tu-154B-1		85335	Tu-154B-2	
85257	Tu-154B-1		85336	Tu-154B-2	
85259	Tu-154B-1		85337	Tu-154B-2	
85260	Tu-154B-1		85338	Tu-154B-2	
85261	Tu-154B-1		85339	Tu-154B-2	
85263	Tu-154B-1		85340	Tu-154B-2	
85264	Tu-154B-1		85341	Tu-154B-2	
85265	Tu-154B-1		85343	Tu-154B-2	
85266	Tu-154B-1		85344	Tu-154B-2	
85267	Tu-154B-1		85346	Tu-154B-2	
85268	Tu-154B-1		85347	Tu-154B-2	
85269	Tu-154B-1		85348	Tu-154B-2	
85270	Tu-154B-1		85349	Tu-154B-2	
85271	Tu-154B-1		85350	Tu-154B-2	
85272	Tu-154B-1		85351	Tu-154B-2	
85273	Tu-154B-1		85352	Tu-154B-2	
85274	Tu-154B-1		85353	Tu-154B-2	
85275	Tu-154B-1		85354	Tu-154B-2	
85276	Tu-154B-1		85355	Tu-154B-2	
85277	Tu-154B-1		85356	Tu-154B-2	
85278	Tu-154B-1		85357	Tu-154B-2	
85279	Tu-154B-1		85358	Tu-154B-2	
85280	Tu-154B-1		85359	Tu-154B-2	
85281	Tu-154B-1		85360	Tu-154B-2	
85282	Tu-154B-1		85361	Tu-154B-2	
85283	Tu-154B-1		85362	Tu-154B-2	
85284	Tu-154B-1		85363	Tu-154B-2	
85285	Tu-154B-1		85364	Tu-154B-2	
85286	Tu-154B-1		85365	Tu-154B-2	
85287	Tu-154B-1		85366	Tu-154B-2	
85288	Tu-154B-1		85367	Tu-154B-2	
85289	Tu-154B-1		85368	Tu-154B-2	
85290	Tu-154B-1		85369	Tu-154B-2	
85291	Tu-154B-1		85370	Tu-154B-2	
85292	Tu-154B-1		85371	Tu-154B-2	
85293	Tu-154B-1		85372	Tu-154B-2	
85294	Tu-154B-1		85373	Tu-154B-2	
85295	Tu-154B-1		85374	Tu-154B-2	
85296	Tu-154B-1		85375	Tu-154B-2	
85297	Tu-154B-1		85376	Tu-154B-2	
85298	Tu-154B-1		85377	Tu-154B-2	
85299	Tu-154B-1		85378	Tu-154B-2	
85300	Tu-154B-2		85379	Tu-154B-2	
85301	Tu-154B-2		85380	Tu-154B-2	
85302	Tu-154B-2		85381	Tu-154B-2	
85303	Tu-154B-2		85382	Tu-154B-2	
85304	Tu-154B-2		85383	Tu-154B-2	
85305	Tu-154B-2		85384	Tu-154B-2	
85306	Tu-154B-2		85385	Tu-154B-2	
85307	Tu-154B-2		85386	Tu-154B-2	
85308	Tu-154B-2		85387	Tu-154B-2	
85309	Tu-154B-2		85388	Tu-154B-2	
85310	Tu-154B-2		85389	Tu-154B-2	
85311	Tu-154B-2		85390	Tu-154B-2	
85312	Tu-154B-2		85391	Tu-154B-2	
85313	Tu-154B-2		85392	Tu-154B-2	
85314	Tu-154B-2		85393	Tu-154B-2	
85315	Tu-154B-2		85394	Tu-154B-2	
85316	Tu-154B-2		85395	Tu-154B-2	
85317	Tu-154M		85396	Tu-154B-2	
85318	Tu-154B-2		85397	Tu-154B-2	
85319	Tu-154B-2		85398	Tu-154B-2	
85321	Tu-154B-2		85399	Tu-154B-2	
85322	Tu-154B-2		85400	Tu-154B-2	
85323	Tu-154B-2		85401	Tu-154B-2	
85324	Tu-154B-2		85402	Tu-154B-2	
85325	Tu-154B-2		85403	Tu-154B-2	
85328	Tu-154B-2		85404	Tu-154B-2	

Notes	Reg.	Type	Notes	Reg.	Type
	85405	Tu-154B-2		85487	Tu-154B-2
	85406	Tu-154B-2		85489	Tu-154B-2
	85407	Tu-154B-2		85490	Tu-154B-2
	85409	Tu-154B-2		85491	Tu-154B-2
	85410	Tu-154B-2		85492	Tu-154B-2
	85411	Tu-154B-2		85494	Tu-154B-2
	85412	Tu-154B-2		85495	Tu-154B-2
	85413	Tu-154B-2		85496	Tu-154B-2
	85414	Tu-154B-2		85497	Tu-154B-2
	85416	Tu-154B-2		85498	Tu-154B-2
	85417	Tu-154B-2		85499	Tu-154B-2
	85418	Tu-154B-2		85500	Tu-154B-2
	85419	Tu-154B-2		85501	Tu-154B-2
	85421	Tu-154B-2		85502	Tu-154B-2
	85423	Tu-154B-2		85503	Tu-154B-2
	85424	Tu-154B-2		85504	Tu-154B-2
	85425	Tu-154B-2		85505	Tu-154B-2
	85426	Tu-154B-2		85506	Tu-154B-2
	85427	Tu-154B-2		85507	Tu-154B-2
	85429	Tu-154B-2		85508	Tu-154B-2
	85430	Tu-154B-2		85509	Tu-154B-2
	85431	Tu-154B-2		85510	Tu-154B-2
	85432	Tu-154B-2		85511	Tu-154B-2
	85433	Tu-154B-2		85512	Tu-154B-2
	85434	Tu-154B-2		85513	Tu-154B-2
	85435	Tu-154B-2		85514	Tu-154B-2
	85436	Tu-154B-2		85515	Tu-154B-2
	85437	Tu-154B-2		85516	Tu-154B-2
	85438	Tu-154B-2		85517	Tu-154B-2
	85439	Tu-154B-2		85518	Tu-154B-2
	85440	Tu-154B-2		85519	Tu-154B-2
	85441	Tu-154B-2		85520	Tu-154B-2
	85442	Tu-154B-2		85521	Tu-154B-2
	85443	Tu-154B-2		85522	Tu-154B-2
	85444	Tu-154B-2		85523	Tu-154B-2
	85445	Tu-154B-2		85524	Tu-154B-2
	85446	Tu-154B-2		85525	Tu-154C-2
	85448	Tu-154B-2		85526	Tu-154B-2
	85449	Tu-154B-2		85527	Tu-154B-2
	85450	Tu-154B-2		85528	Tu-154B-2
	85451	Tu-154B-2		85529	Tu-154B-2
	85452	Tu-154B-2		85530	Tu-154B-2
	85453	Tu-154B-2		85531	Tu-154B-2
	85454	Tu-154B-2		85532	Tu-154B-2
	85455	Tu-154B-2		85533	Tu-154B-2
	85456	Tu-154B-2		85534	Tu-154B-2
	85457	Tu-154B-2		85535	Tu-154B-2
	85458	Tu-154B-2		85536	Tu-154B-2
	85459	Tu-154B-2		85537	Tu-154B-2
	85460	Tu-154B-2		85538	Tu-154B-2
	85461	Tu-154B-2		85539	Tu-154B-2
	85462	Tu-154B-2		85540	Tu-154B-2
	85463	Tu-154B-2		85541	Tu-154B-2
	85464	Tu-154B-2		85542	Tu-154B-2
	85465	Tu-154B-2		85544	Tu-154B-2
	85466	Tu-154B-2		85545	Tu-154B-2
	85467	Tu-154B-2		85546	Tu-154B-2
	85468	Tu-154B-2		85547	Tu-154B-2
	85469	Tu-154B-2		85548	Tu-154B-2
	85470	Tu-154B-2		85549	Tu-154B-2
	85471	Tu-154B-2		85550	Tu-154B-2
	85472	Tu-154B-2		85551	Tu-154B-2
	85475	Tu-154B-2		85552	Tu-154B-2
	85476	Tu-154B-2		85553	Tu-154B-2
	85477	Tu-154B-2		85554	Tu-154B-2
	85478	Tu-154B-2		85555	Tu-154B-2
	85479	Tu-154B-2		85556	Tu-154B-2
	85480	Tu-154B-2		85557	Tu-154B-2
	85481	Tu-154B-2		85558	Tu-154B-2
	85482	Tu-154B-2		85559	Tu-154B-2
	85483	Tu-154B-2		85560	Tu-154B-2
	85484	Tu-154B-2		85561	Tu-154B-2
	85485	Tu-154B-2		85562	Tu-154B-2
	85486	Tu-154B-2			

Reg.	Type	Notes	Reg.	Type	Notes
85563	Tu-154B-2		85718	Tu-154M	
85564	Tu-154B-2		85719	Tu-154M	
85565	Tu-154B-2		85720	Tu-154M	
85566	Tu-154B-2		85721	Tu-154M	
85567	Tu-154B-2		85722	Tu-154M	
85568	Tu-154B-2		85723	Tu-154M	
85570	Tu-154B-2		85724	Tu-154M	
85571	Tu-154B-2		85725	Tu-154M	
85572	Tu-154B-2		85726	Tu-154M	
85573	Tu-154B-2		85727	Tu-154M	
85574	Tu-154B-2		85728	Tu-154M	
85575	Tu-154B-2		85729	Tu-154M	
85577	Tu-154B-2		85730	Tu-154M	
85578	Tu-154B-2		85731	Tu-154M	
85579	Tu-154B-2		85732	Tu-154M	
85580	Tu-154B-2		85733	Tu-154M	
85581	Tu-154B-2		85734	Tu-154M	
85582	Tu-154B-2		85735	Tu-154M	
85583	Tu-154B-2		85736	Tu-154M	
85584	Tu-154B-2		85737	Tu-154M	
85585	Tu-154B-2		85738	Tu-154M	
85586	Tu-154B-2		85739	Tu-154M	
85587	Tu-154B-2		85740	Tu-154M	
85588	Tu-154B-2		85741	Tu-154M	
85589	Tu-154B-2		85742	Tu-154M	
85590	Tu-154B-2		85743	Tu-154M	
85592	Tu-154B-2		85744	Tu-154M	
85594	Tu-154B-2		85745	Tu-154M	
85595	Tu-154B-2		86000	IL-86	
85596	Tu-154B-2		86002	IL-86	
85600	Tu-154B-2		86003	IL-86	
85601	Tu-154B-2		86004	IL-86	
85602	Tu-154B-2		86005	IL-86	
85604	Tu-154B-2		86006	IL-86	
85605	Tu-154B-2		86007	IL-86	
85606	Tu-154B-2		86008	IL-86	
85607	Tu-154B-2		86009	IL-86	
85608	Tu-154B-2		86010	IL-86	
85609	Tu-154M-2		86011	IL-86	
85610	Tu-154B-2		86012	IL-86	
85611	Tu-154B-2		86013	IL-86	
85612	Tu-154B-2		86014	IL-86	
85613	Tu-154B-2		86015	IL-86	
85614	Tu-154B-2		86016	IL-86	
85615	Tu-154B-2		86017	IL-86	
85616	Tu-154B-2		86018	IL-86	
85617	Tu-154B-2		86022	IL-86	
85618	Tu-154B-2		86025	IL-86	
85619	Tu-154B-2		86050	IL-86	
85620	Tu-154B-2		86051	IL-86	
85621	Tu-154B-2		86052	IL-86	
85622	Tu-154B-2		86053	IL-86	
85623	Tu-154B-2		86052	IL-86	
85624	Tu-154B-2		86053	IL-86	
85625	Tu-154B-2		86054	IL-86	
85626	Tu-154B-2		86055	IL-86	
85700	Tu-154M		86056	IL-86	
85701	Tu-154M		86057	IL-86	
85702	Tu-154M		86058	IL-86	
85703	Tu-154M		86059	IL-86	
85704	Tu-154M		86060	IL-86	
85705	Tu-154M		86061	IL-86	
85706	Tu-154M		86062	IL-86	
85707	Tu-154M		86063	IL-86	
85708	Tu-154M		86064	IL-86	
85709	Tu-154M		86065	IL-86	
85710	Tu-154M		86066	IL-86	
85711	Tu-154M		86067	IL-86	
85712	Tu-154M		86068	IL-86	
85713	Tu-154M		86069	IL-86	
85714	Tu-154M		86070	IL-86	
85715	Tu-154M		87071	IL-86	
85716	Tu-154M		86072	IL-86	
85717	Tu-154M		87073	IL-86	

Reg.	Type		Reg.	Type
86074	IL-86		86517	IL-62MK
86075	IL-86		86518	IL-62M
86076	IL-86		86519	IL-62M
86077	IL-86		86520	IL-62MK
86078	IL-86		86521	IL-62M
86079	IL-86		86522	IL-62M
86080	IL-86		86523	IL-62M
86081	IL-86		86524	IL-62M
86082	IL-86		86528	IL-62MK
86083	IL-86		86530	IL-62MK
86084	IL-86		86531	IL-62M
86085	IL-86		86532	IL-62MK
86086	IL-86		86533	IL-62M
86087	IL-86		86534	IL-62MK
86088	IL-86		86535	IL-62M
86450	IL-62		86536	IL-62M
86451	IL-62		86555	IL-62M (VIP)
86452	IL-62M		86605	IL-62
86453	IL-62M		86606	IL-62
86454	IL-62M		86607	IL-62M
86455	IL-62M		86608	IL-62
86456	IL-62M		86609	IL-62
86457	IL-62M		86610	IL-62
86458	IL-62M		86611	IL-62
86459	IL-62M		86612	IL-62
86460	IL-62		86613	IL-62
86461	IL-62		86615	IL-62
86462	IL-62M		86616	IL-62
86463	IL-62M		86617	IL-62
86464	IL-62M		86618	IL-62M
86465	IL-62M		86619	IL-62M
86466	IL-62M		86620	IL-62M
86469	IL-62M		86621	IL-62M
86471	IL-62M		86622	IL-62M
86472	IL-62M		86623	IL-62M
86473	IL-62M		86624	IL-62
86474	IL-62M		86648	IL-62
86475	IL-62M		86649	IL-62
86476	IL-62M		86650	IL-62
86477	IL-62M		86652	IL-62
86478	IL-62M		86653	IL-62
86479	IL-62M		86654	IL-62
86480	IL-62M		86655	IL-62
86481	IL-62M		86656	IL-62M
86482	IL-62M		86657	IL-62
86483	IL-62M		86658	IL-62M
86484	IL-62M		86661	IL-62
86485	IL-62M		86662	IL-62
86486	IL-62M		86663	IL-62
86487	IL-62M		86664	IL-62
86488	IL-62M		86665	IL-62
86489	IL-62M		86666	IL-62
86491	IL-62M		86667	IL-62
86492	IL-62M		86668	IL-62
86493	IL-62M		86669	IL-62
86494	IL-62M		86670	IL-62
86497	IL-62M		86672	IL-62
86498	IL-62M		86673	IL-62M
86499	IL-62M		86674	IL-62
86500	IL-62M		86675	IL-62
86501	IL-62M		86676	IL-62
86502	IL-62M		86677	IL-62
86503	IL-62M		86678	IL-62
86505	IL-62M		86679	IL-62
86506	IL-62M		86680	IL-62
86507	IL-62M		86681	IL-62
86508	IL-62M		86682	IL-62
86509	IL-62M		86683	IL-62
86510	IL-62M		86684	IL-62
86511	IL-62M		86685	IL-62
86512	IL-62M		86686	IL-62
86513	IL-62M		86687	IL-62
86514	IL-62M		86688	IL-62
86516	IL-62M		86689	IL-62

Reg.	Type	Notes	Reg.	Type	Notes
86690	IL-62		86700	IL-62M	
86691	IL-62		86701	IL-62M	
86692	IL-62M		86702	IL-62M	
86693	IL-62M		86703	IL-62	
86694	IL-62		86704	IL-62	
86695	IL-62		86705	IL-62M	
86696	IL-62		86706	IL-62M	
86697	IL-62		86707	IL-62M	
86698	IL-62		86710	IL-62MK	
86699	IL-62		86711	IL-62M	

CN (Morocco)

Reg.	Type	Owner or Operator	Notes
CN-CCF	Boeing 727-2B6	Royal Air Maroc *Fez*	
CN-CCG	Boeing 727-2B6	Royal Air Maroc *L'Oiseau de la Providence*	
CN-CCH	Boeing 727-2B6	Royal Air Maroc *Marrakech*	
CN-CCW	Boeing 727-2B6	Royal Air Maroc *Agadir*	
CN-RMB	Boeing 707-351C	Royal Air Maroc *Tangier*	
CN-RMC	Boeing 707-351C	Royal Air Maroc *Casablanca*	
CN-RME	Boeing 747-2B6B (SCD)	Royal Air Maroc	
CN-RMH	Boeing 737-2T5	Royal Air Maroc	
CN-RMI	Boeing 737-2B6	Royal Air Maroc *El Ayoun*	
CN-RMJ	Boeing 737-2B6	Royal Air Maroc *Oujda*	
CN-RMK	Boeing 737-2B6	Royal Air Maroc *Smara*	
CN-RML	Boeing 737-2B6	Royal Air Maroc	
CN-RMM	Boeing 737-2B6C	Royal Air Maroc	
CN-RMN	Boeing 737-2B6C	Royal Air Maroc	
CN-RMO	Boeing 727-2B6	Royal Air Maroc	
CN-RMP	Boeing 727-2B6	Royal Air Maroc	
CN-RMQ	Boeing 727-2B6	Royal Air Maroc	
CN-RMR	Boeing 727-2B6	Royal Air Maroc	
CN-RMS	Boeing 747SP-44	Royal Air Maroc	
CN-RMT	Boeing 757-2B6	Royal Air Maroc	
CN-RMZ	Boeing 757-2B6	Royal Air Maroc	

CS (Portugal)

CS-TBC	Boeing 707-382B	TAP — Air Portugal *Cidade de Luanda*	
CS-TBG	Boeing 707-382B	TAP — Air Portugal *Fernao de Magalhaes*	
CS-TBJ	Boeing 707-373C	TAP — Air Portugal *Lisboa*	
CS-TBK	Boeing 727-82	TAP — Air Portugal *Acores*	
CS-TBL	Boeing 727-82	TAP — Air Portugal *Madeira*	
CS-TBM	Boeing 727-82	TAP — Air Portugal *Algarve*	
CS-TBO	Boeing 727-82C	TAP — Air Portugal *Costa do Estoril*	
CS-TBS	Boeing 727-282	TAP — Air Portugal *Lisboa*	
CS-TBT	Boeing 707-3F5C	TAP — Air Portugal *Humberto Delgado*	
CS-TBU	Boeing 707-3F5C	TAP — Air Portugal *Jaime Cortesao*	
CS-TBW	Boeing 727-282	TAP — Air Portugal *Coimbra*	
CS-TBX	Boeing 727-282	TAP — Air Portugal *Faro*	
CS-TBY	Boeing 727-282	TAP — Air Portugal *Amadora*	
CS-TCH	Boeing 727-232	TAP — Air Atlantis *Ponta de Sagres*	
CS-TCI	Boeing 727-232	TAP — Air Atlantis *Praia da Rocha*	
CS-TCJ	Boeing 727-232	TAP — Air Atlantis *Monte Gordo*	
CS-TEA	L.1011-385 TriStar 500	TAP — Air Portugal *Luis de Camoes*	
CS-TEB	L.1011-385 TriStar 500	TAP — Air Portugal *Infante D. Henrique*	
CS-TEC	L.1011-385 TriStar 500	TAP — Air Portugal *Gago Coutinho*	
CS-TED	L.1011-385 TriStar 500	TAP — Air Portugal *Bartolomeu de Gusmao*	
CS-TEE	L.1011-385 TriStar 500	TAP — Air Portugal *St Antonio de Lisboa*	
CS-TEK	Boeing 737-282	TAP — Air Portugal *Ponta Delgada*	
CS-TEL	Boeing 737-282	TAP — Air Portugal *Funchal*	
CS-TEM	Boeing 737-282	TAP — Air Portugal *Setubal*	
CS-TEN	Boeing 737-282	TAP — Air Portugal *Braga*	
CS-TEO	Boeing 737-282	TAP — Air Portugal *Evora*	
CS-TEP	Boeing 737-282	TAP — Air Portugal *Oporto*	
CS-TEQ	Boeing 737-282C	TAP — Air Portugal *Vila Real*	

Notes	Reg.	Type	Owner or Operator
	CS-TER	Boeing 737-230	TAP — Air Portugal
	CS-TES	Boeing 737-230	TAP — Air Portugal
	CS-T	Boeing 737-230	TAP — Air Portugal
	CS-T	Boeing 737-230	TAP — Air Portugal
	CS-T	Boeing 737-2K9	Air Atlantis
	CS-T	Boeing 737-2K9	Air Atlantis
	CS-T	Airbus A.310-304	TAP — Air Portugal
	CS-T	Airbus A.310-304	TAP — Air Portugal
	CS-T	Boeing 737-3Q8	TAP — Air Portugal
	CS-T	Boeing 737-3Q8	TAP — Air Portugal
	CS-T	Boeing 737-3Q8	TAP — Air Portugal
	CS-T	Boeing 737-3Q8	TAP — Air Portugal
	CS-T	Boeing 737-3Q8	TAP — Air Portugal

CU (Cuba)

	CU-T1208	Ilyushin IL-62M	Cubana *Capt Wifredo Perez*
	CU-T1209	Ilyushin IL-62M	Cubana
	CU-T1215	Ilyushin IL-62M	Cubana
	CU-T1216	Ilyushin IL-62M	Cubana
	CU-T1217	Ilyushin IL-62M	Cubana
	CU-T1218	Ilyushin IL-62M	Cubana
	CU-T1225	Ilyushin IL-62M	Cubana
	CU-T1226	Ilyushin IL-62M	Cubana
	CU-T1252	Ilyushin IL-62M	Cubana
	CU-T1259	Ilyushin IL-62M	Cubana

D (German Federal Republic)

	D-AAST	S.E.210 Caravelle 10R	Aero Lloyd
	D-ABAK	S.E.210 Caravelle 10R	Aero Lloyd
	D-ABFA	Boeing 737-230	Lufthansa *Regensburg*
	D-ABFB	Boeing 737-230	Lufthansa *Flensburg*
	D-ABFC	Boeing 737-230	Lufthansa *Würzburg*
	D-ABFD	Boeing 737-230	Lufthansa *Bamberg*
	D-ABFF	Boeing 737-230	Lufthansa *Gelsenkirchen*
	D-ABFH	Boeing 737-230	Lufthansa *Pforzheim*
	D-ABFK	Boeing 737-230	Lufthansa *Wuppertal*
	D-ABFL	Boeing 737-230	Lufthansa *Coburg*
	D-ABFM	Boeing 737-230	Lufthansa *Osnabrück*
	D-ABFN	Boeing 737-230	Lufthansa *Kempton*
	D-ABFP	Boeing 737-230	Lufthansa *Offenbach*
	D-ABFR	Boeing 737-230	Lufthansa *Solingen*
	D-ABFS	Boeing 737-230	Lufthansa *Oldenburg*
	D-ABFU	Boeing 737-230	Lufthansa *Mülheim a.d.R*
	D-ABFW	Boeing 737-230	Lufthansa *Wolfsburg*
	D-ABFX	Boeing 737-230	Lufthansa *Tübingen*
	D-ABFY	Boeing 737-230	Lufthansa *Göttingen*
	D-ABFZ	Boeing 737-230	Lufthansa *Wilhelmshaven*
	D-ABGE	Boeing 737-230C	Lufthansa
	D-ABGI	Boeing 727-230	Lufthansa *Leverkusen*
	D-ABHA	Boeing 737-230	Lufthansa *Koblenz*
	D-ABHB	Boeing 737-230	Lufthansa *Goslar*
	D-ABHC	Boeing 737-230	Lufthansa *Friedrichshafen*
	D-ABHD	Boeing 737-230	Condor Flugdienst (*to Air Portugal 11/88*)
	D-ABHE	Boeing 737-230C	Lufthansa
	D-ABHF	Boeing 737-230	Lufthansa *Heilbronn*
	D-ABHH	Boeing 737-230	Lufthansa *Marburg*
	D-ABHI	Boeing 727-230	Lufthansa *Mönchengladbach*
	D-ABHK	Boeing 737-230	Lufthansa *Bayreuth*
	D-ABHL	Boeing 737-230	Lufthansa *Worms*
	D-ABHM	Boeing 737-230	Lufthansa *Landshut*
	D-ABHN	Boeing 737-230	Lufthansa *Trier*
	D-ABHP	Boeing 737-230	Lufthansa *Erlangen*
	D-ABHR	Boeing 737-230	Lufthansa *Darmstadt*
	D-ABHS	Boeing 737-230	Lufthansa *Remscheid*
	D-ABHU	Boeing 737-230	Lufthansa *Konstanz*
	D-ABHW	Boeing 737-230	Lufthansa *Baden Baden*

Reg.	Type	Owner or Operator	Notes
D-ABKA	Boeing 727-230	Lufthansa *Heidelberg*	
D-ABKB	Boeing 727-230	Lufthansa *Augsburg*	
D-ABKC	Boeing 727-230	Lufthansa *Braunschweig*	
D-ABKD	Boeing 727-230	Lufthansa *Freiburg*	
D-ABKE	Boeing 727-230	Lufthansa *Mannheim*	
D-ABKF	Boeing 727-230	Lufthansa *Saarbrücken*	
D-ABKG	Boeing 727-230	Lufthansa *Kassel*	
D-ABKH	Boeing 727-230	Lufthansa *Karlsruhe*	
D-ABKI	Boeing 727-230	Lufthansa *Bremerhaven*	
D-ABKJ	Boeing 727-230	Lufthansa *Wiesbaden*	
D-ABKK	Boeing 727-230	Condor Flugdienst	
D-ABKL	Boeing 727-230	Condor Flugdienst	
D-ABKM	Boeing 727-230	Lufthansa *Hagen*	
D-ABKN	Boeing 727-230	Lufthansa *Ulm*	
D-ABKP	Boeing 727-230	Lufthansa *Krefeld*	
D-ABKQ	Boeing 727-230	Lufthansa *Mainz*	
D-ABKR	Boeing 727-230	Lufthansa *Bielefeld*	
D-ABKS	Boeing 727-230	Lufthansa *Oberhausen*	
D-ABKT	Boeing 727-230	Lufthansa *Aachen*	
D-ABLI	Boeing 727-230	Lufthansa *Ludwigshafen a.Rh.*	
D-ABMA	Boeing 737-230	Lufthansa *Idar-Oberstein*	
D-ABMB	Boeing 737-230	Lufthansa *Ingolstadt*	
D-ABMC	Boeing 737-230	Lufthansa *Norderstedt*	
D-ABMD	Boeing 737-230	Lufthansa *Paderborn*	
D-ABME	Boeing 737-230	Lufthansa *Schweinfurt*	
D-ABMF	Boeing 737-230	Lufthansa *Verden*	
D-ABMI	Boeing 727-230	Condor Flugdienst	
D-ABNI	Boeing 727-230	Lufthansa	
D-ABPI	Boeing 727-230	Lufthansa	
D-ABQI	Boeing 727-230	Lufthansa *Hildesheim*	
D-ABRI	Boeing 727-230	Lufthansa *Esslingen*	
D-ABSI	Boeing 727-230	Lufthansa *Hof*	
D-ABTI	Boeing 727-230	Condor Flugdienst	
D-ABVA	Boeing 747-430	Lufthansa	
D-ABVB	Boeing 747-430	Lufthansa	
D-ABVC	Boeing 747-430	Lufthansa	
D-ABVD	Boeing 747-430	Lufthansa	
D-ABVE	Boeing 747-430	Lufthansa	
D-ABVF	Boeing 747-430	Lufthansa	
D-ABVI	Boeing 727-230	Condor Flugdienst	
D-ABWA	Boeing 737-330	Condor Flugdienst	
D-ABWB	Boeing 737-330	Condor Flugdienst	
D-ABWC	Boeing 737-330	Condor Flugdienst	
D-ABWD	Boeing 737-330	Condor Flugdienst	
D-ABWE	Boeing 737-330	Condor Flugdienst	
D-ABWI	Boeing 727-230	Condor Flugdienst	
D-ABXA	Boeing 737-330	Lufthansa *Giessen*	
D-ABXB	Boeing 737-330	Lufthansa *Passau*	
D-ABXC	Boeing 737-330	Lufthansa *Delmenhorst*	
D-ABXD	Boeing 737-330	Lufthansa *Siegen*	
D-ABXE	Boeing 737-330	Lufthansa *Hamm*	
D-ABXF	Boeing 737-330	Lufthansa *Minden*	
D-ABXH	Boeing 737-330	Lufthansa *Cuxhaven*	
D-ABXI	Boeing 737-330	Lufthansa *Berchtesgaden*	
D-ABXK	Boeing 737-330	Lufthansa *Ludwigsburg*	
D-ABXL	Boeing 737-330	Lufthansa *Neuss*	
D-ABXM	Boeing 737-330	Lufthansa	
D-ABXN	Boeing 737-330	Lufthansa	
D-ABXO	Boeing 737-330	Lufthansa	
D-ABXP	Boeing 737-330	Lufthansa	
D-ABXR	Boeing 737-330	Lufthansa	
D-	Boeing 737-3Q8	Lufthansa	
D-	Boeing 737-3Q8	Lufthansa	
D-	Boeing 737-3Q8	Lufthansa	
D-ABYJ	Boeing 747-230B (SCD)	Lufthansa *Hessen*	
D-ABYK	Boeing 747-230B (SCD)	Lufthansa *Rheinland-Pfalz*	
D-ABYL	Boeing 747-230B (SCD)	Lufthansa *Saarland*	
D-ABYM	Boeing 747-230B (SCD)	Lufthansa *Schleswig-Holstein*	
D-ABYN	Boeing 747-230B	Lufthansa *Baden-Wurttemberg*	
D-ABYO	Boeing 747-230F (SCD)	Lufthansa *America*	
D-ABYP	Boeing 747-230B	Lufthansa *Niedersachen*	

|---|---|---|---|
	D-ABYQ	Boeing 747-230B	Lufthansa *Bremen*
	D-ABYR	Boeing 747-230B (SCD)	Lufthansa *Nordrhein-Westfalen*
	D-ABYS	Boeing 747-230B (SCD)	Lufthansa *Bayern*
	D-ABYT	Boeing 747-230B (SCD)	Lufthansa *Hamburg*
	D-ABYU	Boeing 747-230F	Lufthansa *Asia*
	D-ABYW	Boeing 747-230B (SCD)	Lufthansa *Berlin*
	D-ABYX	Boeing 747-230B (SCD)	Lufthansa *Köln*
	D-ABYY	Boeing 747-230B (SCD)	Lufthansa *München*
	D-ABYZ	Boeing 747-230B (SCD)	Lufthansa *Frankfurt*
	D-ABZA	Boeing 747-230B (SCD)	Lufthansa *Dusseldorf*
	D-ABZB	Boeing 747-230F	Lufthansa *Europa*
	D-ABZC	Boeing 747-230B (SCD)	Lufthansa *Hannover*
	D-ABZD	Boeing 747-230B	Lufthansa *Kiel*
	D-ABZE	Boeing 747-230B (SCD)	Lufthansa *Stuttgart*
	D-ABZF	Boeing 747-230F (SCD)	Lufthansa *Africa*
	D-ABZH	Boeing 747-230B	Lufthansa *Bonn*
	D-ABZI	Boeing 747-230F	Lufthansa
	D-ACVK	S.E.210 Caravelle 10R	Aero Lloyd *Otto Trump*
	D-ADAO	Douglas DC-10-30	Lufthansa
	D-ADBO	Douglas DC-10-30	Lufthansa *Bochum*
	D-ADCO	Douglas DC-10-30	Lufthansa
	D-ADDO	Douglas DC-10-30	Lufthansa *Duisburg*
	D-ADFO	Douglas DC-10-30	Lufthansa *Fürth*
	D-ADGO	Douglas DC-10-30	Lufthansa
	D-ADHO	Douglas DC-10-30	Lufthansa
	D-ADJO	Douglas DC-10-30	Lufthansa *Essen*
	D-ADKO	Douglas DC-10-30	Lufthansa
	D-ADLO	Douglas DC-10-30	Lufthansa *Nurnberg*
	D-ADMO	Douglas DC-10-30	Lufthansa *Dortmund*
	D-ADPO	Douglas DC-10-30	Condor Flugdienst
	D-ADQO	Douglas DC-10-30	Condor Flugdienst
	D-ADSO	Douglas DC-10-30	Lufthansa
	D-ADUA	Douglas DC-8-73CF	German Cargo
	D-ADUC	Douglas DC-8-73AF	German Cargo
	D-ADUE	Douglas DC-8-73CF	German Cargo
	D-ADUI	Douglas DC-8-73AF	German Cargo
	D-ADUO	Douglas DC-8-73CF	German Cargo
	D-AELB	F.27 Friendship Mk 600	WDL
	D-AERA	L.1011-385 TriStar 1	LTU
	D-AERE	L.1011-385 TriStar 1	LTU
	D-AERI	L.1011-385 TriStar 1	LTU
	D-AERL	L.1011-385 TriStar 500	LTU
	D-AERM	L.1011-385 TriStar 1	LTU
	D-AERN	L.1011-385 TriStar 200	LTU
	D-AERP	L.1011-385 TriStar 1	LTU
	D-AERT	L.1011-385 TriStar 500	LTU
	D-AERU	L.1011-385 TriStar 100	LTU
	D-AERY	L.1011-385 TriStar 1	LTU
	D-AFKA	Fokker 50	D.L.T.
	D-AFKB	Fokker 50	D.L.T.
	D-AFKC	Fokker 50	D.L.T.
	D-AFKD	Fokker 50	D.L.T.
	D-AFKE	Fokker 50	D.L.T.
	D-AFKF	Fokker 50	D.L.T.
	D-AFKG	Fokker 50	D.L.T.
	D-AGEA	Boeing 737-35B	Germania
	D-AGEB	Boeing 737-35B	Germania
	D-AGEC	Boeing 737-35B	Germania
	D-AG	Boeing 737-35B	Germania
	D-AG	Boeing 737-35B	Germania
	D-AG	Boeing 737-35B	Germania
	D-AHLC	Airbus A.300B4	Hapag-Lloyd
	D-AHLD	Boeing 737-2K5	Hapag-Lloyd
	D-AHLG	Boeing 737-2K5	Hapag-Lloyd
	D-AHLH	Boeing 737-2K5	Hapag-Lloyd
	D-AHLI	Boeing 737-2K5	Hapag-Lloyd
	D-AHLM	Boeing 727-81	Hapag-Lloyd
	D-AHLT	Boeing 727-2K5	Hapag-Lloyd
	D-AHLU	Boeing 727-2K5	Hapag-Lloyd
	D-AHLV	Airbus A.310-304	Hapag-Lloyd
	D-AHLW	Airbus A.310-304	Hapag-Lloyd

Reg.	Type	Owner or Operator	Notes
D-AH	Airbus A.310-304	Hapag-Lloyd	
D-AH	Boeing 737-4K5	Hapag-Lloyd	
D-AH	Boeing 737-4K5	Hapag-Lloyd	
D-AH	Boeing 737-4K5	Hapag-Lloyd	
D-AH	Boeing 737-4K5	Hapag-Lloyd	
D-AH	Boeing 737-4K5	Hapag-Lloyd	
D-AH	Boeing 737-4K5	Hapag-Lloyd	
D-AHSA	H.S.748 Srs 2B	D.L.T.	
D-AHSB	H.S.748 Srs 2B	D.L.T.	
D-AHSC	H.S.748 Srs 2B	D.L.T.	
D-AHSD	H.S.748 Srs 2B	D.L.T.	
D-AHSE	H.S.748 Srs 2B	D.L.T.	
D-AHSF	H.S.748 Srs 2B	D.L.T.	
D-AIAH	Airbus A.300-603	Lufthansa *Lindau/Bodenzee*	
D-AIAI	Airbus A.300-603	Lufthansa *Erbach/Odenwald*	
D-AIAK	Airbus A.300-603	Lufthansa *Kronberg im Taunus*	
D-AIAL	Airbus A.300-603	Lufthansa *Stade*	
D-AIAM	Airbus A.300-603	Lufthansa *Rosenheim*	
D-AIAN	Airbus A.300-603	Lufthansa *Boeblingen*	
D-AIAP	Airbus A.300-603	Lufthansa *Bingen*	
D-AICA	Airbus A.310-203	Lufthansa *Neustadt an der Weinstrausse*	
D-AICB	Airbus A.310-203	Lufthansa *Garmisch-Partenkirchen*	
D-AICC	Airbus A.310-203	Lufthansa *Kaiserslauten*	
D-AICD	Airbus A.310-203	Lufthansa *Detmold*	
D-AICF	Airbus A.310-203	Lufthansa *Rüdesheim am Rhein*	
D-AICH	Airbus A.310-203	Lufthansa *Lüneburg*	
D-AICK	Airbus A.310-203	Lufthansa *Westerland-Sylt*	
D-AICL	Airbus A.310-203	Lufthansa *Rothenburg ob der Tauber*	
D-AICM	Airbus A.310-203	Condor Flugdienst	
D-AICN	Airbus A.310-203	Condor Flugdienst	
D-AICP	Airbus A.310-203	Condor Flugdienst	
D-AICR	Airbus A.310-203	Condor Flugdienst	
D-AICS	Airbus A.310-203	Lufthansa *Recklinghausen*	
D-AICT	Airbus A.310-203	Lufthansa	
D-AICU	Airbus A.310-203	Lufthansa	
D-AICW	Airbus A.310-203	Lufthansa	
D-AICX	Airbus A.310-203	Lufthansa	
D-AICY	Airbus A.310-203	Lufthansa	
D-AICZ	Airbus A.310-203	Lufthansa	
D-AIDA	Airbus A.310-304	Condor Flugdienst	
D-AIDB	Airbus A.310-304	Condor Flugdienst	
D-AIDC	Airbus A.310-304	Lufthansa	
D-AIDD	Airbus A.310-304	Lufthansa	
D-ALLA	Douglas DC-9-32	Aero Lloyd	
D-ALLB	Douglas DC-9-32	Aero Lloyd	
D-ALLC	Douglas DC-9-32	Aero Lloyd	
D-ALLD	Douglas DC-9-83	Aero Lloyd	
D-ALLE	Douglas DC-9-83	Aero Lloyd	
D-ALLF	Douglas DC-9-83	Aero Lloyd	
D-AL	Douglas DC-9-87	Aero Lloyd	
D-AL	Douglas DC-9-87	Aero Lloyd	
D-AMAY	Airbus A.300B4	Hapag-Lloyd	
D-AMUS	Boeing 757-2G5	LTU-Sud	
D-AMUT	Boeing 757-2G5	LTU-Sud	
D-AMUV	Boeing 757-2G5	LTU-Sud	
D-AMUW	Boeing 757-2G5	LTU-Sud	
D-AMUX	Boeing 757-2G5	LTU-Sud	
D-BAAA	Aerospatiale ATR-42-300	Nürnberger Flugdienst (NFD)	
D-BAKA	F.27 Friendship Mk 100	WDL	
D-BAKI	F.27 Friendship Mk 100	WDL	
D-BAKO	F.27 Friendship Mk 100	WDL	
D-BAKU	F.27 Friendship Mk 200	WDL	
D-BCRM	Aerospatiale ATR-42-300	R.F.G.	
D-BCRN	Aerospatiale ATR-42-300	R.F.G.	
D-BEST	D.H.C.8 Dash Eight	Contactair	
D-B	D.H.C.8 Dash Eight	Contactair	
D-B	Aerospatiale ATR-42-300	R.F.G.	
D-B	Aerospatiale ATR-42-300	Nürnberger Flugdienst (NFD)	
D-B	Aerospatiale ATR-42-300	Nürnberger Flugdienst (NFD)	
D-CABA	Swearingen SA227AC Metro III	Nürnberger Flugdienst (NFD)	

Notes	Reg.	Type	Owner or Operator
	D-CABB	Swearingen SA227AC Metro III	Nürnberger Flugdienst (NFD)
	D-CABD	Swearingen SA227AC Metro III	Nürnberger Flugdienst (NFD)
	D-CABE	Swearingen SA227AC Metro III	Nürnberger Flugdienst (NFD)
	D-CABF	Swearingen SA227AC Metro III	Nürnberger Flugdienst (NFD)
	D-CABG	Swearingen SA227AC Metro III	Nürnberger Flugdienst (NFD)
	D-CABH	Swearingen SA227AC Metro III	Nürnberger Flugdienst (NFD)
	D-CABI	Swearingen SA227AC Metro III	Nürnberger Flugdienst (NFD)
	D-CDIA	Saab SF.340A	Delta Air
	D-CDIB	Saab SF.340A	Delta Air
	D-CDIZ	Dornier Do.228-201	Delta Air
	D-CEMA	EMB-120RT Brasilia	D.L.T.
	D-CEMB	EMB-120RT Brasilia	D.L.T.
	D-CEMC	EMB-120RT Brasilia	D.L.T.
	D-CEMD	EMB-120RT Brasilia	D.L.T.
	D-CEME	EMB-120RT Brasilia	D.L.T.
	D-CEMF	EMB-120RT Brasilia	D.L.T.
	D-CEMG	EMB-120RT Brasilia	D.L.T.
	D-CEMH	EMB-120RT Brasilia	D.L.T.
	D-CEMI	EMB-120RT Brasilia	D.L.T.
	D-CEMJ	EMB-120RT Brasilia	D.L.T.
	D-CEMK	EMB-120RT Brasilia	D.L.T.
	D-CEML	EMB-120RT Brasilia	D.L.T.
	D-CEMM	EMB-120RT Brasilia	D.L.T.
	D-CEMN	EMB-120RT Brasilia	D.L.T.
	D-CEZH	Dornier Do.228-201	Hanse Express
	D-CONA	BAe Jetstream 3102	Contactair/D.L.T.
	D-CONE	BAe Jetstream 3102	Contactair
	D-CONI	BAe Jetstream 3102	Contactair
	D-CONU	BAe Jetstream 3102	Contactair/D.L.T.
	D-ICFB	Swearingen SA226AT Merlin IV	R.F.G.
	D-ICRJ	Swearingen SA226TC Metro II	R.F.G.
	D-ICRK	Swearingen SA226TC Metro II	R.F.G.
	D-ICRL	Swearingen SA226TC Metro II	R.F.G.
	D-IDOM	Dornier Do.228-100	Hanse Express
	D-IHCW	Swearingen SA226TC Metro II	R.F.G.
	D-IHRB	Swearingen SA226TC Metro II	Hanse Express
	D-INWK	Swearingen SA226AT Merlin IV	Naske Air

DDR (German Democratic Republic)

	DDR-SCF	Tupolev Tu-134	Interflug
	DDR-SCH	Tupolev Tu-134	Interflug
	DDR-SCI	Tupolev Tu-134A	Interflug
	DDR-SCK	Tupolev Tu-134A	Interflug
	DDR-SCL	Tupolev Tu-134A	Interflug
	DDR-SCN	Tupolev Tu-134A	Interflug
	DDR-SCO	Tupolev Tu-134A	Interflug
	DDR-SCP	Tupolev Tu-134A	Interflug
	DDR-SCR	Tupolev Tu-134A	Interflug
	DDR-SCS	Tupolev Tu-134A	Interflug
	DDR-SCT	Tupolev Tu-134A	Interflug
	DDR-SCU	Tupolev Tu-134A	Interflug
	DDR-SCV	Tupolev Tu-134A	Interflug
	DDR-SCW	Tupolev Tu-134A	Interflug
	DDR-SCX	Tupolev Tu-134A	Interflug
	DDR-SCY	Tupolev Tu-134A	Interflug
	DDR-SDC	Tupolev Tu-134A	Interflug
	DDR-SDE	Tupolev Tu-134A	Interflug
	DDR-SDF	Tupolev Tu-134A	Interflug
	DDR-SDG	Tupolev Tu-134A	Interflug
	DDR-SDU	Tupolev Tu-134A	Interflug
	DDR-SEB	Ilyushin IL-62	Interflug
	DDR-SEC	Ilyushin IL-62	Interflug
	DDR-SEF	Ilyushin IL-62	Interflug
	DDR-SEG	Ilyushin IL-62	Interflug
	DDR-SEH	Ilyushin IL-62	Interflug
	DDR-SEI	Ilyushin IL-62M	Interflug
	DDR-SEK	Ilyushin IL-62M	Interflug
	DDR-SEL	Ilyushin IL-62M	Interflug

Reg.	Type	Owner or Operator	Notes
DDR-SEM	Ilyushin IL-62M	Interflug	
DDR-SEO	Ilyushin IL-62M	Interflug	
DDR-SEP	Ilyushin IL-62M	Interflug	
DDR-SER	Ilyushin IL-62M	Interflug	
DDR-SES	Ilyushin IL-62M	Interflug	
DDR-SET	Ilyushin IL-62M	Interflug	
DDR-SEU	Ilyushin IL-62M	Interflug	
DDR-STA	Ilyushin IL-18D	Interflug	
DDR-STB	Ilyushin IL-18D	Interflug	
DDR-STC	Ilyushin IL-18D	Interflug	
DDR-STD	Ilyushin IL-18D	Interflug	
DDR-STE	Ilyushin IL-18D	Interflug	
DDR-STF	Ilyushin IL-18D	Interflug	
DDR-STG	Ilyushin IL-18D	Interflug	
DDR-STH	Ilyushin IL-18D	Interflug	
DDR-STI	Ilyushin IL-18D	Interflug	
DDR-STK	Ilyushin IL-18D	Interflug	
DDR-STM	Ilyushin IL-18D	Interflug	
DDR-STN	Ilyushin IL-18D	Interflug	
DDR-STO	Ilyushin IL-18D	Interflug	
DDR-STP	Ilyushin IL-18D	Interflug	

EC (Spain)

Reg.	Type	Owner or Operator	Notes
EC-BIG	Douglas DC-9-32	Iberia *Villa de Madrid*	
EC-BIH	Douglas DC-9-32	Aviaco *Ciudad de Barcelona*	
EC-BIJ	Douglas DC-9-32	Iberia *Santa Cruz de Tenerife*	
EC-BIK	Douglas DC-9-32	Aviaco *Castillo de Guanapa*	
EC-BIL	Douglas DC-9-32	Iberia *Ciudad de Zaragoza*	
EC-BIM	Douglas DC-9-32	Iberia *Ciudad de Santander*	
EC-BIN	Douglas DC-9-32	Iberia *Palma de Mallorca*	
EC-BIO	Douglas DC-9-32	Iberia *Villa de Bilbao*	
EC-BIP	Douglas DC-9-32	Aviaco *Castillo de Monteagudo*	
EC-BIQ	Douglas DC-9-32	Aviaco *Castillo de Argueso*	
EC-BIR	Douglas DC-9-32	Iberia *Ciudad de Valencia*	
EC-BIS	Douglas DC-9-32	Iberia *Ciudad de Alicante*	
EC-BIT	Douglas DC-9-32	Iberia *Ciudad de San Sebastian*	
EC-BIU	Douglas DC-9-32	Iberia *Ciudad de Oviedo*	
EC-BPF	Douglas DC-9-32	Iberia *Ciudad de Almeria*	
EC-BPG	Douglas DC-9-32	Iberia *Ciudad de Vigo*	
EC-BPH	Douglas DC-9-32	Iberia *Ciudad de Gerona*	
EC-BQA	CV-990A Coronado	Spantax (*stored/Palma*)	
EC-BQQ	CV-990A Coronado	Spantax (*stored/Palma*)	
EC-BQT	Douglas DC-9-32	Iberia *Ciudad de Murcia*	
EC-BQU	Douglas DC-9-32	Iberia *Ciudad de La Coruna*	
EC-BQV	Douglas DC-9-32	Iberia *Ciudad de Ibiza*	
EC-BQX	Douglas DC-9-32	Iberia *Ciudad de Valladolid*	
EC-BQY	Douglas DC-9-32	Aviaco *Ciudad de Cordoba*	
EC-BQZ	Douglas DC-9-32	Iberia *Ciudad de Santa Cruz de La Palma*	
EC-BRQ	Boeing 747-256B	Iberia *Calderon de la Barca*	
EC-BYD	Douglas DC-9-32	Iberia *Ciudad de Arrecife de Lanzarote*	
EC-BYE	Douglas DC-9-32	Iberia *Ciudad de Mahon*	
EC-BYF	Douglas DC-9-32	Iberia *Ciudad de Granada*	
EC-BYG	Douglas DC-9-32	Iberia *Ciudad de Pamplona*	
EC-BYH	Douglas DC-9-32	Aviaco *Castillo de Butron*	
EC-BYI	Douglas DC-9-32	Iberia *Ciudad de Vitoria*	
EC-BYJ	Douglas DC-9-32	Iberia *Ciudad de Salamanca*	
EC-BYK	Douglas DC-9-33RC	Iberia *Ciudad de Badajoz*	
EC-BYL	Douglas DC-9-33RC	Iberia *Cuidad de Albacete*	
EC-BYM	Douglas DC-9-33RC	Iberia *Ciudad de Cangas de Onis*	
EC-BYN	Douglas DC-9-33RC	Iberia *Ciudad de Caceres*	
EC-BZO	CV-990A Coronado	Spantax (*stored/Palma*)	
EC-BZP	CV-990A Coronado	Spantax (*stored/Palma*)	
EC-CAI	Boeing 727-256	Iberia *Castilla la Neuva*	
EC-CAJ	Boeing 727-256	Iberia *Cataluna*	
EC-CAK	Boeing 727-256	Iberia *Aragon*	
EC-CBA	Boeing 727-256	Iberia *Vascongadas*	
EC-CBB	Boeing 727-256	Iberia *Valencia*	
EC-CBC	Boeing 727-256	Iberia *Navarra*	

Notes	Reg.	Type	Owner or Operator
	EC-CBD	Boeing 727-256	Iberia *Murcia*
	EC-CBE	Boeing 727-256	Iberia *Leon*
	EC-CBF	Boeing 727-256	Iberia *Gran Canaria*
	EC-CBG	Boeing 727-256	Iberia *Extremadura*
	EC-CBH	Boeing 727-256	Iberia *Galicia*
	EC-CBI	Boeing 727-256	Iberia *Asturias*
	EC-CBJ	Boeing 727-256	Iberia *Andalucia*
	EC-CBK	Boeing 727-256	Iberia *Baleares*
	EC-CBL	Boeing 727-256	Iberia *Tenerife*
	EC-CBM	Boeing 727-256	Iberia *Castilla La Vieja*
	EC-CBO	Douglas DC-10-30	Iberia *Costa del Sol*
	EC-CBP	Douglas DC-10-30	Iberia *Costa Dorada*
	EC-CEZ	Douglas DC-10-30	Iberia *Costa del Azahar*
	EC-CFA	Boeing 727-256	Iberia *Jerez Xeres Sherry*
	EC-CFB	Boeing 727-256	Iberia *Rioja*
	EC-CFC	Boeing 727-256	Iberia *Tarragona*
	EC-CFD	Boeing 727-256	Iberia *Montilla-Moriles*
	EC-CFE	Boeing 727-256	Iberia *Penedes*
	EC-CFF	Boeing 727-256	Iberia *Valdepenas*
	EC-CFG	Boeing 727-256	Iberia *La Mancha*
	EC-CFH	Boeing 727-256	Iberia *Priorato*
	EC-CFI	Boeing 727-256	Iberia *Carinena*
	EC-CFK	Boeing 727-256	Iberia *Riberio*
	EC-CGN	Douglas DC-9-32	Aviaco *Martin Alonso Pinzon*
	EC-CGO	Douglas DC-9-32	Aviaco *Pedro Alonso Nino*
	EC-CGP	Douglas DC-9-32	Aviaco *Juan Sebastian Elcano*
	EC-CGQ	Douglas DC-9-32	Aviaco *Alonso de Ojeda*
	EC-CGR	Douglas DC-9-32	Aviaco *Francisco de Orellana*
	EC-CID	Boeing 727-256	Iberia *Malaga*
	EC-CIE	Boeing 727-256	Iberia *Esparragosa*
	EC-CLB	Douglas DC-10-30	Iberia *Costa Blanca*
	EC-CLD	Douglas DC-9-32	Aviaco *Hernando de Soto*
	EC-CLE	Douglas DC-9-32	Aviaco *Jaun Ponce de Leon*
	EC-CNH	CV-990A Coronado	Spantax *(stored/Palma)*
	EC-CSJ	Douglas DC-10-30	Iberia *Costa de la Luz*
	EC-CSK	Douglas DC-10-30	Iberia *Cornisa Cantabrica*
	EC-CTR	Douglas DC-9-34CF	Aviaco *Hernan Cortes*
	EC-CTS	Douglas DC-9-34CF	Aviaco *Francisco Pizarro*
	EC-CTT	Douglas DC-9-34CF	Aviaco *Pedro de Valdivia*
	EC-CTU	Douglas DC-9-34CF	Aviaco *Pedro de Alvarado*
	EC-CZE	Douglas DC-8-61	Spantax
	EC-DCC	Boeing 727-256	Iberia *Albarino*
	EC-DCD	Boeing 727-256	Iberia *Chacoli*
	EC-DCE	Boeing 727-256	Iberia *Mentrida*
	EC-DDV	Boeing 727-256	Iberia *Acueducto de Segovia*
	EC-DDX	Boeing 727-256	Iberia *Monasterio de Poblet*
	EC-DDY	Boeing 727-256	Iberia *Cuevas de Altamira*
	EC-DDZ	Boeing 727-256	Iberia *Murallas de Avila*
	EC-DEA	Douglas DC-10-30	Iberia *Rias Gallegas*
	EC-DGB	Douglas DC-9-34	Aviaco *Castillo de Javier*
	EC-DGC	Douglas DC-9-34	Aviaco *Castillo de Sotomayor*
	EC-DGD	Douglas DC-9-34	Aviaco *Castillo de Arcos*
	EC-DGE	Douglas DC-9-34	Aviaco *Castillo de Bellver*
	EC-DHZ	Douglas DC-10-30	Iberia *Costas Canarias*
	EC-DIA	Boeing 747-256B	Iberia *Tirso de Molina*
	EC-DIB	Boeing 747-256B	Iberia *Cervantes*
	EC-DLC	Boeing 747-256B SCD	Iberia *Francisco de Quevedo*
	EC-DLD	Boeing 747-256B SCD	Iberia *Lupe de Vega*
	EC-DLE	Airbus A.300B4	Iberia *Doana*
	EC-DLF	Airbus A.300B4	Iberia *Canadas del Teide*
	EC-DLG	Airbus A.300B4	Iberia *Tablas de Daimiel*
	EC-DLH	Airbus A.300B4	Iberia *Aigues Tortes*
	EC-DNP	Boeing 747-256B	Iberia *Juan Ramon Jimenez*
	EC-DNQ	Airbus A.300B4	Iberia *Islas Cies*
	EC-DNR	Airbus A.300B4	Iberia *Ordesa*
	EC-DTR	Boeing 737-2K5	Spantax
	EC-DUB	Boeing 737-2K5	Spantax
	EC-DVB	Douglas DC-8-61	Spantax
	EC-DVC	Douglas DC-8-61	Spantax
	EC-DXV	Boeing 737-2L9	Hispania
	EC-DYY	Douglas DC-8-61	Canafrica

Reg.	Type	Owner or Operator	Notes
EC-DZA	Douglas DC-8-61	Canafrica	
EC-DZB	Boeing 737-248C	Hispania (*until June 1988*)	
EC-EAK	Boeing 737-3Q8	Air Europa	
EC-EAM	Douglas DC-8-61	Spantax	
EC-EBX	Boeing 737-3Z9	Hispania	
EC-EBY	Boeing 737-3Z9	Hispania	
EC-ECM	Boeing 737-3QA	Air Europa	
EC-ECN	Douglas DC-9-83	Canafrica	
EC-ECO	Douglas DC-9-83	Canafrica	
EC-ECQ	Boeing 737-3QA	Air Europa	
EC-ECR	Boeing 737-3YO	Air Europa	
EC-ECS	Boeing 737-375	Air Europa	
EC-ECU	Douglas DC-9-32	Iberia	
EC-EDM	Boeing 737-3Q8	Universair	
EC-EEG	Boeing 737-229	Spantax	
EC-EEK	Boeing 747-256B	Iberia *Garcia Lorca*	
EC-EFJ	Douglas DC-9-83	Spantax	
EC-EFK	Douglas DC-9-83	Lineas Aereas Canarias	
EC-EFL	Douglas DC-9-83	Spantax	
EC-	Douglas DC-9-83	Spantax	
EC-	Douglas DC-9-83	Spanair	
EC-	Douglas DC-9-83	Spanair	
EC-	Douglas DC-9-83	Spanair	
EC-	Douglas DC-9-83	Spanair	
EC-	Douglas DC-10-30	Spantax	
EC-EFU	Douglas DC-9-83	Lineas Aereas Canarias	
EC-EFY	Boeing 757-2G5	LTE	
EC-	Douglas DC-9-83	Andalusair	
EC-	Boeing 737-300	Chiasa	
EC-	Boeing 737-300	Chiasa	
EC-	Boeing 737-3Q8	Viva	
EC-	Boeing 737-3Q8	Viva	
EC-	Boeing 737-3Q8	Viva	

Note: With the delivery of the DC-9-83s Spantax will release all its 737s. A pair of Boeing 767s will also be in service to replace the DC-8-61s.

EI (Republic of Ireland)

Including complete current Irish Civil Register

EI-ABI	D.H.84 Dragon	Aer Lingus *Iolar* (EI-AFK)	
EI-ADV	PA-12 Super Cruiser	R. E. Levis	
EI-AFF	B.A. Swallow 2 ★	J. McCarthy	
EI-AFN	B.A. Swallow 2 ★	J. McCarthy	
EI-AGB	Miles M.38 Messenger 4 ★	J. McLoughlin	
EI-AGD	Taylorcraft Plus D ★	H. Wolf	
EI-AGJ	J/1 Autocrat	W. G. Rafter	
EI-AHA	D.H.82A Tiger Moth ★	J. H. Maher	
EI-AHR	D.H.C.1 Chipmunk 22 ★	C. Lane	
EI-AKM	Piper J-3C-65 Cub	Setanta Flying Group	
EI-ALH	Taylorcraft Plus D	N. Reilly	
EI-ALP	Avro 643 Cadet	J. C. O'Loughlin	
EI-ALU	Avro 631 Cadet	M. P. Cahill	
EI-AMK	J/1 Autocrat	Irish Aero Club	
EI-AMO	J/1B Aiglet	R. Hassett	
EI-AND	Cessna 175A	Jack Braithwaite (Ireland) Ltd	
EI-ANE	BAC One-Eleven 208AL	Aer Lingus *St Mel*	
EI-ANF	BAC One-Eleven 208AL	Aer Lingus *St Malachy*	
EI-ANG	BAC One-Eleven 208AL	Aer Lingus *St Declan*	
EI-ANH	BAC One-Eleven 208AL	Aer Lingus *St Ronan*	
EI-ANR	Lake LA.4-200 Buccaneer	R. G. Baker & F. Dubbin	
EI-ANT	Champion 7ECA Citabria	P. Ryan	
EI-AOB	PA-28 Cherokee 140	J. Surdival & ptnrs	
EI-AOK	Cessna F.172G	R. J. Cloughley & N. J. Simpson	
EI-AOO	Cessna 150E	R. Hassett	
EI-AOP	D.H.82A Tiger Moth ★	Institute of Technology/Dublin	
EI-AOS	Cessna 310B	Joyce Aviation Ltd	
EI-APF	Cessna F.150F	L. O. Kennedy	

Notes	Reg.	Type	Owner or Operator
	EI-APS	Schleicher ASK 14	G. W. Connolly & M. Slazenger
	EI-ARH	Currie Wot/S.E.5 Replica	L. Garrison
	EI-ARM	Currie Wot/S.E.5 Replica	L. Garrison
	EI-ARW	Jodel D.R.1050	M. Mannion
	EI-ASA	Boeing 737-248	Aer Lingus St Jarlath
	EI-ASD	Boeing 737-248C	Aer Lingus St Ide
	EI-ASE	Boeing 737-248C	Aer Lingus St Fachtna
	EI-ASF	Boeing 737-248	Aer Lingus St Nathy
	EI-ASG	Boeing 737-248	Aer Lingus St Cormack
	EI-ASH	Boeing 737-248	Aer Lingus St Eugene
	EI-ASI	Boeing 747-148	Aer Lingus St Colmcille
	EI-ASJ	Boeing 747-148	Aer Lingus St Patrick
	EI-ASL	Boeing 737-248C	Aer Lingus St Killian
	EI-AST	Cessna F.150H	Liberty Flying Group
	EI-ATC	Cessna 310G	Iona National Airways Ltd
	EI-ATK	B.121 Pup 1	Wexford Aero Club
	EI-ATK	PA-28 Cherokee 140	Mayo Flying Club Ltd
	EI-ATS	M.S.880B Rallye Club	O. Bruton & G. Farrar
	EI-AUC	Cessna FA.150K Aerobat	Flying Fifteen Aero Club Ltd
	EI-AUE	M.S.880B Rallye Club	Kilkenny Flying Club Ltd
	EI-AUG	M.S.894 Rallye Minerva 220	Weston Ltd
	EI-AUJ	M.S.880B Rallye Club	P. Mulhall
	EI-AUM	J/1 Autocrat	J. G. Rafter
	EI-AUO	Cessna FA.150K Aerobat	Kerry Aero Club
	EI-AUP	M.S.880B Rallye Club	Limerick Flying Club
	EI-AUS	J/5F Aiglet Trainer	T. Stephens & T. Lennon
	EI-AUT	Forney F-1A Aircoupe	Joyce Aviation Ltd
	EI-AUV	PA-23 Aztec 250	Shannon Executive Aviation
	EI-AUY	Morane-Saulnier M.S.502	Historical Aircraft Preservation Group
	EI-AVB	Aeronca 7AC Champion	G. G. Bracken
	EI-AVC	Cessna F.337F	337 Flying Group
	EI-AVM	Cessna F.150L	P. Kearney
	EI-AVN	Hughes 369HM	Helicopter Maintenance Ltd
	EI-AWE	Cessna F.150M	Third Flight Group
	EI-AWH	Cessna 210J	Southern Air Ltd
	EI-AWP	D.H.82A Tiger Moth	A. Lyons
	EI-AWR	Malmo MFI-9 Junior	G. Fawcett
	EI-AWU	M.S.880B Rallye Club	Longford Aviation Ltd
	EI-AWW	Cessna 414	Ace Coin (Ireland) Ltd (stored)
	EI-AYA	M.S.880B Rallye Club	D. Bothwell & ptnrs
	EI-AYB	GY-80 Horizon 180	Westwing Flying Group
	EI-AYD	AA-5 Traveler	P. Howick & ptnrs
	EI-AYF	Cessna FRA.150L	Garda Flying Club
	EI-AYI	M.S.880B Rallye Club	Irish Air Training Group
	EI-AYK	Cessna F.172M	S. T. Scully
	EI-AYL	A.109 Airedale	J. Ronan
	EI-AYN	BN-2A Islander	Aer Arran
	EI-AYO	Douglas DC-3A ★	Science Museum, Wroughton
	EI-AYR	Schleicher ASK-16	Kilkenny Airport Ltd
	EI-AYS	PA-22 Colt 108	Messrs Skelly & Hall
	EI-AYT	M.S.894A Rallye Minerva	R. C. Cunningham
	EI-AYV	M.S.892A Rallye Commodore 150	P. Murtagh
	EI-AYW	PA-23 Aztec 250	Chutewell International Ltd
	EI-AYY	Evans VP-1	M. Donoghue
	EI-BAF	Thunder Ax6-56 balloon	W. G. Woollett
	EI-BAJ	Stampe SV-4C	Dublin Tiger Group
	EI-BAO	Cessna F.172G	Kingdom Air Ltd
	EI-BAR	Thunder Ax8-105 balloon	J. Burke & V. Hourihane
	EI-BAS	Cessna F.172M	Falcon Aviation Ltd
	EI-BAT	Cessna F.150M	J. Barrow
	EI-BAV	PA-22 Colt 108	J. P. Montcalm
	EI-BAY	Cameron V-77 balloon	F. N. Lewis
	EI-BBC	PA-28 Cherokee 180C	Rathcoole Flying Group
	EI-BBD	Evans VP-1	Volksplane Group
	EI-BBE	Champion 7FC Tri-Traveler (tailwheel)	R. Sharpe
	EI-BBF	EAA P-2 Biplane	B. Feeley
	EI-BBG	M.S.880B Rallye Club	Weston Ltd
	EI-BBI	M.S.892 Rallye Commodore	Kilkenny Airport Ltd

Reg.	Type	Owner or Operator	Notes
EI-BBJ	M.S.880B Rallye Club	Weston Ltd	
EI-BBK	A.109 Airedale	H. S. Igoe	
EI-BBM	Cameron O-65 balloon	Dublin Ballooning Club	
EI-BBN	Cessna F.150M	Sligo N.W. Aero Club	
EI-BBO	M.S.893E Rallye 180GT	J. G. Lacey & ptnrs	
EI-BBV	Piper J-3C-65 Cub	F. Cronin	
EI-BBW	M.S.894A Rallye Minerva	J. J. Ladbrook	
EI-BCE	BN-2A-26 Islander	Aer Arann	
EI-BCF	Bensen B.8M	T. A. Brennan	
EI-BCH	M.S.892A Rallye Commodore 150	The Condor Group	
EI-BCJ	F.8L Falco 1 Srs 3	D. Kelly	
EI-BCK	Cessna F.172K	Iona National Airways	
EI-BCL	Cessna 182P	Iona National Airways	
EI-BCM	Piper J-3C-65 Cub	Kilmoon Flying Group	
EI-BCN	Piper J-3C-65 Cub	Snowflake Flying Group	
EI-BCO	Piper J-3C-65 Cub	J. Molloy	
EI-BCR	Boeing 737-281	Aer Lingus St Oliver Plunkett	
EI-BCS	M.S.880B Rallye Club	J. Murphy	
EI-BCT	Cessna 411A	Avmarm (Ireland) Ltd	
EI-BCU	M.S.880B Rallye Club	Weston Ltd	
EI-BCV	Cessna F.150M	Hibernian Flying Club Ltd	
EI-BCW	M.S.880B Rallye Club	H. Clarke & D. Lodge	
EI-BCY	Beech 200 Super King Air (232)	Minister of Defence	
EI-BDH	M.S.880B Rallye Club	Munster Wings Ltd	
EI-BDK	M.S.880B Rallye Club	Limerick Flying Club Ltd	
EI-BDL	Evans VP-2	J. Duggan	
EI-BDM	PA-23 Aztec 250D	Executive Air Services	
EI-BDP	Cessna 182P	182 Flying Group	
EI-BDR	PA-28 Cherokee 180	Cork Flying Club	
EI-BEA	M.S.880B Rallye 100ST	Weston Ltd	
EI-BEB	Boeing 737-248	Aer Lingus Teo St Eunan	
EI-BEC	Boeing 737-248	Aer Lingus Teo St Fiacre	
EI-BED	Boeing 747-130	Aer Linte Eireann Teo St Kieran	
EI-BEE	Boeing 737-281	Aer Lingus Teo St Cronin	
EI-BEI	—	Aer Lingus Teo	
EI-BEJ	—	Aer Lingus Teo	
EI-BEK	Short SD3-60	Aer Lingus Teo St Eithne	
EI-BEL	Short SD3-60	Aer Lingus Teo	
EI-BEN	Piper J-3C-65 Cub	Capt J. J. Sullivan	
EI-BEO	Cessna 310Q	Iona National Airways	
EI-BEP	M.S.892A Rallye Commodore 150	H. Lynch & J. O'Leary	
EI-BEY	Naval N3N-3	Huntley & Huntley Ltd	
EI-BFF	Beech A.23 Musketeer	E. Hopkins	
EI-BFH	Bell 212	Irish Helicopters Ltd	
EI-BFI	M.S.880B Rallye 100ST	J. O'Neill	
EI-BFJ	Beech A.200 Super King Air (234)	Minister of Defence	
EI-BFM	M.S.893E Rallye 235GT	NDM Aviation	
EI-BFO	Piper J-3C-90 Cub	M. Slattery	
EI-BFP	M.S.800B Rallye 100ST	Weston Ltd	
EI-BFR	M.S.880B Rallye 100ST	Galway Flying Club	
EI-BFS	FRED Srs 2	G. J. McGlennon	
EI-BFV	M.S.880B Rallye 100T	Ormond Flying Club	
EI-BGA	SOCATA Rallye 100ST	J. J. Frew	
EI-BGB	M.S.880B Rallye Club	G. N. Atkinson	
EI-BGD	M.S.880B Rallye Club	N. Kavanagh	
EI-BGG	M.S.892E Rallye 150GT	C. Weldon	
EI-BGH	Cessna F.172N	Iona National Airways	
EI-BGJ	Cessna F.152	Hibernian Flying Club	
EI-BGK	Cessna P206D	Press 22 Aviation Ltd	
EI-BGO	Canadair CL-44D-4J ★	Irish Airports Authority/Dublin	
EI-BGP	Cessna 414A	Iona National Airways	
EI-BGS	M.S.893B Rallye 180GT	M. Farrelly	
EI-BGT	Colt 77A balloon	K. Haugh	
EI-BGU	M.S.880B Rallye Club	M. F. Neary	
EI-BGV	AA-5 Traveler	J. Crowe	
EI-BHB	M.S.887 Rallye 125	Hotel Bravo Flying Club	
EI-BHC	Cessna F.177RG	P. J. McGuire & B. Palfrey	
EI-BHD	M.S.893E Rallye 180GT	Epic Flying Group	

Notes	Reg.	Type	Owner or Operator
	EI-BHF	M.S.892A Rallye Commodore 150	B. Mullen
	EI-BHI	Bell 206B JetRanger 2	J. Mansfield
	EI-BHK	M.S.880B Rallye Club	J. Lawlor & B. Lyons
	EI-BHL	Beech E90 King Air	Stewart Singlam Fabrics Ltd
	EI-BHM	Cessna 337E	The Ross Flying Group
	EI-BHN	M.S.893A Rallye Commodore 180	K. O'Driscoll & ptnrs
	EI-BHO	Sikorsky S-61N	Irish Helicopters Ltd
	EI-BHP	M.S.893A Rallye Commodore 180	G. Atkinson
	EI-BHT	Beech 77 Skipper	Waterford Aero Club
	EI-BHV	Champion 7EC Traveler	Condor Group
	EI-BHW	Cessna F.150F	Shannon Executive Aviation
	EI-BHY	SOCATA Rallye 150ST	D. Killian
	EI-BIB	Cessna F.152	Galway Flying Club
	EI-BIC	Cessna F.172N	Oriel Flying Group Ltd
	EI-BID	PA-18 Super Cub 95	D. MacCarthy
	EI-BIG	Zlin 526	P. von Lonkhuyzen
	EI-BIJ	AB-206B JetRanger 2	Irish Helicopters Ltd
	EI-BIK	PA-18-180 Super Cub	Dublin Gliding Club
	EI-BIM	M.S.880B Rallye Club	D. Millar
	EI-BIO	Piper J-3C-65 Cub	Monasterevin Flying Club
	EI-BIR	Cessna F.172M	P. O'Reilly
	EI-BIS	Robin R.1180TD	Robin Aiglon Group
	EI-BIT	M.S.887 Rallye 125	City Aviation
	EI-BIU	Robin R.2112A	Wicklow Flying Group
	EI-BIV	Bellanca 8KCAB Citabria	Aerocrats Flying Group
	EI-BIW	M.S.880B Rallye Club	E. J. Barr
	EI-BJA	Cessna FRA.150L	Blackwater Flying Group
	EI-BJC	Aeronca 7AC Champion	R. J. Bentley
	EI-BJE	Boeing 737-275	Air Tara Ltd
	EI-BJG	Robin R.1180	N. Hanley
	EI-BJJ	Aeronca 15AC Sedan	A. A. Alderdice & S. H. Boyd
	EI-BJK	M.S.880B Rallye 110ST	P. Slazenger
	EI-BJL	Cessna 550 Citation II	Helicopter Maintenance Ltd
	EI-BJM	Cessna A.152	Leinster Aero Club
	EI-BJN	Cessna 500 Citation	Tool & Mould Steel (Ireland) Ltd
	EI-BJO	Cessna R.172K	P. Hogan & G. Ryder
	EI-BJS	AA-5B Tiger	P. Morrisey
	EI-BJT	PA-38-112 Tomahawk	Shannon Executive Aviation
	EI-BJW	D.H.104 Dove 6 ★	Waterford Museum
	EI-BKC	Aeronca 115AC Sedan	G. Treacy
	EI-BKD	Mooney M.20J	Limerick Warehousing Ltd
	EI-BKF	Cessna F.172H	M. & M. C. Veale
	EI-BKK	Taylor JT.1	Waterford Aero Club
	EI-BKM	Zenith CH.200	B. McGann
	EI-BKN	M.S.880B Rallye 100ST	Weston Ltd
	EI-BKP	Zenith CH.200	L. McEnteggart
	EI-BKS	Eipper Quicksilver	Irish Microlight Ltd
	EI-BKT	AB-206B JetRanger 3	Irish Helicopters Ltd
	EI-BKU	M.S.892A Rallye Commodore 150	Limerick Flying Club
	EI-BLB	Stampe SV-4C	J. E. Hutchinson & R. A. Stafford
	EI-BLD	Bolkow Bo 105C	Irish Helicopters Ltd
	EI-BLE	Eipper Microlight	R. P. St George-Smith
	EI-BLG	AB.206B JetRanger 3	Anglo Irish Meat Co Ltd
	EI-BLN	Eipper Quicksilver MX	O. J. Conway & B. Daffy
	EI-BLO	Catto CP.16	R. W. Hall
	EI-BLR	PA-34-200T Seneca II	R. Paris
	EI-BLU	Evans VP-1	A. Bailey
	EI-BLW	PA-23 Aztec 250	Shannon Executive Aviation
	EI-BLY	Sikorsky S-61N	Irish Helicopters Ltd
	EI-BMA	M.S.880B Rallye Club	Trinity Aviation Ltd
	EI-BMB	M.S.880B Rallye 100T	Clyde Court Development Ltd
	EI-BMC	Hiway Demon Skytrike	S. Pallister
	EI-BMD	Eagle Microlight	E. Fitzgerald
	EI-BMF	F.8L Falco	M. Slazenger
	EI-BMH	M.S.880B Rallye Club	N. J. Bracken
	EI-BMI	SOCATA TB.9 Tampico	Weston Ltd
	EI-BMJ	M.S.880B Rallye 100T	Weston Ltd
	EI-BMK	Cessna 310Q	Iona National Airways Ltd
	EI-BML	PA-23 Aztec 250	Bruton Aircraft Engineering Ltd
	EI-BMM	Cessna F.152 II	Iona National Airways Ltd

Reg.	Type	Owner or Operator	Notes
EI-BMN	Cessna F.152 II	Iona National Airways Ltd	
EI-BMO	Robin R.2160	L. Gavin & ptnrs	
EI-BMS	Cessna F.177RG	A. M. Smyth	
EI-BMU	Monnet Sonerai II	P. Forde & D. Connaire	
EI-BMV	AA-5 Traveler	R. C. Cunningham	
EI-BMW	Vulcan Air Trike	L. Maddock	
EI-BMY	Boeing 737-2L9	Air Tara Ltd	
EI-BNA	Douglas DC-8-63CF	Aer Turas	
EI-BNB	Lake LA-4-200 Buccaneer	L. McNamara & M. Ledwith	
EI-BNC	Cessna F.152	Iona National Airlines	
EI-BND	Conroy CL-44-0	HeavyLift Cargo Airlines Ltd/Stansted	
EI-BNF	Goldwing Canard	T. Morelli	
EI-BNG	M.S.892A Rallye Commodore 150	Shannon Executive Aviation	
EI-BNH	Hiway Skytrike	M. Martin	
EI-BNJ	Evans VP-2	G. A. Cashman	
EI-BNK	Cessna U.206F	Irish Parachute Club Ltd	
EI-BNL	Rand KR-2	K. Hayes	
EI-BNN	SC.7 Skyvan	Shannon Executive Aviation	
EI-BNP	Rotorway 133	R. L. Renfroe	
EI-BNR	AA-5 Traveler	Victor Mike Flying Group	
EI-BNT	Cvjetkovic CA-65	B. Tobin & P. G. Ryan	
EI-BNU	M.S.880B Rallye Club	P. A. Doyle	
EI-BOA	Pterodactyl Ptraveller	A. Murphy	
EI-BOE	SOCATA TB.10 Tobago	E. L. Symmons	
EI-BOH	Eipper Quicksilver	L. Leech	
EI-BOK	PA-23 Aztec 250	K. A. O'Connor	
EI-BOM	Boeing 737-2T4	Air Tara Ltd (*leased in US*)	
EI-BON	Boeing 737-2T4	Air Tara Ltd (*leased in US*)	
EI-BOO	PA-23 Aztec 250	P. Mercer	
EI-BOR	Bell 222	V. O'Brien	
EI-BOT	AS.350B Ecureuil	J. Kelly	
EI-BOV	Rand KR-2	G. O'Hara & G. Callan	
EI-BOX	Duet	K. Riccius	
EI-BPB	PA-28R Cherokee Arrow 200	G. P. O'Gorman	
EI-BPD	Short SD3-60	Aer Lingus Teo *St Gall*	
EI-BPE	Viking Dragonfly	G. Bracken	
EI-BPH	Boeing 747-133	Air Tara Ltd (*leased in US*)	
EI-BPI	EMB-110P1 Bandeirante	Ryan Air	
EI-BPJ	Cessna 182A	J. Matthews & V. McCarthy	
EI-BPL	Cessna F.172K	Phoenix Flying	
EI-BPM	AS.350B Ecureuil	Helicopter Maintenance Ltd	
EI-BPO	Puma Skytrike	A. Morelli	
EI-BPP	Quicksilver MX	J. A. Smith	
EI-BPR	Boeing 737-2S3	Air Tara Ltd (*leased in US*)	
EI-BPS	PA-30 Twin Comanche 160	Group Air	
EI-BPT	Skyhook Sabre	T. McGrath	
EI-BPU	Hiway Demon	A. Channing	
EI-BRB	Boeing 737-2S3	Air Tara Ltd	
EI-BRG	H.S.125 Srs 600	Anglo-Irish Meats	
EI-BRH	Mainair Gemini Flash	F. Warren & T. McGrath	
EI-BRK	Flexiform Trike	L. Maddock	
EI-BRM	Cessna 172Q	Iona National Airways	
EI-BRO	Cessna F.152	Iona National Airways	
EI-BRP	Canadair CL-44J	Aer Turas	
EI-BRS	Cessna P.172D	D. & M. Hillery	
EI-BRT	Flexwing M17727	S. Pallister	
EI-BRU	Evans VP-1	C. Quinn	
EI-BRV	Hiway Demon	M. Garvey & C. Tully	
EI-BRW	Ultralight Deltabird	A. & E. Aerosport	
EI-BRX	Cessna FRA.150L	P. O'Donnell	
EI-BSC	Cessna F.172N	Colby Investments Ltd	
EI-BSD	Enstrom F-28A	R. Moffet	
EI-BSE	H.S.748 Srs 1	Ryanair Ltd *Spirit of Ireland*	
EI-BSF	H.S.748 Srs 1	Ryanair Ltd *Spirit of Tipperary*	
EI-BSG	Bensen B.80	J. Todd	
EI-BSH	Colt 77A balloon	T. MacCormack	
EI-BSI	Douglas C-47B	Apple Air Services Ltd	
EI-BSK	SOCATA TB.9 Tampico	Weston Ltd	
EI-BSL	PA-34-220T Seneca	E. L. Symons	
EI-BSN	Cameron O-65 balloon	W. Woollett	
EI-BSO	PA-28 Cherokee 140B	D. Rooney	

Notes	Reg.	Type	Owner or Operator
	EI-BSP	Short SD3-60	Aer Lingus Teo
	EI-BSQ	Thundercolt Ax6-56Z balloon	D. Hooper
	EI-BSR	Lake LA.4-200 Buccaneer	Avmark Ltd
	EI-BSS	RomBac One-Eleven 561RC	Ryanair Ltd
	EI-BST	Bell 206B JetRanger	Celtic Helicopters Ltd
	EI-BSU	Champion 7KCAB	R. Bentley
	EI-BSV	SOCATA TB.20 Trinidad	J. Comdron
	EI-BSW	Solar Wings Pegasus XL-R	E. Fitzgerald
	EI-BSX	Piper J-3C-65 Cub	J. & T. O'Dwyer
	EI-BSY	BAC One-Eleven 525T	Ryanair Ltd *Spirit of Tipperary*
	EI-BSZ	BAC One-Eleven 525T	Ryanair Ltd *Spirit of Dublin*
	EI-BTB	Douglas DC-9-82	Irish Aerospace Ltd
	EI-BTC	Douglas DC-9-82	Irish Aerospace Ltd
	EI-BTD	Douglas DC-9-82	Irish Aerospace Ltd
	EI-BTF	Boeing 737-3Y0	Air Tara Ltd (*leased to Corse Air*)
	EI-BTN	L.1101-385 TriStar 1	Air Tara Ltd (*leased to Air America*)
	EI-BTQ	Boeing 747-2R7F	Flying Tiger Line
	EI-BTR	Boeing 737-2QR	Air Tara Ltd (*leased in US*)
	EI-BTS	—	Air Tara Ltd
	EI-BTT	—	Air Tara Ltd
	EI-BTU	—	Air Tara Ltd
	EI-BTV	—	Air Tara Ltd
	EI-BTW	—	Air Tara Ltd
	EI-BTX	—	Air Tara Ltd
	EI-BTY	—	Air Tara Ltd
	EI-BTZ	—	Air Tara Ltd
	EI-BUA	Cessna 172M	B. Norton
	EI-BUC	Jodel D.9	L. Maddock
	EI-BUD	Boeing 737-348	Aer Lingus *St Lawrance O'Toole*
	EI-BUE	Boeing 737-348	Aer Lingus *St Ciara*
	EI-BUF	Cessna 210N	210 Group
	EI-BUG	SOCATA ST.10 Diplomate	Diplomate Flying Group
	EI-BUH	Lake LA.4-200 Buccaneer	Translift Ltd
	EI-BUJ	M.S.892A Rallye Commodore 150	S. Bruton
	EI-BUK	Cessna 402B	D. Hillary
	EI-BUL	MW-5 Sorcerer	J. Green
	EI-BUM	Cessna 404	Iona National Airways Ltd
	EI-BUN	Beech 76 Duchess	S. Ryle
	EI-BUO	Lavery Sea Hawker	C. Lavery & C. Donaldson
	EI-BUP	Boeing 727-46	Club Travel Air Rentals Ltd
	EI-BUQ	RomBac One-Eleven 561RC	Ryanair Ltd
	EI-BUR	PA-38-112 Tomahawk	Avmark Ltd
	EI-BUS	PA-38-112 Tomahawk	Avmark Ltd
	EI-BUT	M.S.893A Commodore 180	T. Keating
	EI-BUU	Solar Wings Pegasus XL-R	R. L. T. Hudson
	EI-BUV	Cessna 172RG	J. J. Spollen
	EI-BUW	Noble Hardman Snowbird IIIA	Weston Ltd
	EI-BUX	—	—
	EI-BUY	Cessna 551 Citation 2	Tool & Mould Steel (Ireland) Ltd
	EI-BUZ	Robinson R-22	Avmark Ltd
	EI-BVA	Cessna 404	Iona National Airways Ltd
	EI-BVB	Whittaker MW.6 Merlin	R. England
	EI-BVC	Cameron N-65 balloon	E. Shepherd
	EI-BVD	—	—
	EI-BVE	Jodel D.9	J. Greene
	EI-BVF	Cessna F.172N	Ryan Air Ltd
	EI-BVG	—	—
	EI-BVH	—	—
	EI-BVI	—	—
	EI-BVJ	—	—
	EI-BVK	—	—
	EI-BVL	—	—
	EI-BWH	Partenavia P.68C	K. Buckley
	EI-EDR	PA-28R Cherokee Arrow 200	E. Ryan
	EI-GPA	Canadair CL-601S Challenger	Air Tara Ltd
	EI-XMA	Robinson R-22B	Spectra Photographic Laboratories Ltd

EP (Iran)

Reg.	Type	Owner or Operator	Notes
EP-IAA	Boeing 747SP-86	Iran Air *Fars*	
EP-IAB	Boeing 747SP-86	Iran Air *Kurdistan*	
EP-IAC	Boeing 747SP-86	Iran Air *Khuzestan*	
EP-IAD	Boeing 747SP-86	Iran Air	
EP-IAG	Boeing 747-286B (SCD)	Iran Air *Azarabadegan*	
EP-IAH	Boeing 747-286B (SCD)	Iran Air *Khorasan*	
EP-IAM	Boeing 747-186B	Iran Air	
EP-ICA	Boeing 747-2J9F	Iran Air	
EP-ICB	Boeing 747-2J9F	Iran Air	
EP-ICC	Boeing 747-2J9F	Iran Air	
EP-ICE	Boeing 707-3J9C	Iran Air	
EP-ICF	Boeing 747-131F (SCD)	Iran Air	
EP-IRK	Boeing 707-321C	Iran Air	
EP-IRL	Boeing 707-386C	Iran Air *Apadana*	
EP-IRM	Boeing 707-386C	Iran Air *Ekbatana*	
EP-IRN	Boeing 707-386C	Iran Air *Pasargad*	
EP-NHD	Boeing 747-131F	Iran Air	
EP-NHK	Boeing 747-131F	Iran Air	
EP-NHN	Boeing 747-2J9F	Iran Air	
EP-NHP	Boeing 747-131F	Iran Air	
EP-NHR	Boeing 747-131F	Iran Air	
EP-NHS	Boeing 747-131	Iran Air	
EP-NHT	Boeing 747-131F	Iran Air	
EP-NHV	Boeing 747-131F	Iran Air	

ET (Ethiopia)

Reg.	Type	Owner or Operator	Notes
ET-ACQ	Boeing 707-379C	Ethiopian Airlines	
ET-AIE	Boeing 767-260ER	Ethiopian Airlines	
ET-AIF	Boeing 767-260ER	Ethiopian Airlines	
ET-AIV	Boeing 707-327C	Ethiopian Airlines	
ET-AIZ	Boeing 767-260ER	Ethiopian Airlines	

F (France)

Reg.	Type	Owner or Operator	Notes
F-BEIG	Douglas DC-3	Stellair *Le Petit Prince*	
F-BIUK	F.27 Friendship Mk 100	Uni-Air	
F-BJEN	S.E.210 Caravelle 10B	Air Charter/E.A.S.	
F-BJTU	S.E.210 Caravelle 10B	Air Charter/E.A.S.	
F-BLHX	Nord 262A	Compagnie Aérienne du Languedoc	
F-BMKS	S.E.210 Caravelle 10B	Air Charter/E.A.S.	
F-BNOG	S.E.210 Caravelle 12	Air Inter	
F-BNOH	S.E.210 Caravelle 12	Air Inter	
F-BOJA	Boeing 727-228	Air France	
F-BOJB	Boeing 727-228	Air France	
F-BOJC	Boeing 727-228	Air France	
F-BOJD	Boeing 727-228	Air France	
F-BOJE	Boeing 727-228	Air France	
F-BOJF	Boeing 727-228	Air France	
F-BPJG	Boeing 727-228	Air France	
F-BPJH	Boeing 727-228	Air France	
F-BPJI	Boeing 727-228	Air France	
F-BPJJ	Boeing 727-228	Air France	
F-BPJK	Boeing 727-228	Air France	
F-BPJL	Boeing 727-228	Air France	
F-BPJM	Boeing 727-228	Air France	
F-BPJN	Boeing 727-228	Air France	
F-BPJO	Boeing 727-228	Air France	
F-BPJP	Boeing 727-228	Air France	
F-BPJQ	Boeing 727-228	Air France	
F-BPJR	Boeing 727-228	Air France	
F-BPJS	Boeing 727-228	Air France	
F-BPJT	Boeing 727-228	Air France	
F-BPJU	Boeing 727-214	Air Charter	

Notes	Reg.	Type	Owner or Operator
	F-BPJV	Boeing 727-214	Air Charter
	F-BPNC	F.27 Friendship Mk 500	Air Inter
	F-BPND	F.27 Friendship Mk 500	Air Inter
	F-BPNE	F.27 Friendship Mk 500	Air Inter
	F-BPNG	F.27 Friendship Mk 500	Brit Air
	F-BPNI	F.27 Friendship Mk 500	Brit Air
	F-BPPA	Aero Spacelines Guppy-201	Airbus Industrie _Airbus Skylink 2_
	F-BPUA	F.27 Friendship Mk 500	Air France
	F-BPUB	F.27 Friendship Mk 500	Air France
	F-BPUC	F.27 Friendship Mk 500	Air France
	F-BPUD	F.27 Friendship Mk 500	Air France
	F-BPUE	F.27 Friendship Mk 500	Air France
	F-BPUF	F.27 Friendship Mk 500	Air France
	F-BPUG	F.27 Friendship Mk 500	Air France
	F-BPUH	F.27 Friendship Mk 500	Air France
	F-BPUI	F.27 Friendship Mk 500	Air France
	F-BPUJ	F.27 Friendship Mk 500	Air France
	F-BPUK	F.27 Friendship Mk 500	Air France
	F-BPUL	F.27 Friendship Mk 500	Air France
	F-BPVA	Boeing 747-128	Air France
	F-BPVB	Boeing 747-128	Air France
	F-BPVC	Boeing 747-128	Air France
	F-BPVD	Boeing 747-128	Air France
	F-BPVE	Boeing 747-128	Air France
	F-BPVF	Boeing 747-128	Air France
	F-BPVG	Boeing 747-128	Air France
	F-BPVH	Boeing 747-128	Air France
	F-BPVJ	Boeing 747-128	Air France
	F-BPVK	Boeing 747-128	Air France
	F-BPVL	Boeing 747-128	Air France
	F-BPVM	Boeing 747-128	Air France
	F-BPVN	Boeing 747-128	Air France
	F-BPVO	Boeing 747-228F (SCD)	Air France
	F-BPVP	Boeing 747-128	Air France
	F-BPVQ	Boeing 747-128	Air France
	F-BPVR	Boeing 747-228F (SCD)	Air France
	F-BPVS	Boeing 747-228B (SCD)	Air France
	F-BPVT	Boeing 747-228B (SCD)	Air France
	F-BPVU	Boeing 747-228B (SCD)	Air France
	F-BPVV	Boeing 747-228F (SCD)	Air France
	F-BPVX	Boeing 747-228B (SCD)	Air France
	F-BPVY	Boeing 747-228B	Air France
	F-BPVZ	Boeing 747-228F (SCD)	Air France
	F-BRGU	S.E.210 Caravelle VI-N	Minerve
	F-BRUN	Beech 99	T.A.T.
	F-BSUM	F.27 Friendship Mk 500	Air France
	F-BSUN	F.27 Friendship Mk 500	Air France
	F-BSUO	F.27 Friendship Mk 500	Air France
	F-BTDB	Douglas DC-10-30	Union de Transports Aériens (UTA)
	F-BTDC	Douglas DC-10-30	Union de Transports Aériens (UTA)
	F-BTDD	Douglas DC-10-30	Union de Transports Aériens (UTA)
	F-BTDE	Douglas DC-10-30	Union de Transports Aériens (UTA)
	F-BTDG	Boeing 747-3B3 (SCD)	Union de Transports Aériens (UTA)
	F-BTDH	Boeing 747-3B3 (SCD)	Union de Transports Aériens (UTA)
	F-BTGV	Aero Spacelines Guppy-201	Airbus Industrie _Airbus Skylink 1_
	F-BTMA	Beech 99	T.A.T.
	F-BTMD	Mercure 100	Air Inter
	F-BTMJ	Beech 99A	T.A.T.
	F-BTMK	Beech 99A	T.A.T.
	F-BTOA	S.E.210 Caravelle 12	Air Inter
	F-BTOB	S.E.210 Caravelle 12	Air Inter
	F-BTOC	S.E.210 Caravelle 12	Air Inter
	F-BTOD	S.E.210 Caravelle 12	Air Inter
	F-BTOE	S.E.210 Caravelle 12	Air Inter
	F-BTSC	Concorde 101	Air France
	F-BTSD	Concorde 101	Air France
	F-BTTA	Mercure 100	Air Inter
	F-BTTB	Mercure 100	Air Inter
	F-BTTC	Mercure 100	Air Inter
	F-BTTD	Mercure 100	Air Inter

Reg.	Type	Owner or Operator	Notes
F-BTTE	Mercure 100	Air Inter	
F-BTTF	Mercure 100	Air Inter	
F-BTTG	Mercure 100	Air Inter	
F-BTTH	Mercure 100	Air Inter	
F-BTTI	Mercure 100	Air Inter	
F-BTTJ	Mercure 100	Air Inter	
F-BUAE	Airbus A.300B2	Air Inter	
F-BUAF	Airbus A.300B2	Air Inter	
F-BUAG	Airbus A.300B2	Air Inter	
F-BUAH	Airbus A.300B2	Air Inter	
F-BUAI	Airbus A.300B2	Air Inter	
F-BUAJ	Airbus A.300B2	Air Inter	
F-BUAK	Airbus A.300B2	Air Inter	
F-BUAL	Airbus A.300B4	Air Inter	
F-BUAM	Airbus A.300B2	Air Inter	
F-BUAN	Airbus A.300B2	Air Inter	
F-BUAO	Airbus A.300B2	Air Inter	
F-BUAP	Airbus A.300B2	Air Inter	
F-BUAQ	Airbus A.300B4	Air Inter	
F-BUOR	Douglas DC-8-55F	SFAIR	
F-BUTI	F-28 Fellowship 1000	T.A.T./Air France	
F-BVFA	Concorde 101	Air France	
F-BVFB	Concorde 101	Air France	
F-BVFF	Concorde 101	Air France	
F-BVFG	Nord 262A	Air Limousin *Lac de Vassivière*	
F-BVFH	Nord 262A	Air Limousin	
F-BVFI	Nord 262A	Air Limousin	
F-BVFJ	Nord 262A	Air Limousin *Val de Briance*	
F-BVGA	Airbus A.300B2	Air France	
F-BVGB	Airbus A.300B2	Air France	
F-BVGC	Airbus A.300B2	Air France	
F-BVGD	Airbus A.300B2	Air Inter	
F-BVGE	Airbus A.300B2	Air Inter	
F-BVGF	Airbus A.300B2	Air Inter	
F-BVGG	Airbus A.300B4	Air France	
F-BVGH	Airbus A.300B4	Air France	
F-BVGI	Airbus A.300B4	Air France	
F-BVGJ	Airbus A.300B4	Air France	
F-BVGL	Airbus A.300B4	Air France	
F-BVGM	Airbus A.300B4	Air France	
F-BVGN	Airbus A.300B4	Air France	
F-BVGO	Airbus A.300B4	Air France	
F-BVGP	Airbus A.300B4	Air France	
F-BVGQ	Airbus A.300B4	Air France/Air Jamaica	
F-BVGR	Airbus A.300B4	Air France	
F-BVGS	Airbus A.300B4	Air France	
F-BVGT	Airbus A.300B4	Air France	
F-BVJL	Beech 99A	T.A.T.	
F-BVPZ	S.E.210 Caravelle VI-N	Corse Air *Golfe du Valinco*	
F-BVSF	S.E.210 Caravelle VI-N	Corse Air *Golfe de Porto Vecchio*	
F-BYAB	F.27 Friendship Mk 600	Air Jet	
F-BYAO	F.27 Friendship Mk 100	Uni-Air	
F-BYAP	F.27 Friendship Mk 100	Uni-Air	
F-BYCJ	BN-2A-III-2 Trislander	Europe Aero Fret	
F-BYFM	Douglas DC-8-53	Minerve	
F-GAOT	F.27 Friendship Mk 100 (SCD)	Uni-Air	
F-GAPA	S.E.210 Caravelle VI-N	Minerve	
F-GATS	EMB-110P2 Bandeirante	Air Littoral *Hérault*	
F-GATZ	S.E.210 Caravelle VI-N	Minerve	
F-GBBR	F.28 Fellowship 1000	T.A.T./Air France	
F-GBBS	F.28 Fellowship 1000	T.A.T./Air France	
F-GBBT	F.28 Fellowship 1000	T.A.T./Air France	
F-GBBX	F.28 Fellowship 1000	T.A.T./Air France	
F-GBEA	Airbus A.300B2	Air Inter	
F-GBEB	Airbus A.300B2	Air Inter	
F-GBEC	Airbus A.300B2	Air Inter	
F-GBEI	Nord 262B	Compagnie Aérienne du Languedoc	
F-GBEJ	Nord 262B	Compagnie Aérienne du Languedoc	
F-GBEK	Nord 262A	Air Littoral	
F-GBGA	EMB-110P2 Bandeirante	Brit Air	

Notes	Reg.	Type	Owner or Operator
	F-GBLE	EMB-110P2 Bandeirante	Brit Air
	F-GBME	EMB-110P2 Bandeirante	Air Littoral *Aquitaine*
	F-GBMF	EMB-110P2 Bandeirante	Compagnie Aérienne du Languedoc/ Air Littoral
	F-GBMG	EMB-110P2 Bandeirante	Brit Air
	F-GBOX	Boeing 747-2B3F	Union de Transports Aériens (UTA)
	F-GBRM	EMB-110P2 Bandeirante	Brit Air
	F-GBRQ	FH.227B Friendship	T.A.T.
	F-GBRU	F.27J Friendship	T.A.T.
	F-GBRV	F.27J Friendship	T.A.T.
	F-GBTO	SA.226TC Metro II	Compagnie Aèrienne du Languedoc
	F-GBYA	Boeing 737-228	Air France
	F-GBYB	Boeing 737-228	Air France
	F-GBYC	Boeing 737-228	Air France
	F-GBYD	Boeing 737-228	Air France
	F-GBYE	Boeing 737-228	Air France
	F-GBYF	Boeing 737-228	Air France
	F-GBYG	Boeing 737-228	Air France
	F-GBYH	Boeing 737-228	Air France
	F-GBYI	Boeing 737-228	Air France
	F-GBYJ	Boeing 737-228	Air France
	F-GBYK	Boeing 737-228	Air France
	F-GBYL	Boeing 737-228	Air France
	F-GBYM	Boeing 737-228	Air France
	F-GBYN	Boeing 737-228	Air France
	F-GBYO	Boeing 737-228	Air France
	F-GBYP	Boeing 737-228	Air France
	F-GBYQ	Boeing 737-228	Air France
	F-GCBA	Boeing 747-228B	Air France
	F-GCBD	Boeing 747-228B (SCD)	Air France
	F-GCBH	Boeing 747-228B (SCD)	Air France
	F-GCBI	Boeing 747-228B (SCD)	Air France
	F-GCDA	Boeing 727-228	Air France
	F-GCDB	Boeing 727-228	Air France
	F-GCDC	Boeing 727-228	Air France
	F-GCDD	Boeing 727-228	Air France
	F-GCDE	Boeing 727-228	Air France
	F-GCDF	Boeing 727-228	Air France
	F-GCDG	Boeing 727-228	Air France
	F-GCDH	Boeing 727-228	Air France
	F-GCDI	Boeing 727-228	Air France
	F-GCFC	FH.227B Friendship	T.A.T.
	F-GCFE	SA.226TC Metro II	Compagnie Aérienne du Langudoc
	F-GCGH	FH.227B Friendship	T.A.T.
	F-GCGQ	Boeing 727-227	Europe Aero Service *Normandie*
	F-GCJL	Boeing 737-222	Euralair/Air Charter
	F-GCJO	FH.227B Friendship	T.A.T.
	F-GCJT	S.E.210 Caravelle 10B	Europe Aero Service *Alsace*
	F-GCJV	F.27 Friendship Mk 400	Air Jet
	F-GCLA	EMB-110P1 Bandeirante	Aigle Azur
	F-GCLL	Boeing 737-222	Euralair/Air Charter
	F-GCLM	FH.227B Friendship	T.A.T.
	F-GCLN	FH.227B Friendship	T.A.T./Air France
	F-GCLO	FH.227B Friendship	T.A.T.
	F-GCLQ	FH.227B Friendship	T.A.T.
	F-GCMQ	EMB-110P2 Bandeirante	Air Littoral *Provence*
	F-GCMV	Boeing 727-2X3	Air Charter
	F-GCMX	Boeing 727-2X3	Air Charter
	F-GCPG	SA.226TC Metro II	Compagnie Aérienne du Languedoc
	F-GCPS	FH.227B Friendship	T.A.T.
	F-GCPT	FH.227B Friendship	T.A.T.
	F-GCPU	FH.227B Friendship	T.A.T.
	F-GCPV	FH.227B Friendship	T.A.T.
	F-GCPX	FH.227B Friendship	T.A.T./Air France
	F-GCPY	FH.227B Friendship	T.A.T.
	F-GCPZ	FH.227B Friendship	T.A.T.
	F-GCSL	Boeing 737-222	Euralair/Air Charter
	F-GCTE	SA.226TC Metro II	Compagnie Aérienne du Languedoc
	F-GCVI	S.E.210 Caravelle 12	Air Inter
	F-GCVJ	S.E.210 Caravelle 12	Air Inter
	F-GCVK	S.E.210 Caravelle 12	Air Inter

Reg.	Type	Owner or Operator	Notes
F-GCVL	S.E.210 Caravelle 12	Air Inter	
F-GCVM	S.E.210 Caravelle 12	Air Inter	
F-GDAQ	L.100-30 Hercules	SFAIR	
F-GDCI	EMB-110P2 Bandeirante	Air Littoral *Comté de Nice*	
F-GDFC	F.28 Fellowship 4000	T.A.T./Air France	
F-GDFD	F.28 Fellowship 4000	T.A.T./Air France	
F-GDFY	S.E.210 Caravelle 10B	Air Charter/Europe Aero Service	
F-GDFZ	S.E.210 Caravelle 10B	Air Charter/Europe Aero Service	
F-GDJK	Douglas DC-10-30	Lineas Aereas de Mocambique (LAM)	
F-GDJM	Douglas DC-8-62CF	Minerve	
F-GDJU	S.E.210 Caravelle 10B	Europe Aero Service *Lorraine*	
F-GDMR	SA.226TC Metro II	Compagnie Aérienne du Languedoc	
F-GDPM	Douglas DC-8-53	Minerve	
F-GDPP	Douglas DC-3	ACE Transvalair	
F-GDPS	Douglas DC-8-61	Pointair *Les Trois Voltas*	
F-GDRM	Douglas DC-8-73	Minerve	
F-GDSG	UTA Super Guppy	Airbus/Air France Industrie *Airbus Skylink 3*	
F-GDSK	F.28 Fellowship 4000	T.A.T./Air France	
F-GDUS	F.28 Fellowship 2000	T.A.T.	
F-GDUT	F.28 Fellowship 2000	T.A.T./Air France	
F-GDUU	F.28 Fellowship 2000	T.A.T./Air France	
F-GDUV	F.28 Fellowship 2000	T.A.T./Air France	
F-GDUY	F.28 Fellowship 4000	T.A.T./Air France	
F-GDUZ	F.28 Fellowship 4000	T.A.T./Air France	
F-GDXL	Aerospatiale ATR-42-300	Brit Air	
F-GDXP	Douglas DC-3	ACE Transvalair	
F-GEAI	UTA Super Guppy	Airbus Industrie *Airbus Skylink 4*	
F-GEBD	Boeing 747-228B	Air France	
F-GEBU	SA.226TC Metro II	Compagnie Aérienne du Languedoc	
F-GECK	F.28 Fellowship 1000	T.A.T./Air France	
F-GEDR	EMB-110 P1 Bandeirante	Air Littoral	
F-GEDZ	Aerospatiale ATR-42-300	Air Littoral/Air France	
F-GEGD	Aerospatiale ATR-42-300	Air Littoral/Air France	
F-GEGE	Aerospatiale ATR-42-300	Air Littoral/Air France	
F-GEGF	Aerospatiale ATR-42-300	Air Littoral/Air France	
F-GEJE	V952F Vanguard	EAS Intercargo Service	
F-GEJF	V953F Vanguard	EAS Intercargo Service	
F-GELG	Saab SF.340A	Europe Air	
F-GELH	Saab SF.340A	Europe Air	
F-GELP	S.E.210 Caravelle	Europe Aero Service	
F-GEMA	Airbus A.310-203	Air France	
F-GEMB	Airbus A.310-203	Air France	
F-GEMC	Airbus A.310-203	Air France	
F-GEMD	Airbus A.310-203	Air France	
F-GEME	Airbus A.310-203	Air France	
F-GEMF	Airbus A.310-203	Air France	
F-GEMG	Airbus A.310-304	Air France	
F-GEMH	Airbus A.310-304	Air France	
F-GEOM	Douglas DC-3	Stellair	
F-GEPC	S.E.210 Caravelle 10B	Corse Air *Golfe de Porto Marina*	
F-GERV	SA226TC Metro II	Air Vendee	
F-GESB	Douglas DC-3	Stellair	
F-GESM	Douglas DC-8-73CF	Minerve	
F-GETA	Boeing 747-3B3 (SCD)	Union de Transports Aériens (UTA)	
F-GETB	Boeing 747-3B3 (SCD)	Union de Transports Aériens (UTA)	
F-GETM	Douglas DC-8-61	Minerve *Ville de Nimes*	
F-GEXI	Boeing 737-2L9	Europe Aero Service	
F-GEXJ	Boeing 737-200	Europe Aero Service	
F-GEXP	Nord 2501 Noratlas	ACE Transvalair	
F-GEXR	Nord 2501 Noratlas	ACE Transvalair	
F-GEXS	Nord 2501 Noratlas	ACE Transvalair	
F-GEXT	F.28 Fellowship 1000	T.A.T./Air France	
F-GEXU	F.28 Fellowship 1000	T.A.T./Air France	
F-GEXX	F.28 Fellowship 1000	T.A.T./Air France	
F-GFAE	D.H.C.6 Twin Otter 310	T.A.T.	
F-GFAF	D.H.C.6 Twin Otter 310	T.A.T.	
F-GFAG	D.H.C.6 Twin Otter 310	T.A.T.	
F-GFAJ	D.H.C.6 Twin Otter 310	T.A.T.	
F-GFAS	L-100-30 Hercules	SFAIR	
F-GFBA	S.E.210 Caravelle 10R	Europe Aero Service	

	F-GFBZ	Saab SF.340A	Brit Air
	F-GFEN	EMB-120 Brasilia	Air Littoral/Air France
	F-GFEO	EMB-120 Brasilia	Air Littoral/Air France
	F-GFEP	EMB-120 Brasilia	Air Littoral/Air France
	F-GFEQ	EMB-120 Brasilia	Air Littoral/Air France
	F-GFER	EMB-120 Brasilia	Air Littoral/Air France
	F-G	Saab SF.340A	Air Limousin
	F-G	Saab SF.340A	Air Limousin
	F-GFGE	SA226TC Metro II	T.A.T.
	F-GFGF	SA226TC Metro II	T.A.T.
	F-GFJH	Aerospatiale ATR-42-300	Brit Air
	F-GFJP	Aerospatiale ATR-42-300	Brit Air
	F-GFJS	F.27 Friendship Mk 600	Air Jet
	F-GFKA	Airbus A.320-110	Air France
	F-GFKB	Airbus A.320-110	Air France
	F-GFKC	Airbus A.320-110	Air France
	F-GFKD	Airbus A.320-110	Air France
	F-GFKE	Airbus A.320-110	Air France
	F-GFKF	Airbus A.320-110	Air France
	F-GFKG	Airbus A.320-110	Air France
	F-GGAV	Dornier Do.228-201	Air Vendee
	F-GGBJ	Saab SF.340A	Air Limousin
	F-GGBV	Saab SF.340A	Air Limousin
	F-GGEA	Airbus A.320-110	Air Inter
	F-GGEB	Airbus A.320-110	Air Inter
	F-GGEC	Airbus A.320-110	Air Inter
	F-GGED	Airbus A.320-110	Air Inter
	F-GGEE	Airbus A.320-110	Air Inter
	F-GGEF	Airbus A.320-110	Air Inter
	F-GGEG	Airbus A.320-110	Air Inter
	F-GGEH	Airbus A.320-110	Air Inter
	F-GGEI	Airbus A.320-110	Air Inter
	F-GGGV	Dornier Do.228-201	Air Vendee
	F-GGLR	Aeritalia ATR.42	Brit Air
	F-GGMA	Douglas DC-9-83	Minerve
	F-GGMB	Douglas DC-9-83	Minerve
	F-GGMC	Douglas DC-9-83	Minerve
	F-G	Boeing 737-300	Corse Air
	F-GHBM	Boeing 747-283B	Minerve
	F-GMFM	Douglas DC-8-71	Pointair *Region Reunion*
	F-GMOL	F.28 Fellowship 1000	T.A.T.
	F-GPAN	Boeing 747-2B3F	Air France
	F-GTNT	BAe 146-200QT	Euralair (TNT)
	F-OGQC	Douglas DC-10-30	Air Zaire

Note: Air France also operates four more Boeing 747s which retain the US
registrations N1289E, N4506H, N4508E and N4544F. UTA also operates two
DC-10-30s registered N54629 and N54649.

HA (Hungary)

HA-LBE	Tupolev Tu-134	Malev
HA-LBF	Tupolev Tu-134	Malev
HA-LBG	Tupolev Tu-134	Malev
HA-LBH	Tupolev Tu-134	Malev
HA-LBI	Tupolev Tu-134A-3	Malev
HA-LBK	Tupolev Tu-134A-3	Malev
HA-LBN	Tupolev Tu-134A-3	Malev
HA-LBO	Tupolev Tu-134A-3	Malev
HA-LBP	Tupolev Tu-134A	Malev
HA-LBR	Tupolev Tu-134A	Malev
HA-LCA	Tupolev Tu-154B-2	Malev
HA-LCB	Tupolev Tu-154B-2	Malev
HA-LCE	Tupolev Tu-154B-2	Malev
HA-LCG	Tupolev Tu-154B-2	Malev
HA-LCH	Tupolev Tu-154B-2	Malev
HA-LCM	Tupolev Tu-154B-2	Malev
HA-LCN	Tupolev Tu-154B-2	Malev
HA-LCO	Tupolev Tu-154B-2	Malev

Reg.	Type	Owner or Operator	Notes
HA-LCP	Tupolev Tu-154B-2	Malev	
HA-LCR	Tupolev Tu-154B-2	Malev	
HA-LCS	Tupolev Tu-154B-2	Malev	
HA-LCT	Tupolev Tu-154B-2	Malev	

HB (Switzerland)

HB-AHA	Saab SF.340A	Crossair	
HB-AHB	Saab SF.340A	Crossair	
HB-AHC	Saab SF.340A	Crossair	
HB-AHD	Saab SF.340A	Crossair	
HB-AHE	Saab SF.340A	Crossair	
HB-AHF	Saab SF.340A	Crossair	
HB-AHG	Saab SF.340A	Crossair	
HB-AHH	Saab SF.340A	Crossair	
HB-AHI	Saab SF.340A	Crossair	
HB-AHK	Saab SF.340A	Crossair	
HB-AHL	Saab SF.340A	Crossair	
HB-AHM	Saab SF.340A	Crossair	
HB-AHN	Saab SF.340A	Crossair	
HB-A	Saab SF.340A	Crossair	
HB-A	Saab SF.340A	Crossair	
HB-A	Saab SF.340A	Crossair	
HB-A	Saab SF.340A	Crossair	
HB-A	Saab SF.340A	Crossair	
HB-A	Saab SF.340A	Crossair	
HB-ICI	S.E.210 Caravelle 10B1R	CTA	
HB-ICJ	S.E.210 Caravelle 10B	Air City	
HB-ICO	S.E.210 Caravelle 10B1R	CTA Romandie	
HB-IFH	Douglas DC-9-32	Swissair Baden	
HB-IFU	Douglas DC-9-32	Swissair Chur	
HB-IFV	Douglas DC-9-32	Swissair Bülach	
HB-IGC	Boeing 747-357 (SCD)	Swissair Bern	
HB-IGD	Boeing 747-357 (SCD)	Swissair Basel	
HB-IGG	Boeing 747-357 (SCD)	Swissair Ticino	
HB-IHC	Douglas DC-10-30	Swissair Obwalden	
HB-IHD	Douglas DC-10-30	Swissair Thurgau	
HB-IHE	Douglas DC-10-30	Swissair Vaud	
HB-IHF	Douglas DC-10-30	Swissair Nidwalden	
HB-IHG	Douglas DC-10-30	Swissair Graubünden	
HB-IHH	Douglas DC-10-30	Swissair Schaffhausen	
HB-IHI	Douglas DC-10-30	Swissair Fribourg	
HB-IHK	Douglas DC-10-30	Balair	
HB-IHL	Douglas DC-10-30ER	Swissair Ticino	
HB-IHM	Douglas DC-10-30ER	Swissair Valais-Wallis	
HB-IHN	Douglas DC-10-30ER	Swissair St Gallen	
HB-IHO	Douglas DC-10-30ER	Swissair Uri	
HB-IKL	Douglas DC-9-82	Alisarda (Italy)	
HB-INA	Douglas DC-9-82	Swissair Höri	
HB-INB	Douglas DC-9-82	Balair	
HB-INC	Douglas DC-9-81	Swissair Lugano	
HB-IND	Douglas DC-9-81	Swissair Bachenbülach	
HB-INE	Douglas DC-9-81	Swissair Rümlang	
HB-INF	Douglas DC-9-81	Swissair Appenzell a.Rh.	
HB-ING	Douglas DC-9-81	Swissair Winkel	
HB-INH	Douglas DC-9-81	Swissair Winterthur	
HB-INI	Douglas DC-9-81	Swissair Kloten	
HB-INK	Douglas DC-9-81	Swissair Opfikon	
HB-INL	Douglas DC-9-81	Swissair Jura	
HB-INM	Douglas DC-9-81	Swissair Lausanne	
HB-INN	Douglas DC-9-81	Swissair Bülach	
HB-INO	Douglas DC-9-81	Swissair Bellinzona	
HB-INP	Douglas DC-9-81	Swissair Oberglatt	
HB-INR	Douglas DC-9-82	Balair	
HB-INS	Douglas DC-9-81	Swissair Meyrin	
HB-INT	Douglas DC-9-81	Swissair Grand-Saconnex	
HB-INU	Douglas DC-9-81	Swissair Vernier	
HB-INV	Douglas DC-9-81	Swissair Dubendorf	
HB-INW	Douglas DC-9-82	Balair	

Notes	Reg.	Type	Owner or Operator
	HB-INX	Douglas DC-9-81	Swissair
	HB-INY	Douglas DC-9-81	Swissair
	HB-INZ	Douglas DC-9-81	Swissair
	HB-IPA	Airbus A.310-221	Swissair *Aargau*
	HB-IPB	Airbus A.310-221	Swissair *Neuchatel*
	HB-IPC	Airbus A.310-221	Swissair *Schwyz*
	HB-IPD	Airbus A.310-221	Swissair *Solothurn*
	HB-IPE	Airbus A.310-221	Swissair *Basel-Land*
	HB-IPF	Airbus A.310-322	Swissair *Glarus*
	HB-IPG	Airbus A.310-322	Swissair *Zug*
	HB-IPH	Airbus A.310-322	Swissair *Appenzell i. Rh*
	HB-IPI	Airbus A.310-322	Swissair *Luzern*
	HB-IPK	Airbus A.310-322	Balair
	HB-ISV	Douglas DC-9-51	Swissair *Basserdorf*
	HB-ISW	Douglas DC-9-51	Swissair *Dubendorf*
	HB-IUA	Douglas DC-9-87	CTA
	HB-IUB	Douglas DC-9-87	CTA
	HB-IUC	Douglas DC-9-87	CTA
	HB-IUD	Douglas DC-9-87	CTA
	HB-IVA	Fokker 100	Swissair *Aarau*
	HB-IVB	Fokker 100	Swissair *Biel/Bienne*
	HB-IVC	Fokker 100	Swissair *Chur*
	HB-IVD	Fokker 100	Swissair *Dietlikon*
	HB-IVE	Fokker 100	Swissair *Baden*
	HB-IVF	Fokker 100	Swissair *Sion*
	HB-IVG	Fokker 100	Swissair *Basserdorf*
	HB-IVH	Fokker 100	Swissair *Wallisellen*
	HB-LNE	SA.227AC Metro III	Crossair
	HB-LNO	SA.227AC Metro III	Crossair

Note: Swissair also operates two Boeing 747-357s which retain their US registrations N221GE and N221GF and are named *Genève* and *Zurich* respectively. The remaining DC-9-32/51s will be withdrawn during 1988.

HK (Colombia)

	HK-2900	Boeing 747-124F	Avianca
	HK-2980X	Boeing 747-259B	Avianca *Cartagena de Indias*

HL (Korea)

	HL7315	Douglas DC-10-30	Korean Air
	HL7316	Douglas DC-10-30	Korean Air
	HL7317	Douglas DC-10-30	Korean Air
	HL7328	Douglas DC-10-30	Korean Air
	HL7431	Boeing 707-321C	Korean Air
	HL7435	Boeing 707-321B	Korean Air
	HL7440	Boeing 747-230B	Korean Air
	HL7441	Boeing 747-230F	Korean Air
	HL7443	Boeing 747-2B5B	Korean Air
	HL7447	Boeing 747-230B	Korean Air
	HL7451	Boeing 747-2B5F (SCD)	Korean Air/Saudia
	HL7452	Boeing 747-2B5F (SCD)	Korean Air
	HL7454	Boeing 747-2B5B	Korean Air
	HL7458	Boeing 747-2B5B	Korean Air
	HL7459	Boeing 747-2B5F (SCD)	Korean Air
	HL7463	Boeing 747-2B5B	Korean Air
	HL7464	Boeing 747-2B5B	Korean Air
	HL7468	Boeing 747-3B5	Korean Air
	HL7469	Boeing 747-3B5	Korean Air
	HL7471	Boeing 747-273C	Korean Air
	HL7474	Boeing 747-2S4F (SCD)	Korean Air

HS (Thailand)

Reg.	Type	Owner or Operator	Notes
HS-TGA	Boeing 747-2D7B	Thai Airways International *Visuthakasatriya*	
HS-TGB	Boeing 747-2D7B	Thai Airways International *Sirisobhakya*	
HS-TGC	Boeing 747-2D7B	Thai Airways International *Dararasmi*	
HS-TGD	Boeing 747-3D7	Thai Airways International	
HS-TGE	Boeing 747-3D7	Thai Airways International	
HS-TGF	Boeing 747-2D7B	Thai Airways International *Phimara*	
HS-TGG	Boeing 747-2D7B	Thai Airways International *Sriwanna*	
HS-TGJ	Boeing 747-3D7	Thai Airways International	
HS-TGS	Boeing 747-2D7B	Thai Airways International *Chainarai*	
HS-TGV	Boeing 747-3D7	Thai Airways International	
HS-TME	Douglas DC-10-30ER	Thai Airways International	
HS-TMF	Douglas DC-10-30ER	Thai Airways International	
HS-T	Douglas DC-10-30ER	Thai Airways International	

HZ (Saudi Arabia)

HZ-AHA	L.1011-385 TriStar 200	Saudia — Saudi Arabian Airlines	
HZ-AHB	L.1011-385 TriStar 200	Saudia — Saudi Arabian Airlines	
HZ-AHC	L.1011-385 TriStar 200	Saudia — Saudi Arabian Airlines	
HZ-AHD	L.1011-385 TriStar 200	Saudia — Saudi Arabian Airlines	
HZ-AHE	L.1011-385 TriStar 200	Saudia — Saudi Arabian Airlines	
HZ-AHF	L.1011-385 TriStar 200	Saudia — Saudi Arabian Airlines	
HZ-AHG	L.1011-385 TriStar 200	Saudia — Saudi Arabian Airlines	
HZ-AHH	L.1011-385 TriStar 200	Saudia — Saudi Arabian Airlines	
HZ-AHI	L.1011-385 TriStar 200	Saudia — Saudi Arabian Airlines	
HZ-AHJ	L.1011-385 TriStar 200	Saudia — Saudi Arabian Airlines	
HZ-AHL	L.1011-385 TriStar 200	Saudia — Saudi Arabian Airlines	
HZ-AHM	L.1011-385 TriStar 200	Saudia — Saudi Arabian Airlines	
HZ-AHN	L.1011-385 TriStar 200	Saudia — Saudi Arabian Airlines	
HZ-AHO	L.1011-385 TriStar 200	Saudia — Saudi Arabian Airlines	
HZ-AHP	L.1011-385 TriStar 200	Saudia — Saudi Arabian Airlines	
HZ-AHQ	L.1011-385 TriStar 200	Saudia — Saudi Arabian Airlines	
HZ-AHR	L.1011-385 TriStar 200	Saudia — Saudi Arabian Airlines	
HZ-AIA	Boeing 747-168B	Saudia — Saudi Arabian Airlines	
HZ-AIB	Boeing 747-168B	Saudia — Saudi Arabian Airlines	
HZ-AIC	Boeing 747-168B	Saudia — Saudi Arabian Airlines	
HZ-AID	Boeing 747-168B	Saudia — Saudi Arabian Airlines	
HZ-AIE	Boeing 747-168B	Saudia — Saudi Arabian Airlines	
HZ-AIF	Boeing 747SP-68	Saudia — Saudi Arabian Airlines	
HZ-AIG	Boeing 747-168B	Saudia — Saudi Arabian Airlines	
HZ-AIH	Boeing 747-168B	Saudia — Saudi Arabian Airlines	
HZ-AII	Boeing 747-168B	Saudia — Saudi Arabian Airlines	
HZ-AIJ	Boeing 747SP-68	Saudia — Saudi Arabian Airlines	
HZ-AIK	Boeing 747-368	Saudia — Saudi Arabian Airlines	
HZ-AIL	Boeing 747-368	Saudia — Saudi Arabian Airlines	
HZ-AIM	Boeing 747-368	Saudia — Saudi Arabian Airlines	
HZ-AIN	Boeing 747-368	Saudia — Saudi Arabian Airlines	
HZ-AIO	Boeing 747-368	Saudia — Saudi Arabian Airlines	
HZ-AIP	Boeing 747-368	Saudia — Saudi Arabian Airlines	
HZ-AIQ	Boeing 747-368	Saudia — Saudi Arabian Airlines	
HZ-AIR	Boeing 747-368	Saudia — Saudi Arabian Airlines	
HZ-AIS	Boeing 747-368	Saudia — Saudi Arabian Airlines	
HZ-AIT	Boeing 747-368	Saudia — Saudi Arabian Airlines	
HZ-AJA	Airbus A.300-620	Saudia — Saudi Arabian Airlines	
HZ-AJB	Airbus A.300-620	Saudia — Saudi Arabian Airlines	
HZ-AJC	Airbus A.300-620	Saudia — Saudi Arabian Airlines	
HZ-AJD	Airbus A.300-620	Saudia — Saudi Arabian Airlines	
HZ-AJE	Airbus A.300-620	Saudia — Saudi Arabian Airlines	
HZ-AJF	Airbus A.300-620	Saudia — Saudi Arabian Airlines	
HZ-AJG	Airbus A.300-620	Saudia — Saudi Arabian Airlines	
HZ-AJH	Airbus A.300-620	Saudia — Saudi Arabian Airlines	
HZ-AJI	Airbus A.300-620	Saudia — Saudi Arabian Airlines	
HZ-AJJ	Airbus A.300-620	Saudia — Saudi Arabian Airlines	
HZ-AJK	Airbus A.300-620	Saudia — Saudi Arabian Airlines	

Note: Saudia also operates other aircraft on lease.

I (Italy)

Notes	Reg.	Type	Owner or Operator
	I-ATIE	Douglas DC-9-32	Aero Trasporti Italiani (ATI) *Toscana*
	I-ATIH	Douglas DC-9-32	Aero Trasporti Italiani (ATI) *Lido degli Estensi*
	I-ATIJ	Douglas DC-9-32	Aero Trasporti Italiani (ATI)
	I-ATIQ	Douglas DC-9-32	Aero Trasporti Italiani (ATI) *Sila*
	I-ATIU	Douglas DC-9-32	Aero Trasporti Italiani (ATI)
	I-ATIW	Douglas DC-9-32	Aero Trasporti Italiani (ATI) *Lazio*
	I-ATIY	Douglas DC-9-32	Aero Trasporti Italiani (ATI) *Lombardia*
	I-ATJA	Douglas DC-9-32	Aero Trasporti Italiani (ATI) *Sicilia*
	I-ATJB	Douglas DC-9-32	Aero Trasporti Italiani (ATI) *Riviera de Conero*
	I-BUSB	Airbus A.300B4	Alitalia *Tiziano*
	I-BUSC	Airbus A.300B4	Alitalia *Botticelli*
	I-BUSD	Airbus A.300B4	Alitalia *Caravaggio*
	I-BUSF	Airbus A.300B4	Alitalia *Tintoretto*
	I-BUSG	Airbus A.300B4	Alitalia *Canaletto*
	I-BUSH	Airbus A.300B4	Alitalia *Mantegua*
	I-BUSJ	Airbus A.300B4	Alitalia *Tiepolo*
	I-BUSL	Airbus A.300B4	Alitalia *Pinturicchia*
	I-DAVA	Douglas DC-9-82	Aero Trasporti Italiani (ATI) *Cuneo*
	I-DAVB	Douglas DC-9-82	Alitalia *Ferrara*
	I-DAVC	Douglas DC-9-82	Aero Trasporti Italiani (ATI) *Lucca*
	I-DAVD	Douglas DC-9-82	Aero Trasporti Italiani (ATI) *Mantova*
	I-DAVF	Douglas DC-9-82	Aero Trasporti Italiani (ATI) *Oristano*
	I-DAVG	Douglas DC-9-82	Aero Trasporti Italiani (ATI) *Pesaro*
	I-DAVH	Douglas DC-9-82	Aero Trasporti Italiani (ATI) *Salerno*
	I-DAVI	Douglas DC-9-82	Alitalia *Assisi*
	I-DAVJ	Douglas DC-9-82	Alitalia
	I-DAVK	Douglas DC-9-82	Alitalia
	I-DAVL	Douglas DC-9-82	Aero Trasporti Italiani (ATI)
	I-DAVM	Douglas DC-9-82	Alitalia
	I-DAVN	Douglas DC-9-82	Alitalia
	I-D	Douglas DC-9-82	Alitalia
	I-D	Douglas DC-9-82	Alitalia
	I-DAWA	Douglas DC-9-82	Alitalia *Roma*
	I-DAWB	Douglas DC-9-82	Alitalia *Cagliari*
	I-DAWC	Douglas DC-9-82	Alitalia *Campobasso*
	I-DAWD	Douglas DC-9-82	Alitalia *Catanzaro*
	I-DAWE	Douglas DC-9-82	Alitalia *Milano*
	I-DAWF	Douglas DC-9-82	Alitalia *Firenze*
	I-DAWG	Douglas DC-9-82	Alitalia *L'Aquila*
	I-DAWH	Douglas DC-9-82	Alitalia *Palermo*
	I-DAWI	Douglas DC-9-82	Alitalia *Ancona*
	I-DAWJ	Douglas DC-9-82	Alitalia *Genova*
	I-DAWL	Douglas DC-9-82	Alitalia *Perugia*
	I-DAWM	Douglas DC-9-82	Alitalia *Patenza*
	I-DAWO	Douglas DC-9-82	Alitalia *Bari*
	I-DAWP	Douglas DC-9-82	Alitalia *Torino*
	I-DAWQ	Douglas DC-9-82	Alitalia *Trieste*
	I-DAWR	Douglas DC-9-82	Alitalia *Venezia*
	I-DAWS	Douglas DC-9-82	Alitalia *Aosta*
	I-DAWT	Douglas DC-9-82	Aero Trasporti Italiani (ATI) *Napoli*
	I-DAWU	Douglas DC-9-82	Alitalia *Bologna*
	I-DAWV	Douglas DC-9-82	Aero Trasporti Italiani (ATI) *Trento*
	I-DAWW	Douglas DC-9-82	Aero Trasporti Italiani (ATI) *Riace*
	I-DAWY	Douglas DC-9-82	Aero Trasporti Italiani (ATI) *Agrigento*
	I-DAWZ	Douglas DC-9-82	Aero Trasporti Italiani (ATI) *Avellino*
	I-DEMC	Boeing 747-243B (SCD)	Alitalia *Taormina*
	I-DEMD	Boeing 747-243B (SCD)	Alitalia *Cortina d'Ampezzo*
	I-DEMF	Boeing 747-243B (SCD)	Alitalia *Portofino*
	I-DEMG	Boeing 747-243B	Alitalia *Cervinia*
	I-DEML	Boeing 747-243B	Alitalia *Sorrento*
	I-DEMN	Boeing 747-243B	Alitalia *Portocervo*
	I-DEMP	Boeing 747-243B	Alitalia *Capri*
	I-DEMR	Boeing 747-243F (SCD)	Alitalia *Stresa*

Reg.	Type	Owner or Operator	Notes
I-DEMS	Boeing 747-243B	Alitalia *Monte Argentario*	
I-DEMT	Boeing 747-243B (SCD)	Alitalia *Monte Catini*	
I-DEMV	Boeing 747-243B	Alitalia *Sestriere*	
I-DEMW	Boeing 747-243B	Alitalia *Spoleto*	
I-DIBC	Douglas DC-9-32	Alitalia *Isola di Lampedusa*	
I-DIBD	Douglas DC-9-32	Alitalia *Isola di Montecristo*	
I-DIBJ	Douglas DC-9-32	Alitalia *Isola della Capraia*	
I-DIBN	Douglas DC-9-32	Alitalia *Isola della Palmaria*	
I-DIBO	Douglas DC-9-32	Aero Trasporti Italiani (ATI) *Conca d'Ora*	
I-DIBQ	Douglas DC-9-32	Alitalia *Isola di Pianosa*	
I-DIBR	Douglas DC-9-32	Alitalia *Isola di Capri*	
I-DIBS	Douglas DC-9-32	Alitalia *Isola d'Elba*	
I-DIBT	Douglas DC-9-32	Alitalia *Isola di Murano*	
I-DIBU	Douglas DC-9-32	Alitalia *Isola di Pantellaria*	
I-DIBV	Douglas DC-9-32	Alitalia *Isola d'Ischia*	
I-DIBW	Douglas DC-9-32	Alitalia *Isola del Giglio*	
I-DIBX	Douglas DC-9-32	Alitalia *Isola di Giannutri*	
I-DIBY	Douglas DC-9-32	Alitalia *Isola di Panarea*	
I-DIBZ	Douglas DC-9-32	Alitalia *Isola di Lipari*	
I-DIKM	Douglas DC-9-32	Alitalia *Isola di Positano*	
I-DIKP	Douglas DC-9-32	Alitalia *Isola di Marettimo*	
I-DIKR	Douglas DC-9-32	Alitalia *Piemonte*	
I-DIKS	Douglas DC-9-32	Aero Trasporti Italiani (ATI) *Isola di Filicudi*	
I-DIKT	Douglas DC-9-32	Aero Trasporti Italiani (ATI) *Isola d'Ustica*	
I-DIKV	Douglas DC-9-32	Alitalia *Isola di Vulcano*	
I-DIKY	Douglas DC-9-32	Aero Trasporti Italiani (ATI) *Puglia*	
I-DIKZ	Douglas DC-9-32	Alitalia *Isola di Linosa*	
I-DIZA	Douglas DC-9-32	Alitalia *Isola di Palmarola*	
I-DIZC	Douglas DC-9-32	Aero Trasporti Italiani (ATI)	
I-DIZE	Douglas DC-9-32	Alitalia *Isola della Meloria*	
I-DIZF	Douglas DC-9-32	Aero Trasporti Italiani (ATI) *Dolomiti*	
I-DIZI	Douglas DC-9-32	Aero Trasporti Italiani (ATI)	
I-DIZO	Douglas DC-9-32	Aero Trasporti Italiani (ATI) *Liguria*	
I-DIZU	Douglas DC-9-32	Aero Trasporti Italiani (ATI) *Valle d'Aosta*	
I-SMEA	Douglas DC-9-51	Alisarda	
I-SMEI	Douglas DC-9-51	Alisarda	
I-SMEK	Douglas DC-9-82	Alisarda	
I-SME	Douglas DC-9-82	Alisarda	
I-SMET	Douglas DC-9-82	Alisarda	
I-SMEU	Douglas DC-9-51	Alisarda	

Note: Alisarda also uses a DC-9-82 which retains its Swiss registration HB-IKL. Two of the Alitalia DC-9-32s have been re-registered N515MD and N516MD. Similarly ATI uses N871UM, N872UM and N873UM.

J2 (Djibouti)

Note: Air Djibouti leases a Boeing 737 from Sobelair or Sabena.

JA (Japan)

JA8101	Boeing 747-146	Japan Air Lines	
JA8104	Boeing 747-246B	Japan Air Lines	
JA8105	Boeing 747-246B	Japan Air Lines	
JA8106	Boeing 747-246B	Japan Air Lines	
JA8107	Boeing 747-146F (SCD)	Japan Air Lines	
JA8108	Boeing 747-246B	Japan Air Lines	
JA8110	Boeing 747-246B	Japan Air Lines	
JA8111	Boeing 747-246B	Japan Air Lines	
JA8112	Boeing 747-146A	Japan Air Lines	
JA8113	Boeing 747-246B	Japan Air Lines	
JA8114	Boeing 747-246B	Japan Air Lines	
JA8115	Boeing 747-146A	Japan Air Lines	
JA8116	Boeing 747-146A	Japan Air Lines	

Notes	Reg.	Type	Owner or Operator
	JA8122	Boeing 747-246B	Japan Air Lines
	JA8123	Boeing 747-246F (SCD)	Japan Air Lines
	JA8125	Boeing 747-246B	Japan Air Lines
	JA8127	Boeing 747-246B	Japan Air Lines
	JA8129	Boeing 747-246B	Japan Air Lines
	JA8130	Boeing 747-246B	Japan Air Lines
	JA8131	Boeing 747-246B	Japan Air Lines
	JA8132	Boeing 747-246F	Japan Air Lines
	JA8140	Boeing 747-246B	Japan Air Lines
	JA8141	Boeing 747-246B	Japan Air Lines
	JA8144	Boeing 747-246F (SCD)	Japan Air Lines
	JA8149	Boeing 747-246B	Japan Air Lines
	JA8150	Boeing 747-246B	Japan Air Lines
	JA8151	Boeing 747-246F (SCD)	Japan Air Lines
	JA8154	Boeing 747-246B	Japan Air Lines
	JA8155	Boeing 747-246B	Japan Air Lines
	JA8160	Boeing 747-221F (SCD)	Japan Air Lines
	JA8161	Boeing 747-246B	Japan Air Lines
	JA8162	Boeing 747-246B	Japan Air Lines
	JA8163	Boeing 747-346	Japan Air Lines
	JA8165	Boeing 747-221F (SCD)	Japan Air Lines
	JA8166	Boeing 747-346	Japan Air Lines
	JA8169	Boeing 747-246B	Japan Air Lines
	JA8171	Boeing 747-246F (SCD)	Japan Air Lines
	JA8173	Boeing 747-346	Japan Air Lines
	JA8177	Boeing 747-346	Japan Air Lines
	JA8178	Boeing 747-346	Japan Air Lines
	JA8179	Boeing 747-346	Japan Air Lines
	JA8180	Boeing 747-246F (SCD)	Japan Air Lines
	JA8185	Boeing 747-346	Japan Air Lines
	JA8535	Douglas DC-10-40	Japan Air Lines
	JA8538	Douglas DC-10-40	Japan Air Lines
	JA8539	Douglas DC-10-40	Japan Air Lines
	JA8541	Douglas DC-10-40	Japan Air Lines
	JA8542	Douglas DC-10-40	Japan Air Lines
	JA8543	Douglas DC-10-40	Japan Air Lines
	JA8544	Douglas DC-10-40	Japan Air Lines
	JA8545	Douglas DC-10-40	Japan Air Lines
	JA8547	Douglas DC-10-40	Japan Air Lines

Note: Japan Air Lines also operates a Boeing 747-221F which retains its US
registration N211JL and two 747-346s N212JL and N213JL.

JY (Jordan)

	JY-ADP	Boeing 707-3D3C	Royal Jordanian Airline
	JY-AEB	Boeing 707-384C	Gamair
	JY-AEC	Boeing 707-384C	Royal Jordanian Airline *Um Qais*
	JY-AFA	Boeing 747-2D3B	Royal Jordanian Airline *Prince Ali*
	JY-AGA	L.1011-385 TriStar 500	Royal Jordanian Airline *Abas Bin Firnas*
	JY-AGB	L.1011-385 TriStar 500	Royal Jordanian Airline *Ibn Battouta*
	JY-AGC	L.1011-385 TriStar 500	Royal Jordanian Airline *Al Jawaheri*
	JY-AGD	L.1011-385 TriStar 500	Royal Jordanian Airline *Ibn Sina*
	JY-AGE	L.1011-385 TriStar 500	Royal Jordanian Airline *Princess Aysha*
	JY-AGH	L.1011-385 TriStar 500	Royal Jordanian Airline/Sudan Airways
	JY-AGI	L.1011-385 TriStar 500	Royal Jordanian Airline/*Prince Faisal*
	JY-AGJ	L.1011-385 TriStar 500	Royal Jordanian Airline *Princess Zein*
	JY-CAD	Airbus A.310-304	Royal Jordanian Airline *Prince Hashem*
	JY-CAE	Airbus A.310-304	Royal Jordanian Airline
	JY-CAF	Airbus A.310-304	Royal Jordanian Airline
	JY-C	Airbus A.310-304	Royal Jordanian Airline
	JY-C	Airbus A.310-304	Royal Jordanian Airline
	JY-C	Airbus A.310-304	Royal Jordanian Airline

LN (Norway)

Reg.	Type	Owner or Operator	Notes
LN-AKA	F.27 Friendship Mk 200	Busy Bee	
LN-AKB	F.27 Friendship Mk 200	Busy Bee	
LN-AKC	F.27 Friendship Mk 200	Busy Bee	
LN-AKD	F.27 Friendship Mk 200	Busy Bee	
LN-BSC	F.27J Friendship	Swedair	
LN-BSD	F.27F Friendship	Malmo Aviation	
LN-BWG	Convair 580	Partnair	
LN-BWN	Convair 580	Partnair	
LN-FOG	L-188AF Electra	Fred Olsen Airtransport	
LN-FOH	L-188AF Electra	Fred Olsen Airtransport	
LN-FOI	L-188CF Electra	Fred Olsen Airtransport	
LN-KLK	Convair 440	Norsk Metropolitan Fly Klubb	
LN-KOA	Beech 200 Super King Air	Norsk Air	
LN-KOB	Beech 200 Super King Air	Norsk Air	
LN-KOC	EMB-120 Brasilia	Norsk Air	
LN-KOD	EMB-120 Brasilia	Norsk Air	
LN-KOE	EMB-120 Brasilia	Norsk Air	
LN-MOA	Cessna 441 Conquest	Morefly	
LN-MOB	Beech 200 Super King Air	Morefly	
LN-MOD	Beech 200 Super King Air	Morefly	
LN-MOF	Douglas DC-8-63	S.A.S./Scanair *Bue Viking*	
LN-MOT	Douglas DC-8-63	S.A.S./Scanair	
LN-MOW	Douglas DC-8-62	S.A.S./Scanair *Roald Viking*	
LN-NFT	Beech 200 Super King Air	Norsk Air	
LN-NOR	Boeing 737-33A	Norway Airlines	
LN-	Boeing 737-33A	Norway Airlines	
LN-NPB	Boeing 737-2R4C	Busy Bee	
LN-NPC	F-27 Friendship Mk 100	Busy Bee	
LN-NPD	F-27 Friendship Mk 100	Busy Bee	
LN-NPH	F.27 Friendship Mk 300	Busy Bee/Gambia Air Shuttle	
LN-NPI	F.27 Friendship Mk 100	Busy Bee	
LN-NPM	F.27 Friendship Mk 100	Busy Bee	
LN-NVD	Saab SF.340A	Norving Air Services	
LN-NVE	Saab SF.340A	Norving Air Services (*leased as PH-KJH*)	
LN-NVF	Saab SF.340A	Norving Air Services	
LN-PAA	Convair 580	Partnair	
LN-PAD	Beech 200 Super King Air	Partnair	
LN-PAE	Beech 200 Super King Air	Partnair	
LN-PAF	Beech 200 Super King Air	Partnair	
LN-PAG	Beech 200 Super King Air	Partnair	
LN-PAJ	Beech 100 King Air	Partnair	
LN-PAO	Beech 100 King Air	Partnair	
LN-RKA	Douglas DC-10-30	S.A.S. *Olav Viking*	
LN-RKC	Douglas DC-10-30	S.A.S. *Leif Viking*	
LN-RKD	Douglas DC-10-30	S.A.S.	
LN-RLA	Douglas DC-9-41	S.A.S. *Are Viking*	
LN-RLB	Douglas DC-9-41	S.A.S. *Arne Viking*	
LN-RLC	Douglas DC-9-41	S.A.S. *Gunnar Viking*	
LN-RLD	Douglas DC-9-41	S.A.S. *Torleif Viking*	
LN-RLE	Douglas DC-9-81	S.A.S. *Trygve Viking*	
LN-RLF	Douglas DC-9-82	S.A.S. *Finn Viking*	
LN-RLG	Douglas DC-9-82	S.A.S. *Trond Viking*	
LN-RLH	Douglas DC-9-41	S.A.S. *Einar Viking*	
LN-RLJ	Douglas DC-9-41	S.A.S. *Stein Viking*	
LN-RLK	Douglas DC-9-41	S.A.S. *Erling Viking*	
LN-RLL	Douglas DC-9-21	S.A.S. *Guttorm Viking*	
LN-RLN	Douglas DC-9-41	S.A.S. *Halldor Viking*	
LN-RLO	Douglas DC-9-21	S.A.S. *Gunder Viking*	
LN-RLP	Douglas DC-9-41	S.A.S. *Froste Viking*	
LN-RLR	Douglas DC-9-82	S.A.S. *Kettil Viking*	
LN-RLS	Douglas DC-9-41	S.A.S. *Asmund Viking*	
LN-RLT	Douglas DC-9-41	S.A.S. *Audun Viking*	
LN-RLU	Douglas DC-9-41	S.A.S. *Eivind Viking*	
LN-RLW	Douglas DC-9-33AF	S.A.S./Air de Cologne *Rand Viking*	
LN-RLX	Douglas DC-9-41	S.A.S. *Sote Viking*	
LN-RLZ	Douglas DC-9-41	S.A.S. *Bodvar Viking*	
LN-RMA	Douglas DC-9-81	S.A.S.	
LN-RMB	Douglas DC-9-83	S.A.S.	

Notes	Reg.	Type	Owner or Operator
	LN-RMC	Douglas DC-9-51	S.A.S. *Turgeis Viking*
	LN-RMD	Douglas DC-9-82	S.A.S.
	LN-RNX	F.27 Friendship Mk 200	S.A.S. *Vikar Viking*
	LN-RNY	F.27 Friendship Mk 600	S.A.S. *Vatnar Viking*
	LN-RNZ	F.27 Friendship Mk 600	S.A.S. *Vemund Viking*
	LN-SUA	Boeing 737-205	Braathens SAFE
	LN-SUB	Boeing 737-205	Braathens SAFE *Magnus Den Gode*
	LN-SUD	Boeing 737-205	Braathens SAFE *Olav Tryggvason*
	LN-SUE	F.27 Friendship Mk 100	Busy Bee
	LN-SUF	F.27 Friendship Mk 100	Busy Bee
	LN-SUG	Boeing 737-205	Braathens SAFE *Harald Gille*
	LN-SUH	Boeing 737-205	Braathens SAFE *Sigurd Jorsalfar*
	LN-SUI	Boeing 737-205	Braathens SAFE *Haakon den Gode*
	LN-SUJ	Boeing 737-205	Braathens SAFE *Magnus Barfot*
	LN-SUK	Boeing 737-205	Braathens SAFE *Magnus Erlingsson*
	LN-SUL	F.27 Friendship Mk 100	Busy Bee
	LN-SUM	Boeing 737-205	Braathens SAFE *Magnus Lagaboter*
	LN-SUP	Boeing 737-205	Braathens SAFE *Haakon IV Hakonsson*
	LN-SUQ	Boeing 737-205	Braathens SAFE
	LN-SUS	Boeing 737-205	Braathens SAFE *Haakon V Magnusson*
	LN-SUT	Boeing 737-205	Braathens SAFE *Oystein Magnusson*
	LN-SUU	Boeing 737-205	Braathens SAFE
	LN-SUV	Boeing 737-205	Braathens SAFE
	LN-SUZ	Boeing 737-205	Braathens SAFE

LV (Argentina)

	LV-MLO	Boeing 747-287B	Flying Tiger Line
	LV-MLP	Boeing 747-287B	Aerolineas Argentinas
	LV-MLR	Boeing 747-287B	Aerolineas Argentinas
	LV-OEP	Boeing 747-287B	Aerolineas Argentinas
	LV-OHV	Boeing 747SP-27	Aerolineas Argentinas
	LV-OOZ	Boeing 747-287B	Aerolineas Argentinas
	LV-OPA	Boeing 747-287B	Aerolineas Argentinas

Note: Services to the UK are suspended.

LX (Luxembourg)

	LX-ACV	Boeing 747-271C (SCD)	Cargolux
	LX-BCV	Boeing 747-271C (SCD)	Cargolux
	LX-DCV	Boeing 747-2R7F	Flying Tiger Line
	LX-ECV	Boeing 747-271C (SCD)	Cargolux
	LX-LGA	F.27 Friendship Mk 100	Luxair *Prince Henri*
	LX-LGB	F.27 Friendship Mk 100	Luxair *Prince Jean*
	LX-LGD	F.27 Friendship Mk 600	Luxair *Princess Margaretha*
	LX-LGH	Boeing 737-2C9	Luxair *Prince Guillaume*
	LX-LGI	Boeing 737-2C9	Luxair *Princess Marie-Astrid*
	LX-LGJ	F.27 Friendship Mk 200	Luxair
	LX-LGK	F.27 Friendship Mk 200	Luxair
	LX-LGL	Swearingen SA.227AC Metro III	Luxair
	LX-LGM	Swearingen SA.227AC Metro III	Luxair
	LX-LGP	Airbus A.300B4	Luxair

LZ (Bulgaria)

	LZ-BEA	Ilyushin IL-18D	Balkan Bulgarian Airlines
	LZ-BEK	Ilyushin IL-18V	Balkan Bulgarian Airlines
	LZ-BEL	Ilyushin IL-18V	Balkan Bulgarian Airlines
	LZ-BEO	Ilyushin IL-18D	Balkan Bulgarian Airlines
	LZ-BEU	Ilyushin IL-18V	Balkan Bulgarian Airlines
	LZ-BEV	Ilyushin IL-18V	Balkan Bulgarian Airlines
	LZ-BTA	Tupolev Tu-154B	Balkan Bulgarian Airlines
	LZ-BTC	Tupolev Tu-154B	Balkan Bulgarian Airlines
	LZ-BTD	Tupolev Tu-154B	Balkan Bulgarian Airlines

Reg.	Type	Owner or Operator	Notes
LZ-BTE	Tupolev Tu-154B	Balkan Bulgarian Airlines	
LZ-BTF	Tupolev Tu-154B	Balkan Bulgarian Airlines	
LZ-BTG	Tupolev Tu-154B	Balkan Bulgarian Airlines	
LZ-BTI	Tupolev Tu-154M	Balkan Bulgarian Airlines	
LZ-BTJ	Tupolev Tu-154B-1	Balkan Bulgarian Airlines	
LZ-BTK	Tupolev Tu-154B	Balkan Bulgarian Airlines	
LZ-BTL	Tupolev Tu-154B	Balkan Bulgarian Airlines	
LZ-BTM	Tupolev Tu-154B	Balkan Bulgarian Airlines	
LZ-BTO	Tupolev Tu-154B-1	Balkan Bulgarian Airlines	
LZ-BTP	Tupolev Tu-154B-1	Balkan Bulgarian Airlines	
LZ-BTQ	Tupolev Tu-154M	Balkan Bulgarian Airlines	
LZ-BTR	Tupolev Tu-154B-2	Balkan Bulgarian Airlines	
LZ-BTS	Tupolev Tu-154B-2	Balkan Bulgarian Airlines	
LZ-BTT	Tupolev Tu-154B-2	Balkan Bulgarian Airlines	
LZ-BTU	Tupolev Tu-154B-2	Balkan Bulgarian Airlines	
LZ-BTV	Tupolev Tu-154B-2	Balkan Bulgarian Airlines	
LZ-BTW	Tupolev Tu-154M	Balkan Bulgarian Airlines	
LZ-BTX	Tupolev Tu-154M	Balkan Bulgarian Airlines	
LZ-TUA	Tupolev Tu-134	Balkan Bulgarian Airlines	
LZ-TUC	Tupolev Tu-134	Balkan Bulgarian Airlines	
LZ-TUD	Tupolev Tu-134	Balkan Bulgarian Airlines	
LZ-TUE	Tupolev Tu-134	Balkan Bulgarian Airlines	
LZ-TUG	Tupolev Tu-134A-3	Balkan Bulgarian Airlines	
LZ-TUK	Tupolev Tu-134A	Balkan Bulgarian Airlines	
LZ-TUL	Tupolev Tu-134A-3	Balkan Bulgarian Airlines	
LZ-TUM	Tupolev Tu-134A-3	Balkan Bulgarian Airlines	
LZ-TUN	Tupolev Tu-134A-3	Balkan Bulgarian Airlines	
LZ-TUO	Tupolev Tu-134	Balkan Bulgarian Airlines	
LZ-TUP	Tupolev Tu-134A	Balkan Bulgarian Airlines	
LZ-TUS	Tupolev Tu-134A	Balkan Bulgarian Airlines	
LZ-TUT	Tupolev Tu-134A-3	Balkan Bulgarian Airlines	
LZ-TUU	Tupolev Tu-134A-3	Balkan Bulgarian Airlines	
LZ-TUV	Tupolev Tu-134A-3	Balkan Bulgarian Airlines	
LZ-TUZ	Tupolev Tu-134A-3	Balkan Bulgarian Airlines	

N (USA)

Reg.	Type	Owner or Operator	Notes
N10ST	L-100-30 Hercules	Southern Air Transport	
N11ST	L-100-30 Hercules	Southern Air Transport	
N12ST	L-100-30 Hercules	Southern Air Transport	
N16ST	L-100-30 Hercules	Southern Air Transport	
N18ST	L-100-30 Hercules	Southern Air Transport	
N19ST	L-100-30 Hercules	Southern Air Transport	
N20ST	L-100-30 Hercules	Southern Air Transport	
N21ST	L-100-30 Hercules	Southern Air Transport	
N23ST	L-100-30 Hercules	Southern Air Transport	
N37ST	L-100-30 Hercules	Southern Air Transport	
N38ST	L-100-30 Hercules	Southern Air Transport	
N39ST	L-100-30 Hercules	Southern Air Transport	
N67AB	Boeing 737-3Y0	Air Berlin	
N92TA	L-1011-385 TriStar 100	Gulf Air	
N92TB	L-1011-385 TriStar 100	Gulf Air	
N106WA	Douglas DC-10-30CF	World Airways	
N107WA	Douglas DC-10-30CF	World Airways	
N108AK	L-100-30 Hercules	Markair	
N108WA	Douglas DC-10-30CF	World Airways	
N112WA	Douglas DC-10-30CF	World Airways	
N116KB	Boeing 747-312	Singapore Airlines	
N117KC	Boeing 747-312	Singapore Airlines	
N118KD	Boeing 747-312	Singapore Airlines	
N119KE	Boeing 747-312	Singapore Airlines	
N120KF	Boeing 747-312	Singapore Airlines	
N121AE	Canadair CL-44D-4	Aeron International *City of Stamford*	
N121KG	Boeing 747-312	Singapore Airlines	
N122AE	Canadair CL-44D-4	Aeron International *Dixie*	
N122KH	Boeing 747-312	Singapore Airlines	
N123KJ	Boeing 747-312	Singapore Airlines	
N124KK	Boeing 747-312	Singapore Airlines	
N125KL	Boeing 747-312	Singapore Airlines	

| --- | --- | --- | --- |
	N133TW	Boeing 747-156	Trans World Airlines
	N134TW	Boeing 747-156	Trans World Airlines
	N136AA	Douglas DC-10-30	American Airlines
	N137AA	Douglas DC-10-30	American Airlines
	N138AA	Douglas DC-10-30	American Airlines
	N139AA	Douglas DC-10-30	American Airlines
	N140AA	Douglas DC-10-30	American Airlines
	N141AA	Douglas DC-10-30	American Airlines
	N141US	Douglas DC-10-40	Northwest Airlines
	N142AA	Douglas DC-10-30	American Airlines
	N143AA	Douglas DC-10-30	American Airlines
	N144AA	Douglas DC-10-30	American Airlines
	N145US	Douglas DC-10-40	Northwest Airlines
	N146US	Douglas DC-10-40	Northwest Airlines
	N147US	Douglas DC-10-40	Northwest Airlines
	N148US	Douglas DC-10-40	Northwest Airlines
	N149US	Douglas DC-10-40	Northwest Airlines
	N150US	Douglas DC-10-40	Northwest Airlines
	N151US	Douglas DC-10-40	Northwest Airlines
	N152US	Douglas DC-10-40	Northwest Airlines
	N153US	Douglas DC-10-40	Northwest Airlines
	N154US	Douglas DC-10-40	Northwest Airlines
	N155US	Douglas DC-10-40	Northwest Airlines
	N156US	Douglas DC-10-40	Northwest Airlines
	N157US	Douglas DC-10-40	Northwest Airlines
	N158US	Douglas DC-10-40	Northwest Airlines
	N159US	Douglas DC-10-40	Northwest Airlines
	N160US	Douglas DC-10-40	Northwest Airlines
	N161US	Douglas DC-10-40	Northwest Airlines
	N162US	Douglas DC-10-40	Northwest Airlines
	N163AA	Douglas DC-10-30	American Airlines
	N164AA	Douglas DC-10-30	American Airlines
	N185AT	L-1011 TriStar 1	American Trans Air
	N186AT	L-1011 TriStar 1	American Trans Air
	N187AT	L-1011 TriStar 1	American Trans Air
	N188AT	L-1011 TriStar 1	American Trans Air
	N189AT	L-1011 TriStar 1	American Trans Air
	N190AT	L-1011 TriStar 1	American Trans Air
	N191AT	L-1011 TriStar 1	American Trans Air
	N192AT	L-1011 TriStar 1	American Trans Air
	N193AT	L-1011 TriStar 1	American Trans Air
	N195AT	L-1011 TriStar 1	American Trans Air
	N211JL	Boeing 747-221F	Japan Air Lines
	N212JL	Boeing 747-346	Japan Air Lines
	N213JL	Boeing 747-346	Japan Air Lines
	N221GE	Boeing 747-357	Swissair Geneve
	N221GF	Boeing 747-357	Swissair Zurich
	N250SF	L-100-30 Hercules	Southern Air Transport
	N251SF	L-100-30 Hercules	Southern Air Transport
	N301FE	Douglas DC-10-30CF	Federal Express
	N301TW	Boeing 747-282B	Trans World Airlines
	N301US	Boeing 747-451	Northwest Airlines
	N302FE	Douglas DC-10-30CF	Federal Express
	N302TW	Boeing 747-282B	Trans World Airlines
	N302US	Boeing 747-451	Northwest Airlines
	N303FE	Douglas DC-10-30CF	Federal Express
	N303TW	Boeing 747-257B	Trans World Airlines
	N303US	Boeing 747-451	Northwest Airlines
	N304FE	Douglas DC-10-30CF	Federal Express
	N304TW	Boeing 747-257B	Trans World Airlines
	N304US	Boeing 747-451	Northwest Airlines
	N305FE	Douglas DC-10-30CF	Federal Express
	N305TW	Boeing 747-284B	Trans World Airlines
	N305US	Boeing 747-451	Northwest Airlines
	N306FE	Douglas DC-10-30AF	Federal Express
	N306US	Boeing 747-451	Northwest Airlines
	N307FE	Douglas DC-10-30AF	Federal Express
	N307US	Boeing 747-451	Northwest Airlines
	N308FE	Douglas DC-10-30AF	Federal Express
	N308US	Boeing 747-451	Northwest Airlines
	N309FE	Douglas DC-10-30AF	Federal Express

Reg.	Type	Owner or Operator	Notes
N309US	Boeing 747-451	Northwest Airlanes	
N310FE	Douglas DC-10-30AF	Federal Express	
N311FE	Douglas DC-10-30AF	Federal Express	
N311US	Boeing 747-451	Northwest Airlines	
N312FE	Douglas DC-10-30AF	Federal Express	
N313FE	Douglas DC-10-30AF	Federal Express	
N314FE	Douglas DC-10-30AF	Federal Express	
N315FE	Douglas DC-10-30AF	Federal Express	
N316FE	Douglas DC-10-30AF	Federal Express	
N317FE	Douglas DC-10-30AF	Federal Express	
N318FE	Douglas DC-10-30AF	Federal Express	
N319AA	Boeing 767-223ER	American Airlines	
N320AA	Boeing 767-223ER	American Airlines	
N321AA	Boeing 767-223ER	American Airlines	
N322AA	Boeing 767-223ER	American Airlines	
N323AA	Boeing 767-223ER	American Airlines	
N324AA	Boeing 767-223ER	American Airlines	
N325AA	Boeing 767-223ER	American Airlines	
N327AA	Boeing 767-223ER	American Airlines	
N328AA	Boeing 767-223ER	American Airlines	
N329AA	Boeing 767-223ER	American Airlines	
N330AA	Boeing 767-223ER	American Airlines	
N332AA	Boeing 767-223ER	American Airlines	
N334AA	Boeing 767-223ER	American Airlines	
N335AA	Boeing 767-223ER	American Airlines	
N336AA	Boeing 767-223ER	American Airlines	
N338AA	Boeing 767-223ER	American Airlines	
N339AA	Boeing 767-223ER	American Airlines	
N345HC	Douglas DC-10-30ER	Finnair	
N351AA	Boeing 767-323ER	American Airlines	
N352AA	Boeing 767-323ER	American Airlines	
N353AA	Boeing 767-323ER	American Airlines	
N354AA	Boeing 767-323ER	American Airlines	
N355AA	Boeing 767-323ER	American Airlines	
N357AA	Boeing 767-323ER	American Airlines	
N358AA	Boeing 767-323ER	American Airlines	
N359AA	Boeing 767-323ER	American Airlines	
N360AA	Boeing 767-323ER	American Airlines	
N361AA	Boeing 767-323ER	American Airlines	
N362AA	Boeing 767-323ER	American Airlines	
N363AA	Boeing 767-323ER	American Airlines	
N390EA	Douglas DC-10-30	Continental Airlines	
N508MD	Douglas DC-9-32	Aero Transporti Italiani (ATI)	
N515MD	Douglas DC-9-32	Alitalia	
N516MD	Douglas DC-9-32	Alitalia *Isola di Ponza*	
N520SJ	L-100-20 Hercules	Southern Air Transport	
N521SJ	L-100-20 Hercules	Southern Air Transport	
N522SJ	L-100-20 Hercules	Southern Air Transport	
N601BN	Boeing 747-127	Tower Air	
N601TW	Boeing 767-231ER	Trans World Airlines	
N601US	Boeing 747-151	Northwest Airlines	
N602FF	Boeing 747-124	Tower Air	
N602TW	Boeing 767-231ER	Trans World Airlines	
N602US	Boeing 747-151	Northwest Airlines	
N603FF	Boeing 747-130	Tower Air	
N603P	Boeing 767-201ER	Piedmont Airlines *Pride of Piedmont*	
N603PE	Boeing 747-143	Continental Airlines	
N603TW	Boeing 767-231ER	Trans World Airlines	
N603US	Boeing 747-151	Northwest Airlines	
N604P	Boeing 767-201ER	Piedmont Airlines *City of London*	
N604PE	Boeing 747-243B	Continental Airlines	
N604TW	Boeing 767-231ER	Trans World Airlines	
N604US	Boeing 747-151	Northwest Airlines	
N605PE	Boeing 747-243B	Continental Airlines	
N605TW	Boeing 767-231ER	Trans World Airlines	
N605US	Boeing 747-151	Northwest Airlines	
N606PE	Boeing 747-143	Continental Airlines	
N606TW	Boeing 767-231ER	Trans World Airlines	
N606US	Boeing 747-151	Northwest Airlines	
N607P	Boeing 767-201ER	Piedmont Airlines *City of Charlotte*	
N607PE	Boeing 747-238B	Continental Airlines	

Notes	Reg.	Type	Owner or Operator
	N607TW	Boeing 767-231ER	Trans Wordd Airlines
	N607US	Boeing 747-151	Northwest Airlines
	N608P	Boeing 767-201ER	Piedmont Airlines
	N608PE	Boeing 747-238B	Continental Airlines
	N608TW	Boeing 767-231ER	Trans World Airlines
	N608US	Boeing 747-151	Northwest Airlines
	N609PE	Boeing 747-238B	Continental Airlines
	N609TW	Boeing 767-231ER	Trans World Airlines
	N609US	Boeing 747-151	Northwest Airlines
	N610PE	Boeing 747-238B	Continental Airlines
	N610TW	Boeing 767-231ER	Trans World Airlines
	N610US	Boeing 747-151	Northwest Airlines
	N611US	Boeing 747-251B	Northwest Airlines
	N612US	Boeing 747-251B	Northwest Airlines
	N613US	Boeing 747-251B	Northwest Airlines
	N614P	Boeing 767-201ER	Piedmont Airlines
	N614US	Boeing 747-251B	Northwest Airlines
	N615US	Boeing 747-251B	Northwest Airlines
	N616US	Boeing 747-251F (SCD)	Northwest Airlines
	N617P	Boeing 767-201ER	Piedmont Airlines
	N617US	Boeing 747-251F (SCD)	Northwest Airlines
	N618US	Boeing 747-251F (SCD)	Northwest Airlines
	N619US	Boeing 747-251F (SCD)	Northwest Airlines
	N620US	Boeing 747-135	Northwest Airlines
	N621US	Boeing 747-135	Northwest Airlines
	N622US	Boeing 747-251B	Northwest Airlines
	N623US	Boeing 747-251B	Northwest Airlines
	N624US	Boeing 747-251B	Northwest Airlines
	N625US	Boeing 747-251B	Northwest Airlines
	N626US	Boeing 747-251B	Northwest Airlines
	N627US	Boeing 747-251B	Northwest Airlines
	N628US	Boeing 747-251B	Northwest Airlines
	N629US	Boeing 747-251F (SCD)	Northwest Airlines
	N630US	Boeing 747-2J9F	Northwest Airlines
	N631US	Boeing 747-251B	Northwest Airlines
	N632US	Boeing 747-251B	Northwest Airlines
	N633US	Boeing 747-227B	Northwest Airlines
	N634US	Boeing 747-227B	Northwest Airlines
	N635US	Boeing 747-227B	Northwest Airlines
	N636US	Boeing 747-251B	Northwest Airlines
	N637US	Boeing 747-251B	Northwest Airlines
	N638US	Boeing 747-251B	Northwest Airlines
	N639US	Boeing 747-251F (SCD)	Northwest Airlines
	N640US	Boeing 747-251F (SCD)	Northwest Airlines
	N652PA	Boeing 747-121	Pan Am *Clipper Mermaid*
	N653PA	Boeing 747-121 (SCD)	Pan Am *Clipper Pride of the Ocean*
	N655PA	Boeing 747-121 (SCD)	Pan Am *Clipper Sea Serpent*
	N656PA	Boeing 747-121	Pan Am *Clipper New Horizons*
	N657PA	Boeing 747-121	Pan Am *Clipper Seven Seas*
	N659PA	Boeing 747-121	Pan Am *Clipper Voyager*
	N703TT	L.1101-385 TriStar 1	Air America
	N707ZS	Boeing 707-309C	Jet Cargo *Miritza*
	N723PA	Boeing 747-212B	Pan Am *China Clipper II*
	N724DA	L.1011-385 TriStar 200	Delta Air Lines
	N724PA	Boeing 747-212B	Pan Am *Clipper Fairwind*
	N725DA	L.1011-385 TriStar 1	Delta Air Lines
	N725PA	Boeing 747-132 (SCD)	Pan Am *Clipper Mandarin*
	N726PA	Boeing 747-212B	Pan Am *Clipper Belle of the Skies*
	N727PA	Boeing 747-212B	Pan Am *Clipper Cathay*
	N728PA	Boeing 747-212B (SCD)	Pan Am *Clipper Water Witch*
	N729PA	Boeing 747-212B (SCD)	Pan Am *Clipper Wild Wave*
	N730PA	Boeing 747-212B (SCD)	Pan Am *Clipper Gem of the Ocean*
	N733PA	Boeing 747-121	Pan Am *Clipper Pride of the Seas*
	N734PA	Boeing 747-121 (SCD)	Pan Am *Clipper Champion of the Seas*
	N735PA	Boeing 747-121	Pan Am *Clipper Spark of the Ocean*
	N737DA	L.1011-385 TriStar 100	Delta Airlines
	N737PA	Boeing 747-121	Pan Am *Clipper Ocean Herald*
	N739PA	Boeing 747-121 (ScD)	Pan Am *Clipper Maid of the Seas*
	N740DA	L.1011-385 TriStar 100	Delta Airlines
	N740PA	Boeing 747-121	Pan Am *Clipper Ocean Pearl*
	N741DA	L.1011-385 TriStar 100	Delta Airlines

Reg.	Type	Owner or Operator	Notes
N741PA	Boeing 747-121	Pan Am *Clipper Sparkling Wave*	
N741PR	Boeing 747-2F6B	Philippine Airlines	
N742PA	Boeing 747-121	Pan Am *Clipper Neptune's Car*	
N742PR	Boeing 747-2F6B	Philippine Airlines	
N743PA	Boeing 747-121 (SCD)	Pan Am *Clipper Black Sea*	
N743PR	Boeing 747-2F6B	Philippine Airlines	
N744PA	Boeing 747-121	Pan Am *Clipper Ocean Spray*	
N744PR	Boeing 747-2F6B	Philippine Airlines	
N747PA	Boeing 747-121	Pan Am *Clipper Juan J. Trippe*	
N748PA	Boeing 747-121	Pan Am *Clipper Crest of the Wave*	
N749PA	Boeing 747-121	Pan Am	
N749WA	Boeing 747-273C	Evergreen International Airlines	
N750PA	Boeing 747-121	Pan Am *Clipper Ocean Rose*	
N751DA	L-1011-385 TriStar 500	Delta Air Lines	
N751PA	Boeing 747-121	Pan Am *Clipper Gem of the Seas*	
N752DA	L-1011-385 TriStar 500	Delta Air Lines	
N753DA	L-1011-385 TriStar 500	Delta Air Lines	
N753PA	Boeing 747-121	Pan Am *Clipper Queen of the Seas*	
N754DL	L.1011-385 TriStar 500	Delta Air Lines	
N755DL	L.1011-385 TriStar 500	Delta Air Lines	
N756DR	L.1011-385 TriStar 500	Delta Air Lines	
N762BE	L.1011-385 TriStar 1	Hawaiian Air	
N763BE	L.1011-385 TriStar 1	Hawaiian Air	
N765BE	L.1011-385 TriStar 1	Hawaiian Air	
N766BE	L.1011-385 TriStar 1	Hawaiian Air	
N791FT	Douglas DC-8-73CF	Emery Worldwide	
N792FT	Douglas DC-8-73CF	Emery Worldwide	
N795FT	Douglas DC-8-73CF	Emery Worldwide	
N796FT	Douglas DC-8-73CF	Emery Worldwide	
N801PA	Airbus A.310-222	Pan Am *Clipper Berlin*	
N802PA	Airbus A.310-222	Pan Am *Clipper Frankfurt*	
N803FT	Boeing 747-132F (SCD)	Flying Tiger Line	
N803PA	Airbus A.310-222	Pan Am *Clipper Munich*	
N804FT	Boeing 747-132F (SCD)	Flying Tiger Line	
N804PA	Airbus A.310-222	Pan Am *Clipper Hamburg*	
N805FT	Boeing 747-132F (SCD)	Flying Tiger Line	
N805PA	Airbus A.310-222	Pan Am *Clipper Miles Standish*	
N806FT	Boeing 747-249F (SCD)	Flying Tiger Line *Robert W. Prescott*	
N806PA	Airbus A.310-222	Pan Am *Clipper Betsy Ross*	
N807FT	Boeing 747-249F (SCD)	Flying Tiger Line *Thomas Haywood*	
N807PA	Airbus A.310-222	Pan Am *Clipper Kit Carson*	
N808FT	Boeing 747-249F (SCD)	Flying Tiger Line *William E. Bartlett*	
N810FT	Boeing 747-249F (SCD)	Flying Tiger Line *Clifford G. Groh*	
N811FT	Boeing 747-245F (SCD)	Flying Tiger Line	
N811PA	Airbus A.310-324	Pan Am *Clipper Constitution*	
N812FT	Boeing 747-245F (SCD)	Flying Tiger Line	
N812PA	Airbus A.310-324	Pan Am *Clipper Freedom*	
N813FT	Boeing 747-245F (SCD)	Flying Tiger Line	
N813PA	Airbus A.310-324	Pan Am *Clipper Great Republic*	
N814FT	Boeing 747-245F (SCD)	Flying Tiger Line	
N814PA	Airbus A.310-324	Pan Am *Clipper Liberty Bell*	
N815EV	Douglas DC-8-73CF	Evergreen International Airlines	
N815FT	Boeing 747-245F (SCD)	Flying Tiger Line *W. Henry Renniger*	
N815PA	Airbus A.310-324	Pan Am *Clipper Mayflower*	
N816EV	Douglas DC-8-73CF	Air India Cargo	
N816FT	Boeing 747-245F (SCD)	Flying Tiger Line *Henry L. Heguy*	
N816PA	Airbus A.310-324	Pan Am *Clipper Meteor*	
N817FT	Boeing 747-121F (SCD)	Flying Tiger Line	
N817PA	Airbus A.310-324	Pan Am *Clipper Midnight Sun*	
N818FT	Boeing 747-121F (SCD)	Flying Tiger Line	
N818PA	Airbus A.310-324	Pan Am *Clipper Morning Star*	
N819FT	Boeing 747-121F (SCD)	Flying Tiger Line	
N819PA	Airbus A.310-324	Pan Am *Clipper Northern Light*	
N820FT	Boeing 747-121F (SCD)	Flying Tiger Line	
N820PA	Airbus A.310-324	Pan Am *Clipper Plymouth Rock*	
N821PA	Airbus A.310-324	Pan Am *Clipper Ship of the Sky*	
N822PA	Airbus A.310-324	Pan Am *Clipper Victory*	
N846TW	Boeing 727-31	Trans World Airlines *City of Berlin*	
N865F	Douglas DC-8-63	Emery Worldwide	
N870TV	Douglas DC-8-73	Emery Worldwide	
N901PA	Boeing 747-123F	Pan Am *Clipper Telegraph*	

Notes	Reg.	Type	Owner or Operator
	N902PA	Boeing 747-132	Pan Am *Clipper Seaman's Bridge*
	N906R	Douglas DC-8-63CF	Emery Worldwide
	N921R	Douglas DC-8-63CF	Emery Worldwide
	N929R	Douglas DC-8-63AF	Emery Worldwide
	N950R	Douglas DC-8-63	Emery Worldwide
	N951R	Douglas DC-8-63F	Emery Worldwide
	N952R	Douglas DC-8-63CF	Emery Worldwide
	N957R	Douglas DC-8-63CF	Emery Worldwide
	N959R	Douglas DC-8-63CF	Emery Worldwide
	N961R	Douglas DC-8-73CF	Emery Worldwide
	N964R	Douglas DC-8-63CF	Emery Worldwide
	N1289E	Boeing 747-228B	Air France
	N1295E	Boeing 747-306	K.L.M. *The Ganges*
	N1298E	Boeing 747-306	K.L.M. *The Indus*
	N1301E	Boeing 747SP-27	CAAC
	N1304E	Boeing 747SP-J6	CAAC
	N1309E	Boeifg 747-306	K.L.M. *Admiral Richard E. Byrd*
	N1738D	L.1011-385 TriStar 250	Delta Airlines
	N1739D	L.1011-385 TriStar 250	Delta Airlines
	N1804	Douglas DC-8-62	Rich International Airways
	N1805	Douglas DC-8-62	Rich International Airways
	N1808E	Douglas DC-8-62	Rich International Airways
	N2674U	Douglas DC-8-73CF	Emery Worldwide
	N3016Z	Douglas DC-10-30	Zambia Airways *Nkwazi*
	N3140D	L.1011-385 TriStar 500	B.W.I.A.
	N3878P	Douglas DC-10-30	Aeromexico
	N4201G	Aerospatiale ATR-42-300	Pan Am Express
	N4202G	Aerospatiale ATR-42-300	Pan Am Express
	N4203G	Aerospatiale ATR-42-300	Pan Am Express
	N4204G	Aerospatiale ATR-42-300	Pan Am Express
	N4501Q	Boeing 747-283B	Philippine Airlines
	N4502R	Boeing 747-283B	Philippine Airlines
	N4506H	Boeing 747-228B	Air France
	N4508E	Boeing 747-228F	Air France
	N4508H	Boeing 747SP-09	China Airways
	N4522V	Boeing 747SP-09	China Airways
	N4544F	Boeing 747-228B	Air France
	N4548M	Boeing 747-306	K.L.M. *Sir Frank Whittle*
	N4551N	Boeing 747-306	K.L.M. *Sir Geoffrey de Havilland*
	N4703U	Boeing 747-122	Pan Am *Clipper Nautilus*
	N4704U	Boeing 747-122	Pan Am *Clipper Belle of the Sea*
	N4710U	Boeing 747-122	Pan Am *Clipper Sea Lark*
	N4711U	Boeing 747-122	Pan Am *Clipper Witch of the Waves*
	N4712U	Boeing 747-122	Pan Am *Clipper Tradewind*
	N4731	Boeing 727-235	Pan Am *Clipper Alert*
	N4732	Boeing 727-235	Pan Am *Clipper Challenger*
	N4733	Boeing 727-235	Pan Am *Clipper Charger*
	N4735	Boeing 727-235	Pan Am *Clipper Daring*
	N4736	Boeing 727-235	Pan Am *Clipper Dashaway*
	N4738	Boeing 727-235	Pan Am *Clipper Electric*
	N4739	Boeing 727-235	Pan Am *Clipper Electric Spark*
	N4740	Boeing 727-235	Pan Am *Clipper Endeavour*
	N4741	Boeing 727-235	Pan Am *Clipper Defender*
	N4742	Boeing 727-235	Pan Am *Clipper Defender*
	N4743	Boeing 727-235	Pan Am *Clipper Good Hope*
	N4745	Boeing 727-235	Pan Am *Clipper Invincible*
	N4746	Boeing 727-235	Pan Am *Clipper Intrepid*
	N4747	Boeing 727-235	Pan Am *Clipper Lookout*
	N4748	Boeing 727-235	Pan Am *Clipper Progressive*
	N4751	Boeing 727-235	Pan Am *Clipper Competitor*
	N4754	Boeing 727-235	Pan Am *Clipper Resolute*
	N7035T	L.1011-385 TriStar 100	Trans World Airlines
	N7036T	L.1011-385 TriStar 100	Trans World Airlines
	N8034T	L.1011-385 TriStar 100	Trans World Airlines
	N8955Y	Boeing 707-321B	Skystar International
	N9670	Boeing 747-123	Pan Am *Clipper Empress of the Skies*
	N9674	Boeing 747-123	Tower Air
	N12061	Douglas DC-10-30	Continental Airlines *Richard M. Adams*
	N13066	Douglas DC-10-30	Continental Airlines
	N14062	Douglas DC-10-30	Continental Airlines
	N14063	Douglas DC-10-30	Continental Airlines

Reg.	Type	Owner or Operator	Notes
N17125	Boeing 747-136	Trans World Airlines	
N17126	Boeing 747-136	Trans World Airlines	
N19072	Douglas DC-10-30	Continental Airlines	
N31018	L.1011-385 TriStar 50	Trans World Airlines	
N31019	L.1011-385 TriStar 50	Trans World Airlines	
N31021	L.1011-385 TriStar 50	Trans World Airlines	
N31022	L.1011-385 TriStar 50	Trans World Airlines	
N31023	L.1011-385 TriStar 50	Trans World Airlines	
N31024	L.1011-385 TriStar 50	Trans World Airlines	
N31029	L.1011-385 TriStar 100	Trans World Airlines	
N31030	L.1011-385 TriStar 100	Trans World Airlines	
N31031	L.1011-385 TriStar 100	Trans World Airlines	
N31032	L.1011-385 TriStar 100	Trans World Airlines	
N31033	L.1011-385 TriStar 100	Trans World Airlines	
N39356	Boeing 767-323ER	Amerian Airlines	
N39364	Boeing 767-323ER	American Airlines	
N39365	Boeing 767-323ER	American Airlines	
N41020	L.1011-385 TriStar 50	Trans World Airlines	
N46965	L-100-30 Hercules	Southern Air Transport	
N53110	Boeing 747-131	Trans World Airlines	
N54629	Douglas DC-10-30	U.T.A.	
N54649	Douglas DC-10-30	U.T.A.	
N68060	Douglas DC-10-30	Continental Airlines *Robert F. Six*	
N68065	Douglas DC-10-30	Continental Airlines	
N68066	Douglas DC-10-30	Continental Airlines	
N81025	L.1011-385 TriStar 100	Trans World Airlines	
N81026	L.1011-385 TriStar 100	Trans World Airlines	
N81027	L.1011-385 TriStar 50	Trans World Airlines	
N81028	L.1011-385 TriStar 100	Trans World Airlines	
N93104	Boeing 747-131	Trans World Airlines	
N93105	Boeing 747-131	Trans World Airlines	
N93106	Boeing 747-131	Trans World Airlines	
N93107	Boeing 747-131	Trans World Airlines	
N93108	Boeing 747-131	Trans World Airlines	
N93109	Boeing 747-131	Trans World Airlines	
N93119	Boeing 747-131	Trans World Airlines	

Note: Continental Airlines will be re-registering the aircraft acquired during the course of various takeovers. As a result the ex-People Express 747s which previously carried N603PE to N610PE inclusive will become N17010, N16020, N33021, N17011, N50022, N10023, N10024 and N17025 respectively.

OD (Lebanon)

Reg.	Type	Owner or Operator	Notes
OD-AFD	Boeing 707-3B4C	Middle East Airlines	
OD-AFE	Boeing 707-3B4C	Middle East Airlines	
OD-AFM	Boeing 720-023B	Middle East Airlines	
OD-AFN	Boeing 720-023B	Middle East Airlines	
OD-AFY	Boeing 707-327C	Trans Mediterranean Airways	
OD-AFZ	Boeing 720-023B	Middle East Airlines	
OD-AGB	Boeing 720-023B	Middle East Airlines	
OD-AGD	Boeing 707-323C	Trans Mediterranean Airways	
OD-AGF	Boeing 720-047B	Middle East Airlines	
OD-AGO	Boeing 707-321C	Trans Mediterranean Airways	
OD-AGP	Boeing 707-321C	Trans Mediterranean Airways	
OD-AGS	Boeing 707-331C	Trans Mediterranean Airways	
OD-AGU	Boeing 707-347C	Middle East Airlines	
OD-AGV	Boeing 707-347C	Middle East Airlines	
OD-AGX	Boeing 707-327C	Trans Mediterranean Airways	
OD-AGY	Boeing 707-327C	Trans Mediterranean Airways	
OD-AHB	Boeing 707-323C	Middle East Airlines	
OD-AHC	Boeing 707-323C	Middle East Airlines	
OD-AHE	Boeing 707-323C	Middle East Airlines	

OE (Austria)

Notes	Reg.	Type	Owner or Operator
	OE-ILF	Boeing 737-3Z9	Lauda-Air *Bob Marley*
	OE-ILG	Boeing 737-3Z9	Lauda-Air
	OE-ILH	Boeing 737-3Z9	Lauda Air
	OE-	Boeing 767-3Z9ER	Lauda Air
	OE-LAA	Airbus A.310-322	Austrian Airlines
	OE-LAI	Airbus A.310-322	Austrian Airlines
	OE-LDF	Douglas DC-9-32	Austrian Airlines
	OE-LDG	Douglas DC-9-32	Austrian Airlines
	OE-LDH	Douglas DC-9-32	Austrian Airlines
	OE-LDI	Douglas DC-9-32	Austrian Airlines *Bregenz*
	OE-LDP	Douglas DC-9-81	Austrian Airlines *Wien*
	OE-LDR	Douglas DC-9-81	Austrian Airlines *Niederösterreich*
	OE-LDS	Douglas DC-9-81	Austrian Airlines *Burgenland*
	OE-LDT	Douglas DC-9-81	Austrian Airlines *Kärnten*
	OE-LDU	Douglas DC-9-81	Austrian Airlines *Steiermark*
	OE-LDV	Douglas DC-9-81	Austrian Airlines *Oberösterreich*
	OE-LDW	Douglas DC-9-81	Austrian Airlines *Salzburg*
	OE-LDX	Douglas DC-9-81	Austrian Airlines *Tirol*
	OE-LDY	Douglas DC-9-81	Austrian Airlines *Vorarlberg*
	OE-LDZ	Douglas DC-9-81	Austrian Airlines *Bregenz*
	OE-LLP	D.H.C.8-103 Dash Eight	Tyrolean Airways
	OE-LLR	D.H.C.8-102 Dash Eight	Tyrolean Airways *Stadt Graz*
	OE-LLS	D.H.C.7-102 Dash Seven	Tyrolean Airways *Stadt Innsbruck*
	OE-LLT	D.H.C.7-102 Dash Seven	Tyrolean Airways *Stadt Wien*
	OE-LMA	Douglas DC-9-81	Austrian Airlines *Linz*
	OE-LMB	Douglas DC-9-81	Austrian Airlines *Eisenstadt*
	OE-LMC	Douglas DC-9-81	Austrian Airlines *Baden*
	OE-LMK	Douglas DC-9-87ER	Austrian Airlines *Bad-Aussee*
	OE-LML	Douglas DC-9-87ER	Austrian Airlines *Velden*
	OE-LMM	Douglas DC-9-87	Austrian Airlines
	OE-LMN	Douglas DC-9-87	Austrian Airlines

Note: The four DC-9-32s are leased by Austrian pending delivery of the DC-9-87s.

OH (Finland)

	OH-LAA	Airbus A.300B4-203	Kar-Air
	OH-LAB	Airbus A.300B4-203	Kar-Air
	OH-LHA	Douglas DC-10-30ER	Finnair *Iso Antti*
	OH-LHB	Douglas DC-10-30ER	Finnair
	OH-LHD	Douglas DC-10-30ER	Finnair
	OH-LMA	Douglas DC-9-87	Finnair
	OH-LMB	Douglas DC-9-87	Finnair
	OH-LMC	Douglas DC-9-87	Finnair
	OH-LMD	Douglas DC-9-87	Finnair
	OH-	Douglas DC-9-87	Finnair
	OH-	Douglas DC-9-87	Finnair
	OH-	Douglas DC-9-87	Finnair
	OH-	Douglas DC-9-82	Finnair
	OH-LMN	Douglas DC-9-82	Finnair
	OH-LMO	Douglas DC-9-82	Finnair
	OH-LMP	Douglas DC-9-82	Finnair
	OH-LMR	Douglas DC-9-83	Finnair
	OH-LMS	Douglas DC-9-83	Finnair
	OH-LNB	Douglas DC-9-41	Finnair
	OH-LNC	Douglas DC-9-41	Finnair
	OH-LND	Douglas DC-9-41	Finnair
	OH-LNE	Douglas DC-9-41	Finnair
	OH-LNF	Douglas DC-9-41	Finnair
	OH-LYH	Douglas DC-9-15MC	Finnair
	OH-LYN	Douglas DC-9-51	Finnair
	OH-LYO	Douglas DC-9-51	Finnair
	OH-LYP	Douglas DC-9-51	Finnair
	OH-LYR	Douglas DC-9-51	Finnair
	OH-LYS	Douglas DC-9-51	Finnair
	OH-LYT	Douglas DC-9-51	Finnair

Reg.	Type	Owner or Operator	Notes
OH-LYU	Douglas DC-9-51	Finnair	
OH-LYV	Douglas DC-9-51	Finnair	
OH-LYW	Douglas DC-9-51	Finnair	
OH-LYX	Douglas DC-9-51	Finnair	
OH-LYY	Douglas DC-9-51	Finnair	
OH-LYZ	Douglas DC-9-51	Finnair	

Note: Finnair also operates a DC-10-30ER whach retains its US registration N345HC.

OK (Czechoslovakia)

OK-AFA	Tupolev Tu-134A	Ceskoslovenske Aerolinie	
OK-AFB	Tupolev Tu-134A	Ceskoslovenske Aerolinie	
OK-CFC	Tupolev Tu-134A	Ceskoslovenske Aerolinie	
OK-CFE	Tupolev Tu-134A	Ceskoslovenske Aerolinie	
OK-CFF	Tupolev Tu-134A	Ceskoslovenske Aerolinie	
OK-CFG	Tupolev Tu-134A	Ceskoslovenske Aerolinie	
OK-CFH	Tupolev Tu-134A	Ceskoslovenske Aerolinie	
OK-DBE	Ilyushin IL-62	Ceskoslovenske Aerolinie *Brno*	
OK-DFI	Tupolev Tu-134A	Ceskoslovenske Aerolinie	
OK-EBG	Ilyushin IL-62	Ceskoslovenske Aerolinie *Banska Bystrica*	
OK-EFJ	Tupolev Tu-134A	Ceskoslovenske Aerolinie	
OK-EFK	Tupolev Tu-134A	Ceskoslovenske Aerolinie	
OK-FBF	Ilyushin IL-62	Ceskoslovenske Aerolinie	
OK-GBH	Ilyushin IL-62	Ceskoslovenske Aerolinie *Usti Nad Labem*	
OK-HFL	Tupolev Tu-134A	Ceskoslovenske Aerolinie	
OK-HFM	Tupolev Tu-134A	Ceskoslovenske Aerolinie	
OK-IFN	Tupolev Tu-134A	Ceskoslovenske Aerolinie	
OK-JBI	Ilyushin IL-62M	Ceskoslovenske Aerolinie *Plzen*	
OK-JBJ	Ilyushin IL-62M	Ceskoslovenske Aerolinie *Hradec Kralové*	
OK-KBK	Ilyushin IL-62M	Ceskoslovenske Aerolinie *Ceske Budejovice*	
OK-KBN	Ilyushin Il-62M	Ceskoslovenske Aerolinie	
OK-	Tupolev Tu-154M	Ceskoslovenske Aerolinie	
OK-	Tupolev Tu-154M	Ceskoslovenske Aerolinie	
OK-	Tupolev Tu-154M	Ceskoslovenske Aerolinie	
OK-	Tupolev Tu-154M	Ceskoslovenske Aerolinie	
OK-	Tupolev Tu-154M	Ceskoslovenske Aerolinie	
OK-OBL	Ilyushin IL-62M	Ceskoslovenske Aerolinie	
OK-PBM	Ilyushin IL-62M	Ceskoslovenske Aerolinie	
OK-YBA	Ilyushin IL-62	Ceskoslovenske Aerolinie *Praha*	

OO (Belgium)

OO-DHB	Convair Cv.580	European Air Transport (DHL)	
OO-DHC	Convair Cv.580	European Air Transport (DHL)	
OO-DHD	Convair Cv.580	European Air Transport (DHL)	
OO-DHL	Convair Cv.580	European Air Transport (DHL)	
OO-DJA	F.27 Fellowship 3000	Delta Air Transport	
OO-DTA	FH-227B Friendship	Delta Air Transport	
OO-DTB	FH-227B Friendship	Delta Air Transport	
OO-DTC	FH-227B Friendship	Delta Air Transport	
OO-DTD	FH-227B Friendship	Delta Air Transport	
OO-DTE	FH-227B Friendship	Delta Air Transport	
OO-	EMB-120 Brasilia	Delta Air Transport	
OO-	EMB-120 Brasilia	Delta Air Transport	
OO-	EMB-120 Brasilia	Delta Air Transport	
OO-HUB	Convair Cv.580	European Air Transport (DHL)	
OO-	Convair Cv.580	European Air Transport (DHL)	
OO-ILF	Boeing 737-3Q8	Air Belgium	
OO-JPA	Swearingen SA226AT Merlin IVA	European Air Transport	
OO-JPI	Swearingen SA226TC Metro II	European Air Transport	
OO-JPK	Swearingen SA226TC Metro II	European Air Transport	
OO-JPN	Swearingen SA226AT Merlin IVA	European Air Transport	

Notes	Reg.	Type	Owner or Operator
	OO-SBQ	Boeing 737-229	Sobelair
	OO-SBS	Boeing 737-229	Sobelair
	OO-SBT	Boeing 737-229	Sobelair
	OO-SBU	Boeing 707-373C	Sobelair
	OO-SBZ	Boeing 737-329	Sobelair
	OO-SCA	Airbus A.310-221	Sabena
	OO-SCB	Airbus A.310-221	Sabena
	OO-SCC	Airbus A.310-322	Sabena
	OO-SDA	Boeing 737-229	Sabena
	OO-SDB	Boeing 737-229	Sabena
	OO-SDC	Boeing 737-229	Sabena
	OO-SDD	Boeing 737-229	Sabena/Spantax
	OO-SDE	Boeing 737-229	Sabena
	OO-SDF	Boeing 737-229	Sabena
	OO-SDG	Boeing 737-229	Sabena
	OO-SDJ	Boeing 737-229C	Sabena
	OO-SDK	Boeing 737-229C	Sabena
	OO-SDL	Boeing 737-229	Sabena
	OO-SDM	Boeing 737-229	Sabena
	OO-SDN	Boeing 737-229	Sabena
	OO-SDO	Boeing 737-229	Sabena
	OO-SDP	Boeing 737-229C	Sabena
	OO-SDR	Boeing 737-229C	Sabena
	OO-SDV	Boeing 737-329	Sabena
	OO-SDW	Boeing 737-329	Sabena
	OO-SDX	Boeing 737-329	Sabena
	OO-SDY	Boeing 737-329	Sabena
	OO-SGA	Boeing 747-129A (SCD)	Sabena
	OO-SGB	Boeing 747-129A (SCD)	Sabena
	OO-SGC	Boeing 747-329 (SCD)	Sabena
	OO-SLA	Douglas DC-10-30CF	Sabena/J.A.T.
	OO-SLB	Douglas DC-10-30CF	Sabena
	OO-SLC	Douglas DC-10-30CF	Sabena
	OO-SLD	Douglas DC-10-30CF	Sabena
	OO-SLE	Douglas DC-10-30CF	Sabena
	OO-TEF	Airbus A.300B1	Trans European Airways *Aline*
	OO-TEH	Boeing 737-2M8	Trans European Airways *Marcus Johannes*
	OO-TEK	Boeing 737-2Q9	Trans European Airways
	OO-TEL	Boeing 737-2M8	Trans European Airways *Antwerpen*
	OO-TEO	Boeing 737-2M8	Trans European Airways *Jonathan*
	OO-	Boeing 737-3B2	Trans European Airways
	OO-	Boeing 737-3B2	Trans European Airways
	OO-TYC	Boeing 707-328B	Trans European Airways
	OO-VGA	Swearingen SA226TC Metro II	European Air Transport
	OO-VGC	Swearingen SA226AT Merlin IV	European Air Transport
	OO-VGD	Swearingen SA226AT Merlin IV	European Air Transport
	OO-VGH	Convair Cv.580	European Air Transport (DHL)
	OO-VGI	Convair Cv.580	European Air Transport (DHL)

OY (Denmark)

Notes	Reg.	Type	Owner or Operator
	OY-APE	F.27 Friendship Mk 600	Starair
	OY-BDD	Nord 262A-21	Cimber Air
	OY-BPH	Swearingen SA227AC Metro III	Metro Airways
	OY-BPJ	Swearingen SA227AC Metro III	Metro Airways
	OY-BPK	Swearingef SA227TT Merlin IIIC	Metro Airways
	OY-CCK	F.27 Friendship Mk 600	Starair
	OY-CCL	F.27 Friendship Mk.600	Starair
	OY-CIB	Aerospatiale ATR-42-300	Cimber Air
	OY-CIC	Aerospatiale ATR-42-300	Cimber Air
	OY-C	Aerospatiale ATR-42-300	Cimber Air
	OY-C	Aerospatiale ATR-42-300	Cimber Air
	OY-CNA	Airbus A.300-320	Conair
	OY-CNK	Airbus A.300-320	Conair
	OY-CNL	Airbus A.300-320	Conair
	OY-DDA	Douglas DC-3	Danish Air Lines
	OY-KAC	F.27 Friendship Mk 600	S.A.S.
	OY-KAD	F.27 Friendship Mk 600	S.A.S.

Reg.	Type	Owner or Operator	Notes
OY-KDA	Douglas DC-10-30	S.A.S. *Gorm Viking*	
OY-KDB	Douglas DC-10-30	S.A.S. *Frode Viking*	
OY-KDC	Douglas DC-10-30	S.A.S.	
OY-KGA	Douglas DC-9-41	S.A.S. *Heming Viking*	
OY-KGB	Douglas DC-9-41	S.A.S. *Toste Viking*	
OY-KGC	Douglas DC-9-41	S.A.S. *Helge Viking*	
OY-KGD	Douglas DC-9-21	S.A.S. *Ubbe Viking*	
OY-KGE	Douglas DC-9-21	S.A.S. *Orvar Viking*	
OY-KGF	Douglas DC-9-21	S.A.S. *Rolf Viking*	
OY-KGG	Douglas DC-9-41	S.A.S. *Sune Viking*	
OY-KGH	Douglas DC-9-41	S.A.S. *Eiliv Viking*	
OY-KGI	Douglas DC-9-41	S.A.S. *Bent Viking*	
OY-KGK	Douglas DC-9-41	S.A.S. *Ebbe Viking*	
OY-KGL	Douglas DC-9-41	S.A.S. *Angantyr Viking*	
OY-KGM	Douglas DC-9-41	S.A.S. *Arnfinn Viking*	
OY-KGN	Douglas DC-9-41	S.A.S. *Gram Viking*	
OY-KGO	Douglas DC-9-41	S.A.S. *Holte Viking*	
OY-KGP	Douglas DC-9-41	S.A.S. *Torbern Viking*	
OY-KGR	Douglas DC-9-41	S.A.S. *Holger Viking*	
OY-KGS	Douglas DC-9-41	S.A.S. *Hall Viking*	
OY-KGT	Douglas DC-9-81	S.A.S. *Hake Viking*	
OY-KGY	Douglas DC-9-81	S.A.S. *Rollo Viking*	
OY-KGZ	Douglas DC-9-81	S.A.S. *Hagbard Viking*	
OY-KHC	Douglas DC-9-81	S.A.S. *Faste Viking*	
OY-KTF	Douglas DC-8-63	Scanair *Mette Viking*	
OY-KTG	Douglas DC-8-63	Scanair *Torodd Viking*	
OY-MBC	D.H.C.7 Dash Seven	Maersk Air	
OY-MBD	D.H.C.7 Dash Seven	Maersk Air	
OY-MBE	D.H.C.7 Dash Seven	Maersk Air	
OY-MBF	D.H.C.7 Dash Seven	Maersk Air	
OY-MBG	D.H.C.7 Dash Seven	Maersk Air	
OY-MBV	Boeing 737-2L9	Maersk Air	
OY-MBZ	Boeing 737-2L9	Maersk Air	
OY-MMG	Fokker 50	Maersk Air	
OY-MMH	Fokker 50	Maersk Air	
OY-MMI	Fokker 50	Maersk Air	
OY-MMJ	Fokker 50	Maersk Air	
OY-MMK	Boeing 737-3L9	Maersk Air	
OY-MML	Boeing 737-3L9	Maersk Air	
OY-MMM	Boeing 737-3L9	Maersk Air	
OY-MMN	Boeing 737-3L9	Maersk Air	
OY-M	Boeing 737-3L9	Maersk Air	
OY-M	Boeing 737-3L9	Maersk Air	
OY-M	Boeing 737-3L9	Maersk Air	
OY-SAT	Boeing 727-2J4	Sterling Airways	
OY-SAU	Boeing 727-2J4	Sterling Airways	
OY-SBE	Boeing 727-2J4	Sterling Airways	
OY-SBF	Boeing 727-2J4	Sterling Airways	
OY-SBG	Boeing 727-2J4	Sterling Airways	
OY-SBH	Boeing 727-2B7	Sterling Airways	
OY-SBI	Boeing 727-2B7	Sterling Airways	
OY-SBJ	Boeing 727-2L8	Sterling Airways	
OY-SBK	Douglas DC-8-63	Scanair	
OY-SBL	Douglas DC-8-63	Scanair	
OY-SBN	Boeing 727-2B7	Sterling Airways	
OY-SBO	Boeing 727-2K3	Sterling Airways	
OY-STC	S.E.210 Caravelle 10B	Sterling Airways	
OY-STD	S.E.210 Caravelle 10B	Sterling Airways	
OY-STF	S.E.210 Caravelle 10B	Sterling Airways	
OY-STH	S.E.210 Caravelle 10B	Sterling Airways	
OY-STI	S.E.210 Caravelle 10B	Sterling Airways	
OY-STM	S.E.210 Caravelle 10B	Sterling Airways	
OY-TOV	Nord 262A-30	Cimber Air	

PH (Netherlands)

PH-AGA	Airbus A.310-203	K.L.M. *Rembrandt*	
PH-AGB	Airbus A.310-203	K.L.M. *Jeroen Bosch*	
PH-AGC	Airbus A.310-203	K.L.M. *Albert Cuyp*	
PH-AGD	Airbus A.310-203	K.L.M. *Marinus Ruppert*	

Notes	Reg.	Type	Owner or Operator
	PH-AGE	Airbus A.310-203	K.L.M. *Nicolaas Maes*
	PH-AGF	Airbus A.310-203	K.L.M. *Jan Steen*
	PH-AGG	Airbus A.310-203	K.L.M. *Vincent van Gogh*
	PH-AGH	Airbus A.310-203	K.L.M. *Peiter de Hoogh*
	PH-AGI	Airbus A.310-203	K.L.M. *Jan Toorop*
	PH-AGK	Airbus A.310-203	K.L.M. *Johannes Vermeer*
	PH-AHB	Boeing 727-2H3	Air Holland
	PH-AHD	Boeing 727-2H3	Air Holland
	PH-AHE	Boeing 757-27B	Air Holland
	PH-AHF	Boeing 757-27B	Air Holland
	PH-AHI	Boeing 757-27B	Air Holland
	PH-BDA	Boeing 737-306	K.L.M. *Willem Barentz*
	PH-BDB	Boeing 737-306	K.L.M. *Olivier van Noort*
	PH-BDC	Boeing 737-306	K.L.M. *Cornelis De Houteman*
	PH-BDD	Boeing 737-306	K.L.M. *Anthony van Diemen*
	PH-BDE	Boeing 737-306	K.L.M. *Abel J. Tasman*
	PH-BDG	Boeing 737-306	K.L.M. *Michiel A. D. Ruyter*
	PH-BDH	Boeing 737-306	K.L.M. *Petrus Plancius*
	PH-BDI	Boeing 737-306	K.L.M. *Maarten H. Tromp*
	PH-BDK	Boeing 737-306	K.L.M. *Jan H. van Linschoten*
	PH-BDL	Boeing 737-306	K.L.M. *Piet Heyn*
	PH-BD	Boeing 737-306	K.L.M.
	PH-BD	Boeing 737-306	K.L.M.
	PH-BFA	Boeing 747-406	K.L.M.
	PH-BFB	Boeing 747-406	K.L.M.
	PH-BFC	Boeing 747-406	K.L.M.
	PH-BFD	Boeing 747-406	K.L.M.
	PH-BFE	Boeing 747-406	K.L.M.
	PH-BFF	Boeing 747-406	K.L.M.
	PH-BUA	Boeing 747-206B	K.L.M. *The Mississippi*
	PH-BUB	Boeing 747-206B	K.L.M. *The Danube*
	PH-BUC	Boeing 747-206B	K.L.M. *The Amazon*
	PH-BUD	Boeing 747-206B	K.L.M. *The Nile*
	PH-BUE	Boeing 747-206B	K.L.M. *Rio de la Plata*
	PH-BUG	Boeing 747-206B	K.L.M. *The Orinoco*
	PH-BUH	Boeing 747-306	K.L.M. *Dr Albert Plesman*
	PH-BUI	Boeing 747-306	K.L.M. *Wilbur Wright*
	PH-BUK	Boeing 747-306	K.L.M. *Louis Blériot*
	PH-BUL	Boeing 747-306	K.L.M. *Charles A. Lindbergh*
	PH-BUM	Boeing 747-306	K.L.M. *Sir Charles E. Kingsford-Smith*
	PH-BUN	Boeing 747-306	K.L.M. *Anthony H. G. Fokker*
	PH-BUO	Boeing 747-306	K.L.M. *Missouri*
	PH-BUW	Boeing 747-306	K.L.M. *Leonardo da Vinci*
	PH-B	Boeing 747-406	K.L.M.
	PH-B	Boeing 747-406	K.L.M.
	PH-CHB	F.28 Fellowship 4000	N.L.M. *Birmingham*
	PH-CHD	F.28 Fellowship 4000	N.L.M. *Maastricht*
	PH-CHF	F.28 Fellowship 4000	N.L.M. *Guernsey*
	PH-CHN	F.28 Fellowship 4000	N.L.M.
	PH-DDA	Douglas DC-3	Dutch Dakota Association
	PH-DNC	Douglas DC-9-15	K.L.M. *City of Luxembourg*
	PH-DNI	Douglas DC-9-32	K.L.M. *City of Istanbul*
	PH-DNK	Douglas DC-9-32	K.L.M. *City of Copenhagen*
	PH-DNL	Douglas DC-9-32	K.L.M. *City of London*
	PH-DNO	Douglas DC-9-33RC	K.L.M. *City of Oslo*
	PH-DNP	Douglas DC-9-33RC	K.L.M. *City of Athens*
	PH-DNR	Douglas DC-9-33RC	K.L.M. *City of Stockholm*
	PH-DNT	Douglas DC-9-32	K.L.M. *City of Lisbon*
	PH-DOA	Douglas DC-9-32	K.L.M. *City of Utrecht*
	PH-DOB	Douglas DC-9-32	K.L.M. *City of Santa Monica*
	PH-DTA	Douglas DC-10-30	K.L.M. *Johann Sebastian Bach*
	PH-DTB	Douglas DC-10-30	K.L.M. *Ludwig van Beethoven*
	PH-DTC	Douglas DC-10-30	K.L.M. *Frédéric François Chopin*
	PH-DTD	Douglas DC-10-30	K.L.M. *Maurice Ravel*
	PH-DTL	Douglas DC-10-30	K.L.M. *Edvard Hagerup Grieg*
	PH-FKT	F-27 Friendship Mk 600	XP Express Parcel System *Monique*
	PH-HVF	Boeing 737-3K2	Transavia *Johan Cruijff*
	PH-HVG	Boeing 737-3K2	Transavia *Wubbo Ockels*
	PH-HVJ	Boeing 737-3K2	Transavia
	PH-HVK	Boeing 737-3K2	Transavia
	PH-KFD	F.27 Friendship Mk 200	N.L.M. *Jan Moll*

Reg.	Type	Owner or Operator	Notes
PH-KFE	F.27 Friendship Mk 600	N.L.M. *Jan Dellaert*	
PH-KFG	F.27 Friendship Mk 200	N.L.M. *Koos Abspoel*	
PH-KFI	F.27 Friendship Mk 500	N.L.M. *Bremen*	
PH-KFK	F.27 Friendship Mk 500	N.L.M. *Zestienhoven*	
PH-KFL	F.27 Friendship Mk 500	N.L.M.	
PH-KJA	BAe Jetstream 3102	Nether Lines	
PH-KJB	BAe Jetstream 3102	Nether Lines	
PH-KJC	BAe Jetstream 3102	Nether Lines	
PH-KJD	BAe Jetstream 3102	Nether Lines	
PH-KJF	BAe Jetstream 3102	Nether Lines	
PH-KJG	BAe Jetstream 3102	Nether Lines	
PH-KJH	Saab SF.340A	Nether Lines	
PH-KLC	Fokker 100	K.L.M. *Gerard Mercator*	
PH-KLD	Fokker 100	K.L.M. *Jan A. Leeghwater*	
PH-KLE	Fokker 100	K.L.M. *Gerard J. Leeuwenhoek*	
PH-KLG	Fokker 100	K.L.M. *Johannes Blaeu*	
PH-KLH	Fokker 100	K.L.M. *Christiaan Huygens*	
PH-KLI	Fokker 100	K.L.M. *Antonie van Leeuwenhoek*	
PH-KLK	Fokker 100	K.L.M. *Chris H. D. Buys Ballot*	
PH-KLL	Fokker 100	K.L.M. *Hendrick A. Lorentz*	
PH-KLN	Fokker 100	K.L.M. *Pieter Zeeman*	
PH-KLO	Fokker 100	K.L.M. *Jan H. Oort*	
PH-MBG	Douglas DC-10-30CF	Martinair *Kohoutek*	
PH-MBN	Douglas DC-10-30CF	Martinair *Anthony Ruys*	
PH-MBP	Douglas DC-10-30CF	Martinair *Hong Kong*	
PH-MBT	Douglas DC-10-30CF	Martinair	
PH-MBZ	Douglas DC-9-82	Martinair *Prinses Juiliana*	
PH-MCA	Airbus A.310-202	Martinair *Prins Bernhard*	
PH-MCB	Airbus A.310-202CF	Martinair	
PH-MCD	Douglas DC-9-82	Martinair *Lucien Ruys*	
PH-MCE	Boeing 747-21AC (SCD)	Martinair	
PH-MCF	Boeing 747-21AC (SCD)	Martinair	
PH-SAD	F.27 Friendship Mk 200	N.L.M. *Evert van Dijk*	
PH-SFA	F.27 Friendship Mk 400	N.L.M.	
PH-SFB	F.27 Friendship Mk 400	N.L.M.	
PH-SFC	F.27 Friendship Mk 400	XP Express Parcel System	
PH-TVC	Boeing 737-2K2C	Transavia *Richard Gordon*	
PH-TVH	Boeing 737-222	Transavia *Neil Armstrong*	
PH-TVR	Boeing 737-2K2	Transavia	
PH-TVS	Boeing 737-2K2	Transavia	
PH-TVU	Boeing 737-2K2	Transavia	
PH-TVX	Boeing 737-2K2	Transavia	

Note: K.L.M. also operates Boeing 747-306s N1295E, N1298E, N1309E, N4548M and N4551N. Sixteen DC-9s have been sold in America for delivery spread over two years starting in January 1987.

PK (Indonesia)

PK-GIA	Douglas DC-10-30	Garuda Indonesian Airways	
PK-GIB	Douglas DC-10-30	Garuda Indonesian Airways	
PK-GIC	Douglas DC-10-30	Garuda Indonesian Airways	
PK-GID	Douglas DC-10-30	Garuda Indonesian Airways	
PK-GIE	Douglas DC-10-30	Garuda Indonesian Airways	
PK-GIF	Douglas DC-10-30	Garuda Indonesian Airways	
PK-GSA	Boeing 747-2U3B	Garuda Indonesian Airways	
PK-GSB	Boeing 747-2U3B	Garuda Indonesian Airways	
PK-GSC	Boeing 747-2U3B	Garuda Indonesian Airways	
PK-GSD	Boeing 747-2U3B	Garuda Indonesian Airways	
PK-GSE	Boeing 747-2U3B	Garuda Indonesian Airways	
PK-GSF	Boeing 747-2U3B	Garuda Indonesian Airways	

PP (Brazil)

PP-VMA	Douglas DC-10-30	VARIG	
PP-VMB	Douglas DC-10-30	VARIG	
PP-VMD	Douglas DC-10-30	VARIG	
PP-VMQ	Douglas DC-10-30	VARIG	

Notes	Reg.	Type	Owner or Operator
	PP-VMS	Douglas DC-10-30	VARIG
	PP-VMT	Douglas DC-10-30F	VARIG Cargo
	PP-VMU	Douglas DC-10-30F	VARIG Cargo
	PP-VMV	Douglas DC-10-30	VARIG
	PP-VMW	Douglas DC-10-30	VARIG
	PP-VMX	Douglas DC-10-30	VARIG
	PP-VMY	Douglas DC-10-30	VARIG
	PP-VMZ	Douglas DC-10-30	VARIG
	PP-VNA	Boeing 747-2L5B (SCD)	VARIG
	PP-VNB	Boeing 747-2L5B (SCD)	VARIG
	PP-VNC	Boeing 747-2L5B (SCD)	VARIG
	PP-VNH	Boeing 747-341 (SCD)	VARIG
	PP-VNI	Boeing 747-341 (SCD)	VARIG
	PP-VOA	Boeing 747-341	VARIG
	PP-VOB	Boeing 747-341	VARIG
	PP-VOC	Boeing 747-341	VARIG

RP (Philippines)

Note: Philippine Airlines operates four Boeing 747-2F6Bs which retain their U.S.
registrations N741PR, N742PR, N743PR and N744PR and two 747-283Bs
N4501Q and N4502R.

S2 (Bangladesh)

	S2-ABN	Boeing 707-351C	Bangladesh Biman *City of Shah Jalal*
	S2-ACE	Boeing 707-351C	Bangladesh Biman *City of Tokyo*
	S2-ACO	Douglas DC-10-30	Bangladesh Biman *City of Hazrat-Shar Makhdoom (R.A.)*
	S2-ACP	Douglas DC-10-30	Bangladesh Biman *City of Dhaka*
	S2-ACQ	Douglas DC-10-30	Bangladesh Biman *City of Hz Shah Jalal (R.A.)*
	S2-	Douglas DC-10-30	Bangladesh Biman

S7 (Seychelles)

	S7-SIS	Douglas DC-8-63	Seychelles International
	S7-	Boeing 707 Super Q	Air Seychelles
	S7-	Boeing 707 Super Q	Air Seychelles

SE (Sweden)

	SE-BSM	Douglas DC-3	Swedair Luftfartsverket
	SE-CFP	Douglas DC-3	S.A.S. *Fridtjof Viking*
	SE-DAK	Douglas DC-9-41	S.A.S. *Ragnvald Viking*
	SE-DAL	Douglas DC-9-41	S.A.S. *Algot Viking*
	SE-DAM	Douglas DC-9-41	S.A.S. *Starkad Viking*
	SE-DAN	Douglas DC-9-41	S.A.S. *Alf Viking*
	SE-DAO	Douglas DC-9-41	S.A.S. *Asgaut Viking*
	SE-DAP	Douglas DC-9-41	S.A.S. *Torgils Viking*
	SE-DAR	Douglas DC-9-41	S.A.S. *Agnar Viking*
	SE-DAS	Douglas DC-9-41	S.A.S. *Garder Viking*
	SE-DAU	Douglas DC-9-41	S.A.S. *Hadding Viking*
	SE-DAW	Douglas DC-9-41	S.A.S. *Gotrik Viking*
	SE-DAX	Douglas DC-9-41	S.A.S. *Helsing Viking*
	SE-DBH	Douglas DC-8-63	Scanair *Dana Viking*
	SE-DBK	Douglas DC-8-63	Scanair *Sigyn Viking*
	SE-DBL	Douglas DC-8-63	Scanair *Bodil Viking*
	SE-DBM	Douglas DC-9-41	S.A.S. *Ossur Viking*
	SE-DBN	Douglas DC-9-33AF	S.A.S./Air de Cologne *Sigtrygg Viking*
	SE-DBO	Douglas DC-9-21	S.A.S. *Siger Viking*
	SE-DBP	Douglas DC-9-21	S.A.S. *Rane Viking*
	SE-DBR	Douglas DC-9-21	S.A.S. *Skate Viking*
	SE-DBS	Douglas DC-9-21	S.A.S. *Svipdag Viking*

Reg.	Type	Owner or Operator	Notes
SE-DBT	Douglas DC-9-41	S.A.S. *Agne Viking*	
SE-DBU	Douglas DC-9-41	S.A.S. *Hjalmar Viking*	
SE-DBW	Douglas DC-9-41	S.A.S. *Adils Viking*	
SE-DBX	Douglas DC-9-41	S.A.S. *Arnljot Viking*	
SE-DDP	Douglas DC-9-41	S.A.S. *Brun Viking*	
SE-DDR	Douglas DC-9-41	S.A.S. *Atle Viking*	
SE-DDS	Douglas DC-9-41	S.A.S. *Alrik Viking*	
SE-DDT	Douglas DC-9-41	S.A.S. *Amund Viking*	
SE-DDU	Douglas DC-8-62	Scanair *Knud Viking*	
SE-DEB	S.E.210 Caravelle 10R	Transwede	
SE-DEH	S.E.210 Caravelle 10B	Transwede	
SE-DEI	BAe 146-200QT	Malmo Aviation (TNT)	
SE-DFD	Douglas DC-10-30	S.A.S. *Dag Viking*	
SE-DFE	Douglas DC-10-30	S.A.S. *Sverker Viking*	
SE-DFF	Douglas DC-10-30	S.A.S. *Solve Viking*	
SE-DFG	Douglas DC-10-30	S.A.S.	
SE-DFH	Douglas DC-10-30	S.A.S./Scanair	
SE-DFN	Douglas DC-9-51	S.A.S.	
SE-DFO	Douglas DC-9-51	S.A.S.	
SE-DFR	Douglas DC-9-81	S.A.S. *Ingsald Viking*	
SE-DFS	Douglas DC-9-82	S.A.S. *Gaut Viking*	
SE-DFT	Douglas DC-9-82	S.A.S. *Assur Viking*	
SE-DFU	Douglas DC-9-82	S.A.S. *Isulv Viking*	
SE-DFX	Douglas DC-9-82	S.A.S. *Ring Viking*	
SE-DFY	Douglas DC-9-81	S.A.S. *Ottar Viking*	
SE-DGA	F.28 Fellowship 1000	Linjeflyg	
SE-DGB	F.28 Fellowship 1000	Linjeflyg	
SE-DGC	F.28 Fellowship 1000	Linjeflyg	
SE-DGD	F.28 Fellowship 4000	Linjeflyg	
SE-DGE	F.28 Fellowship 4000	Linjeflyg	
SE-DGF	F.28 Fellowship 4000	Linjeflyg	
SE-DGG	F.28 Fellowship 4000	Linjeflyg	
SE-DGH	F.28 Fellowship 4000	Linjeflyg	
SE-DGI	F.28 Fellowship 4000	Linjeflyg	
SE-DGK	F.28 Fellowship 4000	Linjeflyg	
SE-DGL	F.28 Fellowship 4000	Linjeflyg	
SE-DGM	F.28 Fellowship 4000	Linjeflyg	
SE-DGN	F.28 Fellowship 4000	Linjeflyg	
SE-DGO	F.28 Fellowship 4000	Linjeflyg	
SE-DGP	F.28 Fellowship 4000	Linjeflyg	
SE-DGR	F.28 Fellowship 4000	Linjeflyg	
SE-DGS	F.28 Fellowship 4000	Linjeflyg	
SE-DGT	F.28 Fellowship 4000	Linjeflyg	
SE-DGU	F.28 Fellowship 4000	Linjeflyg *Ulla*	
SE-DGX	F.28 Fellowship 4000	Linjeflyg	
SE-DHA	S.E.210 Caravelle 10B	Transwede	
SE-DHB	Douglas DC-9-83	Transwede	
SE-D	Douglas DC-9-83	Transwede	
SE-D	Douglas DC-9-87	Transwede	
SE-D	Douglas DC-9-87	Transwede	
SE-IRF	F.27 Friendship Mk 600	S.A.S. *Vinge Viking*	
SE-IRG	F.27 Friendship Mk 600	S.A.S. *Vigge Viking*	
SE-ITH	F.27 Friendship Mk 600	S.A.S. *Visbur Viking*	
SE-ITI	F.27 Friendship Mk 600	S.A.S. *Vidar Viking*	
SE-IVR	L-188CF Electra	Falcon Cargo	
SE-IVS	L-188CF Electra	Falcon Cargo	
SE-IVT	L-188CF Electra	Falcon Cargo	
SE-IVY	V.815 Viscount	Baltic Aviation	

Note: Malmo Aviation operates two Fairchild F.27s registered LN-BSC and LN-BSD.

SP (Poland)

SP-LBA	Ilyushin IL-62M	Polskie Linie Lotnicze (LOT) *Juliusz Sowacki*	
SP-LBB	Ilyushin IL-62M	Polskie Linie Lotnicze (LOT) *Jgnacy Paderewski*	
SP-LBC	Ilyushin IL-62M	Polskie Linie Lotnicze (LOT) *Joseph Conrad-Korzeniowski*	

Notes	Reg.	Type	Owner or Operator
	SP-LBD	Ilyushin IL-62M	Polskie Linie Lotnicze (LOT)
	SP-LBE	Ilyushin IL-62M	Polskie Linie Lotnicze (LOT)
	SP-LBF	Ilyushin IL-62M	Polskie Linie Lotnicze (LOT)
	SP-LBI	Ilyushin IL-62M	Polskie Linie Lotnicze (LOT)
	SP-L	Ilyushin IL-62M	Polskie Linie Lotnicze (LOT)
	SP-LCA	Tupolev Tu-154M	Polskie Linie Lotnicze (LOT)
	SP-LCB	Tupolev Tu-154M	Polskie Linie Lotnicze (LOT)
	SP-LCC	Tupolev Tu-154M	Polskie Linie Lotnicze (LOT)
	SP-LCD	Tupolev Tu-154M	Polskie Linie Lotnicze (LOT)
	SP-LCE	Tupolev Tu-154M	Polskie Linie Lotnicze (LOT)
	SP-LCF	Tupolev Tu-154M	Polskie Linie Lotnicze (LOT)
	SP-LCG	Tupolev Tu-154M	Polskie Linie Lotnicze (LOT)
	SP-LCH	Tupolev Tu-154M	Polskie Linie Lotnicze (LOT)
	SP-LCI	Tupolev Tu-154M	Polskie Linie Lotnicze (LOT)
	SP-LCK	Tupolev Tu-154M	Polskie Linie Lotnicze (LOT)
	SP-LCL	Tupolev Tu-154M	Polskie Linie Lotnicze (LOT)
	SP-LCM	Tupolev Tu-154M	Polskie Linie Lotnicze (LOT)
	SP-LHA	Tupolev Tu-134A	Polskie Linie Lotnicze (LOT)
	SP-LHB	Tupolev Tu-134A	Polskie Linie Lotnicze (LOT)
	SP-LHC	Tupolev Tu-134A	Polskie Linie Lotnicze (LOT)
	SP-LHD	Tupolev Tu-134A	Polskie Linie Lotnicze (LOT)
	SP-LHE	Tupolev Tu-134A	Polskie Linie Lotnicze (LOT)
	SP-LHF	Tupolev Tu-134A	Polskie Linie Lotnicze (LOT)
	SP-LHG	Tupolev Tu-134A	Polskie Linie Lotnicze (LOT)
	SP-LSA	Ilyushin IL-18V (Cargo)	Polskie Linie Lotnicze (LOT)
	SP-LSB	Ilyushin IL-18V	Polskie Linie Lotnicze (LOT)
	SP-LSC	Ilyushin IL-18V (Cargo)	Polskie Linie Lotnicze (LOT)
	SP-LSD	Ilyushin IL-18V	Polskie Linie Lotnicze (LOT)
	SP-LSE	Ilyushin IL-18V	Polskie Linie Lotnicze (LOT)
	SP-LSF	Ilyushin IL-18E	Polskie Linie Lotnicze (LOT)
	SP-LSG	Ilyushin IL-18E	Polskie Linie Lotnicze (LOT)
	SP-LSH	Ilyushin IL-18V	Polskie Linie Lotnicze (LOT)
	SP-LSI	Ilyushin IL-18D	Polskie Linie Lotnicze (LOT)

ST (Sudan)

	ST-AFA	Boeing 707-3J8C	Sudan Airways
	ST-AFB	Boeing 707-3J8C	Sudan Airways
	ST-AIX	Boeing 707-369C	Sudan Airways
	ST-AJD	Douglas DC-8-55F	Trans Arabian Air Transport
	ST-AJR	Douglas DC-8-55F	Trans Arabian Air Transport
	ST-DRS	Boeing 707-368C	Sudan Airways
	ST-NSR	Boeing 707-330B	Sudan Airways

Note: Sudan Airways also uses TriStar 500 JY-AGH on lease from Royal Jordanian.

SU (Egypt)

	SU-AOU	Boeing 707-366C	EgyptAir *Khopho*
	SU-APD	Boeing 707-366C	EgyptAir *Khafrah*
	SU-AVX	Boeing 707-366C	EgyptAir *Tutankhamun*
	SU-AVY	Boeing 707-366C	EgyptAir *Akhenaton*
	SU-AVZ	Boeing 707-366C	EgyptAir *Mena*
	SU-AXK	Boeing 707-366C	EgyptAir *Seti I*
	SU-BCB	Airbus A.300B4	EgyptAir *Osiris*
	SU-BCC	Airbus A.300B4	EgyptAir *Nout*
	SU-BDF	Airbus A.300B4	EgyptAir *Hathor*
	SU-BDG	Airbus A.300B4	EgyptAir *Aton*
	SU-DAA	Boeing 707-351C	Zakani Aviation Services
	SU-DAB	Boeing 707-328C	Zakani Aviation Services
	SU-DAC	Boeing 707-336C	Zakani Aviation Services
	SU-DAE	Boeing 707-338C	Zakani Aviation Services
	SU-DAI	Boeing 707-365C	Zakani Aviation Services
	SU-EAA	Boeing 707-351C	Misr Overseas Airways
	SU-FAA	Boeing 707-138B	Misr Overseas Airways
	SU-FAC	Boeing 707-323C	Misr Overseas Airways
	SU-GAA	Airbus A.300B4	EgyptAir *Isis*

Reg.	Type	Owner or Operator	Notes
SU-GAB	Airbus A.300B4	EgyptAir *Amun*	
SU-GAC	Airbus A.300B4	EgyptAir *Bennou*	
SU-GAH	Boeing 767-266ER	Egyptair *Nefertiti*	
SU-GAI	Boeing 767-266ER	Egyptair *Nefertari*	
SU-GAJ	Boeing 767-266ER	Egyptair *Tiye*	
SU-GAL	Boeing 747-366	Egyptair	
SU-GAM	Boeing 747-366	Egyptair	

SX (Greece)

Reg.	Type	Owner or Operator	Notes
SX-BCA	Boeing 737-284	Olympic Airlines *Apollo*	
SX-BCB	Boeing 737-284	Olympic Airlines *Hermes*	
SX-BCC	Boeing 737-284	Olympic Airlines *Hercules*	
SX-BCD	Boeing 737-284	Olympic Airlines *Hephaestus*	
SX-BCE	Boeing 737-284	Olympic Airlines *Dionysus*	
SX-BCF	Boeing 737-284	Olympic Airlines *Poseidon*	
SX-BCG	Boeing 737-284	Olympic Airlines *Phoebus*	
SX-BCH	Boeing 737-284	Olympic Airlines *Triton*	
SX-BCI	Boeing 737-284	Olympic Airlines *Proteus*	
SX-BCK	Boeing 737-284	Olympic Airlines *Nereus*	
SX-BCL	Boeing 737-284	Olympic Airlines *Isle of Thassos*	
SX-BEB	Airbus A.300B4	Olympic Airways *Odysseus*	
SX-BEC	Airbus A.300B4	Olympic Airways *Achilleus*	
SX-BED	Airbus A.300B4	Olympic Airways *Telemachos*	
SX-BEE	Airbus A.300B4	Olympic Airways *Nestor*	
SX-BEF	Airbus A.300B4	Olympic Airways *Ajax*	
SX-BEG	Airbus A.300B4	Olympic Airways *Diamedes*	
SX-BEH	Airbus A.300B4	Olympic Airways *Peleus*	
SX-BEI	Airbus A.300B4	Olympic Airways *Neoptolemos*	
SX-CBA	Boeing 727-284	Olympic Airways *Mount Olympus*	
SX-CBB	Boeing 727-284	Olympic Airways *Mount Pindos*	
SX-CBC	Boeing 727-284	Olympic Airways *Mount Parnassus*	
SX-CBD	Boeing 727-284	Olympic Airways *Mount Helicon*	
SX-CBE	Boeing 727-284	Olympic Airways *Mount Athos*	
SX-CBF	Boeing 727-284	Olympic Airways *Mount Taygetus*	
SX-DBC	Boeing 707-384C	Olympic Airways *City of Knossos*	
SX-DBD	Boeing 707-384C	Olympic Airways *City of Sparta*	
SX-DBE	Boeing 707-384B	Olympic Airways *City of Pella*	
SX-DBF	Boeing 707-384B	Olympic Airways *City of Mycenae*	
SX-DBO	Boeing 707-351C	Olympic Airways *City of Lindos*	
SX-DBP	Boeing 707-351C	Olympic Airways *City of Thebes*	
SX-OAB	Boeing 747-284B	Olympic Airways *Olympic Eagle*	
SX-OAC	Boeing 747-212B	Olympic Airways *Olympic Spirit*	
SX-OAD	Boeing 747-212B	Olympic Airways *Olympic Flame*	
SX-OAE	Boeing 747-212B	Olympic Airways *Olympic Peace*	

TC (Turkey)

Reg.	Type	Owner or Operator	Notes
TC-AKA	S.E.210 Caravelle 10B1R	Istanbul Airlines	
TC-	S.E.210 Caravelle 10B1R	Istanbul Airlines	
TC-AKD	Boeing 727-2H9	Talia Airways	
TC-	Boeing 737-300	Istanbul Airlines	
TC-	Boeing 737-300	Istanbul Airlines	
TC-	Boeing 737-300	Istanbul Airlines	
TC-ARI	S.E.210 Caravelle 10B1R	Istanbul Airlines	
TC-JAB	Douglas DC-9-32	Turk Hava Yollari (THY) *Bogazici*	
TC-JAD	Douglas DC-9-32	Turk Hava Yollari (THY) *Anadolu*	
TC-JAE	Douglas DC-9-32	Turk Hava Yollari (THY) *Trakya*	
TC-JAF	Douglas DC-9-32	Turk Hava Yollari (THY) *Ege*	
TC-JAG	Douglas DC-9-32	Turk Hava Yollari (THY) *Akdeniz*	
TC-JAK	Douglas DC-9-32	Turk Hava Yollari (THY) *Karadeniz*	
TC-JAL	Douglas DC-9-32	Turk Hava Yollari (THY) *Halic*	
TC-JAU	Douglas DC-10-10	Türk Hava Yollari (THY) *Istanbul*	
TC-JAY	Douglas DC-10-10	Türk Hava Yollari (THY) *Izmir*	
TC-JBF	Boeing 727-2F2	Türk Hava Yollari (THY) *Adana*	
TC-JBG	Boeing 727-2F2	Türk Hava Yollari (THY) *Ankara*	
TC-JBJ	Boeing 727-2F2	Türk Hava Yollari (THY) *Diyarbakir*	

Notes	Reg.	Type	Owner or Operator
	TC-JBK	Douglas DC-9-32	Türk Hava Yollari (THY) *Aydin*
	TC-JBL	Douglas DC-9-32	Türk Hava Yollari (THY) *Gediz*
	TC-JBM	Boeing 727-2F2	Türk Hava Yollari (THY) *Menderes*
	TC-JCA	Boeing 727-2F2	Türk Hava Yollari (THY) *Edirne*
	TC-JCB	Boeing 727-2F2	Türk Hava Yollari (THY) *Kars*
	TC-JCC	Boeing 707-321C	Türk Hava Yollari (THY) *Kervan I*
	TC-JCD	Boeing 727-2F2	Türk Hava Yollari (THY) *Sinop*
	TC-JCE	Boeing 727-2F2	Türk Hava Yollari (THY) *Hatay*
	TC-JCF	Boeing 707-321C	Türk Hava Yollari (THY) *Kervan II*
	TC-JCK	Boeing 727-243	Türk Hava Yollari (THY) *Erciyes*
	TC-JCL	Airbus A.310-203	Türk Hava Yollari (THY) *Seyhan*
	TC-JCM	Airbus A.310-203	Türk Hava Yollari (THY) *Ceyhan*
	TC-JCN	Airbus A.310-203	Türk Hava Yollari (THY) *Dicle*
	TC-JCO	Airbus A.310-203	Türk Hava Yollari (THY) *Firat*
	TC-JCR	Airbus A.310-203	Türk Hava Yollari (THY) *Kizilirmak*
	TC-JCS	Airbus A.310-203	Türk Hava Yollari (THY) *Yesilirmak*
	TC-JCU	Airbus A.310-203	Türk Hava Yollari (THY) *Sakarya*
	TC-JCV	Airbus A.310-304	Türk Hava Yollari (THY)
	TC-JCY	Airbus A.310-304	Türk Hava Yollari (THY)
	TC-JCZ	Airbus A.310-304	Türk Hava Yollari (THY)
	TC-	Airbus A.310-304	Türk Hava Yollari (THY)
	TC-	Airbus A.310-304	Türk Hava Yollari (THY)

TF (Iceland)

	TF-FLB	Douglas DC-8-55F	Icelandair
	TF-FLE	Douglas DC-8-63	Icelandair
	TF-FLG	Boeing 727-185C	Icelandair *Heim Fari*
	TF-FLI	Boeing 727-208	Icelandair *Fronfari*
	TF-FLK	Boeing 727-276	Icelandair
	TF-FLM	F.27 Friendship Mk 200	Icelandair
	TF-FLN	F.27 Friendship Mk 200	Icelandair
	TF-FLO	F.27 Friendship Mk 200	Icelandair
	TF-FLP	F.27 Friendship Mk 200	Icelandair
	TF-FLS	F.27 Friendship Mk 200	Icelandair
	TF-FLT	Douglas DC-8-63	Icelandair
	TF-FLU	Douglas DC-8-63	Icelandair *Austurfari*
	TF-FLV	Douglas DC-8-63	Icelandair *Vesturfari*
	TF-	Boeing 737-408	Icelandair
	TF-	Boeing 737-408	Icelandair
	TF-VLT	Boeing 737-205C	Eagle Air

Note: Icelandair also operates DC-8s on lease.

TJ (Cameroon)

	TJ-CAB	Boeing 747-2H7B (SCD)	Cameroon Airlines *Mont Cameroun*

TR (Gabon)

	TR-LBV	L-100-30 Hercules	Air Gabon Cargo
	TR-LVK	Douglas DC-8-55F	Air Gabon Cargo/Affretair

Note: Air Gabon operates Boeing 747-2Q2B F-ODJG on lease.

TS (Tunisia)

	TS-IMA	Airbus A.300B4	Tunis-Air *Amilcar*
	TS-	Airbus A.300B4	Tunis-Air
	TS-	Airbus A.300B4	Tunis-Air
	TS-IOC	Boeing 737-2H3	Tunis-Air *Salammbo*
	TS-IOD	Boeing 737-2H3C	Tunis-Air *Bulla Regia*
	TS-IOE	Boeing 737-2H3	Tunis-Air *Zarzis*
	TS-IOF	Boeing 737-2H3	Tunis-Air *Sousse*

Reg.	Type	Owner or Operator	Notes
TS-JHN	Boeing 727-2H3	Tunis-Air *Carthago*	
TS-JHQ	Boeing 727-2H3	Tunis-Air *Tozeur-Nefta*	
TS-JHR	Boeing 727-2H3	Tunis-Air *Bizerte*	
TS-JHS	Boeing 727-2H3	Tunis-Air *Kairouan*	
TS-JHT	Boeing 727-2H3	Tunis-Air *Sidi Bousaid*	
TS-JHU	Boeing 727-2H3	Tunis-Air *Hannibal*	
TS-JHV	Boeing 727-2H3	Tunis-Air *Jugurtha*	
TS-JHW	Boeing 727-2H3	Tunis-Air *Ibn Khaldoun*	

TU (Ivory Coast)

Reg.	Type	Owner or Operator	Notes
TU-TAL	Douglas DC-10-30	Air Afrique *Libreville*	
TU-TAM	Douglas DC-10-30	Air Afrique	
TU-TAN	Douglas DC-10-30	Air Afrique *Niamey*	
TU-TAO	Airbus A.300B4-203	Air Afrique *Nouackchott*	
TU-TAS	Airbus A.300B4-203	Air Afrique *Bangui*	
TU-TAT	Airbus A.300B4-203	Air Afrique	
TU-TCF	Douglas DC-8-63CF	Air Afrique *Ndjamena*	

TZ (Mali)

Reg.	Type	Owner or Operator	Notes
TZ-ADR	Boeing 727-173C	Air Mali	

V8 (Brunei)

Reg.	Type	Owner or Operator	Notes
V8-RBA	Boeing 757-2M6ER	Royal Brunei Airlines	
V8-RBB	Boeing 757-2M6ER	Royal Brunei Airlines	
V8-RBC	Boeing 757-2M6ER	Royal Brunei Airlines	

VH (Australia)

Reg.	Type	Owner or Operator	Notes
VH-EBA	Boeing 747-238B	Qantas Airways	
VH-EBB	Boeing 747-238B	Qantas Airways	
VH-EBG	Boeing 747-238B	Qantas Airways *City of Fremantle*	
VH-EBH	Boeing 747-238B	Qantas Airways *City of Parramatta*	
VH-EBI	Boeing 747-238B	Qantas Airways *City of Dubbo*	
VH-EBJ	Boeing 747-238B	Qantas Airways *City of Newcastle*	
VH-EBL	Boeing 747-238B	Qantas Airways *City of Ballart*	
VH-EBM	Boeing 747-238B	Qantas Airways *City of Grosford*	
VH-EBN	Boeing 747-238B	Qantas Airways *City of Albury*	
VH-EBO	Boeing 747-238B	Qantas Airways *City of Elizabeth*	
VH-EBP	Boeing 747-238B	Qantas Airways *City of Adelaide*	
VH-EBQ	Boeing 747-238B	Qantas Airways *City of Bunbury*	
VH-EBR	Boeing 747-238B	Qantas Airways *City of Hobart*	
VH-EBS	Boeing 747-238B	Qantas Airways *City of Longreach*	
VH-EBT	Boeing 747-338	Qantas Airways *City of Canberra*	
VH-EBU	Boeing 747-338	Qantas Airways *City of Sydney*	
VH-EBV	Boeing 747-338	Qantas Airways *City of Melbourne*	
VH-EBW	Boeing 747-338	Qantas Airways *City of Brisbane*	
VH-EBX	Boeing 747-338	Qantas Airways *City of Perth*	
VH-EBY	Boeing 747-338	Qantas Airways *City of Darwin*	
VH-	Boeing 747-438	Qantas	
VH-	Boeing 747-438	Qantas	
VH-	Boeing 747-438	Qantas	
VH-	Boeing 747-438	Qantas	

VR-H (Hong Kong)

Reg.	Type	Owner or Operator	Notes
VR-HIA	Boeing 747-267B	Cathay Pacific Airways	
VR-HIB	Boeing 747-267B	Cathay Pacific Airways	
VR-HIC	Boeing 747-267B	Cathay Pacific Airways	
VR-HID	Boeing 747-267B	Cathay Pacific Airways	

Notes	Reg.	Type	Owner or Operator
	VR-HIE	Boeing 747-267B	Cathay Pacific Airways
	VR-HIF	Boeing 747-267B	Cathay Pacific Airways
	VR-HIH	Boeing 747-267B	Cathay Pacific Airways
	VR-HII	Boeing 747-367	Cathay Pacific Airways
	VR-HIJ	Boeing 747-367	Cathay Pacific Airways
	VR-HIK	Boeing 747-367	Cathay Pacific Airways
	VR-HKG	Boeing 747-267B	Cathay Pacific Airways
	VR-HKK	Boeing 707-336C	Air Hong Kong
	VR-HOL	Boeing 747-367	Cathay Pacific Airways
	VR-HOM	Boeing 747-367	Cathay Pacific Airways
	VR-HON	Boeing 747-367	Cathay Pacific Airways
	VR-HOO	Boeing 747-467	Cathay Pacific Airways
	VR-HOP	Boeing 747-467	Cathay Pacific Airways
	VR-HVY	Boeing 747-236F (SCD)	Cathay Pacific Airways *Hong Kong Jumbo*
	VR-HVZ	Boeing 747-267F (SCD)	Cathay Pacific Airways

VT (India)

Notes	Reg.	Type	Owner or Operator
	VT-EBE	Boeing 747-237B	Air-India *Emperor Shahjehan*
	VT-EBN	Boeing 747-237B	Air-India *Emperor Rajendra Chola*
	VT-EBO	Boeing 747-237B	Air-India *Emperor Nikramaditya*
	VT-EDU	Boeing 747-237B	Air-India *Emperor Akbar*
	VT-EFJ	Boeing 747-237B	Air-India *Emperor Chandragupta*
	VT-EFU	Boeing 747-237B	Air-India *Emperor Krishna Deva*
	VT-EGA	Boeing 747-237B	Air-India *Emperor Samudra Gupto*
	VT-EGB	Boeing 747-237B	Air-India *Emperor Mahendra Varman*
	VT-EGC	Boeing 747-237B	Air India *Emperor Harsha Vardhuma*
	VT-EJG	Airbus A.310-304	Air India *Vamuna*
	VT-EJH	Airbus A.310-304	Air India *Tista*
	VT-EJI	Airbus A.310-304	Air India *Saraswati*
	VT-EJJ	Airbus A.310-304	Air India *Beas*
	VT-EJK	Airbus A.310-304	Air India *Gomti*
	VT-EJL	Airbus A.310-304	Air India *Sabarmati*
	VT-ENQ	Boeing 747-212B	Air India
	VT-	Boeing 747-337	Air India
	VT-	Boeing 747-337	Air India

Note: Air-India Cargo operates Douglas DC-8s and Boeing 747s on lease from various airlines.

XA (Mexico)

Notes	Reg.	Type	Owner or Operator
	XA-DUG	Douglas DC-10-30	Aeromexico *Ciudad de Mexico*
	XA-DUH	Douglas DC-10-30	Aeromexico *Castillo de Chapultepec*

Note: Aeromexico also operates DC-10-30 N3878P on lease.

YI (Iraq)

Notes	Reg.	Type	Owner or Operator
	YI-AGE	Boeing 707-370C	Iraqi Airways
	YI-AGG	Boeing 707-370C	Iraqi Airways
	YI-AGK	Boeing 727-270	Iraqi Airways
	YI-AGL	Boeing 727-270	Iraqi Airways
	YI-AGM	Boeing 727-270	Iraqi Airways
	YI-AGN	Boeing 747-270C (SCD)	Iraqi Airways
	YI-AGO	Boeing 747-270C (SCD)	Iraqi Airways
	YI-AGP	Boeing 747-270C (SCD)	Iraqi Airways
	YI-AGQ	Boeing 727-270	Iraqi Airways
	YI-AGR	Boeing 727-270	Iraqi Airways
	YI-AGS	Boeing 727-270	Iraqi Airways
	YI-AKO	Ilyushin IL-76M	Iraqi Airways
	YI-AKP	Ilyushin IL-76M	Iraqi Airways
	YI-AKQ	Ilyushin IL-76M	Iraqi Airways
	YI-AKS	Ilyushin IL-76M	Iraqi Airways

Reg.	Type	Owner or Operator	Notes
YI-AKT	Ilyushin IL-76M	Iraqi Airways	
YI-AKU	Ilyushin IL-76M	Iraqi Airways	
YI-AKV	Ilyushin IL-76M	Iraqi Airways	
YI-AKW	Ilyushin IL-76M	Iraqi Airways	
YI-AKX	Ilyushin IL-76M	Iraqi Airways	
YI-ALL	Ilyushin IL-76M	Iraqi Airways	
YI-ALM	Boeing 747SP-70	Iraqi Airways *Al Qadissiya*	
YI-ALO	Ilyushin IL-76M	Iraqi Airways	
YI-ALP	Ilyushin IL-76M	Iraqi Airways	
YI-ALQ	Ilyushin IL-76MD	Iraqi Airways	
YI-ALR	Ilyushin IL-76MD	Iraqi Airways	
YI-ALS	Ilyushin IL-76MD	Iraqi Airways	
YI-ALT	Ilyushin IL-76MD	Iraqi Airways	
YI-ALU	Ilyushin IL-76MD	Iraqi Airways	
YI-ALV	Ilyushin IL-76MD	Iraqi Airways	
YI-ALW	Ilyushin IL-76MD	Iraqi Airways	
YI-ALX	Ilyushin IL-76MD	Iraqi Airways	
YI-ANA	Ilyushin IL-76MD	Iraqi Airways	
YI-ANB	Ilyushin IL-76MD	Iraqi Airways	
YI-ANC	Ilyushin IL-76MD	Iraqi Airways	
YI-AND	Ilyushin IL-76MD	Iraqi Airways	
YI-ANF	Ilyushin IL-76MD	Iraqi Airways	
YI-ANG	Ilyushin IL-76MD	Iraqi Airways	
YI-ANH	Ilyushin IL-76MD	Iraqi Airways	

YK (Syria)

Reg.	Type	Owner or Operator	Notes
YK-AGA	Boeing 727-29A	Syrian Arab Airlines *October 6*	
YK-AGB	Boeing 727-294	Syrian Arab Airlines *Damascus*	
YK-AGC	Boeing 727-294	Syrian Arab Airlines *Palmyra*	
YK-AHA	Boeing 747SP-94	Syrian Arab Airlines *16 Novembre*	
YK-AHB	Boeing 747SP-94	Syrian Arab Airlines *Arab Solidarity*	
YK-AIA	Tupolev Tu-154M	Syrian Arab Airlines	
YK-AIB	Tupolev Tu-154M	Syrian Arab Airlines	
YK-AIC	Tupolev Tu-154M	Syrian Arab Airlines	
YK-ATA	Ilyushin IL-76M	Syrian Arab Airlines	
YK-ATB	Ilyushin IL-76M	Syrian Arab Airlines	
YK-ATC	Ilyushin IL-76M	Syrian Arab Airlines	
YK-ATD	Ilyushin IL-76M	Syrian Arab Airlines	

YR (Romania)

Reg.	Type	Owner or Operator	Notes
YR-ABA	Boeing 707-3K1C	Tarom	
YR-ABC	Boeing 707-3K1C	Tarom	
YR-ABM	Boeing 707-321C	Tarom	
YR-ABN	Boeing 707-321C	Tarom	
YR-ADA	Antonov 26	Tarom	
YR-ADB	Antonov 26	Tarom	
YR-ADC	Antonov 26	Tarom	
YR-ADE	Antonov 26	Tarom	
YR-ADG	Antonov 26	Tarom	
YR-ADH	Antonov 26	Tarom	
YR-ADJ	Antonov 26	Tarom	
YR-ADK	Antonov 26	Tarom	
YR-ADL	Antonov 26	Tarom	
YR-BCB	BAC One-Eleven 424EU	Tarom *(stored)*	
YR-BCC	BAC One-Eleven 424EU	Liniile Aeriene Romane (LAR)	
YR-BCD	BAC One-Eleven 424EU	Liniile Aeriene Romane (LAR)	
YR-BCE	BAC One-Eleven 424EU	Tarom *(leased to GAS Air)*	
YR-BCF	BAC One-Eleven 424EU	Liniile Aeriene Romane (LAR)	
YR-BCG	BAC One-Eleven 401AK	Tarom *(stored)*	
YR-BCH	BAC One-Eleven 402AP	Tarom	
YR-BCI	BAC One-Eleven 525FT	Tarom	
YR-BCJ	BAC One-Eleven 525FT	Tarom	
YR-BCK	BAC One-Eleven 525FT	Tarom	
YR-BCL	BAC One-Eleven 525FT	Tarom	
YR-BCM	BAC One-Eleven 525FT	Tarom	

Notes	Reg.	Type	Owner or Operator
	YR-BCQ	BAC One-Eleven 525FT	Tarom
	YR-BRA	RomBac One-Eleven 561RC	Tarom
	YR-BRE	RomBac One-Eleven 561RC	Tarom
	YR-BRG	RomBac One-Eleven 561RC	Tarom
	YR-IMA	Ilyushin IL-18D	Tarom
	YR-IMC	Ilyushin IL-18V	Tarom
	YR-IMD	Ilyushin IL-18V	Tarom
	YR-IME	Ilyushin IL-18V	Tarom
	YR-IMF	Ilyushin IL-18V	Tarom
	YR-IMG	Ilyushin IL-18V	Tarom
	YR-IMH	Ilyushin IL-18V	Tarom
	YR-IMJ	Ilyushin IL-18D	Tarom
	YR-IML	Ilyushin IL-18D	Tarom
	YR-IMM	Ilyushin IL-18D	Tarom
	YR-IMZ	Ilyushin IL-18V	Tarom
	YR-IRA	Ilyushin IL-62	Tarom
	YR-IRB	Ilyushin IL-62	Tarom
	YR-IRC	Ilyushin IL-62	Tarom
	YR-IRD	Ilyushin IL-62M	Tarom
	YR-IRE	Ilyushin IL-62M	Tarom
	YR-TPA	Tupolev Tu-154B	Tarom
	YR-TPB	Tupolev Tu-154B	Tarom
	YR-TPC	Tupolev Tu-154B	Tarom
	YR-TPD	Tupolev Tu-154B	Tarom
	YR-TPE	Tupolev Tu-154B-1	Tarom
	YR-TPF	Tupolev Tu-154B-1	Tarom
	YR-TPG	Tupolev Tu-154B-1	Tarom
	YR-TPI	Tupolev Tu-154B-2	Tarom
	YR-TPJ	Tupolev Tu-154B-2	Tarom
	YR-TPK	Tupolev Tu-154B-2	Tarom
	YR-TPL	Tupolev Tu-154B-2	Tarom

YU (Yugoslavia)

Notes	Reg.	Type	Owner or Operator
	YU-AGE	Boeing 707-340C	Jugoslovenski Aerotransport
	YU-AGG	Boeing 707-340C	Jugoslovenski Aerotransport
	YU-AGI	Boeing 707-351C	Jugoslovenski Aerotransport
	YU-AHJ	Douglas DC-9-32	Adria Airways Ljubljana
	YU-AHL	Douglas DC-9-32	Jugoslovenski Aerotransport
	YU-AHN	Douglas DC-9-32	Jugoslovenski Aerotransport
	YU-AHU	Douglas DC-9-32	Jugoslovenski Aerotransport
	YU-AHV	Douglas DC-9-32	Jugoslovenski Aerotransport
	YU-AHW	Douglas DC-9-33RC	Adria Airways Sarajevo
	YU-AHX	Tupolev Tu-134A-3	Aviogenex Beograd
	YU-AHY	Tupolev Tu-134A-3	Aviogenex Zagreb
	YU-AJA	Tupolev Tu-134A-3	Aviogenex Titograd
	YU-AJD	Tupolev Tu-134A-3	Aviogenex Skopje
	YU-AJF	Douglas DC-9-32	Adria Airways
	YU-AJH	Douglas DC-9-32	Jugoslovenski Aerotransport
	YU-AJI	Douglas DC-9-32	Jugoslovenski Aerotransport
	YU-AJJ	Douglas DC-9-32	Jugoslovenski Aerotransport
	YU-AJK	Douglas DC-9-32	Jugoslovenski Aerotransport
	YU-AJL	Douglas DC-9-32	Jugoslovenski Aerotransport
	YU-AJM	Douglas DC-9-32	Jugoslovenski Aerotransport
	YU-AJT	Douglas DC-9-51	Adria Airways
	YU-AJU	Douglas DC-9-51	Adria Airways Maribor
	YU-AJZ	Douglas DC-9-81	Adria Airways
	YU-AKB	Boeing 727-2H9	Jugoslovenski Aerotransport
	YU-AKD	Boeing 727-2L8	Aviogenex Zagreb
	YU-AKE	Boeing 727-2H9	Jugoslovenski Aerotransport
	YU-AKF	Boeing 727-2H9	Jugoslovenski Aerotransport
	YU-AKG	Boeing 727-2H9	Jugoslovenski Aerotransport
	YU-AKH	Boeing 727-2L8	Aviogenex Beograd
	YU-AKI	Boeing 727-2H9	Jugoslovenski Aerotransport
	YU-AKJ	Boeing 727-2H9	Jugoslovenski Aerotransport
	YU-AKK	Boeing 727-2H9	Jugoslovenski Aerotransport
	YU-AKL	Boeing 727-2H9	Jugoslovenski Aerotransport
	YU-AKM	Boeing 727-243	Aviogenex Pula

Reg.	Type	Owner or Operator	Notes
YU-AMA	Douglas DC-10-30	Jugoslovenski Aerotransport *Nikola Tesla*	
YU-AMB	Douglas DC-10-30	Jugoslovenski Aerotransport *Edvard Rusijan*	
YU-ANB	Douglas DC-9-82	Adria Airways	
YU-ANC	Douglas DC-9-82	Adria Airways	
YU-AND	Boeing 737-3H9	Jugoslovenski Aerotransport	
YU-ANF	Boeing 737-3H9	Jugoslovenski Aerotransport	
YU-ANG	Douglas DC-9-82	Adria Airways	
YU-ANH	Boeing 737-3H9	Jugoslovenski Aerotransport	
YU-ANI	Boeing 737-3H9	Jugoslovenski Aerotransport	
YU-ANJ	Boeing 737-3H9	Jugoslovenski Aerotransport	
YU-ANK	Boeing 737-3H9	Jugoslovenski Aerotransport	
YU-ANL	Boeing 737-3H9	Jugoslovenski Aerotransport	
YU-ANO	Douglas DC-9-82	Adria Airways	
YU-ANP	Boeing 737-2K3	Aviogenex *Zadar*	
YU-ANS	RomBac One-Eleven 561RC	Adria Airways	
YU-ANT	RomBac One-Eleven 561RC	Adria Airways	
YU-ANU	Boeing 737-2K3	Aviogenex	
YU-	Boeing 737-3H9	Jugoslovenski Aerotransport	

Note: JAT also operates DC-10-30s OH-LHA and OO-SLA on lease.

YV (Venezuela)

YV-134C	Douglas DC-10-30	Viasa	
YV-135C	Douglas DC-10-30	Viasa	
YV-136C	Douglas DC-10-30	Viasa	
YV-137C	Douglas DC-10-30	Viasa	
YV-138C	Douglas DC-10-30	Viasa	

Z (Zimbabwe)

Z-WKR	Boeing 707-330B	Air Zimbabwe	
Z-WKS	Boeing 707-330B	Air Zimbabwe	
Z-WKT	Boeing 707-330B	Air Zimbabwe	
Z-WKU	Boeing 707-330B	Air Zimbabwe	
Z-WKV	Boeing 707-330B	Air Zimbabwe	
Z-WMJ	Douglas DC-8-54F	Affretair *Captain Jack Malloch*	

Note: Affretair also operates DC-8-55F TR-LVK.

ZK (New Zealand)

ZK-NZU	Boeing 747-419B	Air New Zealand	
ZK-NZV	Boeing 747-219B	Air New Zealand *Aotea*	
ZK-NZW	Boeing 747-219B	Air New Zealand *Tainui*	
ZK-NZX	Boeing 747-219B	Air New Zealand *Takitimu*	
ZK-NZY	Boeing 747-219B	Air New Zealand *Te Arawa*	
ZK-NZZ	Boeing 747-219B	Air New Zealand *Tokomaru*	

ZP (Paraguay)

ZP-CCE	Boeing 707-321B	Lineas Aéreas Paraguayas	
ZP-CCF	Boeing 707-321B	Lineas Aéreas Paraguayas	
ZP-CCG	Boeing 707-321B	Lineas Aéreas Paraguayas	
ZP-CCH	Douglas DC-8-63	Lineas Aéreas Paraguayas	

ZS (South Africa)

Notes	Reg.	Type	Owner or Operator
	ZS-SAL	Boeing 747-244B	South African Airways *Tafelberg*
	ZS-SAM	Boeing 747-244B	South African Airways *Drakensberg*
	ZS-SAN	Boeing 747-244B	South African Airways *Lebombo*
	ZS-SAO	Boeing 747-244B	South African Airways *Magaliesberg*
	ZS-SAP	Boeing 747-244B	South African Airways *Swartberg*
	ZS-SAR	Boeing 747-244B (SCD)	South African Airways *Waterberg*
	ZS-SAT	Boeing 747-344	South African Airways *Johannesburg*
	ZS-SAU	Boeing 747-344	South African Airways *Cape Town*
	ZS-SPB	Boeing 747SP-44	South African Airways *Outeniqua*
	ZS-SPE	Boeing 747SP-44	South African Airways *Hantam*
	ZS-SPF	Boeing 747SP-44	South African Airways *Soutpansberg*

3B (Mauritius)

	3B-NAE	Boeing 707-344B	Air Mauritius *City of Port Louis*
	3B-NAG	Boeing 747SP-44	Air Mauritius *Chateau du Reduit*
	3B-NAJ	Boeing 747SP-44	Air Mauritius *Chateau Mon Plaigir*
	3B-NAK	Boeing 767-23BER	Air Mauritius
	3B-NAL	Boeing 767-23BER	Air Mauritius

4R (Sri Lanka)

	4R-ULC	L.1011-385 TriStar 100	Air Lanka *City of Jayawardanapura*
	4R-ULE	L.1011-385 TriStar 50	Air Lanka *City of Ratnapura*
	4R-ULJ	L.1011-385 TriStar 1	Air Lanka
	4R-ULK	L.1011-385 TriStar 1	Air Lanka

4W (Yemen)

	4W-ACF	Boeing 727-2N8	Yemen Airways
	4W-ACG	Boeing 727-2N8	Yemen Airways
	4W-ACH	Boeing 727-2N8	Yemen Airways
	4W-ACI	Boeing 727-2N8	Yemen Airways
	4W-ACJ	Boeing 727-2N8	Yemen Airways

4X (Israel)

	4X-ABN	Boeing 737-258	El Al
	4X-ABO	Boeing 737-258	El Al
	4X-ATD	Boeing 707-331B	El Al
	4X-ATR	Boeing 707-358B	El Al
	4X-ATS	Boeing 707-358B	El Al
	4X-ATT	Boeing 707-358B	El Al
	4X-ATX	Boeing 707-358C	El Al
	4X-ATY	Boeing 707-358C	El Al
	4X-AXA	Boeing 747-258B	El Al
	4X-AXB	Boeing 747-258B	El Al
	4X-AXC	Boeing 747-258B	El Al
	4X-AXD	Boeing 747-258C	El Al
	4X-AXF	Boeing 747-258C	El Al
	4X-AXG	Boeing 747-258F (SCD)	El Al
	4X-AXH	Boeing 747-258B	El Al
	4X-AXZ	Boeing 747-124F (SCD)	El Al
	4X-EAA	Boeing 767-258	El Al
	4X-EAB	Boeing 767-258	El Al
	4X-EAC	Boeing 767-258ER	El Al
	4X-EAD	Boeing 767-258ER	El Al
	4X-EBL	Boeing 757-258	El Al
	4X-EBM	Boeing 757-258	El Al
	4X-E	Boeing 757-258	El Al

5A (Libya)

Reg.	Type	Owner or Operator	Notes
5A-DAI	Boeing 727-224	Libyan Arab Airlines	
5A-DAK	Boeing 707-3L5C	Libyan Arab Airlines	
5A-DIA	Boeing 727-2L5	Libyan Arab Airlines	
5A-DIB	Boeing 727-2L5	Libyan Arab Airlines	
5A-DIC	Boeing 727-2L5	Libyan Arab Airlines	
5A-DID	Boeing 727-2L5	Libyan Arab Airlines	
5A-DIE	Boeing 727-2L5	Libyan Arab Airlines	
5A-DIF	Boeing 727-2L5	Libyan Arab Airlines	
5A-DIG	Boeing 727-2L5	Libyan Arab Airlines	
5A-DIH	Boeing 727-2L5	Libyan Arab Airlines	
5A-DII	Boeing 727-2L5	Libyan Arab Airlines	
5A-DIX	Boeing 707-348C	Libyan Arab Airlines	
5A-DIY	Boeing 707-348C	Libyan Arab Airlines	
5A-DJM	Boeing 707-321B	Libyan Arab Airlines	
5A-DJT	Boeing 707-328B	Libyan Arab Airlines	
5A-DJU	Boeing 707-351C	Libyan Arab Airlines	

Note: Services to the UK suspended.

5B (Cyprus)

5B-DAG	BAC One Eleven 537GF	Cyprus Airways	
5B-DAH	BAC One Eleven 537GF	Cyprus Airways	
5B-DAJ	BAC One Eleven 537GF	Cyprus Airways	
5B-DAL	Boeing 707-123B	Cyprus Airways	
5B-DAO	Boeing 707-123B	Cyprus Airways	
5B-DAP	Boeing 707-123B	Cyprus Airways	
5B-DAQ	Airbus A.310-203	Cyprus Airways	
5B-DAR	Airbus A.310-203	Cyprus Airways	
5B-DAS	Airbus A.310-203	Cyprus Airways	
5B-	Airbus A.310-203	Cyprus Airways	
5B-	Airbus A.320-230	Cyprus Airways	
5B-	Airbus A.320-230	Cyprus Airways	
5B-	Airbus A.320-230	Cyprus Airways	
5B-	Airbus A.320-230	Cyprus Airways	
5B-	Airbus A.320-230	Cyprus Airways	
5B-	Airbus A.320-230	Cyprus Airways	
5B-	Airbus A.320-230	Cyprus Airways	
5B-	Airbus A.320-230	Cyprus Airways	

5N (Nigeria)

5N-ABJ	Boeing 707-3F9C	Nigeria Airways	
5N-ABK	Boeing 707-3F9C	Nigeria Airways	
5N-ANN	Douglas DC-10-30	Nigeria Airways	
5N-ANO	Boeing 707-3F9C	Nigeria Airways	
5N-AON	Douglas DC-8-62	Okada Air	
5N-AOQ	Boeing 707-355C	Okada Air	
5N-ARH	Douglas DC-8-55F	Arax Airlines	
5N-ASY	Boeing 707-351C	EAS Cargo	
5N-ATS	Douglas DC-8-55F	EAS Cargo	
5N-ATY	Douglas DC-8-55F	Flash Airlines	
5N-AUE	Airbus A.310-221	Nigeria Airways	
5N-AUF	Airbus A.310-221	Nigeria Airways	
5N-AUH	Airbus A.310-221	Nigeria Airways	
5N-AVO	S.E.210 Caravelle III	Inter Continental Airlines	
5N-AVP	S.E.210 Caravelle III	Inter Continental Airlines	
5N-AVQ	S.E.210 Caravelle III	Inter Continental Airlines	

5R (Madagascar)

5R-MFT	Boeing 747-2B2B (SCD)	Air Madagascar *Tolom Piavotana*	

5X (Uganda)

Notes	Reg.	Type	Owner or Operator
	5X-UAC	Boeing 707-351C	Uganda Airlines *The Flying Crane*
	5X-UBC	Boeing 707-338C	Uganda Airlines *Pearl of Africa*
	5X-UCF	L-100-30 Hercules	Uganda Airlines *The Silver Lady*

5Y (Kenya)

	5Y-AXC	Boeing 707-351C	African Express Airways
	5Y-AXS	Boeing 707-344B	Flash Airlines
	5Y-BBI	Boeing 707-351B	Kenya Airlines
	5Y-BBJ	Boeing 707-351B	Kenya Airlines
	5Y-BBK	Boeing 707-351B	Kenya Airlines
	5Y-BBX	Boeing 720-047B	Kenya Airlines
	5Y-BEL	Airbus A.310-304	Kenya Airlines *Nyayo Star*
	5Y-BEN	Airbus A.310-304	Kenya Airlines *Harambee Star*
	5Y-ZEB	Douglas DC-8-63	African Safari Airways

6O (Somalia)

	6O-SBS	Boeing 707-330B	Somali Airlines
	6O-SBT	Boeing 707-330B	Somali Airlines
	6O-	Airbus A.310-304	Somali Airlines

6Y (Jamaica)

Note: Air Jamaica operates its UK services jointly with British Airways.

7T (Algeria)

	7T-VEA	Boeing 727-2D6	Air Algerie *Tassili*
	7T-VEB	Boeing 727-2D6	Air Algerie *Hoggar*
	7T-VED	Boeing 737-2D6C	Air Algerie *Atlas Saharien*
	7T-VEE	Boeing 737-2D6C	Air Algerie *Oasis*
	7T-VEF	Boeing 737-2D6	Air Algerie *Saoura*
	7T-VEG	Boeing 737-2D6	Air Algerie *Monts des Ouleds Neils*
	7T-VEH	Boeing 727-2D6	Air Algerie *Lalla Khadidja*
	7T-VEI	Boeing 727-2D6	Air Algerie *Djebel Amour*
	7T-VEJ	Boeing 737-2D6	Air Algerie *Chrea*
	7T-VEK	Boeing 737-2D6	Air Algerie *Edough*
	7T-VEL	Boeing 737-2D6	Air Algerie *Akfadou*
	7T-VEM	Boeing 727-2D6	Air Algerie *Mont du Ksall*
	7T-VEN	Boeing 737-2D6	Air Algerie *La Soummam*
	7T-VEO	Boeing 737-2D6	Air Algerie *La Titteri*
	7T-VEP	Boeing 727-2D6	Air Algerie *Mont du Tessala*
	7T-VEQ	Boeing 737-2D6	Air Algerie *Le Zaccar*
	7T-VER	Boeing 737-2D6	Air Algerie *Le Souf*
	7T-VES	Boeing 737-2D6C	Air Algerie *Le Tadmaït*
	7T-VET	Boeing 727-2D6	Air Algerie *Georges du Rhumel*
	7T-VEU	Boeing 727-2D6	Air Algerie
	7T-VEV	Boeing 727-2D6	Air Algerie
	7T-VEW	Boeing 727-2D6	Air Algerie
	7T-VEX	Boeing 727-2D6	Air Algerie
	7T-VEY	Boeing 737-2D6	Air Algerie *Rhoufi*
	7T-VEZ	Boeing 737-2T4	Air Algerie *Monts du Daia*
	7T-VJA	Boeing 737-2T4	Air Algerie *Monts des Babors*
	7T-VJB	Boeing 737-2T4	Air Algerie *Monts des Bibons*
	7T-VJC	Airbus A.310-203	Air Algerie
	7T-VJD	Airbus A.310-203	Air Algerie
	7T-	Airbus A.310-203	Air Algerie
	7T-	Airbus A.310-203	Air Algerie

9G (Ghana)

Reg.	Type	Owner or Operator	Notes
9G-ANA	Douglas DC-10-30	Ghana Airways	

9H (Malta)

9H-AAO	Boeing 720-047B	Air Malta	
9H-ABA	Boeing 737-2Y5	Air Malta	
9H-ABB	Boeing 737-2Y5	Air Malta	
9H-ABC	Boeing 737-2Y5	Air Malta	
9H-ABE	Boeing 737-2Y5	Air Malta	
9H-ABF	Boeing 737-2Y5	Air Malta	
9H-ABG	Boeing 737-2Y5	Air Malta	

Note: Air Malta also operates two Boeing 727s on lease from Gulf Air (US).

9J (Zambia)

9J-ADY	Boeing 707-349C	Zambia Airways	
9J-AEB	Boeing 707-351C	Zambia Airways	
9J-AEL	Boeing 707-338C	Zambia Airways	
9J-AEQ	Boeing 707-321C	Zambia Airways	

Note: Zambia Airways also operates DC-10-30 N3016Z which is expected to be allocated a 9J registration.

9K (Kuwait)

9K-ADA	Boeing 747-269B (SCD)	Kuwait Airways *Al Sabahiya*	
9K-ADB	Boeing 747-269B (SCD)	Kuwait Airways *Al Jaberiya*	
9K-ADC	Boeing 747-269B (SCD)	Kuwait Airways *Al Murbarakiya*	
9K-ADD	Boeing 747-269B (SCD)	Kuwait Airways *Al Salmiya*	
9K-AHA	Airbus A.310-222	Kuwait Airways *Al-Jahra*	
9K-AHB	Airbus A.310-222	Kuwait Airways *Gharnada*	
9K-AHC	Airbus A.310-222	Kuwait Airways *Kadhma*	
9K-AHD	Airbus A.310-222	Kuwait Airways *Failaka*	
9K-AHE	Airbus A.310-222	Kuwait Airways *Burghan*	
9K-AHF	Airbus A.300-620C	Kuwait Airways *Wafra*	
9K-AHG	Airbus A.300-620C	Kuwait Airways *Wara*	
9K-AHI	Airbus A.300-620C	Kuwait Airways *Ali-Rawdhatain*	
9K-AIA	Boeing 767-269ER	Kuwait Airways *Alriggah*	
9K-AIB	Boeing 767-269ER	Kuwait Airways *Algrain*	
9K-AIC	Boeing 767-269ER	Kuwait Airways *Garouh*	

9L (Sierra Leone)

Sierra Leone Airways' services between Freetown and London are operated by using a Royal Jordanian TriStar.

9M (Malaysia)

9M-MHI	Boeing 747-236B	Malaysian Airline System	
9M-MHJ	Boeing 747-236B	Malaysian Airline System	
9M-MHK	Boeing 747-3H6 (SCD)	Malaysian Airline System	

9Q (Zaïre)

9Q-CKQ	Canadair CL-44-6	Volcanair *(stored)*	
9Q-CLG	Douglas DC-8-63CF	Air Zaire	

Notes	Reg.	Type	Owner or Operator
	9Q-CLH	Douglas DC-8-63AF	Air Zaire (*stored*)
	9Q-CVG	Boeing 707-329C	Katale Aero Transport
	9Q-CZF	Boeing 707-344	Air Region

Note: Air Zaire operates Douglas DC-10-30 F-OGQC.

9V (Singapore)

	9V-SKA	Boeing 747-312	Singapore Airlines
	9V-SKM	Boeing 747-312 (SCD)	Singapore Airlines
	9V-SKN	Boeing 747-312 (SCD)	Singapore Airlines
	9V-SKP	Boeing 747-312 (SCD)	Singapore Airlines
	9V-	Boeing 747-412	Singapore Airlines
	9V-	Boeing 747-412	Singapore Airlines
	9V-	Boeing 747-412	Singapore Airlines
	9V-	Boeing 747-412	Singapore Airlines
	9V-SQL	Boeing 747-212B	Singapore Airlines
	9V-SQM	Boeing 747-212B	Singapore Airlines
	9V-SQN	Boeing 747-212B	Singapore Airlines
	9V-SQO	Boeing 747-212B	Singapore Airlines
	9V-SQP	Boeing 747-212B	Singapore Airlines
	9V-SQQ	Boeing 747-212B	Singapore Airlines
	9V-SQR	Boeing 747-212B	Singapore Airlines
	9V-SQS	Boeing 747-212B	Singapore Airlines
	9V-	Boeing 747-212F	Singapore Airlines

Note: Singapore Airlines also operates Boeing 747-312 N116KB, N117KC, N118KD, N119KE, N120KF, N121KG, N122KH, N123KJ, N124KK and N125KL.

9XR (Rwanda)

	9XR-JA	Boeing 707-328C	Air Rwanda

9Y (Trinidad and Tobago)

	9Y-TGJ	L.1011 TriStar 500	B.W.I.A. *Flamingo*
	9Y-TGN	L.1011 TriStar 500	B.W.I.A.
	9Y-THA	L.1011 TriStar 500	B.W.I.A.

Note: B.W.I.A. also operates a TriStar 500 which retains its US registration N3140D.

Overseas Registrations

Aircraft included in this section are those based in the UK but which retain their non-British identities.

Reg	Type	Owner or Operator	Notes
A4O-AB	V.1103 VC10 ★	Brooklands Museum (G-ASIX)	
CF-EQS	Boeing-Stearman PT-17 ★	Imperial War Museum/Duxford	
CF-KCG	Grumman TBM-3E Avenger AS.3 ★	Imperial War Museum/Duxford	
CS-ACQ	Fleet 80 Canuck ★	Visionair Ltd (stored)/Coventry	
D-IFSB	D.H.104 Dove 6★	Mosquito Aircraft Museum	
EI-AYO	Douglas DC-3 ★	Science Museum/Wroughton	
F-BDRS	Boeing B-17G (231983) ★	Imperial War Museum/Duxford	
F-BGNR	V.708 Viscount ★	Air Service Training/Perth	
LX-NUR	Falcon 50	Kingson Investments/Heathrow	
N1MF	Cessna 421B	Pelmont Aviation Inc/Cranfield	
N2FU	Learjet 35A	Motor Racing Developments Inc	
N3TV	Douglas DC-3	Hibernian Dakota Flight Ltd	
N14CP	Beech C90 King Air	Scholl Inc	
N14KH	Christen Eagle II	R. Frohmayer	
N15AW	Cessna 500 Citation	A. W. Alloys Ltd	
N15SC	Learjet 35A	Sea Containers Associates/Luton	
N18F	Boeing 247D ★	Science Museum/Wroughton	
N18V	Beech D.17S Traveler (PB1)	R. Lamplough	
N47DD	Republic P-47D Thunderbolt ★	Imperial War Museum/Duxford	
N51JJ	P-15 Mustang (463221)	B.-J. S. Grey/Duxford	
N58GG	Cessna 551 Citation II	Business Real Estate Corporation	
N59NA	Douglas C-47A	Aces High Ltd (G-AKNB)/North Weald	
N71AF	R. Commander 680W	Metropolitan Aviation	
N88ZK	Boeing Stearman	R. Hanna/Duxford	
N122DU	G.1159 Gulfstream 2	Jet Services Corporation	
N145ST	G.1159 Gulfstream 2	Kalair USA Corporation	
N158C	S.24 Sandringham (VH-BRC) ★	Southampton Hall of Aviation	
N167F	P-51D Mustang (473877)	RLS 51 Ltd/Duxford	
N230ET	PA-30 Twin Comanche 160	P. Bayliss (G-ATET)	
N260QB	Pitts S-2S Special	D. Baker	
N333MP	C.A.S.A. 1.131E Jungmann	M. Plecenik (G-BECV)	
N415FS	F-100F Super Sabre	Flight Refuelling Ltd/Bournemouth	
N417FS	F-100F Super Sabre	Flight Refuelling Ltd/Bournemouth	
N418FS	F-100F Super Sabre	Flight Refuelling Ltd/Bournemouth	
N419FS	F-100F Super Sabre	Flight Refuelling Ltd/Bournemouth	
N425EE	Cessna 425	J. W. MacDonald	
N444M	Grumman G.44 Widgeon (1411)	M. Dunkerley/Biggin Hill (To be G-AHEC)	
N490CC	Cessna 551 Citation II	A. W. Alloys Ltd	
N500LN	Howard 500	D. Baker	
N535SM	R. Commander 680	J. E. Tuberty	
N804CC	G.159 Gulfstream 1	American Trans Air/Gatwick	
N900FR	Dassault Falcon 20DC	Flight Refuelling Ltd/Bournemouth	
N900MD	Learjet 36A	MMFI/Gatwick	
N901FR	Dassault Falcon 20DC	Flight Refuelling Ltd/Bournemouth	
N902FR	Dassault Falcon 20DC	Flight Refuelling Ltd/Bournemouth	
N903FR	Dassault Falcon 20DC	Flight Refuelling Ltd/Bournemouth	
N904FR	Dassault Falcon 20DC	Flight Refuelling Ltd/Bournemouth	
N905FR	Dassault Falcon 20DC	Flight Refuelling Ltd/Bournemouth	
N906FR	Dassault Falcon 20DC	Flight Refuelling Ltd/Bournemouth	
N907FR	Dassault Falcon 20DC	Flight Refuelling Ltd/Bournemouth	
N908FR	Dassault Falcon 20DC	Flight Refuelling Ltd/Bournemouth	
N909FR	Dassault Falcon 20DC	Flight Refuelling Ltd/Bournemouth	
N1344	Ryan PT-22	H, Mitchell	
N1447Q	Cessna 150L	US Embassy Flying Club	
N1621G	Champion 7KCAB Citabria	M. Butcher	
N2700	Fairchild C-119G	Aces High Ltd (G-BLSW)/North Weald	
N2929W	PA-28-151 Warrior	R. Lobell	
N3600X	Dassault Falcon 10	Xerox Corporation/Heathrow	
N3851Q	Cessna 172K	Bentwaters Aero Club/Woodbridge	
N3983N	Agusta A.109A	NSM Aviation	
N4306Z	PA-28 Cherokee 140	USAF Aero Club/Upper Heyford	
N4712V	Boeing Stearman PT-13D	Wessex Aviation & Transport Ltd	
N4727V	Spad S.VII (S4523)	Imperial War Museum/Duxford	
N4806E	Douglas A-26C Invader ★	R. & R. Cadman/Southend	
N5063N	Beech D.18S (HB275)	Harvard Formation Team (G-BKGM)	
N5237V	Boeing B-17G (483868) ★	RAF Bomber Command Museum/Hendon	

263

Notes	Reg	Type	Owner or Operator
	N5246	Nieuport 28	A. Graham-Enock
	N6268	Travel Air Model 2000	Personal Plane Services Ltd
	N7614C	B-25J Mitchell	Imperial War Museum/Duxford
	N7777G	L.749A Constellation ★	Science Museum (G-CONI)/Wroughton
	N8035H	Stinson L-5C	Keenair Services Ltd/Liverpool
	N8155E	Mooney M.20A	D. Skans
	N8297	FG-1D Corsair (88297)	B. J. S. Grey/Duxford
	N9012P	C.A.S.A. 352L (1Z+EK)	Junkers Ju.52/3M Flight
	N9089Z	TB-25J Mitchell (HD368)★	Aces High Ltd (G-BKXW)/North Weald
	N9115Z	TB-25N Mitchell (429366) ★	RAF Bomber Command Museum/ Hendon
	N9455Z	TB-25N Mitchell (30210)	Visionair Ltd
	N9606H	Fairchild M.62A Cornell ★	Rebel Air Museum/Earls Colne
	N11824	Cessna 150L	Lakenheath Aero Club
	N26178	Cessna 550 Citation II	A. W. Alloys Ltd
	N26634	PA-24 Comanche 250	P. Biggs (G-BFKR)
	N30228	Piper J-3C-65 Cub	C. Morris
	N33600	Cessna L-19A Bird Dog (111989) ★	Museum of Army Flying/ Middle Wallop
	N41836	Cessna 150A	US Embassy Flying Club (G-ARFI)
	N43069	PA-28-161 Warrior II	Lakenheath Aero Club
	N54558	Cessna F.152	J. J. Baumhardt
	N54922	Boeing Stearman	Yugo Cars
	N54607	Douglas C-47A	J. Keen *Maggie May*/Liverpool
	N60626	Cessna 150J	Lakenheath Aero Club
	N88972	B-25D-30-ND Mitchell (KL161)	Fighter Collection/Duxford
	N91437	PA-38-112 Tomahawk	Lakenheath Aero Club
	N91457	PA-38-112 Tomahawk	Lakenheath Aero Club
	N91590	PA-38-112 Tomahawk	Lakenheath Aero Club
	N94466	Curtiss P-40E Kittyhawk 1 (SU-E)	J. R. Paul/Duxford
	N96240	Beech D.18S	J. Hawke (G-AYAH)
	N99153	T-28C Trojan ★	Norfolk & Suffolk Aviation Museum/ Flixton
	N99225	Dornier Do.24T-3 (HD.5-1) ★	RAF Museum/Hendon
	NC517N	Lockheed 10A Electra ★	Science Museum (G-LIOA)/Wroughton
	NC15214	Waco UKC-S	P. H. McConnell/White Waltham
	NL1009N	Curtiss P-40M Kittyhawk (FR870)	B. J. S. Grey/Duxford
	NL1051S	P-51D-25-NA Mustang (511371)	Myrick Aviation/Southend
	NL9494Z	TB-25N Mitchell (151632)	Visionair Ltd
	NX47DD	Republic P-47D Thunderbolt (226671)	B. J. S. Grey/Duxford
	NX700H	Grumman F8F-2B Bearcat (121714)	B. J. S. Grey/Duxford
	NX1337A	Vought F4U-7 Corsair (133722)	L. M. Walton/Duxford
	VH-BRC	*See N158C*	
	VH-SNB	D.H.84 Dragon ★	Museum of Flight/E. Fortune
	VH-UTH	GAL Monospar ST-12 ★	Newark Air Museum (*stored*)
	VR-BEP	WS.55 Whirlwind 3 ★	East Midlands Aeropark (G-BAMH)
	VR-BET	WS.55 Whirlwind 3 ★	British Rotorcraft Museum (G-ANJV)
	VR-BEU	WS.55 Whirlwind 3 ★	British Rotorcraft Museum (G-ATKV)
	VR-BJI	Lockheed Jetstar	Denis Vanguard International Ltd
	VR-CBE	Boeing 727-46	Resebury Corporation
	VR-CBI	BAC One-Eleven 401	Bryan Aviation Ltd
	5N-ABW	Westland Widgeon 2 ★	British Rotorcraft Museum (G-AOZE)

Radio Frequencies

The frequencies used by the larger airfields/airports are listed below. Abbreviations used: TWR — Tower, APP — Approach, A/G — Air-ground advisory. It is possible for changes to be made from time to time with the frequencies allocated which are all quoted in Megahertz (MHz).

Airfield	TWR	APP	A/G	Airfield	TWR	APP	A/G
Aberdeen	118.1	120.4		Inverness	122.6	122.6	
Aldergrove	118.3	120.0		Ipswich	118.32		
Alderney	123.6			Jersey	119.45	120.3	
Andrewsfield			130.55	Kidlington	119.8	130.3	
Barton			122.7	Land's End			122.3
Barrow			123.2	Leavesden	122.15	122.15	
Belfast Harbour	130.75	130.85		Leeds	120.3	123.75	
Bembridge			123.25	Leicester			122.25
Biggin Hill	129.4	118.42		Liverpool	118.1	119.85	
Birmingham	118.3	120.5		Long Marston			130.1
Blackbushe			122.3	Luton	120.2	129.55	
Blackpool	118.4	118.4		Lydd	120.7	120.7	
Bodmin			122.7	Manchester	118.7	119.4	
Booker			126.55	Manston	124.9	126.35	
Bourn			129.8	Netherthorpe			123.5
Bournemouth	125.6	118.65		Newcastle	119.7	126.35	
Bristol	120.55	127.75		North Denes			120.45
Cambridge	122.2	123.6		Norwich	118.9	119.35	
Cardiff	121.2	125.85		Panshanger			120.25
Carlisle			123.6	Perth	119.8	122.3	
Compton Abbas			122.7	Plymouth	122.6	123.2	
Conington			123.0	Popham			129.8
Coventry	119.25	119.25		Prestwick	118.15	120.55	
Cranfield	123.2	122.85		Redhill			123.22
Denham			130.72	Rochester			122.25
Doncaster			122.9	Ronaldsway	118.9	120.85	
Dundee	122.9	122.9		Sandown			123.5
Dunkeswell			123.5	Seething			122.6
Dunsfold	124.32	122.55		Sherburn			122.6
Duxford			123.5	Shipdham			123.05
East Midlands	124.0	119.65		Shobdon			123.5
Edinburgh	118.7	121.2		Shoreham	125.4	123.15	
Elstree			122.4	Sibson			122.3
Exeter	119.8	128.15		Sleap			122.45
Fairoaks			123.42	Southampton	118.2	128.85	
Felthorpe			123.5	Southend	119.7	128.95	
Fenland			123.05	Stansted	118.15	126.95	
Filton	124.95	130.85		Stapleford			122.8
Gamston			130.47	Staverton	125.65	125.65	
Gatwick	124.22	118.95		Sumburgh	118.25	123.15	
Glasgow	118.8	119.1		Swansea	119.7	119.7	
Goodwood	122.45			Swanton Morley			123.5
Guernsey	119.95	128.65		Sywell			122.7
Halfpenny Green			123.0	Teesside	119.8	118.85	
Hatfield	130.8	123.35		Thruxton			130.45
Haverfordwest			122.2	Tollerton			122.8
Hawarden	124.95	123.35		Wellesbourne			130.45
Hayes Heliport			123.65	Weston	122.5	129.25	
Headcorn			122.0	West Malling			130.42
Heathrow	118.7	119.2		White Waltham			122.6
	118.5	119.5		Wick	119.7		
Hethel			122.35	Wickenby			122.45
Hucknall			130.8	Woodford	126.92	130.05	
Humberside	118.55	123.15		Yeovil	125.4	130.8	
Ingoldmells			130.45				

Airline Flight Codes

Three-letter flight codes are now in general use. Those listed below identify both UK and overseas carriers appearing in the book.

Code	Airline		Code	Airline		Code	Airline	
AAG	Air Atlantique	G	ECS	Air Ecosse	G	MSO	Somali A/L	6O
AAL	American A/L	N	EGY	Egypt Air	SU	NAA	National A/W	G
ABB	Air Belgium	OO	EIA	Evergreen Intl	N	NET	NetherLines	PH
ABR	Air Bridge	G	EIN	Aer Lingus	EI	NEX	Northern Executive	G
ACA	Air Canada	C	ELY	El Al	4X	NFD	NFD	D
ACF	Air Charter Intl	F	ETH	Ethiopian A/L	ET	NGA	Nigeria A/W	5N
AEA	Air Europa	EC	EUI	Euralair	F	NLM	NLM	PH
AEF	Aero Lloyd	D	EYT	Europe Aero Service	F	NWA	Northwest A/L	N
AEL	Air Europe	G	FAZ	Sfair	F	NXA	Nationair	C
AFL	Aeroflot	CCCP	FDE	Federal Express	N	OAL	Olympic A/L	SX
AFR	Air France	F	FGT	Fairflight	G	OCT	Octavia Air	G
AFW	Air Furness	G	FIN	Finnair	OH	ORN	Orion A/W	G
AGX	Aviogenex	YU	FOF	Fred Olsen	LN	OYC	Conair	OY
AHD	Air Holland	PH	FTL	Flying Tiger	N	PAA	Pan Am	N
AIC	Air India	VT	GBL	GB Airways	G	PAI	Piedmont	N
ALK	Air Lanka	4R	GEC	German Cargo	D	PAL	Philippine A/L	RP
AMC	Air Malta	9H	GER	Guernsey A/L	G	PAR	Partnair	LN
AMM	Air 2000	G	GFA	Gulf Air	A40	PAT	Paramount A/W	G
AMT	American Trans Air	N	GFG	Germania	D	PSS	Peregrine A/S	G
ANC	Anglo Cargo	G	GHA	Ghana A/W	9G	QFA	Qantas	VH
ANZ	Air New Zealand	ZK	GIA	Garuda	PK	RAM	Royal Air Maroc	CN
ATI	ATI	I	GIL	Gill Air	G	RBA	Royal Brunei	V8
ATT	Aer Turas	EI	GMP	Transwede	SE	RFG	RFG	D
AUA	Austrian A/L	OE	HBD	Hubbardair	G	RIA	Rich Intl	N
AUR	Aurigny A/S	G	HLA	HeavyLift	G	RJA	Royal Jordanian	JY
AVD	Air Vendee	F	HLF	Hapag-Lloyd	D	ROT	Tarom	YR
AYC	Aviaco	EC	HSL	Hispania	EC	RWD	Air Rwanda	9XR
AZA	Alitalia	I	IAA	Adria A/W	YU	RYR	Ryan Air	EI
AZI	Air Zimbabwe	Z	IAW	Iraqi A/W	YI	SAA	South African A/W	ZS
AZR	Air Zaire	9Q	IBE	Iberia	EC	SAB	Sabena	OO
BAF	British Air Ferries	G	ICE	Icelandair	TF	SAS	SAS	SE OY LN
BAL	Britannia A/L	G	IFL	Interflug	DDR	SAW	Sterling A/W	OY
BAW	British Airways	G	IKA	Tradewinds	G	SDI	Saudi	HZ
BBB	Balair	HB	INS	Instone A/L	G	SEE	South East Air	G
BBC	Bangladesh Biman	S2	IRA	Iran Air	EP	SEY	Air Seychelles	S7
BCA	British Caledonian	G	ISL	Eagle Air	TF	SIA	Singapore A/L	9V
BCS	European A/T	OO	ISS	Alisarda	I	SJM	Southern A/T	N
BEE	Busy Bee	LN	ITF	Air Inter	F	SLA	Sierra Leone A/W	9L
BER	Air Berlin	N	IYE	Yemen A/W	4W	SLA	Sobelair	OO
BEX	Birmingham Executive	G	JAL	Japan A/L	JA	STR	Stellair	F
BIH	British Intl Heli	G	JAT	JAT	YU	SUD	Sudan A/W	ST
BIS	British Island A/W	G	JEA	Jersey European A/W	G	SWE	Swedair	SE
BKT	British Airtours	G	KAC	Kuwait A/W	9K	SWR	Swissair	HB
BMA	British Midland	G	KAL	Korean Air	HL	SYR	Syrian Arab	YK
BRA	Braathens	LN	KAR	Kar-Air	OH	TAP	Air Portugal	CS
BRW	Capital Air	G	KIS	Contactair	D	TAR	Tunis Air	TS
BRY	Brymon A/W	G	KLM	KLM	PH	TAT	TAT	F
BWA	BWIA	9Y	KND	Kondair	G	TEA	Trans European A/W	OO
BXS	Spantax	EC	KQA	Kenya A/W	5Y	THA	Thai A/W Intl	HS
BZH	Brit Air	F	LAA	Libyan Arab A/L	5A	THG	Tal-Air	G
CAI	Cal Air Intl	G	LAZ	Bulgarian A/L	LZ	THY	Turkish A/L	TC
CAX	Connectair	G	LDA	Lauda Air	OE	TMA	Trans Mediterranean	OD
CCA	CAAC	B	LGL	Luxair	LX	TOW	Tower Air	N
CFG	Condor	D	LIM	Air Limousin	F	TRH	Transavia	PH
CLX	Cargolux	LX	LIN	Linjeflyg	SE	TWA	TWA	N
COA	Continental A/L	N	LIT	Air Littoral	F	TYR	Tyrolean	OE
CPX	Cathay Pacific	VR-H	LOG	Loganair	G	UAE	Emirates A/L	A6
CRL	Corse Air	F	LOT	Polish A/L (LOT)	SP	UGA	Uganda A/L	5X
CRX	Crossair	HB	LTU	LTU	D	UKA	Air UK	G
CSA	Czech A/L	OK	MAH	Malev	HA	UPA	Air Foyle	G
CTA	CTA	HB	MAL	McAlpine	G	UPA	Euroair	G
CYM	A/W Intl Cymru	G	MAS	Malaysian A/L	9M	UTA	UTA	F
CYP	Cyprus A/W	5B	MAU	Air Mauritius	3B	UYC	Cameroon A/L	TJ
DAH	Air Algerie	7T	MEA	Middle East A/L	OD	VIA	Viasa	YV
DAL	Delta A/L	N	MEE	Mediterranean Exp	G	VIR	Virgin Atlantic	G
DAN	Dan-Air	G	MIN	Minerve	F	VKG	Scanair	SE OY LN
DAT	Delta Air Transport	OO	MNX	Manx A/L	G	VRG	Varig	PP
DLH	Lufthansa	D	MON	Monarch A/L	G	WDL	WDL	D
DLT	DLT	D	MOR	Morefly	LN	WOA	World A/W	N
DMA	Maersk Air	OY	MPH	Martinair	PH	WWC	Worldways	C
DQI	Cimber Air	OY						

British Aircraft Preservation Council Register

The British Aircraft Preservation Council was formed in 1967 to co-ordinate the works of all bodies involved in the preservation, restoration and display of historical aircraft. Membership covers the whole spectrum of national, Service, commercial and voluntary groups, and meetings are held regularly at the bases of member organisations. The Council is able to provide a means of communication, helping to resolve any misunderstandings or duplication of effort. Every effort is taken to encourage the raising of standards of both organisation and technical capacity amongst the member groups to the benfit of everyone interested in aviation. To assist historians, the B.A.P.C. register has been set up and provides an identity for those aircraft which do not qualify for a Service serial or inclusion in the UK Civil Register.

Aircraft on the current B.A.P.C. Register are as follows:

Reg.	Type	Owner or Operator	Notes
1	Roe Triplane Type IV (replica)	Now G-ARSG	
2	Bristol Boxkite (replica)	Now G-ASPP	
3	Blériot XI	Now G-AANG	
4	Deperdussin Monoplane	Now G-AANH	
5	Blackburn Monoplane	Now G-AANI	
6	Roe Triplane Type IV (replica)	Greater Manchester Museum of Science & Technology	
7	Southampton University MPA	The Shuttleworth Trust	
8	Dixon ornithopter	The Shuttleworth Trust	
9	Humber Monoplane (replica)	Airport Terminal/Birmingham	
10	Hafner R.II Revoplane	Museum of Army Flying/Middle Wallop	
11	English Electric Wren	Now G-EBNV	
12	Mignet HM.14	Museum of Flight/E. Fortune	
13	Mignet HM.14	Brimpex Metal Treatments	
14	Addyman standard training glider	N. H. Ponsford	
15	Addyman standard training glider	The Aeroplane Collection Ltd	
16	Addyman ultra-light aircraft	N. H. Ponsford	
17	Woodhams Sprite	The Aeroplane Collection Ltd	
18	Killick MP Gyroplane	N. H. Ponsford	
19	Bristol F.2b	Anne Lindsay	
20	Lee-Richards annular biplane (replica)	Newark Air Musem	
22	Mignet HM.14 (G-AEOF)	Aviodome/Schiphol, Holland	
25	Nyborg TGN-III glider	Midland Air Museum	
27	Mignet HM.14	M. J. Abbey	
28	Wright Flyer (replica)	RAF Museum/Cardington	
29	Mignet HM.14 (G-ADRY)	Brooklands Museum	
31	Slingsby T.7 Tutor	S. Wales Aircraft Preservation Soc	
32	Crossley Tom Thumb	Midland Air Museum	
33	DFS.108-49 Grunau Baby IIb	Russavia Collection/Duxford	
34	DFS.108-49 Grunau Baby IIb	D. Elsdon	
35	EoN primary glider	Russavia Collection	
36	FZG-76 (V.1) (replica)	Imperial War Museum/Duxford	
37	Blake Bluetit	The Shuttleworth Trust	
38	Bristol Scout replica (A1742)	Historical Aircraft Museum/RAF St Athan	
40	Bristol Boxkite (replica)	Bristol City Museum	
41	B.E.2C (replica) (6232)	Historical Aircraft Museum/RAF St Athan	
42	Avro 504 (replica) (H1968)	Historical Aircraft Museum/RAF St Athan	
43	Mignet HM.14	Lincolnshire Aviation Museum	
44	Miles Magister (L6906)	G. H. R. Johnston (G-AKKY)	
45	Pilcher Hawk (replica)	Stanford Hall Museum	
46	Mignet HM.14	Alan McKechnie Racing Ltd	
47	Watkins Monoplane	Historical Aircraft Museum/RAF St Athan	
48	Pilcher Hawk (replica)	Glasgow Museum of Transport	
49	Pilcher Hawk	Royal Scottish Museum/Edinburgh	
50	Roe Triplane Type 1	Science Museum	
51	Vickers Vimy IV	Science Museum	
52	Lilienthal glider	Science Museum Store/Hayes	
53	Wright Flyer (replica)	Science Museum	
54	JAP-Harding monoplane	Science Museum	
55	Levavasseur Antoinette VII	Science Museum	
56	Fokker E.III (210/16)	Science Museum	
57	Pilcher Hawk (replica)	Science Museum	
58	Yokosuka MXY-7 Ohka II (15-1585)	FAA Museum/Yeovilton	
59	Sopwith Camel (replica) (D3419)	Historical Aircraft Museum/RAF St Athan	

Notes	Reg.	Type	Owner or Operator
	60	Murray M.1 helicopter	The Aeroplane Collection Ltd
	61	Stewart man-powered ornithopter	Lincolnshire Aviation Museum
	62	Cody Biplane (304)	Science Museum
	63	Hurricane (replica) (L1592)	Torbay Aircraft Museum
	64	Hurricane (replica)	Kent Battle of Britain Museum
	65	Spitfire (replica) (QV-K)	Hawkinge Aeronautical Trust
	66	Bf 109 (replica) (1480)	Hawkinge Aeronautical Trust
	67	Bf 109 (replica) (14)	Midland Air Museum
	68	Hurricane (replica) (H3426)	Midland Air Museum
	69	Spitfire (replica) (QV-K)	Torbay Aircraft Museum
	70	Auster AOP.5 (TJ472)	Aircraft Preservation Soc of Scotland
	71	Spitfire (replica) (P9390)	Norfolk & Suffolk Aviation Museum
	72	Hurricane (replica) (V7767)	N. Weald Aircraft Restoration Flight
	73	Hurricane (replica)	Queens Head/Bishops Stortford
	74	Bf 109 (replica) (6)	Torbay Aircraft Museum
	75	Mignet HM.14 (G-AEFG)	Nigel Ponsford
	76	Mignet HM.14 (G-AFFI)	Bomber County Museum/Cleethorpes
	77	Mignet HM.14 (G-ADRG)	P. Kirby/Innsworth
	78	Hawker Hind (K5414)	Now G-AENP
	79	Fiat G.46-4 (MM53211)	British Air Reserve/Lympne
	80	Airspeed Horsa (TL659)	Museum of Army Flying
	81	Hawkridge Dagling	Russavia Collection/Duxford
	82	Hawker Hind (Afghan)	RAF Museum
	83	Kawasaki Ki-100-1b	Aerospace Museum/Cosford
	84	Nakajima Ki-46 (Dinah III)	RAF St Athan
	85	Weir W-2 autogyro	Museum of Flight/E. Fortune
	86	de Havilland Tiger Moth (replica)	Yorkshire Aircraft Preservation Soc
	87	Bristol Babe (replica) (G-EASQ)	Bomber County Museum
	88	Fokker Dr 1 (replica) (102/18)	Fleet Air Arm Museum
	89	Cayley glider (replica)	Greater Manchester Museum of Science & Technology
	90	Colditz Cock (replica)	Torbay Aircraft Museum
	91	Fieseler Fi 103/FZG.76 (V.1)	Lashenden Air Warfare Museum
	92	Fieseler Fi 103/FZG.76 (V.1)	RAF Museum/Henlow
	93	Fieseler Fi 103/FZG.76 (V.1)	Imperial War Museum/Duxford
	94	Fieseler Fi 103/FZG.76 (V.1)	Aerospace Museum/Cosford
	95	Gizmer autogyro	—
	96	Brown helicopter	N.E. Aircraft Museum
	97	Luton L.A.4A Minor	Nene Valley Aviation Soc
	98	Yokosuka MXY-7 Ohka II	Greater Manchester Museum of Science & Technology
	99	Yokosuka MXY-7 Ohka II	Aerospace Museum/Cosford
	100	Clarke glider	RAF Museum/Hendon
	101	Mignet HM.14	Lincolnshire Aviation Museum
	103	Pilcher glider (replica)	Personal Plane Services Ltd
	104	Blériot XI (replica)	Now G-AVXV/Duxford
	105	Blériot XI (replica)	Aviodome/Schiphol, Holland
	106	Blériot XI (164)	RAF Museum
	107	Blériot XXVII (433)	RAF Museum
	108	Fairey Swordfish IV (HS503)	RAF Museum/Henlow store
	109	Slingsby Kirby Cadet TX.1	RAF Museum/Henlow store
	110	Fokker D.VII replica (static) (5125)	Leisure Sport Ltd/Thorpe Park
	111	Sopwith Triplane replica (static) (N5492)	FAA Museum/Yeovilton
	112	D.H.2 replica (static) (5984)	Museum of Army Flying/Middle Wallop
	113	S.E.5A replica (static) (B4863)	Leisure Sport Ltd/Thorpe Park
	114	Vickers Type 60 Viking (static)	Leisure Sport Ltd/Thorpe Park
	115	Mignet HM.14	Essex Aviation Group/Andrewsfield
	116	Santos-Dumont Demoiselle (replica)	Brooklands Museum
	117	B.E.2C (replica)	N. Weald Aircraft Restoration Flight
	118	Albatros D.V. (replica)	N. Weald Aircraft Restoration Flight
	119	Bensen B.7	N.E. Aircraft Museum
	120	Mignet HM.14 (G-AEJZ)	Bomber County Museum/Cleethorpes
	121	Mignet HM.14 (G-AEKR)	S. Yorks Aviation Soc
	122	Avro 504 (replica)	British Broadcasting Corp
	123	Vickers FB.5 Gunbus (replica)	A. Topen (*stored*)/Cranfield
	124	Lilienthal Glider Type XI (replica)	Science Museum
	125	Clay Cherub (G-BDGP)	Midland Air Museum
	126	D.31 Turbulent (static)	Midland Air Museum store
	127	Halton Jupiter MPA	Shuttleworth Trust
	128	Watkinson Cyclogyroplane Mk IV	British Rotorcraft Museum
	129	Blackburn 1911 Monoplane (replica)	Cornwall Aero Park/Helston store

Reg.	Type	Owner or Operator	Notes
130	Blackburn 1912 Monoplane (replica)	Cornwall Aero Park/Helston store	
131	Pilcher Hawk (replica)	C. Paton	
132	Blériot XI (G-BLXI)	Aerospace Museum/Cosford	
133	Fokker Dr 1 (replica) (425/17)	Torbay Aircraft Museum	
134	Pitts S-2A static (G-RKSF)	Torbay Aircraft Museum	
135	Bristol M.1C (replica) (C4912)	Leisure Sport Ltd/Thorpe Park	
136	Deperdussin Seaplane (replica)	Leisure Sport Ltd/Thorpe Park	
137	Sopwith Baby Floatplane (replica) (8151)	Leisure Sport Ltd/Thorpe Park	
138	Hansa Brandenburg W.29 Floatplane (replica) (2292)	Leisure Sport Ltd/Thorpe Park	
139	Fokker Dr 1 (replica) 150/17	Leisure Sport Ltd/Thorpe Park	
140	Curtiss R3C-2 Floatplane (replica)	Leisure Sport Ltd/Thorpe Park	
141	Macchi M.39 Floatplane (replica)	Leisure Sport Ltd/Thorpe Park	
142	SE-5A (replica) (F5459)	Cornwall Aero Park/Helston	
143	Paxton MPA	R. A. Paxton/Staverton	
144	Weybridge Mercury	Cranwell Gliding Club	
145	Oliver MPA	D. Oliver (*stored*)/Warton	
146	Pedal Aeronauts Toucan MPA	Shuttleworth Trust	
147	Bensen B.7	Norfolk & Suffolk Aviation Museum	
148	Hawker Fury II (replica) (K7271)	Aerospace Museum/Cosford	
149	Short S.27 (replica)	FAA Museum (*stored*)/Yeovilton	
150	SEPECAT Jaguar GR.1 (replica) (XX718)	RAF Exhibition Flight	
151	SEPECAT Jaguar GR.1 (replica) (XZ363)	RAF Exhibition Flight	
152	BAe Hawk T.1 (replica) (XX163)	RAF Exhibition Flight	
153	Westland WG.33	British Rotorcraft Museum (*stored*)	
154	D.31 Turbulent	Lincolnshire Aviation Museum	
155	Panavia Tornado GR.1 (replica) (ZA600)	RAF Exhibition Flight	
156	Supermarine S-6B (replica) (S1595)	Leisure Sport Ltd	
157	Waco CG-4A	Pennine Aviation Museum	
158	Fieseler Fi 103/FZG.76 (V.1)	Joint Bomb Disposal School/Chattenden	
159	Fuji MXY-7 Ohka II	Joint Bomb Disposal School/Chattenden	
160	Chargus 108 hang glider	Museum of Flight/E. Fortune	
161	Stewart Ornithopter Coppelia	Bomber County Museum	
162	Goodhart Newbury Manflier MPA	Science Museum/Wroughton	
163	AFEE 10/42 Rotabuggy (replica)	Museum of Army Flying/Middle Wallop	
164	Wight Quadruplane Type 1 (replica)	Wessex Aviation Soc/Wimborne	
165	Bristol F.2b (E2466)	RAF Museum/Hendon	
166	Bristol F.2b	Now G-AANM	
167	S.E.5A replica	Torbay Aircraft Museum	
168	D.H.60G Moth static replica (G-AAAH)	Hilton Hotel/Gatwick	
169	SEPECAT Jaguar GR.1 (static replica) (XX110)	No 1 S. of T.T. RAF Halton	
170	Pilcher Hawk (replica)	A. Gourlay/Strathallan	
171	BAe Hawk T.1 (replica) (XX297)	RAF Exhibition Flight/Abingdon	
172	Chargus Midas Super 8 hang glider	Science Museum/Wroughton	
173	Birdman Promotions Grasshopper	Science Museum/Wroughton	
174	Bensen B.7	Science Museum/Wroughton	
175	Volmer VJ-23 Swingwing	Greater Manchester Museum of Science & Technology	
176	SE-5A (replica) (A4850)	S. Yorkshire Aircraft Preservation Soc	
177	Avro 504K (replica) (G1381)	(*Stored*)/Henlow	
178	Avro 504K (replica) (E373)	(*Stored*)/Henlow	
179	Sopwith Camel (replica)	N. Weald Aircraft Restoration Flight	
180	McCurdy Silver Dart (replica)	RAF Museum/Hendon	
181	RAF B.E.2b (replica)	RAF Museum/Cardington	
182	Wood Ornithopter	Greater Manchester Museum of Science & Technology	
183	Zurowski ZP.1	Newark Air Museum	
184	Spitfire IX (replica) (EN398)	Aces High Ltd/North Weald	
185	Waco CG-4A (243409)	Museum of Army Flying/Middle Wallop	
186	D.H.82B Queen Bee (K3584)	Mosquito Aircraft Museum	
187	Roe Type 1 biplane (replica)	Brooklands Museum	
188	McBroom Cobra 88	Science Museum/Wroughton	
189	Bleriot XI (replica)	—	

Note: Registrations/Serials carried are mostly false identities. MPA = Man Powered Aircraft.

Addenda

New or restored British registrations

Notes	Reg.	Type	Owner or Operator
	G-BLFI	PA-28-181 Archer II	Leavesden Flight Centre Ltd
	G-BMOR	Boeing 737-2S3	Air UK Leisure Ltd/Stansted
	G-BOFD	Cessna U.206G	R. M. McCarthy
	G-BOFE	—	—
	G-BOFF	Cameron N-77 balloon	Systems-80 Double Glazing Ltd
	G-BOFG	Short SD3-60	Short Bros PLC/Sydenham
	G-BOFH	Short SD3-60	Short Bros PLC/Sydenham
	G-BOFI	Short SD3-60	Short Bros PLC/Sydenham
	G-BOFJ	Short SD3-60	Short Bros PLC/Sydenham
	G-BOFK	Short SD3-60	Short Bros PLC/Sydenham
	G-BOFL	Cessna 152	Coventry (Civil) Aviation Ltd
	G-BOFM	Cessna 152	Coventry (Civil) Aviation Ltd
	G-BOFN	Beech 100 King Air	Essex Leasing
	G-BOFP	Slingsby T.67M-200	Slingsby Aviation Ltd/Kirkbymoorside
	G-BOFR	Slingsby T.67M-200	Slingsby Aviation Ltd/Kirkbymoorside
	G-BOFS	Slingsby T.67M-200	Slingsby Aviation Ltd/Kirkbymoorside
	G-BOFT	Slingsby T.67M-200	Slingsby Aviation Ltd/Kirkbymoorside
	G-BOFU	Slingsby T.67M-200	Slingsby Aviation Ltd/Kirkbymoorside
	G-BOFV	PA-44-180 Seminole	K. A. Summers
	G-BOFW	—	—
	G-BOFX	—	—
	G-BOFY	PA-28 Cherokee 140	Bristol & Wessex Aeroplane Club Ltd
	G-BOFZ	—	—
	G-BOGA	Cessna 500 Citation	World Courier Aviation Ltd
	G-BOGB	Hawker Tempest II replica	D. L. Riley
	G-BOGC	Cessna 152	Skyviews & General Ltd
	G-BOGD	Cameron 80 Dinosaur SS balloon	Cameron Balloons Ltd
	G-BOGE	Cessna 152	Seal Executive Aircraft Ltd
	G-BOGF	—	—
	G-BOGG	—	—
	G-BOGH	Cameron N-160 Balloon	Cameron Balloons Ltd
	G-BOGX	AS.355F-2 Twin Squirrel	McAlpine Helicopters Ltd/Hayes
	G-BOHE	Cameron O-120 balloon	H. R. Evans
	G-BRYD	D.H.C.7-110 Dash Seven	Brymon Aviation Ltd/Plymouth
	G-BSAT	PA-28-181 Archer II	Astro Technology Ltd
	G-BTSL	Cameron Glass SS balloon	Bass & Tennent Sales Ltd
	G-BZWW	BAe 748ATP	British Aerospace PLC (to be N375AE)
	G-CSJH	BAe 146-200	Air UK Ltd/Norwich
	G-CVAN	Cessna F406 Caravan 2	Bob Crowe Aircraft Sales Ltd
	G-DSGN	Robinson R-22B	William Towns Ltd
	G-ETON	Maule M5-235C Lunar Rocket	J. R. Hatton (G-BHDB)
	G-FTFT	Colt Financial Times balloon	Financial Times Ltd
	G-HWKN	PA-31P-325 Navajo	Crosbyglow Ltd
	G-IBET	Cameron 70 Can SS balloon	Bass & Tennent Sales Ltd
	G-IFLP	PA-34-200T-2 Seneca	Golf-Sala Ltd
	G-JETX	Bell 206B JetRanger	Tripgate Ltd
	G-JMDD	Cessna 340A	Thoroughbred Technology Ltd
	G-LAGR	Cameron N-90 balloon	Bass & Tennent Sales Ltd
	G-OFAB	Bell 206B JetRanger	J. L. Leonard
	G-OOOD	Boeing 757-28A	Air 2000 Ltd/Manchester
	G-OOOO	Mooney M.20J	Creedair International Ltd
	G-OPMB	Cessna P.210N	Policy Master Ltd
	G-PDSI	Cessna 172N	Quick Logic Ltd
	G-PELE	Cameron 80 Pele SS balloon	Cameron Balloons Ltd
	G-SALI	Cessna 421C	Rapid 3864 Ltd
	G-SJGM	Cessna 182R	Crystal Air Ltd
	G-STYL	Pitts S-1S Special	B. MacMillan
	G-TINS	Cameron N-90 balloon	Bass & Tennent Sales Ltd
	G-TOMY	Mitsubishi Mu.300 Diamond	Lynton Aviation Ltd
	G-WRCF	Beech 200 Super King Air	W. R. C. M. Foyle
	G-XIIX	Robinson R-22B	Defence Products Ltd
	G-YUPI	Cameron N-90 balloon	West Country Marketing & Advertising Ltd

New overseas registrations

Notes	Reg.	Type	Owner or Operator
	B-2452	Boeing 747SP-J6	CAAC (ex-N1304E)
	C-FWDX	Airbus A310-304 (802)	Wardair Canada H. W. Harry Hayter

Reg.	Type	Owner or Operator	Notes
C-FXWD	Airbus A310-304	Wardair Canada	
C-GBWD	Airbus A310-304 (806)	Wardair Canada *C. C. Carl Agar*	
C-GCWD	Airbus A310-304	Wardair Canada	
C-GDWD	Airbus A310-304	Wardair Canada	
C-GIWD	Airbus A310-304	Wardair Canada	
C-GJWD	Airbus A310-304	Wardair Canada	
C-GKWD	Airbus A310-304	Wardair Canada	
C-GLWD	Airbus A310-304	Wardair Canada	
CS-TET	Boeing 737-2K9	Air Atlantis	
D-AHLZ	Airbus A310-204	Hapag-Lloyd	
D-AMUY	Boeing 757-2G5	LTU	
EC-EGI	Boeing 757-236	Air Europa/Air Europe (G-BKRM)	
F-BPJR	Boeing 727-228	Air Charter International	
F-G	Boeing 737-2K5	Air France (ex-EC-DTR)	
F-G	Boeing 737-2K5	Air France (ex-EC-DUB)	
HS-TMA	Douglas DC-10-30ER	Thai International	
HS-TMB	Douglas DC-10-30ER	Thai International	
LN-NOS	Boeing 737-33A	Norway Airlines	
LN-RMF	Douglas DC-9-83	S.A.S.	
LX-LGN	Boeing 737-229	Luxair (ex-OO-SDA)	
OE-LAU	Boeing 767-3Z9	Lauda Air (ex-OE-LAA)	
OO-ILH	Boeing 737-4Q8	Air Belgium	
OY-KHF	Douglas DC-9-87	S.A.S. *Ragnar Viking*	
OY-KHG	Douglas DC-9-81	S.A.S. *Alle Viking*	
SE-DIA	Douglas DC-9-81	S.A.S. *Ulrik Viking*	
SE-DIB	Douglas DC-9-87	S.A.S. *Varin Viking*	
SE-DIC	Douglas DC-9-87	S.A.S. *Grane Viking*	
SE-DID	Douglas DC-9-82	S.A.S. *Spjute Viking*	
9Q-CBS	Boeing 707-329C	Scibe Air	
9Q-CSB	Boeing 707-373C	Sicotra Aviation (ex-CS-TBJ)	
9V-SKQ	Boeing 747-212F	Singapore Airlines	

Future Allocations Log
(Out-of-Sequence)

This grid can be used to record out-of-sequence registrations as they are issued or seen. The first column is provided for the ranges prefixed with G-B, ie from G-BOxx to G-BZxx. The remaining columns cover the sequences from G-Cxxx to G-Zxxx and in this case it is necessary to insert the last three letters in the appropriate section.

G-B	G-C	G-E	G-G	G-I	G-L	G-N	G-O	G-P	G-S	G-U
										G-V
				G-J						
										G-W
	G-D	G-F	G-H		G-M	G-O		G-R		
									G-T	
										G-X
				G-K						
										G-Y
										G-Z